# SAS
# STORIES OF HEROES II

SHAUN CLARKE

DAVID MONNERY

BLITZ EDITIONS

This edition published 1994

Published by Blitz Editions
an imprint of Bookmart Limited
Registered Number 2372865
Trading as Bookmart Limited
Desford Road, Enderby
Leicester, LE9 5AD



ISBN 1 85605253 2

Typeset by Hewer Text Composition Services, Edinburgh
Printed in Great Britain by Cox & Wyman, Reading

# SOLDIER D: SAS

# THE COLOMBIAN COCAINE WAR

David Monnery

# Prelude

Joss Wynwood reinserted the magazine into the Browning High Power 9mm pistol, and put the pistol back in the cross-draw holster at his belt. After checking that the two spare magazines were in his windcheater pocket, he leaned back on the bench and grinned at his partner.

As usual Richard Anderson was struggling with the shoulder holster, which he, almost alone in 22 SAS Regiment, preferred to the cross-draw. Wynwood got up and helped straighten out the strapping across his back. 'You need a mother,' he added helpfully as he resumed his seat.

'Don't we all,' Anderson agreed, zipping up his windcheater. 'You know what this place reminds me of?' he said, looking round. 'One of those recreation-ground dressing rooms we used on Sunday mornings when I was a kid.'

Wynwood followed Anderson's gaze round the barracks ante-room. 'We used to change behind a tree,' he said, consciously exaggerating the Welsh lilt to his voice.

'What, the whole team, behind one tree?'

Wynwood laughed. His partner seemed in better spirits today, after spending most of the previous day bemoaning the fact that it was Christmas Eve and he was 10,000 kilometres away from Beth and the kids.

The thought was premature.

'What a way to spend Christmas Day,' Anderson said, as if he'd read Wynwood's mind.

The Welshman sighed. 'This *was* your idea.'

'You agreed.'

Yes, he had. After training the Colombian unit for six weeks it had seemed like a good idea to watch them in action. A sort of end-of-term master-class, with two SAS masters and the first Colombian Special Forces Anti-Narcotics Unit as the class. A practical exam. And then he and Andy would be homeward bound in time to welcome in the nineties, Hereford-style.

It was not soon enough for Anderson. 'It just doesn't seem right, not seeing the kids on Christmas Day,' he protested.

'So you keep telling me,' Wynwood said, letting a slight edge into his own voice. He could understand Anderson missing home, but he needed no reminding of what was probably going on in his own house on this particular Christmas Day.

Anderson looked at him. 'What's got into you?'

'Oh, nothing,' he sighed. 'Happy Christmas.'

'Yeah.' It was Anderson's turn to sigh. 'Where the fuck is Gómez?' he growled, getting up and stretching his arms above his head.

As if in reply, footsteps could be heard coming their way.

'I think Gómez the fuck is here,' Wynwood murmured.

The door opened to reveal a smiling officer. He was tall for a Colombian, with typical slicked-back raven hair and neat moustache, and a row of the neat white teeth which Anderson and Wynwood had come to see as the badge of the Colombian middle class. He was, the two Britons thought, an OK guy.

'We're ready,' Wynwood said, getting up.

'*Un momento*' Captain Gómez said, holding his palms face forward. 'I have to say something you may not . . .' He searched for the right word. 'Appreciate?' he asked.

'Tell us in Spanish.'

Gómez nodded gratefully. 'Señor Muñoz has expressed concern about your presence at the meeting . . . You must understand' – the Colombian shrugged – 'two gringo guards – it makes him look like a tool of the Americans, like he is only saying what he says for the sake of foreigners, that he does not really have the interests of this nation at heart . . .'

'So what's the score?' Anderson interrupted.

'He is happy for you to be there, provided you keep a – how you say in English – a narrow profile?'

'A low profile. OK, we'll be as invisible as we can. Can we go now?'

'Of course.'

The two Britons swapped grimaces as Gómez led them outside into the barracks yard, where the procession was coiled like a snake, its motorcycle head by the closed gate. Behind this three ordinary saloons were sandwiched between the two armoured personnel carriers (APCs) into which Gómez's unit was being loaded.

'You will travel in the third car,' Gómez told them. 'I will be in the first with Señor Muñoz.'

'Which suckers are travelling in the middle car?' Wynwood wondered out loud.

'Oh, just some journalists,' Gómez said absentmindedly. He ushered them into the Toyota's back seat and closed the door.

'Neat,' Anderson said. 'If it all goes well, the journalists will be full of praise, and it if fucks up there's a fair chance they'll all be dead. That's what I call news management.'

Wynwood grinned. 'How did an Englishman get so cynical?' he murmured.

'Just paying attention, my son. You ought to try it sometime.'

Up front the motorcycles burst into life, the barracks gates were drawn open and the convoy slowly unwound itself to emerge onto the streets of Cali. It was dusk now, the north-running Calle Ramona deep in shadow, the fading glow of the sunset visible above the mountains to the east at each intersection. For the moment they were heading towards the centre of the city, but their ultimate destination was the sprawling slum barrio of Malverdes on the city's north-western outskirts. There, in a local sports hall, Señor Muñoz would deliver an election speech to the downtrodden and the dispossessed.

Wynwood examined the view through the open window. He saw lots of concrete, the occasional palm tree, shuttered cafés, rubble, children interrupting their play to watch the convoy go past. Colombia was unfinished, Wynwood decided. The thing about England was that they had had two thousand years to fill in all the spaces, to do the place up properly, to finish the job. Here they had only had a few hundred, and it had been a big place to start with. It would not be finished for a while yet.

Thinking about England took his thoughts back, reluctantly but inexorably, to Susan. The thought of her and her boyfriend – whatever his goddamn name was – sent a shaft of anger surging from his stomach to his throat. It would be about eleven o'clock in England; they would probably be in the middle of a Christmas fuck, probably on his living-room carpet, under the Christmas tree he and Susan had successfully replanted last January. Well, he hoped the bastard got pine needles in his prick.

Why did he think about her? Why torture himself? He didn't want her back any more than she wanted him back. But it stuck somehow, stuck in his throat.

Andy was jogging his arm gently. 'Wake up,' he said.

The convoy was slowing down in the early evening traffic, making it an easier target. But the only immediate threat Wynwood could see was the plumes of toxic waste from the bus exhausts. 'No one's going to attack us before we pick up the Big Cheese,' he said.

'True,' Anderson agreed. 'You know, I don't think I could ever get used to hot weather at Christmas. It's perverse.'

'It's hot in Australia.'

'Everything's perverse in Australia.'

'It was probably hot in Bethlehem.'

'I'm talking Christmas here, not religion.'

'Sorry.'

They were halted at traffic lights, and Wynwood

was watching a young boy – he could not have been more than six or seven – juggling balls between the cars on the front row. He had no sooner stopped juggling and offered his battered baseball cap for monetary reward than the lights changed. As they pulled away Wynwood saw first the balls then the cap escape from his clutch. And then the boy was kneeling on the street, tyres hissing past his ear, reaching for the silver pesos scattered on the tarmac.

Wynwood did not know why he always felt moved by such obvious evidence of poverty. Maybe his mother was right when she said it was a good heart. Maybe it just tugged at memories of his family's struggle to stay afloat when he was a kid in Pontarddulais. It did not matter either way, he concluded.

They were threading the more prosperous *avenidas* of the downtown section now, passing rows of shops with armed guards where laundered cocaine money could buy you Japanese technology and French fashions. A few minutes more and the convoy came to a halt in the semicircular forecourt of the high-rise Hotel Torre de Cali. All save the lead car, which had dived down into the underground parking lot to collect its political cargo. It emerged two minutes later, resumed its place as the convoy rolled out onto the Avenida de las Americas, and they were heading north-west again, out of the city centre, towards the wall of mountains which marked the western side of the Cauca valley.

The tropical night had fallen with its usual swiftness, and the dim yellow streetlamps were doing battle with a moonless sky. By contrast the occasional shrieking neon sign seemed to possess an eye-aching intensity. As always in Colombia, Wynwood found the change a forbidding one. Such a friendly place by day, but by night . . .

Away to the left, as if to reassure him, the large white illuminated statue of Jesus which stood on the slopes above the city was intermittently visible through gaps in the buildings.

The streetlamps grew rarer and seemingly dimmer, but it was still possible in the gloom to detect a progressive deterioration in the quality of life. Wynwood wondered what Señor Muñoz was thinking to himself two cars ahead. How did you come out to a place like this in a sharp suit and find something to say that anyone would listen to? It would be like Tory politicians turning up in Pontardulais the day a local mine closed down. Not that they had, needless to say.

The lights seemed to be getting brighter. And there were more people on the sides of the road. They had reached another world.

The convoy moved down a crowded street and came to a halt outside a large, garishly lit concrete hall. Across the street the words 'Pool! Pool! Pool!' were flashing in alternate yellow and green neon, and youths with cues were visible through the windows. Spanish-American pop music, which Wynwood had decided was easily the worst music known to man, was blaring overlapping rhythms from several different directions. Children were already gathering round the armoured personnel carriers, some open-mouthed, some happily taking the piss out of the disembarking soldiers. One child had discovered Wynwood and Anderson, and was clinging Garfield-like to the rear passenger window of their car.

'What d'you reckon?' Wynwood asked.

'Sit it out a few minutes before we show our honky faces?'

'Yeah.'

The two of them watched Muñoz hustled professionally past the welcoming horde and in through the doors of the sports hall. He seemed taller than they had expected from photographs, bespectacled, silvering hair glinting in the artificial light. His suit was sharp enough though.

'What do you know about him?' Anderson asked.

'Not a lot. He doesn't seem to have been around long. But he's been gunning for the drug cartels for the last few months . . .'

'So now they're gunning for him,' Anderson said dryly.

Wynwood shrugged. 'Who knows what makes those bastards tick. They may think they're so fucking powerful that people like Muñoz here aren't worth the time and trouble.'

'Well, we're probably going to get an earful this evening.' He reached for the door handle. 'Miss Brodie, shall we go and check out our pupils?'

'Miss Brodie was a fucking Scot.'

They clambered out into the warm air. Cali was slightly less than a thousand metres above sea level, high enough to take the edge off of the humidity, low enough not to get too cool at night. The smell of cooking filled the street.

'Makes you feel hungry, doesn't it?' Wynwood murmured.

'Anything makes *you* feel hungry. You're going to spread like a balloon in a few years' time.'

Wynwood smacked himself in the stomach with both hands. 'Pure muscle,' he said. 'At least I'm not a borderline anorexic,' he added, eyeing Anderson's willowy frame.

Anderson grunted. 'Ever feel you were in a Western movie?' he asked, surveying the scene around them.

'All the time,' Wynwood said, 'but I know what you mean.'

The street they were standing on arrowed off

into distant darkness in both directions, and the bustling, brightly lit restaurants across the street seemed to have nothing behind them. It felt like a film set.

'Let's get inside.'

They went in through the main doors, exchanging grins with several of the men they had been training for the previous six weeks. In the main hall, wooden-floored and marked out for basketball, five-a-side football and other sports, several hundred plastic chairs had been arranged. Most were now occupied by a talking, shouting, laughing, screeching audience. Children roamed wild around and under the seats, though none had as yet got in among the ceiling beams. At the far end, on a raised platform made by pushing about twenty wooden tables together, Carlos Muñoz and a couple of local political heavies were sitting talking in another row of plastic chairs. The red, blue and yellow flags of Muñoz's political party were draped everywhere that flags could be draped.

The two SAS men made their way through to the area beside and slightly behind the stage, where another door led through to what looked like offices.

'When the talking starts I'll do the rounds,' Anderson said.

'You mean I have to listen to the speech?'

'I shall expect a full report.'

They did not have long to wait. One of the local men got to his feet, and after spending several minutes in a vain attempt to secure silence from the audience, finally managed to coax several ear-piercing shrieks from the PA system. That did the trick.

A few introductory words elicited more catcalls, and then Muñoz was on his feet. He knew how to handle an audience, Wynwood soon realized. It was not so much what he was saying as the simple way he had of saying it. The content was mostly predictable – corruption in government, the evil of the drug lords, the malign hand of Washington. All three supported each other, no matter how much they wished or claimed to do otherwise. While the American banks controlled the Colombian economy, drugs were the only way to pay for development. While the drug lords controlled all the profits from the trade the politicians were powerless and even the best of them liable to become corrupted.

In fact, Wynwood decided, Muñoz seemed to be arguing for the nationalization of the cocaine industry. Which did have a bizarre logic to it.

'I don't like it,' Anderson's voice sounded in his ear.

'What, the speech?' Wynwood asked, knowing he meant something else.

'Arsehole.'

Wynwood waited for Anderson to say something else, but he didn't. 'Sixth sense?'

Anderson sighed. 'Yeah.'

'Which way did you go? I'll take a look.'

'Out the front, round to the right and through the back door, which brings you into the office beyond this one. The exits are all covered. I just . . .' He shrugged.

'I'll do it in reverse,' Wynwood decided. He walked through the offices to the back door, where Jaime Morales, one of the friendlier Colombians in the Gómez unit, was in charge of a four-man team. 'No problems?' Wynwood asked him in Spanish.

'No.'

Wynwood eased himself out of the door and into a dark, narrow street. Night goggles would have been useful, he thought. Not that there seemed to be anything to see, even with night goggles. Still, he took Andy's sixth sense as seriously as he took his own, and any other SAS man's. 'The senses take in more stuff than the brain can deal with,' the instructor had told them in one of Hereford's classrooms, 'so it comes back lacking clarity, more of a feeling than a thought. Don't ignore something because you can't quite work out where it's coming from or what it is. It may be nemesis coming to call.'

At which point Ben Young had asked whether

nemesis wasn't the first book in the Bible. Ben, a long time gone now, was one of those lost to the freezing South Atlantic waters during the Falklands War.

You're getting maudlin in your old age, Wynwood, he thought to himself. A true son of Owain Glyndwr.

He gingerly turned the corner off the hall and padded down the alley which ran along its side to the main street. The latter looked the same, but it did feel different. Or was he imagining it because of Andy? There seemed to be a stillness in the air, a tension. The three cars shining by the front door seemed vulnerable, the group of soldiers smoking by the armoured patrol car complacently cocky. Wynwood couldn't *see* anything, but . . .

He went back indoors. Muñoz was still talking, the audience still listening with what seemed like interest.

Anderson looked at him quizzically.

'Yeah, I think we should talk to Gómez.'

'And tell him what?'

'That he's going to need some help.'

'Rather you than me.'

'OK.' Wynwood looked round. 'Where is he?'

'Out the back, I think.'

Wynwood walked through one office and into the other. Gómez was sitting on a table, talking on the phone to someone, and at that moment something happened, because he stopped talking, shook the phone and then tried listening. 'It's . . .' he started to say, but the rest of his sentence was swallowed by the sound of the explosion.

Anderson did not just hear the explosion – he saw it. And he had a pretty good idea what had caused it too – a rocket, fired from a mobile launcher, impacting on the front APC outside.

The explosion had blown the windows in, and bits of at least one trooper with them. The flying glass had hit the audience side on, and the sound of a huge collective scream seemed to be rending the air in its wake. Anderson, half behind the makeshift platform on the side farthest from the door, was unhurt, save for a small cut on his cheek. He was just starting forward to check out what had happened to Muñoz when, through the blasted window frames, silhouetted against the lighted windows on the other side of the main street, he saw several figures appear, arms stretched to throw. Recognizing the cylindrical missiles while they were in mid-air, he dropped to his knees, covering eyes and ears with his arms.

The dozen or so stun grenades exploded, searing the eyes with their flaring magnesium, lashing the eardrums with overlapping blasts of sound. Even with his eyes and ears covered it felt to Anderson like the end of the world.

The silence which followed was almost as complete, but only for a moment, as whimpers rose to wails and wails to screams for help. Anderson looked round for Wynwood, but found only Muñoz, kneeling not two metres away, shaking badly and looking round blindly, blood flowing from a cut above his eye. Above him, above the whole ghastly scene, the row of phosphorescent lights that hung from the beams were flickering like demented telegraph machines.

The shout 'Fire!' penetrated Anderson's brain, and he turned to see a second shower of missiles rain in through the windows, followed, seconds later, by the hiss of gas.

The echoes of the initial rocket attack were still humming in the air when a shout from the guards on the back door announced the presence of enemies in the alley at the rear. A succession of shots followed. Gómez and Wynwood exchanged glances. 'Take the back door,' the Colombian said, and without waiting for agreement hurried back through the other office towards the hall.

Wynwood was drawing the Browning from its holster when a figure burst through the door in question, carrying a Heckler & Koch MP5 sub-machine-gun. At the same moment the stun grenades detonated in the hall behind him. Which was lucky for Wynwood. The newcomer was facing the flash, and even through two doorways this gave him enough pause for Wynwood to fire a double tap through his forehead.

'Shut the door!' he screamed at one of the troops. 'And keep it covered.'

Wynwood turned and walked swiftly – the temptation to run was almost irresistible, but only Clint Eastwood could aim a pistol on the run. Gómez was struggling to his feet, trying to shake the blindness out of his eyes; behind him Andy was looking round. Gas canisters were coming through the window.

'Andy,' he screamed.

'Yeah.' Anderson was grabbing Muñoz by the shoulder. 'Let's take the prize home ourselves,' he shouted.

Wynwood went to help him, holding his breath as the gas billowed round the hall. Already his nose and eyes seemed to be running. Now he knew what the terrorists in the Iranian Embassy must have felt like.

They managed to pull the politician into the first office, and to slam the door behind them against the gas.

'Where now, Tonto?' Anderson asked. He seemed to be having the time of his life. The sound of gunfire now seemed to be coming from all round the building.

'Out of here,' Wynwood suggested.

'Sounds good.'

Beside them Muñoz seemed to be coming out of the disorientation caused by the stun grenades. 'What is happening? What do you want?' He wiped his face with the back of his hand, looked at the blood as if surprised it was there.

'We're the British trainers of this unit,' Wynwood explained. And not too proud of it at the moment, he thought to himself. 'And we're getting you out of here,' he continued.

'But . . .'

'No buts,' Anderson interrupted, hustling Muñoz towards the back door and almost tripping over the Colombian Wynwood had killed a few minutes earlier. 'Nice shooting, partner,' he murmured, noticing the twin holes in the forehead. 'What now. Shall we ring for a taxi?'

Wynwood ignored him. 'We're taking El Señor out of here,' he told Morales. 'Straight across the alley and through the door that's dead opposite. You and Jesús here can give us covering fire.' He thought for a second, then knelt down and extricated the MP5 from the dead Colombian's hands.

'OK,' he said, 'open the door.'

Morales pushed it outwards, and a volley of fire stitched a pattern on the inner face. Then there was silence.

'Go!' shouted Wynwood.

The two Colombians almost flew through the door, into the rolls the SAS trainers had taught them, coming to rest face down in the middle of the alley, their M16s opening up in opposite directions.

Wynwood was proud of them. 'I'll take the door,' he told Anderson.

Anderson just nodded. 'Get ready,' he told Muñoz, as Wynwood half ran, half rolled across the alley and landed in the opposite doorway with a thud. Ricochets echoed down the walls.

'Shit,' Wynwood muttered. He was getting too old for this. He allowed his eyes a few seconds to adjust to the darkness, and then searched the door for the lock. But there seemed not to be one. He tried the handle and the door opened. 'Our lucky day,' he murmured, and beckoned to Anderson.

At that moment a volley of fire seemed to kick up dust in front of one of the spread-eagled Colombians. It was Jesús. He seemed to cough apologetically as the rifle dropped from his hands.

'Go!' Anderson told Muñoz on the other side of the great divide.

Muñoz looked at him like he was mad. 'No!' he shouted, turning away towards the door leading back towards the hall. As he did so a gas canister bounced off his foot, rolled away and exploded.

With a sound like a moan Muñoz turned and ran

straight out through the door, across the alley and in through the open door opposite, bullets whining round his head. Anderson was right behind him, taking the more professional approach, trying to vary the speed and profile of his body as he made the dash.

'I'll check the back,' Wynwood said, and was gone.

'What now?' Muñoz asked Anderson, who ignored him. 'Keep it slow,' he was whispering to Morales, who was edging snakewise towards the doorway. Jesús's body had the limpness of death.

On the far side someone was unwise enough to silhouette himself against the lighted office. For a second Anderson thought it was Gómez, but the man shouted something to others out of sight in a voice the SAS man did not recognize, and just for safety's sake he put a 'double tap' through the man's trunk. He sank to his knees clutching his stomach.

Morales reached the relative safety of the doorway. 'Two,' Anderson said out loud, counting his shots expended. From each direction down the alley he could hear men gathering; he hoped to God Wynwood had found another way out.

He had. 'This way,' the Welshman shouted, and Anderson half pushed Muñoz after him, Morales bringing up the rear. The building seemed to be disused, just a series of empty rooms bisected by a corridor. Wynwood led them out across a freshly flattened back door, through an overgrown yard to a dilapidated corrugated fence. Through one of the many gaps they could see a steep bank leading down to a river.

There was no time for consideration. Wynwood half scrambled, half fell down the slope and into the water. It was deeper, colder and faster-flowing than he had expected, and for a second he had troubling keeping the MP5 clear of the water without losing his balance. The lack of light was a further complication; from the deep channel cut by the river he could see only the stars above and a far bank which might be ten metres away – or fifty.

Muñoz arrived with a splash beside him, followed by Morales and Anderson. The politician started to say something, but Anderson's finger in front of his mouth made him aware of the virtues of silence. Wynwood struck out across the river, the water up to his chest, the current tugging at his body.

The river was about fifteen metres wide. Once the others were all safely across Wynwood started pulling himself up the steep slope, and was just about to breast the rise when noises across the river told him that pursuers had reached the top of the bank they had clambered down. He froze, conscious that he and the others would be masked by the darkness, praying the enemy did not have a torch.

They didn't. But neither did they seem inclined to retrace their steps. Instead, one of them lit a cigarette, giving a snapshot of his face in the glow of the match, and the two of them started an inaudible conversation.

After half a minute of this Wynwood began to wonder whether it might be worth trying to take them both out with the MP5. It would be noisy, but not exactly difficult, even in light like this . . .

The drone of a helicopter insinuated its way into his attention. It had to be behind him, coming towards them. Was it the police? The Army? The enemy?

'Whatever,' he murmured to himself. The helicopter seemed almost overhead now. Wynwood pulled the MP5 into firing position, and as the helicopter passed across the river, about fifty metres downstream of their position and not much higher, he raked the two silhouettes on the far bank. Both were thrown back into the corrugated fence with a crash, the lighted cigarette flying up and forward before extinguishing itself in the river.

Wynwood turned and climbed over the rim of the bank. In front of him he could see several empty railway tracks running parallel to the gentle curve of the river. Beyond them what looked like a large warehouse stretched for about fifty metres in either direction. Two loading docks were built into its side, and one of them was open, letting out the dimmest glow. There had to be a road beyond it all.

By the time he had taken all this in the others had scrambled up the bank to join him. Above the buildings on the far bank the helicopter's lights were now moving across the sky. It was circling. Wynwood no longer had any doubts about whose it was.

'I'll recce,' he told Anderson, and without waiting for an answer struck off along the tracks to the right.

'You OK?' Anderson asked Muñoz, who was crouching beside him.

The Colombian managed a wry smile. 'Yes,' he answered. 'I think so.'

'Jaime?'

'Yes, boss.'

The helicopter was coming almost directly towards them now, its drone growing louder. As it crossed the river someone switched on its spotlight, just too late to catch the huddled group.

Wynwood was not so lucky. He was just recrossing the tracks when the light went on, catching him almost in mid-spot for one brief, revealing second. Then the helicopter had overshot, and he was invisible again. But not for long. It was already banking, and Wynwood had only a few seconds. 'I'll lead them off,' he shouted in English to Anderson. 'There's a way through to a road off to your right. You look after the Big Cheese!'

The helicopter was flying towards them along the tracks, throwing its circle of light forward like a single huge headlamp beam, reaching out for the running Wynwood, catching him and holding him. But only for a second. As someone opened up with a sub-machine-gun the SAS man swerved away to the right, launched himself up off the nearest rail onto the loading stage and disappeared through the open doorway.

Anderson led the others to the right, round the corner of the warehouse and up a rutted alley to the road. On its far side single-storey houses stretched away up the slope, like a hillside of oversized shoeboxes. Some windows showed a dim light, but there were no other signs of life. It was not yet eight o'clock and the district seemed half dead. Or simply keeping its collective head under the pillow.

Anderson could hear but not see the helicopter. At that moment a wash of light advanced along the wall opposite and then stopped – a car had pulled up round the bend to the left.

Muñoz and Morales were standing waiting in

the shadows, both looking as though they would rather be somewhere else. If it had been Cup Final day, Anderson thought, their manager would say they had 'frozen'. Both men were certainly shivering, but then sopping clothes and a cool breeze were hardly a recipe for warmth.

Anderson beckoned with a finger, and the three of them started off to the right, leaving behind the wash of light. Morales was limping, he noticed. And Muñoz just seemed exhausted by the night's excitement.

There was no way they were all going to walk out of here, Anderson realized. They needed transport.

Pausing to look back he could see the helicopter some half a kilometre away, almost motionless in the air, its light shining down like one of those beams flying saucers in movies always used to pull up their helpless prey. As he watched another helicopter appeared in the distance, also trailing its spotlight like a net.

'Boss,' Morales whispered loudly. 'Look'.

It was a car.

Wynwood's building had turned out to be an abattoir. He ran headlong down a long corridor, past rows of what looked like refrigerated rooms, out into an office area, through to another landing dock. At its edge, watching his rapid approach like startled rabbits caught in a headlight, were two Colombian men – presumably the nightwatchmen. Wynwood had no sooner taken in their presence than he saw another man, better dressed and gun in hand, halfway between a parked car and the loading dock.

Ignoring the first two men, Wynwood went over the loading dock, into a double roll and opened up with the MP5. The man with the gun sank to his knees, surprise on his face.

As a bullet clattered off the corrugated warehouse wall behind him, and as the helicopter appeared round the rim of the warehouse roof, Wynwood rolled once more, sending a concentrated burst through the windscreen of the waiting car. Then, as the pilot struggled to flood the yard with light, he outran it, out through the gate, across the road and into the alleys of the slum quarter opposite.

The car looked new, and what it was doing sitting on the verge of a minor road with its doors wide open Anderson had no idea.

Morales did. 'Riders of joy,' he said in Spanish. It was obvious really. 'They couldn't take it home' – he indicated the hillside across the road – 'but they saved themselves a long walk.'

Muñoz got in the back, Morales in the front, and Anderson demonstrated one of the many skills he had learned at Hereford – hot-wiring. He started the car, and eased it back onto the road, hoping the sound of the engine would be masked by the two helicopters hovering above them. The windscreen was filthy, and he was just wondering whether to get out and wipe it when lights appeared behind him.

He eased the car forward, and for something like fifty metres the car behind simply followed them. Then, suddenly, as if a decision had been taken, the trailing car accelerated forward, flashing its lights for them to stop.

Anderson reckoned from his rear-view mirror that there were at least three men in it. He pressed down on the accelerator, thinking: Christ, what a place! It was like a mixture of Chicago gangsters, *Miami Vice* and the fucking IRA – and all in a foreign language.

Wynwood made his way carefully through the darkened alleys of the slum barrio. He could feel people all around him, twitching their paper curtains, staring out through candlelit cracks in their doors, muttering to each other. They knew he was passing through, all right.

The real enemy still did not, if the activities of the helicopters were anything to go by. One was sweeping the valley bottom, its spotlight turning the rails into silver arcs and the waters of the river to boiling ink. The other was still hovering above the warehouse. Then, as Wynwood watched, it suddenly veered away to the south, as if yanked by a sudden signal.

He turned and carried on up the hill, a rank smell growing slowly stronger in his nostrils. Reaching the crest a few minutes later, he discovered its source. Here the houses abruptly ended, and in the valley below there was only rubbish, mountains of it, stretching as far as his eyes could see.

A couple of kilometres to the south Anderson accelerated down another dark street, the car like a bucking bronco on the potholed surface. Behind them the pursuit was neither gaining nor losing ground. 'Which way?' he asked Morales and Muñoz. Neither answered. Glancing in the rear-view mirror, he noticed that Muñoz seemed to be praying.

Anderson squealed the car round another corner. Above the buildings on the right-hand side of the road the dark shape of a helicopter loomed across the stars. Why didn't the bastards open fire?

And then it occurred to him how they had managed to get this far. The bastards wanted Muñoz alive. Which had to give him some sort of edge. All he had to do was stay ahead.

Another intersection was approaching. And

bright lights. He slowed marginally, decided on a left turn and took the corner on two wheels.

A familiar-looking convoy of cars appeared in front of him, headed by a wrecked APC. Outside the hall the road was covered in people, presumably those brought out since the original attack.

All this took a second to take in. He swung the wheel to the right, towards a side-street opening, just as two children stepped out to cross. Another wrench of the wheel missed them but not the corner building. The front right of the car struck it at an angle, catapulting Jaime Morales out through the windscreen, and slamming Anderson's head against the roof as it slammed his chest again the steering wheel. He had one last glimpse of gunmen walking carefully towards the car before he blacked out.

Wynwood found a mound that seemed suitable and started to dig himself into it. The garbage was fresh, which carried a twofold advantage. For one thing it had not had time to congeal, which would make made it easier to penetrate without leaving obvious signs. For another the stink was so bad it would deter anyone from looking too closely.

The downside was only too obvious to

Wynwood as he worked himself into and under the putrid heap. The famed ditch at Hereford, filled with animal entrails, was lavender compared with this.

# 1

It was a minute past midnight in Bogotá. President Juan Estrada was happily settled in front of the TV in that part of the Presidential Palace reserved for his personal use. His wife had finally gone to bed, and he had three back-to-back episodes of *Dallas* to watch on his video. He was not sure what vintage they were – they might even be from the series which had turned out to be only Pam Ewing's dream – but that didn't matter.

In fact these days the further he got from reality the better Estrada liked it. So he was not particularly pleased when his Filipino houseboy brought news that his Minister of the Interior had arrived to see him on urgent business.

'I suppose you'd better show him up,' the President said reluctantly, freezing the video on the Miss Ellie who had come back from the dead. He smiled to himself.

Luis Quintana was not smiling. 'Juan,' he began, 'I'm sorry to interrupt your Christmas, but this couldn't wait.' He looked across at the drinks tray. 'Can I help myself?' he asked.

'What can't wait?' Estrada asked.

'Carlos Muñoz has been kidnapped.'

A faint smile appeared on the President's face.

Quintana poured himself a large neat whisky. 'In Cali. He was out in some slum barrio, talking to the poor, and . . .' He shrugged. 'They snatched him.'

'Who?'

'Not sure. But it looks like either the Escobars or the Amarales. Whoever it was, they managed to kill about twenty people in the process.'

Estrada grunted. 'Ransom, you think?'

'Probably.' Quintana took a large hit of whisky.

'Who'd pay?'

'His family,' Quintana suggested.

Estrada grimaced. Muñoz was standing against him in three months' time for the Party's Presidential nomination. And as matters stood lately it looked like the bastard had a chance of winning, regardless of the fact that Estrada was the incumbent president of the country. 'I could always pay the bastards to keep him,' he said sardonically.

'Some people may think you paid the bastards to snatch him,' Quintana replied mildly. 'And there's more. One of the two English Special Forces people was taken with him. You know, the ones your favourite Mrs Thatcher let you borrow.'

'She's not my favourite! I just enjoyed annoying the Americans by taking English soldiers as advisers.'

'Well, she's not going to be pleased.'

'So she won't be pleased.' He thought for a moment. 'What about the other Englishman?'

'He's missing.'

'Wonderful,' Estrada said wryly.

'Anyway, in a few hours your favourite will probably be on the phone asking you what steps are being taken to find one soldier and release the other.'

'I'll take the phone off the hook.'

Quintana sat down opposite Estrada. 'Juan, I agree it doesn't matter a damn what the British want or think. But Muñoz is another matter. You know as well as I do that this nation is like a house of cards. Take one out, any one, and the whole thing's liable to come down on our heads. Muñoz is the acceptable face of our system. You know and I know that he's just a stupid dreamer who wouldn't recognize the real world if it bit him . . .'

'It looks like it just has,' Estrada interjected sourly.

'Maybe. As far as Washington and a lot of our own people are concerned, the Muñozes are the only reason they give us any credibility at all. Muñoz is proof that the cartels don't run the nation.'

'They do, near as damn it.'

Quintana suppressed his exasperation. 'Yes, but as long as it looks like they have some opposition the Americans are not going to turn the country into a free-fire zone to protect their bored children from cocaine and our own people are still going to pay taxes to us as well as the cartels. We may not need Muñoz but we need people like him, and it has to look like we're trying to get him back.'

'It'd be nice to fail.'

'I agree we could find a more satisfactory opponent for you for the election, but . . .'

'So, find me the biggest idiot of a general you can and we'll send him off.'

'No. It would have to be our best people. But anyway I have another idea. Why not let the British do it for you? Their men need rescuing too, and if they fail we have a convenient scapegoat, no?'

'Could they even attempt such an operation so far from England?'

'The Malvinas?' Quintana said dryly.

'That was a full-scale military operation.'

'I know. But they have the capacity, believe me.'

'They might refuse.'

Quintana laughed. 'They are far too arrogant

to refuse. Particularly when it's pointed out – tactfully of course that their men's incompetence was responsible for the success of the kidnap attempt.'

'Was it?'

'They trained the unit who were supposed to be protecting Muñoz.'

Estrada thought about it. 'You said if they fail we have a scapegoat. What if they succeed?'

'We'd be no worse off. In fact, when I think about it, we'd be better off. Who will be able to claim the credit for bringing them in? You. What selflessness! All that ingenuity and effort, just to rescue your main opponent from the cartels. Everyone will be impressed.'

Estrada shook his head. 'I still think I'd rather have Muñoz in a box.'

Quintana was looking at his watch. 'It's 5 a.m. in London. No point in waking them up. You can talk to your favourite first thing in the morning.'

'OK,' the President agreed. 'Now go away and let me watch TV.'

With almost infinite patience Wynwood eased his head out through the top layer of fetid rubbish. For at least a minute he held the same position, not moving his head, eyes growing accustomed to the darkness, ears straining for any sounds of human activity. There seemed to be none. With the same patience he slowly swivelled his head. There was darkness all around. Tilting his head upwards he discovered, thankfully, that the stars he would need for navigation were still twinkling in a clear sky.

Still conscious of the need to make as little noise as possible, he eased himself out of the flank of the rubbish mountain and gingerly descended to the firmer ground around its base. To his surprise he could hardly smell it any more. Doubtless anyone else would be able to smell him a mile away.

There did not seem to be a shower handy.

He brushed himself off as best as he could, thinking it had been worth it. Several times over the last eight hours he had heard dogs not far off, but no dog alive would have been able to trail him through the *mélange* of smells in this place.

His watch, guaranteed to withstand two hundred metres of water – so useful for a time-conscious manta ray, Wynwood thought – had managed to survive one metre of Colombian refuse. It was four after four, which gave him around two hours more of darkness. He had decided against going back into Cali – there was just no way of knowing who could be trusted. No, it had to be Bogotá, where at least the presence of embassies induced a notional sense of one law for everyone. And anyway, it was on the way home to Blighty.

So which way? Memory told Wynwood that Malverdes was north-north-west of the city centre, and that the main north road out of Cali actually ran due north-east across the valley before heading due north along the bottom of the mountains. So, eight kilometres north would take him clear of the city, then the same distance east should bring him to that road. Sixteen kilometres in two hours should not be beyond him, not travelling as light as he was. Keeping one eye on the Pole Star, which nestled close to the horizon this far south, he started wending his way through the valley of rubbish.

It covered another two kilometres before giving way to a stretch of bare hillside presumably earmarked as an extension. Beyond this he found himself pushing through steeply sloping cornfields, the tumbledown shacks of their owners often visible as a dim square of black in the valley below. These in turn gave way to less broken slopes, mostly bare, which reminded him, in the dark at least, of the Brecon Beacons.

For once his SAS training seemed almost too apt. His thoughts went back to that day in Initial Training almost ten years before, crawling on all fours through the trench filled with water and sheeps' intestines and God knew what else. At the end of that day they had pulled the trick of having the waiting lorries drive off just when you thought the agony was over. He had been almost swinging his arm back to belt the officer when someone else had beaten him to it. And had of course been RTU'd – Returned To Unit. Not SAS material.

Wynwood grinned to himself. First the Brecon Beacons, then Mount Kent in the Falklands campaign, now the fucking Andes. Next year, Nepal!

He walked on, gradually swinging his line of march east of north and downhill. Over the next few kilometres he crossed several small dirt roads, passed many small homesteads and one larger-looking *estancia*, reaching the shallow banks of the River Cauca at almost exactly 05.30. To the east he thought he could make out the faintest seepage of light above the mountains. Full daylight was less than an hour away.

As he sat on his haunches a light crossed his line of vision to the east. A car or truck. As he watched another glow moved in the opposite direction. It had to be the main highway, three kilometres away at most.

Wynwood slid into a river for the second time that night. This one seemed even colder, but the current was leisurely, and he had no difficulty traversing its thirty metres with the two guns held above his head. After examining the lie of the land on the far side – an orchard stretching off into the distance – he left the guns on the bank and went back into the water to thoroughly wash himself and his clothes.

He climbed out feeling a lot cleaner. Hot water would have been nice, not to mention a bar of soap, but beggars can't be choosers. Especially after dark in Colombia. He picked up the two guns, thought for a moment, then turned and hurled the MP5 up and out into the centre of the river. It was just a trifle conspicuous for daylight.

A long walk up through orchards and more cornfields eventually brought him to the side of the highway. He waited in the half-light for a few minutes, watching two cars, one bus and one truck go by, then hurried across and up the opposite slope. While the invisible sun rose beyond the mountains he followed a course out of sight of, but parallel to, the highway. After about five kilometres he found what he was looking for – a roadside eating-place. On the slope above it he stripped, laid his clothes out to dry in the sun, and settled down to wait and watch. It was just past nine o'clock.

In London it was already four in the afternoon. Barney Davies was not sorry to leave the house in Bloomsbury where his wife, their three children and her new husband were celebrating Boxing Day. In fact the mixture of polite chatter, unserious drinking and repressed anger was likely to give celebration a bad name. It was all for the kids, of course, and predictably enough they had shown their appreciation of this sacrificial get-together by disappearing into the remotest corners of the house. Happy families.

It was a cold day, and not exactly bright, but the clouds were high enough to ward off a depressing gloom. And at least it was a pleasure to drive through London's near-deserted streets. The city had an almost post-holocaust feel to it – all that was really needed was a few cars skewed across the pavement, the odd body.

You cheerful bastard, Davies told himself, guiding the BMW down the half-empty Strand. He wondered if any more news of Joss and Andy had come in, and whether their disappearance was the reason he had been summoned to the Whitehall conference room. He would soon find out.

He parked off Horse Guards Road and walked through the maze of buildings and covered walkways towards the back of Downing Street. His pass was examined three times, the final time by a doorkeeper who recognized him from his last visit. That had been several years ago, and his lads had ended up taking back an African country for its rightful government. Whatever that might be in Africa.

He climbed the stairs to Conference Room B, wondering, as last time, where Conference Room

A might be. Two men he did not know were already sitting on one side of the table. Unlike him they were wearing suits and ties. He smiled at them and sat down. Half a minute later a more familiar figure arrived – one of the Foreign Office ministers, Davies knew, though he could not remember the name. And on his heels the Prime Minister, who treated them all to a wide smile and a hint of gardenia.

She took her seat at the head of the rectangular walnut table, and introduced everyone. Across from Davies were Pennington (young and studious-looking, from the Foreign Office's Latin America section) and Spenser (fair and harassed-looking, from MI6). The tall, patrician man he had recognized was Alan Holcroft, a junior minister at the Foreign Office.

'And you all know who I am,' the Prime Minister added without apparent humour.

'Very well,' she went on, 'I'm sorry to have to drag you all in here on Boxing Day' – she looked about as sorry as a cat with a bowl of fresh cream, Davies thought – 'but something has come up that requires immediate attention. All of you, except perhaps Lieutenant-Colonel Davies here' – she gave him a brief smile – 'have some idea of what this is about, but for the Lieutenant-Colonel's sake I'll summarize what we know for certain at this moment. Please correct me if I make any mistakes.'

She glanced around, as if daring anyone to show such temerity.

'Two of Lieutenant-Colonel Davies's men, Sergeants Wynwood and Anderson, both I believe of 22 SAS's Training Wing . . .?' She gave him a questioning look.

'That is correct,' Davies agreed. So it was about Joss and Andy.

'These two men have been on secondment in Colombia, training a new Anti-Narcotics Unit at the express invitation of the Colombian President. As you know, this is the sort of job the SAS has fulfilled, with great success, in many parts of the world over the last thirty years. And of course it's in all our interests to strengthen the forces fighting against the drug trade in South America.'

She paused for breath. 'Their ten-week term of secondment was due to end this coming weekend. However, yesterday – Christmas Day – they accompanied the Anti-Narcotics Unit on an operation. This had nothing to do with drugs apparently – it involved ensuring the security of a prominent politician' – she checked the memorandum in front of her – 'one Carlos Muñoz, at a meeting in the town of Cali. This meeting was attacked, either by guerrillas or gangsters of the drug trade, and at least fifteen people have been killed. Muñoz and the two SAS men were apparently not among them. They have simply disappeared, and the presumption is that they have been kidnapped.

'Are there questions at this stage?' she asked.

'What do we know about this Muñoz?' Holcroft asked his minion from the Latin American section.

Pennington adjusted his glasses and started off on what seemed a prepared speech. 'He is a prominent member of the Colombian Liberal Party, and the signs are that he intends to challenge Juan Estrada, the current national President, for their Party's nomination for the next Presidential election this summer. He's a liberal with a small "l" too, almost a social democrat by Colombian standards, so he's critical of the current Government, and he's also talked a lot about the need for stronger action against the drug cartels. In fact, more than once he's hinted at high-level connections between the current Government and the cartels . . .'

'How do the Americans feel about him?' Holcroft interrupted.

'Er . . . That's hard to say. They distrust him because he's rather left-wing, but they like his anti-drug stance, so . . .'

'So they haven't got a clue,' Holcroft half sneered.

The Prime Minister frowned at him.

'If he's such a threat why wasn't he simply killed?' the MI6 man asked Pennington.

'He may have been by now. But there's a long history of kidnapping politicians for ransom in Colombia. They – whoever they are – may just want money. Or they may want to use possession of Muñoz as a means of exerting pressure on his liberal friends.'

'And our SAS men?' the Prime Minister asked, taking the words out of Davies's mouth.

'Again they may simply want money. Or perhaps they intend to use the SAS men as bargaining counters. We have several minor cartel people in prison here. They may want them released.'

'Well, they can forget that idea,' the Prime Minister said, half to herself. 'Thank you, Mr Pennington. Now, there is one further fact of which you are all unaware. This afternoon, an hour or so after the first news had come through from our embassy in Bogotá, I received a personal call from the Colombian President. He expressed his regrets, but doubted whether the forces at his disposal would prove equal to the task of rescuing either Muñoz or our men . . .'

'That seems likely,' Pennington muttered.

'. . . and then, well, not to put too fine a point on it, he invited us' – her glance came to rest on Davies – 'to go and get our men back ourselves.'

'What?' Holcroft half spluttered.

She shot him a withering glance. 'Before we ask whether this *should* be done, I'd like an opinion on whether it *could* be done. Lieutenant-Colonel Davies?'

All Davies's military instincts revolted against giving a snap judgement. He knew next to nothing about either Colombia in particular or South America in general. But he also knew this was a crucial moment, that the Prime Minister expected a yes, perhaps even needed one to get the possibility past people like Holcroft. And damn it, if anyone could do it, 22 SAS could.

These thoughts occupied about two seconds. 'Yes, it could be done,' he said. 'With one obvious proviso – we'd have to know where they're being held.'

'What base would you use?' Holcroft asked.

'Belize,' Davies said, almost without thinking. It was probably close enough. If not, they would have to think again. But in the ops room at Hereford, not in Conference Room B with the PM looming over the table.

'Will finding them prove a problem?' the Prime Minister was asking the MI6 man.

'Hard to say,' he said diffidently. 'We have a reasonable network in Colombia, and our friends have an even better one.'

'I wouldn't like to be the one to tell the Americans we're envisaging military action in Colombia,' Holcroft said.

The Prime Minister stared at her memorandum

for a few seconds. 'Very well,' she said at last. 'Let us assume it could be done. What do we risk and what do we potentially gain, apart from the rescue of our men, by trying? Alan, could you describe the risks. Then perhaps Mr Pennington could describe the potential gains.' She smiled at the latter, as if to encourage him.

Holcroft was silent for a moment, wondering, Davies guessed, how to present his case in the light most likely to please his boss. 'I don't wish to cast doubts on our forces' ability to overcome the military problems inherent in such an operation,' the Foreign Office man began, 'but I have to point out that the perils of failure would be immense. For one thing we would look like a colonial power all over again, undoing all the good repair work our people have done in Latin America since the Falklands. The cost in trade would probably be severe . . .'

'Even if we're there by invitation?' the MI6 man asked.

'It won't be by *public* invitation,' Holcroft said acidly. 'I repeat, the trade consequences will be severe. Secondly, our relations with the Americans will be damaged whatever happens. Latin America is *their* backyard, and they never forget it. If we inform them of any upcoming operation it will probably be leaked, and if we don't they'll accuse us of not even having the courtesy to tell them when we're trespassing on their turf.'

He leant back in his chair. 'I need hardly add that we will be risking the lives of many soldiers for the sake of two men whose lives, as far as we know at this moment, are not in immediate danger.'

The Prime Minister nodded. 'Mr Pennington?'

'I agree with everything Mr Holcroft has just said,' he started diplomatically. 'However, Colombia is potentially one of our most important trading partners in South America, and gaining the goodwill of the next President – whether it be Estrada or Muñoz – would be worthwhile in this respect. If successful, the operation would add to the prestige of both Britain and the SAS. The latter, if I may put it so' – he glanced almost apologetically at Davies – 'is a saleable commodity in its own right these days, and new demonstrations of prowess and efficiency make it more so. I realize such an operation won't be front-page news, but I imagine those who matter will hear of it. And, with all due respect' – another nod in Davies's direction – 'the same can be said of what appears to be yesterday's failure . . .'

'Señor Estrada seemed to hold the same opinion,' the Prime Minister said dryly.

Pennington shrugged. 'As for the Americans, such an operation would doubtless irritate some of them, but I think the added respect we'd get from others would probably more than compensate.' He too leant back in his chair.

'Do you have anything to add, Mr Spenser?' the Prime Minister asked.

'No.'

'I do,' she said. 'I think the successful conduct of such an operation would increase our respect for ourselves. But, we cannot reach a final decision at this moment. In the meantime – Mr Spenser, please get your people in Colombia moving. Thank you, gentlemen, that is all.' She got to her feet. 'If you could stay behind, Lieutenant-Colonel Davies.'

Davies looked at the framed picture of a tea schooner as the others filed out. In Victorian times Palmerston would just have sent a gunboat, he thought to himself. Nowadays they'd send the SAS. It felt desperately old-fashioned, and it made him feel proud just the same.

'Lieutenant-Colonel . . . Barney,' she corrected herself with a smile. 'Start planning. And assume it's on unless and until I tell you it's off.'

'Yes, Ma'am,' Davies said to her disappearing back.

He walked thoughtfully back to his car, and sat staring out through the windscreen at the tops of the bare trees in St James's Park. 'Hereford!' he said suddenly to himself. He'd ring the kids on the car phone once he was on the M40. It was only a couple of hours since he had seen them – they would still remember who he was.

Joss Wynwood, now dressed in dry clothes, albeit ones that looked like they had been danced on by horses, carefully descended the hill beyond the roadside restaurant, taking care to keep whatever tree cover there was between him and the back windows. For three hours he had been waiting and watching a long line of trucks pull into the parking area, and at last one had parked in the exact place which he had been hoping for.

Reaching the foot of the hill Wynwood found he had got his angles right. Anyone crossing the ground between the trees and the truck's cab could not be seen from the restaurant's windows. He walked swiftly across, found the cab door open, and slid into the sleeping space behind the two seats.

About twenty minutes later the driver returned, opening the door and pausing to belch loudly before climbing up into the driving seat. He pulled the door to, belched again, rather more softly, and caught sight of Wynwood in the his rear-view mirror.

'*Qué*?!' he exclaimed, turning round angrily. '*Qué* . . .?' he started again, breaking off abruptly when he saw the Browning.

'I need a lift,' Wynwood said softly in Spanish.

'Sure, sure,' the driver said, his hand reaching almost involuntarily for the door. 'But please, no guns.'

'If you open the door I shall shoot you,' Wynwood said steadily. 'Now start the engine, and let's go.'

'Yes, yes. Where? Where do we go?'

'Where are you headed?' Wynwood asked.

A look of cunning flashed across the driver's face. 'Cali,' he said. 'Cali.'

'You just came from Cali,' Wynwood said patiently. 'You're going north. Where to?'

'Ibagué.'

'That will do fine. Drive. In the meantime . . .' He reached past the Colombian for the paper bag. 'I think my need is greater than yours.'

'If you are hungry I can go back for more.'

'Nice try, bozo. Drive.'

'I am Manuel,' the driver said indignantly.

'Figures,' said Wynwood.

'*Qué*?'

'Drive!'

Manuel pulled the truck out onto the highway.

'Jesus, she's gorgeous!' Kilcline almost groaned.

'You could say that,' Bourne agreed, licking the Guinness head off his upper lip and following his partner's gaze. Its object was sitting at a table on the other side of the Slug and Pellet: a girl in her late teens with pale skin and lipstick which matched her billowing dark-red hair. Her black dress seemed to be unravelling at both ends, revealing extra yardage of both creamy breast and black-tighted thigh with each subtle shift of position.

'Jesus!' Kilcline repeated. He was on his fourth pint and it was beginning to show. The Killer just could not take his drink like he used to, Bourne thought. Which was hardly surprising: their wives only let them out like this on Boxing Days.

Kilcline groaned again, causing the girl to flash him a smile.

'Down, boy!' Bourne said, but he need not have bothered. The girl's boyfriend, a large and probably harmless oaf, had had enough. He approached their table, looking like a wing forward come to investigate a suspicious ruck.

He leaned forward across the table, hands palm down, his face no more than a foot away from Kilcline's. 'You want a photograph, grandad?' he said with a startling lack of originality.

Kilcline smiled at him. 'Naked?' he asked.

The boy's face tightened still further. 'OK,' he sneered. 'I know you're probably too old to get it up any more, but I think I'm gonna kick the shit out . . .' His friend was tugging at his sleeve. 'What?!'

'We need to talk,' the friend told him, offering Bourne and Kilcline the hint of an apologetic smile.

'Now?!'

'Yes, now!' He pulled him away.

'I'll be back in a minute,' he snarled over his shoulder.

'Mine's a pint of Dark Star,' Kilcline shouted after him.

'Why do boys that age think boys our age are beyond sex?' Bourne asked himself out loud. The letters 'SAS' could be heard in the conversation taking place across the bar.

'I'm almost inclined to kick the shit out of him anyway,' Kilcline mused. 'I don't like being called grandad.'

'You'll be one in a few months.'

'Maybe, but I've only been forty for a few weeks, and I could still wrap that shithead round a lamppost.'

'That's what they've just told him,' Bourne observed. The offended party, friends and girlfriends were on their way out, all eyes on the door, save for the vision in red and black, who could not resist giving them a farewell smile.

'I was enjoying that,' Kilcline said.

'It's called voyeurism,' Bourne said. 'She's a lot younger than your daughter.'

'So was Lolita.'

'How's the other one?'

'The other daughter? Oh, Kate's fine – she won a couple of medals last weekend at the county championship. Four hundred metres and long jump. It's the West of England next. I think she could go all the way.'

'Sounds good. And Jill?'

'I thought wives were out of bounds on this occasion.' He sighed. 'She's fine – sent her love. How's Lynn?'

'Same. Are we getting old, do you think?'

'Yes, grandad. One more for the road, I think . . . Same again?'

Bourne nodded, and watched his friend shoulder his way through the scrum to the bar. Nearly twenty years they had known each other. They had met in Oman, high on the Jebel Massif in the middle of an operation against the *adoo* terrorists. Kilcline had been working his way through every known Elvis song at the time, and if the *adoo* had not shot him his own side probably would have. It was not a serious injury though, and through later months of fly-blown boredom they had become good friends. Both had spent three terms in the SAS before returning to their original units – in his case the Royal Signals, in Kilcline's the Royal Engineers – and they had wound up back together in the SAS, both Majors, commanding the Counter Revolutionary Warfare and Training Wings respectively. Bourne still preferred Otis Redding to Elvis, but otherwise they got on pretty well.

Kilcline was on his way back, when Bourne felt

a hand on his shoulder. For a second he thought it was the oaf come back, but it wasn't.

'This is the fifth pub I've tried,' Barney Davies said, sitting down.

'Hi, boss,' Bourne greeted him, with that lack of formality which characterized most SAS conversations between ranks.

'What would you like, boss?' Kilcline asked, placing the pints of Guinness and Dark Star on the table.

'Nothing, thanks,' Davies said. 'I need to talk to you both.' He looked round. 'But not here. Can I invite you back to my place? For a coffee perhaps,' he added, watching Kilcline's difficulty in completing the journey from upright to seated.

'Now?' Bourne asked.

'Yes, if you don't mind.'

It was not exactly a request, and within a minute they were emerging from the pub into the cold air, then diving into the warmth of the CO's BMW. Jazz came on with the ignition, and no one spoke during the ten-minute drive to his cottage on the western outskirts of the town.

Davies deposited them in the living room, apologized for there being no fire – 'I've just got back from London' – and went out to the kitchen to make coffee. Kilcline and Bourne exchanged glances. 'What the fuck's happened?' Kilcline murmured.

'I expect he'll tell us when you're sober enough.'

'I'm not that pissed!'

Davies came back with three mugs of black coffee and a packet of sugar. 'Right,' he said, sitting down. 'Sergeants Wynwood and Anderson have gone AWOL in Colombia. Probably kidnapped. At least, we hope so because if they haven't been then they're probably dead.' He stirred two spoonfuls of sugar into his coffee.

Bourne and Kilcline waited for him to continue, suddenly feeling much soberer.

Davies recounted what was known of the events in Cali.

'I don't suppose the Government are going to *do* anything about this,' Kilcline said bitterly.

'That was my expectation,' Davies agreed, 'but for once we may be wrong. The possibility of action *was* discussed.' He went over the political arguments that had been put for and against. 'As far as I could tell the PM is determined that we should take action. She told me the rescue operation – *our* rescue operation – would be on until such time as she called it off . . .'

'That's great,' Bourne said.

'Brilliant,' Kilcline agreed.

'Yes, but I also got the feeling that she's going to need all the help she can get. The Foreign Office don't like the idea – that was obvious enough – and God knows what the Cabinet will say, if she ever puts it to them. I think she'd like a little help . . . What do the Israelis call it when they plant a few more settlements on the West Bank? – "establishing facts". The more "on" we make this, the harder it'll be for anyone to call it off.'

For a moment there was silence.

'A four-man team inserted by land, right away,' Bourne said, as if to himself. 'Then anything up to a couple of dozen troops for insertion by air, depending on what the ground team reports back.'

'Sounds good,' Davies said. 'Now go home and get some sleep, both of you. I want something on my desk by noon tomorrow.'

The road ahead seemed clear of both other traffic, houses and possible phones. The last sign had announced that Ibagué was only eight kilometres away. 'Pull over,' Wynwood said.

'Why?' Manuel wanted to know.

'Just do it.'

The truck shuddered to a halt. Manuel looked distinctly nervous.

'Do you know the bus station in Ibagué?' Wynwood asked him.

'Of course. It is my town. I will take you to it,' he added eagerly.

'No. I'm afraid this is where we part company.'

'You are leaving?' the Colombian asked hopefully.

'No, you are. I'm afraid you're going to have to walk the rest of the way.'

'*Qué*?!'

'It's not far.' He reached into his pocket, and counted out the peso equivalent of twenty pounds, which he guessed would be a week's wages to someone like Manuel. 'This is for your trouble,' he said. 'Of course if I'm arrested I'll have to tell them I gave it to you,' he added, hoping that would prove a sufficient deterrent should Manuel find a phone round the next corner.

'But my truck!' the Colombian protested.

'I'll leave it as close to the bus station as I can,' Wynwood promised. 'Now out!'

Manuel got reluctantly to the ground, and looked up woefully at Wynwood as he slammed the truck into gear. Glancing in the rear-view mirror as he pulled back onto the road Wynwood could see the Colombian busily counting the money.

It was beginning to grow dark now, and the lights actually flickered on beside the road as he drove in through the outskirts of Ibagué. They had come less than three hundred and twenty kilometres in eight hours, but like every cross-country Colombian journey Wynwood had ever taken, it had seemed like there was a mountain to cross every couple of kilometres, and most of them seemed at least that high.

He parked the truck as promised, no more than a hundred metres from the bus station, bought a ticket for Bogotá on the fast night bus and found a table at the back of an anonymous-looking restaurant. Steak, cassava and potatoes restored his sense of well-being, and over a large cup of coffee he thought about Susan for the first time that day.

Damn the woman! He wondered where and how Anderson was. A phone on the wall suggested the possibility of calling the embassy in Bogotá and finding out, not to mention telling someone he was alive himself, but the risk, though probably minimal, did not seem worth taking. He would be in the capital by six in the morning and, if he had any say in the matter, on a plane for home not many hours after that.

# 2

A freight train rumbled across the North London Line girder bridge as Eddie Wilshaw jogged towards it along the River Lea towpath. The diesel wore a different livery from that of his childhood train-spotting days, but he still recognized it as a Class 47. The train was probably on its way from the freight terminal at Felixstowe to the marshalling yard at Willesden.

It was strange what crap the brain kept filed away, he thought, passing under the bridge. A couple of hundred metres ahead of him three black youths were standing in a circle astride the path, apparently deep in conversation with each other.

Eddie wondered. This stretch of the towpath between Carpenter's Road and the Eastway was notorious for muggings and – if you were female – worse. There was no exit between the two roads, just the canalized river on one side, high wire fences on the other. There weren't even any homes overlooking the river, just grimy industrial premises. If he were the nervous type, Eddie thought to himself, he would do a rapid U-turn and get the hell out of there.

As it was, he had never really been afraid of anyone in his life, and two and a half years in the SAS had done nothing to undermine such confidence. He jogged on, wondering if the boys on the path ahead had suffered a worse Christmas than he had.

He was twenty metres away when the tallest of the youths turned in his direction. A long, unbuttoned black trenchcoat revealed red baggy trousers and a bright-green sweater. Dreadlocks spilled out of a Rasta beret to frame a handsome face. The mouth broke into a wide smile. 'Edward, my man!'

Eddie laughed. 'Lloyd, my man,' he echoed, offering his palms for the ritual greeting.

'These is Martin and Stokely,' Lloyd said, introducing the others, who nodded without much enthusiasm. 'You still defending the British Empire?' Lloyd asked.

'You still worshipping a dead Ethiopian president?'

'I reckon,' Lloyd said, smiling. 'You home for Christmas?'

'Yeah. See my dad, you know.'

'He still live in Keir Hardie?' Lloyd asked, looking back over his shoulder at the tower blocks rising beyond the Eastway bridge.

'Yeah. There's no way he can get out.'

'No job?'

'You're kidding. My dad was unemployed when there was full employment.'

Lloyd laughed.

'How're you doing?' Eddie asked.

'Not too bad, you know.' He waved one hand in the air, seemed about to say something, but decided against it.

He was realizing his friends were uncomfortable, Eddie thought. 'I'll see you around,' he said.

'Yeah. Hey, there's a party tonight, at Brian's. Brian Richards – you remember him? Why don't you come? Two-four-five Graham Road.'

'Dalston?'

'Yeah.'

'I might well.' He probably would – anything was better than another evening in front of the TV with his stoned father.

'Right, man, we'd gotta be going,' Lloyd said, giving him another huge smile. The other two were already walking on. 'See you tonight.'

'Yeah.' Eddie stood there for a minute, then turned and broke into a jog, then slowed to a halt again. He had had enough exercise for one morning, and had no great desire to be back at his dad's flat. Instead he walked on, under the Eastway and Homerton Road, before turning off onto the vast grassy expanse of Hackney Marshes. He found a seat and sat down, staring across the river at the tower block he had once lived in, along with his parents and sister.

Clare was long gone, all the way to Epping with her solicitor wanker of a husband. And his mother had died three years ago, just before he had been tested for the SAS. So now there was just him and his dad, two males who had never known how to talk to each other and never would. Football was their only mutual topic of conversation, and since both of them were Tottenham supporters that tended to be just one long moan.

Which reminded him. Yesterday the stupid bastards had thrown away a two-goal lead in the last four minutes. He thought about Lloyd Walker. The two of them had gone to both primary and secondary school together. Lloyd's family had also lived in Keir Hardie, three floors further up. His father had been a porter at Homerton Hospital, probably still was. Assuming – a big assumption these days – that the hospital was still there.

He and Lloyd had really become friends because they had shared a secret – each knew the other was clever. It was not the sort of thing you wanted spread around, not in Homerton Grove Comprehensive. It got you resented, the way being good at football or good with your fists did not.

If you were clever you hid it well, sometimes even from yourself.

Despite everything Eddie could have gone on to higher education. He had managed enough 'O' levels to get into a Sixth Form College, and after eighteen months there he had landed interviews at several universities. At the first of these he had found himself in front of two snotty wankers who wanted his views on multiculturalism. That had not been so bad – at least he had wiped the smiles off their faces – but a cup of tea in the student canteen afterwards had killed any scholastic ambition he had. A group of students – middle class, every last one of them – had been arguing about politics in general and the causes of poverty in particular. He had listened, with interest at first, and then with growing anger. The conversation was full of long words and complex sociological theories, but it had not made him feel inferior. On the contrary, it had made him realize that he had already learnt more about the real world growing up in Hackney than this bunch were likely to do in their whole lives. He had taken the train back to London, spent the weekend brooding about it, and on Monday morning walked through the doors of the Army Recruiting Office that he had so often sneered his way past.

The Welsh Guards had taken him on. Three

years later he had made it into the SAS. And he had not regretted a minute of it.

Wynwood's bus pulled in to Bogotá's central bus station soon after seven in the morning. He had not had much sleep, but there had been no major scares either. The one military roadblock had been manned by soldiers who seemed more asleep than he was, and once again the habit of carrying his passport with him at all times had proved its worth.

He clambered stiffly down to the ground and went looking for a coffee in the bus station. Two cups and a stale pastry later he found a telephone that worked. It seemed to ring for ever. Didn't the goddamn embassy have a twenty-four-hour answering service? At last someone picked it up. Wynwood asked for the Military Attaché.

'Who's calling?' the voice asked.

'Wynwood's the name,' he said.

'Hold on, please,' the voice said. With rather more interest, Wynwood thought.

Another voice appeared. 'Sergeant Wynwood?' it asked.

'Yeah, look . . .'

'Where are you?'

'The bus station . . .'

'In Bogotá?'

'Yeah.' Who was this moron?

'Are you OK?'

'I'm still standing.'

'Is Sergeant Anderson with you?'

'No. Why. . .?'

'When did you last see him?'

'About thirty-six hours ago. In gali.'

'Right. Can you call again in fifteen minutes, please?'

'What!? Look . . .'

The line had gone dead.

Kilcline strode into Bourne's office with a wide grin on his face. 'Wynwood's OK,' he said. 'He's in Bogotá.'

'Fantastic!' Bourne agreed. 'But no sign of Anderson?'

Kilcline perched himself on the corner of Bourne's desk. 'No, it looks like Andy's in the bag. Still, one's a bloody sight better than none. How are you doing?' he asked, surveying the various files and books strewn across Bourne's desk.

'Not bad. There's only one real problem, as far as we can see. Getting them out.'

'Not an insignificant part of the operation.'

Bourne smiled sardonically. 'No.'

'What are the options?'

'Helicopters off a British carrier, helicopters out of Panama or off a US carrier, helicopters out of a Colombian airfield.'

'You seem to have a helicopter fixation,' Kilcline said.

'I suppose they could walk to Brazil,' Bourne added sarcastically.

'OK, I just don't like helicopters.'

'I'm not that fond of them myself,' Bourne conceded, his mind going back, as it too often did, to the nightmare minutes that had followed the crash in San Carlos Water seven years before. Both he and Kilcline had survived – many friends had not. And all because some stupid bird had chosen to commit hara-kiri in the rotor blade.

'Is there any British carrier available?' Kilcline asked.

'Nope. At least not in the timespan we're looking at. And anyway we could hardly send one through the Panama Canal without attracting attention.'

'American?'

'Probably not, and in any case it's not an attractive option. For one thing it would put them right in the picture, with all that would do for security . . .'

'What security?'

'Exactly. For another, it wouldn't fit too well with the PM's DIY approach to sorting out the world. And lastly, they'd probably turn us down anyway. Or spend so long thinking through the diplomatic collaterals that Anderson would have died of old age before we got to him.'

'The Colombian airfield.'

'Yeah,' Bourne sighed. 'It all depends on the sort of guarantees we could get. And I don't just mean from the Colombian Government. I want to hear from whatever security people we have out there. I'd want *them* to say we can trust the military.'

'There must be some good guys in the Colombian military, or why were Joss and Andy out there in the first place?'

Bourne shrugged. 'The problem is knowing who they are. Still, if we get some satisfaction there, then the logistics aren't a problem. The Colombians can provide the transport, and ride shotgun if they think it's necessary. And there won't be any range problem.'

'What about insertion?'

'Depends on the terrain, but probably HAHO out of a Hercules from Belize.'

Kilcline nodded. 'No word of where yet?'

'Nope. Are those the files on Anderson and Wynwood?'

'Yep.' He passed them across.

'I'll bring 'em back over when I've read them,' Bourne said, 'and ask you any questions then. OK?'

'Sure.'

Kilcline disappeared, and Bourne started working his way through the top file. Richard Anderson was twenty-nine, and a Staff Sergeant in the

Training Wing. His primary area of expertise was engineering, but he also specialized in weaponry, signalling, and was reasonably fluent in Spanish.

Impressive, Bourne thought.

Anderson had served in the Falklands as a para, winning a mention in dispatches for Goose Green, and joined the SAS the following year. He had several tours of service in Northern Ireland, and had been one of the back-entrance team in Operation Nimrod – the breaking of the Iranian Embassy occupation. He had just begun his third three-year term with promotion to his current rank.

After completing his second tour in Ulster he had undergone a brief course of psychiatric counselling. Successfully.

His background was middle class: the third son of a Congregationalist minister in Southport. He had attended a minor public school, joining the Parachute Regiment straight from there at eighteen. He was now married with two children, one of each gender. His hobbies were listed as rugby, cricket, motorcycles, opera and stamp-collecting.

Bourne closed the file. Given that the man was being held in God-knew-what conditions the reference to counselling was somewhat worrying. Though of course it could work the other way. The people who survived best in such circumstances were usually those who knew themselves best.

Maybe Anderson had learnt something about himself.

The photograph showed a pale-skinned Germanic face with rapidly thinning hair. Joss Wynwood's, by contrast, showed a face torn between rugged and cheeky, with almost twinkling brown eyes peering out from a mass of dark, curly hair. He was thirty-two, and also a Staff Sergeant in the Training Wing, now approaching the end of his third term in the SAS.

His first major action had been as a member of the three-man team sent into the Gambia to rescue the deposed President's family in 1981. He had served with the Regiment in the Falklands, taking part in both the recapture of South Georgia and the Long Yomp from San Carlos to Port Stanley. Since then he had done the usual tours in Ireland, without, Bourne noted, any need for psychiatric counselling. He was married too, but without children. His hobbies were rugby, photography and music. A nice mixture, Bourne thought. Somehow he had confidence in Wynwood.

He gathered up the files, left the office and building, and walked through the sunlight to the adjoining building where the Training Wing administration was housed. Kilcline was gazing moodily out of his window. 'Wish I was going,' he said to no one in particular.

'Yes, grandad,' Bourne said, placing the files on

Kilcline's desk and taking a seat. 'Tell me, should I be worrying about the fact that Anderson had psychiatric counselling?'

'I've been thinking about that, and I'm not sure. I don't think so. You won't find a cooler man under pressure, but he does tend to bottle things up. He had nightmares for a long time after his second tour in Ireland – couldn't express what was getting to him any other way.' He paused. 'I guess a lot depends on how he's being treated. It sounds crazy, but I'd say he'll hang together better if he's treated badly. Within limits, of course.' He looked up. 'But does it really matter – you've only got to drag him out and throw him into a helicopter, haven't you?'

Bourne sighed. 'I guess so.'

'Do I detect signs of compulsive perfectionism? Maybe *you* should have some psychiatric counselling.'

'Maybe I should,' Bourne agreed with a smile. 'Is Wynwood as together as he seems to be?'

'Pretty much. I can't think of anyone I'd rather have with me in the wilds of Colombia.'

'Good.' Bourne started to get up.

'Except . . .' Kilcline paused.

'What?'

'This is only hearsay, and it may have nothing to do anything, but his marriage seems to be in trouble.'

'Whose isn't?'

'Mine isn't. Neither's yours, you cynical bastard. I just have the feeling that – if it's true – Wynwood's someone who'd take it badly, that's all. It's just a feeling.'

'OK,' Bourne agreed. 'Thanks. I'll see you later.'

He walked back to his own office, where an orderly was placing four new files on his desk. Bourne looked through them, extracted one and handed it back to him. 'Even the SAS doesn't send men with broken legs on overseas missions,' he said.

'No, boss,' the orderly agreed and made a swift exit.

Bourne looked at the three photographs pinned to the front covers. The first showed a pleasantly ugly face, with blue eyes, fair hair and a large mouth. The expression was almost insolent. That was Trooper Edward Wilshaw.

The second showed a more compact face, with almost hooded dark eyes and short, straight, black hair. There was hardly any expression, just the hint of an embarrassed smile. That was Trooper Damien Robson.

The third showed a slightly Slavic face beneath spiky hair, smiling cheerfully at the camera as if he didn't have a care in the world. That was Corporal Chris Martinson.

They looked so young, Bourne thought.

* * *

Wynwood rang back twenty minutes later – it took him that long to find someone prepared to admit they had any change.

'Listen,' the same voice told him. 'Your partner's missing, probably kidnapped by one of the cartels. The Government's response – our Government's, that is – is still being discussed in London, and until we have some clearer idea what's going on we think you'd better not come to the Embassy. So we've got you a room at the Segovia Hotel on Carrera 7. It's paid for. Can you afford a taxi into the centre?'

'Yeah, just about.' He'd given most of his money to Manuel.

'I'll have some cash sent round. As soon as we know anything I'll let you know. OK?'

'I guess so . . .'

The line went dead again.

Chris Martinson raised the binoculars to his eyes and lowered them again. They were only redshanks on the distant mudflats; he thought he had caught a hint of green. Below him a posse of oyster-catchers were drawing crazy patterns in the mud; in the sky above a huge flock of Brent geese was swirling out towards Northey Island.

He remembered his great-grandfather's stories of the island, of the temperance colony which had settled there early in the century, and how a thriving local trade had grown up to supply the inhabitants with illicit liquor. 'You could hardly move at night for rowing boats crammed with bottles,' the old man had used to say, before cackling himself into a coughing fit.

At least, that was how Chris remembered it – his great-grandfather had died in 1969, aged ninety-two. Chris had been seven.

The sun was at its zenith now, the wide expanse of the Blackwater a piercing silver-blue. It was time to head home for lunch, though he was not sure he had room yet for another helping of his mother's cooking. Three days of overindulgence had left their mark.

He started walking along the path which followed the winding northern shore of the estuary towards Maldon. In the first couple of kilometres he encountered several family parties and a couple of lone men; all greeted him with a smile, echoing the day perhaps, but also the simple friendliness of country life. Whenever he was at home, and particularly on days like today when he was out walking, Chris offered a silent prayer of thanks for having grown up in a place like this.

Eddie had called it 'a mudflat too far', but then how would someone from Hackney know any better? He'd liked The Carpenters well enough, and given time . . . You couldn't understand the countryside by making day trips into it.

Chris's parents had not liked Eddie – that was certain enough. Too clever, they had thought; too pleased with himself. The killer had been the last argument with his father, and Eddie calling patriotism a heap of crap. Hearing something like that from one of the town's token socialists was one thing; getting it from an SAS man was another. It had not so much annoyed his father as shaken his sense of the world, Chris thought. Eddie had some strange views.

He did not like animals either, which Chris, who loved just about all of them without reservation, found almost stranger than strange. The two of them were so different in so many ways, yet they were friends. And it was not just being in the SAS together. There was something else they had in common, something about who they were which he could not put his finger on.

He would like a dog himself, he thought, as a couple with a huge golden retriever walked by in the opposite direction. But not for a few years yet. You could hardly keep a dog properly in the Army, and he intended to spend most of his annual leave outside England. The previous year he had blown most of his savings on a fortnight in Costa Rica, visiting all the wildlife reserves. It had been like heaven. So many different species of bird. Such beautiful colours. Six months later he was still revelling in mental flashbacks of the trip.

The best thousand pounds he had ever spent. The only thousand pounds he had ever spent. He had even got a Spanish proficiency mark on his skills dossier for his troubles.

Where could he go this year? He fancied Lapland, but it would probably be too expensive.

Another flock of Brent geese smudged the sky as he passed The Ship and started up the canal. He thought about Molly, and their date that evening. He had met her only three days before, at a Christmas Eve party in Goldhanger, but somehow he already expected something good. She was older than him, about thirty-four he guessed from things she had said, but what did a seven-year age gap mean these days?

One thing it meant was that he did not feel she needed him – or the 'relationship' – to make sense of the world for her, the way so many of the younger women he had known seemed to. And finding out that he was in the Army had not thrown her in either of the two usual directions. She had neither been impressed nor appalled – just taken it on board.

And she had let him talk. No, now he thought about it, she had actually encouraged him to talk. And having several pints inside him, he had obliged. About being in the Army, being in the SAS. 'I love it,' he had said. 'It stretches me.' And it did. Like nothing else he had ever come across. Stretched him physically, mentally, every which way.

'Are you married to it?' she had asked, and to his surprise he had realized that he was not. It had been his life for eight years, and would be for a few more yet, but it was not the limit of his ambition. Another five years perhaps, and then he would quit, spend a couple of years seeing all the wild places of the world while he was still young enough, find the few places people had not managed to fuck up yet. And he would not just be in the way: with the medical experience he had picked up in the Army he could make himself useful.

'I think you're the first man I've met who knows what he wants to do,' Molly had said. She had also had rather a lot to drink. It had not affected her kissing, though.

Chris smiled at the memory. It promised to be a good evening. He strode up Chilton Street, remembering his mother had asked him to buy bread.

Damien Robson – 'the Dame' to all his comrades in the SAS – inserted the last inch of Mars bar into his mouth and stared out of the Renault's window. The drizzle was still coming down – a cold drizzle – he imagined standing out there in the street would be like standing under a half-hearted cold shower. Which was almost attractive when you had been cooped up in a car seat for four hours with nothing to do but watch and wait.

It would be better if he was alone, but the guy from 14 Intelligence was sitting next to him, also eating a Mars bar. The Dame had already forgotten the man's second name – his first was Alan – but at least he had finally got the message and stopped trying to start conversations.

Through the drizzle the lights of the Turf Lodge estate were dimly visible above the roofs of the terraced houses on the other side of Kenneally Street. Out of sight, round the corner at the end of the street, two more 14 Intelligence men were sitting in a battered Fiat. Another three were staked out inside number 36, where the terrorist arms cache awaited collection.

And tonight was the night, according to some-one or other's tout. The Dame doubted it, but he was only playing the odds. For every successful stake-out he had been on in Northern Ireland, he had been on half a dozen wastes of time. And this was beginning to look like one of those.

A pair of young girls walked past on the pavement, laughing under their shared umbrella, apparently oblivious to the watchers in the car, though you could never be sure. In a few minutes they might be telling their Provo brothers that two suckers were asking for it in a Renault on Kenneally Street.

Or they might be watching *Coronation Street*, like his sisters back in Sunderland. Innocent people living innocent lives, no threat to anyone.

The Dame had to admit it though – he liked Belfast. He did not like working there, and he felt sorry for all the people who had to live with it the way things were, but just as a town, as a bunch of people, it reminded him of Sunderland. The same brick streets and derelict docks, the same smell of the sea on the breeze. Like Sunderland it sometimes felt a bit sorry for itself, but the people were not beaten, not really. They held their strength inside, only brought it out when they needed to. Which was the way it should be.

His companion nudged him, and pointed over his shoulder. In the rear-view mirror he could see a youngish man in a leather jacket making his way up the other side of the street. He did not recognize him.

'No,' he said.

'Our man's darker, right?' Alan asked.

'Yes. And older than that.' The Dame was only there, rather than sitting around the TV in Sunderland with his mother and sisters, because the year before he had been one of the few to clock a sight of – and live to remember – the Provo that the tout had claimed would be coming for the cache. His name was Eamonn O'Hanlon, and he was wanted for three murders and more kneecappings than anyone could count.

The Dame had almost been the fourth victim, and he was not about to forget O'Hanlon's face.

It was almost half-past eight – half-time at Filbert Street. Jesus, Sunderland could do with three points . . .

The sound of a motor accelerating drew his eyes to the rear-view mirror. A Toyota van was accelerating up the street, rather fast . . . If this was the men coming to pick up the Armalites surely they would be trying to look less conspicuous . . .

An explosion spun the Dame's head round. The air seemed to be full of flying objects, and number 36 was hidden by a billowing cloud of smoke. As he watched, a flowerpot, still containing its spider plant, landed right way up in the road ahead, and stood there shaking, as if traumatized by its flight.

The Toyota!

He turned his eyes right just at the moment it scraped past and round the front wing of the Renault, squealing to a halt almost dead in front of them, not five yards away, the back doors swinging open. The Dame threw himself down as two hooded figures were revealed, each holding a sub-machine-gun. The windscreen blew away and Alan sank back into his seat with a deep sigh.

The Dame extracted the Browning from its

cross-draw holster and waited for the sound of the Toyota moving away. It did not come. Instead there were footsteps.

He had less than a second to make a decision, but it was not difficult. To do nothing was to die.

Using one foot on the bottom of the nearside door as leverage, he pushed himself up and across the dead Alan, the Browning aiming out through the windscreen. Like a duck coming into the sight of a fairground rifle, aim and target came miraculously together. The Dame pressed the trigger twice in quick succession, and whirled the Browning round in search of the other target just as something seemed to hiss across the shoulder of his windcheater. The sounds of the terrorist's shots were still echoing when the Dame sent two bullets through the upper centre of his body.

A third man appeared around the side of the van, and disappeared just as quickly. The Dame could see nothing through the open back doors of the van, but he fired anyway, and thought he heard a cry of pain. The van roared away into the drifting smoke and disappeared.

Sirens seemed to be opening up from all directions. An ambush, he thought. An ambush within an ambush. The cache had been bait, planted over a bomb, which someone had detonated at exactly the right moment to disorientate those in the watching cars.

He wondered whether the occupants of the other car had been any quicker than Alan.

He checked the latter's heart just to make sure, then cautiously climbed out of the car. The two men he had shot were lying a few feet apart. Both were young – young as he was. The first had died instantly, the second had taken time to spill a trickle of blood onto the wet road.

Neither of them was Eamonn O'Hanlon.

'You look sharp,' Eddie's dad remarked from the living-room doorway.

'Yeah,' Eddie said, examining his tie-knot in the hallway mirror. 'What are you doing this evening?'

'Oh nothing. You know. There's a good film on the TV – one of the *Star Treks*. *Five*, I think. Not that it makes much difference.'

Eddie smiled at him. Behind his father he could see the papers, tobacco and dope tin all laid out on the arm of the sofa. 'Don't get busted while I'm out,' he said.

'Some chance,' his father said. 'They'd have to mend the lifts first.'

That was probably true, Eddie thought, as he walked down the seven floors to the ground. His dad's car, a second-hand Nissan Cherry, still had all its wheels. The local kids probably knew whose it was.

He pulled out into Glyn Road and headed west towards Mare Street. He had told his father the party started at eight, but one in the morning was more like it. First off he would have a decent meal in a wine bar he knew under the railway arches.

It was the third time he had been there over the furlough week and this time the waitress recognized him. She was quite small, with dark hair tied back in a bun, and a face that managed to be both decidedly European and vaguely oriental. And she had a lovely walk, Eddie thought, watching her cross the room.

He wondered what her name was.

He studied the menus, and decided on Chicken Chasseur with a Portuguese red. He could really get into wine, he thought. If he ever had any money, building up a good cellar would be really interesting.

The waitress took his order.

'Can I ask your name?' Eddie asked.

'Lisa,' she said. 'As in Mona.'

He liked that. When she brought the meal he asked her when she got off. Midnight, she said. And yes she did fancy a party. But he would have to put up with her dressed the way she was.

Eddie took his time with the bottle of wine, watching the other customers of the wine bar – mostly yuppie wankers as far as he could see – and enjoying Lisa's occasional passage across the room. He would put up with her dressed the way she was, he thought, but he would rather have her naked.

Who knows, he thought. He visited the men's toilet and found a condom machine that actually worked, which had to be a good omen.

She was not just sexy, he discovered on the way to the party. She was a student at Hackney College, planning on going round the world for a year when she was finished, and on an eventual career in some area of conservation.

Despite his fears the party was already in full swing when they arrived, and after sinking two glasses of wine in quick succession Lisa announced her desire to dance. They danced. First like dervishes, then like robots, finally in each other's arms.

She smelt good. Too good. He could feel an erection coming between them. So could she, and pulled him closer. They kissed for a while.

'Do you have a home we could go to?' she asked.

''Fraid not. Do you?'

She giggled. 'No. Can we go for a drive?'

'Sure.'

'I have to go somewhere first.'

He waited in the hall, looking around him. There was no sign of Lloyd, but maybe it was too early for him. The party seemed about seventy per cent black and thirty per cent white. But no Pakis, Eddie thought. They just did not mix, the Asians. Funny that – everyone had this bugbear about the blacks, the West Indians, but most of them were quite happy to be British. They were pissed off about being poor, not about being British. The Asians, on the other hand, just wanted to keep to themselves. Which pissed everyone else off.

'I'm ready,' Lisa said behind him.

It was cold outside now, and it took the car heater a while to warm up. Eddie drove east, her hand on his thigh.

'Where are we going?' she asked.

'Somewhere quiet?' he said. A tiny voice in his head told him she should not be putting herself at the mercy of a stranger like this. He would tell her so. Afterwards.

He found the industrial lane he knew, and drove to the end where a circular turning space fronted a corner of the Marshes. There was no one else there. Eddie had never been very enamoured of back-seat fucking, but Lisa made it a very pleasant experience. By this time the car heater had done its job, they had managed to strip each other of everything but socks, and Tina Turner's 'Steamy Windows' was playing in Eddie's head.

'I liked that,' she said, as they helped pull each other's trousers on.

'Yeah,' he agreed. Seeing her again would be nice, he thought. He had four more days to survive in Keir Hardie Tower. 'Where do you live?' he asked.

'Stoke Newington.'

'I'll take you home.'

'Oh.'

'I didn't mean it as an insult. I'd like to see you again. Soon.'

'Yeah, OK.'

They climbed back into the front seats.

'I don't do this all the time, you know,' she said.

'What?'

'What do you think? Fuck perfect strangers.'

'OK.'

'But I noticed you when you came in on Christmas Eve, and . . .'

'I'm glad.'

'What do you do, anyway?'

Eddie hesitated. He often lied at this point, because the true answer usually led the questioner to draw all the wrong conclusions about him. But this time he decided on being straight. 'I'm in the Army,' he said.

She said nothing.

He looked at her in the half-light. 'Surprised?' he asked.

'Yes,' she said.

'The Army's like most things,' he said. 'Everyone's different, and everyone's in it for a different reason.'

'What's yours?' she asked.

'I wanted to get away from Hackney,' he said. When he knew her better he could try and explain it properly.

She smiled. 'It'll take some getting used to,' she said. 'Most of the people I know think the Army's just a bunch of trained thugs.'

'They're wrong there,' Eddie said. 'We're *highly* trained thugs.' He started the engine, turned the car and slowly drove back down the lane to the road. 'Whereabouts in Stoke Newington?' he asked, wondering whether to tell her he was SAS. No, he decided.

She didn't seem too worried about his occupation, leaning her head on his shoulder all the way back to Shacklewell Lane, where she shared a first-floor room with another girl. He took down her telephone number, and they kissed with a tenderness which almost surprised him.

He took the drive back to Hackney slowly, realizing he had to be over the limit. He was nearly home, stopped at the lights on Chatsworth Road, when a familiar figure burst out of the road to his left, and stood, holdall in hand, looked wildly around, not five metres away.

'Lloyd!' he shouted.

His friend almost jumped out of his skin. The swelling whine of a siren suggested an explanation for the nervousness.

'Give us a lift, man?' Lloyd asked.

Eddie sighed. 'Get in,' he said.

Lloyd climbed in with alacrity, but still almost managed to fall out again as Eddie accelerated away up the road.

'What's in the bag?' he asked.

'Er, party things.'

'Try again.' The police car had swung round behind them.

'Just a few watches.'

'Shit!' Eddie gripped the wheel harder. 'OK, they're going out the window.'

'No, man . . .'

'Either the bag goes, or you and the bag. Choose.'

'All right man, don't get your white knickers in a twist.'

'Open the window. Once we're round the next corner.' They took it on squealing tyres. 'Here, look, there's a skip.'

Lloyd leant out and propelled the bag with perfect accuracy. 'Magic Johnson – eat your heart out,' he said exultantly, falling back into his seat.

Eddie took another tight turn, then another, then dramatically slowed down as he reached

Chatsworth Road again. Which was fortunate, because a police car was flagging them down.

'Evening, officer,' Eddie said.

The constable stared at him while another stared at Lloyd from the other side. 'Can I show you some ID?' Eddie asked, finger poised over his pocket.

'How kind,' the constable said sarcastically. 'Mind if we look in the back?'

'Not at all.'

The second constable had a look, while Eddie showed his 22 SAS identity card.

'One used condom on the floor,' the second constable reported.

'Couldn't you afford one each?' the first one said with a grin. 'Go on, get out of here.'

'I must have one of those magic cards printed,' Lloyd said as they drove off.

Eddie turned a corner and pulled over. 'Why don't you go robbing in Hampstead or somewhere like that?' he demanded.

'I'd get caught, brother, that's why.'

'You'll get caught here.'

'Yeah, I know. But a black boy gotta do what a black boy gotta do. We can't all play Lone Ranger for Queen and Cunt. And besides, if every poor black boy went over Hampstead it'd be like the Notting Hill Carnival every night of the week.'

Eddie smiled. 'Yeah, right. Have you ever considered planning anything?'

'I had the brick with me, didn't I?'

They both burst out laughing.

Eddie was still grinning as he began the climb to Flat 26, but somewhat less cheery when he let himself in. The TV was still on, the smell of marijuana thick on the air. His dad looked at him with glazed eyes. 'Message by the phone,' he said.

Eddie went and looked. 'Report Back Hereford Souness,' it said.

So either the Glasgow Rangers manager was getting messages, his dad could not spell 'soonest', or it was a joke.

There was a stoned giggle from the living-room.

# 3

Eddie's alarm went off at 7.30. He had a quick shower, and sat in the kitchen with a bowl of cereal and a cup of coffee. The whole flat still smelt of dope, but if he opened a window his dad would probably die of hypothermia. At ten to eight he switched on the local radio to get the weather forecast – clear but cold – and find out which BR and Underground lines were fucked that morning. The answer was none that he intended to use. At eight o'clock, with his father still snoring loudly in the bedroom, Eddie left a note saying 'Gone To War' on the kitchen table and started down the fourteen flights of stairs which led to the outside world.

It seemed deserted – as usual the people of Britain had decided that the period between Boxing Day and New Year's Eve was a national holiday. The trains were running though, and Eddie took the overland to Liverpool Street, changing there onto the Circle Line for Paddington. He arrived with more than half an hour to spare before the Hereford train, and was in the queue for a coffee in Casey Jones when a hand grabbed his shoulder.

He turned to find a familiar, cheery face. 'Christ, I thought they might want me for something important,' Eddie said. 'But if they want you as well . . .'

'Get me a coffee while I get my ticket,' Chris said. 'And watch my bag,' he added, dropping it within an inch of Eddie's foot.

'Yes, Corporal.'

'Bollocks,' Chris said over his shoulder.

He came back five minutes later. Eddie handed him his coffee.

Chris examined the cup, then the giver. 'Christ, you must have had a good Christmas. You look bloody awful.'

'Thanks. I didn't get much sleep last night, that's all. I'll kip on the train.'

'And why didn't you get much sleep?'

'I was deep in sexual ecstasy. There were these four nymphomaniacs – one blonde, one Chinese, one black and one Arab princess – and they were passing me round.'

'I expect they were all trying to get rid of you.'

Eddie laughed. 'How was yours? You don't look that good yourself.'

'I think I'm in love.'

Eddie groaned. 'Not again. Another simple peasant girl, is it? A shepherdess, something like that?'

'Something like that. She works at Essex University, some sort of admin job, I think. We didn't have much time for talking.'

'Well, country folks do speak slowly. Funny that – you'd think with a smaller vocabulary it'd be easier to find the right words, not harder.'

Chris eyed him with affection. 'Have you finished? Molly is about as slow up top as Nigel Mansell's gear-stick. And gorgeous.'

'Breasts like peaches?'

'Yep.'

'Thighs to die for?

'Yep.'

'And you're in love.'

'Yep.'

'How'd she take the news of your sudden departure?' Eddie asked.

Chris grimaced. 'She doesn't know yet. I'll ring her from Hereford.' He sighed. 'We were going out tonight.'

Eddie patted him on the shoulder. 'Cheer up. Let's go and find this train.' He picked up his bag, thinking he would ring Lisa when they arrived.

* * *

Ramón Amarales was watching from the upper verandah when the red car came into view on the valley road. He had a shrewd idea why his brother was paying him a visit so early in the morning, and was not exactly looking forward to the confrontation.

Not that he ever really looked forward to seeing Miguel. Or his sister Victoria, who was due back in Popayán from Bogotá that day. Though he, Ramón, was the head of the family, neither sibling had ever given him any respect. They just spent the money he made for them.

Miguel was supposedly the good-looking one, the sociable one. And, by his own reckoning, the intelligent one. Ramón did not deny his brother was handsome, but anyone with any intelligence would have thought twice about tying himself to that Escobar bitch. He wondered if the woman stopped shopping when they were in bed. She had to have more dresses than Imelda Marcos had shoes. Victoria, he admitted, was intelligent. But what had she done with her brains? She had married an idiot too, albeit one who was rather more useful to the family than Maria Escobar. He bored her, and presumably she had affairs. Otherwise, as far as Ramón could see, she did nothing but read French magazines, ski and paint her toenails.

He poured himself another coffee from the silver

jug on the tray, added two spoons of sugar and resumed his position, leaning against one of the verandah supports.

Miguel's car was being allowed through the outer perimeter gate. Against the sweep of green mountains the red car seemed almost like an insult. But then Miguel had always preferred the city to the real Colombia. Maybe he was intelligent in his way, but he had about as much wisdom as his wife.

'Juanita,' Ramón called through the open door. 'Fetch Chirlo for me.' He liked having his chief *sicario* with him at such times, mostly because he knew Miguel disliked the man.

The car cruised up through the paddock towards the second gate, causing the two Arabian horses to canter away towards the stream.

'Yes, *patrón*,' a soft voice said behind Ramón.

'Chirlo, have some coffee. Miguel has come.'

Rodrigo Sepulveda smiled and helped himself. He was twenty-four years old and looked younger, with clear blue eyes that looked out from under long, light-brown hair. The scar which gave him the nickname Chirlo ran horizontally across his left cheek like an African tribal mark. He sat down in one of the two rocking chairs, idly stirring his coffee.

The sound of footsteps on the stairs preceded Miguel Amarales's appearance in the doorway.

He looked, Ramón thought, more than ever like a male model. Long black hair framed his Castilian features, the luxuriant moustache was cut to perfection, the sleeves of his white shirt were rolled up to reveal a gold watch on one wrist, a gold bracelet on the other. He might not have been a resounding academic success at UCLA, but his fashion sense had been honed to perfection.

'Why?' he asked angrily, shaking his head and causing a snake-shaped gold earring to dance out from under his hair.

'Have some coffee,' Ramón suggested. Maybe he should grow a moustache himself, he thought.

'Why didn't you consult me first?' Miguel demanded to know.

'You were in Miami, and . . .'

'I was on my way back.'

Ramón shrugged. 'We couldn't wait.'

Miguel poured himself a cup, scowling first at his brother, then at Chirlo. 'So why?' he asked.

'Leverage,' Ramón said. 'And example. If we send Muñoz back he'll think twice about sounding off quite so much in future. Whatever we do with him, others will think twice.' He tinkled the ice in his glass. 'Everyone knows deep down that there's two sources of power in this country, but we have to remind them occasionally, bring it to the surface of their minds, so to speak. The moment politicians think they can ignore us with impunity we're finished.' He shrugged. 'It was an exercise in *realpolitik*. And an interesting military exercise, too.'

'Was that the real reason?'

'I've given you the real reason,' Ramón said angrily.

Miguel half smiled. 'OK, OK.' He knew his brother too well. 'But what made it interesting?'

Ramón smiled. 'We based it on the British SAS attack on that embassy in London,' Ramón said. 'Which turned out to be somewhat ironic. We caught an SAS man with Muñoz.'

'What are you going to do with him?'

'I don't know. Maybe ransom him back to the British. Maybe offer him work helping to train our men. The SAS are the best, you know.'

'Better than the Americans?' Miguel asked, surprised.

'Oh yes.'

Miguel looked round. 'Where are they?'

'Upstairs. They only arrived this morning.'

'Have you talked with Noguera?'

'Of course. He and Victoria should be coming to dinner tonight.'

Miguel grimaced. 'With an open pocket, no doubt. Our brother-in-law's needs seem to keep rising.'

Ramón smiled. 'He's the only Military Governor of the province we have. At least for the moment.'

'Maybe. How much are you asking for Muñoz?'

'I haven't decided yet. Chirlo, what do you think?'

'*Patrón*?'

Ramón repeated the question and Chirlo allowed half his mind to consider it. The other half was still busy absorbing the news that his mistress would be coming to the ranch that evening.

Eddie and Chris took a taxi from the station to Stirling Lines, the SAS headquarters in the Hereford suburb of Redhill. On arrival soon after two they were told there would be a preliminary briefing at 1600 hours in the 'Kremlin'.

'Who else has been called back?' Chris asked the orderly sergeant.

'Just you two, the Dame and Monkey. But . . .'

'They here yet?'

'No. The Dame's being flown in from Belfast. But it looks like Monkey's not going to make this one. He broke a leg playing rugby yesterday.'

'Probably on someone's teeth,' Eddie murmured. He got on OK with Monkey on a superficial level, but he had never been in a tight spot with the man, and he was not sure he wanted to be. He might be wrong – others had found him all right – but he had no great desire to find out. The myth about the SAS – that all three hundred of them got on with each other like best buddies – was just that, a myth. They got on with each other because they all had the self-discipline not to let the ones they did not like get too far up their noses.

'You know what this is about, boss?' Chris was asking the order sergeant.

'Yes thanks,' the sergeant said with a smile. 'And so will you come 1600 hours.'

'C'mon,' Eddie said. 'Let's do an hour in the gym.'

They walked back to their adjoining rooms, and met outside again ten minutes later in shorts and singlets.

'If Monkey's kaput we'll need another signaller,' Chris mused.

'Looks like it.' Each four-man team had a specialist signaller, medic, engineer and linguist. Most had an array of secondary skills, more so with each year of service.

Eddie was the linguist in this proposed team – thanks to two long summers in his teens working as a bouncer on the Costa del Sol – but he had also acquired a good grounding in communications during a stint in Northern Ireland the previous year. Chris was primarily the medic, but there was not much he didn't know about boats, and he had more than a smattering of Spanish. Damien – the Dame – was the engineer, with special expertise in laying and defusing explosives.

'The Dame's got Spanish too, hasn't he?' Eddie said, as he set the weights on the backbreaker.

'I hope to Christ it's not Gibraltar,' Chris said.

Wynwood climbed out of the shower, pulled on his shorts, carefully sniffed himself, and pronounced himself satisfied. The stiff nail-brush someone had abandoned in his hotel bathroom had removed the last traces of the Cali rubbish mountains.

He unfastened the window and examined the outside world. The sky was clear, the air delightfully warm, like an early summer day on the Gower. He had grown to like Bogotá in the two or three days he and Andy had spent there after their arrival back in November. Maybe they had only seen the nice bits, but the place had a good feel to it.

If he could only get his wife out of his head he could enjoy his last few days there as well.

Having something to do would help. He checked his watch – twenty minutes till he was supposed to meet the man from the British Embassy. Oliver his name was, though whether that was his first name or last Wynwood did not know.

Wynwood dressed, left his room and made his way downstairs. The man on the desk gave him a cheerful '*buenos dias*'. He smiled back and walked out onto Carrera 7. Across the street a white-towered church almost blazed in the sunlight.

The Museum of Gold was only a ten-minute walk away. Oliver had said it opened at ten, and a queue had already formed by the time Wynwood arrived. Rather than join it he sat down on a wrought-iron seat in the square across the street, watching for anyone who might look like his contact.

He had only been there a few seconds when a soft voice echoed in his ear: 'Wynwood?' He turned to find a slightly plumper version of Bobby Charlton, a smattering of long fair hairs twisting in the wind above a bald pate. 'That's me,' he replied.

'Oliver,' the man introduced himself, with what sounded like a faint West Country accent. 'Pleased to meet you. And congratulations on your escape,' he added dryly. 'Shall we go in,' he said, indicating the museum across the street.

'We could just talk here.'

'Have you been already?' Oliver asked, sounding disappointed.

'No, but . . .'

'Well, in that case . . .' The embassy man got to his feet. 'No one should miss the Museum of Gold – it's Bogotá's one great attraction.'

Oh well, in that case, Wynwood thought sarcastically.

At least Oliver paid for both of them. 'I have money for you,' he said as the two walked past a posse of armed guards and up the wide flight of stairs which led to the first-floor galleries.

'Good,' Wynwood said, and waited for more.

He waited in vain as Oliver examined an exhibit. Inside a large glass cabinet a skeleton reclined on the earth floor of a tomb, grinning at the ceiling. Gold trinkets hung from its neck, small gold ornaments lay all around – the treasure it had taken, literally, to the grave. And as if to underline the dead man's failure to buy the intended immortality, spindly roots were writhing in through the walls and ceiling. It was strangely moving, Wynwood thought. It made him think of his father.

Oliver was already moving on to the next exhibit, a life-sized model of two Indians heating gold in a crucible. A few feet away a mixed group of tourists were having a selection of gold-filigree ear ornaments explained to them in both English and Spanish. Beyond them, ten or more uniformed guards toting automatic weapons and communication devices paced up and down in front of a huge mural of palms and mountains.

I wouldn't fancy trying to rob this place, Wynwood thought; though planning such a robbery would make a good exercise for continuation training back home. Getting hold of the plans might be somewhat difficult.

'I don't have much to tell you,' Oliver was saying

by his side. They were now standing in front of the mummified remains of a pre-Columbian woman, who could not have been much more than four feet tall. 'There is a good chance that your people will be attempting a rescue,' Oliver continued, so quietly that Wynwood was not sure he had heard him correctly.

'Did you say rescue?' he asked after a moment.

'Yes. I'm sure you'll have at least as much idea of what that entails as I do. I'm to tell you that nothing is finally decided. If, I repeat *if*, London gives the green light, I understand that three men will be sent in to join you for surveillance and preparation. In the meantime, you're to stay out of sight. Be a tourist.' He looked at his watch. 'Come, they only open the Sun Room once an hour.'

Wynwood followed him up the stairs, absorbing the information he had just been given, working out which questions he should ask. There seemed only one that was relevant. 'Do you know when the final decision is being taken?' he asked.

'Probably today,' Oliver said. 'There's a meeting this evening – 8 p.m. London time – so if a decision is taken the embassy should be informed today.'

The Sun Room occupied the centre of the third floor, and a small crowd was already gathering at its doors. A host of uniformed schoolchildren, all with shining black hair and bright-red uniforms, giggled and poked at each other. Several paler-skinned tourists, most of them looking significantly shabbier than the Colombians in the crowd, chatted to each other in English and German.

His mind still racing through the possibilities, Wynwood waited with Oliver for the doors to open, then filed in with everyone else. The doors clanged shut behind them, causing one of the tourists to gasp, but a split second later the lights came on in the glass cabinets that lined the walls. Each was top-lit, revealing a shining, beautifully crafted gold headpiece against a blue-black surround.

Wynwood had to admit to himself it was magical. He turned to find Oliver watching him, a faint smile on his face. 'OK,' the SAS man said, 'you were right, it's amazing.'

Oliver half bowed.

On their way round the rest of the third floor he asked if Wynwood had recognized any of the opposition in Cali.

'Didn't see a single face,' Wynwood said. 'You don't have any news of Andy – Sergeant Anderson?'

'Not yet. But I'm expecting something on that today as well.'

'Where from?' Wynwood asked innocently.

'Sources,' Oliver said curtly. 'I shall be leaving you now. Your hotel is all right? Good. I'll be in touch.'

'Today?'

'If I have anything to tell you,' Oliver said over his shoulder.

Wynwood spent another ten minutes desultorily examining the exhibits, but his heart was not in it. He made his way outside into the sunshine and started walking. Down a nearby street he found an outdoor café, with several metal tables in primary colours spilling across the pavement. He sat down, absent-mindedly studied the menu and watched the world go by.

Oliver, he guessed, was better at his job than he looked. And Colombian women tended to be on the plump side. How the hell was he going to fill up the rest of the day?

His mind was a blank, he just sat there. As usual, thoughts of Susan came to fill the vacant space. The two of them were through, and they both knew it, and though both felt sad about it – at least he thought she did – neither of them really wanted to turn back the clock. The marriage had run its course – that was all there was to it. They had both accepted it in their heads, and she seemed to have accepted it in her heart as well. Why the fuck couldn't he?

She can accept it, a voice in his head reminded him, because she's fucking that bastard teacher she met at her fucking watercolour fucking painting fucking evening class.

'What would you like, sir?' a waiter asked, apparently not noticing the anger still infusing his customer's eyes.

Wynwood ordered a black coffee. It was the sense of failure that he found hard to cope with, he decided. And losing Andy as well. Oliver had congratulated him on his escape, but he knew better. They had fucked up somewhere along the line, and he had had the luck which had obviously deserted his partner. He wanted the chance to do something right.

Several shoeshine boys inspected his boots with optimistic interest, but he sent them all away – there was something he didn't like about the idea of someone kneeling at his feet. Something demeaning, though who it demeaned he was not sure. The boys certainly showed no signs of embarrassment – in fact they carried their little wooden boxes with a definite swagger.

A trio of Colombian girls – young women really – probably secretaries – sat down at a nearby table. An Indian walked by, wearing a black hat with an embroidered headband. He stopped to look back at the woman trailing twenty metres behind him, who was carrying a huge pile of similar hats in a polythene sack on her back. The noble savage, Wynwood thought.

Yellow taxis went by in profusion. A man suddenly appeared alongside his table, one arm outstretched towards him, the other cut off in a neat stump. 'No,' he said instinctively.

The coffee finally arrived.

'How are you doing, lads?' a voice said from the doorway.

Eddie and Chris turned to greet the owner of the Wearside accent. The Dame plonked himself down on Eddie's bed.

'You just got in?' Eddie asked.

'Yeah. Just come over from fuckin' Belfast.'

'I thought you were on leave like the rest of us.'

The Dame sighed. 'I was. Enjoying it too, getting looked after hand and foot by my sisters. But the bosses needed me for a special job . . .'

'Oh, listen to him – special job!' Chris said.

'We're not fit to tie his shoelaces,' Eddie agreed.

'It was tied up with something happened over there last year,' the Dame said placidly. 'What are we doing here, anyway? I thought I'd be back in Sunderland tonight, not listening to you two wankers mouthing off.'

'Fuck only knows.' Chris looked at his watch. 'It's five to six – we'd better get down there.'

The Kremlin's briefing room boasted all the usual paraphernalia associated with such rooms, plus a huge mounted water buffalo's head which dated back to the regiment's time in Malaya, and whose large, serene eyes gazed down benevolently on Eddie, Chris and the Dame as they took their seats. It was a minute before six, and Chris's stomach was already rumbling. It had to be true, he reflected – the more you eat, the more you need.

'Did I hear thunder?' the Dame asked.

'I doubt it,' Chris said.

'Do you know how Major Bourne got the name "Roy"?' Eddie asked.

The other two shook their heads.

'When he was in the Oman the food used to make him fart like there was no tomorrow. So first they called him "Bourne on the Wind" – get it? – and that got shortened to "Roy" 'cos it's a song by Roy Orbison.'

'That sounds almost stupid enough to be true,' the Dame observed.

'It is true.'

'Have I died and gone to hell?' Chris asked the ceiling.

'You should be so lucky, Trooper,' Bourne said, brushing past him and putting his papers on the table next to the overhead projector. Another four men filed in: Captains Mike Bannister and Rory Atkins, officers commanding C Squadron's Air and Mountain Troops respectively, Training

Wing's Major Kilcline, and a man in civilian clothes whom Bourne introduced as 'Mr Pennington from the Foreign Office'.

Bourne started things off. 'Right, unless our security's even worse than I think it is, you four' – he indicated Eddie, the Dame, Chris and Mike Bannister – 'have no idea why you've been dragged out of the bosom of your families halfway through the season of good cheer. I'm sure your families are glad to be rid of you, but . . .'

'Is it true you need a diploma in stand-up to be an officer here, boss?' Eddie asked.

'Yes, Trooper, it is. But to get serious . . .' Bourne went through what they knew of what had happened in Cali. 'We thought Joss Wynwood had been taken as well,' he admitted. 'We only heard this morning that he's alive and well in the capital.'

'That big Welsh bastard would survive a night with Cilla Black,' Kilcline observed.

'Perhaps,' Bourne agreed, 'but what sort of shape would she be in?'

Everyone laughed.

'So,' Bourne went on, 'the job is to get Sergeant Anderson back. And, if we can, recover Muñoz as well.'

'Any particular reason?' Chris asked. 'For Muñoz, I mean.'

'Yes, there is. The unit which was supposed to

be protecting him from something like this blew it. Since they were at least partly trained by us, *we* blew it. OK?'

'Yes, boss.'

'OK. Colombia. I don't suppose any of you have been there?'

They all shook their heads.

'Or know anything about the place?'

'Wasn't that where Bobby Moore got accused of stealing a bracelet or something?' the Dame asked.

'Very useful,' Bourne said. 'Well, Bobby can't be with us today . . .'

'We could give him a buzz, boss,' Eddie suggested.

Bourne ignored him. 'But we do have Mr Pennington here from the Foreign Office.'

Pennington was pinning up a large-scale map of northern South America. 'Colombia,' he said, a little nervously, pointing it out on the map. 'It's a big country. About thirty-five million people in an area five times that of the UK. The vast majority of the population, about seventy per cent, are *mestizos* – people of mixed Spanish/Indian descent. Another twenty per cent would consider themselves of pure Spanish blood, while seven per cent are pure Indian and three per cent negro. Nearly all the power is in the hands of the pure Spanish twenty per cent, but the country doesn't have a race problem the way we would understand it. The majority is in the middle, so to speak, which makes for stability, at least in that regard.

He turned to the map. 'As you can see, Colombia is only just north of the Equator, so those areas close to sea level, the coastal plains and this huge area of jungle in the south-east, have a tropical climate – hot and humid the whole year round.'

Eddie groaned.

'But don't despair,' Pennington went on with a smile. 'About ninety-five per cent of the population live in these mountains' – he ran his finger down the map – 'which give the country a kind of dual spine running north to south. Most of the population lives over 1200 metres above sea level, where the climate is much kinder.

'One last point, before I abandon the geography lesson. You can see from the way the country's made up how hard overland communication must be. And of course this has made it almost impossible for anyone or any government to stamp its authority on the whole country. So instead of a powerful centre you have regional powers. Warlords. Or these days, drug lords.

'So you should always remember – law is local in Colombia. You may be on territory controlled by the local arm of the military or by the local representative of central government or by some local bigwig or by some guerrilla group – and there are plenty of those – or by one of the drug cartels. If someone offers you any help, try and make sure they can deliver what they say they can.'

'It sounds like a nightmare,' Chris said.

'In some ways it is. It's probably the most lawless country in the world. And yet most people who visit it also think it's one of the friendliest.' Pennington shrugged. He was beginning to enjoy himself.

'That's enough geography,' he went on. 'We don't yet know which group has Carlos Muñoz and Sergeant Anderson, but it's likely to be one of the major drug cartels. I'm using the word "cartels" because they're often called that in the media, but usually they're just phenomenally successful family businesses. And being successful they can each afford an army of hired guns – *sicarios* in local parlance.

'I'm probably telling you things you already know, but . . . cocaine is made from coca leaves. The coca bush doesn't grow in Colombia, only in a few high Andean valleys in Peru and Bolivia. The leaves are picked and reduced to a paste there, and then this is flown north to hundreds of hidden airstrip laboratories in the Colombian backwoods where it is further refined into pure cocaine. From there it's moved by sea and air, mostly across the Caribbean to the States. Over the last few years a growing amount has reached Europe, often via West Indian transit points.

'As you'd expect, the governments of the West are keen to at least reduce the flow, if not stop it. There are several obvious ways of going about this. They can try and stop the Peruvians and Bolivians from growing the leaf, try to intercept the shipments en route, or try to stop our kids wanting to use the stuff. They've tried all three and they're still trying, but the success rate isn't encouraging. The fourth option is to try and help the Colombian Government put its own house in order. Which I assume is why Anderson and Wynwood were out there helping to train an Anti-Narcotics Unit.

'I should add that a lot of people in the Colombian Government and Military have got their own snouts in the trough, and that the anti-cartel noises they make are strictly for show. They need to impress their own people at election time, and the rest of the world whenever there's trade or aid deals in the offing.

'Right. That's the place you're going to. It's a wild place, wild like the Falls Road rather than wild like the Falklands. But then again, it's probably the most beautiful country you'll ever see in your lives. The phrase "a land of contrasts" is pretty much a cliché, but it fits Colombia better than most.'

He sat down.

'Any questions?' Bourne asked.

'What kind of government is it?' the Dame wanted to know.

'What difference does it make?' Eddie muttered.

'There are regular elections, but it would be stretching it more than a little to call Colombia a real democracy,' Pennington said. 'The same groups tend to take turns in power.'

'Sounds like Hackney Council,' Eddie said.

Chris was trying to remember how far north the giant condors lived. He would give a lot to see one of them.

'OK,' Bourne said. 'Since we don't yet know where the prisoners are being held it's more a matter of getting you as near the likely action as possible.' He paused. 'Now this isn't the Falklands, and this isn't a military operation in that sense. You won't be going in armed.'

'What?!' Eddie and the Dame said in unison.

Bourne just smiled at them.

'Nothing?'

'You've been trained to look after yourselves without any technological help . . .'

'Yes, boss, but . . .'

'We don't know if you'll be expected. We don't know the connections between the Government, the Military and the cartels. We do know that Englishmen turning up at the Colombian border in the next few days armed to the teeth may make someone suspicious.'

'Border, boss?'

'This one.' Bourne pointed out the border with Ecuador. 'We don't want to fly you into Bogotá for exactly the reasons I've just stated – in the circumstances any English arrivals are liable to be deemed suspicious. So we're going to fly you into Quito, on a regular flight. By thc time you get there we may have more information. Either way we'll take a decision about where you should rendezvous with Wynwood inside Colombia. The three of you will then make your way across the border. This is a travellers' trail – lots of Americans, Europeans, Australians, you name it – will be travelling in each direction. You'll just be three more. Your clothing and packs should be chosen accordingly – I don't want three standard-issue bergens in a row. Once you're inside Colombia we can see about getting you properly kitted up.'

'That's a relief.'

'Wynwood will be arranging for a cache.' Bourne looked at them. 'So all you three comics have to do is meet him without drawing attention to yourselves. That's all. Almost a joyride.'

'Thanks, boss,' Chris said with a smile.

'What's the weather like?' Eddie wanted to know. 'Should we take umbrellas?'

* * *

It was just past half-past eleven in Bogotá. Wynwood nursed his whisky chaser and stared blankly at the rows of bottles behind the bar of the Intercontinental Hotel. The only other customers were a group of middle-aged Germans in a booth behind him. Every now and then their guttural tones would impinge on Wynwood's consciousness, reminding him how much he disliked them and their nation. When it came down to it, the Germans had all the worst characteristics of the English and none of the latter's few redeeming features. Arrogant, humourless sods!

Wynwood had been propping up the bar since sundown, except for a brief interlude in the adjoining restaurant. He was not particularly drunk – he had been drinking too slowly for that – but neither was he the soberest man in South America.

The same thoughts were circling his brain like Indians round a wagon train. In fact they seemed to be drawing the circle tighter as the evening went on. The sheer absurdity of it was beginning to really piss him off. It all seemed so bloody unreal.

'So make it real,' he murmured to himself. Break the spell, talk to the bitch. Remind yourself why you're better off without her. Call her up.

He called the barman over. The barman told him he could make an international call from reception. Reception told him it would take about ten minutes, if he could wait in the booth. 'Sir does realize it is the middle of the night in England?'

Sir had forgotten that, but what the hell. Wynwood waited by the phone booth, deliberately avoiding any premeditated thought of what he was going to say, until the receptionist indicated he should pick up the phone. It was ringing. Amazing, he thought. All that distance. It was a fucking miracle.

The phone kept ringing. Twenty times, thirty times. It gradually dawned on Wynwood that his wife was not at home.

He could not remember ever feeling so frustrated in his whole life.

He put the phone down with dreadful care and left the booth. The receptionist was saying something, but he ignored him, walking down the three steps and out through the swing doors onto the busy avenue. He stopped for a second, then spun round to the right and broke into a brisk walk. He had no idea where he was going and he didn't much care.

The Colombians filling the crowded pavement – the ones that saw him coming – stepped judiciously out of his way. Some were not so lucky, and simply got shoved aside. Their curses followed him, but he hardly heard them.

The city was like white noise. He went past food stalls doing a brisk trade, cafés with music pouring from their doorways, groups of men gathered round a spinning wheel of faces, coins clattering on a board. He saw none of them.

It was a mile or more before he let the world back in, absent-mindedly agreeing to buy some chewing gum from a child who should have been in bed hours ago. The child's delight was like some sort of switch. Suddenly Wynwood was aware of his surroundings again, and they left something to be desired. The swish shops and elegant squares of the city centre had given way to an altogether harsher environment, full of seedy-looking pool halls, rusty cars and groups of aimless-looking young men.

This was not the safest place in Bogotá, Wynwood realized. Thanks to his dark hair and sun-tanned skin his presence had so far not been noticed. So far. But he had come out without either the Browning or his knife.

'Dumbo,' he muttered to himself, looking round for a taxi to get him the hell out of there.

And then he saw her. She was really something: slimmer than most Colombian women he had seen, with dark hair spilling across brown shoulders, a tight-waisted red cotton dress emphasizing the rounded swell of breasts and hips.

And she was looking at him.

'Would you like some love?' she asked, or at least that was what he thought she said.

And somehow the question made him feel both

sorry for himself and angry for feeling it. Yes, he thought, he'd like some love. Who wouldn't? Plus, it would get him off the street. 'What did you have in mind?' he asked.

'Come with me and I'll show you,' she said, offering him her hand. He took it, and she led him away down the side street.

She smelled of soap and water. Christ, he thought, he had not been with a prostitute since he was a teenager. And they didn't look like this round King's Cross. While a voice in his head told him how stupid he was being, his eyes were taking in the smooth brown skin of her shoulders and upper breasts. She stopped at a door and smiled up at him. 'This is my house,' she said.

They went in through an open door and up two flights of stairs to a door with paint peeling off it. She took a key from her purse and opened it. The sound of a crying baby was coming from somewhere inside.

'Go through there,' she said, pointing to another door, 'I will be only a moment.' He did as he was told, and found himself in a surprisingly large room. A large bed took up the far corner, and the only other furniture was a chair and table. On the latter were several books – two of them English primers.

She came in, closing the door behind her. 'You are American, yes,' she said carefully in English.

'British,' Wynwood said. Telling people you were Welsh in Colombia was guaranteed to elicit only puzzlement.

'I learn,' she said.

'So I see,' Wynwood said. This was getting more difficult.

As if sensing this she went to the window and opened the shutters, bathing the far wall with an orange-neon glow from some invisible outside source. Then she turned the room lighting off, removed her belt and, with one simple movement, stepped out of her dress. She was wearing nothing underneath it.

'You like?' she asked.

Wynwood took a deep breath. 'Yep,' he said.

She smiled and walked across to him. She put one hand around his neck, while the other searched for and found the bulge his cock was beginning to make in his jeans. 'Twenty dollars for everything,' she said, her palm lightly stroking him as she waited for his reply.

'Cheap at the price,' Wynwood murmured.

'*Qué*?'

'*Sí*, twenty dollars.'

Her fingers unfastened his shirt, then his jeans. He stepped out of them, and she pulled down his shorts, took his cock in both hands and began to massage it.

Christ, it felt good.

'I have condom,' she said.

'Great,' Wynwood said. It was a good thing one of them had some sense.

She rummaged in a drawer full of clothes while Wynwood enjoyed the graceful lines of her behind, found the packet of condoms and extracted one for him. Then she lay back across the bed, her legs crossed, with one hand on her stomach, the other holding the condom on the pillow behind her head.

Wynwood lay down beside her and ran his hand down her body.

She handed him the condom and watched while he put it on.

'Would you like me on top?' she asked.

'No,' he said, gently pushing her legs apart and pulling himself on top of her.

She took him in her hand and guided him inside with a practised motion.

He tried to kiss her, and though she didn't refuse it, she didn't take much part in the exercise either. Her body was moving energetically enough. Trying to get it over as quickly as possible, a small voice said in the back of Wynwood's mind. And it worked. His two months of celibacy ended in a satisfying rush.

He lay there on top of her, other thoughts crowding into his mind, hardly noticing as she gently disengaged them and rolled him onto his side.

But he did notice the door slam open.

There were two of them. Both were in their late teens or early twenties, wearing almost identical clothes – T-shirts, tight jeans and trainers. The differences lay in the messages emblazoned on the T-shirts: while one proclaimed the superiority of Pepsi the other endorsed Madonna's claim to be 'Like A Virgin'.

Wynwood swung his legs off the bed and sat on its edge, looking up at them. He made no move to reach for his clothes – that would be seen as a sign of weakness.

'*Buenas noches*,' one of them said with a smile.

Wynwood looked round at the girl to see if she was part of this. Her face betrayed nothing.

'What do you want, *compadres*?' he asked them

The one who had smiled, laughed. The other looked tough. They had seen too many movies. But they were both big for Colombians, Wynwood admitted to himself. And he was not in the best state he had ever been in. He wondered if they were armed.

As if in reply to the unspoken question, Smiler pulled a gun from his jeans pocket, and his partner a flick-knife, pressing the switch as he did so, causing the blade to leap out dramatically.

'I bet you practise that in front of the mirror,' Wynwood said.

The frown deepened. Obviously he did.

'We want everything you have, gringo,' Smiler said. 'It's only fair – you come here and fuck our women and fuck our country. You should pay for all this. It's only fair.'

'And you're Robin Hood and Little John, I suppose?' Wynwood was beginning to realize just how bad this was going to be if he fucked up. Andy was relying on him, and what the fuck was he doing?

'Your money, gringo. And a specimen of your signature with the credit cards of course.'

Wynwood reached for his trousers, pulled out his wallet and handed it up. Frowner stepped forward three paces, taking care not to get between his partner's gun and Wynwood, took the wallet and passed it to his partner.

Smiler's smile widened. With this act of submission Wynwood had removed any anxiety they might have had. Smiler moved the gun from one hand to the other to examine the wallet. Frowner did not bother to retreat the full three paces he had advanced, and his attention was divided between Wynwood and what bounties the wallet might contain.

This was the moment. Wynwood rose and took a step towards Frowner in one swift movement, then continued on, bringing the other foot up in a vicious arc between the man's legs, and the right arm down across the subclavian artery as he buckled.

It took two seconds. Smiler was still trying to juggle the gun from one hand to the other when Wynwood's fist slammed into his throat. He fell back, breath rasping and still clutching the gun. Wynwood trod on his wrist and extricated it from his fingers.

He turned to see the girl looking at him with a mixture of awe and . . . contempt?

He felt suddenly naked.

Frowner was groaning on the floor, Smiler wheezing. Wynwood watched them as he dressed, keeping the gun within easy reach. He handed the girl her twenty dollars, which she took and placed under a pillow without saying a word.

She had made no effort to dress herself. She looked, Wynwood thought, like a fallen madonna, or was he just being sentimental. She also looked about sixteen. Why hadn't she looked that young before?

He turned back to the youths. 'Get up!' he said.

They did so, humiliation and frustration sharing the pain in their expressions.

'Now go away,' Wynwood said. 'And don't bother this girl any more.'

'She is our sister,' Frowner said. It was the first time Wynwood had heard him speak.

He laughed without humour. 'Get lost,' he said.

They went. She looked at him as if she was expecting him to take his money back.

'How do I get back to the centre?' he asked.

'There are taxis,' she said reluctantly.

'Where?'

'Round the corner. Everywhere.'

He picked up her dress and threw it to her. 'Show me. And I'll give you another five dollars.'

'Big deal,' she said. But she pulled the dress on.

They went back down to the street. There was no sign of her two 'brothers'. Three taxis were waiting round the first corner, outside what looked, from the tickets littering the pavement, like a betting joint.

Wynwood climbed in, and they drove off. Looking back he could see her standing on the pavement, just staring into space.

Back at his hotel the night clerk gave him his key and a quizzical look. He ignored the man, wearily climbed the stairs and tried to unlock the door of his room. It was already unlocked. He cautiously pushed it open.

'It's only me,' Oliver's voice said from inside.

Wynwood closed the door behind him. The embassy man was sitting in the only chair, an open bottle of aguardiente on his lap. 'Well?' Wynwood asked, sitting on the edge of the bed.

'You look like you've been out on the town,' Oliver commented.

'You could say that.'

Oliver grunted. 'Well, there's no news from London, and in this case no news is good news. It seems to be on.'

Wynwood let his head fall back onto the bed. 'Brilliant,' he said.

'And I think I've located Anderson and Muñoz,' Oliver went on.

Wynwood sat up again. 'Even better. Where are they?'

'Outside Popayán – you know where that is? – about a hundred and thirty kilometres south of Cali. The Amarales family have them. Theirs is probably the third largest of the cartels. Their headquarters is a ranch called Totoro, some thirty kilometres outside Popayán, and that's where my information says they've taken Anderson and Muñoz.'

'This is probably a naïve question, but if it's just a ranch not far from a major town, why . . .'

'Why can't the authorities do something?' Oliver smiled. 'It is a naïve question. The whole area is in their pocket – police, military, you name it . . . that province belongs to the Amarales.' He poured Wynwood an inch of aguardiente. 'And the ranch itself is like a fortress,' he added cheerfully.

# 4

It felt strange going off like this, without so much as a knife. It was more like going on holiday, Eddie thought, surveying all the bodies spread around the Gatwick departure lounge who were planning on just that – waiting to be jetted away for a week in the sun. Mind you, he thought, in the old days he usually had taken a knife on holiday.

Their scheduled departure time was still an hour away. Chris had disappeared, the Dame was deep into a Wilbur Smith, and he was bored. Why not ring her, he thought. What harm could it do?

'You're on bag detail,' he told the Dame, and went looking for a phone. It rang just once before she picked up.

'Hi,' he said.

'I knew it was you,' Lisa said.

'No, you didn't,' he retorted. Somehow things like that made him uneasy.

'Yes, I did. Don't be so grumpy. Where are you?'

'At the airport.'

'What airport? Why?'

'I'm going away for a bit. That's why I'm ringing.'

'Oh.'

'I didn't want you to think I'd just disappeared,' he said, surprising himself.

'How long will you be?'

'Don't know. Couple of weeks, maybe a month.'

'Send us a postcard . . .'

'Yeah, look, I haven't got any more money,' he lied. 'I'll be in touch when I get back, OK?'

'OK. I . . .'

The line went dead. 'I' what? Eddie wondered. He stood there for a moment, thinking. She had a nice voice. And she was . . . straight, that was it. She was straight. He liked that. She said what she thought. No bullshit. He liked her. He thought about the time in his back seat and felt something stir in his trousers.

Across the departure lounge he could see Chris and the Dame talking to a young man in a suit. The latter had disappeared by the time he had rejoined them. 'Who was he?' Eddie asked Chris.

'Foreign Office,' Chris said. 'He brought us this.' He handed him a book: *The South American Handbook 1990.*

'In case we get lost?'

'The chaps thought we might find it useful,' Chris said with an upper-class accent. 'Where've you been?' he asked.

'On the phone. I suddenly remembered I hadn't broken a woman's heart yet today.'

'Mission accomplished?'

'I expect she's knee-deep in tears by now.'

'Of gratitude, I expect,' Chris said. He had rung Molly the night before, and she had been downright cool. Still, they hadn't exactly got to know each other yet. 'You got anyone to ring, Dame?' he asked.

'Nope.'

'It's all those sisters,' Eddie observed. 'They weaken a man.'

'I thought that was against the law,' Chris observed.

'Not up north – they're used to sleeping four to a bed up there. And you know, one thing leads to another and . . .

'They're sleeping five to a bed.'

'Exactly.'

The Dame observed them tolerantly. 'What you two know about the North could be written on a rabbit turd.'

'I expect everything anyone needs to know about the North could be written on a rabbit turd,' Chris said.

'Maybe it's not the sisters,' Eddie mused.

'Maybe it's not even the pictures of Virginia Bottomley he keeps under his pillow.'

'What then?'

'I think our friend here has made a great discovery. He's realized that there's only one person he really wants to make love to, only one person who won't complain about his appalling technique or embarrass him in the morning by demanding a spoon with the cornflakes . . .'

'Who can this be?' Chris wondered out loud.

'Himself, of course.'

The Dame gave them an ironic round of applause, slammed his Wilbur Smith shut and got to his feet. 'Boarding Gate 22,' he said.

'Sit down, John,' Barney Davies said.

Kilcline obliged.

'I've just been talking to the PM.' He thought about this statement and amended it. 'Listening to her might be a better way of putting it.'

'She's not called it off!?'

'No. It's still on . . .'

'Thank God for that!'

'Yes. There's one fly in the ointment, though. We've had to involve the Americans . . .'

'Why for Christ's sake?'

'Two reasons. One, MI6 insisted they needed CIA help inside Colombia. Two, the Foreign Office insisted that using the Colombian military to pull the lads out was unnecessarily risky. MI6 supported them. So the Americans will do it from Panama.'

'Have they got the range?' Kilcline asked doubtfully.

'They say so. And before you ask, they're restricting it to a Need to Know.'

'Oh good,' Kilcline said sarcastically. 'It won't be in the papers till tomorrow then.'

'I don't think so. They're only helping with a weapons cache for the patrol *in situ* and providing a taxi service. And there's no organizational connection between the two jobs.' He shrugged. 'Anyway, ours not to reason why, etcetera. Let's look on the bright side. It's on. Our man in Bogotá – name of Oliver – will be on a scrambled line to you at 1600 hours our time. He'll be your liaison with Wynwood and the patrol. So set up contact procedures. And make it clear to him that whatever Wynwood wants he should get.' He paused, then smiled. 'I don't need to tell you that, do I? No. OK. How soon can we get our lads away?'

'First thing tomorrow.'

'Good. Let's do it.'

Two hours later Oliver was ushering Wynwood down Carrera 7 towards lunch. Wynwood felt more hung-over than hungry, but Oliver had insisted. They found the restaurant the embassy man was looking for halfway up one of the streets leading down to the Plaza Bolivar.

It was called the Indian Cultural Museum, which did not seem such a strange name for an eating-place once they got inside. The room had more Indian artefacts in it than people, and it was dark, with candles burning brightly on each table. The long wall of windows might have admitted more of the noon sunlight, but the courtyard it overlooked was filled with a dense jungle of foliage, and only the slimmest line of blue sky was visible above the tall plants, creating the momentary impression that they were sitting at the bottom of a well.

There seemed to be only one dish on the menu, so Oliver ordered it for both of them and then disappeared in the direction of the toilets. Wynwood was left to nurse his head. Strangely enough, in every other way he felt better than he had the day before. The events of the previous evening had somehow exorcized something.

Oliver returned to the table. 'Nice, isn't it?' he observed, looking round. 'And quiet. I've just been talking to one of your superiors – a Major Kilcline.'

'Killer.'

Oliver looked at him askance. 'If you say so. I have instructions for you.' He paused while the waiter arrived with a half carafe of Chilean wine, took an appreciative sip, and continued. 'You are to rendezvous with three other men – Martinson, Wilshaw and Robson – tomorrow in the Plaza de Armas in Popayán. At 1900 hours. If either party is late then try again two hours later, then at 0900 hours the next morning and at two hour intervals throughout the day. Is that all clear?'

'Yep.' A good choice of men, Wynwood thought. He had worked with Chris Martinson before, and he had heard good things about both Eddie Wilshaw and Damien Robson.

'Next thing . . . ah, we'll have to wait.'

The food was arriving, but not on plates. Each steak was presented on a wooden board, with a selection of vegetables arranged around it – one potato, one cassava, one dumpling-like object which Oliver said was called an *arepa*. A circular hollow in the board held a small quantity of highly spiced liquid.

Hungry or not Wynwood found it all delicious, and he said so. Oliver gave him a slight bow, as if he was the chef receiving compliments, and refilled their wine glasses. 'Back to business,' he said. 'The four of you are to place Totoro under observation. The cache should be in place soon, and once you have recovered it you will of course be able to talk directly to your people in Belize on the radio. Until then your only link is with me by telephone, and it shouldn't be used by you except in an emergency.

I will call you each day with news of your mother. When she comes out of the coma the cache is ready for collection. Understood?'

'What's in the cache?'

Oliver reached into his pocket. 'This is the list I was given by Hereford, with the understanding that I'd ask you if there was anything needed adding.'

Wynwood scanned the list. Everything seemed to be there. Except . . . 'Add a couple of Claymores,' he said, 'with all the usual trimmings.' He read through the list once more, and handed it back. 'Plus I need a car.'

'Here or in Popayán?'

'Here would be better – I'd feel less conspicuous travelling down that way. But I'm really thinking of there – it'll give us some flexibility.'

'I can't see any problem. Any particular make?'

'A Rolls?'

'How about a Fiat?'

'Long as it's not red.'

'I'll see what I can do.' Oliver gestured to the waiter. 'Let's continue this conversation outside,' he suggested to Wynwood.

They left the restaurant and strolled slowly down the bustling Carrera 7 to the Plaza Bolivar.

'This should be safe enough,' Oliver said, taking a seat on a low wall in the centre of the square. 'See that empty space,' he said conversationally, pointing out a large gap in the buildings surrounding the square. 'That's where the Palace of Justice used to stand. Guerrillas occupied it a few years ago, taking about thirty hostages, and the Army decided that the best way to deal with the situation was to level the building. With the guerrillas and the hostages still inside.' He smiled. 'There aren't many races capable of giving lessons in ruthlessness to the Spanish.'

Wynwood could believe it.

'Anyway,' Oliver said, rubbing his hands together, 'two of your troops will be arriving in Belize tomorrow. They'll be ready to drop in on the Amarales family at your invitation.'

'Who's taking us out?' Wynwood wanted to know.

'The Americans.'

Wynwood was not surprised. 'From Panama?'

'Yes. They're also filling your weaponry order and getting satellite shots of Totoro to supplement your work on the ground.'

Wynwood nodded. 'So when can I get the car?'

'You don't need to leave till tomorrow morning.'

'I'd rather get off today.' He looked round to where the twin towers of the cathedral seemed to be almost glowing against the background of dark hills and darkening sky. 'I've had enough of Bogotá,' he said.

'That I can understand,' Oliver said. 'I'll see what I can do.'

Richard Anderson pushed away the lunch tray and went to the window. It was the fourth morning of his captivity, and the lack of information as to his captors' intentions was beginning to get to him. Neither he nor Muñoz had been badly treated – in fact, in many ways, they were almost being pampered. Anderson imagined most prisoners the world over would settle for nicely furnished single rooms with a shared bathroom, three good meals and two hours of outside exercise a day. One of the guards had even lent him one of the pornographic comics which Colombian men loved so much: '"*Would she do that for him?*" *the handsome Rodrigo asked.*' You bet she would.

No, there was no material discomfort – it was just not knowing what was happening. Not knowing when or whether he would ever see Beth and the kids again.

The view from the window certainly did not tell him much. It faced slightly north of east – that much he knew from the sun – but all he could see was the small yard where they took their exercise, the wall which bounded it and forested slopes rising in the distance beyond it. He could have been in Wales if it was not for the heat.

He wondered where Wynwood was now. Either dead or back in England, he supposed.

A key sounded in the lock. Thinking it was the guard come to get the breakfast tray, Anderson did not bother to turn round.

'Señor,' said a voice he had not heard before. It belonged to a young man with blue eyes and a scar that split his left cheek. 'Come with me, please,' he said. The voice seemed almost liquid, Anderson thought irrelevantly. But polite, he added to himself. If he was being invited to his execution at least he was being invited politely. He walked past the pale blue eyes and out through the door.

'This way,' Chirlo said, leading him down a corridor, past what looked like a security centre, and up a flight of stairs to the first floor. Another short corridor led out onto a wide upper verandah where a man was pouring coffee into three cups from a silver jug. Beyond him lay a panoramic view of the valley leading down to the river.

'*Buenos dias*, Señor Anderson – that is your name, yes?' the man said in Spanish. 'Please have a seat. I am Ramón Amarales and this,' he added, indicating Anderson's escort, 'is Chirlo.'

Anderson sat down. Perhaps at last he was going to be told something of his future.

He accepted the proffered cup of coffee and suddenly noticed the book on the table. It was a

Spanish translation of a well-known British book on the SAS.

Amarales noticed his look of surprise. 'I am a great fan of the SAS,' he said, stirring his own coffee. Chirlo, as usual, had taken a seat in the shadows. 'Did you not notice anything familiar about our operation in Malverdes?'

'The SAS doesn't usually attack political rallies,' Anderson said.

'But the method – it was borrowed from your own attack on the Embassy of Iran in London in 1980.'

Anderson smiled. 'We didn't leave an escape route open at the back.'

'Of course not. I am not claiming our men are trained to anything like the SAS's level of efficiency. Yet. But I would like them to be. This is why we are having this talk. I would like you to help train my men.'

'You must . . .'

'Before you say anything, Señor Anderson, let me finish. I have made some enquiries as to how much you are being paid in the SAS – very little, it seems to me, for all that you are prepared to do and risk. I will give you five times your annual salary for a mere ten weeks of your time as an adviser.'

'I . . .'

'One more thing. You will doubtless have one of two major objections to this. If you are a typical honest Englishman you will not want to work for a "drug baron", is that not so? Well, I think once you know more about the realities of our situation here in Colombia you may find it hard to see any great moral difference between working for the Amarales family and working for the families who run the Government in Bogotá. At one level we are all what you would call crooks, at another we are all just trying to make our way in a jungle that is not of our making.

'If, on the other hand, you are not so "honest", then you may be wondering how you will explain deserting your unit for ten weeks to earn a fortune. But you need not worry about that. It can be easily worked out, believe me. For all anyone knows, you are our prisoner. And there are many ways to arrange payment.'

Anderson smiled. 'You have not reminded me of the great objection to refusing you – what will happen to me if I do refuse.'

'Nothing. At present your embassy in Bogotá is considering a demand for half a million US dollars as the price of your return. I expect you have more idea than me whether they will agree to this . . .'

'No,' Anderson said. He did not have a clue.

'Well,' Amarales continued, 'if they are prepared to spend billions on recovering the Malvinas for a thousand shepherds, then it would seem sensible to pay half a million for a highly trained officer like yourself. But . . .' He shrugged. 'I am offering no threats. As you can imagine, money like that is always welcome, but I would rather have your services for those ten weeks if possible.'

Anderson was not sure how to respond. 'Can I think it over?' he asked.

'Of course.'

'And what about Señor Muñoz?'

'I don't think there's much *he* can teach us . . .' Amarales said.

Chirlo laughed, making his presence felt for the first time since the conversation began.

'So it's just a matter of ransom,' Amarales continued. 'A million dollars in his case. He comes from a very wealthy family,' he added. 'The ones who care so much about the poor usually do.' He looked at Anderson. 'Were you in the Malvinas, by the way?'

'Yes,' Anderson said, seeing no reason to deny it.

'Excellent,' Amarales said. 'I would like to talk to you about the reconquest some evening. I have read many accounts of the battles, but there are several questions which never seem to be answered.'

Anderson said nothing.

'Very well then,' Amarales said in dismissal. Chirlo rose from his seat and accompanied the SAS man back downstairs, not saying a word. The key turned in the lock once more, leaving Anderson feeling the need for someone to talk to.

He walked through to the adjoining room, where Muñoz was lying on his head gazing at another pornographic comic. 'They want a million dollars for you,' he told the Colombian. 'The man himself just told me.'

'Amarales?' Muñoz pulled himself up to lean against the headboard. 'I expect my father will pay,' he said. 'What about you?'

'He only wants half as much for me. But he'd rather pay me to stay on voluntarily to train his goons.'

'I shouldn't put too much store by any promises he makes,' Muñoz said. 'And don't make the mistake of thinking that because he's a well-spoken Spaniard he won't just have you killed. These people only understand the law of the jungle, my friend.'

That's what he said about you, Anderson thought. Jesus, what a country. He would swap all these fucking mountains for one square foot of Morecambe Bay mud. If he ever got the chance.

It was soon after five when their plane completed its descent into the mountain bowl which housed the capital of Ecuador.

The first flight, across the Atlantic, had been uneventful. Chris had drunk, slept and browsed through *The South American Handbook*; Eddie had drunk, slept and watched the movie; the Dame had drunk and read Wilbur Smith. Shortly after noon US Eastern Time they had landed in a grey-skied Miami, and spent another two hours in a departure lounge.

The AeroPeru flight to Ecuador was notable only for the identical gorgeousness of two of the hostesses. They had eaten their third major meal in nine hours and watched an American movie with Spanish subtitles that featured an English torturer working for a corrupt Latino crime syndicate. It had not seemed like a particularly good omen, but the twins had smiled at them as they left the plane.

Customs and Immigration took an irritating amount of time, but otherwise there were no problems. It was almost dark by the time they had found a taxi for the ride into the city.

London had booked three rooms for them at the Hotel Valencia. The receptionist seemed blissfully unaware of this, and after fifteen minutes of argument tiredness was turning irritation into anger. Fortunately, at this moment someone arrived from the embassy, a few notes changed hands, and the reservation was discovered. They went up to their rooms, which were in a line on the second floor front, overlooking the park.

They all trooped into Chris's room. The man

from the embassy – 'just call me Stephen' – underlined what the briefers at Hereford had told them, that they would need a couple of hours' rest before their bodies were ready to cope properly with 2700 metres of altitude.

'No problem,' they all agreed.

Stephen arranged to come back at nine that evening, and the three SAS men went to their rooms and laid themselves out.

Eddie could not rest. And he felt fine. He decided that as long as he did nothing too strenuous he would not have any problems. They would probably be heading north in the morning, and who knew when he would ever get to see Quito again. It was not exactly next door to Hackney.

He pushed a note under Chris's door and went out. The streets seemed fuller than when they had driven in, as if everyone had suddenly come out for an evening stroll. There were eating-places everywhere, and walking along the pavements of the old city was like moving through a long line of delicious smells. It was almost enough to make him feel hungry.

He reached a square where a small band was playing, surrounded by a large circle of onlookers. In a farther corner of the same square three jugglers were practising, throwing tenpins between them. It all seemed extraordinarily alive.

Down a narrow side street he got a surprise –

pride of place on a stall selling posters belonged to a large picture of a topless Samantha Fox. 'And they say our exports are shrinking,' Eddie murmured to himself. Almost as incomprehensibly, most of the other posters seemed to be of Swiss scenery. He had been under the impression that Ecuador had mountains of its own.

It was gone eight now, yet the shops were all still open. A bookshop had a window display devoted to the Galápagos Islands, which made him think of Chris and his wildlife fetish. Chris had been moaning all day that he had not had time to get a book about South American birds.

They had one inside. It was heavy, would cost most of his cash, but looked good. He bought it and started back for the hotel.

Chris was waiting for him. 'If you collapse from altitude sickness don't expect me to carry you,' he said angrily.

'You'll be too busy carrying this,' Eddie said handing him the book.

Chris looked at it. 'Oh you bastard,' he said. 'You beautiful bastard.' He grabbed Eddie and kissed him on the forehead.

'I thought you two were only into women,' the Dame said from the doorway.

'And goats,' Eddie corrected him.

'Gentlemen,' Stephen said from over the Dame's shoulder.

He shut the door behind him, paused theatrically, and gave them the same time and place Oliver had given Wynwood.

'How long will it take us?' Chris wanted to know.

Stephen considered. 'Four hours to the border, two to get across, five or six more to Popayán.'

'Looks like an early start,' Eddie said.

Wynwood had been woken from his siesta that afternoon by the phone. 'Your car's in the hotel parking lot,' Oliver told him. 'A green Fiat Uno, registration 6785 B 34. It's on hire from Hertz. There are some maps in the glove compartment which I thought you'd find useful. The keys are at the desk.'

'Is the hotel bill paid,' Wynwood asked.

'Until tomorrow lunchtime.'

'OK . . .'

'Only call me if you have to,' Oliver reiterated. 'I'll be in touch.'

'Over and out,' Wynwood said and hung up. He sat on the side of the bed for a moment. 'No time like the present,' he murmured to himself. He gathered up his belongings, packed them into the blue holdall he had brought from England, and left the hotel by the back exit. He found the car, threw the holdall in the back seat, re-entered the hotel by the back door, picked up the key and left again through the front.

In the car he spent several minutes examining a large-scale road map of the country, and made a snap decision. The quickest route to Popayán was via Ibagué and Cali, but he did not fancy retracing his route of three days before. The route via Neiva had dubious roads and would probably be an even longer drive than it looked, but he had plenty of time and it felt safer. It was the way to go.

He pulled the Fiat out into the afternoon traffic. Twenty minutes later he was skirting the ridge of the bowl which contained the city, and heading south on the aptly named Carretera del Sur.

At what seemed the last major intersection before the city fell away he found what he was looking for – a fellow-Caucasian hitchhiker. And a female one to boot.

She had to be crazy, he thought as he pulled over, a single woman hitching in a country as macho as it was lawless. And she was certainly not unattractive, he discovered as she climbed gratefully into the front seat. Her hair was long and blonde, framing a face that seemed instantly welcoming. 'Hi,' she said in the American accent he had expected, stretching long legs to hoist her rucksack into the back seat.

'Hi,' he said.

'Where you headed?' she asked.

'Neiva,' he said. 'That do you?'

'It's great. I've been standing there nearly an hour – anywhere's great. But Neiva's on my way.'

'To where?' Wynwood asked. He could hardly credit she had been there that long. Maybe it was National Celibacy Week in Colombia.

'San Agustín, you know?'

'No, what's there?'

'Wow, don't you know?' she said, unable to believe his ignorance. 'It's like the biggest tourist attraction in Colombia almost. After Cartagena, maybe. There's lots of old statues – really old statues, from before Columbus, you know – and they're spread out on green hills in this gorgeous valley. But that's not all – it's like a kind of place where there's a lot of, you know, travelling people living there. Some have been there for twenty years, ever since the hippie trail started down to Peru in the sixties. It's a really peaceful place.'

'You've been there before?'

'No, but I know people who have. Everyone says it's the one place in Colombia you have to see.'

'Maybe I'll get there,' Wynwood said.

'Where do you come from?' she asked. 'Are you English?'

'Welsh,' he said. 'My name's Joss.'

'I'm Bobbie,' she said. 'From San Diego. How far is it to Neiva?'

'Just over three hundred kilometres.'

She absorbed the information. 'I'll have to stay the night there,' she thought out loud. 'Do you know anywhere good to stay?'

'No,' Wynwood said absent-mindedly. The black Merc two cars behind him seemed to have been there as long as he could remember. Or was he just getting paranoid? He would find out when they stopped for a drink.

'Shall we have some music?' Bobbie was asking.

'I don't have any,' Wynwood said.

'I do,' she said, leaning back over the seat again and rummaging in her rucksack.

He had been afraid of that. A few seconds later Mick Hucknall's voice was echoing round the car. It could have been worse, Wynwood thought. At least it wasn't grunge or Barry Manilow. And it might stop her talking. It didn't, but he didn't really mind.

She was quite entertaining, brighter than she was knowledgeable, and older than she looked. Closer to thirty than twenty, a lot closer. As they swapped tales of their countries and families and travels he began to get the sense that she had been pretty bruised by something or someone, and for some reason that made him like her the more. He had always been a sucker for wounded birds.

Through Fusagasuga he drove, and down from

the mountains and into the Magdalena valley, the heat rising to meet them like a damp mist. They crossed the river at Girardot and headed south up its valley, passing the turn-off to Ibagué and Cali as the sun disappeared beyond the western crest. Behind them the black Merc kept its hundred-metre distance, only passing them when Wynwood stopped at a small and grubby roadside stall for two bottles of coke. Three kilometres farther on it pulled back onto the road behind them.

So who was it, Wynwood wondered. Amarales family goons? That seemed the best bet, but how the hell had they traced him? It did not say much for Oliver's security, or for any hopes of achieving surprise in any action against the drug lords. For all he knew the men in the Merc – he assumed there was more than one – were Colombian police or security people in the pay of one of the drug cartels.

Either way, he had to shake them off. His thoughts turned to when, where and how. If it had not been for Bobbie he would have opted for somewhere near and soon. Picking her up to give him protective colouring might have been a good idea, but it looked like he had picked up the tail before her. Now the protective colouring was more like a millstone. He could always just dump her somewhere, but he would have found it hard to dump his worst enemy by a Colombian highway at nightfall, let alone a pretty American blonde with a faith in humanity that verged on the suicidal.

But once in Neiva both he and the car would be more exposed and more vulnerable. And whatever happened he did not want it to happen in front of witnesses. He needed to stay as invisible as a Welshman could in Colombia; he needed to reach Popayán with no one in pursuit.

And even if he had been willing to let his presence be known there was no way he could trust the local authorities. God only knew whose side those in Neiva were on – he might find himself arrested on some trumped-up charge that night and handed over to the Amarales tomorrow.

It had to be before Neiva. And he had to get Bobbie out of the way. A good-sized roadside restaurant, he thought. He had not given his pursuers much warning of his departure from Bogotá, so unless they kept a picnic hamper permanently stashed in their back seat they were probably as hungry as he was. He started watching out for one.

Bobbie, he discovered, had fallen asleep to her Joan Armatrading tape, her mouth slightly open, revealing a pink tongue and perfect American teeth.

He found the restaurant half an hour later, and pulled in to the large parking lot. He nudged her awake. 'Dinner time,' he said. 'My treat.'

'That's very nice of you,' she said, eyes shining.

'Can you go in and get us a table,' he said. 'I'll be with you in a few minutes.'

She looked surprised but said OK.

Once she was gone he recovered the cross-draw holster from the holdall and put it on. He slipped the Browning in, and pulled the windcheater on over his shirt.

Outside the car the air was hot and sticky. The restaurant was perched between the highway and the Magdalena, whose wide dark waters rolled majestically along fifty metres to his right. Wynwood walked across to the front door, brushing insects from his face.

At the door he turned to see the Merc pulling up on the other side of the lot, close to the river. Inside, Bobbie had chosen an ideal table, close enough to the door that he would get a good view of the enemy when they came in. If they came in.

They did. There were three of them, two fairly young and one who looked around forty. The two young ones were both wearing tight-fitting suits which had not been tailored to take account of the shoulder holsters they were wearing. If the older one was carrying a gun it was at his waist. As the three of them walked across to a table on the far side of the restaurant, none of them cast so much as a glance in Wynwood's direction.

He and Bobbie both chose steak and eggs. The

waiter delivered their order at the serving hatch, then went to take the threesome's. The older man asked him something, and the waiter cast a quick glance back at Wynwood's table. He had been asked what the gringos had ordered, Wynwood guessed – they did not want to order a good meal themselves and then have to abandon it half-eaten.

He smiled to himself.

'Aren't you hot in that jacket?' Bobbie asked.

'No,' he lied.

They chatted about Bogotá until the food arrived. It was good, and there was lots of it. Bobbie cleared her plate with relish. No fears of anorexia for this one, Wynwood thought.

The threesome across the room were still in mid-meal. Wynwood loudly ordered coffees, and just as vociferously asked where the men's toilet might be. Out the back, he was told, as expected.

He went through the doorway indicated, and found himself in a corridor leading to a back entrance. Once outside he broke into a run, reaching the Merc in a few seconds. He had been intending to shoot out its tyres, but the door was open and it took only a second to take off the handbrake, get round the front and start pushing the car towards the river. As he strained to push it across the slightly raised area of ground by the river bank he wondered if he was doing the right thing. His pursuers would just steal another car . . .

What the hell, he thought, and with one last heave tipped the £20,000 car over the rim of the bank and down into the water. The car slid in up to its roof before the current started to tug it away.

He turned away to find the three men walking towards him, all with guns in hand.

'Gringo!' the older one shouted.

Wynwood remembered Andy's question: 'Do you ever feel like you're in a Western?'

'I think we will have to use your car now,' one of the younger ones said.

There seemed to be no grounds for compromise, Wynwood thought. And they had made a stupid mistake – he would be almost invisible against the darkness of the far bank, while they were silhouetted against the light from the restaurant.

He pulled the Browning from its holster, raised it with both arms and aimed at the younger man on the right. Not at the head, his training told him – it's too dark. He put a double tap through the upper torso, another through the same portion of the older man in the centre, then sank to one knee as the third man fired wildly over his head. Wynwood fired again and the third man went down.

He walked carefully across to the three prone figures. They were all dead. He took a deep breath and started pulling them one by one to the edge of the river. Once he had done that he tipped each one in beside the rapidly disappearing Merc, then walked back towards the restaurant, wondering how much had been heard.

His Browning was silenced, but they would have had to be deaf to miss the shot fired by the Colombian.

Maybe they were, maybe they weren't. No one seemed to be calling the police or cowering behind the hatch.

'You've been a long time,' Bobbie said as he rejoined her. 'I was beginning to get worried. And I thought I heard a shot.'

'They say gunfire is the national music of Colombia,' Wynwood said. 'Shall we go?'

They reached Neiva two hours later. Bobbie asked him if he wanted to share a hotel room. 'Just friends,' she added hastily, in case he had misunderstood. Why not, he thought. He found her about as sexually stimulating as a teddy bear, and he had kind of grown to like her over the last eight hours.

## 5

Troopers Sam 'Blackie' Blackman and Charles 'Bonnie' McCall sat side by side in the belly of the Hercules C-130. Somewhere beneath them was the Gulf of Mexico. They seemed to have been flying for ever, but according to Bonnie's watch it was only thirteen hours.

'We must be running out of fuel,' Blackie said, running a hand through what the barber had left of his hair. He was a tall Liverpudlian, with a body that looked more gangling than it actually was.

'No such luck.' Bonnie tried to make himself more comfortable for the umpteenth time. He was slightly smaller than Blackie, a ginger-haired Scot with an abundance of freckles. 'I joined the Army to see inside exotic women's blouses,' he complained, 'not the inside of some ugly transport plane.'

'You'd enjoy Oman,' Blackie said. 'The women are exotic and they don't even wear blouses. It's the Arab tradition – they wear veils across their faces and nothing else.'

'Bollocks!'

'It's true. You ask the boss here.'

Mike Bannister was just making his way past them en route for the forward section. 'Ask me what?'

'Is it true that the women in Oman wear nothing but veils, boss?' Bonnie asked.

'Absolutely,' Bannister said with a straight face, winking at Blackie as he moved on.

'Told yer,' Blackie said, rubbing it in.

'Still sounds like bollocks to me. The place would be knee-deep in tourists.'

'It is.'

'I never knew anyone who went there.'

'Majorca – that's in Oman.'

'No, it fucking isn't.'

One of the older troopers across the plane opened his eyes. 'Will you two stop filling the air with bullshit!' he half roared.

Bonnie and Blackie looked at each other and burst out laughing.

'Kids!' the older trooper said vehemently, and closed his eyes once more.

'Sorry, grandad,' Blackie muttered under his breath. Both he and Bonnie were only twenty-two, which might well have made them the youngest men on the plane. They had only returned from jungle training in Brunei a few days before Christmas, and had been expecting a couple of weeks' leave before resuming normal duties in Hereford. Neither of them had seen active service since winning their SAS badges the previous summer. And their nervousness at the prospect, as both were more than half aware, was what was making them behave even more like idiots than usual.

'How much longer?' Blackie asked Bannister, who was passing them again, this time in the opposite direction.

'About an hour,' he told them. 'But it'll seem like three,' he added cheerfully. He had been on enough flights like this to know how long they seemed to the uninitiated.

'One hour,' Bonnie repeated, after Bannister had moved on. 'Thank Christ for that. Do you have any idea where this place is that we're going?' he asked Blackie.

'Belize?'

'No, the place in Colombia.'

Blackie shook his head. 'We'll get briefed soon enough.'

'It's a nice feeling, though, knowing that if you get taken by the enemy, the Regiment'll come and get you back. Makes you feel wanted, don't you think.'

'I doubt if the Regiment would come looking

for you plonkers,' observed the veteran with closed eyes.

'I don't think he likes us,' Blackie said.

'He's just a bit nervous,' Bonnie suggested. 'He doesn't want to let us down when the time comes.'

'Your time'll come sooner than you expect if you don't shut the fuck up!'

'See, I told you. He's all heart really.'

'Who did you ring from Heathrow?' Chris asked Eddie. They were only an hour out of Quito, but it felt like a world away as their bus ground its way up the road towards the distant mountain pass. To their left the land dropped away like a stone, down to where a toy river flashed silver in the morning sun.

'Her name's Lisa,' Eddie admitted. 'I only met her this week,' he added, as if that absolved him from further questioning.

'Where?' Chris asked.

'In a wine bar. She's a student, but she waitresses to help pay the bills.'

'Uh-huh. What's she look like?'

'Er, lovely body, dark hair – long, nice smile.'

'Well that narrows it down.'

'Christ, I don't know. How do you describe someone? I guess her face is a bit cat-like, if you know what I mean.'

'Yeah. What colour eyes?'

'Dunno.'

'Don't know!?'

'Brown, probably. I never notice the colour of people's eyes.'

'Bet you noticed how big her tits were.'

'Yep.' He smiled at the memory. 'Perfect,' he added.

'You sound . . .' Chris hesitated. 'How can I put this without you feeling insulted . . . You sound *interested* in this one.'

'Could be.'

Chris laughed. 'Mr Commitment.'

Eddie grinned. 'You know what it's like in this job. You never get the time.'

'I know. I sometimes think that's why some of us do it.'

'You?'

'I sometimes wonder. You gonna see her again?'

'Hope so. We gotta get home first.'

'Yeah,' Chris agreed.

They sat in silence for a minute or so. 'But look at it,' Chris said eventually, staring out at the vista of mountains receding into mountains beneath a pure blue sky. 'Fucking beautiful. It just makes me want to get out. Moments like this I love the SAS and I hate it. Love it for bringing me out here and hate it for rushing me through it at a hundred miles an hour.'

Eddie followed his gaze. 'It's an improvement on the Falls Road,' he said.

Four seats back the Dame was staring out at the same scenery. Before leaving Quito they had agreed not to travel as a threesome, even on the Ecuadorian leg of the journey, and it had not been hard deciding who would be the odd man out. All of them knew that in any group of three loners the Dame would out-loner the other two. So, unless there was some sort of emergency, he would not be communicating with Chris and Eddie until they all 'accidentally' checked into the same hotel in Popayán. Which suited him fine. He liked the two of them, but he liked his own company better.

Wilbur Smith's was not bad either, but the suspension on the bus was so bad that reading was impossible. He supposed the landscape was beautiful, but he was bored with looking at it. Trying to traverse it on foot would be something; cruising through it on a bus, no matter how uncomfortable the seats, was no challenge to anyone.

But the Dame had to admit there was something else too. He had always found landscapes like this – gargantuan bloody landscapes – made him feel a bit uneasy. He remembered feeling that way, feeling vaguely threatened by it all, when he was about ten and the family had gone to Scotland for their summer holiday. Maybe that was why he wanted to get out and show it who was boss, he thought suddenly. Yeah, maybe that was it.

He had a sudden mental picture of the two Provo bodies lying in Kenneally Street, the blood and the rain. He had done that. Shown them who was boss. He had had no choice. But was that all it meant? Could you just walk away? Or did it leave some invisible mark on you? Some patch of darkness somewhere.

His dad had always laughed at religion, even though his mother had always gone to church on Sundays. 'She only goes for the singing,' his dad used to tell them, but she didn't. 'Somebody must have dreamt all this up' she would say, and it was hard to imagine anyone other than God dreaming up the Garth flats in Sunderland.

His dad had been unimpressed by the logic. He had 'better things to do than pray to some bearded old fart the rich had invented to make the poor feel better'. Like drinking himself into his usual Sunday stupor with his mates.

'You'll roast,' his mother used to say, and maybe that was what his dad was doing. But the Dame could not really believe it – just about everybody who knew the man had loved him, and that had to count for something.

His mother and his sisters loved the Dame, but would that go on one side of some balance sheet, the bodies in the rain on the other? Was that how it worked? If so, how did they measure it all, the good and the evil? It all seemed crazy.

But he had killed eight people now, and though every one of them had been trying to kill him, it still seemed a lot. Maybe that was how you measured it, by how it felt. In which case Hitler must have gone to heaven. Which was nuts.

There was no way of knowing. Maybe you did just walk away.

'The British Ambassador,' the President's personal secretary announced from the door. The President rose somewhat reluctantly to his feet and ushered the Queen's representative in Bogotá into the ornate Spanish chair which faced his desk. He checked the office door was properly closed and reseated himself in the rather more comfortable product of a modern Swedish manufacturer.

'Good morning, Mr President,' the Ambassador began. 'I have some good news.'

'Yes?' Estrada said, his palms together in front of his chin.

'The operation will soon be under way.'

Estrada lifted his eyebrows. 'How soon?'

'I'm afraid I don't have that information as

yet. But of course as soon as I do, you will be informed.'

Before or after it's all over, Estrada asked himself. 'Thank you, Mr Ambassador,' he said.

'I have also been advised that the United States Government has been apprised of the situation to date, and that it is possible there may be limited United States participation in the operation,' the Ambassador went on. 'But,' he added, 'I am asked to convey to you personally the assurance of both my Government and the United States Government that no United States troops will set foot on Colombian soil.'

Estrada grunted. 'Is that all?' he asked.

'That is all,' the Ambassador agreed, getting to his feet.

'I would appreciate as much notice as possible of the actual operation,' Estrada said, his hand on the doorknob.

'Of course.' The Ambassador bowed and left.

'Get me Señor Quintana,' Estrada told his secretary. 'I'll be upstairs.'

They reached the border town of Tulcan soon after eleven. From there it was a taxi ride to the border itself, which was marked by a river at the bottom of a small valley. Border posts had been set up on either end of the river bridge. The Ecuadorians just waved them through, and they walked across to where the Colombian border guards, all toting sub-machine-guns, were waiting to herd them into a long, low building. Inside an officer was waiting to examine their passports. He had a sub-machine-gun lying carelessly on the desk beside him.

Chris and Eddie were behind an American couple in the queue, and this turned out to be good news. After aggressively asking the two Americans a string of questions in staccato Spanish, and nearly reducing the woman to tears before finally letting them through with ill-concealed reluctance to the paradise that was Colombia, the officer greeted the two SAS men with a wide smile and enquiries about the health of Mrs Thatcher and Gary Lineker.

Eddie told him how much he admired the Colombian player Carlos Valderama, which made the officer's day. 'Enjoy your stay in Colombia!' he said, waving them through with a flourish.

They watched from a distance as the Dame came through, hoping he didn't think he had time to convince the Colombian that Sunderland were a football team.

Another fleet of taxis carried everyone on into the town of Ipiales, where they climbed reluctantly into another bus for the six-hour trip to Popayán. So far so good, Eddie thought, as they started off on the first leg to Pasto, climbing a valley that seemed large and deep enough to lose the Grand Canyon in. He could see what Chris meant, sort of. He almost felt like getting out himself. Almost.

Luis Quintana was shown into the President's private quarters, and was pleased to find that just for once no American soap opera was flooding the room with 'sound and fury signifying nothing'. Where did that line come from? he wondered. He couldn't remember.

The TV was on, but with the sound turned down, and the obvious delight of the local game-show contestants was mercifully muted. The President was staring into space, a look of frozen anxiety on his face. Looking at him, Quintana wondered if his own ambitions for the presidency were at all sensible. He did not want to end up like Juan Estrada, perpetually unsure of himself, a virtual prisoner in his own palace, only ever at ease in front of televised fantasies from North America.

'*Buenas tardes*, Juan,' he said, lowering himself onto the other sofa without waiting to be asked.

Estrada grunted and bit his thumb. 'The English are on their way,' he said unhappily.

'I thought that was what you wanted.'

'I'm not so sure any more. In fact I'm beginning to regret letting you talk me into it.'

Quintana smiled thinly, but did not bother

trying to correct this minor revision of history. 'It was a good idea last Monday, why is it not a good idea today?'

'Perhaps it was not a good idea on Monday.'

Quintana tried a change of tack. 'What do you mean – they are on the way? When? How many of them?'

'Oh, they don't tell me that. You know what the English are like – they tell you nothing very politely and at great length. "Soon" – that's what it comes down to. "Soon". A few days? A week? They say they will give me exact times and dates when they have them, but I wouldn't put it past them to tell me after it's all over.'

Quintana could not help thinking that if he was in the English commander's shoes he would do just that. He went back to the first problem. 'I still do not understand why it is a bad idea,' he said calmly.

'What if it *fails*?' Estrada said. 'I know these SAS men are supposed to be supermen, but they must fuck up sometimes. What if they fuck up here? We'll have a pile of English bodies that we can't explain away. Everyone will know that the Government must have been involved, and the cartels will be screaming that I am just a foreign stooge and they are the only true Colombians.' He looked coldly at Quintana, unaware that the opening credits for *Knot's*

*Landing* were rolling silently across the screen behind him.

Quintana reprcssed a smile. 'If by any chance it should fail – I still think the odds must be heavily on success, but just supposing it does fail – things will not be that bad. Muñoz will presumably be dead, which would be a plus, particularly since it would be obvious to everyone what lengths you were prepared to go to try and save him.'

Estrada was impressed despite himself. 'Perhaps,' he admitted. 'In any case it's too late to change our plans now.' He turned to glance at the screen, and turned back to Quintana. 'Just one more thing. The negotiations for the ransom – how are they proceeding?'

'They have given us until Wednesday to agree the terms.' He shrugged. 'If the English mean what they say it will probably be all over by then.'

'Good. Thank you, Luis.'

It was a dismissal. Quintana was only halfway to the door when the TV sound boomed back on.

He walked down the stairs which led from Estrada's private quarters to the Presidential offices, going back over what he had just said to reassure Estrada. It had been half true, he thought, but only half. Certainly Muñoz would be gone, but would Estrada receive the benefit? The President was probably right in thinking he would be damaged by the revelation of British involvement – after all, the Malvinas War was still fresh in many minds, and gringos were gringos.

Reaching his own office, Quintana sat thinking by his window for several minutes. With both Muñoz and Estrada out of the running he could not think of anyone with a better prospect of succeeding the latter than himself.

Somewhere in the distance a bell chimed nine o'clock. Eddie and Chris were slowly working their way round Popayán's Plaza de Armas, looking out for a large tousle-headed Welshman. It was their second circuit; on the first they had passed the Dame sitting on one of the benches, deep in conversation with two young women whose rucksacks bore Australian flag badges.

'Finds sisters wherever he goes,' Chris observed.

'It's obscene,' Eddie agreed.

The three of them had arrived in the Popayán bus station soon after dark, found a middling hotel courtesy of the handbook, and had found time to shower and change before coming out to keep their appointment with Wynwood. Popayán itself, insofar as they could tell by night, was exactly what the handbook said it was: an attractive old colonial town full of narrow streets, white buildings and university students.

'Here comes Ivor the Engine,' Eddie murmured.

Wynwood was strolling across the square towards them. 'Eddie, Chris!' he almost shouted in his sing-song voice.

'Hello b . . .' Chris bit off the word 'boss'.

'Hiya, Taff,' Eddie said brazenly, offering Wynwood a hand to shake. 'And what brings you to sunny Popayán?'

Wynwood grinned. 'Same as you, I expect – the peaceful climate. Have you two eaten?' he asked. 'I'm starving, and there's a place just down there . . .' He pointed across the square. 'Where's your friend, by the way?' he asked Chris.

'He's watching us now,' Chris said quietly. 'Just lead off and he'll follow.'

'Right.' Wynwood led them across the square and a few yards up Calle 5 to a restaurant named La Plazuela.

The Dame arrived at their table a few moments later.

Wynwood examined his three new partners. With his own mass of dark curls, Eddie's unruly blonde mop, Chris's shock of spikes and the Dame's near-skinhead cut, the four of them did not stand out as an obvious team. Which was not only good, but a marked improvement on the early eighties, when so many SAS men had adopted unruly long hair for undercover work that it had become like a new uniform.

Clothes-wise the differences were few. Chris was

wearing a shirt and jeans, the rest of them T-shirts and jeans. All wore some sort of windcheater and boots. Too bad, Wynwood thought – travellers were not known for their originality of dress.

They ordered food and kept the conversation to impressions of Colombia and what was going on back home. After paying the bill they found a store selling beer and took the bottles back to Wynwood's room at the nearby Hotel Acapulco. It was somewhat swisher than their own hotel.

'I thought it was important that we weren't all staying in the same squalor,' Wynwood explained.

'It's being so old,' Eddie explained to the Dame. 'He needs his comforts more.'

The Dame smiled and opened a bottle of beer. 'Not bad,' he reckoned, after a first taste. 'Not Newcastle Brown, but not bad.'

'OK,' Wynwood said, sitting himself down on the floor with his back to the wall. 'To business. How did Man U do on Boxing Day?'

'Lost 7–0 to City,' Eddie offered.

'Uh-huh.'

'They drew 1–1 with Everton,' the Dame said.

'That sounds better. You lot didn't have any trouble getting here?' he asked Chris.

'Nope.'

'There were the twins on the plane,' the Dame suggested. 'We had to hose Eddie down after the flight.'

'And then we had to spend a week in Quito looking for some bird-watching book,' Eddie added.

'Well, I did have a minor problem or two,' Wynwood said, and told them the story of the car that had trailed him from Bogotá.

They listened in silence, jokes forgotten.

'So who knows?' Wynwood concluded. 'The operation may be blown. I'll call Bogotá tonight, pass on the information, then wait and see if Hereford or London have any news or suggestions.'

'OK, boss,' Chris agreed. Each SAS patrol tended to operate much of the time as a group of equals regardless of rank, but in this case there was no doubt in anyone's mind who was boss. Apart from anything else, Wynwood knew the territory.

'What do we do in the meantime?' Eddie asked.

'Tomorrow I want to get a look at Totoro – that's the name of the estate or ranch or whatever it is where we think Andy and Muñoz are being held. Chris can drop me off a few kilometres out and pick me up later. You two can just amuse yourselves. Separately would be best. Get rested up, get used to the altitude. I have the distinct feeling this one is not going to be a picnic.'

'There's just one other thing, boss,' Eddie asked deadpan.

'What?'

'Did you give Bobbie one?'

Wynwood eyed him tolerantly. 'Let's just say she's been given a standard by which to judge other men.'

'Maybe she wanted more than an evening paper, boss.'

# 6

'Are there are any *people* in Belize?' Blackie asked.

'Doesn't look like it, does it?' Bonnie agreed. They were walking across the strip of tarmac which separated the barrack from the HQ building. To their right two Hercules C-130 transport planes were being busied over by ground staff, and beyond them a quartet of Harriers were parked in line. And that was about it. In every direction the airfield seemed to end in a wall of jungle. The sky was a uniform blue-white, the air thick and humid. They were in the tropics all right, but if they had not been told where they would have had no way of knowing. It didn't *feel* any different to Brunei.

They were on their way to the morning briefing, along with the other thirty members of C Squadron's Mountain and Air Troops. Judging by the eyes turned their way as they entered the briefing room they were the last ones there.

'Sorry to drag you away from your pleasures,'

Major Bourne greeted them sarcastically. 'I'll try and make sure this doesn't take too long.'

'They were only tossing each other off,' a voice said.

'Some of us have heard of women,' Blackie said.

Bourne waited as the laughter subsided. Sometimes he wished that he could get through just one briefing, just one, without a parallel seminar in sexual innuendo. But when all was said and done, it was just a way of releasing tension. As the actress said to the bishop, he thought to himself.

Thirty pairs of eyes were watching him.

'I thought you might all like some clear idea of what you're doing here,' he began. 'As things stand at the moment, one of our number – Sergeant Anderson of the Training Wing staff – I'm sure you all remember him from Basic Training . . .'

There were several groans.

'Sergeant Anderson is being held for ransom by a Colombian criminal organization – one of the cocaine cartels. A well-known Colombian politician is being held with him, for the same reason . . .'

'I bet they want more for him than Andy Anderson,' someone remarked.

'Twice as much,' Bourne replied. 'The villains in question are the Amarales family. They have a fortified estate just outside Popayán, which, for all you geographic illiterates' – he turned to the large-scale map of Colombia behind him – 'is here in the southern mountains.' He turned back to face them. 'Negotiations are under way,' he went on, 'between the two Governments and the villains, but that needn't concern us. We're going in to get Andy back. And the local politician too while we're at it.'

'Boss, what happens if our politicians pull the plug on us at the last moment?'

'I don't think there's much chance of that. Of course, if it happens, it happens. No matter what you and I might think of our politicians, we're here to carry out their decisions, not question them.'

There were more groans, this time of resignation.

Bourne smiled. 'Stop getting your knickers in a twist,' he advised them. 'I think this is a Go, and you might as well believe likewise until you hear otherwise. Now' – he took hold of the map and flipped it over to reveal a blown-up satellite photograph of Totoro – 'you've each got a copy of this in front of you as part of the briefing pack. I want you to take it away and memorize the layout. And of course everything else in the pack. Someone's working on a model as I speak, and tomorrow we should be able to start some detailed planning. By then we may have additional information from our surveillance patrol. Most of you probably know the men concerned – Joss Wynwood from Training Wing and Chris Martinson, Eddie Wilshaw and Damien Robson from B Squadron's Mountain Troop.'

'Not B Squadron, boss!'

'I'm afraid it was the best we could come up with at short notice, Trooper. The four of them should be *in situ* sometime tonight.'

'Do we have a date yet, boss?'

'If today is D1, we want to be ready to go by the evening of D3. That's all I can tell you, at present. And we haven't yet decided between HAHO and HALO for insertion. Nor has it been decided whether we need to send in two Troops or just the one.'

Some heartfelt groans were heard.

'I know you'd all love to go,' Bourne said. 'We'll see. For the moment, go through the briefing packs, and spend some time considering the advantages and disadvantages of each insertion method in these circumstances. Right, any questions?'

'How are we getting home, boss?'

'That's a remarkably pertinent question, Trooper. Since it's only approximately two hundred kilometres across this 4000-metre mountain range to the Ecuadorian border we considered turning the whole business into an endurance exercise. However, it was felt that that would be unfair to the Colombian politician. So you're being lifted out by our allies.'

'Not the Yanks, boss? They couldn't even lift their own men out of Iran.'

'This is a rather easier proposition for them, Trooper. This time we have the cooperation of the local Government.'

'But do the local military always listen to their Government?' someone wanted to know.

It was an intelligent question, and Bourne could not help feeling a little proud of the questioner, even though he had been put on the spot. 'No, not always,' he admitted. He would not insult the men in front of him by telling them anything less than the truth as he understood it. 'We're not expecting any trouble from that direction,' he went on, 'and we'll take all steps to make it even more unlikely, but we won't be ignoring the possibility either.' He waited for a follow-up but none came. 'Any more?' he asked.

There were no more questions.

'OK, get all the information we have packed in among your brain cells – I'm sure there's plenty of spare space. And I know it's New Year's Eve, but try not to wash away everything you've learned on a tide of beer tonight. Enjoy yourselves, but remember, we may be in action the day after tomorrow. If any of you have ever tried free-falling with a hang-over you'll know what I mean.'

There were a couple of assenting murmurs.

Bourne left the room. In the back row Blackie and Bonnie looked at each other. 'Hey-ho,' Blackie sighed.

'Or hey-lo,' Bonnie said. 'I don't know which is worse – floating around next to the moon getting frostbite, or plummeting down at about a hundred miles an hour hoping the bastard who made your parachute had his mind on the job that day.'

'You're an inspiration, you are,' Blackie said.

'I always thought Colombia was a record label,' Bonnie said sourly.

Wynwood and Chris got an early start, driving out of the city soon after eight. It was a beautiful day, the sun rising through an almost clear blue sky. In the far distance mere wisps of cloud sat on the shoulders of the mountains. They followed the main highway to Cali for the first few kilometres, then turned off onto the lesser road Wynwood had traversed from Neiva the previous morning. Chris was driving, Wynwood examining Oliver's large-scale maps as he applied camouflage cream to his face and neck.

After another few kilometres they crossed a bridge over the energetic waters of the upper Cauca, and turned right again, up the river valley. The road was paved, but seemed little used. Cocaine money, Wynwood guessed.

Ten minutes later he told Chris to pull over. They were in a relatively narrow section of the valley, where the Cauca and the road shared most of the flat ground and forested slopes rose quite steeply on either side towards invisible heights.

"Totoro is about two kilometres further up the valley," Wynwood said, "and since this road doesn't seem quite as busy as the M25, I think it would be better if you went back the way we came rather than drive past the entrance." He looked at his watch. "Eight forty-seven," he said. Chris checked his and nodded. "Eight hours should do it," Wynwood reckoned. "So let's say here at 17.00. If I don't show, two-hour intervals until I do. Or until Man U win the League."

"Christ, we're not hanging around that long."

Wynwood smiled, checked the binoculars and the Browning in his cross-draw.

"Do you want to take this?" Chris asked, offering him the bird book.

"The book to spot 'em, the Browning to shoot 'em? I don't think so, Chris. You go and sit on a mountain with it." He reached for the door. "I'll see you at two."

The sound of the car receded as he started climbing the eastern slope of the valley. There was little undergrowth beneath the trees, so the going was not particularly hard, and he had to remind himself to stop every few minutes because of the altitude. After about half an hour he found himself on a kind of shelf and, reckoning he was now high enough, started following it southwards. So far he had seen no sign of human life – no path, cigarette ends, litter, traps. The forest seemed as virgin as the day it was born.

He climbed in and out of two valleys cut by streams running down to join the Cauca. It was in the third such valley, he judged from his map, that he would find Totoro. He consciously slowed his pace, eyes and ears straining for any sign of danger.

Another kilometre went by. He was too far east, he judged. He would have to do some tree-climbing, which was not an activity he took much pleasure in. It was worth it though. Swaying in the top of a thirty-metre tree he could see a thin line of smoke rising into the western sky. He was too far to the east.

He took a compass bearing, clambered down and started off again. Twenty minutes later he found himself about to emerge from the trees at the head of a broad valley. The source of the smoke was laid out below him, no more than a kilometre away. Totoro.

It took him almost half an hour to find a good viewing position where an old landslide had created a gap in the screen of trees. Laid out behind tufts of grass he could bring his binoculars to bear on the whole complex.

The valley below was almost rectangular, only narrowing to a sudden point just beneath his position. The stream which had made it clung to the foot of the eastern slope – to the left as Wynwood looked. Both slopes were steep, rearing up at something close to forty-five degrees. They were tree-covered, with the notable exception of the lowest hundred metres or so, which had been stripped, presumably for security reasons.

The two lines of trees faced each other across a valley floor some five hundred metres wide. From where Wynwood lay to the confluence of the stream with the north-south-flowing Cauca it was about three times as far. Beyond the Cauca another steep, tree-covered slope blocked the natural horizon.

Man's work in the valley was not quite so tidy. The road ran alongside the river, crossing it just before disappearing away to the north. A paved entrance road left it amid a copse of trees and curved up towards the ranch, passing between gates set in a high wire fence after a hundred metres, and more gates set in a high stone wall four hundred metres farther on, before ending in a wide circular parking space at the heart of the inner compound.

The outer compound, that area surrounded by

the high wire fence, took up more than half the valley floor, ending at the tree-line to the right and just beyond the stream to the left. It had been largely denuded of trees. Wynwood could see two horses standing together away near the main gate.

The inner compound, surrounded by a stone wall some three metres high, was almost square, with each side about two hundred metres long. The main house – a two-storey villa with flat roof and first-floor verandah – was at Wynwood's end. It had two single-storey wings that had obviously been added at a later date. Three more buildings – one of two storeys, the others of one – stretched along the inside of the northern wall. Beyond them there was a helipad, but no helicopter. The south-western corner was mostly lawn, and boasted a couple of canopied tables.

There were several armed guards in evidence, some stationary and some moving. Wynwood watched one of the latter slowly walking the southern fence. When he reached the far corner he took something from his pocket and seemed to speak into it. There was obviously a security centre somewhere in the complex.

Wynwood got out a pencil and began sketching the layout as accurately as he could. He worked quickly, knowing that the squadron in Belize would be getting satellite blow-ups, and that his main job that day was to find the surveillance patrol an observation post and a hide location. He found them both within the next two hours.

Retreating uphill from his vantage point, he had drawn a wide circle round to the south and west before cresting the ridge of the slope that rose up from the stream due south of the compound. About a third of the way down the slope he found a climbable tree that offered an almost uninterrupted view of the estate. There was a swimming pool behind the eastern wall which had not been visible from his previous position.

On the other side of the ridge, one valley away from Totoro, he found the ideal spot for their hide: a wide gully in the valley side which boasted the extra protection of a large uprooted tree.

He could see no disadvantages to this site, but it was not yet two o'clock, and he might still have time to look for something better once he had found somewhere for the helicopters to land.

Eddie walked across the arched bridge, then down some steps to the park which stretched out alongside the river. There were lots of students sitting on the grass and under the palms, while others paced up and down murmuring to themselves. Maybe here they had exams at Christmas, he thought.

A couple of hundred metres on he came across a huge open-air blackboard, with a dozen or so students busy drawing equations on it. The whole thing made him smile, though he was not sure why.

There were lots of trees, though few of them seemed particularly tropical; in fact most seemed not that different from the sort you would find in Epping Forest. He stopped to watch two art students having their photographs taken with their paintings, huge canvases covered in abstract designs which, like the trees, seemed just a little strange. It occurred to him that this was a difficult place for Europeans to understand; it was different but not really different enough. You felt like a foreigner but at the same time you didn't.

Still, none of the locals had any trouble identifying him as one. As he walked through the park the word "gringo" came at him in a bewildering mixture of mutters, growls and simple observations. The park ended, and away across two blocks he could see a statue on a hill. He walked up the road, and found a path which spiralled up towards the summit.

The statue turned out to be a large and suitably aggressive-looking conquistador. From its base Eddie could see the town spread out below him – a grid pattern of mostly white buildings in a wide plain bounded by distant mountains. It didn't look like Hackney. In fact it looked damn peaceful.

Appearances could be deceptive, of course. Two teenagers were coming up the path he had climbed, carrying a ghetto-blaster between them. Loud and distorted heavy metal blared from its speakers. They took one look at Eddie and disappeared from sight round the other side of the statue. Not out of earshot, however. Their ghetto-blaster, apparently aimed at Ecuador and Peru, still strained at its speakers like a wooden boat in a thunderstorm.

Home sweet home, Eddie thought. He wondered what Lisa was doing. "Happy New Year," he murmured.

On the other side of the town the Dame was walking round the block which contained the Cathedral. It looked like a fortress, with its high walls and corner tower, but the Dame didn't think that was why he found it forbidding. B Squadron could be over those walls in fifteen seconds.

He stopped at the front entrance and stared up at the sun-shadowed stonework and the dome floating in the blue sky. There seemed to be a stork or something like it nesting under the eaves. Chris would know.

He crossed the road and entered through the small door which had been made in the larger ones. After the bright sunlight it seemed almost lightless inside, but after a while his eyes began to adjust and he started walking slowly down a side aisle, watching those sitting in the pews, their pleading faces turned upwards towards the stricken Christ.

He looked away, and tried to make out details of the dimly lit paintings on the walls. Surely the men who had painted them would have wanted them seen more clearly than this. A sign caught his eye, telling visitors, in English, not to use flash.

Dull gold gleamed everywhere; it was like being swallowed by a huge golden whale. And yet . . . his eyes were drawn back unwillingly to the upturned faces. So much need. And he knew what for. He could not put words to it, but he knew what for.

He got to his feet, aware again of the church around him. The thought crossed his mind that death would be like this golden darkness. He shook his head and started back down the aisle, towards where a thin wash of light was seeping in from the invisible doorway.

Chris did what Wynwood had told him to do – went and sat on a mountain. Once back on the main road he simply turned the car uphill, and watched as the view through the windscreen grew ever more spectacular. After an hour or so he emerged onto a vast, rolling plateau. For what seemed like thirty kilometres in every direction palm-studded fields and hills stretched away towards purple mountains. Above it all myriad banks of cloud rolled across an enormous sky. It seemed like a land custom-made for giants.

He parked the car and walked up to the crest of

a nearby knoll, book in hand, and had no sooner sat down than a hawk-like bird appeared almost directly above him, drawing lazy circles in the air. It was white with prominent black markings either side of the neck. A black-shouldered kite, the book told him.

The next few hours went by like minutes, and it was with some reluctance that Chris abandoned his perch to collect Wynwood.

The upper slopes of the Cauca valley were still bathed in sunshine, but the light had already deserted the road in its bottom, and Wynwood seemed to almost leap from the shadows at the arranged spot.

"Well?" Chris asked as they drove back down.

Wynwood told him about the layout of the estate and the potential hide. "There's a pretty wide flat clearing about a kilometre to the north-east which should do for the pick-up," he added.

"Great."

"Yeah, but dropping in isn't going to be so easy. It's all forest."

"What about the front garden?"

"It may come to that."

His New Year soirée was going well, Luis Quintana thought. A fair slice of the cream of Colombian society was there, which not only reflected well on the respect in which he was held, but also on the wealth of the coffers which would be available to him for financing a presidential campaign.

Noticing his wife across the room he thought she looked almost desirable. Perhaps, he thought sourly, the two of them could start speaking to each other again in the coming year.

At that moment he noticed Rafael Lamizares standing alone, and took the opportunity he had been waiting for all evening.

"Could I have a word, Rafael?" he asked.

"Of course, Luis. A private word?"

Quintana nodded. "The garden, perhaps?"

Lamizares followed Quintana out onto the terrace and down into the shadows of the path which circled the lawn. The two men had known each other for twenty years, ever since they had attended the same college in the United States, and both had risen high in the Party. Quintana was an important minister, and though Lamizares had no official Government post, those well versed in Colombian politics considered him one of the most powerful men in the country. He was the Liberal Party's kingmaker. Or, more accurately, its President-maker.

"I have a question for you, Rafael," Quintana began, once they had moved far enough away from the house. "A hypothetical question, of course."

"Of course," Lamizares said, smiling. Over the

distant centre of Bogotá a firework flashed red stars into the sky.

"If Estrada was not to stand or not to be selected by the Party, do you think I would stand a chance of the nomination?" Quintana asked.

"Is he thinking of not standing?"

"Not that I know of."

"Then he will be selected." Another rocket showered stars into the sky, this time green ones.

"It looks that way. But six months is a long time – something might happen to undermine his popularity. Who can tell?"

Lamizares stopped and looked at him closely. "Who indeed?" he said sardonically. "Well, in this highly hypothetical situation, and assuming that whatever it is that undermines Estrada's popularity does not also undermine your own, then . . . well, I would make you second favourite to Muñoz. Always assuming his family agrees to pay the ransom, of course. A long way second though, Luis, I'm afraid to say. This is not my personal preference, you understand. It's what I suspect would be the Party's preference."

Quintana said nothing, savouring the possibility.

'Of course,' Lamizares went on, 'if Muñoz didn't come back, I suspect the radicals would find it hard to agree on his successor. In which case I don't think there's much doubt you would be the favourite.'

It was what Quintana had wanted to hear. 'Thank you, Rafael,' he said with more than his usual sincerity, 'for indulging a few New Year daydreams. Let's go back in.'

The phone rang in Wynwood's room. 'There's a long-distance call for you, Señor Wynwood,' the receptionist told him.

'Fine,' Wynwood said.

Oliver's voice came down the line, but there was no click to suggest the receptionist had hung up.

'Hi, Joss,' Oliver said. 'I just called to tell you I can't make it. Would you believe five of our people are down with colds, which only leaves two to man the phones.'

'I'm sorry to hear that, Jim.'

'Yeah, well, can't be helped. I'd still like to see you on the sixteenth if that's possible?'

'Sure. What number's your apartment again?'

'Seventy-three.'

'I remember now. OK, see you then. Bye Jim.'

Wynwood hung up, picked up the list of numbers he had just made, and went out to use one of the public phones in the Plaza de Armas. He chose one as far from prying ears as possible, punched out the code for Bogotá and the numbers Oliver had just given him – 521673.

The embassy man answered immediately. 'Hi,' he said, 'everything OK?'

'No,' Wynwood said. He told Oliver about the men in the Merc.

'Oh hell' was the first response; 'I'd better get on to London' the second.

Wynwood waited for more.

'Did you check them for ID?' Oliver asked.

'There wasn't time.' Had there been? he wondered.

'No matter, it probably wouldn't have told us anything.'

'Seems to me,' Wynwood said, 'the best place to find out whether it's blown is Totoro. I think we should establish the surveillance operation right now.' He told Oliver about the recon that day. 'It didn't look like they were preparing a reception committee. And if they do, then if we're *in situ* we'll know about it.'

'There's a problem with that – your cache. We were going to deliver to certain map coordinates and let you collect, but it's been decided that such an operation would be unnecessarily complicated. Instead, we intend to deliver direct.'

'To the hotel room?'

'No, of course not. But the delivery is tonight, which is why I say there's a problem with establishing the surveillance immediately.'

'Where?'

'A lay-by off the Cali-Popayán highway, three kilometres north of the turn-off to Silvio, about ten kilometres south of Pescador. On the west side of the road. A blue and cream coffee truck, bearing the name Café Liberador. You got that?'

'Yeah, we stop for coffee.'

'The driver's name is Manolo Ochoa.'

'When?'

'Ten this evening.'

'We could pick up the stuff and then establish surveillance.'

'If you say so. I thought . . .'

'Always assuming the night vision equipment is on board.'

'It is.'

'And everything else?' Wynwood was thinking how good it was going to feel to be a soldier again.

'Even the Claymores.'

'Great. Thanks, Oliver. Hope to see you in some other life.'

'Good luck.'

Wynwood put the phone down and walked back across the square and up Calle 6 to the others' hotel. He found the Dame reading, took him down to where Chris and Eddie were playing cards, told them what he had just discussed with Oliver, and asked them what they thought.

The decision was unanimous.

'What are we going to do with the car, boss?' Chris asked.

'It's either hide it close by or one of us has got to hide it some way off and walk all the way back in.'

They thought about it for a moment. 'What are the chances of hiding it close by?' Eddie asked.

'I don't really know,' Wynwood admitted. 'I didn't see any obvious places.'

'Neither did I,' Chris said.

'Then I vote for a long way off,' Eddie said. 'If it's found close by then the thing's blown, it's as simple as that.'

'He's right,' the Dame agreed.

'OK, who's going to take the long walk?' Wynwood wanted to know.

'I will,' Chris said. 'Anyone else is liable to get lost.'

Eddie sprayed him with the pack of cards.

'What about the hotel?' the Dame asked.

'We'll check out. Tell 'em we're taking the night bus,' Chris suggested.

'Where to?'

'Wherever it's going.'

Wynwood looked at his watch. We've got an hour and a half. I'll pick you up out front in half an hour, OK?'

'Yes, boss.'

* * *

Thirty-two minutes later Wynwood was piloting the car past the bus station and onto the Cali road. Chris was sitting beside him in the front, examining a photocopy of the large-scale map which Wynwood had just made in one of the town's numerous student shops. Eddie and the Dame sat behind, each keeping an eye on the view from his window. As far as they could tell the town was indifferent to their departure – no suspicious eyes seemed to be following the Fiat.

Wynwood was pleased. Male gringo foursomes in cars were not unknown, but they were not exactly common either. Now all they had to worry about was running into a military checkpoint.

They drove north along the dark highway, mostly in silence, as each man subconsciously prepared himself for action.

Wynwood almost missed the lay-by specified by Oliver: in the moonless dark it seemed to jump in and out of his headlights in an instant. He pulled over, and all four men got out.

The road was deep in a wooded valley, and the only illumination came from the stars and their own sidelights. 'I'll wait by the car,' Wynwood said. 'I think two of you should stay in the trees here, one across the road, yes?'

They all agreed.

'Chris, you take the Browning,' Wynwood said. He looked at his watch. 'Twelve minutes. Let's go.'

The delivery was early. Chris and Eddie had only just taken up position in the trees, and the Dame was barely across the highway, when headlights breasted the hill to the north and a truck rumbled down the incline and pulled across into the lay-by.

The legend 'Café de Liberador' adorned the sides.

There were two men in the cab. The driver climbed down and walked towards their car, leaving his mate behind. '*Buenas noches*,' he said. 'You are American?'

'No, British.'

'Good, good. I am Ochoa. He raised a hand to his comrade, who also got down, gun in hand.

'What's the gun for?' Wynwood asked urgently.

'*De nada*,' Ochoa said. 'Manuel,' he shouted, '*el fusil*!'

The other man laughed and put the gun back up on the seat. Wynwood wondered if he would have found being shot amusing. It must have been a pretty close thing.

'Come,' Ochoa said. He led Wynwood round to the back of the truck, into which his mate had disappeared. Behind the sacks of coffee beans they could hear him. A moment later his head emerged and then the rest of him, humping a large canvas bag out across the pungent cargo.

'There are two,' he said, dumping the first on the tailgate. Wynwood looked inside and found gleaming metal.

Two minutes later the truck was pulling out onto the highway and disappearing in the direction of Popayán. The four SAS men reconvened by their car.

'This doesn't seem like a very good place to check the contents,' Wynwood observed.

'Let's do it on the move,' Eddie suggested.

'Yeah,' Wynwood agreed.

They piled back into the car. Wynwood turned it round and headed back towards Popayán as Eddie and the Dame, more than half-hidden by the bags on their laps, went through the contents.

'What should there be in here, boss?' Eddie asked.

'Four MP5SDs, three Browning High Powers, one L96A1 sniper rifle with a nightscope, two Claymores, four sets of night-vision goggles, a PRC 319 radio and two spades. Food supplies for a week.'

'It looks OK, but it's hard to tell without unpacking everything.'

'If it's not all there, there's not much we can do about it anyway,' Chris said. 'The turn-off's coming up,' he added.

'I know,' Wynwood said curtly. He was feeling the adrenalin beginning to flow. They were no longer just four tourists – they were four heavily armed soldiers behind enemy lines. Always assuming you could find a line in Colombia.

He turned off the main road, and it was like leaving the world behind. There seemed to be no traffic on the mountain road to Neiva, and there was likely to be even less on the Cauca valley road. For the next fifteen minutes they would be somewhat conspicuous. And there was nothing, Wynwood thought, that the SAS hated more than that.

The fifteen minutes dragged slowly by, Wynwood driving, the others just sitting, in a tense silence.

'This is it,' Chris said softly.

Wynwood pulled the car over and killed the lights. They all got out, ears and eyes straining for danger.

The only sounds came from the rushing river, the only light, and a ghostly one at that, from the crescent moon rising above the hills ahead and the sparks of silver it struck on the water.

Eddie and the Dame pulled the canvas bags from the back seat and boot. 'I'll take one of the Brownings,' Chris said, and did so, with a spare magazine of ammunition. He looked at his watch. 'Twenty-two forty-eight,' he said. 'I'll try and dump this at least ten kilometres away, so' – he did a rough mental calculation – 'you should see me before dawn.' He climbed back into the driving seat. 'Enjoy your digging, lads,' he added, and started the engine.

As he turned the car the other three shifted the canvas bags off the road and into the trees. By the time the noise of its engine had faded into nothing they were about thirty metres up the slope. A convenient area of nearly flat ground offered a chance to rationalize the baggage.

First they picked out the night goggles and put them on. The world was suddenly a stranger, greener and more visible place. Next they emptied out the canvas bags, and while the Dame went to work burying one of them in the roots of a tree Wynwood and Eddie divided its contents into roughly equal weights for their rucksacks and bodies. Everything Wynwood had asked for was there. He offered Oliver a silent vote of thanks.

The three of them applied camouflage cream to their faces and wrists, checked each other's artwork, and started off, Wynwood picking out the trail, Eddie and the Dame carrying the large bag between them. At first they seemed to be making an incredible amount of noise, but as they climbed a breeze blew up, rustling the trees and helping to hide the sounds of their passage. The ambient light also increased, and they were able to dispense with the night goggles.

With the compass and his experience earlier in the day Wynwood had no trouble finding the way, and it was only the weight and awkwardness of what they were carrying which prevented a really brisk pace. As it was, they covered the three kilometres to Wynwood's first observation post in just over an hour, and the other two got their first sighting of Totoro.

By night it looked more like a prison, Wynwood thought. Arc lights covered both the outer fence and inner wall; floodlights bathed the buildings. There seemed to be more guards than there had been by day, but it might well have been that they had been less visible in mere daylight. Wynwood hoped to God they had no thermal imaging devices. It did not seem likely, but then not much about the cocaine cartels did.

The last lap, circling round to the hide position Wynwood had found beyond the ridge of the valley's southern slope, took another hour, mostly because they were sacrificing speed in the interests of silence.

It was now 01.15, and their work was far from over. Eddie and the Dame went immediately to work with their spades, digging out a hide-cum-sleeping area in the form of a cross some five metres wide. Each arm had space for one of them to lie down, leaving the central hub for their equipment.

While the troopers dug, Wynwood took out the PRC 319 and set up the two tuning antennae.

Once he had the right frequency he typed out the call-sign on the small keypad, checked it through, and sent: 'Condor calling Hummingbird.'

The magic message came back: 'Hummingbird receiving.'

Wynwood passed on the information that they were in the process of establishing the observation post outside Totoro. 'Hummingbird' told him that they had good daytime satellite photographs of the area, and that, based on these, they had a list of queries needing answers. The words 'Do you have a pencil?' appeared on Wynwood's display.

He smiled to himself in the darkness and took down the list, half wondering why he was bothering, since everything on it – details of the defensive structures, security guard patterns, lighting, power sources – would have occurred to him in any case.

After arranging to call at 22.00 the next day he signed off.

'Watch out for tarantulas – over and out' was the last incoming message.

Bastard, Wynwood thought. He packed away the PRC 319 and went across to where the other two were still digging. 'Looks soft enough,' he observed.

'It's so easy I'm reluctant to give up my spade,' Eddie said.

'Good,' Wynwood agreed. 'I'll go over the ridge

and cut some wood for the roof. And I'll take those.' He indicated the two rucksacks already filled with earth for dumping at a reasonable distance from the hide.

It had been a long day. It was going to be a long night.

'Hey, boss,' Eddie said quietly, 'before you go. It's New Year. How about a silent rendition of "Auld Lang Syne".'

Wynwood grinned. 'Why not,' he said, linking up arms. The Dame looked at them as if they were both mad, sighed, and walked over to complete the circle. And for a minute or more the three men gently raised and lowered their arms on the dark Andean hillside, miming the words in silent harmony.

# 7

The small amount of dawn light filtering through the roof of their star-shaped hide was a good sign, Wynwood thought, as he lay on his back in one of its arms. Above him rows of cut branches supported the waterproof sheeting they had brought with them, and above that a thin layer of turf with vegetation cover had been added. An unsuspecting stranger might fall in, but someone looking out for it would have to search the small dip in the slope with a very suspicious eye to spot anything.

Raising his head, Wynwood could see Eddie's feet just protruding from one of the arms at right angles to his. A low snoring could be heard, which was not so good. He looked at his watch. It was 06.15. Time to get moving. He crawled towards the centre of the star, and raised his head up through the hollow ball of vegetation they had placed there.

'Morning, boss.' The Dame's voice was so low he only just heard it. Looking up he could see him perched astride the split trunk of a tree.

Wynwood scrambled out and walked across, taking care to vary the route. 'No sign of Chris?' he asked.

'He arrived about twenty minutes ago. He's gone down to wash.'

'I'll do the same when he comes back.' It was important to keep clean – the less they smelled, the more chance they had of remaining undetected, particularly by dogs.

Chris appeared, so silently that he almost made Wynwood jump. Another good sign, he thought. This had the makings of an excellent patrol. The two men smiled at each other. 'Wake Eddie up,' Wynwood told the Dame. 'We'd better have a meeting. Oh, and tell him to bring the make-up.'

'A pleasure,' the Dame said.

'No problems?' Wynwood asked, squatting down next to Chris.

'Nope. The car's in a bush about twelve kilometres away. It's about fifty metres from the road, and I did my best to cover up the tracks. It's hard to tell in the dark . . .' He looked around. 'Shouldn't we have someone on lookout?'

'We will soon. As far as I can tell, no human has set foot in this valley for months. Or on any of the slopes overlooking Totoro. They may be armed to the teeth down there, but the notion of active defence seems to have passed them by, thank Christ. So I think we can do without a lookout for ten minutes. We need to talk about the day's work.'

Chris nodded his agreement. 'I could do with a few hours' sleep.'

'You're first in the queue. Ah, here comes Sleeping Beauty.'

Eddie and the Dame made a circle with the other two. 'Where's breakfast?' Eddie asked.

Everyone ignored him.

'This is the plan for the day,' Wynwood said. 'We'll do four-hour shifts in the observation post, starting with Eddie, then me, then Chris. By then it'll be dark again and we'll re-evaluate. After Eddie's done his shift and the Dame has had some sleep the two of you can go up the mountain and look for a decent landing zone.' He looked round at them all. 'How's that sound?'

'Sounds good, boss.'

'Right, you two get some sleep. Next shift is 10.30 hours.'

Chris and the Dame disappeared into the hide. Wynwood and Eddie took out the tubes of camouflage cream and started work. First they applied a light base coat to dull the shine on all exposed areas of skin, then a second coat of darker streaks in random patterns. Each checked the other to make sure neither had missed anywhere.

Then they turned to the MP5s, swathing them in strips of green and brown cloth that Wynwood had torn from a shirt bought for that purpose on his arrival in Popayán. More strips were tied round the binoculars.

'You've got the veil?' Wynwood checked.

Eddie pulled the sheet from a pocket. Using the binoculars behind it would have a minimal influence on vision, but would eliminate any chance of tell-tale reflective flash.

Lastly the two men each walked a few paces to check for sound. Neither rustled, jingled or clattered.

'Let's go,' Wynwood said, and led off up the slope. At the top of the ridge they approached with caution, advancing on their stomachs, but beyond the crest was nothing more than empty forest and the distant roofs of Totoro in the valley below. They crossed over and worked their way downhill, constantly alert and as silent as they could make themselves, careful to leave no trace of their presence, and on the lookout for traces of anyone else's.

They found none. At the observation tree Wynwood waited while Eddie climbed up, returned his eventual thumbs up and then climbed back over the ridge to their camp, where he took his place in the tree some thirty metres from the hide, and spent much of the next four hours considering their options for rescuing Anderson.

Kilcline leant back in the his chair and grimaced at the taste of the tea in his mug. How many times did he have to tell the stupid bastard that stewing the stuff didn't improve its taste?

He put the mug down with a thump that sent tea slopping over the side, and with reflexes that did credit to a man of his years managed to yank the report from Bogotá out of the way in time. He read it through again, then gazed gloomily out of the window at the dull grey winter day.

If he was reading between the lines correctly, then Joss Wynwood seemed to be using up his lives rather fast at the moment. Not to mention the lives of others.

The men who had followed the big Welshman southwards from Bogotá worried Kilcline. They could have been under orders from any number of authorities, legal or otherwise – always assuming you could tell the difference in Colombia – and there was no way of finding out which. If they had been working for the Government, that was probably OK. If the cartels, then it might be, or might not be. It depended on which cartel. It might even have been some damn-fool game of the Americans.

The bottom line, Kilcline thought to himself,

was simple enough. Had the operation been blown? Did the Amarales family know they were coming? And the answer to that could only be discovered by surveillance. If this Totoro ranch was being made ready to face a major attack it should be obvious enough. And if that was what Wynwood's patrol reported back then they would have to abort and think again.

He tried another sip of the tea. It was colder.

There was another way of improving the odds. Assuming that any leaker would have to be high in Colombian Government circles, then some judicious misinformation might be in order. The place was a given, so it could only be the time.

A day later, Kilcline thought. If they told the Colombian Government the operation was set for a day later than it actually was, and that information was leaked, then Totoro might have some forewarning, but there would still be at least some element of surprise. Of course, the British Government might not want to tell porkies to the Colombian Government. He had better find out.

At 10.30 Chris relieved Wynwood, Wynwood went to relieve Eddie, and Eddie came back to check the Dame's make-up. Satisfied, they took the large-scale map and began working their way east up the slope.

According to the map, the road below Totoro

ran roughly parallel to the 2000-metre contour, and the slopes above eventually ended in peaks nearly 5000 metres above sea level, but the two SAS troopers were not aiming to climb that far. About three hundred metres above them there seemed to be a wide ledge on the mountainside, almost a plateau, which might offer a suitable LZ. There was no way of knowing without having a look.

At first the going was not particularly difficult, the vegetation not particularly tropical. In fact, Colombia above 2000 metres did not seem that dissimilar to Wales at sea level. Until you looked back, that was, and found yourself watching clouds floating along in the valley beneath you.

After half an hour or so, as the slope steepened into a tumbling mess of broken rock, the vegetation began to thin. Another fifteen minutes and they were over a rise and onto the ledge. Here, on a space about the size of two football fields, small palms that resembled enormous pineapples and the occasional outcrop of stone were all that dotted a grassy heath.

The valleys below, which held Totoro and their hide, were completely invisible from where they stood. The slopes on the far side of the Cauca valley rose up in the distance towards rocky heights and blue sky.

'What do you think?' the Dame asked, squatting on his haunches.

'It'll do,' Eddie said. 'Though I wouldn't fancy landing in one of those pineapples.'

Wynwood started his watch by surveying the entire panorama and noting down the position of every man and vehicle he could see. Then he went through Eddie's notes.

No one had arrived from the outside world during the last four hours, and no one had left the valley either. The movements of the Amarales's security guards – those that could be seen, at least – had all been neatly noted down. It did not look like they operated to any rigid pattern. This, though predictable, was unfortunate.

One man and one woman, the first answering to their description of the elder Amarales brother, Ramón, had sat on the verandah drinking coffee. The woman had been a 'stunner'.

Wynwood smiled to himself and went on reading. There had been no sign of either Anderson or Muñoz.

He went through another survey of the panorama before concentrating on the inner compound. Always assuming Andy and Muñoz were here, and the embassy in Bogotá had not been given the runaround, where would they be? There was no way of guessing, but somehow they had to find out.

And not only the building, but also the room. It was going to be hard enough penetrating the inner compound; if they had to conduct a room-by-room search of all the buildings they might as well give up now.

The morning wore on. Wynwood carried on noting the movements in the valley below and scouring the set-up for any other information that might prove relevant. Shortly after midday he was watching the space between the compound wall and the main house when he thought he caught a movement on the wall's white inner face. The shadows of people moving, perhaps.

Taking an instant decision, he clambered down from the tree and made his way two hundred metres or so diagonally up the slope to the east. There he shinned up another suitable tree and aimed his binoculars at the space which had previously been invisible.

'Geronimo!' he murmured. Two men were walking in the space – Andy and Carlos Muñoz. Both looked fit and well.

Seconds later they were being ushered in through a door in the back of the main house. Wynwood had not seen them a moment too soon. Now all he needed to know was which room. There seemed to be a lot to choose from.

* * *

Back in the tree close to their hide, Chris was cleaning his weapons, unloading and breaking them down, wiping off any moisture they had acquired from the dew, checking the movement of all the moving parts, finally reloading the magazines bullet by bullet. Every now and then he would stop to listen or watch a bird in a nearby tree, and wish that he could check an unfamiliar plumage or physiognomy with the book he had left in the hide. Books, though, were among the most visible things made by man, and he was too much of a professional to risk shiny white pages in a tree. He would just have to remember the blue-green breast, the badger-like face with its white streaks on black. Anyway, what did it matter what it was called? A name would hardly make it any more beautiful.

'Are you suggesting we deliberately mislead the Colombian President as to the timing of our operation?' Alan Holcroft asked.

'Yes,' Barney Davies said. His heart had sunk when he had discovered Holcroft on the other end of the line, but he supposed he should not have been surprised.

'This operation is being mounted at the President's request,' Holcroft said, as though he was talking to a particularly obtuse schoolboy.

'Then he'll want it to be a success,' Davies came

back. 'Come on, you're not telling me that "Need To Know" criteria haven't reached the Foreign Office yet?'

'That's hardly the point . . .'

'I think it's exactly the point,' Davies said, grabbing what looked like an advantage. 'But I'm not sure that's what we're talking about here.'

'I don't follow you,' Holcroft said haughtily.

'You were against this operation from the beginning. I can respect your opinion in the matter. But I think you may be in danger of letting your antipathy to the operation seriously undermine its chances of success.'

'Lieutenant-Colonel,' Holcroft said, 'military success can be quickly and easily measured. Diplomatic success is harder to measure and never certain, because the game is never over.'

'I understand that.'

'Good. I in turn can appreciate your concern for your men. I will recommend that the deception you suggest be implemented. With any luck we can explain it away later as the result of someone's incompetence.'

It had been dark for almost half an hour when Chris returned from the observation post. He fed himself while Wynwood read through the notes he had made over the last four hours. Then the two of them joined the Dame in the nearby tree for a conference.

'It seems like we have a reasonably efficient, but not very well armed, outfit to deal with,' Wynwood began. 'There's usually between five and six guards outside, probably another three or four inside. They seem to do an eight-hour shift, which would mean one shift on duty, one in reserve and one sleeping. Thirty men, of whom twenty can be deployed immediately. They're all carrying automatic weapons, mostly M16s, though we've noted at least four Kalashnikovs. We haven't seen any grenade-launcher attachments but that doesn't mean they haven't got any. We haven't seen any heavier guns, which probably does mean they haven't got any. Agreed?'

'Yeah,' Chris said. 'I seem to remember reading something about how much these guys like grenade-launchers – so maybe we should assume they have them.'

'OK. We think Andy and Muñoz are in the main house. But whatever building they're in, the best entry point for a rescue party has to be through the wire on the far side, yes? If we can persuade our incoming lads to make a big noise on this side, that should help. Plus, a sniper on the far side to take out as many guards as possible.' He turned to the Dame. 'I'm told you can shoot.'

'All those hours at the fair on Sunderland beach,' the Dame sighed.

'Well, after we've finished this chatting, you can work your way up and round the head of the valley and onto the far slope. Find a good position. And while you're at it, take the International's nightscope with you. See if you can see anything of our boy through the back windows.'

The Dame nodded.

'Well, that's one rough plan,' Wynwood said. 'Either of you got anything better?'

They hadn't. The Dame collected the nightscope and melted away into the forest.

'If the Ops HQ buy this,' Chris asked, 'how are we going to divide it up? Am I going in with you?'

'No. I'll go in with Eddie.' He saw the signs of mutiny gathering in Chris's eyes. 'You're the only one here I would trust not to get lost in a blackout in a licorice factory. If we don't get the incoming lads down here as fast and as quietly as possible then everything else is down the chute.' He held Chris's eyes. 'Agreed?'

'Agreed.' The word came out reluctantly, but it came out.

'And I want to see if Eddie's as good as he thinks he is.'

'He is.'

They sat in silence for a few moments. Wynwood

broke it. 'You get some sleep,' he said. 'When I relieve Eddie at 22.30 he can take you up to the LZ they found.'

'What are you thinking?' Blackie asked. Bonnie was gazing down at his steak and kidney pie, looking unusually serious.

'I don't know really. Thinking about home. My mum and dad. Friends I went to school with. Dunfermline.'

'Any particular reason?'

Bonnie absent-mindedly dragged a chip through the gravy on the end of his fork. 'You'll think it's stupid. I mean, I think it's stupid.' He looked round to make sure no one else was listening. The airbase canteen was almost empty.

'What is, for Christ's sake?'

'We're not very old, are we?'

'You noticed.'

'You know what I mean. It sort of gets real when you think about what could happen.'

'Like not beating the clock?'

'Yeah. You know that stupid thing they say in films – "I'm too young to die!" Well, fuck it, Blackie – I *am* too young to die! Know what I mean?'

'Course. But you know, my great-grandad died last year, and he was ninety-four. And I reckon if he'd had the energy he'd have got up and shouted out the same thing: "I'm too young to die!" He wasn't ready, I'll tell you that. Only a couple of months before that, he was still trying to feel up the nurses in the hospital.'

Bonnie grinned. 'Yeah. I know. It's not that I'm scared. At least I don't think that's it. I'd just be really pissed off if I got killed by . . . well, you've seen 'em in *Miami Vice* – all those sleazeball Colombians with fancy earrings and half a ton of gel on their heads. Getting killed by another soldier would be bad enough but . . . You know? There's too much to do. It'd be a waste.'

Blackie leaned across and stole a chip. 'Like they say – Who dares wins.'

Half an hour before relieving Eddie in the observation tree Wynwood set up the PRC 319 and started to transmit. Belize acknowledged. He relayed all the information the patrol had gathered since the last transmission, and then offered them a précis of his proposed plan of attack.

This turned out to be a dead ringer for the provisional plan that the 'green slime' – Intelligence – in Belize had drawn up on the basis of their satellite photographs. Wynwood was somewhat less pleased to be told that the operation would be under way in less than twenty-four hours. He reminded them that they had not yet discovered the exact location of the hostages.

They asked him what he had planned for the following day – a picnic?

# 8

As on the previous morning, the patrol abandoned their continual surveillance of the valley for a brief dawn meeting. 'I just want to check everyone knows what's going on,' Wynwood said. 'Sometimes in situations like this it's hard to remember who you've told what to.' He looked round. 'You all know when we're expecting company. But we have a lot of jobs to get through before then. First off, we have to try and pinpoint which room or rooms Andy and Muñoz are being held in. Second, I want to check out our approach to the compound from the far side of the valley in daylight. Third, we have to keep a watch on Totoro, particularly for any incoming reinforcements. Fourth, we have to make sure we all get enough sleep during the day to be on top form tonight. Show those goons from C Squadron what real SAS soldiers can do.' He looked round again. 'All right, so far?'

The other three nodded. 'Yes, boss.'

* * *

It had been light outside for well over an hour. Luis Quintana knew this because his brain had refused to stop thinking long enough for him to get back to sleep. He checked his watch on the bedside table – it was almost eight. It was time to get up. He got no farther than the edge of the bed, sitting there naked, still thinking.

'Luis,' a small voice said behind him.

Julia's face was mostly hidden by her tumbling hair, but her arms were reaching up to him, her nipples peeking above the top of the sheet.

Quintana was tempted, but . . . He took her hands, kissed them and recrossed her arms across the breasts. 'I have work to do,' he said. Her smile turned into a yawn.

He put on a dressing-gown and walked through into the other room of the apartment he rented for her. As usual it was strewn with the clothes they had discarded with abandon the night before. He placed water and coffee in the filter machine and stood there watching it bubble.

Yes, he decided. Yes.

Two things had kept him awake most of the night – a slightly queasy conscience and a fear of being caught. The former was easier to deal with. Why should he worry about a bunch of gringos, who by all accounts were not much more than highly trained thugs? He would have no compunction about the death of Colombian thugs, so why agonize about a few Englishmen? Soldiers died, it was as simple as that.

The second problem was more acute. For all he knew, he and Estrada were the only two men in Colombia who knew about the operation. If that was the case then it would not be hard to pinpoint the source of a future leak. Still, he could not believe that was the case. Estrada was incapable of keeping his mouth shut, and there would be others in the know – the English and American embassies almost certainly.

He had worked out that the Americans would have to be involved – there was no one else in a position to extract the English soldiers. And if the cartels did not have informants in all the significant American military and police agencies then his name was not Luis Quintana.

Yes, he told himself. Yes.

He took a small book from his pocket and reached for the phone. There was no guarantee that the call could not be traced, but the number was unlisted and would be difficult to trace back to him. He had to take *some* risks, he told himself. He looked up the Popayán number and dialled it. After several rings a male voice answered, its anger tempered by sleepiness.

'Am I speaking to Miguel Amarales?' Quintana asked.

'Yes, who . . .'

'Just listen, please. This is a warning. I know Carlos Muñoz and an English officer are being held at Totoro . . .'

'Who the fuck are you?'

'Just listen. I am a friend. A military operation is being planned against Totoro, by the English and Americans. President Estrada has given them his permission. The attack is scheduled for 1 a.m. on the fourth – that's tomorrow night.'

There was silence at the other end. 'How do you know this?' a calmer voice asked.

'Just believe it,' Quintana said, and put the phone down. He took a sip of coffee and realized he was sweating. Just one more call, he told himself.

This time he called the international operator and asked for a number in Panama City. The saying was that it paid to kill two birds with one stone, but Quintana saw no harm in throwing two stones at the same bird.

Major Bourne brought the briefing room to some semblance of order. 'Gentlemen, the first piece of news is that we have the green light for tonight . . .'

A raucous outburst of cheering followed.

'But I have bad news for half of you. It has been decided that only one Troop will be used – and Air Troop has been chosen . . .'

The room divided into expressions of delight and disgust.

'After our discussions yesterday,' Bourne continued, 'and due consideration of all that was said, it has been decided to use a HAHO drop. Air Troop's much greater experience in using this technique is the reason it has been chosen.'

There were murmurs of grudging comprehension.

'Of course this HAHO drop will mean longer in the air, but the overriding priority with this infiltration is secrecy. Air Troop will leave the aircraft twenty kilometres to the north-west of the target, free-fall for ten seconds, deploy at around 8500 metres and glide' – he smiled at their side of the room – 'gracefully as birds for an anticipated fifty-five minutes before reaching the LZ. You'll need oxygen of course. You'll be taking a couple of CADS with the 81mm mortars.

'The C-130 will depart at 18.30 hours, and will be refuelled en route by a tanker. You will exit the aircraft beginning at 23.05 hours, and will be airborne, as I said, for approximately fifty-five minutes, landing here' – he pointed out the landing zone's location on the large-scale map – 'at approximately 24.00 hours. The LZ itself is basically a bald patch on the mountain, one of the few, I might add, so aim yourselves well. The ground surface is relatively flat but broken, so watch out. One of the surveillance team will be there to meet you, listen to your bullshit about what great parachutists you are, and then guide you down the mountain to the target. It's a two-kilometre walk, all downhill, through medium forest. Not difficult, even for you lot. Any questions so far?'

No one had any. It had suddenly got through to them that it was real, Bourne thought.

He continued. 'The weather forecast is good. At jumping altitude the wind will be around ten knots and the visibility upward of sixteen kilometres.'

'And it'll be bloody cold,' a voice muttered.

'Bloody cold,' Bourne agreed. 'But you can warm up on the ground. It should be around fourteen degrees centigrade when you land. No rain is expected. The moon is only four days old, so the ambient light will be limited. You will in any case all be carrying PNGs.' He looked round inviting questions.

One arrived. 'Are we likely to meet anyone between the LZ and the target, and if we do, what are we supposed to do with them?'

'It'll probably be my mother,' another voice said.

'I wouldn't want to do anything with her,' replied a third.

'It's extremely unlikely you'll meet anyone. Even Trooper Peacock's mother. But if you do, there are no hard and fast rules. Use your discretion. It shouldn't be too hard to tell the difference between a shepherd and a Colombian gunman.'

It was not a very good answer. Bourne knew it, and he suspected quite a few of the men did too. But there was not a better one, and they all knew that as well.

'What about the local authorities?' someone else asked. 'Are there any military bases in the area?'

'I was coming to that. Both the Army and Air Force have bases here in Popayán' – he indicated the place on the map – 'the 17th Brigade and the Juan Pinero Squadron. And no, I don't know who Juan Pinero was. The army brigade is an infantry unit, about six hundred men, armed with automatic weapons but not much else. The Air Force squadron only consists of a few modified UH-1 helicopters. If they're being properly maintained, which is doubtful, they might be effective by day, but their crews have no night-fighting experience.

'Basically, we don't expect any problems from either of these sources. First, someone would have to alert them, and whether the Amarales would even want to is a moot point. Second, the military commanders would have to respond immediately, without obtaining any sanction from higher up. Third, even if the two units' reaction times were a quarter of what we think they are, they'd be hard pushed to bring any force to bear in the two hours you'll be on the ground.

'One thing you won't like, though,' Bourne admitted, 'you'll be wearing helmets throughout this one.'

A chorus of groans erupted. The SAS tradition was never to wear helmets except during parachute drops.

'And American helmets to boot,' Bourne continued, rubbing salt in the wound. 'They've been borrowed from US Special Forces for a trial, and you all look just like guinea pigs, so . . .' He grinned. 'These helmets have built-in radios,' he went on, 'for transmitting and receiving. And they should be ideal for coordinating a night action like this one. Which, by the way, is now officially designated Operation Snowstorm. Snow, for those of you who've been living a truly sheltered life, is slang for cocaine. Right. Any questions at this stage?'

'Who thinks up these names, boss?'

'We get them from TV cartoons, Trooper. And I forgot to say, you will have a test session with the helmets this afternoon. Now, where had we got to . . .'

'We were being led like lambs to the slaughter by some no-hoper from B Squadron,' a voice from the back suggested.

'They've been there for days now,' another

voice added. 'They've probably started buggering llamas.'

'Your knowledge of the world's fauna does you credit, Trooper,' Bourne said after the groans and laughter had subsided. 'But to continue. Once you reach this area' – Bourne placed a finger on the map – 'the force will be split, with two patrols heading this way . . .'

Miguel Amarales decided against the telephone; he wanted to convey this information to his older brother in person. The arrogant oaf had really landed them in it this time – a visit from the goddamn English Special Forces. What priceless irony. The very people Ramón was always prattling on about! His heroes!

It took him just under the usual half hour to reach Totoro, five minutes to pass on the anonymous warning and express his own anger.

Ramón ignored the latter and derided the former. 'Where would they come from?' he asked incredulously. 'A British aircraft carrier in the Pacific? Ascension Island? Heathrow? This is a fantasy. Someone is trying . . .' Even as he listened to himself speak, Ramón was beginning to wonder. Could they really be coming?

'You are not listening, brother,' Miguel was saying. 'If they have Estrada's approval then why not Air Force transport?'

'We would know,' Ramón said firmly.

'Or they could call on American support,' Miguel persisted. The Americans are only four hundred miles away in Panama.'

Ramón could not deny the possibility. 'But for one soldier – it's absurd. Paying the ransom would cost them a tenth as much as mounting such an operation.'

'Whoever said politicians were intelligent?' Miguel wanted to know. Having got his brother on the defensive, he was willing to let his anger abate somewhat. 'Does it matter in any case? Let's assume the information is genuine. Why not just move Muñoz and the Englishman somewhere else, and let the British know we have done so? We can phone their embassy in Bogotá.'

'No.' Ramón was firm. 'If they are coming here, I at least want some bargaining cards.'

'OK,' Miguel agreed. That at least made sense. 'They can't land the whole British Army out there' – a sweep of his arm took in the valley – 'and they will rely on surprise, yes? Well, they won't get that. Jesus, Ramón, if there's anyone in Colombia knows more about these bastards, it's you. How will they come? How do we defend ourselves?'

Ramón looked marginally more cheerful. 'We even have an expert on the premises,' he murmured.

'The Englishman.'

'Of course. We can ask him.'

'You mean Chirlo can ask him.'

'Yes.'

The two men who came for Anderson did not look him in the eye. It was a bad sign, the SAS man thought, though he could not begin to think of any reason.

He was taken out of the main house, along a path in front of the low building adjoining it, and into the next building down. His final destination proved to be a room with no furnishing save an electric socket. The wires which ran through some sort of amplifier to a pair of clip-on electrodes had not yet been plugged in. The man with the scar was standing waiting by the window. Bad news was an understatement.

'Sit down,' Chirlo said in his soft, liquid voice.

Anderson did so. The two men who had brought him stood either side of the closed door, guns in hand.

'Do you know what these are?' Chirlo said, walking across and picking up the electrodes, letting the wires slide through his fingers as if they were a girl's hair.

'Yes,' Anderson said.

Chirlo seemed to address the floor. 'Señor Amarales has received news that men from your unit – the SAS, is that right?' – he raised his blue eyes questioningly – 'are planning to attack us here tomorrow night.'

'I don't believe it,' Anderson said.

'I find it hard myself,' Chirlo agreed. 'But it doesn't really matter one way or the other. We are going on the assumption, you and I, that it is true, and we are going to work out exactly how to go about defeating such an attack.'

Anderson struggled with himself to keep calm. 'If I tell you to fuck off,' he said, 'you're going to attach those to my balls, aren't you?'

Chirlo nodded.

'How will you know if I'm telling the truth?' Anderson asked.

Chirlo looked at him for a moment. 'That's not really your worry, is it?'

'It isn't?'

'If you tell me your friends are going to come over the hill in tanks I may find it hard to believe. Then I will fry your balls. Keep making sense and – who knows . . .' He smiled. 'Do you have children?'

'Yes,' Anderson said, knowing what was coming.

'It's as well. There are two other things you should bear in mind, gringo. One, Señor Amarales knows a lot about your methods already – he won't be easy to fool. And two, I have no problem inflicting pain. I don't need to and I don't need not to. Now, before we begin . . .' He gestured to one of the men, who came forward, undid Anderson's trousers and pulled both them and his underpants down to his knees.

Chirlo gazed at Anderson's genitals with admiration. 'You are a lucky man,' he said.

'Size isn't everything,' Anderson murmured in English. He felt the cold metal clips fastened to his scrotal sack. A second later a shaft of agony coursed through him, forcing him to arch his back.

'Just to show you the price of not being frank,' Chirlo said.

Anderson was breathing fast, sweat running into his eyes. 'I'll tell you whatever you want to know,' he said through gritted teeth. An inner voice was telling him: keep lucid, keep calm. Tell them as much as you can of what they could work out or find out for themselves.

'Good. How many men do you think your people might send. Ten, twenty, forty?'

'A squadron,' Anderson said. 'Sixty-four.'

'How will they get here?'

'By plane. They will parachute in.'

'Where to?'

'I couldn't say . . .' He saw Chirlo's hand move towards the switch. 'I couldn't . . .' he insisted quickly, starting to take in fast and shallow breaths again. One of the tricks taught at Hereford was to pretend to hyperventilate in these situations. 'I have seen nothing of the area. If everywhere else is steep and forested they could choose to land in front of the house.'

Chirlo walked away from the switch, running both hands through his hair. 'So how will they get away again?' he asked.

'There will have to be a helicopter pick-up,' Anderson said. Even a child could work that out, he thought.

'From where?'

'That would depend on what they intend and how confident they are. If they don't intend leaving anyone alive here then the pick-up could be from your helipad. If they're just coming for me, then it could be any flat space big enough and secluded enough. Maybe somewhere down that road I could see from the verandah.'

Chirlo looked at him thoughtfully. 'You have not told me anything I could not guess,' he said.

'That's true,' Anderson admitted, 'but I have answered all your questions.'

The Colombian thought some more, then suddenly signalled the guard to remove the clips. Anderson tried not to look too relieved.

'I will pass on your answers to Señor Amarales,' Chirlo said. 'Tomorrow there will be new questions. More precise questions.' He opened the door, told the guards to take Anderson back to the main house, and disappeared.

Anderson walked back across the tarmac trying hard not search the forested slopes too obviously. Chirlo had not asked him the key question – would there be a patrol already keeping the estate under surveillance? If they really were coming to get him – and he still found it hard to believe – then there would be. Somewhere up on those slopes a fellow SAS soldier would be watching him at this very minute.

What would they need to know, Anderson wondered as he was led through the house and back to his room. Of course! His and Muñoz's whereabouts. Which building, which room. Well, they should know which building by now. He would have to think of some way to let them know which room.

High in the observation tree Eddie watched Anderson being led back across the tarmac and into the main house. There was something about the way the SAS man was walking – he seemed to be dragging his feet slightly – which made Eddie uneasy. Maybe Anderson had been walking the same way half an hour earlier, and he just had not noticed it. Maybe the man was ill. Or maybe something had been done to him in the other building.

Why would they want to torture Anderson? For fun? Or because he could tell them something? What could he tell them? It seemed doubtful that Anderson knew Terry Wogan's personal number, or that the Amarales family would want it. No, much as he disliked the thought, Eddie could only think of one thing the Amarales would want from Anderson – help in planning a defence against the Englishman's comrades. Which meant the operation was blown.

As he considered this, Eddie saw the long-haired brother, Miguel, leave the house, almost leap into his red sports car and roar off towards the inner gate. It swung open to let him out, as did the gate in the outer fence.

Eddie noted the departure in his log. Miguel had been at the house for an hour and forty minutes. Could his arrival have had anything to do with Anderson's trip across the yard? There was no way of knowing. Certainly, if the Amarales were now expecting an imminent attack they were not showing any urgency in preparing to meet it. Perhaps he was jumping to the wrong conclusions.

He hoped he was. If half the Colombian Army suddenly showed up down below then the operation would be called off, and they would have to slink back out of Colombia the way they had come in. Which might be a lot less risky than going in for

Anderson and Muñoz, but who the hell joined the SAS for a less risky life.

Eddie shifted his cramped limbs and carefully examined the watch beneath his sleeve. Another forty minutes. He sighed and lifted the binoculars again. Having come this far, he thought, it would be a real pain in the arse not to get a crack at entering the evil coke barons' lair.

'He seemed as surprised by the idea as you were,' Chirlo told Ramón, his eyes straying across the room to where Victoria was half sitting, half lying on the leather couch. She had arrived alone the previous day, but had so far made no attempt to communicate with him; or anyone else, for that matter. She had spent most of the last twenty-four hours sitting on the verandah and staring into space. At that moment she caught his eye and smiled. It was with some difficulty that he brought his mind back to the business in hand.

'If it's true we'll get confirmation from someone,' Ramón was saying. 'In the meantime . . .' His voice trailed off, and he stood there, massaging his chin between thumb and forefinger.

Chirlo waited, stealing another glance at Victoria.

'How many men did he think?' Ramón asked him.

'He said sixty-four, but he would be bound to

exaggerate. It doesn't really matter, does it? – they are coming for him and Muñoz, and presumably they want them alive. We have all the cards.'

Ramón grunted. 'That's what the terrorists at the London embassy thought,' he said. 'I want some men on the roof,' he added suddenly, 'Permanently. And I'm going to call your husband,' he said to Victoria, 'I think it's time he fulfilled some of his family obligations.'

'Just don't bring him up here unless there's a good chance of getting him killed,' she said coldly.

Chirlo felt a warm glow of anticipation in his heart.

'I think this might be a good time for us to exhibit some solidarity,' Ramón said curtly, dialling a Popayán number.

Victoria did not bother to reply.

'Armando,' Ramón said into the phone, 'we may have a problem here . . .'

Raul Meneres wiped his brow with his handkerchief and put the results of his handiwork carefully to one side. A beer, he thought, and headed for the fridge. The cold Budweiser was on the way down his throat when the telephone rang.

It was Alfonsín, who worked in the fuel depot at the airbase, asking him if he would fancy a ride down to Balboa, in Panama, the following evening. There was a good dogfight on at the Boneyard.

Meneres wondered why Alfonsín would not be working on the special op. 'I thought you were working tomorrow night,' he said casually.

'No . . .'

'That idiot Corles told me there was some special op.'

'That's tonight . . . and anyway Corles should try learning to keep his mouth shut.'

'Be like you trying to stop screwing women.'

'Yeah, maybe,' Alfonsín agreed, obviously pleased with this comment on his sexual profligacy.

'Yeah, Balboa is good,' Meneres said. 'But I'll probably see you this evening anyway . . . I've got some work to catch up on . . .'

He hung up and took another swig of the Bud. The *sicario* had told him the wrong day, he thought. He had said it was Wednesday night. Well, maybe technically it was, but five past midnight was still Tuesday night as far as anyone with any common sense was concerned. It would serve the fuckers right if he pretended he had never heard otherwise.

But then they would not pay him.

Out on the slopes the day wore slowly on. Chris stood lookout over the hide as Eddie and Wynwood slept, then took his own turn in the hide as the Dame took over at the observation post and Wynwood went to reconnoitre the north slope.

By dusk Wynwood had satisfied himself as to where he and Eddie would sit out the waiting hours, and how they would approach the compound. He started working his way back round the head of the valley to where he could get the clearest sight of the back windows of the main house.

Reaching the point where he had first put Totoro under observation, Wynwood settled back into the undergrowth just beneath the ridge. In the valley below he could see the now familiar outlines of the floodlit compound, the fleeting shadows of the guards, the empty helipad. There were now two guards on the roof. Wynwood had listened to Eddie's suspicions and guesswork, and hoped the former were ill-founded, the latter simply wrong. These two guards were the first evidence he had been right.

Wynwood methodically scanned the inner and outer compound for corroboration. He could not find any. Perhaps the guards on the roof were just a whim. He went back to the job he had come for – looking for Anderson.

The main house was a patchwork of lit and darkened windows, but all were covered by either blinds or curtains. Wynwood took out the nightscope and started examining them one by one. The lit squares were almost blinding, the dark ones just that.

'You beautiful bastard!' Wynwood murmured to himself. Through the fourth window from the right, but only with the aid of the nightscope, he could make out a light flashing on and off. A message in the SAS's favourite Morse code: N-E-R-O-O-M-N-O-R-T-H-C-O-M-E-A-N-D-G-E-T-M-E-M-U-N-O-Z-O-N . . .

'I'll buy you a pint in the Slug,' Wynwood murmured. Feeling like a load had been lifted from his mind he resumed his return journey. In half an hour he would be back at the hide.

In the observation post Chris had watched the sun sink behind the western mountains, the light swiftly fade in the valley below. Then the switches had been pulled, flooding the compound with artificial light.

Beyond the reach of the floodlights and arc lights it was now fully dark, and darker than it would be for most of the coming night, since the crescent moon would be making its appearance in a hour or so.

He had now been perched in the tree for over three and half hours, but he was not bored. He rarely was these days. One of the great things he had learnt in the SAS, and particularly in situations like this, was to make every moment count. Every sight, sound, smell, touch and taste could be experienced, enjoyed, even relished. In the civvy world everyone was too hooked on motion, speed and cheap sensation. His old friends from school, they only seemed happy when they were either pissed out of their skulls or being entertained by something or someone. None of them could sit still for more than a moment. It was really sad.

The wind seemed to be getting up. No, it was not the wind – it was the sound of a vehicle. A heavy one. With a sinking sensation in his stomach, Chris trained his binoculars on the point where the Amarales entry road reached the valley highway. An armoured car swam into focus, and behind it another one. They rumbled in through the two pairs of gates and pulled up on either side of the parking space at the heart of the inner compound. Both were armed with M60 machine-guns. A man emerged from the main house to greet the two crews and escort them across and into one of the side buildings. He came out again almost immediately and went back into the main house. Silence reasserted itself.

Strange, Chris thought. The arrival of the armoured cars suggested real concern, but there was still no sign of any real urgency. It was as if the men in the house were expecting trouble, but only at some later date. Chris wondered if the green slime had been dabbling in misinformation.

It was two minutes to seven. His relief should arrive at any moment. He strained his ears, but could hear nothing before Eddie's face appeared in the tree below him.

'Problems,' Chris said, handing him the binoculars.

Eddie looked and grunted. 'I thought I heard something as I came over the hill,' he said. 'There's not much action down there though.'

'That's what I thought,' Chris confirmed. 'I'll get back and report.'

'You think they'll call it off?' Eddie asked.

'They'd better not.'

Wynwood agreed. His euphoria at finding Anderson was somewhat dented by news of the armoured cars, but not totally diminished. 'I think you could well be right,' he said, when Chris offered his theory of an attack expected at a later date. 'And we'll soon know,' he added, as he set up the PRC 319 for transmission.

The Ops HQ was apologetic. The patrol should have been told before of the decision to mislead the Colombian Government over the date of Operation Snowstorm.

'Bloody typical,' Chris muttered, when Wynwood told him. 'But good news, I take it. They must have taken the odd reinforcement into account?'

'It's still on. They'll be leaving Punta Gordas' – he looked at his watch – 'in twenty-seven minutes. But there's one change to the plan. 'They've borrowed a job lot of Yank helmets for the op, with state-of-the-art radio fitted. And they want us to be wearing them too, so Eddie will have to be at the LZ with you, and bring ours over to the north slope while you lead the troop down the other side.'

'Makes sense,' Chris observed. 'You three being out of communication for over two hours before the balloon went up always did seem a touch on the risky side.'

'A touch,' Wynwood conceded. 'Though from what we've seen the last couple of nights there's not a lot going on around here between one and three in the morning.'

Captain Mike Bannister watched the second hand of his watch move its way round to the appointed moment. 'Gentlemen,' he said loudly, as it reached it.

The other fourteen men sitting on either side of the C-130's swaying belly turned their faces in his direction. Each of them was wearing an unzipped one-piece thermal suit over the usual jungle-camouflaged fatigues. Elasticated straps held the Passive Night Goggles (PNGs) around the communication helmets, ready for lowering over the visors when the time came.

'Time to get rigged up,' Bannister said.

The Hercules, which until then had resembled a hall full of thoughtful statues, became a writhing mass of activity, as the chutes, primary and reserve, were passed along the two rows. The fourteen men zipped up their thermal suits and split into seven pairs for rigging the 'chutes, checking each strap on their partner's rig as if his life depended on it – which it did.

Blackie and Bonnie were one of the pairs. They counted off and checked each other's connectors, rigged each other's reserve 'chutes in front, with each man's MP5 tucked in behind it. The bergens were then hooked underneath the back-mounted main parachutes, making each man look rather like an oversized child whose trousers had fallen down.

'You're done,' Blackie told Bonnie.

'So are you.'

Bannister started working his way down the plane, testing each and every strap with a hefty tug, and giving each man the thumbs up when he had finished with him. Once he had passed everyone fit to jump, he submitted to being rigged by one of the NCOs.

'How long now?' Bonnie asked.

'Another half an hour.'

* * *

Wynwood lay just behind a slight lip in the north slope, his head masked by ground foliage. The crescent moon, now high in the sky above and behind him, cast a thin wash of light into the surrounding forest, but nothing like enough to render the PNGs redundant once the time came to move.

It was now nearly one o'clock and while one piece of Wynwood's brain would have rather liked the reassurance of hearing a distant C-130 and catching a glimpse of far-off parachutists, the sensible side was hoping that his first news of their arrival would come from the returning Eddie. And soon.

Below him the guards went about their random pacings and the house lights were mostly out. For the first time in days the thought of Susan crossed his mind. To his surprise it did not come accompanied with the usual empty feeling in the pit of his stomach. Instead he found himself remembering some of the good times they had shared together. That hurt too, but in a different way. Regret, he guessed, was the price of just about everything which could be won and lost. Anger was just denial; regret was about accepting that something was gone.

A couple of hundred metres to his right, perched in a tree which almost overhung the outer fence, the Dame scanned the compound through the Schmidt & Bender telescopic sight. The adjustable rubber butt pad of the L96A1 sniper rifle rested comfortably against his shoulder. The subsonic 7.62-calibre ammunition rested in a convenient niche of the tree.

He aligned the crossed hairs of the sight on the head of the taller roof guard and gently squeezed the trigger. 'Pooff,' he said to himself. If there had been a bullet in the chamber the man would have been be dead.

In a couple of hours' time there would be a bullet in the chamber. The man's life depended on what time they changed shifts, and that did not seem much in the way of life insurance. The Dame wondered why these thoughts never worried him when the time came for action.

Blackie and Bonnie watched as the two of the air crew manoeuvred the Controlled Air Delivery System (CADS) chutes into position. These, which would carry the 81mm mortars, were radio-controlled chutes. Two of the troop would have the task of guiding them down through the Colombian night by hand-held transmitters. Blackie was glad he was not one of them – he had the feeling his hands were full enough already.

Three metres away Bannister's watch reached

another deadline. 'Gentlemen,' he said loudly. 'Time to hook up.'

Each man leant forward and attached the plastic hose from his mask to one of the two oxygen consoles in the centre of the gangway. 'This is the bit I hate,' Bonnie murmured to himself a few seconds later as the pilot began depressurizing the plane and his ears popped. It slowly grew colder.

Bannister's eyes were almost continuously on his watch now. Blackie stared at him, wondering what would happen if the watch suddenly stopped. He was beginning to feel the adrenalin flow. Though he had made only a dozen or so jumps he was not afraid – far from it. In fact he found it hard to think of anything that for sheer thrills could begin to compete. And yet he wondered if you ever got used to these last minutes of waiting or that moment on the ramp with the whole bloody world waiting to watch you drop. He doubted it.

'Time to switch to personal,' Bannister's voice came in loud and clear through the helmet. Each man shifted the hose connector from the console to the bottle at his belt. There was about thirty minutes of oxygen in each bottle, more than enough to reach breathable air, barring some catastrophe like landing on a giant condor's back.

The Hercules was slowing down. 'On your feet,' Bannister told them. There was a low rumble and the night sky suddenly appeared in the widening gap as the back of the plane divided to make the jumping ramp.

'We'll check the helmets,' Bannister said.

'One,' said the first voice. The numbers two to fourteen followed. 'Fifteen,' Bannister finished off. 'Break your partner's light.'

Each of the American helmets had a chemical light set in its upper rear face which was activated by cracking its shell. As seen through the PNGs, they would help guide the troop down in a tight formation.

The ramp was fully down now, the lead jumper waiting beneath the glowing red light. Behind him thirteen other troopers, two CADS and, bringing up the rear, Mike Bannister.

The light turned green.

As usual the last few seconds waiting his turn to jump seemed eternal to Blackie, but once he was out on the ramp there was no time for thought. He followed Bonnie into space, straight into the free-falling position, facing down but with the body arched back, arms and legs stretching out. Meanwhile the eyes were homing in on Bonnie's light below, and the body was struggling to stabilize itself before the brain finished counting to ten and the hand pulled the ripcord.

The chute's release jerked him upright. So far so good. Blackie grasped hold of the control toggles and started to turn a fall into a glide. Beneath him, ahead and slightly to the right, the red chemical light on the back of Bonnie's helmet was clearly visible through the PNGs. Blackie manoeuvred himself into line and, for the first time in a crowded half minute, had time to think.

'I'm going to South America,' were the words that came into his mind. He would have laughed out loud if the oxygen mask had not made it impossible.

For the next few minutes Blackie concentrated on breathing and flying his chute, watching Bonnie below and taking glances at the altimeter built into his reserve chute. The land below was still an undifferentiated black mass, showing no shadows from the moon he knew was behind him. Despite the thermal suit he felt bitterly cold.

It could only get warmer, he reminded himself. They were below 8000 metres already, and for the first time things were beginning to take on shape below. The circular horizon was slowly rising towards them, the air *was* getting warmer.

Flying the chute became a pleasure only alloyed by the slight anxiety which went with any imminent landing. Ahead of him the team was descending in a long graceful curve to the left as Number 1 corrected their course to compensate for either an error of navigation or an unexpected wind strength. They were heading due south down towards and along the spine of a mountain range.

If Blackie's memory served him well the drop-zone was a meadow somewhere on the western side of these mountains at around 2300 metres. So far he could see nothing but sheer faces and steep slopes. But his altimeter had only just gone through 5500 metres, and the highest peaks were still rushing up to meet them.

The line swayed again, this time to the right, passing the peaks on its left, gliding diagonally down across the upper western slopes.

A kilometre and a half from Totoro, and at least three hundred metres closer to God, Chris and Eddie were huddled together beneath a slight hillock on the edge of the landing zone. In front of them half the world seemed to be silhouetted against a violet sky. Above them the moon shone white and razor-edged, and the stars seemed closer and clearer than they ever did in England.

'Visibility is approximately ten light-years, Captain,' Eddie murmured.

'Thank you, Mr Spock,' Chris said. Even with a view like the one in front of him, the adrenalin was beginning to pump through his veins.

He looked at his watch again. It was forty-nine minutes since Belize had told them over the PRC 319 that the jump was in progress. Any minute now.

But it was Eddie who saw them first. 'Here they come!' he said, a sense of excitement seeping out through the laconic Cockney accent.

And there they were, looking like a string of widely spaced pearls in the northern sky, slowly growing into a long line of Tinkerbells floating down towards Never-Never Land, and finally revealing themselves as fully equipped SAS soldiers swinging down towards the plateau.

Blackie could see the meadow now – a large light patch on the dark slopes – and gingerly applied his air brakes as he began swinging out slightly to the left of the direction Bonnie was taking below him. The one great peril of landings like this was landing on top of the man in front, so even numbers had been assigned the right-hand approach, odd numbers the left. This effectively doubled the time between landings.

Blackie corrected his course slightly, moving himself farther away from the forested slope to his left, then released the air brakes and slid down towards the meadow, aiming for a straight run of grass between darker growths of vegetation. He hit the ground running, almost tripped, but managed to stay upright.

He got out of his harness, folded the canopy

and packed it into his bergen, and looked up just in time to see Captain Bannister cover the last few feet to earth.

They were down.

# 9

In the bathroom attached to his private rooms Chirlo lay half-submerged, thinking about Victoria Amarales. All evening, while Ramón had quizzed him on the state of their defences, and how they could be be improved the next day, she had been destroying his concentration by giving him the eye. And when she had finally announced to Ramón that she was staying the night she had given Chirlo a look which could hardly be misinterpreted.

They had never slept together here at Totoro; all their past assignations had been in hotels in Popayán or Bogotá or Cartagena. Either she was tired of subterfuge or so bored that she hoped to precipitate a family crisis. It did not make much difference either way. She knew he would go along, and she was right.

He was probably not being very wise, but so what? She was ten years older than him, probably cleverer than him, and certainly boasted a finer lineage. The Amarales were as near pure Spaniard as you could get, whereas he could trace Spanish, German and Indian blood in his own veins. He thought Ramón and Miguel would probably be outraged by his sleeping with their sister. Miguel would, certainly. Ramón might be more amused. But her husband would not care. Armando Noguera was not interested in anything over the age of fourteen.

Not that Noguera caring would matter anyway – like Chirlo, he was just an employee of the Amarales. But he supposed Ramón and Miguel did matter. He had done well out of working for them – half a million dollars in the Bogotá branch of the Bank of Venezuela. He could probably double that in the next two years and retire a millionaire at the age of twenty-six.

On the other hand, he thought, he was pretty sure he could find similar employment elsewhere, if he wanted it. He didn't, but he could. He didn't need the Amarales any more than they needed him – it was a relationship of equals, regardless of whose blood was the purest. And it was not as if he would be raping their sister; she enjoyed it every bit as much as he did. He stood up and reached for the towel.

Five minutes later he was in the security room, making sure that everything was running smoothly. 'I don't want to be interrupted for an hour unless it's absolutely necessary,' he told the duty officer.

'Sí, boss,' the man said, and went to answer one of the routine call-ins from the guards outside.

Chirlo walked upstairs, past the guard at the head of the stairs, and checked that the two guards outside the prisoners' rooms were awake. Satisfied, he turned and walked back along the long corridor, passing Ramón's rooms and the ones Miguel used when he was staying. The light was still on under the door of Victoria's suite, which did not surprise him.

He stood there a second, wondering if love and lust was driving him into a major mistake, and decided they were not. He knocked softly.

'Come in,' she said.

He closed the door behind him. The room in front of him was lit but empty; her voice came from the one beyond. 'You took your time,' she said.

'I had duties to finish,' he replied stiffly, walking through. She was lying on the bed, a book lying open and face down across her breasts, but otherwise completely naked.

Her body was everything he remembered it was.

She put the book aside, exposing her beautifully formed breasts. 'Take your clothes off,' she said.

He did so, pleasantly conscious of her eyes on him, then came across and leant over her, kissing her on the lips. She responded for a second, then gently pushed his mouth down till he was sucking on her nipple.

He tried to shift his body astride hers, but with a smooth shift of her legs she trapped him between them, and in almost the same motion started pushing his head further down, running his tongue across her stomach and down. With one final push and a tightening of her legs around his back she had him where she wanted him. 'Now you can start kissing me,' she said.

Chris and Mike Bannister had known each other for years, and they greeted each other warmly. The two of them might have just run into each other in a Hereford pub, Eddie thought watching them, rather than halfway up a Colombian mountain, still with a house-call to make on a drug baron. He only hoped Bannister did not ask Chris about the bird-life, or they would be stuck up in the meadow till dawn.

C Squadron's Air Troop were packing away their chutes and oxygen equipment, helping to unload the two remote-controlled CADS, and generally preparing themselves to march. Eddie exchanged silent smiles with those men he had run into before, some in his training intake, others in the Stirling Lines canteen or the pubs of Hereford.

Chris and Bannister talked for only a couple of minutes. Eddie was given a bergen containing radio helmets for himself, Wynwood and the Dame. They synchronized watches, checked that everyone was ready and started off down the mountain.

Seventeen Brits, Eddie thought. The Stray Cats' 'Sexy and 17' started playing in the back of his brain. The silvery light of the crescent moon danced on the single file of helmeted heads below him. It was on nights like this that a man felt really alive.

With silence more important than speed, Chris did not try to force the pace. In addition he was mindful that the line of troops behind him were carrying a lot more than he was, had just spent almost an hour engaged in the exhausting business of guiding a parachute down from 10,000 metres, and had not walked this route before in daylight, let alone by the feeble light of a ten-per-cent moon.

In London it was shortly after six in the morning. The Prime Minister was working her way through one of several waiting red boxes in her private office when the telephone rang.

'It's Lieutenant-Colonel Davies, Prime Minister,' the secretary told her.

'Put him through.'

'I thought you'd like to know,' Barney Davies said, after they had exchanged good mornings, 'our troops are on the ground in Colombia.'

'That's splendid. How long will they be . . . on the ground?'

'Four hours is the period we've allowed for.'

'I'd like to be kept informed, Colonel.'

'Of course, Ma'am.'

She thoughtfully replaced the receiver and went to look out of the small window. At that moment a ray of sunlight seemed to alight on the roof opposite. It seemed like a good sign.

It took them a little over an hour to reach the head of Totoro's valley. Here Eddie's path diverged from the Troop's, and he could afford to speed up his progress. Another twenty minutes brought him to the Dame's tree. The Wearsider received the news of the Air Troop's successful arrival in his usual phlegmatic way. He had no news – the valley below had apparently gone to sleep.

Wynwood was more obviously relieved by Eddie's tidings. He put on the helmet and listened to the younger man's explanation of how it operated. 'Bannister will call you up when he's in position,' Eddie concluded.

On the other side of the valley Chris led the Air Troop along an imaginary contour line about a hundred metres up from the edge of the forest. Dropping off Puma patrol with the first mortar due south of the inner compound, the remaining eleven men walked on another four hundred metres to a position near the edge of the trees level with the outer gate. Jaguar, comprising Bannister and seven other men, were to remain here. Bannister would coordinate the entire diversionary action, using the seven men under his command to intervene if and when it seemed useful.

This left Ocelot, comprising Chris, Bonnie, Blackie and a South Londoner who bore the endearing nickname of Dopey, to continue on to the road. They emerged from the trees a few minutes later and there it was, skirting the feet of the hill. By Chris's reckoning the intersection with Totoro's entry road was out of sight round the next bend, about four hundred metres to their right. 'Ocelot to Jaguar,' he said quietly into the helmet mike, 'road clear.'

They waited for a full minute, listening to the light breeze in the foliage above them and the steady chatter of the river that lay just beyond the road. Then Chris led them down, moving slightly to the left to take advantage of the cover offered by a lone copse of trees.

They crossed the road and reached the river's edge. The water ran fast, but not deep. It looked cold. It was cold. The patrol carried the mortar across and advanced down the left bank, all wearing their PNGs.

The outer gate came into sight through another line of trees. Two men were standing chatting just beyond it by an unlit gatehouse. They did not look like they were expecting anything other than boredom.

Invisible against the dark slope and inaudible against the rushing water, the patrol moved forward until it found a sighting of the gates that was uninterrupted by trees. Chris hand-signalled for them to set up the mortar. When Blackie's thumbs up announced completion of this task he spoke softly into the helmet mike once more: 'Ocelot to Jaguar: ready to go.'

Crouched on his haunches about four hundred metres to the east, looking down along the front line of fence which contained the main gate, Bannister acknowledged the message. He had already received the same message from Puma patrol. He looked at his watch. It was 01.55 hours. Ten minutes behind schedule, so far. 'Jaguar to Condor,' he said, 'Are you ready to go?'

'Condor to Jaguar,' Wynwood said, 'we're ready.'

Bannister took a deep breath, thinking for a second how silent it all was. 'Jaguar to all units,' he said succinctly. 'Time to party. You have two minutes, Condor. Ocelot, prepare to fire at the end of those two minutes.'

'We're on our way,' Wynwood replied. He and Eddie raised themselves from their prone position and began to edge their way down through the trees. At the forest's edge, thirty metres of bare ground away from the high wire fence, they stopped and waited and watched. Neither had their PNGs down over their eyes: the lights were far too bright.

About now, Eddie thought to himself.

On the other side of the river Bonnie dropped the shell into the mortar tube and covered his ears. The explosion shook the valley. As it died away another followed echo-like on its heels, and the fence below them seemed to shiver with fright. Wire-cutters at the ready, Wynwood ran down the bare slope, Eddie right behind him.

Wynwood set to work cutting a flap in the de-electrified fence, while Eddie kept watch. Several bursts of gunfire reverberated in the distance, then all was silent again.

No more than five seconds after the first mortar had landed, the Dame took out the farther of the two guards on the roof with the silenced sniper rifle. The guard had been standing right on the edge, and the bullet through his brain knocked him off the roof and out of sight behind the building. His partner must have heard him hit the ground because he turned, saw no one there, and looked wildly round before the Dame's second shot brought his life to a sudden, anticlimactic end.

Having removed these four eyes from the roof, the Dame started scanning the outer compound, ready to take out anyone who threatened to interrupt Wynwood and Eddie's forced entry.

A guard was walking their way, more to get a view of what had caused the explosions by the gate than because he had seen any intruders. The Dame aligned the cross-hairs in the scope and squeezed the trigger.

In Victoria Amarales's bedroom the light of the explosions flashed across the sky just as she and Chirlo were blissfully skirting round the edges of a mutual orgasm.

'What the fuck?' he asked breathlessly, as the booms rattled the window panes.

'Oh no,' she groaned, as he slid himself out of her and scrambled naked to the window in time to see the second mortar round land close to the guardpost by the outer gate. 'We're being attacked,' he said, as much to himself as to her. He grabbed his trousers and pulled them on, snatched the automatic from the bedside table and started for the door. As he went through it he shouted 'Stay there!' over his shoulder.

* * *

'Enemy on your left down,' the Dame's calm voice said in their helmets as Wynwood and Eddie raced across open ground towards the stone wall which enclosed the inner compound.

Wynwood made a stirrup for Eddie, boosted him up onto the top of the wall, and then waited while the younger man assessed the situation. It was not easy to assess. Since they were behind the main building, Eddie's only view of the inner compound was through a narrow gap between it and one of the barracks-like buildings on his right. The only certainty was that the place was in a slowly growing uproar. Lights were going on, people shouting, feet running.

Of more immediate import, he could see no one in a position to stop them penetrating the main house.

At the other end of the corridor from his lover's bedroom, Chirlo found the faces of the hostages' guards brimming with questions.

'I don't know what's happening,' Chirlo snapped. 'Just stay at your posts. And keep alert if you want to see the morning.' He headed for the stairs, descended them three at a time and turned left into the security centre.

Fernández was at the microphone, with two other *sicarios* standing behind him on either side of his chair, like courtiers behind a throne.

They all looked up with relief when Chirlo appeared.

'Are we being attacked?' one of the men asked.

'Yes,' Chirlo said curtly, biting back the more sarcastic reply that came to mind. 'What the fuck's happening?' he calmly asked Fernández.

'I don't know, chief. Pérez came on, but then he disappeared again . . .'

'Try the gatehouse.'

Fernández did so. 'Nothing,' he said.

'Chief?' a voice came in. Chirlo recognized Pérez's voice.

'What's happening, Manuel?' he asked, leaning across Fernández.

'Christ knows. Mario is dead, and Cayano is wounded. Not seriously. Some sort of bomb, mortar maybe? There were two of them.'

'What's happening now?'

'Nothing, that's what crazy. We can't see anything or anybody. If there's anyone out there they're not moving . . . It could have been dropped from a plane, I suppose, but I didn't hear one . . .'

Was that possible, Chirlo asked himself. Could the British be dropping bombs on them? Or some other cartel? What for? No, it was a crazy idea.

Another thought crossed his mind. 'Start calling round,' he told Fernández. 'You,' he told one of the others, 'wake up the sleeping shift. No,' he corrected himself, 'first get the Army guys up and in their armoured car – that's what they're supposed to be here for. Then wake the others. Move!'

Eddie was just reaching an arm down to Wynwood when a guard came running round the corner of the building. Eddie twisted onto his side, bringing up the MP5, but it was not necessary. Before the man had even seen the figure on the wall a bullet took half of his head away.

'You're clear,' the Dame was saying in his helmet. Eddie gave him a wry wave of the hand and turned once more to help Wynwood up onto the wall.

'You're still clear,' the Dame's voice said.

They both dropped down to the ground, waited a few seconds, and headed out across the inner yard to the side wall of the main building's north wing.

'Good luck, lads,' the Dame said.

They had some immediately. The side door opened, admitting them into a long dimly lit corridor. Doors stood open on either side with darkened rooms behind them. They each took a doorway and waited for any sound nearby. There was none. The corridor was still empty. About forty metres down there was a pool of brighter light surrounding what looked like the bottom of a staircase. As Wynwood examined it a figure appeared and disappeared. Now they could hear the low buzz of conversation.

Wynwood gave Eddie the hand signal to advance, and the two of them inched their way forward along the corridor.

On the edge of the trees to the south Mike Bannister checked his watch and spoke into the radio mike: 'Jaguar to Puma: your turn.' Ten seconds later a mortar bomb landed twenty metres away from the inner gate. Another twenty seconds and the second bomb straddled it.

'Someone tell me where that landed,' Chirlo said into the mike. Why the fuck had Ramón insisted on putting the security centre in the bowels of the house?

Two voices began answering him together.

'Pérez,' Chirlo insisted.

'A bomb on the inner gate. It is a mortar – somewhere in the trees, I think.'

'Are the armoured cars moving?'

'Not yet.'

Chirlo stood there for a moment, thinking furiously.

The *sicario* returned with four soldiers, the two armoured car teams. Chirlo grabbed the front one and almost pulled him towards the front door.

'There's a mortar up on that hillside,' he said. 'Go and get it.' The officer seemed about to argue, but the Walther PPK in Chirlo's hand seemed to convince him. The four men hurried across the yard towards their vehicles.

The Dame had been waiting for them. The problem was they only had fifty metres to run, and once the first of the four went down they ran extremely fast. Two made it into the shelter of their car, engaged the engine, and started rolling it down the drive towards the inner gate.

Ramón's wife always said he slept the sleep of the dead, and it was true that the combination of wine and barbiturates did not make him the lightest sleeper in the world. That was the idea. There was not much point in hiring an army to defend yourself if you were going to be woken up by any little problem.

The four bombs which landed on and around the inner and outer gates were neatly absorbed into a recurring dream he had of arriving with the conquistadors five hundreds years earlier, with Hereford's 81mm mortars standing in for Balboa's cannon. It was only his sister shaking him violently by the shoulders which brought him back to the twentieth century.

* * *

Where the hell was Ramón? Chirlo thought.

'There's no answer from Ruiz, or either of the Romales brothers,' Fernández said.

'Where were they on duty?'

'The Romales brothers were on the roof.'

Chirlo had another thought. 'Get me Pérez again.'

'Yes, chief.' Fernández made the connection.

'Is the fence still switched on?' Chirlo asked Pérez.

'No, the first bomb blew a hole in it – the power's down.'

'Shit.' Chirlo brought his fist down towards the table, then aborted the motion in mid-air. At least it was beginning to make sense. 'Fall back to the inner gate,' he told Pérez. 'You,' he told the remaining *sicario*, 'come with me.'

He moved cautiously out of the security centre and towards the bottom of the stairs. If he knew anything at all about military tactics they would be somewhere in the house by now.

Eddie and Wynwood had passed within five metres of the security centre's open door two minutes earlier. Now upstairs, Eddie placed a single eye round the corner of the corridor, saw the two guards and was seen by them. He stepped out and fired the silenced MP5 from the hip, cutting them both down. 'OK, boss,' he said softly.

The pair of them moved down the corridor, checking each room was empty of possible opposition, until they stood over the two dead guards. Each had a pair of keys in his pocket. Eddie opened the first door, and the two of them went in commando-style.

Muñoz was sitting beneath the window, looking none too happy. Seeing Wynwood's familiar figure, he sighed.

'Your partner is next door,' he said in Spanish.

Wynwood edged back into the corridor, found it was still clear, and unlocked the final door.

Anderson was behind it, holding a torn length of sheet. 'I expected you to abseil in through the window,' he said disappointedly.

'There are bars across it.'

'I know.'

Wynwood handed the other man his Browning and smiled. 'Just shut up and follow me,' he said. 'Condor to Jaguar,' he told the helmet, 'we're on our way out with Tom and Jerry.'

'All clear boss,' Eddie's voice came from outside. He fell in behind the two sergeants as they started back down the corridor.

Chirlo hurled himself up the stairs, his bare feet making next to no noise on the carpeted stairs. The men in the corridor above did not hear him coming, but it was someone else who paid for their mistake. Chirlo's brain took in the four men, the guns, reckoned the odds and crashed his body through the door opposite, all in a tenth of a second.

The bursts from Eddie's and Wynwood's MP5s would have encountered only empty air if Victoria Amarales had not chosen that instant to emerge from her brother's room further down the corridor. Wynwood's took her in the upper torso, Eddie's in the head. She was dead before she hit the door-frame.

Ramón slammed the door shut on her lifeless body.

The three SAS men and Muñoz were left in command of an empty corridor. Somewhere ahead of them was the enemy. It seemed sensible to find another way out.

'You two, check in there,' Wynwood told Eddie and Anderson, pointing out the room opposite the one in which Anderson had been held. 'I'll hold the fort.'

The two men went in one after the other, slamming their backs against the wall. The room was empty save for an array of body-building equipment. French windows led out onto the verandah.

Outside they could see an armoured car which was a dark shape in the outer compound, sending sparks into the night as it fired blindly at the southern slope. An essay in utter futility, Eddie thought.

The inner compound, by contrast, seemed empty. He hand-signalled Wynwood the all-clear.

The Welshman fired one last burst at a door down the corridor which was inching open, then walked swiftly through to the verandah, and headed down towards its far end behind the others. No one seemed to be looking their way. The plan was working perfectly, Wynwood thought. They know there are soldiers out there, but they can't see them, and they can't stop trying to see them.

Eddie clambered down to the ground and Muñoz was lowered to join him. Wynwood and Anderson followed with rather more agility. In spaced single file they rounded the building where Anderson had been tied to the chair. The inner wall was twenty metres away.

'All clear,' the Dame told them.

For Bonnie and Blackie down on the road it had all seemed a bit of a doddle. Once their patrol had fired its planned mortar rounds they had been reduced to keeping watch for any sign of unexpected arrivals on the valley road.

The news of the prisoners' release had come over the radio helmets a few minutes earlier. The next message would be the order for withdrawal to the pick-up zone. It looked all over bar the drinking, Bonnie thought; he would have to fail to beat the clock some other time.

And then he saw the lights, or rather their glow beyond the bend down the valley. 'Incoming,' he said.

'Lights on the road to the north,' Chris was telling Bannister. 'No visual sighting as yet.'

Blackie was recalibrating the mortar to the prearranged setting for the bridge across the river, some four hundred metres away to the north.

One headlight, two headlights, appeared round the distant shoulder of the hill. A rumbling sound added confirmation that the lights were not tricks of the imagination.

'Ocelot to Jaguar: these are not friendlies,' Chris was telling Bannister, though how he could see anything through the nightscope against the brightness of the headlights Bonnie had no idea. Nor did he much care. 'Prepare to fire,' Chris told him and Blackie.

The lead lorry was fifty metres from the bridge, twenty-five . . .

'Fire.'

The mortar went off with a whoosh, the bomb landing almost under the front wheels of the truck, filling the cab with flames.

Bonnie dropped another bomb into the tube.

Another whoosh, and he thought he could see shadowy figures breaking out in both directions from behind the burning truck.

'Jaguar to Ocelot: what strength?' Bannister was asking.

Chris examined the scene through his PNGs. 'Ocelot to Jaguar. As far as I can tell, just two truckloads of men. They're carrying automatic weapons, but I can't see anything heavier.'

'Jaguar to Ocelot: disengage,' Bannister said. 'Start making your way home.'

'Roger. Let's move,' Chris told the others.

They collapsed the mortar, and started working their way back along the river bank. Behind them the new arrivals were still lying low, waiting for more incoming fire, oblivious of their retreat up the river bank. Somewhere further up the valley a heavy machine-gun was firing.

They recrossed the river, which seemed even colder the second time round, and slipping across the empty road, moved up the slope into the dark and welcoming embrace of the forest.

Chirlo looked down at the bloody, broken body. 'What is happening?' Ramón was asking him, but Chirlo ignored him.

'She is dead,' Ramón said. 'We cannot help her now. We must help ourselves.'

Chirlo went down on one knee, swept her

up in his arms, and carried her off down the corridor, back to her room. There he lay her on the bed, careless of the robe falling open to reveal the bullet-raddled body to which he had been making love only an hour before. He leaned down and placed his cheek against the stomach, his tears coursing down to mingle with the still-slippery blood.

After a few minutes he slowly raised his head, pulled the robe closed and stared down at the ruined face. The men who did this will die, he said to himself. If he had to travel the length and breadth of the earth they would die. And not easily.

Familiarity with the ground ensured that Wynwood, Eddie, the Dame and the two ex-prisoners arrived at the landing zone well ahead of the others. Bannister's last contact with the incoming helicopters suggested they were on schedule, and confirmation of their 0400 hours Estimated Time of Arrival came through as the three of them set out the four infrared landing lights.

A couple of minutes later they could hear the faint scraping rhythms of the blades. Another minute and first one, then a second dark shape appeared round the shoulder of the mountain slope, dim silhouettes against the night sky.

'Condor to Jaguar,' Wynwood asked. 'Our transport is in sight. Where are you?'

Chris's voice replied. 'Ten minutes away. Tell them to wait.'

Wynwood was halfway into a smile when the leading helicopter exploded in a ball of flame.

# 10

The second Blackhawk seemed to fly straight through the destruction of the first, but touched down apparently unscathed just a few seconds later. Everyone in the valley was aware of the explosion. Even inside the main house at Totoro they were aware of a momentary flash, like distant sheet lightning or the flicker of a fluorescent bulb. Chirlo looked up, sudden hope in his eyes.

The units still climbing towards the landing zone had a closer view – one moment the hills above them were dark against the stars, the next a blaze of orange fire.

'What was it?' Bannister asked, more calmly than he felt.

'One of the choppers has gone,' Wynwood answered in the same tone.

'Crashed?'

'Exploded.'

'What about the other one?'

'We're checking it out now.'

Or rather the Dame was. As the patrol's explosives specialist he had not even bothered to volunteer, but just shouted to the others to stay back and got on with it. He was underneath it now, inching along on his back examining its belly with his torch.

He did not know how long he had, but it could not be that long. While his eyes scanned every likely hiding place and the sweat gathered on his chest, his mind seemed to stand apart, utterly detached. He had the strange feeling that the men he had killed that evening were there rooting for him.

Maybe the fear of death made brothers of everyone, he thought.

And there was the bomb, taped almost directly beneath the cockpit. It seemed to be ticking up a storm – just like Captain Hook's crocodile, the Dame thought. Probably a cheap alarm clock.

It looked like a parcel wrapped tightly in plastic sheeting, with nothing other than the noise to indicate that it was a bomb, let alone what type. There was no sense in trying to unwrap it. The light was too poor, and time was doubtless on the bomb's side.

He gingerly pulled at the tape holding it to the helicopter's skin, which came off with more ease than he had expected. He let the bomb down onto his stomach, then wriggled his way out from under the helicopter, clutching it with one hand, and slowly got to his feet.

The temptation to throw it was almost irresistible, but such violent motion might well set it off. Breathing deeply he started walking towards the trees. The tick seemed to be growing louder by the moment, but he knew that was just a trick of the mind. Some twenty metres into the shelter of the trees he stopped and lowered the bomb gently to the ground behind a large trunk. And then, finally giving way to normal human fear, he ran like the blazes back the way he had come.

'The second bomb has been removed,' Wynwood was saying into his mike. 'Brilliant,' he told the Dame. 'I . . .'

The bomb exploded before he could finish the sentence, leaving an impression of bars across purple light on the retina, the sound of trees collapsing into one another, and a blazing fire in the overhead foliage.

'That was the second bomb,' Wynwood told Bannister via the helmet. 'No one was hurt.'

'Shee-it,' one of the American crew said under his breath.

The Dame looked at the burning trees, and said nothing.

Eddie and Anderson were coming back from their examination of the first chopper's remains. 'Both pilots are dead,' Anderson confirmed.

The two Americans seemed to wake up to the fact that the bodies had not been brought down. 'Hey, we can't leave them here,' the senior man said aggressively.

'Were they friends?' Anderson asked.

'That's not what I'm saying . . .'

'It would take all night and most of the day to find all the pieces,' Anderson said.

'The bombs were under the cockpit,' the Dame added.

'But . . .'

'How many men can you carry?' Wynwood interrupted.

The pilot gulped and took a second to compose himself. 'OK,' he said, 'sorry. These birds can take two crew plus eleven fully loaded troops.'

'How many without loads?'

'The official weight limit is 1200 kilos, so sixteen, maybe even seventeen . . .' He shrugged. 'With the external tanks fitted we can't afford to push it. The fuel situation's tight enough as it is . . .'

'Twenty-one's out of the question?'

The pilot looked at him. 'I'd love to. But no way. Even if we got the damn thing over the mountains, we'd never make the border.'

It was what Wynwood had expected. He turned to Anderson. 'I think you and Muñoz should go with the guys who just came in. The four of us got here without any help. We can get out the same way.'

'Forget it,' Anderson said. 'I'm not getting on that helicopter with fifteen overfed gorillas from C Squadron. If they don't bring the thing down they'll fart each other to death in the confined space. I'm coming with you.'

'Andy, we're here to rescue you. Maggie's orders.'

'Tough. I know this country, Joss. Fifteen will have a better chance than sixteen in the chopper, and five of us will have a better chance than four on the ground. Especially if I'm one of the five. OK?'

Wynwood sighed. 'OK, but Bannister will have to go along.'

'Let's just tell him.'

'Lack of rank has its privileges?'

'Something like that.'

'You two'd like to see some more of Colombia, wouldn't you?' Wynwood asked Eddie and the Dame.

'Sure,' the Dame said casually.

'I was wondering how I was going to tear myself away,' Eddie said. 'Here come the unlucky ones.'

The fifteen men of C Squadron's Air Troop were filing into the clearing behind Chris. Wynwood waited for Bannister, then took him aside and explained the situation. 'Haven't you contacted Belize?' the Captain wanted to know.

'What for? We're in the best position to make the judgements that need making.' It was a typical SAS answer – rank was all very well in its place, but it should not be allowed to get in the way of correct decisions. 'And there's no time for fucking around,' Wynwood added, pushing his advantage. 'They'll have seen the fireball down in the valley, there's less than two hours till dawn, and Christ knows who or what's been alerted. Just take Muñoz and your lads and get the fuck out of here. Personally,' he added with a grim smile, 'I'd rather take my chances with the Amarales than have to tell the Yanks two of their pilots have been spread all over the landscape.'

'It's their security that was blown . . . but yeah, OK, it makes sense . . . Do you want anything left.'

'You'll have to leave it all behind anyway for weight reasons. We'll take what we need. Let's go.'

Bannister went off to organize his troops. Wynwood sent Eddie and Chris back down the path to keep a lookout for possible pursuit, and set the Dame to work putting together the travelling kits they had not been expecting to need. Anderson went to explain the situation to Muñoz, who had sat out the entire episode of the bomb in a kind of suspended disbelief on a rock at the edge of the landing zone.

Leaving the Colombian with the American pilot, Anderson rejoined Wynwood over a map. 'Which way?' he asked.

'Good question. I'm not even sure it matters. As long as we can put a decent distance between ourselves and here tonight, we can get the Yanks to pick us up tomorrow night.'

Anderson laughed. 'You reckon? I wouldn't like to count on it. Do you think the Americans are going to send another helicopter just like that? I mean, how are they going to explain the loss of this one? They can hardly deny it was in Colombian airspace illegally – not with the pieces all over a Colombian mountain.'

'What are you saying?' Wynwood wanted to know.

'That we may well be on our own. That we have to assume we are. That we have to get the hell out of this country without any help. That it matters which way we walk.'

Wynwood grunted his assent. 'So which way?' he wanted to know.

'From here? Over the mountains to San Agustín.'

'Why not head for the coast?' Wynwood wanted to know. He wondered if Bobbie would still be in San Agustín.

'Because, like they say in the best movies – that's the way they'll expect us to go.'

'If they think we're still here.'

'We have to assume they can recognize a disaster when they see one.'

'Yeah, all right . . .'

'And San Agustín is in a different province – the local law and order may not be so hostile. There's lots of tourists, which means that there's less chance of being noticed. And there'll be lots of buses to Bogotá. Everything'll be hunky-dory.'

'Right,' Wynwood agreed sardonically, looking at the map. 'And how far is it to this place of sanctuary?'

'Only a hundred and thirty kilometres or so.'

'Across a 6000-metre mountain range!'

'It's just two long walks across the Brecon Beacons in a row.'

'Jesus!'

Barney Davies was picking up the phone before the first ring had died away.

'Boss?' Kilcline asked.

The intonation of the voice instantly told Davies it was bad news. 'What's happened?' he asked.

'One of the helicopters exploded at the landing zone. It was sabotaged. They both were – but they managed to disarm the bomb on the other one.'

'Casualties?'

'Just the pilot and co-pilot. Dead. But they had to leave the surveillance team behind. And all their equipment.'

The unwelcome thought crossed Davies's mind that British forces these days were in no financial position to leave their equipment behind.

'Anderson insisted on staying with the surveillance team,' Kilcline was saying.

'Christ, what for?' Davies asked, suspecting personal heroics.

'It was either him or someone else. He knows the country, he knows Wynwood.'

Davies offered Anderson a silent apology. 'But we got Muñoz out?'

'Yes, we've done our bit for Colombian democracy.'

Well, at least it had not been a complete waste of time. 'And we've got five men on the ground in Colombia.'

'They got themselves there. Who says they can't get themselves back? I wouldn't bet against Joss Wynwood walking to Panama.'

'Yeah. What about the Americans?'

'I think you'll have to take that up with the Prime Minister.'

'Oh Christ,' Davies said. 'I'd forgotten about her.'

* * *

An hour after dawn an Amarales helicopter arrived from one of their laboratory complexes on the Amazonian slopes of the Andes. Meeting it on the helipad, Chirlo and Carlos Fernández joined the pilot and his Indian passenger in the cockpit.

'Up the mountain,' Chirlo told the pilot, pointing towards the slope silhouetted against the early morning sky. 'It's not far. Carlos here will tell you exactly where.'

The *sicario* directed the pilot to the clearing. They flew in past the slope bearing the remnants of the American helicopter and touched down in almost the same spot the other American had used the night before. Chirlo jumped out and prowled round the site. Everything was exactly as Fernández, the leader of the pre-dawn search party, had told him it was. Only one helicopter had landed here, and it was obviously not the one now scattered across the landscape. So two had come for the enemy, and only one had left. Unable to take all their equipment with them they had made a pile of it and then exploded some device to render it unusable.

Which left one important question unanswered: had there been room for all of the attackers in the one helicopter? A soldier usually weighs considerably more than his equipment, Chirlo told himself. It all depended on how much leeway they had given themselves.

He waited for the Indian, Manomi, to return with the answer, wondering what Ramón's reaction would be to his sister's death once the shock had worn off. Would he just want to wash his hands of the matter, see the loss of the hostages as a lost business opportunity, Victoria's murder as just an unfortunate tragedy? Or would he want to fight back?

He stared at the panorama of mountains all around him, a feeling of great emptiness in his heart.

Twenty minutes later Manomi emerged from the trees and walked towards him, his face expressionless.

'Well?' Chirlo asked.

'There are recent tracks heading up the mountain,' the Indian said. 'Boot tracks.'

'How many?'

'It is hard to say. Four or five, no more. They are either very big men or carrying heavy loads.'

Chirlo looked at his watch. It was 7.45 – the enemy had about three hours' start. 'You can track them?'

Manomi looked surprised. 'Of course.'

'Good. I will send up ten men to accompany you. Yes?'

'They will have to be good walkers.'

Chirlo grimaced. 'I'll do my best. The helicopter can ferry the men up here and then start an aerial search for them. If we get a sighting we can move you up by air.'

The Indian just nodded and sat himself down. 'Send some food,' he added as Chirlo turned to leave him. 'One day's worth. A few gringos should not be hard to catch in these mountains.'

'These are not ordinary gringos,' Chirlo said. 'They have been trained for circumstances like this.'

Manomi looked vaguely interested for the first time. 'Good,' he said. 'Then send two days' food.'

Barney Davies finished talking to Jimbo Bourne in Belize and wondered how 'to prepare himself for the ordeal ahead. A glass of whisky would not go amiss, he decided. And make it a double, he told himself. This, he decided, was exactly what the American who had organized the Tehran hostage raid must have felt like before picking up the phone to call Jimmy Carter.

Oh well, he had better phone her before the Americans did. Or the Colombians. Davies took a stiff gulp of whisky. At least she would not be able to smell his breath down the telephone line.

She was either addressing the Cabinet or on the toilet: it was several minutes before he heard the familiar voice.

'Prime Minister . . .' he began.

'Lieutenant-Colonel Davies,' she almost gushed. 'Have we counted them all back?'

It was a joke, he decided. And not in very good taste considering the circumstances. 'I'm afraid the news is not all good, Prime Minister,' he said.

A cold wind seemed to blow down the line. 'Why, what has happened?'

He told her.

'Let me get this straight. Your troops carried out their mission successfully, and would all be back in Panama by now if the American helicopter had not exploded.'

'That is correct, Prime Minister.'

'Forgive me for asking this,' she continued, 'but will President Bush be telling me the same story when I talk to him.'

Davies decided he would lose nothing by being blunt. 'If his people tell him the truth, and if he tells it to you, then yes, Ma'am.'

Her answering grunt could have meant many things. 'And we have five men still on the ground in Colombia?' she asked after a moment.

'Yes, Ma'am.'

'And what are you doing about getting them out?'

'At present, nothing.'

'Nothing!?'

'With all respect, Ma'am, there's nothing we can do. If we'd had the capacity to airlift our men out of Colombia then we wouldn't have needed help from the Americans in the first place. A request for further help would require a decision from you. From the Government, that is.'

The distinction did not interest her. 'I will talk to the President,' she said.

'But at the moment we don't even know if the enemy realizes that some men were left behind. I would advise that we don't draw attention to the fact . . .'

'Not even the attention of the Colombian Government?'

'With respect, Prime Minister, the details of the operation must have leaked from somewhere, and the Colombian Government seems the most likely source.'

There was silence on the other end.

'I think I should add,' Davies said, 'that even if their presence on the ground is known, these men have a fair chance of extricating themselves from the situation.' He had thought long and hard about saying this, hoping it would not weaken any resolve there might be in the way of providing the five men with outside help, but had decided he had no real choice. At present only five lives were at stake: sending in more to rescue them would raise the ante. And if all the Americans had to offer was exploding helicopters then maybe his men would be better off on their own.

'What are they going to do – walk out of Colombia?'

'If necessary, Prime Minister.'

'I will have to think this over,' she said. 'I will call you back later this morning.'

'Thank you, Prime . . .' he started to say, but she had hung up. He took another gulp of whisky and stared angrily at the wall.

There was hardly any sign that it had happened, Chirlo thought, looking out across the verandah towards the gates. The gatehouse looked undamaged from this distance, the fence whole. The armoured car was still sitting in the middle of the outer compound; presumably its crew was still trying to recover from their failed attempt to shoot the forest. What a farce!

He heard the arrival of Miguel behind him and turned to join the meeting. Victoria's husband Noguera had arrived an hour earlier and had seemed, to no one's great surprise, not exactly devastated by his wife's death. Much the same could be said for her brothers. Ramón still looked pale, but that had more to do with his own brush with death; he had shown no sign of regretting Victoria's. The arriving Miguel seemed equally unmoved, offering his condolences to Noguera with all the emotion of a weather report. Basically, neither brother had ever forgiven Victoria for being the intelligent one of the three.

There was a silence lasting about half a minute, like those they hold at the beginning of football matches to honour someone recently dead. In the Amarales living-room there was no whistle to signal its end, but the participants all came out kicking anyway.

'Well, now we know where your stupidity has taken us, Ramón,' Miguel began. 'Our sister is dead, your hostages are gone, and our family will be a laughing stock throughout the nation.'

'Do you think so little of your sister that you can use her death to score points against me?' Ramón asked angrily. 'Where were you last night while the rest of us were fighting off the gringo soldiers? Not with your family. You have no right to accuse me.'

'Ramón, Miguel,' Noguera said. 'This is no time for blaming each other. What has happened, has happened. We must decide what to do now.'

'What is there to do?' Miguel asked with a cold laugh. 'We cannot bring Victoria back. Or the hostages, come to that. All we can do is learn from our mistakes,' he added, looking straight at Ramón. 'And cut our losses.'

'Our losses are seven men and a sister,' Ramón said quietly. 'How do you *cut* them?'

'Friends . . .' Noguera implored.

'Señores,' Chirlo said. 'I have some new information. Some of the gringo soldiers did not manage to escape in the helicoper.'

Both brothers looked at him as if he had taken leave of his senses.

'It is true. There must have been inadequate space for them all. Four, perhaps five of them, headed into the mountains on foot. Manomi is tracking them.' He looked at the three of them coldly, waiting for their response.

Miguel was the first to react. 'They will have a long walk home. It is of no concern to us . . .'

'No concern?' Chirlo asked, barely managing to keep his anger under control. 'These are the men who murdered your sister, Señor.'

'He is right,' Ramón said. 'We have a family obligation. And' – he insisted, ignoring Miguel's obvious disagreement – 'we can repair the lost prestige you're so concerned about.'

'You're a complete hypocrite,' Miguel told him. 'Victoria may have been our sister and Armando's wife, but none of us will grieve for her and we all know it . . .'

'Miguel!' Noguera said, but he did not deny it.

Chirlo felt Ramón's glance resting on him – the elder brother had obviously not missed the depth of his reaction to Victoria's death the night before. I loved her, Chirlo wanted to say. And she was worth a dozen of you.

'I will see to it that they do not escape,' he said instead.

'Good,' Ramón agreed. 'Armando, we will need your help.'

Noguera seemed less than enthusiastic. 'There are problems,' he said quickly. 'Bogotá will ask questions. I already have two men dead from last night.'

'Exercises,' Ramón said succinctly. 'You will mount exercises.'

'It is not so easy . . .'

'Armando,' Ramón said, 'we have always thought of you as one of the family, and this is a matter of family honour. Do you understand what I'm saying?'

Noguera swallowed. 'Yes, Ramón.' And he did. Victoria was no longer around to protect him from her brothers.

About twenty kilometres from Totoro, and almost a thousand metres higher, the five SAS men were toiling up what might have been a shepherd's path if there had been any sign of sheep. Someone had made it anyway, and Wynwood doubted if it was hikers. The higher they got the more the feeling grew that man had never set foot in these mountains before. Maybe there was an Andean yeti. Or Bigfoot. *Pie grande*. Or something like that.

Wynwood checked the map again. Another

couple of kilometres and they should come to a small pass. From there they would descend into another valley and then start climbing again.

The mountain slopes were still covered with vegetation, though the type of tree had changed from mostly deciduous to mostly coniferous. The important thing was that they had cover if they needed it. Which was one of the reasons for their dawn decision to keep walking, rather than hole up for the day.

'If they're following us and we stop, they'll catch us,' Chris had argued.

'They may not be following us,' Wynwood had countered, mostly from a desire to play the devil's advocate. 'They may just mount a helicopter search, in which case we'd be better off out of sight.'

Both arguments had had something going for them. Wynwood hoped they had guessed right. All of them were very tired, particularly Anderson, who had not slept for almost thirty-six hours. He claimed to have suffered no ill effects from his period of imprisonment but Wynwood was not convinced, for his old partner seemed strangely subdued in those moments when he thought no one was looking.

Walking ahead of Wynwood, lead scout Eddie seemed the most alert of them all, his Cockney swagger somewhat muted but far from suppressed.

Wynwood had been impressed by the Londoner's efficiency over the last few days, but he did not have a clue what made him tick. He seemed too cynical even for the SAS. At least he looked better in his jungle hat than he had in the ridiculous helmet.

Eddie himself was enjoying the morning. Ever since infant-school days – covering every square foot of the pitch Steve-Perryman-style for the school team – he had been known for his incredible physical stamina. He could walk another twenty kilometres yet without really feeling the pace. Only his eyes felt really tired, and that was a consequence of wearing the PNGs for an extended period.

For a while he had wondered why this latest disaster had not fazed him more. But it just had not – that was all there was to it. In this world you took what was coming and you made the best of it. He disliked riding in helicopters anyway. And it really was a beautiful morning. He smiled to himself as he thought of all the millions of men trapped in offices and factories and tube trains and high-rise flats who would never know what this life was like. And he thought about Lisa and wondered if he could ever learn to live without it.

* * *

Two men behind Eddie, Anderson alternated his gaze between Wynwood's back and the patrol's left flank, for which he was responsible. At the moment it consisted of the small and beautiful valley out of which they were slowly climbing. It looked like a Western setting, needing only a cabin with smoke rising from its chimney and a lone rider's horse picking its way across the shallow mountain stream.

This morning he would have been back in the chair with the cold electrodes fastened to his balls. Would he have told the man with the scar what he wanted to know? No, because the man would not have known the truth from the lies. But if he had known . . . He could still feel the moment the pain hit him. Like every other SAS soldier, Anderson had been through the sensory-deprivation and interrogation training sessions, and he had found them as harrowing as anyone else. But what had happened the day before was something else altogether. He had just had the one shock, but still he felt as if his life had been changed, perhaps even fundamentally. How it would affect him in the long run he did not know. But he wanted to, and as soon as possible. This was one reason, he now realized, why he had been loath to get aboard the helicopter. There was no exorcism available in Hereford, only in real action.

* * *

Behind Anderson, Chris was responsible for the patrol's right flank. This consisted of an overhanging slope rising to invisible heights above their line of march. He scanned what he could of it, despite the near-certainty that the enemy was extremely unlikely to be above them. Amarales men – or Colombian Army men come to that – could only have got ahead of them by air, and only once that morning had they caught the distant sound of a helicopter, and that far away to their rear.

Chris did have another reason for scanning the heights to their right. If he remembered correctly what he had read in his book there were Andean Condors in these mountains. Not many of them, but some. He would happily give a months' pay to see one on the wing.

Behind Chris, officially designated 'Tail-end Charlie', the Dame regularly swung round on his heel to check that there was no danger to the patrol from the rear. There was almost a hundred metres between him and Eddie, and the spaces between each man and his neighbours were deliberately irregular. They were a professional outfit, the Dame thought proudly. They did things *well.* And when they got home they would have some story to tell.

Yet he wondered why he never told his sisters anything of his experiences as an SAS soldier. It was not security – they would never breathe a word if he told them not to. And it was not that he felt ashamed of anything, or that they needed protecting from the real world. If you lived in the Garth flats you knew about the real world, all right.

No, it was just that they were women, and women were not interested in the same things as men. His sisters would be interested in his experiences because they were his, not because of the experiences themselves. They would want to know what señoritas he had met. He would tell them about Barbara on the bus and the two Australian girls in the square at Popayán, and they would tease him about them for months. He smiled to himself and turned round on his heel. Behind him there was only Colombia, spread out like a huge geography lesson.

The pilot returned for fuel and lunch. Chirlo gave him the former, and told him to get back in the air.

'If they are in the area you described they are hiding, Chief.'

'Look again, then widen the area,' Chirlo told him.

'What do you think?' Wynwood asked Anderson. Ahead of them the pass stretched at least a kilometre and a half into the distance, before disappearing over its rim and into the wide blue sky. A small stream bubbled its way down between long slopes of mixed grass and scree. Cover was non-existent.

'What's the choice?' Anderson asked.

'Dig in here until dark.'

'There's not much more cover here.'

That was true enough, Wynwood thought. 'OK, let's go on.'

Luis Quintana waited for the President to stop preening himself in front of the window and tell him the detail he had just received from the military in Popayán.

'There are several Englishmen somewhere in the mountains,' Estrada said with a faint smile on his face. He suddenly laughed. 'You have to hand it to the Americans,' he said. 'They take the minimum number of helicopters and then crash one. What morons! If I was Mrs Thatcher I think I'd bomb Washington.'

Quintana smiled too. At least no one seemed to be publicly raising the question of sabotage. The Americans must know, but that did not matter. 'What are you going to do about these Englishmen?' he asked.

'Me? Nothing. The Amarales are looking for them, and since the Military Commander in Popayán is their brother-in-law I expect they're getting some unofficial help. Officially, I don't even know these Englishmen exist. When I talked to London and Washington this morning no mention was made of them.'

'What did London and Washington tell you?'

'That they'd rescued Muñoz and lost a helicopter and its pilot in the process.'

'Yes, we will soon have Muñoz back,' Quintana agreed. He could not understand why Estrada was in such a good mood.

'He's finished,' Estrada asserted blandly. 'I shall talk to the nation tonight,' he added, passing across a rough draft of what he intended to say.

Quintana read it through, and realized what was plastering the smile across Estrada's face. The whole business had played right into the President's hands. On the one hand he would welcome Muñoz's release on humanitarian grounds, while on the other he would condemn the foreign incursion as a violation of Colombia's sovereignty, an insult to the nation. Without even mentioning the two in the same breath, Muñoz would be tarred with the American brush and Estrada's place would be secure in the coming nomination fight.

'It reads well,' Quintana said mildly, handing the draft back. Why, he thought to himself, did political luck always seem to bless those who deserved it least?

* * *

They were more than halfway up the pass now, though whether the far side would offer more cover was a moot point. Chris had said it would – west-facing slopes got more rain, and therefore had more vegetation – but Wynwood tended to put more faith in Sod's Law than in geography textbooks.

He really was beginning to feel tired now. Even Eddie's legs were showing some signs of strain. Another few kilometres and they would get under cover, sleep a few hours and then push on after dark.

There was even a buzzing in his ears.

'Chopper,' Eddie shouted, and there it was, appearing in the V of the pass ahead.

'Spread out,' he yelled, but he need not have bothered. The members of the patrol split off to the right and left like a well-oiled machine, searching for whatever cover they could find.

Wynwood threw himself 'behind' a shelf of rock which only protruded about three inches above the grass and searched the sky for the helicopter. For a few seconds he could hear it but not see it, and then it emerged from over the ridge behind him, swooping down across the shallow valley. A man in the passenger seat was half leaning out, sub-machine-gun at the ready, and as the craft swooped above Wynwood, its rotors sweeping the grass into his face, the crack of automatic fire resounded above the engine.

Answering fire came from across the valley. Andy and Eddie had opened up with their MP5s.

The helicopter swooped round in a wide arc and then slowed to a virtual hover above the valley a couple of hundred metres ahead of them, as if uncertain what to do. And then the pilot's head suddenly jerked away, the helicopter reared up like a bucking bronco, seemed to hover again for a moment, and then dropped like a stone to the ground. The explosion seemed to wash around the valley like water trapped in a maelstrom. Flames and black smoke gushed into the blue sky.

Looking round, Wynwood saw the Dame still holding the sniper rifle cradled against his shoulder.

'The boy can shoot,' Wynwood murmured to himself. He lay still for a few seconds, straining his ears for the sound of another helicopter, then got slowly to his feet.

All five men walked forward towards the burning helicopter. In the cockpit two Colombians had lost their chance to choose between burial and cremation.

'The pilot was talking into his mike,' The Dame said.

'So they'll probably know how many of us there are,' Chris observed.

'With any luck they won't have any more helicopters to spare,' Anderson said.

Wynwood grunted. 'With any luck they'll think twice about risking another one.'

'Why are they bothering?' the Dame wanted to know. 'What good will it do them?'

'I think they've taken it personally,' Wynwood said. 'We killed a woman back at the house,' he went on, turning to the three who did not know. 'She just stepped out of a doorway into the line of fire,' he added, and shrugged. 'So they may not be worrying too much about risk-evaluation. This may be a matter of family honour. Or something like that.'

'Great,' Anderson murmured. 'We come all this way, and you start a family feud. Just like the bloody Welsh!'

Wynwood gave him a cold stare. He did not feel guilty about the woman's death, any more than he would have done if she had stepped out in front of his car on the M4. But he did not like the fact that it had happened, and he did not feel like making a joke of it.

'Let's get on,' Chris said, trying to fill the breach. 'I need some sleep, and I'd like some sort of roof over my head, even if it's only a tree.'

Wynwood, though, was extricating the PRC 319 from his pack. 'I think we ought to let Belize know we've been spotted,' he said.

* * *

Estrada and Quintana had just finished working their way through the latest American extradition requests when they were informed of the British Ambassador's request for an audience.

They grinned at one another. 'Bring him up,' Estrada said. 'Guess what he wants to talk about,' he said wryly to Quintana. 'You stay,' he added, as the other man got up to leave.

The Ambassador was shown in. After exchanging greetings with the President and being introduced to his Minister for the Interior, he was ushered into the usual ornate and uncomfortable chair.

'Before you begin,' Estrada said, 'I should tell you Señor Quintana is fully cognisant of last night's events.'

The Ambassador nodded. 'I have just received some additional information in that regard,' he said. 'I regret to tell you this, but five of our soldiers were left behind at the scene.' If he was expecting a shocked reaction he was disappointed.

'That is unfortunate,' Estrada agreed. 'Do you know where they are now?'

'Somewhere in the mountains. I am sure you will not take offence if I say that they are probably reluctant to approach the local authorities.'

'Of course not. I would be reluctant to approach them myself,' Estrada said with a broad smile.

The Ambassador sighed inwardly, smiled outwardly. 'The British Government would like to request your help in finding and escorting these men to safety,' he said formally.

'Of course, of course. We will do everything we can,' Estrada said, turning to Quintana for confirmation. The Minister nodded his agreement. With about as much sincerity as a tea-drinking chimpanzee, the Ambassador thought.

'But, as you know, our powers are somewhat limited,' Estrada went on. 'If they had not been, there would have been no need for your soldiers to be there in the first place, yes? But we will try. Of course we will.'

'There are several guerrilla groups active in those mountains,' Quintana added helpfully.

Just before dusk Chris woke Wynwood for his shift on lookout. 'Come and have a look at this,' he said, leading the Welshman back to the position they were using on a sheltered ledge above the camp. The sun had set beneath the western mountains, leaving the vast expanse beneath them bathed in shadow. 'Down there,' Chris said, handing him the sniper rifle's nightscope and pointing.

Wynwood could see nothing with the naked eye. With the scope he could just pick out a line of figures ascending a slope far below. 'Huh,' he said.

'Who *are* those guys?' Chris murmured.

'How far away do you think they are?' Wynwood asked, ignoring the *Butch Cassidy* reference.

'In distance, about three kilometres. In time, several hours. And it'll be too dark to track soon. I don't think we've got anything to worry about.'

'Yeah?' Wynwood asked, one eyebrow raised.

Chris grinned at the absurdity of what he had just said, and made the necessary correction. 'From them, that is.'

'OK,' Wynwood said, 'I'll keep an eye on 'em. Get some sleep.'

'Yes, boss.'

The news of the helicopter's destruction brought Chirlo a savage satisfaction. All day a little voice in his head had been telling him that Manomi was just an Indian who had seen a chance to make some money, that the tracks he was following were either non-existent or made by someone else entirely at some distant time in the past, and that all the Englishmen were back in Panama or wherever it was they had come from.

The little voice had been wrong. They really were out there in the mountains. Five of them, according to the pilot's last report, including the one who had been a prisoner.

Where the fuck did they think they were going?

He had thought they were just keeping themselves out of harm's way until someone friendly came to collect them, but it was beginning to look like no one was coming.

The way these gringos were going they were either lost or intending to walk right across the mountains. The first possibility did not seem very likely. But if they were trying the second then what was their intended destination? It had to be somewhere in the Magdalena valley.

He left the security centre and walked upstairs to the library, pulled out a map of the area and examined it. They could be aiming for San Agustín, or the airport at Pitalito . . .

Either way they would be making themselves vulnerable again.

Walking back down the corridor, he passed one of the TV lounges. As usual, and despite the circumstances, Ramón was spending the afternoon in front of a Hollywood movie.

Chirlo walked down the stairs, letting his anger cool into something closer to sadness. I was the only one who cared for you, he told the woman who was still living in his head.

# 11

By 22.00 hours all five men had had at least four hours' sleep. It was not exactly enough, but it would have to do. Far beneath them the pursuit had camped for the night, the distant glow of their fire like a flare in the nightscope.

'Look on the bright side, lads,' Anderson said, eliciting groans from Eddie and the Dame. 'If this was the "Long Drag" over the Beacons you'd be having to contend with rain, snow and sadistic bastards from Training Wing like Joss here. And here we are on a beautiful night, sky full of stars, not too hot, not too cold. Perfect walking weather.'

'And *two* sadistic bastards from Training Wing for company,' Eddie observed.

'Let's get started,' Wynwood said.

The first hour was the worst, as the muscles stiffened by the previous day's exercise wreaked their revenge. After that it was just a matter of putting one foot in front of the other. This, they all knew, was exactly what their training had been for, and each man called on those inner reserves he had not known he had before the SAS forced him to find them. It was hard, it hurt, but there was no denying it also brought a deep sense of satisfaction.

It was not a night for talking, and even on their rare rest stops barely a word was exchanged. Each man was too busy inside himself, cajoling himself, getting the best out of himself. The surroundings helped. Walking through this land of lofty peaks, cavernous valleys and endless sky was like walking through a dream, taking each man back to the lost fantasies of childhood, to the roots of his own being.

By the time the first glimmer of dawn appeared over the eastern horizon they were starting their descent into the upper reaches of the Magdalena valley, more than half the journey done. At the foot of a high pass, just below the tree line, they made camp for the day. A mist was rising from the valley below, and for a moment they could all have been in Wales again, waiting for the lorries from Hereford to take them home.

'Your call to the State Department,' his secretary informed Alan Holcroft. He grimaced and picked up the receiver.

'John!' he said jovially. He had always found

that false bonhomie seemed to put Americans at a disadvantage. It was as if one part of them knew it was false, while another part could not bear to believe it.

'Alan,' John Stokes, his American opposite number, responded with rather less enthusiasm.

Already Holcroft knew he was going to get nowhere. Not that he particularly wanted to, or thought he deserved to, but the Prime Minister had other ideas. They had used our air bases to attack Libya, and the least they could do was let us use theirs to . . . well, 'attack Colombia' were the words she had used, but Holcroft had presumed this was only a figure of speech, and that her actual intentions did not go beyond extricating the SAS men. It had been pointed out to her that the US were particularly touchy about their relations with Latin America, and had shown it during the Falklands War, but this had only brought forth a history lesson in Anglo-American cooperation, and how the British had been doing most of the cooperating.

The Americans owed us, and she was confident they would make good the debt. At least, she said she was. Presumably she had *some* fears of an American rebuff, or she would have been on the phone herself, talking direct to the White House.

All this flashed through Holcroft's mind in an instant, flooding his mind with the usual cynicism.

'I think we need your help again, John,' he began. 'What are the chances?'

'Not good,' Stokes said. 'You know what Estrada said on TV yesterday. If we mount another operation he'll have to break off relations . . .'

'Only if the second operation is also a failure,' Holcroft interrupted, half masking the accusation in geniality.

'Could you guarantee your military won't fuck up any particular operation?'

Holcroft winced inwardly at the language. 'I think we could guarantee not to make the same mistake twice in a row,' he said, rather more haughtily than he intended.

'Yeah, well, your guys are doubtless all supermen. The point is, Alan, we're not prepared to put our entire Latin America policy at risk for five men. I sympathize, I hope they make it out. But . . .'

Holcroft heard the mental shrug. 'There is a second possibility,' he said. 'You could simply allow us to use your Panama base facilities to mount the operation ourselves.'

'Same problem,' Stokes said succinctly.

'You got a rather more friendly answer from us when you requested the use of our facilities to attack Libya,' Holcroft said, as unaggressively as he could manage.

'NATO facilities,' Stokes corrected him. 'English soil, I give you that. But you tell me, Alan, did

Gaddafi look on the UK Government as an innocent party because it only supplied the air bases?'

There was no answer to that. 'Touché,' Holcroft replied. 'Well, I tried.'

'I hope they make it,' Stokes said again.

The helicopter touched down in the mountain meadow. Chirlo dropped to the ground and walked across to where an impassive-looking Manomi was doing battle with a mango, tugging at the stringy flesh with his irregular teeth, juice glistening on his chin. The ten *sicarios* he had been leading across the mountains sat and lay in some disarray around him. They all looked like they needed an oxygen tent.

'Well?' Chirlo asked, sitting down next to the Indian.

Manomi smiled, and with a simple contemptuous gesture of one hand passed sentence on his fellow-walkers. 'They will not catch them,' he added unnecessarily.

'But you could?'

Manomi shrugged. 'Probably, but I would not like to bet my life on it. These men can walk.' He popped the mango stone into his mouth and begun to suck on it.

'How far ahead are they?'

Manomi manoeuvred the stone into a cheek.

'Perhaps not so far,' he said. 'They will be sleeping now – they only walk by night.'

'Then why . . .' Chirlo started to ask, but the answer was all around him. These men had nothing left. He was tempted to leave them here.

'If they can keep up the same speed,' Manomi volunteered, 'they will be in San Agustín by tomorrow morning.'

This time they slept through most of the daylight hours, each man taking two hours on lookout and eight hours' sleep. Wynwood could not quite manage the latter, and in the last hour of daylight, prematurely darkened by their position on an eastern slope, he went to find Chris in the lookout position. The bird-watcher had a smile on his face.

'I saw two of them,' he said, almost dreamily.

'Two what?'

'Andean Condors. They circled the valley up there. Enormous, they were – the wingspan must have been ten feet. Sort of wrinkled-looking heads . . .'

'I know how they feel.'

'And these large silvery patches on the black wings. Incredible,' he sighed. 'But they didn't stay long. I think they must have sensed our presence.'

'I don't suppose they see many people up

here,' Wynwood agreed, looking up the pass they had descended that morning. 'No sign of our friends?'

'No. Even if they'd started at dawn and matched our pace they'd still be a couple of hours back. But' – he paused for a moment – 'I was wondering whether we should do something to slow them down even more.'

'Booby-trap the path?'

'Yep. We're still carrying a Claymore. If they lost their lead man it'd slow them down no end.'

Wynwood looked round, thinking it over. The odds against an innocent passer-by being killed seemed pretty remote. But then they hardly knew anything about the place. Maybe in a year, two years, some hiker would come along and . . .

'No,' he decided. 'If we were being really pushed, maybe. But I think we can outwalk this bunch.'

Chirlo stood over Ramón as he made the call.

'Armando, it's me. We have more information about the gringos. They will probably be in San Agustín tomorrow morning . . . What does it matter how they got there? They walked . . . This is not a joke . . . Good. Now you must contact General Castro in Neiva. Tell him there are five gringo criminals on the run from your custody, and you want them apprehended and returned to Popayán. If he is difficult then you can use our name and offer him whichever you think will work better – money or threats. But only if he is difficult . . . Yes, I understand. I hope you do too, Armando. Chirlo will be handling things in San Agustín personally . . . Yes, the police chief there is an old friend . . .'

Ramón replaced the phone. 'He will do as you asked,' he told Chirlo.

'Thank you, *patrón*. I am sure the murder of his wife has been a great shock to him,' Chirlo added, not bothering to keep the bitter irony out of his voice.

'I'm sure,' Ramón agreed, in a more neutral tone.

Chirlo went back to his own suite, where he restlessly paced the floor for several minutes before allowing himself to sit down with a cigarette. He looked around at all the trimmings of luxury – the fine clothes, the excellent Japanese sound system, TV and VCR, even a couple of expensive paintings he had acquired on a whim in the USA. None of it had ever meant much to him. The fact of it was important, the fact that he had pulled himself up from nothing, from less than nothing – the orphaned boy living wild in the Bogotá sewers who had risen through teenage gangs and worse to become chief hired gun, the *sicario jefe*, of the Amarales. He was proud that he had not gone under, like so many others he had known.

If he had ever thought about the morality of what he did, it would have been simply to dismiss the question. Almost all the men he had killed would have killed him if they had been quicker or brighter or stronger. He was a soldier in a war, in two wars really – the Amarales against the other drug cartels, and the war of the cartels against the United States.

The first was just a straight dispute between businesses – they all knew what they were doing, all accepted the lack of rules, all played to win. The second was just as straightforward. The people of Peru and Bolivia wanted to sell coca leaves, and a lot of Americans wanted to smoke or snort cocaine. The cartels were just middlemen, turning raw material into product and retailing it at a profit on the open market. If the American Government could use force to keep markets open then so could the cartels.

No, it was not where he was that worried Chirlo, but where he could not go. The post of chief *sicario* to such a family was the highest a *mestizo* like himself could hope for. There might be no limit to the wealth he could accumulate, but he could never become one of them. They were Spanish purebloods one and all, each with a beautifully drawn genealogical chart on the living-room wall tracing his descent from the conquistadors.

None of that could be his. All he could have

was things, more and more expensive things perhaps, but still things. And his power would always be only that, never true authority. Even as a sixteen-year-old he had seen this emptiness at the heart of his future.

And then he had found Victoria. Now he had lost her, the emptiness seemed so much greater than before.

This time the night's walk seemed easier, but not because their path led mostly downhill – that merely meant a new set of muscles to torture. It was a few good hours of sleep that had made the difference. After the day-long wait outside Totoro, the night's excitement and two long marches, all on only four hours of blissful unconsciousness, their energy reserves had been dangerously low. Now, Wynwood thought, they were fully recovered. Eddie had his jaunty step back, Chris had even seen his birds. All was right with the world, or as right as it could be with a drug cartel on your trail.

Shortly before dawn they reached the forested hills overlooking San Agustín. Only a few lights were showing and it was hard to get any real idea of how big the town was.

The five of them gathered in a circle, barely visible to each other in the still-dark forest.

'The way I see it,' Wynwood began, 'we have to

choose now between staying soldiers or going back undercover. And it doesn't seem much of a choice. We can't fight our way out of this country, so there doesn't seem any point in trying. We could present ourselves to the local authorities and hope they're friendly. Or we could go back to being tourists and try and make it to Bogotá, where at least we'll have people to help us.'

'Like you say, boss, there's no choice,' the Dame agreed.

'I don't like the idea of surrendering ourselves to the local military or police,' Chris said, 'at least not until we have some idea whose pocket they're in.'

There were several murmurs of agreement.

'OK,' Wynwood said. 'But if we're going back undercover we have to ditch most of what we're carrying. The MP5s can go in our rucksacks, and we can wear the Brownings, but that's it. The L96 has to go,' he added, looking at the Dame. 'It's earned a decent burial.'

He looked round at them. 'And it's goodbye jungle fatigues, hello your sartorial best.'

'You're not going to wear that shirt again, are you, boss?' Eddie asked. 'There may be fashion police down there.'

It got both lighter and more misty as Wynwood worked his way downhill towards the town. After about a kilometre he came across the first real fence he had seen since Totoro. Since it was high, and stretched into the distance in both directions, Wynwood simply cut his way through it. Climbing a small hill, he found himself suddenly face to face with four figures. For a moment he thought it was a group of men looming out of the mist, but they were statues, man-high stone statues like large chess pieces with flat, playing-card faces. He remembered what Bobbie had told him about San Agustín. He must have broken into the archaeological park.

He continued on his way, more cautiously now, and found some navigational help from the diagrams set up for tourists to follow. Reaching the main gate, he managed to clamber out without attracting any attention from the lighted office off to one side.

From there a road led downhill for a couple of kilometres into the town, eventually becoming a street bound on both sides by houses and bungalow-style hotels. The first real sign of life came from an establishment with the unexpected name of the Brahama Vegetarian Restaurant. Looking in through the doorway, Wynwood could see one European man eating what looked like a pancake.

He went in. The man turned out to be German, and in response to Wynwood's questions about a quiet hotel suggested the one he was staying at himself. It was only two minutes away. He would show Wynwood after he had finished his breakfast.

Resisting the temptation to waste time by ordering himself a pancake, Wynwood made do with a wonderfully hot cup of coffee.

Outside it was now almost full light, and the sun was breaking through the mist. The German, whose name was Klaus, led him round two corners and into a rapidly disintegrating street. A long, one-storey building carried a sign proclaiming it the Residencias El Cesar.

At first sight it did not seem very prepossessing. The large wooden gates were almost falling off their hinges, and the only visible wall looked like it belonged to a barracks. Inside, though, it was a different matter. Klaus led Wynwood down a short passage, turning right onto a verandah that was at least fifty metres long. On one side doors led into a line of rooms, ten or more of them. On the other a balustrade looked out and down over half an acre of tropical vegetation. Butterflies were dancing in the leaves, two donkeys were rummaging in the earth, and a cock, apparently confused by the mist, was belatedly crowing in the dawn.

The owners occupied the far rooms, and the owner's wife, a plump woman whose dress would have seemed appropriate in a Bogotá nightclub, was drinking coffee at the end of the verandah. She showed Wynwood two empty rooms with six beds, the shower and toilet. '*Aguas calientes*,' she said proudly.

Wynwood took the rooms. He could have left the others sitting in the forest while he investigated the situation, but the sooner they came down the better, while the town was still half-asleep. And here in the hotel they would be able to clean themselves up properly – tourists tended not to have their faces covered in dirt.

It took him half an hour to get back to them, this time by a route which skirted round the edge of the archaeological park. Behind him the town was now basking in the early morning sun. Looking back, he could see that it was perched on a sloping plateau above a gorge, surrounded by green hills. Built to the usual Spanish grid pattern, it was about thirty streets long and six streets wide. Most of the buildings seemed to be of two storeys.

Chris was acting lookout on the forest's edge. The others were half dozing on the forest floor. Wynwood kicked Eddie's foot. 'I've found you a bath,' he said.

An hour later a freshly showered Eddie joined the other four in the room Wynwood was nominally sharing with Anderson. As far as they knew, their passage from the forest to the hotel, spaced out in pairs behind Wynwood, had been unobserved by anyone other than children, dogs and the odd chicken.

It was now 0800 hours, and Wynwood did not think they could count on such invisibility for much longer. 'Andy's the only one they've seen,' he said, 'so he stays in the hotel. In the room,' he added. 'I'm going to try and call Bogotá from the local telephone office . . .'

'Why not from here?' Eddie asked.

Wynwood looked at him pityingly. 'Or we could just run a Union Jack up the TV aerial.'

'Sorry, boss.'

'Like I said, the local office. Depending on what Bogotá says, I'll try the bus station – find out when there's a bus. The rest of you should get out of here, but not together. In ones or twos. And we'll meet back here at noon. OK?'

They nodded.

'Anyone got a book I can read while I'm stuck in here?' Anderson asked.

'*Teach Yourself Plastic Surgery*,' Eddie suggested.

'*South American Birds*?' Chris offered.

Anderson turned to the Dame. 'Some people are interested in birds, and some are interested in *birds*, know what I mean?'

'I'll bring you back a chicken,' Eddie promised.

* * *

It was getting warmer out on the street. Wynwood's description of Klaus's banana and papaya pancake had made both Eddie and the Dame feel decidedly hungry, and they made straight for the restaurant. It was more crowded now, with both Colombians and tourists. They took a corner table, ordered pancakes and coffee and sat watching the other occupants, one wary eye on the door.

A bunch of children were going from table to table with a tape recorder, getting all the foreigners to say something in their own language. 'We are Spanish,' Eddie said apologetically, but they were not spared. 'Real Madrid are the greatest football team in the world,' Eddie told them in their own language.

The children left, and a woman appeared in the doorway, demanding that the man at the next table come with her. He argued for a while, then went, leaving half his breakfast still uneaten. No sooner had he gone than two new children appeared, sat down at his table, each with a fork, and demolished the remaining food, occasionally favouring Eddie and the Dame with conspiratorial smiles.

After they had eaten the two men split up, the Dame heading left back up the hill towards the archaeological park, Eddie turning right and walking towards the centre of town. The locals hardly spared him a glance. Most of them seemed too busy playing pool. He could not believe it: in a town as poor and as small as this one he had already walked past half a dozen pool halls. And they were all bursting with activity at nine in the morning.

He walked the length of the main street, past a couple more hotels and a few shops that were obviously aimed at tourists, past a man lying against a wall, his head covered by a poncho. Eddie presumed the man was sleeping rather than dead. A few yards further on a tethered pig grunted at him – affectionately, he thought.

Eddie walked back through the town and found himself standing in the doorway of one of the pool halls. Why not? he asked himself, and wandered in. He paid for a table and tried a few shots, impressing some of the watching Colombian youths. 'You play me, mister?' one asked in English.

'*Sí, señor*,' Eddie replied. He looked at his watch as the Colombian boy broke. Two and a half hours.

The Dame walked on up a rutted road, with only the occasional bar or home on either side. Chickens wandered in circles, a youth went by on a scooter. He noticed clusters of bananas growing upside down on their palm trees, and wondered why he had always assumed they grew the other way.

The road wound steadily uphill past a large,

empty-looking hotel. A couple of large birds landed on the asphalt some forty metres ahead of them, and showed no sign of moving as they approached and went past. They looked like vultures. Chris would know.

At the archaeological park office he bought a ticket. There were two separate collections of statues to choose from, one on the open hills, the other in the forest. The latter sounded more appropriate for someone trying not be noticed.

After the clear air of the hills the path through the forest seemed darker than it was. The early morning rain was still dripping down through the trees, competing with the incessant birdsong. The statues had been placed at about five-metre intervals, set back from the gravel path.

The first one was a flat stone bas-relief, hardly human yet nothing else, holding what looked like two bread rolls. The second was recognizably non-human, but no less terrifying because of it. Maybe it was a dog, maybe not. The third was of a human figure playing a musical instrument – or maybe swallowing a snake.

A giant flying insect flew low over the Dame's head and disappeared into the forest. He felt a heightened sense of nature's reality, and it seemed to weaken his own, leaving him a half-helpless spectator, almost in thrall to the stone images. The dripping sound went on, like Chinese water torture. A black butterfly with pale-green patches fluttered by. The path wound on between hanging palm fronds twice the length of a man.

Almost all the expressions on the faces of the statues seemed part-made of pain, and they flickered past his eyes like a parade of grotesques, a line of mirrors, nightmares within the nightmare.

The next one was different. For one thing it was off the path, in a small clearing surrounded by white-barked trees and enormous palms. For another it featured two full, almost naturalistic figures. And they seemed to be fucking each other. The Dame stared open-mouthed at it for a second, then suddenly burst out laughing.

Chris sat in one of the rocking chairs on the verandah and watched the sun slowly rise above the distant hills. Two other guests, a Canadian husband and wife, had emerged, introduced themselves as Tom and Amy, taken showers, and disappeared back into their room. Judging from the sounds soon coming through the wall, they seemed to be enjoying each other's company. It made him think of Molly.

In the tree in front of him a bird appeared. It had a long, black, swallow-like tail, a gorgeous emerald-green breast and a long, thin, black beak. As it hovered frenetically, making a soft humming sound, the beak picked at the tree's crimson flowers.

Chris could not remember ever seeing anything more beautiful. He was still sitting more than half entranced when the man walked past him down the verandah to where the owner's wife was on her fifth or sixth breakfast coffee, and started talking to her in a low, insistent voice.

Her replies were equally inaudible, but a single glance towards him told Chris most of what he wanted to know. The only remaining question was what to do about it.

He was still pondering this when their conversation ended and the man walked back towards him. Chris had his hand inside his jacket, resting on the Browning's grip, but the man walked straight past him, looking resolutely ahead. At this moment the owner's wife chose to disappear through the door at the far end of the verandah.

The man was five metres away from the other end. Chris drew the Browning as he got to his feet, took aim with both hands and squeezed the trigger. The man went down with a clatter.

Chris whirled round but no one appeared to investigate the noise. The owner's wife was still out of sight, the lovers still striving towards a muffled climax. Only the hummingbird had sensed the presence of death and flown away.

He reached the body in five strides, grabbed it

by the ankles and dragged it backwards along the verandah and in through the doorway of one of their rooms.

'What the fuck!?' Anderson exclaimed.

'He came for our Poll Tax,' Chris said, closing the door on the outside world and looking through the man's clothes. There was no identification, unless you counted the flick-knife in a pocket and the Walther automatic in the shoulder holster.

Chirlo gazed out into the street from a second-floor window of the San Agustín police headquarters. There seemed to be more gringos than Colombians, and any of the gringo men out there could be one of the ones he was looking for. He had been prepared to look for tidy-looking young men, short-haired and clean-shaven, but Ramón had told him the SAS did not place much importance on external appearance. So any one of these hippie types could have killed Victoria.

And there were so many of them. He could not have them all arrested. No, but all he did have to do was find Anderson. And Anderson would either be with the others or lead him to them.

If he had to put the man's cock through a pencil-sharpener he would lead him to them.

Chirlo looked at his watch. It was only ten minutes since he had sent out the men to check the hotels. The road was blocked. And for all he knew the Englishmen were not even here yet.

He took a sip of the coffee Arevalo's secretary had made for him and lit a cigarette. There was still that empty feeling in the pit of his stomach which had nothing to do with food. And he knew that even killing them all one by one would not begin to fill it.

Wynwood had not had a very successful morning. The woman at the telephone office had been most apologetic but there was a problem with the lines. Both the one running north to Bogotá and the one running west across the mountains were down. It was unheard of that both should be down at once. But . . . Here she had shrugged and smiled prettily and offered the clichéd Spanish response – it would be all right '*mañana*'.

Wynwood doubted it. If the telephone lines were down he did not hold out much hope of the bus station being unwatched. Sure enough, two men he recognized from Totoro were hanging round outside, casting an eye over each European who came to enquire about travel. The Amarales's influence might not stretch to kidnapping them in the middle of San Agustín, but he did not imagine they would think twice about stopping a bus on the open road.

There only seemed one remaining option. He

arrived back at the hotel just before Eddie and just after the Dame. They were all treated to the story of the man now stowed under the bed in the corner.

'Time to leave,' Anderson said, 'before someone comes looking for him.'

'Before he starts to smell,' Eddie added.

'The phones are down and the buses are being watched,' Wynwood told them. 'We'll have to pinch a car. Eddie, you're the expert . . .'

'Thanks, boss,' Eddie said sarcastically. It was true, though – he had stolen more cars in his teens than Tottenham had thrown games away. Which was a lot.

'We'll meet on the road outside town,' Wynwood said as he unfolded the map. 'Here,' he decided, pointing to where the road crossed a stream about a kilometre and a half beyond the outskirts. 'Chris, you and the Dame circle round to the north, me and Andy'll take the south. You take a nice car,' he told Eddie. 'Nothing too flashy.'

'I'll look for a Lada.'

'I said a car.'

'Yes, boss.'

Eddie went back to the pool hall and had one last game. He knew it would take the others up to an hour to reach the rendezvous point, and he wanted to be damn sure he would not have to wait for them in a stolen car out in the open.

With about twenty minutes to go he sauntered into the centre of town, keeping his eyes open for a likely prospect. Nothing appeared. He walked on towards a hotel he had noticed earlier that day which offered escorted trips to the nearby ruins for tourists with money. A group of Americans were just setting out on horseback, two blond men and two brunette women. Eddie casually wandered up the alley which ran down the side of the hotel and looked into the yard at the back. There were three cars: a dark-blue Ford Escort, a black Fiat Uno and a red BMW. There were a couple of upstairs windows overlooking the yard, but only a door on the ground floor. No wonder auto-crime is soaring, Eddie told himself.

The BMW was almost irresistible, but he could imagine Wynwood's face when he drove up in it. And the Escort was a hire car with Bogotá plates. The Americans. They had even left the doors open. He climbed in confidently, took off the handbrake and rolled the car silently out of the yard. No one screamed 'thief' at him. In a blind spot by the side of the hotel he stopped and hot-wired the engine.

His watch said he had four minutes. Good timing, he said to himself. Ticka-ticka.

No one seemed to take any notice as he drove

out of the town and down a long slope towards the bottom of the valley. He stopped on the nearside of the bridge across the stream, and four men appeared out of nowhere and piled into the car.

'You can't move for hitchhikers in this country,' Eddie sighed.

For a few kilometres they motored along, passing only a couple of cars in the opposite direction, feeling it was too good to be true. They were right. About eight kilometres north of San Agustín they crested a rise and saw the roadblock a kilometre ahead in the valley below. Two cars had been parked nose to nose across the road at a place where it was bordered by a wall on one side and a river on the other. At the moment two buses were being inspected, which was fortunate, because it gave Eddie time to halt the car, throw it into reverse and accelerate back up out of sight.

'Did they see us?' Chris asked.

'Don't think so,' Eddie said.

'No way round it?' Anderson asked.

'Nope.'

'Wouldn't help anyway,' Wynwood said. 'Once we're seen they've got nearly 500 kilometres in which to stop us.'

'Plan B, then?' Anderson asked.

'Yep,' Wynwood agreed.

Eddie groaned, and started to turn the car round.

'I hate the fucking *ulu*,' he said, using the SAS name for the jungle.

'Don't expect it's overfond of you,' Chris replied.

# 12

San Agustín and what passed for civilization was disappearing behind them, swallowed by the hills that surrounded it. Their road, already deteriorating, ran uphill towards yet another range of mountains. The last road sign had offered the rather dispiriting information that Florencia was sixty-five kilometres away.

'Where exactly are we going?' Chris asked.

'Like Eddie said,' Wynwood replied, 'the fucking *ulu*.'

'Any particular piece?'

'Give him the map, Andy,' Wynwood said, and waited while Chris found his bearings. 'Once we're over these mountains we're in the Amazon basin and it's all downhill to the Atlantic.'

'About 5000 kilometres' worth,' Eddie said.

Wynwood ignored him. 'If we take the road south from Florencia to Tres Esquinas we'll be on the River Caqueta. From there it's only about two hundred and forty kilometres down river to some place whose name I've forgotten . . .'

'La Tagua,' Chris read off the map. 'And then there's a road to the Peruvian border. About thirty kilometres.'

'Right.'

'Are we going to be any better off in Peru?' the Dame asked.

'No idea. We'll have to talk to Belize. If not, there's always Brazil . . .'

'Which is over 1500 kilometres away.'

'A thousand,' Wynwood corrected him.

'Oh, no problem then,' Eddie said.

Wynwood laughed. 'Where would we be without your cheery optimism?' he asked. 'And I don't want an answer.'

'Yes, boss.'

'Have you always had this natural respect for authority?' Anderson asked Eddie.

'Yeah.'

'What sort of boat do you think we're going to find?' Chris asked. 'Do we have enough money to buy one?'

Anderson grunted. 'Quartermaster's going to love us. We dump all our weapons and then buy a boat.'

'A yacht would be nice,' Eddie observed. 'Maybe we could pick up some luscious cuties en route.'

'The rainforest is full of them. We'll probably

have to make do with gang-banging Sting,' Anderson said.

'Jesus!' the Dame exclaimed.

'I doubt if we'll meet him.'

'Who – Jesus or Sting?'

'You could handle a yacht, could you?' Chris asked Eddie.

'A yacht with a crew, yes. But I shouldn't worry about it – I'm sure the boss here is thinking more of leaky canoes.'

'A mind-reader!'

'Seriously, boss,' Eddie said, 'you're not really thinking of canoeing a thousand kilometres, are you?'

'Got any better ideas?'

'Beam me up, Scottie.'

'Señor Chirlo,' Arevalo said respectfully, despite the fact that Chirlo had his feet on the police chief's desk. 'A car has been reported stolen from one of the hotels . . .'

Pérez came through the door. 'We just found Jorge – dead – in one of the rooms at the Residencias El Cesar. The Englishmen were there this morning – five of them. The owner's wife recognized the description of Anderson.'

'They're gone,' Chirlo said. It wasn't a question. 'Have you checked with your men on the Bogotá road?' he snapped at Arevalo.

'Not yet . . .'

'Do it!'

Thc police chief returned a minute later. 'They have checked every vehicle. And they haven't seen a blue Ford.'

'And there is no way round the block?'

'No, señor.'

'So where are they?' Chirlo asked himself out loud. He got up and walked across to take another look at the map on the wall. If they were not headed for Bogotá, then where? They wouldn't go back into the mountains, surely? And the only other roads led down towards the jungle. There was no way home for them that way. He turned away and stared into space for a moment, the scar livid on his cheek.

'Every policeman in Huila is looking out for them, señor,' Arevalo said.

Chirlo sighed. He would have to be patient.

An idea came to him. 'Spread the word that there's a thousand-dollar reward for the man who spots them,' he said.

'Yes, chief.'

Chirlo turned his eyes back to the streets, the parade of gringo tourists. The reward would come out of his own pocket, which was only right. In the matter of Victoria's killers he would not want anyone else to pay.

* * *

Motoring down the eastern slope of the mountains, telegraph poles flashing past the window, it occurred to Wynwood that the enemy was not the only one who could interfere with communications. They stopped in a deserted lay-by, with more than a kilometre of road visible in each direction, and the Dame shinned up a pole with the wire-cutters.

An hour later they drove into Florencia, a small town close to the feet of the mountains. They had felt both temperature and humidity rising with every one of the last thirty downhill kilometres, and it was now distressingly obvious why most Colombians preferred to live in the mountains. A ten-metre walk in Florencia was enough to stick the shirts to their backs.

They had other, more serious things to worry about. Despite the Dame's work with the wire-cutters, Wynwood had half expected either more roadblocks or an armed deputation of welcome. Neither materialized. In fact the town seemed still becalmed in its afternoon siesta, despite it being nearly five o'clock.

On the journey across the mountains they had compiled a shopping list of what they would need in the jungle, and now they set about trying to fill it. Getting shopkeepers to open up was one problem, finding what they needed in the chaotic shops was another.

They had enough dehydrated food for a week, and collecting and purifying water in the jungle was one of the first things they had learnt during training in Brunei. They were not carrying mosquito nets though, since they had not been expecting to be operating below the altitude at which mosquitoes live. The fair-skinned Eddie was particularly keen that they should make up for this lack of foresight.

After an hour they had filled as much of the list as Wynwood thought they could, and rendezvoused back at the car, which Chris had filled at the petrol station in the centre of town.

He told them the bad news as they drove out along the Montanita road. 'A policeman stood there watching me get her filled,' he said. 'I thought he was going to take a photograph, he was so interested. He asked me where I was headed. I told him San Agustín, tried to act the dumb tourist.'

'That must have been easy,' Eddie observed.

'Would have been easier if I'd had you with me. Anyway, I guess the word hasn't got here yet. But when it does . . . I think Señor Plod will remember me.'

'We'll be on the river by then,' Wynwood said.

'Five men in a boat,' Anderson added.

'The fucking *ulu*,' Eddie said for about the fifth time, though with rather more excuse than the last four. The valley they were now descending was far more thickly vegetated than anything they had seen since the Cauca valley, and the trees were of a different type. Coniferous trees were altogether absent, whereas palms in many shapes and sizes now proliferated among taller deciduous trees of a decidedly unEnglish appearance. They were entering the fringes of the world's greatest rainforest.

'Chirlo wishes to speak with you, *patrón*.'

Ramón put down his magazine and walked slowly across the room to pick up the extension. He had been doing a lot of thinking about Chirlo this last couple of days, wondering whether the family should keep him on. Not because of the discovery that Chirlo had been screwing Victoria – Ramón should have guessed that was happening – but because the chief *sicario* seemed to have been dangerously destabilized by her death.

One thing was certain: if the time did come to dispense with Chirlo's services Ramón wanted a lot of armed help at his shoulder when he handed him the news.

'Yes, Chirlo,' he said into the phone.

'*Patrón*, I have lost the trail of the Englishmen, and I thought you might be able to help.'

Ramón resisted the temptation to tell him to stop wasting his time. 'Of course. But how?'

Chirlo outlined the events of the day, and how the Englishmen had vanished into thin air.

'You say they are not on the road to Bogotá, and they have not doubled back across the mountains towards Popayán?'

'I am certain.'

'Then there is only one possibility . . .'

'Amazonia?'

'Chirlo, we Colombians tend to think that Amazonia has nothing to do with us, even though it is two-thirds of our country. It is just a backwater to us, somewhere where the weather is too hot and humid and a few Indians live . . .'

'This is all true.'

'The SAS are trained in jungle warfare. I forget where – in one of England's old colonies in Asia or Africa. It doesn't matter. The point is they will feel more at home in our jungle than you or I would.'

'I understand,' Chirlo said more thoughtfully. 'But where would they go?'

'Brazil?'

'This is over 1500 kilometres away!'

'So? I tell you, they are taught how to survive in the jungle. And they are not in a hurry. What is to stop them?'

'I am, *patrón*.'

The phone clicked off. It was hardly a respectful goodbye, Ramón thought. Chirlo was either not himself, or his real self was finally breaking through the inhibitions of rank. Either way it did not bode too well for the future.

At the other end of the line Chirlo was busily re-examining the map in the San Agustín police office, Ramón already forgotten. His finger traced possible routes down into Amazonia. There were several, but most of them passed through Florencia.

He spun round on the hapless police chief. 'Get hold of Florencia,' he snapped.

'It is in Caqueta province, chief,' Arevalo said apologetically. 'The lines are the same as for Bogotá. And they will not be mended for an hour or more.'

Chirlo looked at him, trying to repress his growing frustration. Both men knew that the line had been cut just outside the town at Chirlo's instruction, but neither wanted to share the knowledge.

He took a deep breath. It did not matter. If the Englishmen were trying to reach Brazil across Amazonia then time was hardly an issue. He was dealing in weeks, not hours. 'When the lines have been mended,' he told the police chief, 'contact Florencia and ask them to find out if the stolen car has been seen. Anywhere in the province. I will be there in an hour myself.'

'Yes, chief,' the police chief said, managing to

repress his sigh of relief. One day with this man had been enough.

They were still about a hundred kilometres from Tres Equinas on the River Caqueta when darkness fell, and the appalling state of the road made their progress slower than it might have been. A third hazard was the stream of heavy lorries travelling in the opposite direction, carrying timber at a pace which suggested the drivers' confidence in their ability to flatten anything they hit. Flashing their lights at them, far from inducing caution, seemed akin to waving a red rag at a bull. The only safe course was to turn out the lights and, if possible, pull off the road. The frequent need to take such evasive action considerably slowed the Ford's rate of progress.

It was 8.30 before they reached Tres Equinas, which seemed to consist of several tumbledown shacks, the sawmill source of the lorries and a hotel which would only have deserved the adjective 'cheap' if the proprietor had paid the guests. This last, which overlooked the river, was also the only source of boats in the village, and Wynwood suspected the worst as the proprietor, none too pleased at being dragged away from doing nothing on his verandah, led them down to the landing stage complaining about the lateness of the hour.

For once Wynwood's pessimism was unjustified. The boats, all identical, looked both river-worthy and considerably better looked after than the hotel or its proprietor. Though shaped like large canoes, they had greater stability in the water and were made of sterner stuff, clinker-built from overlapping planks. There were places for two paddlers, one in the bow and one in the stern, with ample space for two non-paddling passengers and baggage in between them.

The haggling began. At first the proprietor had assumed that they were eccentrics come to rent boats in the middle of the night. The news that they wanted to buy two of them seemed to throw him off his stride, and much bluster was brought forth to cover his confusion.

Wynwood's first reaction was to regret not having simply asked to rent them; his second was to consider just taking them at gunpoint. Still, this would probably have been unwise even if he could have squared it with his conscience – he had no idea what police posts there might be downriver, and he did not want to start a jungle-wide watch for gringo boat-stealers.

A price for two boats was eventually agreed, one which should probably have bought them the hotel as well. They had the choice of which two, and as the patrol's boat specialist, Chris did the choosing.

The owner then offered to show them to their rooms, and was surprised to discover that they intended to set out immediately. Consoling himself with the large wad of pesos in the back pocket of his trousers, he went back to the verandah, muttering '*loco*' to himself at regular intervals.

With this litany vaguely audible in the background the five SAS men loaded their gear aboard the boats. Andy, Chris and the Dame would take one craft, Wynwood and Eddie the other. Since none of them had had more than four hours' sleep in the previous thirty-six, the plan was to get a few kilometres downstream and set up camp for the night.

They eased the two boats out onto the dark river, discovering a strong slow current in the centre of the stream. The river was about a hundred metres across at this point, but widened to almost twice that width before they had gone two kilometres. The jungle came down to the banks on both sides, giving the impression that they were travelling down a chute between two walls, a stationary ceiling of stars above them.

Every now and then what looked like a lighted window would appear in the dark walls to either side, before suddenly shooting off and revealing itself as some sort of luminous insect. The waters were silent save for the swish against their paddles, and the occasional melancholy cry of a bird in the distance seemed to echo all around them all.

After only ten minutes or so the darkness relented and a quarter-moon rose above the trees, turning the deep shades of grey into an altogether more enchanting world of silver and black. To Eddie, sitting in the bow of the lead boat, the scene before him seemed more than a touch unreal after the space and light of the mountains and the mad bustle of their journey from San Agustín. He felt like he had been caught in a time warp and transported back to a world still untouched by men. Real or not, it thrilled him to the marrow.

'There's a sandbank about two hundred metres ahead,' Andy said quietly from the boat behind them. As the only non-paddler he had been entrusted with the nightscope.

'We'll see if it has any rooms,' Wynwood said, and steered towards it.

Closer to, the sandbank resembled a swathe of silver dust someone had thrown in the river. It had no rooms, but the remains of a fire showed it had been used before for camping. They pulled the boats out of the water and each man scraped a trench in the sand for sleeping in.

'A fire?' Anderson suggested.

'What do you think?' Wynwood asked.

'I can't see them sending up planes at night to

look for us. How would they know it was us anyway? Only if old Trusthouse Forte back at the hotel tells them, and if they talk to him they'll know roughly where we are anyway.'

'There you go, then,' Wynwood agreed. 'I'm going to talk to Belize.'

'Ask them for the football results,' Eddie said.

'This is probably the time to tell you about the candiru,' Chris told Eddie.

'Uh-huh. And what's a candiru?'

'It's a tiny fish, which homes in on piss.'

'You're making it up.'

'Nope. And it actually swims up your anus and sticks itself there with barbs so it has to be cut out.'

'Jesus!'

'Why don't you take the boat across and get us some more wood,' Anderson suggested. 'And if you fall in the water try and stay as tight-arsed as possible.'

'OK, OK,' Wynwood said, midway through setting up the PRC 319, 'give me some quiet to think in.' The trouble was, he felt too tired to think straight anyway.

On the other hand, there was not really much need for thought. He told Belize where they were and what their options looked like. Then he requested as much information as possible on what was waiting for the five of them downstream: the navigability of the river, the weather, the numbers and friendliness of the human population, the warmth of their likely reception at the Peruvian or Brazilian border.

Apart from a simple question on the state of their health, the duty officer in Belize restricted himself to acknowledging Wynwood's requests. The latter signed off with a promise to repeat the contact tomorrow at 0800 hours.

By this time Anderson had got a decent fire going with driftwood the Dame had collected on the sandbank, and was in the process of preparing a warm meal from tins they had bought in Florencia. The boat was on its way back with more wood. It was like being a boy scout again, Wynwood thought. He resisted the temptation to start singing 'ging-gang-gooly-gooly'.

They ate their meal, watching the smoke from their fire drift across the stars, and then four of them went to sleep, leaving the apparently inexhaustible Eddie with the first watch.

Just before he slipped into sleep, Wynwood's thoughts were optimistic. He knew they were still in Colombia as the atlases drew it, but he could not help thinking they had escaped from the Colombia of the drug barons. Now it was just them and the *ulu*, and he had won that battle before.

* * *

A hundred and sixty kilometres to the north Chirlo took a swig from the can of Pepsi and watched the light plane aim itself between the parallel lines of fires which marked the jungle airstrip. Almost before it had touched down in the bumpy meadow men were extinguishing the fires in the oil drums by the simple expedient of replacing the lids. It was all probably unnecessary, Chirlo thought, but who knew when the satellites up there were taking pictures?

He waited while the plane turned a tight circle and started taxiing back up towards the group of men who were waiting to unload its cargo of coca paste.

The pilot climbed out. As Chirlo had expected, it was the Frenchman Paul Vadim, one of the few men who had worked for the Amarales longer than he had.

'Vadim,' he called out.

'Who wants me?'

Chirlo walked out of the shadows towards him.

'Chirlo,' Vadim said, surprised and somewhat wary. 'You're a long way from home. Is something wrong?' His hand had moved instinctively into his jacket pocket.

'I need you and your plane,' Chirlo said, wondering if Vadim was stupid enough to think he could outdraw and outshoot him. 'I will explain it to you over a beer.'

He and the Frenchman walked along the path past the lab, the filtering plant and the drying structure to the room adjoining the kitchen which had been fitted up to function as a bar.

The fridge yielded two cans of beer, and Chirlo went through the events of the past few days.

'I've never been able to make up my mind which I loathe most – the English, the Americans or the Germans,' was Vadim's only comment.

'They bought two boats at Tres Equinas,' Chirlo concluded, 'and they're somewhere on the Caqueta. I want you to find them, preferably without them realizing you've done so.'

The Frenchman shrugged. 'That won't be easy. The only way you can see what's on those rivers is by flying directly above them.'

'Can't you fly a zigzag route,' Chirlo suggested.

'That would make it less obvious,' Vadim agreed. He had previously thought of Chirlo as just a highly efficient thug. Perhaps he had underestimated him.

It was five in the morning in Hereford when Kilcline woke the CO with the news from Belize.

'Where are they exactly?' Barney Davies asked sleepily, stretching the telephone cord towards the shelves where he kept his atlases. Even as a boy he had always loved maps, and there were now almost fifty atlases of various vintages in his collection.

He pulled out the most modern and rifled his way through the pages to Colombia. Why was South America always at the back of atlases, he wondered. Was it that the British had traditionally had less interest in it than other continents?

Kilcline gave him the details again. 'Christ, it looks a long way from anywhere,' he murmured, mostly to himself.

'It is,' Kilcline agreed. 'I've set the wheels turning on the information front,' he said, 'but I thought you'd want to deal with the political stuff yourself.'

'Yes, I'll handle it,' Davies agreed.

'They're transmitting again at 1300 our time.'

'OK. I'll get back to you by 1100.' He hung up, spent a few moments staring at the atlas page, shook his head and went to make himself some coffee. The prospect of more contact with the Foreign Office hardly filled him with the joys of spring. In fact he felt a considerable reluctance to divulge the men's whereabouts to anyone outside the Regiment. But he supposed they had to end up in another country at some point, and it would be better to be greeted by a friendly face than a deportation order sending them back to Colombia.

Eddie sat on the far end of the sandbank from his sleeping comrades listening to the soundtrack of the jungle. It had no recognizable rhythm, unless that in itself was a rhythm; the backing track supplied by cicadas and frogs had the seamlessness of disco, but it didn't exactly set the toes tapping. As for the vocalists, they were a strange bunch, not much given to essaying more than a single croak, howl, hiss or cry. The word 'unearthly' flashed through Eddie's mind, and made him laugh. If the natural earth sounded unearthly they were in deep trouble.

It was just an impersonal sound, he decided. Not threatening, not friendly, just there. Rather like being in London, where these days you couldn't even escape from the hum of traffic in the middle of Hampstead Heath. Just the noise of the world.

Where was there still silence? he wondered. In the Arctic maybe, provided two polar bears were not busy at it on a neighbouring ice floe. He wondered what Lisa was doing. Sleeping, he supposed, since it was about five in the morning in England. Sleeping alone, he hoped. He wondered what she would think if she could see him now. Would she be impressed?

In his mind's eye he could see her upturned face in the back of his dad's car, half amused, half nervous. It had been great, but she had been worried that it would not be, that somehow she would not live up to his expectations, or even her own.

The fear of failure seemed to be everywhere, he thought. In sex and love and school and work. Maybe you had to grow up knowing there was no real escape to realize that it was the trying that mattered – stretching yourself, learning new things, going for broke every day of your life.

One day you would lose your bet, but that would not be failure. As long as you were trying you couldn't fail.

# 13

In the hour after dawn the jungle's backing track seemed to fade, offering each soloist their best chance of the day to be heard. A mixture of cries rent the air – high-spirited, mournful, jaunty, melancholic.

'The heat, the flies, the endless drums,' Anderson murmured, gazing at the dark-green wall of vegetation across the dark green water.

'Sounds like the Brixton Academy,' Eddie said.

Anderson eyed him affectionately. He had grown rather fond of Eddie over the last couple of days, though he could not for the life of him think why. The two of them were reloading their gear into the boats, while the Dame filtered river water through the canvas bag they had looked for and bought in Florencia. It was not as efficient as the Millbank bag they normally used but it would have to do. Once filtered, the water would be sterilized with tablets.

Chris was busy removing as many traces as

he could of their night on the sandbank. It was probably a one in a hundred chance that anyone would notice, but it was that chance which the ingraining of good habits was supposed to remove. The SAS did not leave tracks when they could avoid doing so.

Twenty metres away Wynwood was 'talking' to Belize on the PRC 319. Finishing, he collapsed the antennae and walked back across the sandbank to the boats. 'Which would you like first,' he asked them, 'the good news or the bad news?'

'Do we have to have both?' Eddie asked.

'What's the bad news?' Anderson demanded.

'There's a stretch of rapids eighty kilometres downstream, about five kilometres of them, which we'll have to carry the boats past. Tomorrow I guess. There's a portage trail, so the going shouldn't be too difficult.'

'No native bearers?' Eddie wanted to know.

'Only you and the Dame.'

'Ha ha. So what's the good news?'

'It looks like the Peruvian authorities will turn a blind eye to our appearance in their fair country, provided we can get into it without being stopped.'

'That's good news?' Eddie said. 'I was expecting wine and women at the very least.'

'Even a Little Chef with a plump waitress round the next bend would have been something,' Anderson agreed.

'Mmmm,' Chris said, 'I love their cherry pancakes.'

'Have you clowns quite finished?' Wynwood asked politely.

'Yes, boss.'

'Are there any Indians around here?' the Dame asked.

'A few. From the Witoto tribe. But they've been civilized, whatever that means.'

'Bought or killed,' Eddie said dryly.

Wynwood looked at him. Every time he had made up his mind that there really was only cynicism in Eddie's heart, something else would slip out through the protective camouflage. 'Yeah,' he agreed. 'Come on, let's get started.'

They slid the boats off the sand and into the river, and for the next few hours, as the sun climbed into place above them, made steady progress. The river meandered this way and that, but slowly, in giant curves rather than sharp bends, and the wall of forest on either side seemed practically unchanging, as if, like a wallpaper border, it was drawn to a recurring pattern.

If the flora showed little obvious variety, the same could not be said for the fauna. Monkeys chattered and howled in the trees, the occasional alligator snoozed in the shallows, and large fish broke the surface and disappeared again with a splash. Huge blue butterflies floated past like dreams.

And then there were the birds. Chris could hardly believe the variety to be found in any direction he chose to look. There were several species of wading birds, but the ones which drew his attention were the jaburus – white storks almost as tall as men, with red throats and black legs, heads and beaks. They paced up and down the sandbanks with heads slightly bowed, looking for all the world as if they were pondering some deep philosophical problem.

Woodpeckers could be heard and often seen, herons stood watchfully on the banks, hawks circled above the river, kingfishers glided across the water, and bright-coloured macaws flew by, seemingly always in groups of three. The only blots on this tableau of grace and beauty were the flocks of hoatzins, fowls that looked like distant relations of the pterodactyl, and delighted in hissing at the party from the safety of the bank.

The richness of the bird-life contrasted with the almost total lack of any human imprint. The occasional ruin of a landing stage bore testimony to past activity, but no villages came into view, no other boats, no other people. Only a single plane, which flew high across the river behind them, offered visual proof that there were still other humans on the planet.

Wynwood was still wondering about it an hour later. It could have been in this area for any number of reasons, though the most probable was undoubtedly drug-running. And if it had been looking for them it had done a good job of looking like it wasn't. Wynwood mentally shrugged: there was nothing they could do about it if it was, other than keep themselves in a state of constant vigilance.

'Reminds me of my school staff room,' Eddie said in front of him.

Wynwood followed his gaze to where a flock of hoatzins was watching them from the lower branches of a tree. He laughed, and looked back up at the sky. 'Looks like rain,' he said.

He was right. The clouds above grew steadily darker, and finally disgorged themselves just as the five men were pulling the boats up onto the mid-river sandbank Wynwood had chosen for rest and food. Thoughts of seeking shelter lasted about twenty seconds – by which time they were soaked to the skin. They set out receptacles to collect water and sat in the downpour consuming cold the last tins from Florencia.

'I found them,' Vadim said.

'Show me,' Chirlo said, reaching for the map.

'Here,' Vadim said, pointing. 'They were there at quarter past eleven, so . . . well, you can work it out.' He drew on his cigarette. 'Where do you intend to stop them?'

It was Chirlo's turn to point a finger. 'Tomorrow morning, I should think.'

'Couldn't they be there tonight?'

Chirlo shrugged. 'I doubt it, but we will be there just in case.'

'How many of you?'

'Eight men.' Chirlo smiled. 'And an M60 machine-gun.'

The shower had proved as short as it was heavy, and by mid-afternoon the sun had dried them and their clothes as they moved downstream. But towards dusk the sky again darkened and they decided to make a dry camp on the shore rather than risk a cold, wet night on the sandbank.

With the boats secured all five men set to work constructing a waterproof 'basha', using jungle wood – mostly bamboo – to provide the frame, interwoven atap leaves to keep out the water, and various vines and creepers to hold the whole thing together. It was something they had all done before in Brunei, and in not much more than an hour a passable shelter some three metres long and just over two wide had been constructed.

While the Dame prepared some warm food, the others took time to thoroughly clean and dry their Brownings and MP5s. In the jungle, humidity alone could render weapons inoperable, let alone the drenching of a tropical rainstorm.

'Where are we, boss?' Eddie asked.

'About two hours from the rapids by my reckoning,' Wynwood replied. 'So we should get there by 0900 at the latest. Allow three hours for the portage, an hour's rest . . . we should be close to La Tagua by dusk.'

'And then it's what? Sixty-odd kilometres by road to the border?'

'Something like that.'

'Piece of cake,' Eddie said. He looked out through the open wall of the shelter, where the rain was beginning to come down in almost grotesquely large droplets. 'The thought of curried snake for the next thousand kilometres was beginning to get me down.'

'The one I had in Brunei wasn't bad,' Chris said.

They all joined in the discussion, working their way through a long list of things they had never dreamed of eating in pre-SAS days, but which they had eventually found themselves consuming. There was unanimous agreement on the slug's lack of culinary quality.

'McDonald's should try them,' Eddie suggested. 'McSluggets.'

'Just for that you're on first watch,' Wynwood told him.

* * *

It rained most of the night, which surprised Wynwood, whose previous experience of rain in tropical areas suggested one heavy shower in the middle of each day. Maybe it had something to do with their proximity to the mountains.

The rain eventually stopped an hour or so before dawn, and for the last hour of his watch Wynwood listened to the maddeningly irregular drip of water coming down through the foliage overhead. A mist rose from the river, which the first light of day turned into an opaque fog. Another ten minutes and the sun began clearing it away, breaking the mist into patches like some wonder detergent clearing pollution from the sea.

As the jungle birds awoke to the sunlight Wynwood woke the others. Within half an hour they had dismantled the basha, done their ablutions, breakfasted and loaded the boats.

They set off in the same order as before, Eddie and Wynwood in the lead boat, the Dame, Chris and Andy in the second. The jungle seemed subdued by the night's rain, and the first hour was spent in an almost supernatural silence. When the men spoke to each other it seemed louder than it should, and the occasional cry of a nearby bird was almost enough to make them jump.

It was out of the general silence that a low murmur became increasingly audible. 'The rapids,' Wynwood said thankfully.

'We must be on the right river, then,' Eddie said.

Six kilometres downstream, just ahead of where a small, heavily forested island bisected the channel, a landing stage had been built to assist in the unloading of boats for portage past the rapids. Since at this time of the year the river was still running low, anyone landing would have to make use of the rusted iron steps which led down to the surface of the water two metres below.

Behind the landing stage several decrepit houses – huts to anyone but an estate agent – were roughly lined up on either side of a dirt road which led off into the jungle south of the river. Inside these huts were now gathered all but two of the twenty or so Indians whose homes they were. Since there were no locks on the doors, only threats and the patrolling presence of five of Chirlo's eight *sicarios* physically kept them there. What would happen when the time came, and the *sicarios* were needed elsewhere, might be problematic, but Chirlo hoped the presence of their headman and his woman on the landing stage, covered by several guns, would give the villagers reason to stay put. These two hostages also had another part to play in the drama Chirlo was hoping to direct, that of a smiling welcome committee for the Englishmen.

The M60 was mounted immediately behind the

landing stage, with a line of fire right across the river, just in case the Englishmen were foolish or ignorant enough to attempt the rapids in the boats they had bought. They would certainly die if they tried, but out of Chirlo's sight, which was not the preferred solution.

For the moment the machine-gun was not visible from the river. Four walls of rusty corrugated iron had been rescued from the top end of the village, and recycled into what looked like a simple storage hut. At the pull of a string all four walls would collapse outwards, leaving the gun with a full field of fire.

Chirlo was proud of this idea, but hoped it would not need to be used. With any luck he would be able to get the drop on all five men as they came ashore. Killing them with a machine-gun was, after all, not a great improvement on having the river do it for him. And he wanted to know which of them had killed her.

His men had all been given the positions which they were to occupy the moment the signal was given by the man across the river. He and Fernández were already ensconced inside the door of the first house on the right, which had been built close to the river. The hidden machine-gun, manned by Pérez and Cayano, was ten metres away across the road. Out on the landing stage, as the third point of an equilateral triangle, the two Indians sat in apparent silence.

Had he made any mistakes, Chirlo wondered. The helicopter he had used for ferrying in his men had never been closer than three kilometres to the river, so there was no way they could have heard it. They had no real choice but to leave their boats at this point. They did not have any heavy weapons. He had the superior position.

Looking across the river, he wondered whether he should have put more men on the far bank. At that moment his watchman waved the red T-shirt he was using as a signal. The Englishmen were in sight.

'Get everyone in position,' he told Fernández, 'and remind them – if they fuck up they'll wish they hadn't.'

Coming round the wide bend in the river the first thing Eddie saw, about half a kilometre ahead, was an island in midstream. Then the outer edge of the landing stage emerged from the curve of the right bank.

'People,' he announced succinctly.

'They look friendly enough,' Wynwood said, examining the two Indians through the telescopic sight. One man and one woman, neither of them young. He gave a hand signal to Chris to lengthen the gap between the two boats. He could see nothing suspicious but it was better to be safe than sorry.

They were about two hundred metres from the landing stage when something began to nag at the edge of Wynwood's mind. He took a look back at Anderson, to see if his old partner's fabled sixth sense was picking up any of the wrong vibes, but received only a smile in reply.

'The natives are waiting for their beads,' Eddie said facetiously.

The two Indians had stood up and seemed to be grinning inanely in their direction. Wynwood examined their faces through the scope. There really was something odd about them. They looked, well . . . stoned.

He examined the area behind them, the houses, the corrugated hut. Where was everyone else, he wondered. Where were the dogs? This was the moment in the movie, he thought, when someone says: 'It's too quiet.'

Well, it was. He didn't know why but he didn't like it.

One of the Indians said something indecipherable and beckoned them forward.

That was the last straw. Wynwood hand-signalled Chris to take the other boat away to the left, towards the far bank. 'We'll go in alone,' he told Eddie in a soft voice. 'I'll do the paddling. You keep your eyes open.'

Eddie placed his paddle down and took a firm grip on the MP5 which had been hanging across his stomach.

Wynwood suddenly realized that on one of the visible walls of the corrugated hut the streaks of rust ran up rather than down. With sudden ferocity he propelled the boat forward towards the landing stage.

His scream of 'Take cover' echoed across the river.

Chirlo had watched the separation of the two boats with horror. Why hadn't he foreseen such a simple manoeuvre? And what should he do now? If the two in the first boat landed they would have to be taken, leaving the other three dangerously at liberty . . . unless they could all be taken out by the M60 . . . but they were moving to the other side of the river and he was not that confident in his men's accuracy at such range . . . so perhaps he should open fire immediately on the far boat . . . or else . . .

These thoughts uselessly jostled each other in Chirlo's brain. Accustomed to the split-second decision-making of the slum barrio streets, he lost himself in the luxury of whole seconds in which to make up his mind.

Pérez, in charge of the machine-gun, waited for the order that did not come. In a few seconds the first boat would be shielded by the landing stage, but from where he was the chief could not know that. Logic and fear came together – he gave the word to drop the shields at almost the same moment Wynwood's cry split the silence.

They dropped with a clatter just as Wynwood shot the boat forward towards the cover of the steep bank and landing stage. Pérez sent one stitch of bullets straight through the space where Wynwood's head had been a split second before, then pulled back on the gun and set his sight on the second boat across the river.

In the second boat Chris and Andy responded to Wynwood's cry, but their surge forward was cut off almost as soon as it began. A fusillade of machine-gun fire exploded around them, causing the Dame to curse and the boat to suddenly slow. Chris turned to find the Dame holding a bloody arm and Anderson slumped forward, half his head blown away.

Wynwood's sudden surge forward caught Eddie off balance, and he had only just managed to regain it when the front of the boat rammed into the pilings beneath the landing stage. He reached out an arm and grabbed, somehow keeping hold while the stretch tried to pull his arm out of its socket. The crash had spun the boat's stern to the left, almost catapulting Wynwood into the bank. He managed to keep the MP5 out of the water and gain a hold on the bare red earth of the steep slope.

He could see only sky above the rim of the bank, but a quick look back across the river told its own story. The other boat was running for the cover of the island, but already the man in the back – Andy – had his head slumped forward over his chest, and there was another two hundred metres to go.

The machine-gun fire had stopped, but it could open up again at any moment. There was no choice. Wynwood turned back to Eddie, who was lying forward on the slope on the other side of the landing stage, and gave him the hand signal to advance. Eddie gave him a reproachful glance, then grinned, and started wriggling upwards.

Wynwood did the same. Somewhere up above, two men were conducting a half-whispered argument in Spanish. The gun must have jammed, Wynwood thought. He thanked his lucky stars for the previous night's rain.

He now had his head just short of the top of the bank, and searched with his foot for some point of leverage in the slope. Finding one, he shared glances with Eddie, and they launched themselves up across the lip of the bank just as the M60 opened fire once more. Both landed still rolling, their eyes searching for targets.

Wynwood was only eight metres from the machine-gunners, who were still trying to jerk the gun round towards him when he cut both of them in half with the MP5. Hearing a noise behind and to his left, he twisted round. A feeling like fire running up his arm was followed by the crack of an automatic, and as he opened up with the MP5 a head disappeared round the corner of the building.

Eddie's roll had almost rammed him into the side of the building nearest to the water. In the second he took to decide which way to go, a *sicario* incautiously put more than one eye round the corner and acquired a third in the middle of his forehead. Eddie got to his feet, exchanging the Browning for the MP5, and worked his way round the back of the building. He emerged from the last corner in the same roll, ending up this time in a half-kneeling position with two Colombians not ten metres away.

Having turned everything to disaster with his military inexperience, Chirlo now found himself, for the last time in his life, in his element. As the blond Englishman whirled into view, his revolver raised in both hands, Chirlo simply stepped behind Fernández. It had worked on the streets of Bogotá and it worked now. Fernández absorbed the bullets, his arms flying upwards with the impact, leaving Chirlo space through the armpit to send two bullets into the body of the Englishman. He turned, almost in triumph, to find another Englishman's finger tightening on the trigger.

Chirlo's last thought was of the strangeness of it all: to grow up in one kind of jungle, and to die in another.

Wynwood sank to one knee, his eyes sweeping the scene. In the distance two men were running off down the road; on the landing stage the two Indians were looking at him, almost with curiosity. They had been bait, Wynwood realized, and they were still not sure if they were going to be eaten.

He walked over to where Eddie was lying. One bullet had passed through the heart, another centimetres away. The half-insolent smile seemed younger than before. Wynwood closed Eddie's eyes, and turned to the Indians. 'How many of them were there?' he asked in Spanish.

'Eight,' the Indian man replied. 'Bad men,' he added as an afterthought.

There were two dead by the machine-gun, two more in front of him. Two had run off, and there was the one he had forced back under cover. And there was another slumped behind the corner of the building where Eddie had come up the bank.

'They are all gone,' the Indian said, as if he knew Wynwood needed confirmation of the fact.

Wynwood nodded, and signalled across to Chris

to bring the other boat in. As he watched it cross the river his mind played with the hope that Andy was still alive, but his heart was already well into mourning. Behind him the villagers were slowly emerging from their houses. The jungle, shocked into silence by the guns of man, was once more finding its voice.

They buried Eddie and Andy that afternoon, in home-made coffins on the island in midstream, hoping that at some time in the future someone from the British Embassy could arrange for their collection and transport back to England.

The Dame's arm was a mess, but a repairable one, provided they got him out of the jungle before infection had a chance to set in. Wynwood's wound was more superficial, but hurt like blazes just the same.

Leaving, much to the Indians' delight, another large chunk of their gear behind, Wynwood and Chris shouldered one of the boats and what gear they could carry to the foot of the rapids, and by noon next day they were on the road to the Peruvian border. There they found the rough hut on the Colombian side empty of officialdom, that on the Peruvian side full of smiling locals and an irritated man from the British Embassy.

It was over. One Colombian politician had been saved; two SAS men had failed to beat the clock.

# Epilogue

Kilcline and Bourne were sharing a lunchtime drink in the Slug and Pellet. The idea was to celebrate Bourne's return, but somehow celebration seemed inappropriate.

'Have you seen Beth,' Bourne asked.

'Briefly. She . . . well, you can imagine.'

Bourne could. He could remember the times his own wife had given vent to her fears of becoming a soldier's widow. Well, Britain would have to be invaded for him to ever see any more real action. He and Lynn were safe. Or as safe as you could ever be in the kind of world they seemed to be making.

He shook his head, as if to shake away the mood. 'It was an amazing achievement,' he said, almost to himself.

'And by the time anyone gets round to acknowledging it, the lads who did it will all be dead,' Kilcline said matter-of-factly.

'We know what they did,' Bourne said. 'And they know, which is what really counts.'

Kilcline managed a smile. 'Your round,' he said.

In the Andes another morning had broken, and Ramón Amarales was enjoying the early sunlight with his usual silver jug of coffee on Totoro's verandah. That morning Miguel was coming out for a meeting to decide who should take the dead Chirlo's position as chief *sicario*. It should not be difficult: there was no shortage of tough and intelligent candidates.

Ramón had a nice surprise for his brother – according to the statement that had arrived the previous day, the balance in their Swiss bank account had just passed twenty million dollars. The Amarales had to be among the richest ten families in Colombia.

And it was down to him – Ramón. Victoria might have been the intelligent one, Miguel the handsome one, but without him the business would never have become as successful as it had.

His great mistake, Ramón decided, had always been to underestimate his own achievements. And his prospects too, for that matter. Victoria was dead, Miguel married to a noisy leech. He had taken their father's ranch and turned it into twenty million dollars. And unless the youths of America and Europe suddenly lost their appetite for artificial stimulation he would double that money in the next five years.

If that was not success, what was?

Chris walked slowly along the Blackwater estuary, thinking it was not much more than a month since he had walked the same path on the way home to find the order to report in. And the next day he had met Eddie at Paddington, and it had all begun.

He remembered the condors in the mountains above Totoro and the hummingbird in the tree in San Agustín and the flashing kingfishers on the river. He remembered the man at the briefing saying Colombia was probably the most beautiful country in the world. Well, he had not seen its equal.

But then there many more countries to see. He stood looking out over the waters shining silver in the sun, not thinking about Eddie or Anderson or the man he himself had killed in San Agustín – that was all done, all gone, yesterday's world – but about the deep underlying silence of the jungle river in the hour after dawn, the lone screeches of birds he had never heard before.

He was seeing Molly again that evening for the first time since Christmas Eve. She had sounded enthusiastic over the phone, but he had the feeling he was going through the motions, that really he did not want anyone sharing his thoughts and feelings.

Maybe she felt the same. Maybe they could just have fun for a few hours.

'Have you seen today's polls?' Estrada asked Quintana as he came through the door.

'Yes, Rafael,' Quintana said, though he had not. And he did not need to now. If Estrada was in a good mood then they had to be favourable.

'I am going to win,' Estrada said, almost smugly.

'It looks like it,' Quintana agreed.

'And you must take a lot of the credit,' Estrada insisted. 'It was your idea to invite the English in. If Muñoz had simply been ransomed he might have ended up a hero.' He looked straight at Quintana, sincerity written on his face. 'I won't forget it, Luis,' he added.

Estrada had probably been watching some Hollywood tear-jerker, Quintana guessed. He found the thought that his advice had probably secured the man's re-election was almost more than he could bear.

In a Hereford pub Bonnie and Blackie were still trying to decide which women would be favoured with their attentions that evening. There was quite a wide choice on offer, ranging from the teenage gigglers in the corner to the two women in their mid-thirties standing at the bar.

'Bet you they're teachers,' Bonnie said.

'Social workers,' Blackie thought.

'They're over thirty anyway,' Bonnie said. 'So they're probably desperate.'

'I don't know whether they're that desperate,' Blackie said, looking at him. 'Where did you get that jacket – Oxfam?'

'C&A. What's wrong with it?'

'Nothing a good bonfire wouldn't put right. But the wrinklies'll probably like it. Shall we go for them?'

'Why not? There's no substitute for experience.'

Blackie grinned. 'If they think that, you're in trouble.'

'Huh. We've just jumped out of a fucking plane higher than fucking Everest and hang-glided onto a fucking mountain and attacked a drug baron's ranch and got away again. That's experience, isn't it?

'It may not be exactly what they're looking for.'

Bonnie grinned. 'Know what you mean. This is a time for LALO.'

'For what!?'

'Low altitude, low opening, if you get my drift.'

'I do, but I wish I didn't.'

* * *

The Dame stood at the heart of the swaying crowd behind the goal at Roker Park. It was half-time, Sunderland were losing, but years of disappointment still could not quench the hope.

The other half-time scores started coming through on the loudspeaker. Tottenham were losing as well, 2–0 at Everton. The Dame knew he would never hear Tottenham mentioned now without thinking about Eddie.

He had been thinking a lot about him anyway in the last few weeks. The trouble was, in one way he had felt very close to him. Hackney was a long way from Sunderland, but they were closer to each other than they were to most places in England. They had a – 'strength' was the only word that fitted – a strength about them that came from knowing hardship, and knowing it as a real community. And from out of this came the strange mixture of pride and bitterness which he knew in himself and which he had recognized in Eddie.

Of course Eddie had been flash, London flash, and where the Dame used silence and reserve to protect himself, Eddie had used jokes and cynicism. But this was just style. What worried the Dame were the differences between him and Eddie. Try to talk to him about England or the Army or politics or religion – anything other than football and women – and he would just say it was all bullshit. Eddie had seemed content to live for nothing but the SAS, and not because of any pride in the Regiment or because he agreed with the jobs it was asked to do. No, he had loved the SAS because, as he had once said, it kept surprising him. It had kept him ticking over, till the clock beat him.

And if one small part of the Dame would have liked to be like that, a brilliant skater on the surface of life, the rest of him knew he never could be. He needed reasons for the things he did, and some judgement at the end of the line. And after what had happened to Eddie, somehow he needed these things more than ever.

Barney Davies sat in his darkened living-room, glass of brandy in his hand, watching the ten o'clock news. The Prime Minister was wrapping herself in the flag again at the dispatch box – something to do with Iraq – he wasn't really paying attention to the details. But the patriotic tone was unmistakable.

Nine times out of ten he would have gone along with it, even shared the feelings, if not the belligerency of their expression. But tonight it brought a bad taste to his mouth. He remembered Denis Healey's 'glorying in slaughter', a remark he had thought ill-judged in the extreme at the time, but which now seemed almost fair.

He took another sip of brandy and used the remote control to turn off the TV. What was he complaining about? He had read enough history to know that soldiers had been let down by politicians since time began, so why should he be so upset by one more example of an age-old vice. 'Because,' he murmured out loud to himself, 'this time it was me who had to listen to the utter indifference in the politician's voice.' Not even crocodile tears. Not even a wreath.

Barney swallowed the rest of the brandy in one gulp. Sometimes he wondered why the world was run by people with no sense of honour or obligation.

In the neon-lit room in backstreet Bogotá, the girl in the red dress carefully counted out her earnings from the evening. It was enough, she decided. She collected her English primer from the table and sat with it cross-legged on the floor, rubbing her eyes to keep them open.

Joss Wynwood walked slowly along the dark beach, listening to the waves crashing in from the Irish Sea away to his right. It was a clear night and the lights of Portmadoc were visible in the distance, nestling beneath the dark mass of the mountains beyond.

On his return from South America Wynwood

had not gone home to the house he and Susan shared. He wanted to keep it as a place they had been happy in, and so he checked into a small hotel in Hereford and arranged a meeting with her in a restaurant in the town. Both of them had expected a difficult conversation about what was wrong with their marriage and who was to blame, but it was immediately apparent both had been mistaken. There was no point. It was simply over, and both had known it for a long time. So instead they had a strangely affectionate conversation about the mechanics of the split, and parted feeling better disposed to each other than for many years.

Wynwood had decided to take his leave back in Wales, but not with his family. He needed to be alone, and he had always loved the stretch of coastline between Barmouth and Pwllheli, which brought back memories of childhood holidays, of narrow-gauge steam trains and walks in the mountains. This evening he had found a nice pub in Criccieth, enjoyed a game of darts and a few pints, and was now walking back to his Portmadoc hotel along the coast.

Andy had been much on his mind, but he supposed that was natural. They had been like partners for a long time, and the training stint in Colombia had solidified the bond still further. He wondered what Andy would say if he knew that Wynwood was considering quitting the Army.

Why, probably.

I don't really know, Wynwood silently answered his dead friend.

*Decisive as ever, I see.* He could hear Andy say it, felt the tears rising in his eyes.

He fought them back. It was only the booze making him maudlin, he decided.

*Just like the bloody Welsh*!

So bloody what. He tried to organize his thoughts for the imaginary debate.

*Is it because you were boss and Eddie and I didn't beat the clock*?

No. 'I don't think I made any real mistakes,' he said out loud to the sand and the sea. 'You were just unlucky. Eddie . . . Well, soldiers get killed, it's part of the job.'

*Is it because you had to kill more people than you were ready for*?

'Maybe.' The Cali barrio, the car lot by the Magdalena, the jungle village. The woman at Totoro. There had never been any real choice. 'But I don't think so,' he said.

*So what the fuck are you moaning on about*? *You like the job. You like taking young men and showing them how to make the most of what they have. It's a thing worth doing. And you do it well.'*

'Yeah.' It was. He did. He accepted all that. 'It's just . . .' he began, and then fell silent again. He had stopped walking, and a flicker of a smile crossed his face as he realized what he would look like to a stranger. A lunatic on a beach, talking to himself. 'It's just . . .'

*It's just that you're a maudlin Welsh bastard.*

'Just a man,' Wynwood said carefully, 'who wishes that there was no need to bring out the worst in men in order for them to serve the good.'

*You could put that in a Christmas cracker*!

Wynwood laughed. 'Yeah,' he agreed.

He looked out to sea, listened to the waves. 'Goodbye, Andy,' he said at last, and turned away, walking on towards the distant lights.

# SOLDIER E: SAS

# SNIPER FIRE IN BELFAST

Shaun Clarke

# Prelude

Martin was hiding in a shallow scrape when they found him. He plunged into despair when he heard their triumphant shouting, then he was grabbed by the shoulders and jerked roughly up on to his knees.

The rain was lashing down over the wind-blown green fields, and he caught only a glimpse of the shadowy men in olive-green fatigues, carrying a variety of weapons and moving in to surround him, before he was blindfolded, bound by hands and feet, and thrown into the back of their truck like so much dead meat.

'Face down in the fucking mud,' one of them said, 'digging through to Australia.' The others laughed. 'Looks a bit on the damp side, doesn't he? That should save him embarrassment. We won't notice the stains when the bugger starts pissing his pants – and that won't take long, I'll bet.'

Lying on his side on the floor of the truck, feeling the occasional soft kick from the boots of the men sitting above him, Martin had to choke back his panic and keep control of himself.

*After so long*, he thought. *After so much. Don't lose it all now* . . .

The door on the driver's side of the truck slammed shut, then the engine coughed into life and the vehicle rattled across the hilly terrain, bumped over what Martin judged to be the rough edge of the field, then moved straight ahead along a proper road. Still in despair, though knowing he hadn't lost all yet, he took deep, even breaths, forcing his racing heart to settle down.

When someone's body rolled into his and he heard a nervous coughing, he realized with a shameful feeling of relief that he wasn't the only one they had caught.

'Shit!' he whispered.

'What was that, boyo?' one of his captors asked in a mocking manner. 'Did I hear filthy language from down there?'

'Take off this bloody blindfold,' Martin said. 'You don't really need that.'

'Feeling a bit uncomfortable, are you? A bit disorientated? Well, you better get used to it, you stupid prat, because that blindfold stays on. Now shut your mouth and don't speak until you're spoken to.'

The other tethered man rolled away from Martin, coughing uncomfortably. 'We don't have to . . . ' he began.

'Put a sock in it,' the same captor said, leaning down to roll the man over and somehow silence him. Even as Martin was wondering what the man was doing, a cloth was wrapped tightly around his mouth and tied in a knot at the back of his head. 'Now you're dumb as well as blind,' the man said. 'That should teach you not to open your trap when it's not called for.'

'Have you pissed your pants yet?' another voice asked. 'It's hard to tell, you're both so wet all over. Hope you're not feeling cold, lads.'

Some of the men laughed. 'Fucking SAS,' another man said contemptuously. 'Supposed to be impossible to find and these pricks lie there waiting to be picked up. If this is the best they can manage, they must be fit for the Girl Guides.'

The last remark raised a few more laughs and made Martin feel even worse, adding humiliation to his despair and increasing his fear of what might be to come.

*You haven't lost it all yet,* he told himself. *Just try to stay calm, in control. Don't let them get to you. Don't let fear defeat you.*

It was easier to contemplate than it was to put into practice. Indeed, as the truck growled and shook beneath him, its hard boards seeming to hammer him, he became increasingly aware of his blindfold and gag, which in turn made him feel claustrophobic and unbearably helpless. As the blindfold was also covering his ears, he was practically deaf, dumb and blind. That forced him deeper into himself and made him strain to break out. This feeling was not eased by the cruel mockery of his captors as the truck growled and rattled along the road.

'A big, brave British soldier?' one of his captors said, prodding him in the ribs with his boot. 'Found hiding face down in the mud. Not so big and brave now, boys.'

'Might be big in unseen places. Might be brave with what's hidden.'

'That'll be the day. A pair of English nancy boys. A pair of uniformed British poofters tryin' to keep real men down. Well, when we get where we're goin', we'll find out what they're made of. I'm lookin' forward to that.'

*It's not real*, Martin thought, trying to stop himself from shivering, his soaked clothing starting to freeze and his exhaustion now compounded by despair at being caught. *Bear in mind that nothing is real, that nothing can break you. Just don't make a mistake.*

After what seemed like an eternity, the truck came to a halt, the back was dropped down, and Martin was roughly hauled to his feet and dragged down to the ground, where they deliberately rolled him in the mud a few times, then stood him up in the wind and rain. Someone punched him lightly on the back of his neck, urging him forward. But as his ankles were still tethered together, allowing only minimal movement, they lost patience and two of them dragged him by the armpits across what seemed to be an open space – the wind was howling across it, lashing the rain into his face – then up steps, onto a porch. He heard doors squeaking open, felt warmer air reach his face, then was dragged in to where there was no wind or rain and the warmth was a blessing. His boots scraped over what seemed like linoleum, then they dragged him around a corner, along another straight stretch, then through another door – again he heard it squeaking as it opened – and at last pushed him down into a chair.

*Stay calm*, he thought desperately. *Don't make any mistakes. It all depends on what you say or don't say, so don't let them trick you. Don't panic. Don't break.*

'What a filthy specimen,' someone said contemptuously. 'He looks like he's been taking a swim in his own piss and shit.'

'Just mud and rain, sir,' another man said. 'Not the gentleman's fault, his appearance. The natural elements, is all.'

'Where did you find him?'

'Belly down in the mud. Trying to blend in with the earth in the hope that we'd miss him. Fat chance of that, sir.'

'The dumb British shit. He must think we're all halfwits. Do we talk to him now or let him dry out?'

'He won't smell so bad when he dries out.'

'That's true enough. Hood him.'

The cloth was removed from Martin's mouth, letting him breathe more easily. No sooner had he begun to do so than a hood was slipped over his head and tightened around his neck with a cord, making him feel even more claustrophobic. A spasm of terror whipped through him, then passed away again.

*Breathe deeply and evenly*, he thought. *You're not going to choke. They're just trying to panic you.*

'My name is Martin Renshaw,' he said, just to hear the sound of his own voice. 'My rank is . . .'

A hand pressed over his mouth and pushed his head back until the hard chair cut painfully into his neck.

'When we want your name, rank, serial number and date of birth we'll ask for it,' the colder voice said. 'Don't speak again unless spoken to. We'll now leave you to dry out. Understood?'

Martin nodded.

'That's a good start. Now be a good boy.'

Their footsteps marched away, the door opened and slammed shut, then there was only the silence and his own laboured breathing. Soon he thought he could hear his heart beating, ticking off every second, every terrible minute.

As the hours passed he dried out, and his clothing became sticky, though it could have been sweat. Not knowing if it was one or the other only made him feel worse. His exhaustion, already considerable before his capture, was now attacking his mind. His thoughts slipped like faulty gears, his fear alternated with defiance, and when he started drifting in and out of consciousness it was only the cramp in his tightly bound arms that kept him awake.

He was slipping gratefully into oblivion when someone kicked his chair over. The shock was appalling, jolting him awake, screaming, though he didn't hit the floor. Instead, someone laughed and grabbed the back of the chair to tip him upright again. The blood had rushed to his head and the panic had almost made him snap, but he took a deep breath and controlled himself, remembering that the hood was still over his head and that his feeling of suffocation was caused by that, as well as by shock.

'So sorry,' a man said, sounding terribly polite and English. 'A little mishap. Slip of the foot. I trust you weren't hurt.'

'No,' Martin said, shocked by the breathless sound of his own voice. 'Could you remove this hood? Its really . . . '

The chair went over again and stopped just before hitting the floor. This time they held him in that position for some time, letting the blood run to his head, then tipped him upright again and let his breathing settle.

'We ask the questions,' the polite gentleman said, 'and you do the answering. Now could you please tell us who else was with you in that field.'

Martin gave his name, rank, service number and date of birth.

The chair was kicked back, caught and tipped upright, then someone else bawled in Martin's face: 'We don't want to know that!'

After getting his breath back, Martin gave his name, rank, service number and date of birth, thinking, *This isn't real.*

It became real enough after that, with a wide variety of questions either politely asked or bawled, the polite voice alternating with the bullying one, and the chair being thrown back and jerked up again, but getting lower to the floor every time. Eventually, when Martin, despite his surging panic, managed to keep repeating only his name, rank, serial number and date of birth, they gave up on the chair and dragged him across the room to slam him face first into what seemed like a bare wall. There, the ropes around his ankles were released and he was told to spread his legs as wide as possible, almost doing the splits.

'Don't move a muscle,' he was told by the bully.

He stood like that for what seemed a long time, until his thighs began to ache intolerably and his whole body sagged.

'Don't move!' the bully screamed, slamming

Martin's face into the wall again and forcing him to straighten his aching spine. 'Stay as still as the turd you are!'

'We're sorry to be so insistent,' the polite one added, 'but you're not helping at all. Now, regarding what you were doing out there in the fields, do please tell us . . .'

It went on and on, with Martin either repeating his basic details or saying: 'I cannot answer that question.' They shouted, cajoled and bullied. They made him stand in one position until he collapsed, then let him rest only long enough to enable them to pick another form of torture that did not involve beating.

Martin knew what they were doing, but this wasn't too much help, since he didn't know how long it would last, let alone how long he might endure it. Being hooded only made it worse, sometimes making him feel that he was going to suffocate, at other times making him think that he was hallucinating, but always depriving him of his sense of time. It also plunged him into panics based solely on the fact that he no longer knew left from right and felt mentally and physically unbalanced.

Finally, they left him, letting him sleep on the floor, joking that they were turning out the light, since he couldn't see that anyway. He lay there for an eternity – but perhaps only minutes – now yearning just to sleep, too tired to sleep, and whispering his name, rank, serial number and date of birth over and over, determined not to make a mistake when repeating it or, worse, say more than that. The only words he kept in mind other than those were: 'I cannot answer that question.' He had dreams – they may have been hallucinations – and had no idea of how long he had been lying there where they returned to torment him.

They asked Martin if he smoked and, when he said no, blew a cloud of smoke in his face. While he was coughing, they asked him more questions. When he managed, even through his delirium, to stick to his routine answers, one of them threw him back on the freezing floor and said: 'Let's feed the bastard to the dogs.'

They stripped off his clothing, being none too gentle, then left him to lie there, shivering with cold, almost sobbing, but controlling himself by endlessly repeating his name, rank, serial number and date of birth.

He almost lost control again when he heard dogs barking, snarling viciously, and hammering their paws relentlessly on the closed door.

*Was it real dogs or a recording? Surely, they wouldn't . . . Who?* By now he was too tired to think straight, forgetting why he was there, rapidly losing touch with reality, his mind expanding and contracting, his thoughts swirling in a pool of light and darkness in the hood's stifling heat.

*A recording*, was the thought he clung to. *Must not panic or break.*

The door opened and snarling dogs rushed in, accompanied by the shouting of men.

The men appeared to be ordering the dogs back out. When the dogs were gone, the door closed again.

Silence.

Then somebody screamed: 'Where are you based?'

It was like an electric bolt shooting through Martin's body, making him twitch and groan. He started to tell them, wanted to tell them, and instead said: 'I cannot answer that question.'

'You're a good boy,' the civilized English voice said. 'Too stubborn for your own good.'

This time, when they hoisted him back on to the chair, he was filled with a dread that made him forget everything except the need to keep his mouth shut and make no mistakes. No matter what they said, no matter what they did, he would not say a word.

'What's the name of your squadron commander?' the bully bawled.

'I cannot answer that question,' Martin said, then methodically gave his name, rank, serial number and date of birth.

The silence that followed seemed to stretch out for ever, filling Martin with a dread that blotted out most of his past. Eventually the English-sounding voice said: 'This is your last chance. Will you tell us more or not?'

Martin was halfway through reciting his routine when they whipped off the hood.

Light blinded him.

# 1

'I still don't think we should do it,' Captain Dubois said, even as he hung his neatly folded OGs in his steel locker and started putting on civilian clothing. 'It could land us in water so hot we'd come out like broiled chicken.'

'We're doing it,' Lieutenant Cranfield replied, tightening the laces on his scuffed, black-leather shoes and oblivious to the fact that Captain Dubois was his superior officer. 'I'm fed up being torn between Army Intelligence, MI6, the RUC and even the "green slime",' he said, this last being the Intelligence Corps. 'If we come up with anything, as sure as hell one lot will approve, the other will disapprove, they'll argue for months, and in the end not a damned thing will be done. Well, not this time. I'm going to take that bastard out by myself. As for MI5 . . .'

Cranfield trailed off, too angry for words. After an uneasy silence, Captain Dubois said tentatively, 'Just because Corporal Phillips committed suicide . . .'

'Exactly. So to hell with MI5.'

Corporal Phillips had been one of the best of 14 Intelligence Company's undercover agents, infiltrating the most dangerous republican ghettos of Belfast and collecting invaluable intelligence. A few weeks earlier he had handed over ten first-class sources of information to MI5 and within a week they had all been assassinated, one after the other, by the IRA.

Apart from the shocking loss of so many watchers, including Phillips, the assassinations had shown that MI5 had a leak in its system. That leak, as Cranfield easily discovered, was their own source, Shaun O'Halloran, who had always been viewed by 14 Intelligence Company as a hardline republican, therefore unreliable. Having ignored the advice of 14 Intelligence Company and used O'Halloran without its knowledge, MI5, instead of punishing him, had tried to save embarrassment by simply dropping him and trying to cover his tracks.

Cranfield, still shocked and outraged by the death of ten men, as well as the subsequent suicide of the conscience-stricken Phillips, was determined that their betrayer, O'Halloran, would not walk away scot-free.

'A mistake is one thing,' he said, placing his foot back on the floor and grabbing a grey civilian's jacket from his locker, 'but to believe that you can trust someone with O'Halloran's track record is pure bloody stupidity.'

'They weren't to know that he was an active IRA member,' Dubois said, studying himself in the mirror and seeing a drab civilian rather than the SAS officer he actually was. 'They thought he was just another tout out to make a few bob.'

'Right,' Cranfield said contemptuously. 'They *thought*. They should have bloody well checked.'

Though nervous about his famously short-fused SAS officer, Captain Dubois understood his frustration.

For the past year sharp divisions had been appearing between the two main non-military Intelligence agencies: MI6 (the secret intelligence service run by the Commonwealth and Foreign Office, never publicly acknowledged) and MI5, the Security Service openly charged with counter-espionage. The close-knit, almost tribal nature of the RUC, the Royal Ulster Constabulary, meant that its Special Branch was also running its own agents with little regard for Army needs or requirements. RUC Special Branch, meanwhile, was running its own, secret cross-border contacts with the Irish Republic's Gardai Special Branch. Because of this complex web of mutually suspicious and secretive organizations, the few SAS men in the province, occupying key intelligence positions at the military HQ in Lisburn and elsewhere, were often exposed to internecine rivalries when trying to co-ordinate operations against the terrorists.

Even more frustrating was the pecking order.

While SAS officers attempted to be the cement between mutually mistrustful allies, soldiers from other areas acted as Military Intelligence Officers (MIOs) or Field Intelligence NCOs (Fincos) in liaison with the RUC. Such men and women came from the Intelligence Corps, Royal Military Police, and many other sources. The link with each RUC police division was a Special Military Intelligence Unit containing MIOs, Fincos and Milos (Military Intelligence Liaison Officers). An MIO working as part of such a unit could find himself torn by conflicting responsibilities to the RUC, Army Intelligence and MI6.

That is what had happened to Phillips. Though formally a British Army 'Finco' answerable to Military Intelligence, he had been intimidated by members of the Security Service into routeing his information to his own superiors via MI5. In doing so he had innocently sealed his own fate, as well as the fate of his ten unfortunate informants.

No wonder Cranfield was livid.

Still, Dubois felt a little foolish. As an officer of the British Army serving with 14 Intelligence Company, he was Cranfield's superior by both rank and position, yet Lieutenant Cranfield, one of a small number of SAS officers attached to the unit, ignored these fine distinctions and more or less did what he wanted. A flamboyant character, even by SAS standards, he had been in Northern Ireland only two months, yet already had garnered himself a reputation as a 'big timer', someone working out on the edge and possessed of extreme braggadocio, albeit with brilliant flair and matchless courage. While admiring him, for the latter qualities, Dubois was nervous about Cranfield's cocksure attitude, which he felt would land him in trouble sooner or later.

'We'll be in and out in no time,' Cranfield told him, clipping a holstered 9mm Browning High Power handgun to his belt, positioned halfway around his waist, well hidden by the jacket. 'So stop worrying about it. Are you ready?'

'Yes,' Dubois said, checking that his own High Power was in the cross-draw position.

'Right,' Cranfield said, 'let's go.'

As they left the barracks, Dubois again felt a faint flush of humiliation, realizing just how much he liked and admired Cranfield and had let himself be won over by his flamboyance. Though a former Oxford boxing blue and Catholic Guards officer, Dubois was helplessly awed by the fact that his second-in-command, Lieutenant Randolph 'Randy' Cranfield, formerly of the King's Own Scottish Borderers and the Parachute Regiment, had gone to Ampleforth where the founder of the SAS, David Stirling, had also been educated, and was widely admired for his daring – some would say reckless – exploits.

Dubois had his own brand of courage, which he had often displayed in the mean streets of Belfast or the 'bandit country' of Armagh, but he was basically conservative in outlook and helplessly admiring of those less inhibited. He had therefore gradually become Cranfield's shadow, rather than his leader, and recognition of this fact made him uncomfortable.

They entered what looked like a normal army compound, surrounded by high walls of corrugated iron, with watch-towers and electronically controlled gates guarded on both sides with reinforced sangars. These stone walls were high because the IRA's flavour of the month was the Russian-made RPG 7 short-range anti-tank weapon, which could hurl a rocket-propelled grenade in an arc with an effective range of 500 metres. With walls so high, however, the IRA would have to come dangerously close to the base before they could gain the required elevation for such an attack. The walls kept them at bay.

'Another bleak day in Armagh,' Cranfield said. 'God, what I'd give for some sunshine and the taste of sangria!'

'In January in Northern Ireland,' Dubois replied, 'I can't even imagine that. But I know that I'd prefer the heat of Oman to this bloody place.'

'Some of the others arriving next week have just come from there,' Cranfield said, 'which means they'll be well blooded, experienced in desert survival, filled with the humane values of the hearts-and-minds campaign . . .' – he paused for dramatic effect – 'and completely out of sorts here.'

'Yes,' Dubois agreed glumly. 'We'll have to firm them up quickly. And being attached to us won't make them too happy either. They'll think they've been RTU'd back to the regular Army.'

'They should be so lucky!' Cranfield exclaimed, shaking his head and chuckling ruefully. 'We should *all* be so lucky! Instead, we're with 14 Intelligence Company, in the quicksand of too many conflicting groups. We're neither here nor there, Jeremy.'

'No, I suppose not.'

Though 14 Intelligence Company was a reconnaissance unit, it had been given the cover title, 4 Field Survey Troop, Royal Engineers, but was also known as the Northern Ireland Training and Tactics team. Located in the army compound Dubois and Cranfield were visiting, it was equipped with unmarked, civilian 'Q' cars and various non-standard weapons, including the Ingram silenced sub-machine-gun. The camp was shared with a British Army Sapper unit.

'Look,' Cranfield said impatiently as they crossed the parade ground, from the barracks to the motor pool, in the pearly-grey light of morning, 'what we're doing isn't that unusual. I mean, six months ago we crossed the border to pick up an IRA commander and deposit him back in Northern Ireland, to be arrested by the RUC and brought to trial. Though a lot of people cried out in protest, that murderous bastard eventually got thirty years. Was it worth it or not?'

'It was worth it,' Dubois admitted, studying the low grey sky over the green fields of Armagh and longing for a holiday in the sun, as Cranfield had suggested.

'Right,' Cranfield said as they entered the busy motor pool, which reeked of petrol and was, as usual, filled with the roaring of engines being tested. 'Since that damned power struggle between Five and Six, Major Fred has repeatedly crossed the border wearing dirty jeans, bearded, and carrying a false driving licence issued in Dublin. We're not alone in this, Jeremy.'

'Major Fred' was an MI0 attached to Portadown Police HQ. Almost as disdainful of MI5 and MI6 as was Cranfield, he was also as daring in defying both of those organizations and going his own way. As the value of what he was doing had yet to be ascertained, Cranfield's citing of him as an example of what was admirable in the muddy, dangerous waters of intelligence gathering in bandit country was in no way encouraging to Dubois.

'I'm not interested in Major Fred,' he said. 'Let him worry the Portadown lot. I'm only interested in 14 Intelligence Company and how it might be adversely affected by what you're planning to do.'

'There won't be any adverse effects. We've had those already. We can't do any worse than ten murdered and one suicide. At the very least we'll deny the IRA what they think is a propaganda victory. It's not purely personal.'

I'll bet, Dubois thought. 'I just wish the ceasefire hadn't ended,' he said, not wanting his silence to reveal that he was actually nervous.

'Why?' Cranfield replied. 'It was all nonsense anyway, inspired by the usual, idiotic rivalry between MI5 and MI6. I mean, what did it all amount to? During a raid on an IRA headquarters in Belfast, security forces discover a "doomsday" contingency plan for counter-attack on Protestant areas should there be a repetition of August '69. Dismayed, the Foreign Office, including MI6, seeks a political solution that involves secret contacts with the IRA. The IRA plays along. As they do so, MI5 insist that the terrorists are merely seeking a breathing space. Knowledge of the doomsday plan then gives MI5 a perfect chance to discredit political contacts. Bingo! The ceasefire collapses and we're back in business. Pull the plug on MI5 and we'd all live in a better world.'

They stopped by a red Morris Marina, one of the Q cars, equipped with a covert radio and modified to hide a wide variety of non-standard weapons and Japanese photographic equipment. Two British Army sergeants known to Dubois – both in civilian clothes – were leaning against the side of the car, smoking cigarettes. They straightened up when Dubois and Cranfield approached, though neither man saluted.

'Sergeant Blake,' Dubois said, nodding by way of welcome. 'Sergeant Harris.' He nodded in the direction of Cranfield. 'This is Lieutenant Cranfield of the SAS, in charge of this mission.'

Both men nodded at Cranfield, neither saying a word.

'You've been briefed?' Cranfield asked.

'Yes, sir,' Sergeant Harris said. 'We're not bringing him back. It's terminal. He stays where he lies.'

'Correct,' Cranfield said. 'So let's get going.'

Sergeant Harris was the driver, with Cranfield sitting in the front beside him. As Dubois took his seat in the back, beside Sergeant Blake, he thought of just how confused were the issues of this conflict and how easily men like Cranfield, even himself, could be driven to taking matters into their own hands, as they were doing right now.

Still, it *had* been a rather bad year: the humiliating fall of the Tory government; the creation of a non-elected, supposedly neutral power-sharing executive to replace direct rule of Ulster from London; the collapse of that executive under the intimidation of the Ulster Workers' strike and IRA violence, including the horrendous Birmingham pub massacre; the Dublin bombing; an IRA truce through Christmas and New Year of 1974–5, and finally the collapse of that truce. Now the SAS was being officially brought in, hopefully to succeed where the regular Army had failed. Dubois was mildly offended.

Sergeant Harris started the car and headed away from the motor pool, driving past rows of Saracen armoured cars, troop trucks, tanks, as well as other Q cars, most of which were visibly well used. The road led around to where the Lynx, Wessex and Army Westland Scout helicopters were taking off and landing, carrying men to and from the many OPs, observation posts, scattered on the high, green hills of the province and manned night and day by rotating, regular army surveillance teams. It was a reminder to Dubois of just how much this little war in Northern Ireland was costing the British public in manpower and money.

'I still don't see why they had to bring in the SAS,' he said distractedly as the Q car approached the heavily guarded main gate. 'I mean, every Army unit in the province has Close Observation Platoons specially trained for undercover operations – so why an official, full complement of SAS?'

'The main problem with your COPS,' Cranfield replied, meaning the Close Observation Platoons, 'is that the men simply can't pass themselves off as Irishmen, and have, in fact, often got into trouble when trying to. Since our men are specially trained for covert operations, they can act as watchers without coming on with the blarney and buying themselves an early grave.'

There was more to it than that, as Dubois knew

from his Whitehall contacts. The decision to send the SAS contingent had been taken by Edward Heath's government as long ago as January 1974. The minority Labour government elected six weeks later – Harold Wilson's second administration – was *not* informed when elements of B Squadron 22 SAS were first deployed to Northern Ireland at that time.

Unfortunately, on 26 January 1974, a former UDR soldier named William Black was shot and seriously wounded by security forces using a silenced sub-machine-gun. When Black was awarded damages, the SAS came under suspicion. The soldiers, not trained for an urban anti-terrorist role and fresh from the Omani desert, had not been made aware of the legal hazards of their new environment.

Worse was to come. B Squadron's contingent was withdrawn abruptly from Ireland after two of its members attempted to rob a bank in Londonderry. Both men were later sentenced to six years' imprisonment, though their just punishment hardly helped the image of the SAS, which was being viewed by many as a secret army of assassins, not much better than the notorious Black and Tans of old. Perhaps for this reason, the presence of the SAS in Ireland during that period was always officially denied.

Nevertheless, when Dubois had first arrived in the province to serve with 4 Field Survey Troop, he found himself inheriting SAS Lieutenant Randolph 'Randy' Cranfield as his deputy, or second-in-command. At first, Dubois and Cranfield had merely visited Intelligence officers in the Armagh area, including 'Major Fred' in Portadown, lying that they were under the direct orders of SIS (MI6) and Army HQ Intelligence staff. When believed by the naïve, they asked for suggestions of worthwhile intelligence targets. This led them to make illicit expeditions across the border, initially just for surveillance, then to 'snatch' IRA members and return them at gunpoint to Northern Ireland to be 'captured' by the RUC and handed over for trial in the north. Now they were going far beyond that – and it had Dubois worried.

'At least your lot have finally been committed *publicly* to Northern Ireland,' he said to Cranfield as the car passed between the heavily fortified sangars on both sides of the electronically controlled gates. 'That might be a help.' 'It's no more than a public relations campaign by the Prime Minister,' Cranfield said with his customary cynicism as the car passed through the gates, which then closed automatically.

'Paddy Devlin's already described it as a cosmetic exercise, pointing out, accurately, that the SAS have always been here.'

That was true enough, Dubois acknowledged to himself. Right or wrong, the recent decision to publicly commit the SAS to Northern Ireland had been imposed by the Prime Minister without warning, even bypassing the Ministry of Defence. Indeed, as Dubois had learnt from friends, Home Secretary Merlyn Rees had already secretly confessed that it was a 'presentational thing', a melodramatic way of letting the public know that the most legendary group of soldiers in the history of British warfare were about to descend on Northern Ireland and put paid to the IRA.

'What the Downing Street announcement *really* signalled,' Dubois said, still trying to forget his nervousness, 'was a change in the SAS role from intelligence gathering to combat.'

'Right,' Cranfield replied. 'So don't feel too bad about what we're doing. Just think of it as legitimate combat. You'll sleep easier that way.'

'I hope so,' Dubois said.

As the gates clanged shut behind the Q car, Sergeant Harris turned onto the road leading to the border, which was only a few miles from the camp. Once the grim, high walls of corrugated iron were out of sight, the rolling green hills came into view, reminding Dubois of how beautiful Northern Ireland was, how peaceful it always looked, away from the trouble spots.

This illusion of peace was rudely broken when his observant eye picked out the many overt OPs scattered about the hills, with high-powered binoculars and telescopes glinting under makeshift roofs of camouflaged netting and turf, constantly surveying the roads and fields. It was also broken when armoured trucks and tanks, bristling with weapons, trundled along the road, travelling between the border and the army camp.

After driving for about ten minutes they came to the British Army roadblock located two miles before the border. Sergeant Harris stopped to allow the soldiers, all wearing full OGs, with helmets and chin straps, and armed with SA-80 assanlt rifles, to show their papers. Presenting their real papers, as distinct from the false documents they were also carrying for use inside the Republic, they were waved on and soon reached the border. To avoid the Gardai – the police force of the Republic of Ireland – they took an unmarked side road just before the next village and kept going until they were safely over the border. Ten minutes later they came to a halt in the shady lane that led up to O'Halloran's conveniently isolated farmhouse.

'He can't see us or hear from here,' Cranfield said, 'and we're going the rest of the way by foot. You wait here in the car, Sergeant Harris. No one's likely to come along here, except, perhaps, for some innocent local like the postman or milkman.'

'And if he does?'

'We can't afford to have witnesses.'

'Right, sir. Terminate.'

Cranfield glanced back over his shoulder at Captain Dubois, still in the rear seat. 'Are you ready?'

'Yes.'

'Good, let's go. You too, Sergeant Blake.'

Cranfield and Dubois unholstered their 9mm Browning High Power handguns as they got out of the car. Sergeant Blake withdrew a silenced L34A1 Sterling sub-machine-gun from a hidden panel beneath his feet and unfolded the stock as he climbed out of the car to stand beside the other two men. After releasing their safety-catches, the men walked up the lane, away from the Q car, until they arrived at the wooden gate that led into the fields surrounding the farmhouse.

It was not yet 8.30 a.m. and the sun was still trying to break through a thick layer of cloud, casting shadows over the misty green hills on all sides of the house. Birds were singing. The wind was moaning slightly. Smoke was rising from the chimney in the thatched roof, indicating that O'Halloran, known to live alone, was up and about.

His two Alsatians, tethered to a post in the front yard, hadn't noticed the arrival of the men and were sleeping contentedly. The slightest sound, however, would awaken them.

Cranfield nodded at Sergeant Blake. The latter set his L34A1 to semi-automatic fire, leaned slightly forward with his right leg taking his weight and the left giving him balance, then pressed the extended stock of the weapon into his shoulder with his body leaning into the gun. He released the cocking handle, raised the rear assembly sight, then took careful aim. He fired two short bursts, moving the barrel right for the second burst, his body shaking slightly from the backblast. Loose soil spat up violently, silently, around the sleeping dogs, making them shudder, obscuring the flying bone and geyzering blood from their exploding heads. When the spiralling dust had settled down, the heads of the dogs resembled pomegranates. Blake's silenced L34A1 had made practically no sound and the dogs had died too quickly even to yelp.

Using a hand signal, Cranfield indicated that the men should slip around the gate posts rather than open the chained gate, then cross the ground in front of the farmhouse. This they did, moving as quietly as possible, spreading out as they advanced with their handguns at the ready, merely glancing in a cursory manner at the Alsatians now lying in pools of blood.

When they reached the farmhouse, Cranfield nodded at Sergeant Blake, who returned the nod, then slipped quietly around the side of the house to cover the back door. When he had disappeared around the back, Cranfield and Dubois took up positions on either side of the door, holding their pistols firmly, applying equal pressure between the thumb and fingers of the firing hand.

Cranfield was standing upright, his back pressed to the wall. Dubois was on one knee, already aiming his pistol at the door. When the latter nodded,

Cranfield spun around, kicked the door open and rushed in, covered by Dubois.

O'Halloran was sitting in his pyjamas at the kitchen table, about ten feet away, as the door was torn from its hinges and crashed to the floor. Shocked, he looked up from his plate, the fork still to his mouth, as Cranfield rushed in, stopped, spread his legs wide, and prepared to fire the gun two-handed.

'This is for Phillips,' Cranfield said, then fired the first shot.

O'Halloran jerked convulsively and slapped his free hand on the table, his blood already spurting over the bacon and eggs as his fork fell, clattering noisily on the tiles. He jerked again with the second bullet. Trying to stand, he twisted backwards, his chair buckling and breaking beneath him as he crashed to the floor.

Dubois came in after Cranfield, crouched low, aiming left and right, covering the room as Cranfield emptied his magazine, one shot after another in the classic 'double tap', though using all thirteen bullets instead of two.

O'Halloran, already dead, was jerking spasmodically from each bullet as Sergeant Blake, hearing the shots, kicked the back door in and rushed through the house, checking each room as he went, prepared to cut down anything that moved, but finding nothing at all. By the time he reached the kitchen at the front, the double tap was completed.

Sergeant Blake glanced at the dead man on the floor. 'Good job, boss,' he commented quietly.

'Let's go,' Dubois said.

Cranfield knelt beside O'Halloran, placed his fingers on his neck, checked that he was dead, then stood up again.

'Day's work done,' he said.

Unable to return Cranfield's satisfied grin, though feeling relieved, Captain Dubois just nodded and led the three men out of the house. They returned to the Q car, not glancing back once, and let Sergeant Harris drive them away, back to Northern Ireland.

## 2

Martin was leaning on the rusty railing when the ship that had brought him and the others from Liverpool inched into Belfast harbour in the early hours of the morning. His hair was longer than it should have been, windswept, dishevelled. He was wearing a roll-necked sweater, a bomber jacket, blue jeans and a pair of old suede boots, and carrying a small shoulder bag. The others, he knew, looked the same, though they were now in the bar, warming up with mugs of tea.

Looking at the lights beaming over the dark, dismal harbour, he was reminded of the brilliant light that had temporarily blinded him when the Directing Staff conducting the brutal Resistance to Interrogation (RTI) exercises had whipped the hood off his head. Later they had congratulated him on having passed that final hurdle even before his eyes had readjusted to the light in the bare, cell-like room in the Joint Services Interrogation Unit of 22 SAS Training Wing, Hereford. Even as he was being led from the room, knowing he would soon be bound for the last stages of his Continuation Training in Borneo, he had seen another young man, Corporal Wigan of the Light Infantry, being escorted out of the building with tears in his eyes.

'He was the one you shared the truck with,' his Director of Training had told him, 'but he finally cracked, forgot where he was, and told us everything we wanted to know. Now he's being RTU'd.'

Being returned to your unit of origin was doubly humiliating, first through the failure to get into the SAS, then through having to face your old mates, who would know you had failed. Even now, thinking of how easily it could have happened to him, Martin, formerly of the Royal Engineers, practically shuddered at the thought of it.

Feeling cold and dispirited by the sight of the bleak docks of Belfast, he hurried back into the bar where the other men, some recently badged like him, others old hands who had last fought in Oman, all of them in civilian clothing, were sipping hot tea and pretending to be normal passengers.

Sergeant Frank Lampton, who had been Martin's Director of Training during the horrors of Continuation Training, was leaning back in his chair, wearing a thick overcoat, corduroy trousers, a tatty shirt buttoned at the neck, a V-necked sweater and badly scuffed suede shoes. With his blond hair dishevelled and his clothing all different sizes, as if picked up in charity shops, he did not look remotely like the slim, fit, slightly glamorous figure who had been Martin's DT.

Sitting beside Sergeant Lampton was Corporal Phil Ricketts. Their strong friendship had been forged in the fierce fighting of the 'secret' war in Dhofar, Oman, in 1972. Ricketts was a pleasant, essentially serious man with a wife and child in Wood Green, North London. He didn't talk about them much, but when he did it was with real pride and love. Unlike the sharp-tongued, ferret-faced Trooper 'Gumboot' Gillis, sitting opposite.

Badged with Ricketts just before going to Dhofar, Gumboot hailed from Barnstaple, Devon, where he had a wife, Linda, whom he seemed to hold in less than high esteem. 'I was in Belfast before,' he'd explained to Martin a few nights earlier, 'but with 3 Para. When I returned home, that bitch had packed up and left with the kids. That's why, when I was badged and sent back here, I was pleased as piss. I'll take a Falls Road hag any day. At least you know where you stand with them.'

'Up against an alley wall,' Jock McGregor said.

Corporal McGregor had been shot through the hand in Oman and looked like the tough nut he was. Others who had fought with Lampton, Ricketts and Gumboot in Oman had gone their separate ways, with the big black poet, Trooper Andrew Winston, being returned there in 1975. A lot of the men had joked that the reason Andrew had been transferred to another squadron and sent back to Oman was that his black face couldn't possibly pass for a Paddy's. Whatever the true cause, he had been awarded for bravery during the SAS strikes against rebel strongholds in Defa and Shershitti.

Sitting beside Jock was Trooper Danny 'Baby Face' Porter, from Kingswinford, in the West Midlands. He was as quiet as a mouse and, though nicknamed 'Baby Face' because of his innocent, wide-eyed, choirboy appearance, was said to have been one of the most impressive of all the troopers who had recently been badged – a natural soldier who appeared to fear nothing and was ferociously competent with weapons. His speciality was the 'double tap' – thirteen rounds discharged from a Browning High Power handgun in under three seconds, at close range – which some had whispered might turn out useful in the mean streets of Belfast.

Not as quiet as Danny, but also just badged and clearly self-conscious with the more experienced troopers, Hugh 'Taff' Burgess was a broad-chested Welshman with a dark, distant gaze, a sweet, almost childlike nature and, reportedly, a violent temper when aroused or drunk. Throughout the whole SAS Selection and Training course Taff had been slightly slow in learning, very thorough at everything, helpful and encouraging to others, and always even-tempered. True, he had wrecked a few pubs in Hereford, but while in the SAS barracks in the town he had been a dream of good humour and generosity. Not ambitious, and not one to shine too brightly, he was, nevertheless, a good soldier, popular with everyone.

Last but not least was Sergeant 'Dead-eye Dick' Parker, who didn't talk much. Rumour had it that he had been turned into a withdrawn, ruthless fighting machine by his terrible experience in the Telok Anson swamp in Malaya in 1958. According to the eye-witness accounts of other Omani veterans such as Sergeant Ricketts and Gumboot, Parker, when in Oman with them, had worn Arab clothing and fraternized mostly with the unpredictable, violent firqats, Dhofaris who had renounced their communist comrades and lent their support to the Sultan. Now, lounging lazily on a chair in blue denims and a tatty old ski jacket, he looked like any other middle-aged man running slightly to seed. Only his grey gaze, cold and ever shifting, revealed that he was alert and still potentially lethal.

The men were scattered all around the lounge, not speaking, pretending not to know one another. When the boat docked and the passengers started disembarking, they shuffled out of the lounge with them, but remained well back or took up positions on the open deck, waiting for the last of the passengers to disembark.

Looking in both directions along the quayside,

Martin saw nothing moving among the gangplanks tilted on end, scattered railway sleepers and coils of thick mooring cables. The harbour walls rose out of the filthy black water, stained a dirty brown by years of salt water and the elements, supporting an ugly collection of warehouses, huts, tanks and prefabricated administration buildings. Unmanned cranes loomed over the water, their hooks swinging slightly in the wind blowing in from the sea. Out in the harbour, green and red pilot lights floated on a gentle sea. Seagulls circled overhead, crying keenly, in the grey light of morning.

Having previously been told to wait on the deck until their driver beckoned to them, the men did so. The last of the other passengers had disembarked when Martin, glancing beyond the quayside, saw a green minibus leaving its position in the car park. It moved between rows of empty cars and the trailers of articulated lorries, eventually leaving the car park through gates guarded by RUC guards wearing flak jackets and armed with 5.56mm Ruger Mini-14 assault rifles. When the minibus reached the quayside and stopped by the empty gangplank, Martin knew that it had to be their transport.

As the driver, also wearing civilian clothing, got out of his car, Sergeant Lampton made his way down the gangplank and spoke to him. The man nodded affirmatively. A group of armed RUC guards emerged from one of the prefabricated huts along the quayside to stand guard while the men's bergen rucksacks were unloaded and heaped up on the quayside. There were no weapons; these would be obtained from the armoury in the camp they were going to. All of the men were, however, already armed with 9mm Browning High Power handguns, which they were wearing in cross-draw holsters under their jackets.

When the last of the bergens had been unloaded, Lampton turned back and waved the men down to the quayside. Martin went down between Ricketts and Gumboot, following the first into the back of the minibus, where a lot of the men were already seated. Gumboot was the last to get in. When he did so, one of the RUC guards slid the door shut and the driver took off, heading out into the mean streets of Belfast.

'Can we talk at last?' Gumboot asked. 'I can't stand this silence.'

'Gumboot wants to talk,' Jock McGregor said. 'God help us all.'

'He's talking already,' Ricketts said. 'I distinctly heard him. Like a little mouse squeaking.'

'Ha, ha. Merely attempting to break the silence, boss,' retorted Gumboot, 'and keep us awake until we basha down. That boat journey seemed endless.'

'You won't get to basha down until tonight, so you better keep talking.'

'Don't encourage him,' Jock said. 'It's too early to have to listen to his bullshit. I've got a headache already.'

'It's the strain of trying to think,' Gumboot informed him. 'You're not used to it, Jock.'

His gaze moved to the window and the dismal streets beyond, where signs saying NO SURRENDER! and SMASH SINN FEIN! fought for attention with enormous, angry paintings on the walls of buildings, showing the customary propaganda of civil war: clenched fists, hooded men clasping weapons, the various insignia of the paramilitary groups on both sides of the divide, those in Shankill, the Falls Road, and the grim, ghettoized housing estates of West Belfast.

'How anyone can imagine this place worth all the slaughter,' Taff Burgess said, studying the grim, wet, barricaded streets, 'I just can't imagine.'

'They don't think it's worth it.' Jock said. 'They're just a bunch of thick Paddies and murderous bastards using any excuse.'

'Not quite true,' Martin said. Brought up by strictly methodist parents in Swindon, not religious himself, but highly conscious of right and wrong, he had carefully read up on Ireland before coming here and was shocked by what he had learnt. 'These people have hatreds that go back to 1601,' he explained, 'when the Catholic barons were defeated and Protestants from England arrived by boat to begin colonization and genocide.'

'1601!' Gumboot said in disgust. 'The Paddies sure have fucking long memories.'

'The Catholics were thrown out of their own

land,' Martin continued, feeling a little self-conscious. 'When they returned to attack the Protestants with pitchforks and stones, the British hanged and beheaded thousands of them. Some were tarred with pitch and dynamite, then set on fire.'

'Ouch!' Taff exclaimed.

'When the Catholics were broken completely,' Martin continued in a trance of historical recollection, 'their religion was outlawed, their language was forbidden, and they became untouchables who lived in the bogs below the Protestant towns. They endured that for a couple of hundred years.'

'You're still talking about centuries ago,' Gumboot said. 'That's a long time to hold those old grudges. Might as well go back to the garden of Eden and complain that you weren't given a bite of the fucking apple.'

'It's not the same thing,' Martin insisted, feeling embarrassed that he was talking so much, but determined to get his point across. 'We're not talking about something that happened just once, centuries ago, but about something that's never really stopped.'

'So the poor buggers were thrown out of their homes and into the bogs,' Taff Burgess said with genuine sympathy, his brown gaze focused inward. 'So what happened next, then?'

'Over the centuries, Belfast became a wealthy industrial centre, dominated entirely by Protestants.

But the Catholics started returning to the city about 1800, and naturally, as they were still being treated like scum, they were resentful and struck back.'

'Nothing like a bit of the old "ultra-violence" to get out your frustrations,' said Gumboot, grinning wickedly. 'Remember that film, *A Clockwork Orange*? Fucking good, that was.'

'Race riots and pogroms became commonplace,' Martin continued, now getting into his stride. 'It burst out every five or six years, eventually leading to the formation of Catholic and Protestant militia. Civil war erupted in 1920. In 1921 the country was partitioned, with the six provinces of the North becoming a British statelet, ruled by its Protestant majority.'

'Big fucking deal,' Gumboot said as the minibus passed through a street of small terraced houses, many with their windows and doorways bricked up. Here the signs said: PROVOS RULE! and BRITS OUT! Even at this early hour of the morning there were gangs of scruffy youths on the street corners, looking for trouble. 'What was so bad about that?'

'Well, Catholics couldn't get jobs and their slums became worse,' Martin explained. 'The electoral laws were manipulated to favour owners of property, who were mostly Protestants. Even after more riots in the thirties and forties, nothing changed. Finally, in 1969, the Catholics took to the streets again, where they were attacked by Protestant police and vigilantes. This time they refused to lie down and the whole city went up in flames.'

'I remember that well,' Jock said. 'I saw it on TV. Mobs all over the place, thousands fleeing from their homes, and Army tanks in the streets. I could hardly believe what I was seeing. A civil war on British soil!'

'Right,' Ricketts chipped in. 'And by the time they were done, you had Catholics on one side, Protestants on the other, and the British equivalent of the Berlin Wall between.'

He pointed out of the window of the van, where they could see the actual 'Peace Line': a fifteen-foot-high wall topped with iron spikes, cutting across roads, through rows of houses, and, as they had all been informed, right across the city.

'Which led,' Sergeant Lampton added laconically, 'to the birth of the masked IRA terrorist and his opposite number, the loyalist terrorist in balaclava.'

'And here we are, caught in the middle,' Ricketts said, 'trying to keep the peace.'

'Trying to stay alive,' Gumboot corrected him, 'which is all it comes down to. I've only got one aim in this piss-hole – to make sure that none of the bastards on either side puts one in my back. Fuck all the rest of it.'

The minibus was now leaving the city to travel along the M1, through rolling hills which, Martin noticed, were dotted with British Army observation posts. Even as he saw the distant OPs, an AH-7 Lynx helicopter was hovering over one of them to insert replacements and take off the men already there. The OPs, Martin knew, were resupplied with men and equipment only by air – never by road.

'Hard to believe that's a killing ground out there,' Sergeant Lampton said. 'If it wasn't for the OPs on the hills, it would all seem so peaceful.'

'It looked peaceful in Oman as well,' Ricketts said, 'until the *Adoo* appeared. It's the same with those hills – except instead of *Adoo* snipers, you have the terrorists. They look pretty serene from down here, but you're right – those are killing fields.'

Martin felt an odd disbelief as he looked at the lush, serene hills and thought of how many times they had been used to hide torture and murder. That feeling remained with him when the minibus turned off the motorway and made its way along a winding narrow lane to the picturesque village of Bessbrook, where the British army had taken over the old mill. Located only four miles from the border, it was a village with a strongly Protestant, God-fearing community – there was not a single pub – and it was presently living through a grim spate of sectarian killings.

As revenge for the killing by Protestant terrorists of five local Catholics, a splinter group calling itself the South Armagh Republican Action Force had stopped a local bus and gunned down eleven men, most of them from Bessbrook, who were on their way home after work. Only one passenger and the Catholic driver had survived. Since that atrocity, both Protestant and Catholic 'death squads' had been stalking the countryside of south Armagh, killing people wholesale. It was this, Martin believed, that had prompted the British government to publicly commit the SAS to the area. Yet now, as the minibus passed through the guarded gates of the old mill, he could scarcely believe that this pretty village was at the heart of so many murderous activities.

'OK,' Sergeant Lampton said when the minibus braked to a halt inside the grounds of the mill. 'The fun's over. All out.'

The side door of the vehicle slid open and they all climbed out into the Security Forces (SF) base as the electronically controlled gates whined shut behind them. The mill had been turned into a grim compound surrounded by high corrugated-iron walls topped by barbed wire. The protective walls were broken up with a series of regularly placed concrete sentry boxes under sandbagged roofs and camouflaged netting. An ugly collection of Portakabins was being used for accommodation and administration. RUC policemen, again wearing flak jackets and carrying Ruger assault rifles, mingled with regular Army soldiers. Saracen armoured cars and tanks were lined up in rows by the side of the motor pool. Closed-circuit TV cameras showed the duty operator in the operations room precisely who was coming or going through the main gates between the heavily fortified sangars.

'Looks like a fucking prison,' Gumboot complained.

'Home sweet home,' Sergeant Lampton said.

# 3

'Settle down, men,' Lieutenant Cranfield said when he had taken his place on the small platform in the briefing room, beside Captain Dubois and an Army sergeant seated at a desk piled high with manila folders. When his new arrivals had quietened down, Cranfield continued: 'You men are here on attachment to 14 Intelligence Company, an intelligence unit that replaced the Military Reconnaissance Force, or MRF, of Brigadier Kitson, who was Commander of Land Forces, Northern Ireland, from 1970 to 1972. A little background information is therefore necessary.'

Some of the men groaned mockingly; others rolled their eyes. Grinning, Cranfield let them grumble for a moment, meanwhile letting his gaze settle briefly on familiar faces: Sergeants Lampton, Ricketts and Parker, as well as Corporal Jock McGregor and Troopers 'Gumboot' Gillis and Danny 'Baby Face' Porter, all of whom had fought bravely in Oman, before returning to act as Directing Staff at 22 SAS Training Wing,

Hereford. There were also some recently badged new men whom he would check out later.

'In March 1972,' Cranfield at last began, 'shortly after the Stormont Parliament was discontinued and direct rule from Westminster substituted, selected members of the SAS, mainly officers, were posted here as individuals to sensitive jobs in Military Intelligence, attached to units already serving in the province. Invariably, they found themselves in a world of petty, often lethal jealousies and division among conflicting agencies – a world of dirty tricks instigated by Military Intelligence officers and their superiors. The MRF was just one of those agencies, causing its own share of problems.'

Now Cranfield glanced at the newcomer, Martin Renshaw, who had endured Sergeant Lampton's perfect impersonation of an Irish terrorist during the horrendous final hours of the RTI exercises during Continuation Training. What was more, he had done so without forgetting that it was only an exercise, unlike so many others, who were RTU'd as a result. According to his report, Renshaw was a serious young man with good technological training, pedantic tendencies, and heady ambitions.

'As some of you have come straight from Oman,' Cranfield continued, 'it's perhaps worth pointing out that certain members of the MRF were, like the firqats of Dhofar, former enemies who had been turned. Occasionally using these IRA renegades – known as "Freds" – as spotters, the

MRF's Q-car patrols identified many active IRA men and women, sometimes photographing them with cameras concealed in the boot of the car. Too often, however, MRF operations went over the top, achieving nothing but propaganda for the IRA.'

'Just like the green slime,' Gumboot said, copping some laughs from his mates and, as Cranfield noticed, a stony glance from his uneasy associate, the Army intelligence officer Captain Dubois.

'Very funny, Trooper Gillis,' Cranfield said. 'Perhaps you'd like to step up here and take over.'

'No, thanks, boss. Please continue.'

Cranfield nodded, secretly admiring Gumboot's impertinence, which he viewed as a virtue not possessed by soldiers of the regular Army. 'In 1972 a couple of embarrassing episodes led to the disbandment of Kitson's organization. Number one was when a two-man team opened fire with a Thompson sub-machine-gun from a moving car on men standing at a Belfast bus stop. Though both soldiers were prosecuted, they claimed they'd been fired at first. The second was when the IRA assassinated the driver of an apparently innocuous laundry van in Belfast. This led to the revelation that the company that owned the van, the so-called Four Square Laundry, was actually an MRF front, collecting clothing in suspect districts for forensic examination.'

'Proper dirty laundry,' Jock McGregor said, winning a few more laughs.

'Yes,' Cranfield said, 'it was that all right. Anyway, those two incidents caused a stir and brought an end to the MRF, which was disbanded early in 1973. But it soon became apparent that as the police, whether in or out of uniform, were soft targets for gunmen, a viable substitute for the MRF was required. This would require men who could penetrate the republican ghettos unnoticed, and who possessed keen powers of observation, quick wits, and even quicker trigger fingers.'

'That's us!' the normally quiet Danny Porter, 'Baby Face', said with a shy grin.

'Not at that time,' Cranfield replied, 'though certainly the training officer for the new team was then serving with 22 SAS. In fact, the new unit, formed at the end of 1973, was 14 Intelligence Company. While it was the job of that company to watch and gather information about the IRA, the SAS's function was to act on the intelligence supplied by them and take action when necessary.'

'Excuse me, boss,' Taff Burgess asked, putting his hand in the air like an eager schoolboy. 'Are you saying that 14 Intelligence Company never gets involved in overt action against the IRA? That they've never had, or caused, casualties?'

'No. They have suffered, and have caused, casualties – but only when spotted and usually only when the terrorist has fired first. Their function is to gather intelligence – not to physically engage the enemy. That's our job. To do it within the law, however, we have to know exactly who and what we're involved with here in the province.'

Cranfield nodded at the Army sergeant standing beside the intelligence officer. The sergeant started distributing his manila folders to the SAS troopers sitting in the chairs. 'The information I'm about to give you,' Cranfield said, 'is contained in more detail in those folders. I want you to read it later and memorize it. For now, I'll just summarize the main points.'

He paused until his assistant, Sergeant Lovelock, had given out the last of the folders and returned to his desk.

'At present there are fourteen British Army battalions in Northern Ireland, each with approximately 650 men, each unit deployed in its own Tactical Area of Responsibility, or TAOR, known as a "patch". As the RUC's B Special Reserve were highly suspect in the eyes of the Republicans, their responsibilities have been handed over to the Ulster Defence Regiment, a reserve unit composed in the main of local part-timers. Unfortunately the UDR is already deeply unpopular with the Catholics, who view its members as hard-line loyalists. Most Army commanders are no more impressed by the UDR, believing, like me, that it's dangerous to let part-time Protestant reservists into hard Republican areas.'

'Are they reliable otherwise?' Ricketts asked.

'Many of us feel that the Royal Ulster Constabulary is more reliable than the UDR, though we certainly don't believe policemen are capable of taking complete charge of security. This is evidenced by the fact that RUC officers often refuse to accompany the Army on missions – either because they think it's too risky or because they feel that their presence would antagonize the locals even more than the Army does.'

'That sounds bloody helpful,' Jock McGregor said sourly.

'Quite. In fact, in strongly Republican areas the RUC have virtually ceded authority to us. They do, however, have two very important departments: the Criminal Investigations Department, or CID, in charge of interrogating suspects and gathering evidence after major incidents; and the Special Branch, or SB, which runs the informer networks vital to us all. They also have a Special Patrol Group, or SPG, with mobile anti-terrorist squads trained in the use of firearms and riot control. We can call upon them when necessary.'

'What about the police stations?' Lampton asked.

'Sixteen divisions – rather like Army battalions – in total. Some are grouped into each of three specific regions – Belfast, South and North – each with an assistant chief constable in charge, with as much authority as the Army's three brigadiers. Those three chief constables report in turn to the chief constable at RUC HQ at Knock, east Belfast.'

'Who calls the shots?' Jock McGregor asked.

'The regular Army and UDR battalions are divided between three brigade HQs – 29 Brigade in the Belfast area, 8 Brigade in Londonderry and 3 Brigade in Portadown, the latter responsible for covering the border. The Brigade Commanders report to the Commander Land Forces, or CLF, at Lisburn, the top Army man in Ulster. He has to answer to the General Officer Commanding, or GOC, who, though an Army officer, is also in charge of the RAF and Royal Navy detachments in the province. He's also responsible for co-ordination with the police and ministers. The HQNI, or Headquarters Northern Ireland, is located in barracks at Lisburn, a largely Protestant town just outside Belfast that includes the HQ of 39 brigade. Regarding the role of 14 Intelligence Company in all this, I'll hand you over to Captain Dubois.'

Slightly nervous about talking to a bunch of men who would feel resentful about working with the regular Army, Captain Dubois coughed into his fist before commencing.

'Good morning, gentlemen.' When most of the Troop just stared steadily at him, deliberately trying to unnerve him, he continued quickly: 'Like the SAS, 14 Intelligence Company is formed from soldiers who volunteer from other units and have to pass a stiff selection test. It recruits from the Royal Marines as well as the Army, though it looks for resourcefulness and the ability to bear the strain of long-term surveillance, rather than the physical stamina required for the Special Air Service.'

Applause, cheers and hoots of derision alike greeted Dubois' words. Still not used to the informality of the SAS, he glanced uncertainly at Cranfield, who grinned at him, amused by his nervousness.

'The unit has one detachment with each of the three brigades in Ulster,' Dubois continued. 'Each consists of twenty soldiers under the command of a captain. We operate under a variety of cover names, including the Northern Ireland Training Advisory Team, or NITAT, and the Intelligence and Security Group, or Int and Sy Group. Like the original MRF, most of our work involves setting up static OPs or the observation of suspected or known terrorists from unmarked Q cars. These have covert radios and concealed compartments for other weapons and photographic equipment. Most of the static OPs in Belfast are manned by our men and located in both Republican and Loyalist areas, such as Shankill, the Falls Road and West Belfast's Turf Lodge and the Creggan. You men will be used mainly for OPs in rural areas and observation and other actions in Q cars here in Belfast. You will, in effect, be part of 14 Intelligence Company, doing that kind of work, initially under our supervision, then on your own.'

'Armed?' Danny Porter asked quietly.

'Yes. With weapons small enough to be concealed. These include the 9mm Browning High Power handgun and, in certain circumstances, small sub-machine-guns.'

'What's our brief regarding their use?'

'Your job is observation, not engagement, though the latter isn't always avoidable. Bear in mind that you won't be able to pass yourselves off as locals, eavesdropping in Republican bars or clubs. Try it and you'll soon attract the curiosity of IRA sympathizers, some as young as fourteen, looking as innocent as new-born babies, but almost certainly in the IRA youth wing. If one of those innocents speaks to you, you can rest assured that he'll soon be followed by a hard man of more mature years. Shortly after the hard man comes the coroner.'

Thankfully, the men laughed at Dubois' sardonic remark, encouraging him to continue in a slightly more relaxed manner.

'For that reason we recommend that you don't leave your Q car unless absolutely necessary. We also recommend that you don't try using an Irish accent. If you're challenged, say no more than: "Fuck off!" And say it with conviction.' When the men laughed again, Dubois said: 'I know it sounds funny, but it's actually the only phrase that might work. Otherwise, you cut out of there.'

'At what point do we use our weapons?' the new man, Martin Renshaw, boldly asked.

'When you feel that your life is endangered and there's no time to make your escape.'

'Do we shoot to kill?' 'Baby Face' asked.

'Shooting to wound is a risky endeavour that rarely stops a potential assassin,' Lieutenant Cranfield put in. 'You shoot to stop the man coming at you, which means you can't take any chances. Your aim is to down him.'

'Which means the heart.'

'Yes, Trooper.'

'Is there actually a shoot-to-kill policy?' Ricketts asked.

Captain Dubois smiled tightly. 'Categorically not. Let's say, instead, that there's a contingency policy which covers a fairly broad range of options. I should remind you, however, that the IRA don't always display our restraint. London's policy of minimum fire-power, rejecting the use of ground- or air-launched missiles, mines, heavy machine-guns and armour, has contained the casualty figures to a level which no other government fighting a terrorist movement has been able to match. On the other hand, the Provisional IRA alone presently has at least 1200 active members and they've been well equipped by American sympathizers with a few hundred fully automatic 5.6mm Armalites and 7.62mm M60 machine-guns, as well as heavier weapons, such as the Russian-made RPG 7 short-range anti-tank weapon with rocket-propelled grenades. So let's say we have reasonable cause to believe in reasonable force.'

'Does reasonable force include the taking out of former IRA commanders?' Sergeant 'Dead-eye Dick' Parker asked abruptly.

'Pardon?' Dubois asked, looking as shocked as Cranfield suddenly felt.

'I'm referring to the fact that a few days ago a former IRA commander, Shaun O'Halloran, was taken out by an unknown assassin, or assassins, while sitting in his own home in the Irish Republic.'

Already knowing that his assassination of O'Halloran had rocked the intelligence community, as well as outraging the IRA, but not aware before now that it had travelled all the way back to Hereford, Cranfield glanced at Dubois, took note of his flushed cheeks, and decided to go on the attack.

'Are you suggesting that the SAS or 14 Intelligence Company had something to do with that?' he addressed Parker, feigning disbelief.

Parker, however, was not intimidated. 'I'm not suggesting anything, boss,' he replied in his soft-voiced manner. 'I'm merely asking if such an act would be included under reasonable force?'

'No,' Captain Dubois intervened, trying to gather his wits together and take control of the situation.

'I deny that categorically. And as you said, the assassin was unknown.'

'The IRA are claiming it was the work of the SAS.'

'The IRA blame us for a lot of things,' Cranfield put in, aware that Parker was not a man to fool with.

'Is it true,' Ricketts asked, 'that they also blame the SAS for certain actions taken by 14 Intelligence Company?'

When he saw Dubois glance uneasily at him, Cranfield deliberately covered his own temporary nervousness by smiling as casually as possible at Ricketts, who was, he knew, as formidable a soldier as Parker. 'Yes,' he said, 'that's true. It's a natural mistake to make. They know we're involved in surveillance, so that makes us suspect.'

'Who do you think was responsible for the assassination of O'Halloran?'

The questioner was Sergeant Parker again, studying Dubois with his steady, emotionless gaze. Dubois reddened and became more visibly flustered until rescued by Cranfield, who said: 'O'Halloran's assassination wasn't in keeping with the psychological tactics employed by the Regiment in Malaya and Oman. More likely, then, it was committed by one of the paramilitary groups – possibly even the product of internal conflict between warring IRA factions. It certainly wasn't an example of what the SAS – or 14

Intelligence Company – means by "reasonable force".'

'But the IRA,' Parker went on in his quietly relentless way, 'have hinted that O'Halloran may have been involved with a British army undercover agent, Corporal Phillips, who recently committed suicide for unexplained reasons.'

'Corporal Phillips is believed to have been under considerable stress,' Captain Dubois put in quickly, 'which is not unusual in this line of business. May we go on?'

Sergeant Parker stared hard at the officer, but said no more.

'Good,' Dubois went on, determined to kill the subject. 'Perhaps I should point out, regarding this, that while occasionally we may have to resort to physical force, only one in seven of the 1800 people killed in the Province have died at the hands of the security forces, which total around 30,000 men and women at any given time. I think that justifies our use of the phrase "reasonable force".'

Dubois glanced at Lieutenant Cranfield, who stepped forward again.

'We have it on the best of authority that the British government is about to abandon the special category status that's allowed convicted terrorists rights not enjoyed by prisoners anywhere else in the United Kingdom. Under the new rules, loyalist and republican terrorists in the newly built H-blocks at the Maze Prison will be treated as ordinary felons.

The drill parades and other paramilitary trappings that have been permitted in internment camps will no longer be allowed. This is bound to become a major issue in the nationalist community and increase the activities of the IRA. For that reason, I would ask you to remember this. In the past two decades the IRA have killed about 1800 people, including over a hundred citizens of the British mainland, about eight hundred locals, nearly three hundred policemen and 635 soldiers. Make sure you don't personally add to that number.'

He waited until his words had sunk in, then nodded at Captain Dubois.

'Please make your way to the motor pool,' Dubois told the men. 'There you'll find a list containing the name of your driver and the number of your Q car. Your first patrol will be tomorrow morning, just after first light. Be careful. Good luck.'

Still holding their manila folders in their hands, the men filed out of the briefing room, leaving Captain Dubois and Lieutenant Cranfield alone. When the last of the SAS troopers and Sergeant Lovelock had left, Dubois removed a handkerchief from his pocket and wiped sweat from his forehead.

'That was close,' he said. 'Damn it, Cranfield, I knew we shouldn't have done it.'

'Small potatoes,' Cranfield replied, though he didn't feel as confident as he sounded. 'The Irish eat lots of those.'

# 4

They left the camp at dawn, driving out through the high, corrugated-iron gates, between the two heavily reinforced sangars and, just beyond them, on both sides, the perimeter lights and coils of barbed wire. The gates whined electronically as they opened and shut. The car's exit, Martin knew, was being observed and noted by the guard in the operations room via the closed-circuit TV camera. Even before the gates had closed behind the car, the driver was turning into the narrow country road that would take them on the picturesque, winding, five-mile journey through the morning mist to the M1.

Martin had been very impressed with the previous day's briefing and now, sitting in the rear seat beside Gumboot, he was excited and slightly fearful, even though he had his 9mm Browning High Power handgun in the cross-draw position (in a Len Dixon holster over the rib cage, with four 13-round magazines) and had been shown where the other weapons were concealed.

Also concealed was a Pace Communications Landmaster III hand-held transceiver with a webbing harness, miniature microphone, earphone and encoder, located near the floor between the two front seats; and a 35mm Nikon F-801 camera with a matrix metering system, sophisticated autofocus, electronic rangefinder and long exposure. It was hidden under the Ordnance Survey map of Belfast that was spread for the purpose over Ricketts's lap.

The Q car had been specially adapted to carry a variety of concealed non-standard-issue weapons, including the short, compact Ingram 9mm sub-machine-gun with detachable suppressor and pull-out shoulder-and-hip stock, ideal for anti-terrorist work.

All of the men in the car were wearing the same scruffy civilian clothing that they had worn on the night ferry.

As their driver, Sergeant Lovelock, took the A1, which led all the way to the heart of Republican Belfast, Martin unholstered the Browning and held it on his lap, as he had been instructed, hiding it under a folded newspaper. Nevertheless, he held it at the ready, with his thumb on the safety-catch and his trigger finger resting on the trigger guard.

It was an early morning in January, and there was a heavy layer of frost on the ground, with spikes of ice hanging dramatically from the wintry trees. The windscreen was filthy and frosted over again even as it was wiped clean by the automatic wipers. The motorway ran straight as an arrow between hills covered with grass and gorse, on which cows and sheep roamed, disturbed only by the AH-7 Lynx helicopters rising and falling over the Army OPs.

'The early morning resups,' Sergeant Lovelock explained. 'Men and supplies. Don't fancy static OPs myself, stuck up there for hours, either sweltering in the heat or freezing your nuts off under all that turf and netting. Not my idea of fun.'

'You're the man who gave us the manila folders at the meeting,' Ricketts said.

'You're not blind,' Lovelock replied.

'You prefer being in a Q car?' Ricketts asked him.

'That's for sure. I like being able to move around instead of just waiting for something to happen. When my time comes, you can bury me in an OP, but not before then. So what's it like in the SAS?'

'It's great.'

'You guys get to a lot of exciting places.'

Ricketts chuckled. 'Right. Like Belfast. So what do *you* think about the SAS? Does it bother you to have to work with us?'

'Not at all. In fact, I was thinking of applying when I get posted back to the mainland. I was in the Queen's Royal Lancers before being transferred to the Intelligence Corps, posted here for special duties, which meant 14 Intelligence Company. It's OK, but I need something with a little more variety. If your Lieutenant Cranfield's anything to go by, you guys must be all you're cracked up to be. Cranfield's like fucking James Bond! A real tough guy.'

A couple of Saracen armoured trucks, bristling with weapons and troops, passed the Q car, heading the other way, back to Bessbrook.

'A good officer,' Ricketts said. 'Being in Intelligence yourself, you probably appreciate the type.'

'We're not as free and easy in the Army as you are in the SAS. That's the difference between Captain Dubois and your Lieutenant Cranfield, as you probably noticed. Dubois's a good officer, but he tends to take his job pretty seriously. Cranfield, though good as well, is a lot more informal and headstrong. His SAS training, right?'

'More to do with his personality, I'd think,' Ricketts said, glancing at Gumboot and Martin in the mirror and receiving a wink from the first. 'Though he is, undoubtedly, quite a character and well known to be headstrong.'

From Gumboot's wink and Ricketts's tone, Martin sensed that Ricketts was leading to something specific.

'Absolutely,' Lovelock replied. 'Enough to have taken out that fucking IRA tout, no matter what he told you. Christ, Dubois' face was a picture. He *knows* it wasn't the IRA!'

'Is that the word about the place – that Cranfield did it?'

'Sure is. Him and Dubois and a couple of 14 Intelligence Company sergeants, they went out there and took him out. They did it for Phillips and the ten sources knocked off by the IRA. It was a pure revenge hit.'

'That isn't like the SAS,' Ricketts said.

'It's like Cranfield,' Lovelock insisted. 'Believe me, he did it – which is why Dubois was shitting himself when your friend raised the subject.'

'But Cranfield has never admitted he did it.'

'Of course not. He'd be in deep shit if he did. The killing has incensed the IRA and brought a lot of flak down on 14 Intelligence Company in general and the SAS in particular. That's why Dubois and Cranfield can't admit that they did it.'

'So what makes a lot of people think they did it?'

'Because Cranfield and Dubois have often sneaked across the border to snatch members of the IRA and bring them back to be captured, as it were, by the RUC. It's illegal, but they do it. Combine that knowledge with the fact that Cranfield was openly stating that he was going to avenge the suicide of Phillips, as well as the death of his ten sources and . . . Well, what would *you* think?'

'I'd keep my thoughts to myself,' Ricketts replied.

'OK, Sarge, point taken.'

As they neared Belfast, a stretch of mountain loomed up out of the mist. Ricketts checked his

OS map, looked back up at the mountain and said, 'Divis, known locally as the Black Mountain.' Lovelock nodded his agreement as he left the motorway and entered Westlink.

'So this is the guided tour,' he said. 'We're now heading for the Grosvenor Road roundabout. When we get there, we'll drive along Grosvenor Road, past the Royal Victoria Hospital – where most of the kneecapped or otherwise wounded get treated – then head up the Springfield Road towards Turf Lodge, the heart of "Provo Land" – if it has a heart, that is.'

'It's that bad?'

'Fucking right. This is the worst killing ground in Europe and don't ever forget it.'

'What are the rules regarding the killings?'

'There aren't any. Though oddly enough, the Provos are more controlled than the Prods. The IRA are pretty methodical about who they kill or torture, whereas the loyalists tend to work on impulse – usually when they're angry. When they go for it, any victim will do – an innocent shopper, a teenager idling on a street corner, a pensioner in the bookie's – anyone convenient enough to be snatched. As for IRA tortures, they can't be any worse than what loyalists do with baseball bats, butcher's knives, or blowtorches. We find the victims hanging from fucking rafters and they're never a pretty sight. Freedom fighters? Don't even mention that word to me. These bastards are terrorists and psychopaths and should all be put down.'

Lovelock stopped the car at the Grosvenor Road roundabout, which was already busy. Eventually, when he had a clear run, he slipped into the traffic and turned into Grosvenor Road itself. Almost immediately, they passed a police station and regular Army checkpoint, surrounded by high, sandbagged walls and manned by heavily armed soldiers, all wearing DPM (Disruptive Pattern Material) clothing, helmets with chin straps and standard-issue boots. Apart from the private manning the 7.62mm L4 Light Machine Gun, the soldiers were carrying M16 rifles and had stun and smoke grenades on their webbing. The Q car was allowed to pass without being stopped. Further on, a soldier with an SA-80 assault rifle was keeping a Sapper covered while the latter carefully checked the contents of a rubbish bin. 'The Provos have Russian-manufactured RPG 7s,' Lovelock explained, 'which fire rocket-propelled grenades up to about 500 metres. The Provos use them mainly against police stations, army barracks and armoured "pigs" – they're troop carriers – and Saracen armoured cars. They also command-detonate dustbins filled with explosives from across the waste ground, which is why that Sapper's checking all the bins near the police station and the checkpoint. Usually, when explosives are placed in dustbins, it's done during the night, so the Sappers check this area every morning.'

Glancing out of his window, Martin saw that they were passing an enormous Victorian building on the left. When they reached the entrance, which was guarded by RUC officers wearing flak jackets and carrying the ubiquitous 5.56mm Ruger Mini-14 assault rifle, he saw ambulances inside and realized that it was the Royal Victoria Hospital.

'There it is,' Lovelock said sardonically. 'Kneecap Heaven. Go in there and you'll find them sitting or lying on stretchers, just waiting their turn. It's a daily occurrence – just part of the way of life here. It's fucking amazing what those bastards do to their own kind.'

'I thought they only did it to touts and other kinds of traitors,' Martin said, his curiosity aroused.

'No,' Lovelock said. 'They do it for a lot of things. Not wanting cops on their turf, the paramilitaries keep their own law, which means punishing car thieves, burglars, sex offenders, or so-called traitors in their own, rough fashion. Fuck, man, the people in these ghettos are so terrified of the IRA that when they receive a visit from them, saying they have to report for punishment, they actually go to the place selected for punishment of their own accord. Knowing what's going to happen to them, they sometimes try to anaesthetize themselves beforehand by getting pissed or bombed out on Valium. I mean, the whole business has become so routine, so *commonplace*, that the victims are even allowed to remove their pants or other clothing so they won't be damaged by the bullets. When the punishment's over, the paramilitaries will even call for an ambulance to take you away. You end up in that hospital, and often get compensation from the British government. If you do, you receive another visit from the guys who kneecapped you, demanding part of your compensation. Naturally, you hand it over with a big smile, before wobbling back to your bed of pain and nursing your wounds.'

This part of Belfast looked like London after the Blitz: rows of terraced houses with their doors and windows bricked up and gardens piled high with rubble. The pavements outside the pubs and certain shops were barricaded with large concrete blocks and sandbags. The windows were caged in heavy-duty wire netting as protection against car bombs and petrol bombers.

'OK,' Lovelock said. 'A few words of warning before we get into bandit country. Everything that Captain Dubois told you yesterday was true, but here's some more to remember. You can't leave a car in the streets. If you do, either it'll be vandalized by the kids; stolen for joyriding or to be sold or otherwise used by one of the paramilitary groups; or blown up by the Army because it might contain a bomb. Even if you leave it in a secure location, when returning to it you approach it from behind and bounce it on its springs, so as to trigger the small bomb that might have been planted under the driver's seat. Plan all journeys carefully before you leave and avoid enemy territory wherever possible. When driving, keep your windows locked at all times. If you're parked at a red light and someone approaches you, go through the red light and keep going until out of sight. If someone approaches you before you can move off, the only thing to say is: 'Fuck off!' If they don't, take off as quickly as possible. If you're in paramilitary territory and you knock someone down, don't stop. If you do, you'll be killed.'

The Grosvenor Road led across the Falls to Springfield, Ballymurphy and Turf Lodge, where everyone looked poor and suspicious, notably the gangs of young men – the 'dickers' – who stood menacingly on street corners, keeping their eyes out for newcomers or anything else they felt was threatening, particularly the SF patrols. Invariably, with the gangs, there were young people on crutches or with arms in slings, looking proud to be wounded.

'Have they been kneecapped?' Gumboot asked.

'Correct,' Lovelock replied. 'Look, you can even tell what kind of Catholic you're dealing with by checking just how he's been kneecapped. If it's a wound from a dainty little .22, which doesn't shatter bone, and it's either in a fleshy bit of the thigh or in the ankle, then the victim is only a minor thief or police informer. For something more serious he'll be shot in the back of the knee with a high-velocity rifle or pistol, which means the artery is severed and the kneecap blown right off. Now the six-pack, that's the major one, which makes you a real bad lot. With the six-pack he gets a bullet in each elbow, knee and ankle. That puts him on crutches for a long time and lets everyone see that he's a bad 'un. Now if that's what they can do to their own, what the hell do you think they're capable of when they drag an enemy, one of us, into an abandoned warehouse and string us up to the rafters for what they like to imagine is a bit of proper military interrogation?'

'I'd rather not dwell on it,' Martin said.

'Very wise,' Ricketts told him.

'Any quick way of telling the difference between Prods and Catholics?' Gumboot asked.

Lovelock laughed. 'Well, what can I say? A pigeon fancier is probably Protestant. A hurley player is definitely a Catholic, or Taig, as the Prods call them. Both sides play cricket, but only Orangemen are Rangers fans . . . and so on. You'll soon pick up the differences.'

He drove them around Turf Lodge to Andersonstown, then back to the Falls Road, the Provo heartland and one of the deadliest killing grounds in Northern Ireland – or anywhere else in the Western world. The streets of the 'war zone', as Lovelock called it, were clogged with armoured Land Rovers and forbidding army fortresses looming against the sky. British Army barricades, topped with barbed wire and protected by machine-gun crews atop Saracen armoured cars, were blocking off the entrance to many streets, with the foot soldiers well armed and looking like Martians in their DPM uniforms, boots, webbing, camouflaged helmets and chin-protectors. The soldiers were checking everyone entering the barricaded areas and, in many instances, taking them aside to search them roughly.

'This is the heaviest security I've ever seen,' Ricketts said. 'To find it on British soil is just unbelievable.'

'And that's only the *visible* presence,' Lovelock replied. 'There are also static OPs with high-power cameras on the roofs of distant skyscrapers, recording every movement in these streets. There are also spies in the ceilings of suspected IRA buildings and bugs on the telephones. Caught between us and the IRA, ever vigilant in their more direct way, the people in these streets have little privacy, which only makes them more paranoid.'

Looking out and instinctively tightening his grip on his Browning, Martin noticed that the traffic was heading towards the distant Cave Hill. The black taxis were packed with passengers too frightened to use public transport or walk. Grey-painted RUC mobiles and British Army 'pigs' were passing constantly. In both kinds of vehicles, the officers were scanning the upper windows and roofs on either side of the road, looking for possible sniper positions.

'Look at 'em,' Lovelock said, indicating the men and youths loitering on street corners, the overweight housewives trudging wearily in and out of shops, and the grubby children who were clambering over a burnt-out car, smashing its remaining windows with sticks and screaming like banshees. 'Most of 'em don't give a fuck about a United Ireland; they simply give in to the paramilitaries out of fear. Believe me, if you had a nationwide election, Sinn Fein wouldn't stand a prayer of a chance against Fine Gael or Fianna Fáil. If that happened, the Prods would come under the rule of Dublin conservatives who hate the IRA as much as they do. Unfortunately, the dumb fucks don't see it that way. The political wing of the IRA is fighting a centuries-old war and the Prods are convinced that if the IRA wins, they, the loyalists, will be left to the mercy of the bloodthirsty Micks. It's all paranoid nonsense.'

Eventually, Lovelock ended up at the junction of the Falls Road and Springfield Road, back near the Royal Victoria Hospital, where he stopped the car and said: 'Hand me that camera.' When Ricketts passed him the Nikon, he wound the window down and took a lot of shots of the group of youths loitering across the road. Some had long hair, some had heads closely shaven, and all wore an assortment of casual, tatty jackets and had trousers rolled up high enough to reveal their big, unpolished boots. They looked sullen and dangerous.

Lovelock lowered the camera just before one of the youths looked directly at the car, then said something to his mates, all of whom stopped talking to each other and glanced across the road.

'They've seen us,' Lovelock said. 'That's because of this bloody car. The presence of a strange vehicle in these areas is generally noticed quickly – particularly as we mainly use relatively new British-made saloons, which I think is plain stupid. Outsiders, even innocent civilians, also become prey to republican gun law when kids like that, often armed, hijack cars for use by the IRA or INLA, or simply for the thrill of joyriding. Those little fuckers are dangerous.'

'Will they come over to check us out?' Ricketts asked.

'I don't think this particular bunch will. I think they know who we are. If they do, it means they're not a bunch of innocent kids. It means they're dickers – the ones who keep a lookout for the security forces and pass the word on to their superiors. They're probably in the IRA youth wing. No, they're not coming. They've decided to piss off.'

When the youths had moved away, making obscene gestures at the car and shouting insults that Martin, for one, couldn't quite make out, Lovelock wound the window up, then turned down

Grosvenor Road, back to the neutral territory of the city centre.

'Weird, isn't it?' he said, glancing out at the people streaming along the pavements, ignoring the armed soldiers carefully watching them. 'Most of those people out there are on the dole, supported by British money. This whole province is flooded with hand-outs from the British government. It actually pours more cash into here than it does into England. This fucking place is awash with British money. In fact, the whole place would sink if the British government withdrew its support. So these bastards are fighting the very people who keep them afloat. It doesn't make much sense, does it?'

By the time they arrived at the Protestant Shankill district, in the late afternoon, it had begun to rain. The sky was grey, the buildings were grimy, and the roads were lined with shabby shops and people wearing generally dark, unattractive clothing.

At the bottom of Grosvenor Road Lovelock turned into Sandy Row, a stoutly Protestant area, where he stopped the car again. It was a busy road, lined on both sides with shops and pubs, the pavements bustling with down-at-heel shoppers and the same kind of loiterers who had been so prevalent in the Catholic ghettos. Lovelock remained there for ten minutes, just holding his camera at the ready, then suddenly he wound down the window and took several shots of two men entering a pub across the road.

'A UDR watering-hole,' he explained, lowering the camera again. 'Full of hard-line loyalists. They do as much damage as the IRA, so we have to keep tabs on the bastards. I'm here today because this is collection day and those two are collecting protection money for a loyalist splinter group. This whole fucking city thrives on protection rackets, just like Al Capone ran. Anyone in business in the ghettos has to contribute, whether they like it or not. Falls Road cabbies make weekly payments to the IRA. Prods in Shankill pay similar levies to the UFF or UDA. Likewise with the owners of pubs, shops, betting shops, and people in the building trade. Most of the latter are now totally dependent on the work brought in by restoring or rebuilding bombed-out premises. Take away the Troubles, and you remove the livelihood of half of the populace. Truth of the matter is, the Troubles will never end because there's just too much fucking money in it. United Ireland? Freedom for the Irish people? That's all bullshit. It comes down to hard cash.'

When the two men emerged from the pub again, Lovelock took some more pictures, then put the camera down and jotted details in his notebook, including the time. When he had finished, he wound up the window and drove off.

'Fuck this for a lark,' he said. 'Let's go back to the Falls and see if we can get something worthwhile.'

They left Sandy Row, took the Donegal Road, then cut through the Broadway until they were back in the Falls Road. Lovelock parked well away from a dismal block of flats, by a waste ground filled with rubbish, where mangy dogs and scruffy, dirt-smeared children were playing noisily. He lowered the window, took the camera from Ricketts, and pointed to the high roof of the block of flats, which looked like a prison gone to seed. There, on the roof, was a British Army OP, its high-power telescope scanning the many people who loitered on the balconies or on the ground below, one soldier manning a General Purpose Machine Gun, or GPMG, others holding their M16 rifles, with the barrels resting lightly on the sandbagged wall.

'As you can see, they all know they're under surveillance,' Lovelock said.

'Do those overt OPs do any good?' Ricketts asked.

'Yes. They're equipped with computers linked to vehicle registration and suspect-information centres, as well as state-of-the-art surveillance cameras. Also, their high visibility reminds everyone of our presence and therefore places certain constraints on them, while allowing members of regular units and 14 Intelligence Company to observe suspects and see who their associates are. This in turn allows the collators of intelligence at Lisburn and brigade headquarters – including your so-called green slime – to investigate links between meetings of particular individuals and subsequent terrorist activities.'

'Do those OPs have any back-up?' Ricketts asked.

'Yes. Each OP is backed up by another OP consisting of two to four soldiers and located near enough to offer immediate firearms support. Both OPS are in turn backed up by a QRF, or Quick Reaction Force, of soldiers or police, sometimes both, located at the nearest convenient SF base, which will respond immediately to a radio call for help. So, no, they're not alone.'

'It's still fucking dangerous,' Gumboot said.

'Here everything is,' Lovelock replied. 'It's not a place to take lightly.'

Even as he spoke, the barrel of a Webley pistol was poked through the open window by his face and a harsh, youthful Ulster voice yelled: 'Get out of that fucking car!'

# 5

Everyone froze. 'Get out of that fucking car!' the youth screamed again, still aiming the pistol at Lovelock, but also tugging frantically at the locked door with his free hand. As he did so, another youth, just as scruffy in bomber jacket, jeans and big boots, with his head shaved close to the skull to make him look more brutal than perhaps he was, rushed out from behind a mound of rubble and tried to tug Gumboot's door open. Finding it locked, he kicked the car in frustration.

'Fuck off!' Lovelock said and made to start the car, but was stopped when the first youth reached in, grabbed his wrist with one hand and shoved the barrel of the Webley pistol into his face. 'One move and you're dead, you English cunt. Now get out of that fucking car.'

Lovelock removed his hands from the steering wheel and glanced across the waste ground to see another couple of youths running out of the flats, silhouetted in evening light, heading straight for the car. Before long, this few could grow into a crowd.

'OK, OK,' Lovelock said with a sigh. 'My hands are off the wheel. What's the matter with you, lad? We just came to visit some friends on the Falls and we lost our way.'

'Fucking army shite!' The youth tugged at the door again.

'We're not soldiers,' Lovelock lied. 'We're English, but not soldiers. We work in the building trade and we've come over to visit some old mates. We just got lost and pulled in here to check the map. For Christ's sake, be careful with that gun.'

'You lyin' bastard. The English don't have friends in Divis.' The kid tugged at the door again while his friend repeatedly kicked the rear door in a fury of frustration. 'Now open this fucking door or I'll blow your brains out.'

Seeing that another couple of youths were following the ones already racing towards them, Lovelock opened the door and stepped out of the car. The kid with the gun grabbed him by the shoulder and slammed him back against the car, then reached down for the camera, saying: 'Get that fucking back door open as well.'

Gumboot glanced at Martin, who was flushed with excitement, then unlocked his door and pushed it open. Martin did the same on his side and started getting out, though Ricketts remained where he was seated. Gumboot was still clambering out, about to stand upright, when the excited youth by his door punched him violently in the face.

Gumboot turned away from the blow, catching it on his cheek, almost falling back, but managing to stay standing. The other youth was about to grab the camera when he saw Ricketts sliding the OS map off his legs to reveal the Browning High Power on his lap.

'Fuck!' Jerking back to straighten up and fire at Ricketts, the kid banged the back of his head on the door frame and yelped with pain as his mate was taking another punch at Gumboot. The kid with the pistol threw himself away from the door as Ricketts swung up his Browning and Gumboot cross-drew his from its holster and aimed it two-handed at his assailant.

As Lovelock jumped back into the driver's seat, Ricketts rolled backwards out of his side, the kid with the pistol aimed at the car, and the other started running away from Gumboot. Lovelock turned the ignition key and gunned the engine. Ricketts fired a burst single-handed at the kid with the Webley. The burst picked the kid up and flung him on his back even as Martin, feeling extraordinarily bright, steadied his wrists on the roof of the Q car and fired a burst two-handed over the heads of the youths racing to help their mates.

Gumboot let his assailant go, aware that he was unarmed, then he turned towards the youths whom Martin had fired at. Some were scattering, others flinging themselves to the ground. Gumboot fired over their heads to ram Ricketts's message home, then he and Ricketts dived simultaneously back into the car.

Martin just about managed to get back into his seat when Lovelock reversed at high speed, bouncing backwards up over the pavement and smashing into a wall, before doing a sharp, screeching U-turn and racing away from the flats.

'Shit!' he exclaimed.

Looking through the rear window, Martin saw the youths picking themselves up from the rubble and racing towards the one who had been shot by Ricketts. He was lying spread-eagled, not moving, his chest covered in blood.

'I didn't have a choice,' Ricketts said. 'He was aiming right at me.'

'Those fucking kids weren't amateurs,' Lovelock said. 'To see us that quickly the little pricks had to be on the look out. They were dickers.'

Still glancing back, Martin saw some of the youths hurling stones in frustration, knowing that they couldn't possibly hit the car, but feeling impelled to do something. Meanwhile, the others were gathering around the youth shot, and almost certainly killed, by Ricketts.

'Jesus!' Martin whispered.

'He won't help,' Gumboot informed him. 'The only thing that's gonna help us is to get the fuck out of here.'

Ricketts twisted in his seat to glance back over his shoulder as Lovelock took a corner, practically on two wheels. 'You were very good, Martin,' he said. 'You didn't put a foot wrong. You deliberately fired above their heads, didn't you?'

'Yes,' Martin said.

'You've just earned your badge.' Ricketts turned back to the front as Lovelock slowed down, trying to look like a normal driver, and edged into the Falls Road.

Looking out at the bricked-up doorways, boarded shop windows, wired, sandbagged pubs, weary pedestrians, heavily armed soldiers, flak-jacketed RUC officers, barricaded streets and gangs of watchful youths or screaming, destructive children, Martin thought of what Ricketts had said to him and swelled up with pride.

*You've just earned your badge*, he thought to himself.

'Fuck it,' Lovelock said. 'Those kids were on the look out. That means they were in the IRA youth wing and that means we have to know who they are. Did anyone get a good look at them?'

'I got a good look at the fucker who punched me in the face,' Gumboot said, instinctively rubbing his swollen cheekbone with his fingers. 'If I hadn't turned my head, he'd have taken out my teeth, so I'm certainly gonna remember the little shit. I *want* to remember him!'

'And the others?'

'They were close enough for me to recognize a few,' Ricketts said, amazing Martin with how steady he sounded so soon after having killed a man. 'If I saw them again, I could pick them out.'

'A line-up?'

'Sounds good,' Ricketts said.

'Right.' Lovelock, while driving with one hand, removed the Landmaster III transceiver from its webbed harness and contacted the local commander of the Springfield Road Barracks. When the commander identified himself with a broad Ulster accent, Lovelock told him about the incident and requested a sweep of the area to locate and bring in as many youths as possible for a line-up.

'Did you say one dead?' the commander responded.

'Yes,' Lovelock said. 'He was about to fire at us with a Webley pistol, so all options were closed.'

'That could cause a lot of trouble.'

'I repeat: there was no option. The youth was about to fire a round and there was no time for talk.'

'A youth?'

'Yes.'

'Not an adult.'

'No.'

'Are you certain he was dead?'

'Yes,' Ricketts said.

'Then we're in for some trouble.'

'Sorry,' Lovelock said, 'but we still need that sweep.'

'Be at Castlereagh at precisely eight this evening. Until then, stay low.'

'Right,' Lovelock said. 'Over and out.' He switched off the Landmaster III, returned it to its webbing, and checked his wristwatch while still driving along the Falls Road. 'That leaves us with two hours to kill,' he said, 'so what do we do?' When no one replied, he said: 'I have to have a talk with one of my touts, so let's head back to the centre of town. While I'm having my chat, you men can stay in the car and have your sandwiches and coffee. When I'm done, we'll come back here and see how the sweep's progressing, then go on to Castlereagh.'

'Are you fucking crazy?' Gumboot said. 'I mean, coming back here!'

'We'll be OK,' Lovelock said. 'By the time we get back here the sweep will be well under way and the fuckers on that estate will be too busy to take any notice of us. What do you say, Sarge?'

'I agree.'

Lovelock drove them to the centre of Belfast, then on to a pub opposite the Europa Hotel, which, having been bombed a few times, was now guarded like a military camp.

After parking, Lovelock nodded in the direction of the pub. 'It's a neutral pub that gets the fall-out from Sandy Row. I meet my loyalist tout in there. You can come with me, Ricketts.'

When he got out of the car, Ricketts did the same. Lovelock then opened the back door and indicated that Gumboot should get out too. When

Gumboot had done so, Lovelock said: 'Take the driver's seat. You get up front, as well, Martin. Just sit there, enjoying the view, having your hot tea and sandwiches. If you get checked by any army or RUC patrols – which almost certainly you will – show your ID. When they see it, they'll know you're in a Q car and leave you alone. On the other hand, if you're approached by anyone else – a civilian – be prepared for trouble. If you have to take off, give a long toot on your horn, so Ricketts and I will know you're going. If you take off, don't return for us; just go on to Castlereagh. Any questions?'

'Yeah,' Gumboot said, picking his wrapped sandwiches and vacuum flask off the back seat, slamming the door, then sliding into the driver's seat. 'What's in the sandwiches?'

'Mick turd with mayonnaise,' Lovelock said as Martin got out of the back, also holding a pack of sandwiches, and slipped into the seat beside Gumboot. 'Don't forget to keep the doors locked and the windows wound up. If you see anything of interest, the camera's in the glove compartment. The transceiver's on the floor between you. Enjoy your meal, men.'

'Don't drink on duty,' Martin said with a grin.

'Wouldn't dream of it,' Ricketts replied. 'But if I have to have one in the line of duty, I'll be thinking of you.'

'Fuck off,' Gumboot said.

Ricketts automatically checked that his Browning was well concealed beneath his jacket as he followed Lovelock into the pub. It was an expansive Victorian place with lots of tiles, mahogany and stained-glass windows. It had a long bar and plenty of tables spaced well apart. There were few people at the tables and only one man was sitting on a bar stool – at the end near the entrance.

Leading Ricketts up to the middle of the bar, Lovelock loudly asked him what he'd like to drink. The authenticity of his Ulster accent took Ricketts by surprise, but he managed to hide it and ordered a pint of Guinness in low tones. Lovelock ordered the same for himself, still speaking loudly and like an Ulsterman. He glanced at the lone man near the entrance, then paid the barman, handed Ricketts his Guinness, and led him to a table in the far corner of the pub, where a middle-aged man in oily overalls was savouring a whisky while reading the *Belfast Telegraph*.

'It's no use pretending to read, Norman, I know damned well you can't.'

The man looked up, glanced at his wristwatch, then said without a trace of irony: 'Have you arrived?'

'I have.' Lovelock took the chair beside the man, which meant he could keep his eyes on the entrance. He nodded for Ricketts to take the seat at the other side of him, which placed him in view of the toilets and, possibly, the back door. 'This is an English friend, Phil Ricketts. We used to work together in London, before I saw sense and came home. Phil, this is Norman Reid.'

Ricketts nodded.

'Nice to meet ya, Phil. First time in Belfast?'

'Yes,' Ricketts said.

'A queer wee place, right?'

'It takes some getting used to.'

'What's that you're drinking?' Lovelock asked, still using his Ulster accent, but more softly now.

'Bushmills.'

'A dangerous brew.'

'Ach, well, sure it warms the stomach on a winter's evening.' He had another sip, then glanced at the man sitting at the bar near the entrance. 'Now mind what yer sayin'. That one at the end of the bar is from Sandy Row. Be natural, but keep yer voice low, and he won't hear from here.'

'UDA?'

Reid nodded. 'He's an ijit, but he lives for the cause and is here for the money.'

'Protection?'

'Aye. But he's also here to check out who comes in and he can be right nasty. A dunderhead, but dangerous.'

'Anything to tell me?'

'You heard about the shootin' up near Divis?'

'News travels fast.'

'It does in this wee city. They say the Mick was shot by men in plain clothes and now the

Army are sweeping the area for the other lads involved.'

'The men in plain clothes weren't identified?'

'Na. But no doubt you have yer own ideas.'

'Not so far,' Lovelock said.

'So how'd ya hear about it so quickly, like?'

'We heard it over our car radio. So what's happening down Sandy Row way?'

'They're tickled pink over the fact that another Mick has been killed by the Army.'

'Unidentified,' Lovelock reminded him.

'Aye, unidentified – like an Army Q car's unidentified. They all know it was Army. They think it'll lead to Provisional IRA retaliation, which will give them an excuse for another bloodbath. They're all sittin' down there oilin' their guns with big grins on their mugs. It's as good as the killin' of O'Halloran, they say, so you can expect a wee comeback for that.'

'What kind of comeback?'

'Comeback in kind. I'd say the Micks will go for Lieutenant Cranfield, so he'd best watch his wee English arse. He's done youse all some damage, like.'

Reid talked for another twenty or minutes or so, giving Lovelock an update on what was happening in the pubs of Sandy Row between the members of the UDA and other Protestant paramilitary groups. He passed no written information to Lovelock, but dropped a few names for him to place watches on, with details of where they were most likely to be found. When he had finished, Lovelock thanked him, finished his beer, then left the pub with Ricketts, walking past the UDA man sitting at the bar and keeping his eye on the door. The man studied them carefully as they left, but was distracted when another customer entered, allowing Lovelock and Ricketts to leave without questioning.

The Q car was still parked outside, with Gumboot and Martin, having finished their sandwiches and tea, studying the busy road in a bored manner. Darkness had fallen and the street lights were on, as were the headlights of the many cars and buses of the rush-hour traffic. Across the road, the lights of the Europa Hotel burned brightly, beaming down over the fenced-in courtyard and the huts of the private security guards.

Lovelock knocked on the side window of the car with his knuckles, then jerked his thumb towards the rear. 'OK,' he said, 'out!' Gumboot opened the door, clambered out and got in the back as Lovelock took his place in the driver's seat. Martin did likewise, allowing Ricketts to sit beside Lovelock. 'Any problems?' Lovelock asked, turning on the ignition.

'No problems,' Gumboot said, 'but we were questioned by RUC and Army patrols every ten or fifteen minutes. In fact, every patrol that passed stopped to question us.'

'They would. You can't sit in a parked car in Belfast without being questioned. They were OK when you showed them your ID?'

'Yeah, no bother. They just tipped their peaked caps and moved on. All very polite, like.'

'You're beginning to sound Irish already, like.'

Gumboot grinned. 'It's contagious, like.'

Glancing constantly back over his shoulder, Lovelock edged into the dense traffic, cut through to Bedford Street, then drove down Dublin Road. At Shaftesbury Square he turned into Donegal Road and drove from there, through Broadway, to the Falls Road, which, in the darkness, illuminated by the street lights, looked even more dangerous than it had during the day.

The gangs of men, young and old, standing on street corners seemed larger, with many drinking from cans or bottles and clearly aggressive. The bricked-up doorways and boarded-up windows were only rendered more ominous by the light-streaked darkness. Children smashing parked cars without reprimand from frightened passers-by seemed like scavenging animals. The RUC officers in their flak jackets and the heavily armed soldiers at the sandbagged barracks and barricaded streets, all watchful, never smiling, seemed like faceless men in a bad dream.

Even before the tower block came into view, the crimson glow of flames was illuminating the dark, cloudy sky and the sound of sporadic gunfire could be heard. When Lovelock finally turned off the Falls Road and reached the spot where they had almost been hijacked, they saw mobiles and foot patrols trawling the flats, which were being swept eerily by spotlights. The red glow in the sky came from a series of bonfires deliberately started to block the paths of the mobiles and Saracens, as well as frustrate the charges of the soldiers in flak jackets, perspex-visored riot helmets and reinforced leg and arm shields.

Other fires were caused by the Molotov cocktails being thrown by gangs of teenage dickers. People were screaming when struck by rubber bullets. Others were racing out of clouds of CS gas with eyes streaming. Housewives were drumming bin lids on the concrete floors and balconies, children and youths were throwing stones and dropping bricks on the mobiles thwarted by the bonfires, and unseen men were sniping on the soldiers keeping watch while their mates smashed in doors with sledgehammers and dragged out kicking, punching youths for transportation to the detention block at Castlereagh.

'It's a fucking nightmare,' Gumboot said in the back of the parked car as they watched the distant soldiers drag struggling youths from the walkways of the tower block to the waiting RUC vans. By now, however, the youths' ankles were chained together to prevent them from kicking out or running away.

'This is just another night in Belfast,' Lovelock corrected him sardonically. 'See that,' he added, pointing to where the youths were being practically dragged to the waiting vans. 'The housewives here talk about how they've been handcuffed by the feet. It's a wonderful language.'

'We'd better get to Castlereagh,' Ricketts said.

'I think you're right, Sarge.'

Lovelock turned the car around and drove away from the hellish scene, out of the Falls, back through the city centre, across the Albert Bridge, then along the A23 to Castlereagh.

Arriving at the detention barracks just before 8 p.m., they were directed to the rear of the building by an armed, uniformed RUC guard. Lovelock parked the car in what looked like an enormous yard, like an empty car park, with a high brick wall running along one end. He turned the ignition off, then the headlights, leaving them in almost total darkness.

'Now we wait,' he said, checking his watch. 'It should start any minute now.'

Suddenly, a series of arc lights flared into life along the top of the wall the car was facing, bathing the wall and the ground in front in a dazzling white light. Less than a minute later, a couple of armed RUC officers emerged from a door at one end of the wall to take up positions at both ends of the wall, about twenty feet away, covering it with their 5.56mm Ruger Mini-14 assault rifles. When they were in position, first one, then two, then a whole group of dishevelled youths were coaxed out through the door and along the base of the wall by another RUC officer. When some of the youths, either blinded by the light or frightened, took a step back, the RUC officer prodded them forward with his baton. If this failed, he gave them a light blow with it, and this always worked. Eventually the youths, nearly a dozen, were standing along the whole length of the wall, an equal distance apart, figures in an eerily dreamlike chiaroscuro.

'Well?' Lovelock asked. 'Who do we recognize?'

'That little bastard who punched me,' Gumboot said. 'Fifth from the left.'

'Good,' Lovelock said. 'Anyone else?'

'Yes,' Ricketts said. 'I recognize two of the bunch we fired at.'

'Any more?'

'No.'

'Right,' Lovelock said. 'When they step forward, tap me on the shoulder and I'll toot my horn.'

At a barked command from the RUC officer with the baton, the youth who had been first out of the doorway and was now standing at the far left of the line, stepped forward, where he could be seen more clearly. The RUC officer glanced at the car parked in darkness, outside the range of the arc lights. He heard no toot, and ordered the first youth back against the wall, before calling out the second youth. When there was still no response, he ordered the third youth to step forward. When Lovelock tooted his horn, the youth was dragged out of the line-up and led through the doorway by another armed guard. This process continued until Lovelock tooted his horn again and another youth was pulled out of the line-up and taken away. When the third youth was identified and led away, the parade continued until the last youth had stepped forward and been ordered back. Then the remaining members of the line-up were marched back through the doorway for release and return to Belfast.

When the last of the RUC officers had followed the young men through the door, the arc lights blinked out, plunging the wall back into pitch darkness.

'I think we've all earned a beer,' Lovelock said. 'Your first day is finished, lads.'

He turned the car around and drove them back through the dark, stormy night to the camp at Bessbrook.

# 6

Wearing civilian clothing, but with two different sets of ID papers – one genuine, the other false ones for a fictitious Ulster resident – and with his Browning holstered in the cross-draw position under his coat, Lieutenant Cranfield drove halfway along the Falls Road in a car with Belfast number plates. He parked near the Broadway, checked his watch and waited patiently for his tout to arrive.

The Falls was a lot quieter than it had been yesterday when, after the shooting, the commander of the Springfield Road Barracks had instigated a cordon-and-search sweep of the area, thus sparking off another riot on the block of flats on the Divis estate, with the usual bonfires, hurled stones and drumming bin lids. As the dead youth was only sixteen years old, the republican papers had been filled with the usual sanctimonious outrage, including demands for the boy's 'murderer' to be brought to justice. That so-called 'murderer', as Cranfield knew, was the excellent Sergeant Phil Ricketts.

*Well*, Cranfield thought with a grin, *young Martin Renshaw certainly had an interesting first day in Belfast.*

As was customary, when the various Q-car teams had returned to the camp, they had first signed in their weapons, then reported to Captain Dubois and Lieutnant Cranfield in the briefing room. The meeting with Lovelock, Ricketts, Gumboot and young Renshaw had been more tense than most, particularly when Ricketts confessed that he was the unidentified man who had shot and killed the youth on the Divis estate.

Luckily, by the time of that meeting, Dubois had already received identification of the victim, passed it on to Intelligence, and learnt from them that he was an active member of the IRA youth wing. Naturally, this fact would be denied by the IRA, who would want to use the kid's 'murder' for all the propaganda value they could wring from it. Ricketts, a smart man, had been concerned about that possibility, but Cranfield had put him at his ease, accepting that he'd had no choice in the matter and noting in his report that Sergeant Lovelock and the others present had confirmed that this was indeed the case.

Now, gazing across the Falls Road to see the usual sorry mixture of armed soldiers, sullen or taunting youths, screeching children, and wearily shopping housewives, all rendered more depressing in the grey afternoon light, Cranfield, though vigilant and wary, was at ease with himself. His men, he felt, had behaved impeccably in a bad situation. Contrary to the concern expressed by the overly concerned Captain Dubois, the SAS men had done what was necessary.

Five minutes later, dead on time, Cranfield's tout, Michael O'Leary, slipped into the car and said tersely: 'OK, take off.' Cranfield pulled out into the traffic and headed along the Falls Road, away from the Broadway. 'No camera,' O'Leary said. 'No notebook. Drive slowly, but steadily. Don't slow down when I point anything out. Understood?'

'Yes,' Cranfield said.

It annoyed him that O'Leary should give him this redundant advice when they'd done this so many times. On the other hand, the Irishman was probably more nervous than usual.

Still a member of the provisional IRA, O'Leary had been the bookkeeper for his local wing and started fiddling the books when he became involved with an exceptionally attractive, financially demanding lady named Margaret Dogherty. O'Leary was a sexually inexperienced bachelor who couldn't believe his luck when he met Margaret in his favourite Republican club and ended up in her bed. Margaret was not only beautiful, but superb in bed. O'Leary was soon head-over-heels in love and half out of his mind with desire.

Margaret, however, liked the good life and O'Leary had to pay for it, which led to his 'borrowing' from the funds of his local PIRA branch. When he found he couldn't replace the money, he 'borrowed' more and tried to recoup his loss at the bookie's. When this didn't work, he kept borrowing until he was in so deep, he was desperate. Finally, when it was time for an audit of the books and he knew his thefts would be revealed to his PIRA superiors, he tearfully confided in Margaret, who introduced him to a man who could help him.

This man turned out to be a member of British Intelligence, MI5, who had put Margaret on to O'Leary in the first place. MI5 agreed to repay O'Leary before the audit and also finance him on a regular basis in the future on the grounds that he 'turn' and become their tout. Terrified of being punished by PIRA – which for his offence could have been terminal after torture – and also still besotted with Margaret, who was in fact a high-class prostitute operating out of Dublin, O'Leary agreed.

Nevertheless, he was still a troubled man, knowing that the longer he touted, the greater were his chances of being discovered. When the affair with Margaret abruptly ended – having done her job, she returned to Dublin – O'Leary, no longer blinded by love, had become even more frightened. As he had told Cranfield over the phone, he wanted to be 'lifted out' and given a new identity, in return for which he would give Cranfield a 'big one'. He was going to do so today, which is why he was nervous.

'Has it been arranged?' he asked as they drove up the Falls Road.

'It's been agreed,' Cranfield replied. 'We just need to know your final destination and when you want it to be.'

'Australia.'

'Whereabouts?'

'Anywhere.'

'When?'

'Two weeks, like.'

'Why wait that long?'

'I have to have a yarn with someone in Dublin.'

Cranfield smiled. *How wondrous is love*, he thought. 'That could be leaving it too long,' he said, 'if you're as concerned as you sounded on the phone. *Are* you that concerned?'

'Yeah.'

'Why?'

'I think they suspect me. I've been seen in too many places with m'girlfriend, spending the kind of loot I shouldn't have. Sooner or later, they'll want t'know where I got it.'

'If that's true, you better leave next week.'

'I have to have m'wee yarn first.'

Cranfield shrugged. 'As you wish. Two weeks from today?'

'Aye,' O'Leary said, scanning the busy pavements on both sides of the road. 'That'll do a treat.'

They were silent for a moment, then Cranfield asked: 'So, what's the big one?'

'You,' O'Leary replied without the slightest trace of irony. 'They believe you're the one who copped O'Halloran and they're goin' t'get ya.'

'What makes them think I did it?'

'Ach, come on, man! They know you and Dubois have often crossed the border to snatch men and bring 'em back t'the RUC. Knowing that, they figured it had t'be you who did O'Halloran in. If it *wasn't* you, it doesn't matter a damn. They want a high profile and you've got it; so it's you they'll be gunnin' for. It's also retaliation fer that lad shot dead yesterday.'

'Do they have a suspect for that?'

'Na,' O'Leary said. 'They just talk about the British bastard and say he was one of yours – SAS, like.'

The car had stopped at traffic lights and Cranfield glanced out at a group of men and youths loitering threateningly on the street corner, outside a betting shop that had windows caged in heavy-duty wire netting. When Cranfield noticed that one of the men was on crutches, he felt distinctly uneasy and was glad when the car moved on through the lights. 'So what are you offering?'

'The gits chosen t'hit ya.'

'All of them?'

'Aye. It's a PIRA Active Service Unit of four men. Part of the wing I keep the books for. They're the ones that took out your ten sources before Phillips killed himself. You've been wanting them anyway.'

'Damn, yes!' Cranfield whispered.

'The leader, Michael Quinn, lives right opposite me. He and the others meet reg'larly in his house. When they're not there, they're usually in the streets spyin' an' accusin', holdin' summary trials in back rooms, or personally supervisin' the punishments. I'll point them out to ya. Ya can't take pictures or be seen jottin' notes, so remember their mugs as best ya can.'

'I want more than that.'

'Yer goin' t'get it. Just bide yer time.'

When they stopped at the next traffic lights, O'Leary said: 'Have a look at that bunch on the corner without makin' it obvious. D'ya see them?'

Cranfield turned his head left while ostensibly scratching his right cheek. He saw a bunch of men on the street corner. Four were in their teens, all with short-cropped hair, dressed in the usual scruffy bomber jackets, jeans and big boots, and drinking from cans of extra-strong beer. They were listening intently, nervously, to a man in a soiled gaberdine raincoat. Grey-haired and with a hard, angry face, he was jabbing his forefinger at them as he spoke.

'Yes,' Cranfield said, 'I see them.'

'Four kids and an older man, right?'

'Right.'

'Ignore the kids – they're just dickers. The older

man is Michael Quinn. He's the leader of the PIRA unit chosen to take you out – the one who lives opposite me.' The traffic lights changed to green and they drove on, sticking to a relatively slow, steady pace. 'We'll soon be reaching another bookie's,' O'Leary said. 'A few hundred yards up on the left. Don't slow down – just scan 'im as quickly as possible. He's called Patrick Mulgrew. He collects the protection money from that bookie's and he's there to check people comin' in an' out. He's part of the hit team.'

Even before the car reached the betting shop, Cranfield saw the man standing outside, hunched against the wind in his gaberdine raincoat and blowing into his frozen hands. As they passed him, Cranfield studied his profile, then his full face – hollow-cheeked, thin-lipped, dark circles under the eyes.

'I've got him,' he said.

'Right,' O'Leary replied. 'I live in the next street. Everyone enterin' or leavin' is checked by PIRA members workin' on shifts in four-man teams – two men at each end of the street. Today the men at this end are the other two picked t'hit you. Try t'check them as we turn into the street. Drive slowly and don't stare. If ya haven't enough time, turn around and come back out again.'

'OK,' Cranfield said.

As the car reached the corner, Cranfield saw the two men standing at the far side of the street, both smoking and watching those coming and going. 'That's them,' O'Leary confirmed. Cranfield managed to scan their faces and remember the details before the car straightened out and headed along the street.

'OK,' he said. 'Got them.'

'The one on the right – nearest the Falls – was Seamus McGrath. The one on the left, nearest to us, was John Houlihan. Like Quinn, they're hard men. Very experienced. That's why they've been picked.' They drove along the street, past rows of two-up, two-down terraced houses. 'We'll soon be reachin' number thirty-seven,' O'Leary said. 'That's the home of Michael Quinn, the leader of the pack. He lives there with 'is missus – his kids are all married – but he sends her t'the bingo when his mates come around. As I said, they meet regular, like – two or three times a week. The house directly opposite, number thirty-eight, is mine.' Cranfield glanced at both houses as he drove past. 'As you know,' O'Leary said when they had passed, 'I live there alone. So you get the Army to do a sweep of the street as cover while you move some men into m'loft for yer covert OP. While the sweep's on, ya can bug Quinn's house and hide anything else yer goin' t'need. Ya keep tabs on that lot and then move against 'em at yer leisure. Ya have to set it up before I leave. Take 'em out when I'm gone.'

'I will,' Cranfield said.

* * *

Cranfield dropped O'Leary off where he had picked him up, near the Broadway, then drove back to the centre of town to the Europa Hotel. After being thoroughly checked by the private security guards, he was allowed to drive through the electronically controlled gates and park in the part of the forecourt enclosed by heavy-duty wire fencing and used as a car park.

He went straight to the first-floor lounge bar, where he purchased a Bushmills at the counter. As usual, the bar was busy, mostly with journalists from London, male and female, most of whom smoked like trains, drank like fish, and talked in loud voices on the bar stools or in soft chairs and sofas placed around tables spaced well apart.

Not wishing to be engaged in conversation, but always keen to listen, Cranfield sat at the bar until an empty table became available. Shortly afterwards, Captain Dubois entered, wearing an immaculate pinstripe suit, a shirt and tie, and highly polished black shoes. Having ordered a whisky at the bar, he sat down facing Cranfield. He did not look too happy.

'Why do you always insist on meeting here?' he asked. 'This place is swarming with reporters from London.'

'I'm starved for attractive women,' Cranfield replied, 'and Fleet Street has lots of them.'

Dubois glanced automatically around the packed,

smoky bar, taking note of a couple of very appealing ladies, then he turned back to Cranfield.

'Keep your mind on your work,' he said. 'So, what's the business?'

'We kicked up a bit of a dust storm,' Cranfield said, 'and the debris is raining down.'

Dubois glanced right and left, as if nervous about being overhead, then looked directly at Cranfield again. 'O'Halloran?' Cranfield nodded assent. 'So what's the dust storm?' When Cranfield related what he had just learnt from O'Leary, Dubois looked even less pleased. 'Christ,' he said. 'As if it wasn't bad enough with all this flak in the papers about SAS assassinations. I'm beginning to think, Cranfield, that you're causing me more trouble than you're worth.'

'The SAS get blamed for a lot of things they've never done.'

'We all know who topped O'Halloran.'

'I should remind you that you were present.'

'As for that stone-thrower yesterday . . . '

'He was about to fire a Webley pistol.'

'Nevertheless, it was your damned SAS man who . . . '

'Don't forget,' Cranfield interjected, enjoying Dubois' discomfort, 'that it wasn't just the SAS involved. The driver, indeed the man in charge of the team, was your own Sergeant Lovelock.'

Dubois rolled his eyes and glanced across the

room, momentarily distracted from his own concerns by the long, shapely legs of a woman smoking and drinking at the bar. Perhaps remembering that she was almost certainly a journalist, Dubois shook his head again and sipped some whisky.

'Am I included in their hit list?' he asked.

'No.'

'I'm delighted to hear it. They want only you.'

'That appears to be the case.'

'You don't appear to be concerned.'

'I'm not. I'm planning to get them first.'

'How?'

'I know who they are. O'Leary pointed them out to me. He lives directly opposite the house they meet in, so I'm going to call for a cordon-and-search sweep of the street and plant an OP in O'Leary's place. The PIRA house will be bugged at the same time. We keep tabs on them and move when we're good and ready, knowing just where they'll be.'

Dubois thought about it. 'This is getting tricky,' he said. 'I've a feeling that we've stirred up too much with that single cross-border hit.'

'The ones we've stirred up are the bastards who took out our ten sources and caused Phillips's suicide. If we take them out, it'll look like retaliation, which is the kind of language their mates will understand. It'll give us the edge and begin the required cleansing of Belfast and, later, south Armagh.'

Startled, Dubois stared at Cranfield. 'Is that what you're after?'

'Yes,' Cranfield said.

'You're too ambitious for your own good, Lieutenant.'

'Don't ever mention rank in this bar.'

'I'm so sorry, Cranfield, but the accusation stands.'

Cranfield grinned. 'I don't believe in the concept of too much ambition. I believe in doing what's necessary. And whatever's necessary to clean up Northern Ireland, is what I'm willing to do.'

'You're going against the grain of your own Regiment,' Dubois said. 'The Regiment admires initiation, but not big timing – and that's what you're starting to do by taking matters, including the law, into your own hands. A certain independence of spirit has always been admired in the Regiment, but you're wildly overstepping the mark.'

'I don't know what you mean.'

'You shouldn't have crossed the border without permission, let alone put a stop to someone there.

'Then you shouldn't have helped me.'

'That's true.'

'Listen,' Cranfield said, leaning across the table to place his hand on Dubois' wrist and gaze intently at him. 'This bloody business in Northern Ireland has been going on too long, with the whole of the British intelligence and military complex being humiliated by a bunch of former amateurs. Sooner or later this has to be stopped, but it won't be as long as we abide by the rules while the IRA's completely disregarding them. There's no Geneva Convention here. There are no Queensberry rules. We've been sent over here to finally clean out the whole area, and if we have to do what they do to succeed, then damn it, let's do it.'

'Hence O'Halloran and that lad yesterday.'

'O'Halloran was planned, the lad yesterday wasn't, but the two combined have clearly succeeded in bringing those bastards out of the closet. Now that they're out, let's get them and put an end to it.'

'My God!' Dubois said. 'You really mean it. You think you can win this whole war.'

'I can certainly try,' Cranfield said. He sat back in his chair, glanced at the ladies on the bar stools, then returned his steady, hazel-eyed gaze to Dubois. 'Stop worrying about O'Halloran,' he said. 'What we did, did the trick.'

Dubois sipped some whisky, ran his forefinger around the glass, then shook his head again from side to side.

'Damn it,' he said bitterly. 'We shouldn't have done it. My first instincts were right. Now we've got a damned range war on our hands and the blame will lie squarely with the SAS.'

'Or 14 Intelligence Company,' Cranfield reminded him.

'Even worse,' Dubois said.

'You see it as wrong; I see it as right,' Cranfield said. 'Let's have a damned range war. Let them come out of the woodwork. We want to break the IRA in south Armagh and this opens that gate. They're showing their faces at last and we're going to take them out.'

'We'd better,' Dubois said.

# 7

'So what the fuck did *you* do?' Gumboot asked Jock McGregor over a beer in the busy NAAFI canteen in Bessbrook. He was sitting at a long table with Jock, Ricketts, Sergeant Lampton, Danny 'Baby Face' Porter, 'Taff' Burgess, the recently 'blooded' Martin, and the British Army sergeant, Ralph Lovelock.

As usual, Sergeant 'Dead-eye Dick' Parker was drinking all alone at the bar, not smiling at anyone.

'You mean apart from topping fucking teenagers and starting the Third World War?'

'That teenager had a Webley pistol and was ready to use it,' Martin, who was growing bolder, reminded Jock. 'So Ricketts had no choice.'

'You don't aim to wound,' Danny agreed, speaking as quietly, as shyly, as always. 'Lieutenant Cranfield confirmed that.'

'He would,' Sergeant Lampton said. 'Lieutenant Cranfield is a man who likes action and goes looking for it.'

'No bad thing,' Danny replied.

'It can be,' Lampton said. 'This isn't Oman, where the enemy was clear-cut. It's a war on British soil and we're subject to British laws, so certain actions have to be accounted for. If you shoot the wrong man here, you could find yourself on trial with a life sentence hanging over your head. So going to look for action here isn't a wise thing to do.'

'Right,' Ricketts said. 'I agree completely, Frank. I had to shoot that kid – he was getting ready to shoot me – but the local papers, as well as the IRA, are already talking about murderers and demanding justice. You wouldn't get that in Oman, nor in Malaya. So you don't go looking for trouble in this place, and, even if you happen to find it, you certainly have to look before you leap.'

'Correct,' Lampton said. 'In case you break the law, if nothing else. An awful lot of British soldiers have been put on trial just because they lost their cool and shot the wrong bloody person. That's why you don't seek it out.'

'So what did you do, Jock?' Gumboot repeated. 'Apart from jacking off to pass the time?'

'Apart from jacking off, the same as you,' Jock said. 'We just drove around – me, Danny, Dead-eye Dick, and a sergeant from 14 Intelligence Company.'

'Sergeant Hampton,' Lovelock informed them.

'Yeah, right,' Jock agreed. 'Sergeant Hampton.

Good bloke. We saw the sights, took pictures, wrote notes on what we'd seen, and in general got to know the city. What a fucking nightmare! Schoolkids wrecking cars, teenagers grilling you at traffic lights, fat hags spitting at the soldiers and police, all of them acting like they were barefoot on razors. Buildings burnt out, bombed out, boarded up, with their windows, if not smashed, covered in heavy-duty mesh wire. Tanks and armoured pigs. Sniper fire at least once every hour. A maze of backstreets and narrow, dark alleys, perfect for killing. A right piss-hole, in fact.'

'Where on earth did *you* go?' Taff asked.

'Andersonstown, Mountpottinger, the Falls, Whiterock, the Ardoyne, that bloody Ballymurphy Bull Ring – when not wanking, of course. We've seen it all, Taff, and we're really looking forward to our stay here.'

'At least we don't have to deal with flying beetles, hornets, red and black ants, centipedes, camel spiders and scorpions,' Ricketts said. 'Like we did in Oman.'

'I preferred it there,' Lampton said. 'It wasn't a rat's maze of backstreets. It was all out in the open and the enemy couldn't be mistaken. He might pop up from behind a rock, but you knew you could shoot at him without being grilled by the green slime or the RUC CID.'

'Right,' Jock said. 'As our Army sergeant told us, here you're fighting children, teenagers and screaming women, as well as the IRA. Not good, folks. Not helpful.'

'Still,' Gumboot said, 'a man could make a good bit of money on the side here. As Sergeant Lovelock kindly informed us, the whole city's run on graft and protection rackets, so we could form our own little syndicate.'

'Right,' Martin said, beginning to enjoy the sort of banter they always referred to as bullshit. 'We offer protection from the Catholics *and* the Prods.'

'Arrest them, then ask for a hand-out to let the poor bastards go again. That should rake in the shekels!'

'You think it's funny,' Lampton said, 'but this place can corrupt anyone. When the SAS first came here two of them, obviously thinking the whole place was lawless, attempted to rob a bank in Londonderry.'

'I don't believe it!' Taff exclaimed.

'It's true,' Ricketts told him. 'Both of them got six years in prison and the SAS got a reputation it didn't want.'

'I mean, to attempt to rob a bank and then *fail*,' Jock said in disgust. 'They must have been crap-hats.'

Young Danny glanced at Dead-eye Dick, who was silently downing a pint at the bar. 'He's really quiet,' Danny said.

'Just like you,' Martin said.

'He's a cold-blooded killer,' Jock said, 'who requires a wide berth. You remember that bastard in Oman, Gumboot? He was one weird companion!'

'Right,' Gumboot replied. 'Always dressed up in Arab clothes and running around with the *firqats*. They say he is as good with a knife as he is with his rifle.'

Danny stared admiringly at Parker, then gave a slight smile. 'A good soldier,' he said.

'He is that,' Ricketts told him, knowing that Danny admired the silent Dead-eye because the youngster, even in Continuation Training, had shown all the hallmarks of being just like him – a natural fighter and possibly a born killer, baby face or not. Ricketts checked his watch. 'OK, men,' he said. 'Time to go. The Head Sheds await us.'

Some of the men groaned melodramatically, but they finished their drinks, then filed out of the canteen to go to the briefing room.

While the others were leaving, Danny went up to Dead-eye, tapped him on the shoulder, and spoke to him, telling him that the late-night briefing was about to begin. Dead-eye stared stonily at him, then nodded and waved him away. Danny grinned shyly at Ricketts as he left, then Dead-eye finished his drink, slid off the stool and walked up to Ricketts and Lampton.

'Seems like a good kid,' he said.

'Not bad,' Lampton replied.

Dead-eye just nodded.

Outside, in the freezing night air, they hurriedly crossed a stretch of wind-blown ground to the Portakabin used as a briefing room. Mercifully, it was bright and warm inside. Most of the men were already seated, so Ricketts and Lampton sat in the back row. The Head Sheds on the dais, in front of the blackboard, were Captain Dubois and Lieutenant Cranfield, both back in uniform. As before, Sergeant Lovelock was sitting at a desk beside them, guarding another pile of manila folders.

'Evening, gentlemen,' Lieutenant Cranfield said. 'I trust you're all in good spirits.'

'We'd feel better if we were back in the bar, boss,' Jock replied.

Cranfield just grinned. 'You'll have time for one more before closing,' he said. 'Then you have to be good boys. So! Why this emergency, late-night briefing?'

'Do tell us, boss!' Lampton responded.

After glancing automatically at the sombre Captain Dubois, Cranfield turned back to his men. 'The first thing I should say is that you twelve are here only as an advance party. In a few weeks the whole of D Squadron, numbering seventy-five men, is going to be shipped in, but in the meantime you have to carry the load – and over the next couple of weeks that could become rather heavy.'

'Then give it to the British Army,' Gumboot said. 'They're all brawn and no brains.'

Captain Dubois flushed, then managed a tight grin. Cranfield, whose grin was more genuine, waited until the laughter had died down before continuing: 'The second thing I should tell you is that we're not just here for routine patrols. Our brief is to cleanse Belfast and south Armagh of the IRA – completely, once and for all.'

When the surprised murmuring had subsided, Sergeant Lampton said: 'That sounds pretty ambitious, boss.'

'Ambitious, but not impossible. I feel that we're now in a position to poke a hole in the dam wall, then split it wide open. We have some of the most important IRA men in our sights and we're going to take them out. When we've done so, we'll have dealt a decisive blow to their morale and won ourselves a propaganda victory of such dimensions that it could turn the tide wholly in our favour.'

'Just how important are these men, boss?' Ricketts asked. 'And who are they, exactly?'

'We have reason to believe they're the four-man PIRA active service unit that recently topped ten of our best sources.'

Ricketts glanced quizzically at Sergeant Lovelock, who offered a slight, knowing grin. Then Ricketts returned his gaze to Lieutenant Cranfield. 'Is it true that those deaths may have been the cause of Corporal Phillips's suicide?'

'This subject was raised at the last briefing, Sergeant, but it's still not up for discussion. The reason for Corporal Phillips's suicide remains unknown, though we assume it was stress. I'm not at liberty, however, to discuss the work he was doing.' He nodded at Sergeant Lovelock, who stood up, walked around his desk, and distributed the manila folders to all the troopers. 'The men we're after,' Cranfield said, 'are PIRA members Michael Quinn, Patrick Mulgrew, Seamus McGrath and John Houlihan. You'll find photos of them in those folders, along with intelligence reports on each individual. Quinn is the leader of this four-man ASU. Our job is to take them out as soon as possible.'

'And put them in Long Kesh?' Lampton asked.

'No,' Cranfield said, taking a deep breath and slowly letting it out again. 'Our job is to cancel them completely without breaking the law.'

The men glanced at one another, surprised. Some of them tried to cover their discomfort at the silence by studying the photographs in the folders. Eventually Parker broke the silence in his customary flat tones: 'What's the strategy, boss?'

'For this operation,' Captain Dubois said, 'you men are going to be kitted out tomorrow. At dawn the day after, the army is going to do a cordon-and-search sweep of the lower Falls Road, with particular emphasis on the street where Michael Quinn lives. Quite deliberately, we're going to make this sweep more thorough than most, using hundreds of troops and making a great show of scarching every house – after throwing their occupants temporarily out into the street and frisking the men on the pavements, in full view of their wives and kids. While all this is going on, causing a great deal of confusion, a four-man SAS team will take over the attic of the house of one of our touts, located directly opposite Quinn's place. At the same time, army surveillance specialists will be planting miniaturized audio and video recording devices in Quinn's house.'

'Why not just place the OP in Quinn's attic?' Jock asked.

'Because Quinn's a hard man, very experienced, and that's the first place he'll check when we leave. Nor can we bug his phone in the ordinary manner. But he won't think to look for other miniaturized surveillance devices, some of which will be interacting with the surveillance equipment in the OP across the street.'

'Understood, boss,' Jock said. 'What about the rest of us? The remaining eight.'

'Quinn has a country cottage in south Armagh,' Cranfield said, 'not far from here, close to the border. While the covert OP is keeping tabs on his comings and goings in the Falls, including what's said and done inside his house, the remaining eight men will do the same in two rural OPs located near the cottage – one overlooking the road between the cottage and Belfast, the other on the road that leads to Dublin.'

'For what purpose?' Martin asked naïvely.

'Both the cottage and the house in the Falls Road are used for Quinn's ASU meetings. Based on information received from the three OPs regarding his plans and movements, we'll decide just when and where to take him and the other three out. It has to be both lawful and highly public, so the time and place must be right. Any questions?'

'Yes, boss,' Ricketts said. 'Who does what?'

'You'll be told that tomorrow morning when you report to the Quartermaster's stores after breakfast. The rest of the day will be spent on weapons testing, familiarization with the surveillance equipment, and general instructions regarding, in particular, the urban OP. A final weapons and kit inspection will be made tomorrow night, immediately after dinner. After the inspection, no one will be allowed to drink or even visit the NAAFI canteen for any reason.' When the moans and groans had died away, Cranfield asked: 'Any more questions?'

'Yes, boss,' Gumboot said. 'If we're not allowed to drink tomorrow, can we go and get pissed right now?'

'It's your last chance, trooper. Just make sure you put those folders in your lockers before you go out. Also make sure you thoroughly acquaint yourselves with their contents by tomorrow evening. Right? Class dismissed!'

Leaving the briefing room, the men returned to their bashas, where they locked the manila folders in their lockers, then hurried out for a few more pints in the NAAFI canteen.

# 8

Saracen armoured cars, armoured troop carriers, or 'pigs', and RUC paddy-wagons penetrated the lower Falls, headlights beaming into the morning darkness like the flaring eyes of prehistoric beasts. The convoy rumbled ominously past police stations and army barricades along the Falls Road without interference, then broke up into separate columns that turned into three parallel side streets to begin the early morning cordon-and-search sweep. Within minutes the area was surrounded and the three streets were blocked off.

His attention drawn not by the rumble of the advancing vehicles, but by an approaching helicopter, a dicker looked up, saw what was happening, and shouted a warning, his youthful voice echoing eerily in the silence.

Almost immediately, his mates materialized out of dark doorways and narrow, littered alleys of torture and death to add their bellowed warnings to his own.

Even as sleepy citizens started opening their front

doors, many still in their nightwear, British Army and Parachute Regiment troops poured out of the armoured pigs, into dark streets streaked with morning light. Wearing DPM clothing and helmets, but bulked out even more with ArmourShield General Purpose Vests, or GPVs, including ceramic contoured plates, fragmentation vests, and groin panels, they looked like invaders from space. Even worse, they were armed with sledgehammers, SA-80 assault rifles, and Heckler & Koch MP5 sub-machine-guns – the latter particularly effective for use in confined spaces. Others, the 'snatch' teams, there to take in the prisoners, looked just as fearsome in full riot gear, including shields and truncheons.

RUC officers trained at the SAS Counter Revolutionary Warfare Wing at Hereford, wearing flak jackets and carrying either 5.56mm Ruger Mini-14 assault rifles or batons, jumped out of the back of the paddy-wagons and surrounded their vehicles as the soldiers and paratroopers raced in opposite directions along the street, hammering on doors with the butts of their weapons and bawling for the people to come out.

British Army snipers clambered up on to the roofs from lightweight aluminium assault ladders and from there gave cover with Lee Enfield .303-inch sniper rifles. Wearing earphones, they would be warned of any likely trouble spots either by officers on the street or by the Royal Marine Gazelle observation helicopter that was now hovering right above the rooftops, its spinning rotors creating a fierce wind that blew the rubbish in the gutters across the street.

'Get out, you Fenian bastards! On the pavement!'

When Lampton, Ricketts, Gumboot and Taff looked out through the half-open doors of their Saracen, they saw the soldiers roughly pushing angry women and dazed children aside to grab their menfolk and haul them out on to the pavement. Other soldiers were forcing their way inside the houses to begin what would almost certainly be damaging searches of the premises. When front doors were not opened on request, the soldiers with the sledgehammers smashed them open. As the older male residents of the street, most still in pyjamas, were pushed face first against the wall and made to spread their hands and legs for rough frisking, women screamed abuse, children either did the same or burst into tears, and the youthful dickers further along the street hurled stones, lumps of concrete and abuse.

'Shit!' Gumboot burst out inside the safety of the Saracen. 'I thought this was supposed to be a fake raid, just put on for our benefit.'

'They have to make it look real,' Lampton informed him, 'so the only soldiers who know about us are the ones taking us into O'Leary's house. This is the real thing, Gumboot.'

'Bloody nasty,' Taff said.

'Right,' Gumboot replied. 'Those soldiers are acting like fucking thugs.'

'It's because they're frightened,' Taff said. 'They haven't the time for consideration. They can't avoid the women and children, the enemy could be anyone, some of the houses could be booby-trapped, one of the dickers might have a gun – and so on.'

'Right,' Frank Lampton said. 'In this kind of situation you could get shot in the back by an invalid in his bed, stabbed in the stomach by a housewife with a breadknife, or blown up by a booby-trapped bathroom door – you just never know. So their only thought is to get in and out as quickly as possible and to hell with the rest of it.'

'That's why they smash the doors down and tear the houses apart,' Ricketts said. 'They're not gonna hang about being polite or helping to rearrange the furniture afterwards. They go in, take the house apart and leave. It's not nice, but it works.'

Looking out of the Saracen, they saw two of the soldiers grab a suspect in pyjamas, haul him away from the wall where he had been frisked, and push him roughly into the centre of the road, where an RUC guard hit him with a truncheon and forced him up into a paddy-wagon. A single shot rang out, followed immediately by the sound of breaking glass.

'Mick bastard!' a soldier bawled as he cracked a man's head with the butt of his SA-80, making him topple back and drop the pistol he'd just fired wildly in the air, doing damage only to a window.

When he straightened up, the man turned out to be no more than a teenager. He removed his hand from his temple and looked in amazement at the blood on his fingers, before being jerked sideways by the soldier, then kicked brutally towards the RUC officer, who drove him up into the paddy-wagon like someone using an electric prod on a cow.

'Get in there, you murdering Fenian bastard!' the RUC man exploded, giving the youth a last blow with the truncheon as he stumbled into the vehicle. Elsewhere, soldiers with riot shields were herding groups of men against the wall and using truncheons to force their legs apart.

'Hands against the wall!' one soldier was bawling. 'Spread those fucking legs! Now don't make a move!'

As other soldiers poured in and out of houses, sometimes smashing their way in with sledgehammers, housewives in curlers screamed abuse and attacked them with their fists, children ran about like wild animals, some laughing, some crying, and the dickers further along the road kept throwing stones and lumps of concrete at the line of soldiers forming a cordon of riot shields across the street.

Just as another couple of men were prodded up into the paddy-wagon visible outside the Saracen,

Sergeant Lovelock appeared at the half-open doors with a group of paratroopers behind him. 'OK,' he said, waving his right hand. 'Out you get. Half of your kit's already been taken in and we've no time to waste.'

The four-man SAS OP team climbed out of the Saracen. Like most of the regular Army troops, they were wearing DPM clothing, but with camouflaged soft combat caps instead of helmets, and leather and Gore-tex Danner boots instead of standard-issue British Army boots. They did not have their bergens, as these would have been spotted instantly, so were carrying only what kit they could manage on their belts, in their pockets and in their hands. This included fourteen days' high-calorie rations, mostly chocolate and sweets, on the basis of two days per one day's ration. In bivvy bags on their belts they carried spare underwear and a first-aid kit; and, also on the belt, flashlights and binoculars. They carried as well extra ammunition for the only weapons they were allowed on this operation: their standard-issue 9mm Browning High Power handguns and the short 9mm Sterling Mk 5 sub-machine-gun with retractable butt and 34-round magazines, which they were now carrying openly.

However, as this equipment was insufficient for a lengthy urban recce, the rest of their kit was being carried to the OP by an escort patrol of paratroopers. Some had already entered the house opposite and were making their way slowly along the single loft space of the terrace to O'Leary's loft, located right opposite Quinn's house. Those men, and some of the paratroopers, were taking the rest of the kit, including water in plastic bottles; spare radio batteries; medical packs; extra ammunition; 35mm cameras and rolls of film; tape-recorders; thermal imagers and night-vision scopes; an advanced laser audio surveillance transceiver; brown, plastic-backed notebooks and ballpens; sleeping bags; packs of moisturized cloths for cleaning their faces and hands; towels; toilet paper; and sealable plastic bags for their excrement and urine.

'Let's go!' Lovelock said.

Protected by the ring of heavily armed paratroopers, half deafened by the roaring of the helicopter hovering directly above them, Ricketts, Lampton, Gumboot and Taff raced across the road, through bawling RUC officers and watchful soldiers, past Saracens and pigs, up on to the pavement on the opposite side. There, while British Army soldiers dragged reluctant men and women out of their homes, the paratroopers pushed their way into one of the houses. Once inside, a couple of them proceeded to 'search' the place by noisily sweeping ornaments and bric-à-brac off tables and cupboards, removing drawers and tipping their contents on to the floor, and generally smashing the place up. Meanwhile, the others led the four SAS men upstairs to the trapdoor already opened in the floor of the loft.

Forming his hands into a stirrup, a hefty paratrooper said, 'OK, up you get.' One by one, the four SAS men placed a foot in his joined hands and were hoisted up into the dark loft. The rest of the paratroopers followed suit, leaving only the big one standing below the trapdoor, surrounded by the rest of the kit required for the OP. While the paratroopers on the ground floor continued to wreck the house by way of searching it, the big paratrooper below the trapdoor handed up the kit piece by piece. When it was all in the loft, the men divided it between them and then 'mouse-holed' their way along the terrace, practically the whole length of the street, until they met up with the others already in the cramped space in O'Leary's roof.

'This is it,' Sergeant Lovelock said as the paratroopers laid the rest of the kit and equipment down around the edges of the loft space. 'And there's your peep-hole.' He pointed to where a slate nail in the roof had been removed and replaced with a rubber band that allowed the slate to be raised and lowered, thus providing a spy-hole for the naked eye, binoculars, cameras or thermal imagers. 'At this moment one of our specialists is placing a miniature surveillance probe near the ceiling of the adjoining wall in the house next door to Quinn's without the occupants knowing a thing. That, combined with your advanced laser system, should enable you to hear, see and record everything that goes on in Quinn's place. Any questions?'

'No,' Sergeant Lampton said.

'OK. We've got to go now. Good luck.'

Lovelock patted Lampton on the shoulder, then, using a hand signal, ordered the paratroopers to follow him back along the terrace to the open trapdoor by which they had entered. This they did, dropping down one by one through the small, square hole until they had all disappeared. When the last of them had gone, Ricketts, who had followed them this far, replaced the trapdoor, checked that it was secure, then returned to join the others above O'Leary's house.

Lampton was looking through the peep-hole.

'What's happening?' Ricketts asked.

'They've got Michael Quinn out on the pavement and he's going apeshit. The soldiers have just left the house next door, so the probe must be planted. I think the Army will start pulling out now, taking a few prisoners with them for show. Yep, they've just taken Quinn. They'll pretend they came here to get him. They'll take him to Castlereagh, put him through the wringer, then eventually release him and let him come home, thinking he's fooled them again. I don't think he'll even check his own loft. He seems to think this is genuine. The fact that they've also arrested the tout who owns this place will make the raid seem even more genuine.' He turned away from the peep-hole and motioned Ricketts over. 'Here, take a look.'

'Start unpacking this gear,' Ricketts said to Gumboot and Taff. 'And remember that from this moment on we have to be quiet as mice.'

'I thought it was the tout's house,' Taff said.

'It is, which is certainly a help, but loud noises could be heard in the adjoining houses, so we have to keep it down.' He glanced at the adjoining loft to the right and said, 'That's going to be your bog, so be particularly quiet there, as it belongs to the house next door.' Catching Lampton's grin, he went to the peep-hole, raised the slate and looked down on the street.

The hard man he recognized from the intelligence photo as Michael Quinn was struggling vigorously and bawling abuse as two soldiers with truncheons dragged him off the pavement and forced him up into one of the RUC paddy-wagons. At the same time, another man, whom Ricketts suspected was the tout, was being half-dragged from the area directly below the loft to be thrown into the same vehicle.

That, Ricketts reasoned, was a good idea, as the tout would now appear to be one of those high on the Brits' wanted list. It would make him look good in the eyes of his mates and neighbours, including Quinn.

When the doors of the paddy-wagon had been slammed shut on Quinn and the tout, the housewives and children on the pavements bawled even more abuse at the soldiers and RUC officers. The latter, however, were already getting back into their vehicles and the engines were roaring into life.

As the first of the Saracens and pigs moved off along the street, an even louder roaring came from directly above the house. Looking up as high as he could through the peep-hole, Ricketts saw the Gazelle observation helicopter flying directly overhead, heading back to Armagh. By the time it had disappeared beyond row upon row of rooftops, the last of the Saracens, pigs and paddy-wagons had also disappeared from below, leaving the street to the irate or shocked inhabitants.

Some of the women hurried into their houses, only to rush out again, complaining tearfully about the devastation inside.

Disturbed by that sight, Ricketts dropped the slate back over the peep-hole and turned back to face the other three in the loft. Gumboot and Taff had already unpacked a lot of the kit and were balefully examining the plastic bags intended for their own shit and piss. Lampton, meanwhile, was opening the tripod for the audio surveillance transceiver.

'Take off your boots,' he told them as he unfolded

the tripod, 'and don't put them on again until we leave this place.'

'Home sweet home,' Ricketts murmured, gazing around the dark, freezing, cobwebbed loft.

'I've lived in worse,' Gumboot said.

# 9

That evening, close to midnight, with the covert OP already established opposite Michael Quinn's house in Belfast, Sergeant 'Dead-eye Dick' Parker and Troopers Jock McGregor, Danny 'Baby Face' Porter and Martin Renshaw, were driven out of Bessbrook in a dark-blue high-sided van to set up a second covert OP overlooking Quinn's weekend home in the 'bandit country' of south Armagh.

Though normally the overt OPs were manned and resupped by helicopter, this one would be left alone during its existence and was being set up in strict secrecy. The van, therefore, was being driven by a British Army REME corporal in civilian clothing, guarded by a crack marksman paratrooper, also wearing normal clothes. The OP's SAS team, on the other hand, were wearing DPM windproof clothing, Danner boots with Gore-tex lining, and soft, peaked, camouflaged combat caps. The exposed parts of their faces, necks and hands were smeared with stick camouflage, suitable for blending in with local foliage.

Stopped repeatedly by Army roadblocks, the men in the van had to show their IDs, which in this case were genuine. They were always then allowed to proceed. Nevertheless, the many stops slowed them down considerably and it was just after two in the morning when they finally reached their destination.

Quinn's weekend house was in rolling farmlands in Kilevy, surrounded by the hills along the A1 and high enough to afford a glimpse of Carlingford Lough and the Irish Sea. When the REME corporal parked the van and switched off his headlights in a pitch-black winding lane near Kilevy, the men hurriedly climbed out, with Dead-eye Dick, Jock, the paratrooper and the REME driver going into all-round defence as Martin and Danny unloaded the equipment.

No one spoke.

When the unloading was completed, the four SAS men strapped on their heavily laden bergens, distributed the rest of the equipment between them, then clambered over a fence to begin the long march up a dark, windswept, grassy hill. As they did so, the REME driver, still protected by the paratrooper, turned the van around and headed back to Bessbrook.

The men marching uphill were heavily burdened indeed, with overpacked bergens weighing over fifty pounds and the rest of their weapons, ammunition, equipment, water and rations, either fixed to their webbing or carried by hand, thus making an even greater burden. As the weapons included a GPMG, a couple of L42A1 Lee Enfield .303 bolt-action sniper rifles with starlight 'scopes, M16 assault rifles with M203 grenade launchers, and two 5.56mm Colt Commando semi-automatics with 30-round box magazines, and as the equipment included various surveillance systems and recording machines, as well as a PRC 319 radio, it was a daunting load to carry for any distance.

'Donkey soldiers,' Jock whispered to Martin. 'That's what the *firqats* called us in Oman and that's what we are now. Bloody donkeys!'

Martin tried to laugh, but was so breathless he nearly choked, so instead maintained silence.

Ordered apart by Sergeant 'Dead-eye Dick' Parker, the men advanced up the hill in a well-spaced line, with Jock out front as 'point' man, or lead scout, Danny and Martin in the middle to cover both flanks, and Dead-eye bringing up the rear as 'Tail-end Charlie'. They made it to the OP by a zigzagging route that took in a series of pre-designated RVs, or rendezvous points: the gate of a fence, a copse of trees, a particular hill. Though this took up more time, it was a vital part of their anti-ambush tactics. Eventually, however, after a final rendezvous, or FRV, during which they checked the map with the aid of a pencil torch, they arrived at the location chosen for the OP.

'OK,' Dead-eye Dick, the Patrol Commander,

said, lowering his own heavy loads to the ground. 'This is where we dig in.'

The location was the windy summit of a hill with a glimpse of the lough and sea on one side and, on the other, an unobstructed view of Quinn's cottage – necessary not only for eyeball recces, but for the line-of-sight path required for the laser surveillance system. The location had also been chosen because it was on the direct line of a hedgerow that snaked over the crest of the hill and could be used as the protective wall of the OP.

The clouds were low and patchy, showing stars between, and moonlight made strips of sea glint occasionally in the distance. The wind was cold and strong, howling like a banshee, and frost glinted here and there on the grassy ground.

While the other men sorted out their kit, Jock used the PRC 319 to establish communications with the base at Bessbrook. Having confirmed that the OP had 'comms', or communications, from this location, Dead-eye took guard and radio watch, leaving the experienced Jock, with the help of Danny and Martin, to prepare the OP.

While it was unlikely that they would be seen by enemy aircraft, of which there were none, it was possible that a British Army helicopter crew, not knowing of their mission, would mistake them for a PIRA murder squad. For this reason, the first thing they did was put up a hessian screen, with a poncho and camouflage net for overhead cover, supported on wooden stakes, looped at one end over the hedgerow, and held down with iron pickets and rope.

Once this basic form of protection had been raised, the three men used spades and pickaxes to dig out a large rectangular area suitable for a long-term, top-to-tail OP, with one end running under the hedgerow.

Four shallow 'scrapes' were then dug in the main scrape: one for the observer, one for the sentry, and two as 'rest bays'. One of the latter was for the man having a proper sleep in a sleeping bag; the other was for the man resting from guard or observation duties while taking care of his personal administration matters – such as jotting down his observations – or perhaps just having a snack and a rest while remaining awake.

A fifth shallow scrape was dug out of the middle of the triangular OP as a 'kit-well' for water, high-calorie foods, weapons, spare ammunition, batteries, toiletries and other equipment.

The soil from the scrapes was scattered around the ground a good distance away from the OP. The hessian-and-net covering of the OP was then covered in grass, gorse and vegetation torn from the hedgerow.

A camouflaged entry/exit hole was made in the hessian hanging to the ground at the rear end of the OP. Last, but most important, a camouflaged rectangular viewing hole was shaped from the hedgerow and hessian covering the side of the OP overlooking the target – in this case Quinn's cottage and the road passing it, located about 150 metres away, across the road at the bottom of the hill.

With the OP completed, the rest of the equipment was unpacked and prepared for use.

It was now that the newcomer, Martin Renshaw, came into his own. A former electrical research engineer with Marconi, then with the Pilatus Britten-Norman experimental aircraft production company in the Isle of Wight, Martin had joined the army specifically to get into the Royal Corps of Signals and, through that regiment, into the SAS. Immediately after being badged by the latter, he had spent six weeks each at the Hereford and Royal Signals establishments at Catterick and Blandford, where he had learned about the special surveillance requirements of the SAS, with particular regard to Counter-Terrorist (CT) operations in Northern Ireland. He was therefore particularly thrilled to be here at last and about to put all his training to work.

'Let's see what you can do, kid,' Dead-eye said. 'You can play with your toys now.'

The tripod which Martin set up in front of the viewing hole overlooking Quinn's house was not for the GPMG, which would only be used in dire emergency, but for the cumbersome Thorn EMI multi-role thermal imager, including an infrared capability. Looking like an exceptionally large video camera, it could scan outside walls, track body heat, and reveal the position of those inside the building, by day or by night, in smoke or fog.

'If he leaves the room,' Martin said, 'we're all going to know it.'

Complementing the large, tripod-mounted thermal imager were two other items of highly advanced equipment.

Photographs of those entering or leaving Quinn's cottage, whether by day or by night, would be taken with a Davin Optical Modulux image intensifier connected to a Nikon 35mm SLR camera with interchangeable long-distance and binocular lenses.

'It can also be used as a night sight,' Martin explained enthusiastically, 'but it only works in the visible spectrum and its effectiveness is reduced by smoke, fog, and even dense foliage. Nevertheless, for our long-distance, day and night photographic needs it can't really be bettered.'

He also set up a Hawkeye Systems Model HT10 thermal imaging camera capable of detecting men and vehicles at long distances, either in low light or in total darkness, while producing high-quality video pictures with up to seven times magnification. While the thermal picture was displayed automatically on an integral video monitor for direct viewing, it could also be displayed on a separate monitor for remote applications, such as recording for later visual analysis.

'What the hell's that?' Jock asked Martin, when the latter set up two more tripods and fixed what looked like complicated transmitters, or recording devices, to them.

Camouflaged in hessian, the end of the camera-shaped object was poking through the viewing hole. The other object, which looked like a radio receiver, was joined to the first by a complex web of electric cables.

'It's an STG laser surveillance system,' Martin said as he made his adjustments.

'What the fuck's STG?'

'Surveillance Technology Group.'

'So that's a laser gun?'

'No, not a gun. It's a laser surveillance transmitter. We'll use it to record conversations in Quinn's place and transmit them back here. I'm setting the transmitter on what's known as a line-of-sight path to the cottage, to direct an invisible beam on to the front window.'

'An invisible beam?' Jock asked sceptically.

'Yes. Imagine the window as the diaphragm of a microphone with oscillating sound waves. The invisible beam bounces off the window, back to the optical receiver in our OP. The receiver then converts the modulated beam into audio signals, which in turn are filtered, amplified and converted into clear conversation. The conversation can then be monitored through headphones and simultaneously recorded on a tape-recorder. Pretty neat, eh?'

'Fucking *Star Wars*,' Jock said. 'Anything to help us see in the dark if those PIRA fuckers try to take us by surprise?'

'Yes,' Martin said, now in his element and enjoying himself. 'We've got a hand-held thermal imager operating on SWIR – that's short-wavelength infrared. Also, a little number called "Iris", which is an infrared intruder-detection system, remote controlled and effective over up to five kilometres. Each of the two men on guard will have one or the other of those to give them an extra set of eyes and ears.'

'I'm going right back to my childhood,' Jock said. 'Fucking *Flash Gordon*.'

'That was long before your childhood,' Danny told him, 'even though you *do* look that age.'

'Fuck you, kid,' Jock said.

Finally, when the surveillance equipment was set up, Dead-eye took a couple of brown, plastic-backed 'bingo' books out of his bergen and laid them on the ground below the viewing hole, beside the legs of the tripods. Already containing the names of wanted men, missing vehicles and suspected addresses, the notebooks would soon also contain details of everything seen and heard during this lengthy recce.

Dead-eye turned away from the viewing hole and looked directly at Martin.

'Are you ready?' he asked in his curiously chilling monotone.

'Yes,' Martin said.

'OK.' Dead-eye fixed his gaze on Jock and Danny. 'You two stay here. We're going down to Quinn's house, but we'll be back in about an hour. If any of these instruments indicate that someone's coming, check that it's us before you open fire and blow our nuts off.'

'Will do!' Jock chirped. 'But why are you going to Quinn's house at this hour of the morning?'

'We only have coverage of the front of Quinn's place,' Dead-eye explained, 'so while the bastard's being held in Castlereagh detention barracks, this electrical wizard, Trooper Renshaw, is going to plant miniaturized bugs at the side and rear of the cottage. Don't ask me how.'

Before anyone could say anything else, Dead-eye picked up a 5.56mm Colt Commando semi-automatic and a couple of 30-round box magazines, then crawled out of the OP. Seeing him go, Martin hurriedly took an olive-green canvas shoulder bag from the kit-well, slung it over his right shoulder, picked up an M16 assault rifle, then followed him out.

It was still dark and cold outside, with the wind howling across the fields, but they made their way rapidly, carefully, down the hill until they reached the road running past the cottage. After glancing left and right to check that no vehicles were coming, they crossed the road, opened the garden gate, closed it carefully behind them, then hurried up the path, stopping near the front door.

Dead-eye glanced left and right, then cocked his head as if listening. 'No dogs,' he whispered. When Martin nodded his agreement, Dead-eye led him around the side of the cottage and stopped by the kitchen window.

'Here?'

'Yes,' Martin said.

While Dead-eye kept watch with the Colt Commando crooked in his left forearm, in what is known as the Belfast Cradle, Martin found a stepladder in the back garden, placed it against the wall by the window, climbed it, then used a small hand drill to quietly bore a hole through the top of the wooden window frame. When this was done, he pushed a fibre-optic probe camera, less than an eighth of an inch thick, through the hole, fixed its wired end to the outside of the window frame, then attached a miniaturized transmitter to the frame, right next to the probe, and wired the probe to it. Though it would have been visible to a keen eye, it was unlikely that anyone not deliberately looking would see either the tiny probe or the small transmitter.

'One more,' Martin said. Removing the stepladder from the wall and carrying it around to the back of the house, he placed it over the window of what appeared to be a rear living room and fixed another probe and transmitter to the top of the wooden frame. When the job was completed, he returned the ladder to where he had found it and carefully checked that nothing else had been disturbed. Satisfied, he glanced once more at his handiwork, then said: 'OK. The laser surveillance system in the OP will pick up from the front room, the probe in the side will pick up from the kitchen, and the probe at the back will pick up from the other living room. That should just about do it.'

'The bedrooms and the bog?' Dead-eye asked without a flicker of irony.

'We can't have everything,' Martin replied with a broad grin. 'Come on, boss, let's get out of here.'

With Dead-eye again in the lead and still cradling his Colt Commando, they crossed the road and made their way back up the dark hill. A good distance away from the OP, but within speaking range, they stopped and identified themselves, each personally announcing his own presence for voice identification. Given Jock's permission to continue, they made their way up to the summit, slipped through a space in the hedgerow, dropped on to their hands and knees, then crawled breathlessly back into the OP.

'All done,' Dead-eye said. 'Now let's wait for that Irish bastard to come calling.'

Coins were tossed to see who would take first watch. Dead-eye and Danny lost the toss, allowing Jock and Martin to crawl gratefully into the scrapes and catch up on lost sleep.

The OP overlooking Quinn's cottage on the stretch of road that ran to and from Belfast was now a functioning unit. At approximately the same time, as they all knew, a third covert OP was being set up, also overlooking the cottage, but further south, to cover the road leading to Dublin.

Whichever direction Quinn decided to travel in, they had him well covered.

# 10

Life in O'Leary's loft was not very comfortable. By the end of the first day the men realized just how uncomfortable it was; by the end of the first night they felt tired, dirty and cramped, with nerves already stretched to the limit and humiliation added to their general sense of deprivation. By day three they felt grubby, exhausted, claustrophobic and increasingly tense.

It was cold, too. Outside, when they looked through the peep-hole, they could see frost on the pavements and an occasional snow shower. The Belfast winds howled bitterly. In the loft, because of the need to be quiet and not let O'Leary's neighbours suspect their presence, they could not wear their boots and so, though they wore extra layers of socks, their feet were constantly freezing and their bodies, likewise wrapped in extra clothing, nonetheless were cold more often than not.

The main problems, however, were domestic. No food could be cooked, so they were forced to subsist on dry, high-calorie rations, such as biscuits, cheese, chocolate and sweets. Although they had a couple of vacuum flasks of hot tea and coffee, they had to strictly limit themselves to one hot drink a day and, for the rest of the time, drink tepid water from the plastic water bottles. As there was nowhere to wash, they could only clean themselves with moisturized cloths and clean their teeth, or rather freshen their mouths, with chewing gum. Even worse, as the loft of O'Leary's house was not divided from the other lofts, the loft space of the adjoining house was designated as a toilet, with the men using plastic bags for this purpose; which they had to seal and store carefully after use. Since they also had to do this in full view of the other men, Taff found it to be particularly humiliating.

'I was prepared for anything when I was badged,' he whispered, 'except for shitting into plastic bags in front of the other men. I mean, that's too much for me.'

'You've got an anal complex,' Gumboot replied. 'Me? I'll shit anywhere except in my own pants and I don't mind who sees me doing it. A shit is a shit, mate.'

'You're bloody disgusting, Gumboot. I put it down to country living. I've heard a lot of stories about life on the farm and none of them were very nice. Carnal knowledge with animals and suchlike. Did you ever do that?'

'A hole is a hole,' Gumboot said. 'What do *you* think, old mate?'

Taff didn't know what to think. He was too tired to think. They had to sleep sitting upright, against the brick walls of the loft, a blanket wrapped around them for warmth, a cushion under the arse. They rested two at a time, with one sleeping, one just relaxing, though the second was compelled to keep his eye on the first in case he talked or cried out in his sleep, alerting the neighbours on either side of O'Leary.

For that reason, no matter how tired they were, they were all too tense to sleep properly.

'That fucking O'Leary sleeps better than we do,' Lampton said sardonically to Ricketts. 'I could kill for his bed.'

They had learnt from their own surveillance that the tout's name was O'Leary and that he had been released from Castlereagh detention barracks at the same time as Quinn. They knew he had returned to the house because they could hear him moving about below. Of course, he knew they were above him and tried to stay as quiet as possible, but they heard practically everything – his radio and TV, the flushing of his toilet, the opening and shutting of doors, drawers and cupboards, conversations with his unwanted visitors – and this, combined with what they were picking up from the surveillance, rendered what he did below to be entirely superfluous.

More interesting what was O'Leary had done before for Lieutenant Cranfield.

'The more I hear, the more I fear for him,' Lampton said. 'Cranfield's out on a narrow ledge.'

The surveillance was a welcome distraction from the oppressive horrors of daily life in the loft, which inhibited movement and forced them to be unnaturally quiet, talking only in whispers. The surveillance, therefore, was a form of work that acted as therapy and also contained its own fascinations, most of which revolved around Lieutenant Cranfield, who was increasingly revealed as a man unlike other SAS officers.

'He thinks he's playing an exciting game,' Ricketts said, 'but he's going to get into trouble and maybe drag us down with him.'

Since starting the surveillance, Ricketts and Lampton in particular, perhaps with a clearer picture of what was actually going on, felt that they were being sucked into a whirlpool of Cranfield's making. The surveillance itself, apart from being a distraction from the rigours of the loft, was a seductive business, drawing them out of themselves and into the world of Michael Quinn and his fellow PIRA members.

Hidden in the loft, seeing Quinn's world through the peep-hole, concentrated and magnified, as it were, by the use of the Thorn EMI hand-held thermal imager, weighing only five kilograms, which he carried on a string around his neck, Ricketts soon began to feel that he was more familiar with Quinn's world than he was with his own. This sense of extraordinary intimacy, of dissolving into someone else's existence, was only increased by his frequent recourse to the camera, which was a 35mm Nikon F3HP with a heavy-duty titanium body, telescopic lens, and a Davis Minimodulux image intensifier also used as a night-vision scope. Ricketts had taken so many photos, and studied Quinn so many times through the viewfinder of the camera, seeing him magnified, his every blemish exposed, his every expression exaggerated, that he sometimes felt that he was actually becoming the Irishman himself.

Perhaps, Ricketts reasoned, Lieutenant Cranfield hadn't considered just how detailed the surveillance of Quinn could be and, therefore, just how much about himself it would reveal.

'He killed O'Halloran all right,' Ricketts said to Lampton when they had listened to yet another conversation picked up by the tiny fibre-optic probe camera which had been inserted near the ceiling of the wall in the adjoining house when the soldiers were pretending to search it. With its advanced laser system, the tiny probe picked up the minute vibrations created by conversations in Quinn's place and transmitted them to a tape-recorder in O'Leary's loft, thus giving Ricketts and Lampton an invaluable but increasingly hair-raising glimpse into the world of the terrorists and their hunters.

Released from Castlereagh, Quinn had returned to his home and called an immediate meeting with the other three members of his PIRA murder squad. During that meeting, every word of which was picked up by the probe, Quinn confirmed that Captain Dubois and Lieutenant Cranfield together had made numerous illegal trips across the border in Eire to snatch wanted IRA men and bring them back to Northern Ireland to be 'captured' by the RUC and imprisoned. Because of this, it was widely believed that the two men, and certainly Lieutenant Cranfield, had killed O'Halloran as an act of vengeance for the deaths of ten invaluable 14 Intelligence Company 'Freds', or turncoats, and the subsequent suicide of Corporal Phillips. As retaliation for this, as well as for Cranfield's illegal cross-border 'snatches', Quinn was going to assassinate Cranfield and seriously damage British morale into the bargain.

'It's clear from what Quinn says,' Lampton told Ricketts, 'that he doesn't know that O'Leary, his PIRA bookkeeper, is Cranfield's tout.'

'Which means he can't possibly know that O'Leary is setting him up to be taken out by Cranfield, instead of vice versa, and that Cranfield has deliberately used O'Halloran's murder, as well as the death of that boy in the Divis, to make Quinn go for him and give him a legal reason for ambushing him. Cranfield wants a very public hit and propaganda victory, as well as some glory for himself. He wants to be the top man.'

'Which he'll be if he succeeds.'

'Yes, if he succeeds. But if he fails, that failure will also be public and do us serious damage.'

'Shit!' Lampton exclaimed, though in a whisper. 'It goes against the grain of every SAS tenet. It's self-aggrandizement on a monumental scale. What the hell can we do?'

'Nothing,' Ricketts said. 'We can't even get out of this loft on our own. We can only get out when the Army comes back on another phoney cordon-and-search, and neither Dubois nor Cranfield will ask for that until they're good and ready.'

'Are you saying we're trapped here?' Lampton asked.

'I reckon so,' Ricketts said.

Temporary escape from the claustrophobia of the loft came through communication via the Pace Communications Landmaster III hand-held transceiver, operating in the VHF/UHF frequency range, or through the UHG band on their portable radio. Ricketts and Lampton were able to do this even when manning the surveillance equipment, as they were both equipped with Davis M135b covert microphones with standard safety-pin attachment and ear-worn receivers, positioned on the collars of their jackets, with the on/off switches taped to their wrists. One of these was tuned in to the military command network at Lisburn; the other to the surveillance network, including the two OPs in Armagh.

It was also to military HQ in Lisburn, where

Captain Dubois and Lieutenant Cranfield were based for the duration of this surveillance, and to the two OPs in south Armagh that details of Quinn's plans and movements, as picked up by the surveillance equipment, were relayed by Lampton or Ricketts in short-burst transmissions. As Quinn had suddenly taken to commuting almost daily between Belfast and his cottage in south Armagh, for meetings with other PIRA members, when such plans and movements were discussed, the two OPS in south Armagh were sending similar information back to Lisburn. Based on the information received, Cranfield was going to pick his time for taking out Quinn's PIRA ASU.

'What he wants,' Lampton said, 'is to ambush Quinn when he and his mates are embarked on some illegal PIRA activity. That's what all this surveillance is for. Also, you can bet that when the sum total of our intelligence gathering is regurgitated in edited form by 14 Intelligence Company, under the supervision of Cranfield's nervous friend, Captain Dubois, what you'll have is a report indicating that Quinn was plotting to assassinate Cranfield, but not saying exactly why. More likely it'll imply that it's because Cranfield is a supremely efficient SAS officer, deemed as a threat to the IRA in general and PIRA in particular. This will only enhance Cranfield's reputation and give him an excuse to go for Quinn. I bet Cranfield is good at chess.'

'Diabolical,' Ricketts said. 'But if he fails, he's going to do the SAS enormous harm.' He squinted through the viewfinder of the Minimodulux image intensifier on the Nikon and saw only the drawn curtains and closed front door of Michael Quinn's house. 'Let's face it, the SAS haven't exactly done themselves proud here so far. First, two troopers try to rob a bank in Londonderry and get six months for their troubles. Then we get a reputation as a bunch of killers as bad as the Black and Tans. Now we're arriving in force with a lot of men experienced in jungle or desert warfare, but with no Combat Training experience and no knowledge of the law when it comes to fighting a war on British territory. Given all this, it won't take too much to damage our reputation further – and what Cranfield's doing could do just that.'

'If you can't beat 'em, join 'em,' Lampton said. 'So if we can't stop Cranfield – and we can't – then let's make sure he doesn't fail and leave Hereford with egg on its face.'

'Mmmmm,' Ricketts murmured.

For the next couple of days he tried to concentrate on the job in hand, studying the street in general and Quinn's house in particular, by day and by night, with the aid of his hand-held thermal imager, the Minimodulux image intensifier and, most importantly, the fibre-optic probe camera inserted in the wall of the adjoining house and transmitting back to the laser system in the loft. Thus able to see and hear Quinn and his friends at all times, Ricketts and the others were given a comprehensive picture of exactly what they were doing and how they lived.

It was always difficult to know if an IRA or PIRA member truly believed in the cause or was in it for some other motive. While many had suffered either personally or indirectly at the hands of the British in the past and therefore had genuine motives for fighting them, it was an unfortunate truth that many others simply thrived on the Troubles and had good reason to ensure that they continued. Given the nature of the conflict, it was also an unfortunate truth that dedication and exploitation often tended to become muddled until even the sincere individual had forgotten his original motives and surrendered to the corruption inherent in the situation.

Though the Troubles had sprung out of genuine grievances, the hard fact of the matter was that much of Belfast was now ruled by graft, blackmail and purely mercenary violence, with protection rackets in abundance and gangs competing to rule their own patch, rewarding those who pleased them, punishing those who did not, and in general using the Troubles as a route to personal power. In this unsavoury stew, therefore, it was difficult to tell if a man was a genuine 'freedom fighter' or just another crook.

That difficulty presented itself when Ricketts and the others observed Quinn. Certainly, it was evident that he ruled his own street, was given due respect from his neighbours, and received a constant stream of visitors to his modest terraced house. Most of the visitors were men, either seasoned PIRA co-workers or adolescent dickers who came to Quinn for discussion or instruction. It was clear from the conversations that weapons were being handed over and taken back, usually accompanied by murmurs about 'single shot', 'both knees', 'six-pack', 'house call', 'post office' or 'bookie's', suggesting a combination of PIRA punishments, door-stop assassinations and armed robberies of local establishments. It also appeared, from the conversations, that Quinn doled out the weapons and that they had to be returned when the job was done.

Money also changed hands. It was usually brought in by the older men, who would hand it over while mentioning the names of various pubs, fish-and-chip shops, general stores or betting shops, occasionally saying things like: 'We fire-bombed some sense into the stupid git and now he's only too willin'.'

O'Leary, the tout below, had visited Quinn's house once since getting out of Castlereagh, attending a PIRA meeting. During a conversation about 'funds' and 'more money for weapons', the 'books' were mentioned by Quinn and O'Leary said he would have them ready soon. When Lampton observed that O'Leary sounded nervous, Taff Burgess responded: 'I can understand that – what with us being up in his loft and all. How would *you* feel?'

'I guess you're right,' Lampton said.

At least once each day, Quinn drove with some of the others to his house in Armagh. From information picked up by the OPs overlooking the house, it appeared that he was there to receive daily supplies of weapons being brought in from across the border, probably in hidden compartments in the vehicles.

'He can't be using his country place as an ammunition dump,' Lampton said to Ricketts. 'That would be too dangerous.'

'No,' Ricketts replied. 'Not an ammunition dump. Obviously he's preparing for some forthcoming outrage – something pretty big. Let's just pray that we find out about it in time to prevent it.'

'He keeps mentioning Cranfield,' Lampton recalled.

'That's what worries me,' Ricketts said.

Resting in the corner beside the sleeping Taff Burgess, Gumboot suddenly perked up to say: 'This tout down below us. The one letting us use his loft. Being a tout is one thing – you run the risk of kneecapping – but letting Brits into your loft is something else again. In fact, it's practically suicidal. What would make O'Leary do it for Cranfield?'

Lampton shook his head. 'I don't know.'

'It must be something pretty heavy,' Gumboot said, 'for O'Leary to risk that.'

'Right,' Ricketts said.

'Why do men become touts?'

'Disillusionment,' Lampton suggested. 'Moral revulsion. Money, of course.'

'Exactly,' Gumboot said. 'Money. Isn't O'Leary a PIRA bookkeeper?'

'We picked that up from Quinn,' Ricketts said.

'So maybe he needed money really bad.'

'He was fiddling the books?'

'Right. So he somehow gets involved with 14 Intelligence Company and ends up with Cranfield. I say the man's being paid.'

'So, what's your point?'

'If this guy's fiddled PIRA books and is getting Cranfield to bail him out, I'd say that Cranfield's treading tricky water and risking O'Leary's life. Those bastards across the road, if they ever find out we've been here, they're gonna bury O'Leary. That's not the SAS way, folks.'

'It's Lieutenant Cranfield's way,' Lampton said.

'He's certainly let O'Leary go out on a limb,' Ricketts said. 'Out just about as far as you can go without falling off.'

'He must've had something on him,' Gumboot said.

'Blackmail?' Lampton asked.

'What else?' Gumboot replied.

As one day passed into the next and the surveillance intelligence built up, it became clear from what Quinn said, both in Belfast and in Armagh, that he thought of Cranfield as the prime threat to PIRA and was intending to take him out. Equally clear to Ricketts was that Cranfield was virtually using himself as bait to bring Quinn's gang out into the open, where he could legally, and more publicly, put an end to them. Even more disturbing was the fact that he appeared to be using dubious means of accomplishing his mission and was doing so without consulting his superiors in the intelligence community, let alone those in Hereford. It was this that made him dangerous.

Nevertheless, regardless of their personal feelings, Ricketts and Lampton, with the able assistance of Gumboot and Taff, continued to keep watch on the house across the road and transmit what they found to Lisburn and the OPs in Armagh. Which is how they discovered that something had gone wrong with the OP covering the road to Dublin.

They knew that something had happened because communications to that OP were suddenly cut. Before they could make enquiries, they received a communication from Cranfield in Lisburn, informing them that the OP had been dismantled, for reasons which would be explained later. They were, however, to keep in touch with the OP overlooking the Al running between Belfast and Quinn's cottage.

When Lampton asked how long they had to remain in the loft, Cranfield's message was terse: 'Sit tight.'

Given that they could not leave the loft unaided, they had no choice but to do as they were told.

Later that day, however, when listening to a conversation between Quinn and his murder squad, they heard the full story of the terminated OP.

They were still in a state of shock, trying to take it in, when they heard Quinn telling his men that they were going to attack, and take out, the other OP.

Lampton contacted Lisburn.

# 11

'Arrested!' Dubois practically screamed. 'Your damned troopers have actually been arrested! Explain *that* to me, Cranfield!'

Cranfield was standing by the window in an office in Army HQ Lisburn, gazing down on the courtyard surrounded by high brick walls and filled with Saracens, armoured pigs, paddy-wagons, and uniformed British soldiers and paratroopers and RUC officers in flak jackets. It looked like a fortress. Sighing, Cranfield turned back to Dubois.

'You know the score,' he said blandly. 'From time to time, on an unmarked border, soldiers *do* stray into the south.'

'Not *my* soldiers!' Dubois snapped.

'They have done so in the past and you know it, so let's not be so high and mighty about it.'

Dubois lit a cigarette and exhaled a cloud of smoke. 'All right,' he said. 'I'll try to avoid nitpicking, but this incident is rapidly inflating into a diplomatic incident, so tell me exactly what happened and we'll go on from there.'

Cranfield walked to a chair, was about to sit down, changed his mind and went back to the window, though this time standing with his back to it, in order to face the agitated Dubois. 'It happened two days ago,' he said, 'just before midnight on the fifth.' He shrugged. 'I can only put it down to their lack of experience.'

'Just tell me,' Dubois said.

'It was the men in the OP overlooking the road that runs past Quinn's cottage to Dublin. They had observed – as had the other OP overlooking the road to Belfast – that Quinn was visiting the place regularly to receive daily supplies of arms and ammunition brought in from the Free State.'

'How did they know what the supplies were?'

'Through Quinn's conversations with the suppliers. Both OPs were equipped with STG laser surveillance systems and Quinn's cottage is bugged with a fibre-optic probe camera that still transmits back to the remaining OP.'

'Go on.'

Cranfield took a deep breath, then released it again, which was the nearest he had ever come to publicly displaying nervousness. 'After observing this for three or four days, Sergeant Manners, in charge of the OP, became convinced that he was observing major PIRA suppliers and that if he followed them back to where they had come from, he would find their HQ. As the suppliers arrived about the same time every day, Manners called up a Q car from Bessbrook . . .'

'Christ!' Dubois exclaimed involuntarily.

'. . . then, leaving two of his men in the OP, but accompanied by one of his troopers, only recently badged, he went down to where the Q car was parked – out of sight of Quinn's place but with a clear view of it – and waited until that day's supply of arms had been delivered. When the suppliers drove off again, Manners ordered the driver of the Q car to follow them.'

Dubois sucked on his cigarette, screwed up his eyes and blew out a cloud of smoke like a man who can't believe what he is hearing. 'Every rule in the book broken,' he said. 'An absolute cowboy!'

Cranfield nodded. 'Anyway, Manners followed the PIRA suppliers towards Louth until the driver, navigating with the aid of a torch-lit map, took a wrong turning near Carlingford Lough. Please bear in mind that he'd been sent to Northern Ireland direct from Oman, with no chance to retrain for the very different environment of the Irish border with its confusing web of often unmarked country lanes.'

'So he got lost,' Dubois said in a flat voice.

'Yes . . . and the Q car was stopped at a police roadblock near Cornamucklagh, only 600 yards south of the border.'

Dubois leaned across the desk to cover his face with his hands. He had just inhaled again and the smoke from his cigarette drifted out from between his pursed lips.

'Go on,' he said again, more softly this time.

'Questioned by the Gardai, the SAS men claimed they were on a reconnaissance mission and had made a map-reading error. This was greeted with scepticism, and in spite of appeals to let the patrol return north, the Gardai insisted on taking advice from Dundalk. Then matters took a turn for the worse.'

'What could be worse?' Dubois asked pointedly, still cupping his face with his hands.

'When Sergeant Manners and his trooper still hadn't returned to the OP by first light, the other sergeant in the OP, also fresh from Oman, called up another Q car from Bessbrook and, with the remaining trooper, left the OP and went off to find the two missing men.'

'This is horrendous,' Dubois said, looking up and gazing fixedly beyond Cranfield to the window, clearly wishing to take wing and fly away.

'Taking the same route as Manners,' Cranfield continued, 'the second two arrived at the same Gardai checkpoint about 8 a.m. Naturally they were detained as well.'

'Unbelievable!' Dubois exclaimed bitterly.

'Weapons taken from the four men included Sterling sub-machine-guns with silencers, pump-action shotguns and the standard-issue Browning High Power. The Gardai were suitably impressed and ushered all four soldiers into the police office for further questioning. Reportedly, when the SAS men realized they had stumbled across the border and were in the Republic, they all burst out laughing.'

'Did they indeed?' Dubois stubbed his cigarette out with suppressed fury, then looked up at Cranfield. 'Unfortunately, the Irish aren't so amused. In previous cases of accidental border crossings the soldiers were reprimanded and sent back. However, as a man was recently kidnapped in that area, then brought to this side of the border and murdered, the Gardai insisted that your men be held overnight and a forensic test carried out on their weapons, to ascertain if any of them might have been used for that murder.' Pleased to see Cranfield shocked at last, Dubois nodded and said: 'Yes, Cranfield, I know what's going on. I didn't know what your men were doing in the Republic, but I know what's happening now and why your men were held overnight with the personal permission of no less than the Foreign Minister himself.'

Cranfield took a seat, clearly shaken but determined to stay calm. 'So what were the results?'

'Lucky for you, the tests proved negative. Nevertheless, though your men will be released on bail and sent back to Hereford, the Irish are calling for them to be returned eventually for trial. Naturally the British are furious about this, viewing it as a politically motivated act by the Irish government.

They've been compelled, however, to agree to send the men back when a trial can be arranged, which should be a few months from now. In the meantime, please see to it that your men, when returned to Bessbrook, are put on the first plane back to RAF Lyneham.'

'Yes, Captain,' Cranfield said.

'I take it that the OP constructed by those fools has been demolished.'

'Yes, Captain.'

'And the other one? The one overlooking the road to Belfast?'

'It's still there, manned by four good men.'

'You may need them,' Dubois said. 'We've just received a flurry of short-burst transmissions from the OP in the Falls. They were informed by the OP overlooking the Belfast road about the arms deliveries to Quinn's house. Then, listening in to Quinn's conversations, they discovered that he had found out from a source in Dublin that the SAS troops captured by the Gardai had come from an OP overlooking his place in Armagh. Quinn put that area under observation just before one of our Gazelles dropped a team to demolish it. Alerted by this, he had the area checked further and found the second OP – the one overlooking the road to Belfast.'

'Damn!' Cranfield exclaimed in frustration. 'What's he planning to do?'

'As he can't be seen to be involved himself, he

intends sending two PIRA ASUs to Armagh tomorrow – one to attack and take out the remaining OP, the other to spirit the arms out of his country place before we investigate the deaths of our OP team and, subsequently, search that same house. Meanwhile, Quinn himself will remain in the Falls, keeping his hands clean and with lots of witnesses to confirm where he was at the time of the incident.'

'My God,' Cranfield said softly, looking pleased instead of shocked. 'This is just what we need!'

Dubois had been expecting the reaction, but it still shocked him slightly. 'It's just what *you* need,' he emphasized, 'and unfortunately, whether or not I like it, I'll have to go along with it.'

'We have a legitimate excuse – self-defence. That then gives us the excuse to do a cordon-and-search of the whole area, thus finding the cache in Quinn's cottage, which in turn lets us take him in eventually and plant him in Long Kesh. It's perfect!'

'Nothing's perfect,' Dubois said, 'and I still have my doubts, but clearly we can't miss this opportunity. Can your four men handle it?'

'Yes. They took a GPMG with them and are otherwise well armed. If they're warned, they'll be ready.'

'Quinn's men are gathering at his Belfast house tomorrow at noon and leaving in three separate cars at separate times. According to the surveillance report from the OP facing his house, they'll leave Belfast empty-handed and congregate in Quinn's place in Armagh. There, while four of them pack the armaments into a van to take them elsewhere, the other four will pick the weapons they need and then engage in what they imagine will be a surprise attack on the OP. The use of an RPG 7 rocket launcher was mentioned, so your men had better be prepared to leave the OP and set up an ambush.'

'Right,' Cranfield said. He stood up and walked to the door, preparing to take his leave.

'You have a lot to make amends for,' Dubois said.

'I will,' Cranfield replied. Then, smiling brightly, already shucking off his guilt, he opened the door and hurried out, keen to get things organized.

# 12

It was Danny who first saw the light of the helicopter, hovering like a UFO in the dark sky just before dawn.

On watch at the viewing hole shaped out of the hedgerow and camouflaged in hessian, scanning the area around Quinn's cottage with a pair of binoculars instead of the tripod-mounted thermal imager, Danny was really just trying to distract himself until it was time to waken Martin and let him take over the watch.

Being a working-class lad from the Midlands, reticent at the best of times, unwilling to put himself forward, Danny wasn't sure that he liked Martin, who appeared to have the natural confidence of someone well educated and brought up in the security of the middle class.

In fact, Danny thought Martin was a younger version of Lieutenant Cranfield, who was, in Danny's view, a 'big timer' of the kind not normally encouraged by the SAS.

No, Danny preferred Sergeant 'Dead-eye Dick'

Parker, who, strangely enough, seemed to fill other men with dread. That, Danny reasoned, was because Dead-eye was so quiet and tended to keep to himself. Danny didn't mind that. Indeed, he thought it was a virtue. He certainly preferred it to the cockiness of men like Cranfield and Renshaw.

Of course the latter had been badged at the same time as Danny, undergoing the same Selection and Training course and, Danny had to admit, emerging from the ordeal with flying colours. Yet although Danny respected him for this, he still didn't feel comfortable with him – probably because he was intimidated by middle-class self-assurance, particularly in people his own age.

He didn't mind it so much in Cranfield, who was older and, as an officer, not so close to him.

Jock McGregor was OK. A bit of a laugh, in fact. Along with Ricketts and Dead-eye, he had been one of the SAS troopers who, four years earlier, had scaled the mighty Jebel Dhofar in Oman to flush the fierce *Adoo* fighters from the summit. Once a 'secret' war, now a legendary SAS achievement, the Dhofar campaign was exactly the kind of adventure that Danny desperately wanted to have.

Belfast, though gaining him valuable experience, was not quite so exotic. On the other hand, it had at least put him in the company of the notorious Dead-eye. The latter had also been in Oman and, according to Jock and Ricketts, was one of the best marksmen in the Regiment, as well as being deadly with his knife. Also, according to gossip, he had been a normal, fairly sociable young man until he went into the Telok Anson swamp in the Malayan jungle to fight the fierce guerrillas of Ah Hoi, nicknamed the 'Baby Killers'. Dead-eye never discussed what happened in that swamp, but he had emerged from it changed for all time. Now, he was a steely-eyed, introverted, highly efficient soldier who even made many of his fellow SAS men nervous.

Danny, who had wanted to be a soldier since he was a child, admired Dead-eye for that and was dying to know just what kind of experience had changed him so dramatically. In fact, it was Danny's belief that of all the people in the Squadron, Dead-eye was the only one with the 'secret' of how to be a great soldier – which is what he wanted to be.

Danny was thinking such thoughts when he saw a light hovering in the dark sky, like a flying saucer, then gradually taking the shape of a helicopter. At first thinking it was on a resup mission to one of the overt OPs, he soon realized that it was actually passing over the distant hills and coming straight towards him. When the sound of it reached him, growing louder by the second, he glanced back over his shoulder and saw that Dead-eye was already awake and sitting up to find out what was happening.

'Is that a chopper?' Dead-eye asked as Jock and Martin also woke up, rubbing sleepy eyes.

'Yes,' Danny said. 'And it seems to be coming straight at us.'

Dead-eye scrambled across the OP to glance out of the viewing hole. By that time the chopper was identifiable as a Gazelle flying from the direction of Bessbrook and dropping down towards the OP.

'We're supposed to be on a *secret* mission,' Danny said, 'so what are *they* doing here?'

Dead-eye didn't reply. Instead, he watched the chopper descending. It came down towards the OP, hovered above it for a moment, then glided south and landed behind it, just far enough away for its spinning rotors not to sweep the loose grass and gorse off the camouflaged hessian. Dead-eye grabbed a Colt Commando – he never moved without a weapon – and crawled out of the OP. Automatically picking up his M16, Danny followed him.

'We'll stay here,' Jock shouted after him, 'and keep our eye on the target!'

'You do that,' Danny whispered.

As he crawled out of the OP he saw Lieutenant Cranfield hurrying away from the Gazelle, crouched low against the wind generated by the rotors. Wearing DPMs and a beret with badge, he had a Browning High Power holstered on his hip. Danny climbed to his feet as Cranfield straightened up and approached the watchful Dead-eye. He hurried to stand beside his hero and hear what was said.

'Morning, Sergeant,' Cranfield said. Dead-eye just nodded. The spinning rotors of the Gazelle went into neutral, thus reducing the noise considerably and letting the men hear each other speak. 'How are things up here?'

'Fine,' Dead-eye said. 'No problems. Nothing much happening either way.'

'You heard about the other OP team, I gather?'

Dead-eye nodded. 'Fucking twats.'

'Right,' Cranfield said. 'The OP's been demolished and the men are being flown back to Hereford. The Irish, however, are insisting that they be returned later to Northern Ireland to be put on trial. Downing Street has agreed.'

'A show trial.'

'Yes. Not that they don't deserve it. I trust that you men will show more sense.'

Danny glimpsed a flash of anger in Dead-eye, but his voice remained flat. 'What are you doing here, Lieutenant? This is supposed to be a *covert* OP.'

'Your cover's been blown, Sergeant. Someone in Dublin traced that other OP team back to here and Quinn had the area thoroughly searched. Now Quinn knows that this second OP is here and he intends taking it out.'

'When?'

'Today. Two four-man ASUs will soon be on their way here from the Falls – one to take out the OP, leaving no one alive; the other to remove the weapons and ammunition from

Quinn's place, leaving him looking like Mister Clean.'

'You picked that up from the OP in the Falls?'

'Yes.'

'That was useful.'

'Lampton's team is doing a good job.'

'So what do we do about the ASUs? Are we staying or leaving?'

'You're staying. They're expecting to take you by surprise, but instead you're going to be waiting for them to reverse expectations.'

'An ambush.'

'Correct. They're coming with an RPG 7 rocket launcher, so you have to take them out before they can fire a rocket at the OP. If you manage to do it before Quinn's place is cleared, you can then go down and take out the others.'

'You don't want them captured?'

'I didn't say that. I'm merely saying that I want you to inflict as much damage as possible within the strict letter of the law. It's legitimate self-defence.'

Dead-eye gazed steadily at Cranfield in a silence that seemed to last a long time. Eventually, when the officer didn't flinch, he asked: 'What if we succeed?'

'You call Bessbrook with the results of the action. We'll then lift you out and clean up the damage.'

'What about Quinn, all cosy in Belfast?'

'When we catch the others trying to clear out his cottage – which I expect you to do – we can haul him into Crumlin Road jail as the start of his legal journey to Long Kesh. There we'll slam the door on him.'

'When are the ASUs expected to get here?'

'About noon.'

'That gives us plenty of time. Have you come to help out?'

'I'd love to, but I can't,' Cranfield said. 'Unfortunately, this action has to look like self-defence, not something planned, so I can't be seen to be part of it – and this little visit, incidentally, never happened.'

'What's the story?'

'Having had Quinn's cottage under surveillance for some time, you'd seen his men bringing in weapons, ammunition and explosives. You were deciding what to do about it when an ASU hit squad almost took you by surprise. Luckily, you saw them coming and were able to hit them before they hit you. Then you saw another bunch removing the weapons from the cottage, so you went after them as well, to stop them escaping. That's the story. Stick to it.'

'Will do,' Dead-eye said.

'Good luck, Sergeant.'

'Thanks.'

Cranfield returned to the Gazelle and climbed back in. The rotors slipped out of neutral, started spinning faster, soon whipping up a minor storm, then lifted the chopper up off the hill. Dead-eye watched it flying off towards Bessbrook, beyond lush hills now visible in morning light, then he glanced flatly at Danny and nodded towards the OP.

Danny went in first, with Dead-eye following him. Jock was having a breakfast of cheese and biscuits washed down with water. Martin was adjusting the bulky, tripod-mounted, Thorn EMI thermal imager at the viewing hole, but he turned around to face them when they entered.

'Who was it?' Jock asked.

'Lieutenant Cranfield,' Dead-eye replied.

'What the fuck did *he* want?' Jock asked, with no great respect.

Dead-eye filled him in on the situation as explained by Lieutenant Cranfield. 'The ASUs should be here about noon,' he summarized, 'and we have to be ready.'

'So what's the strategy, boss?' Martin asked, sounding excited.

Dead-eye stared steadily at him, then turned slightly aside, speaking mainly to Jock. 'They have an RPG 7 rocket launcher, so my bet is they'll stop part of the way up the hill to lob one into the OP, thinking we're in it. Given the elevation requirements of the RPG 7, they'll have to fire it from near the bottom of the hill, not much higher than the lower slopes, so that's where we'll locate – to take them out before they can fire the missile.'

'Sounds good,' Jock said.

'There's a hedgerow running down the side of the hill, about fifty yards west of the OP. Three of us will dig in there, near to where it levels out, and wait for the bastards to arrive. The fourth man will remain here on the GPMG to give us cover when the fire-fight commences.'

'If we're down that low,' Jock reminded him, 'we'll be close to the road, which puts us within range of the fire-power of the ASU team clearing out Quinn's place.'

'Exactly,' Dead-eye said. 'Which gives us a legitimate excuse to attack them as well and get our hands on the incriminating evidence – the weapons, ammo and explosives from Quinn's cottage.'

'One of Cranfield's little dodges.'

'Pretty damned good,' Martin said. 'He's a hell of an officer, Lieutenant Cranfield. He knows just what he's doing.'

'I'll *bet* he does,' Jock said. 'So who stays in the OP?'

'You,' Dead-eye told him. 'Apart from me, you're the most experienced, so you shouldn't need supervision. I trust you to use your initiative and not make mistakes.'

'Such as shooting us instead of the ASU team,' Martin said with a wide grin.

'If I shoot you,' Jock said, 'it'll be intentional. I don't make mistakes.'

'You two,' Dead-eye said to Martin and Danny, 'will come with me and do what I tell you. We'll need short-handled pickaxes and spades for the scrapes. Attach the M203 grenade launchers to your M16s. At my signal, you'll lay two grenades down on the ASU. When they explode, Jock'll take that as the signal to open up with the GPMG. What damage not inflicted by Jock, will be inflicted by us. OK, let's get going.'

'They're not coming until noon,' Martin reminded him.

'You've got something better to do up here, Trooper?' Dead-eye asked.

'No, boss.'

'Then let's get the fuck down that hill and make sure we're ready. They might get here *before* noon.'

'Yes, boss!' Martin snapped.

'Whatever way it goes,' Jock said, 'this OP is finished, so take that thermal imager away and let me put the machine-gun in its place.'

'Right,' Martin said. 'But I'll leave the Nikon with the image intensifier so that you can take photos when they arrive. They'll be helpful as evidence.'

Jock glanced at Dead-eye who simply nodded, acknowledging that Martin, though cocky, was right.

'Aye,' Jock said, 'you do that.'

Dead-eye and Danny checked their weapons, ensured that they had a plentiful supply of 30-round magazines, then clipped short-handled spades and pickaxes to their belts. As they were doing so,

Jock set up the tripod for the GPMG. Meanwhile, Martin unscrewed the bulky thermal imager from its tripod, then removed it and the tripod from in front of the viewing hole. Martin placed the thermal imager back in its canvas carrier while Jock set the GPMG up on its tripod, with the barrel poking out through the viewing hole, angled down the hill, beside the Nikon with the image intensifier, also mounted on a tripod at the viewing hole. As Jock was feeding the ammunition belt into the GPMG, which normally required a two-man team, Dead-eye slid a spade and a pickaxe towards Martin, saying: 'Here, clip these to your belt and take as many magazines as you can reasonably carry. Plus fragmentation and buckshot grenades for the M203s. Let's give them a sore arse.'

Martin grinned and did as he was told.

'Are you OK, Jock?' Dead-eye asked.

Jock, now sitting on a wooden box behind the GPMG, stuck his thumb up in the air. 'Straight line-of-sight between here and the cottage. Can't miss, boss.'

'You fire when the grenades go off,' Dead-eye reminded him. 'One belt's all you need.'

'No sweat,' Jock said.

'OK,' Dead-eye said to the others. 'Let's get the fuck down that hill. See you later, Jock.'

'Right, boss,' Jock said.

Holding his 5.56mm Colt Commando in the Belfast Cradle, Dead-eye crawled out, followed by

Martin and Danny. Once outside, in the grey light of morning, they straightened up and headed down the hill at a half crouch, zigzagging automatically over the boulder-strewn grass and turf, heading obliquely towards the tall fuchsia hedges that bordered the western side of the field, beyond which was an undulating landscape of green fields and trees. When they had reached the fuchsia hedges, Dead-eye led them further down until they were about fifty metres from the fence separating the hill from the road running across the front of Quinn's cottage – one way to Belfast, the other to Dublin.

'Our patch,' Dead-eye said.

Wearing DPM clothing, and with their weapons wrapped in tape of a similar colouring, they blended into the hedges even before digging out their scrapes. Nevertheless, using their short-handled pickaxes and spades, they made themselves shallow scrapes that extended into the foliage, letting it fall back over them when they crawled in and lay on their bellies. Though not comfortable, they were practically invisible and ready to fire.

Glancing to his right, downhill, Danny could see the road beyond the fence and, behind that, Quinn's cottage. It was a nondescript building, with brick walls and slate roof, two storeys high, but set well back from the road, surrounded by high, rolling fields, with no other houses in sight. A modest but very pleasant country retreat, it was now a warehouse packed with weapons, ammunition and explosives.

*Fire a grenade in there*, Danny thought, *and the whole place will go up in flames. That's not a house; it's an arsenal.*

Lying belly down in his shallow scrape, half buried in the foliage, cradling his M16 with an M203 grenade launcher attached, with Dead-eye on one side of him and Martin Renshaw on the other, Danny suddenly realized that his Selection and Training were over and that this was the real thing.

He had been in the Army for two years, 3rd Battalion, Light Infantry, but this was the first time he'd been involved in an actual conflict, let alone being out of England. His couple of days in Belfast, doing the 'tour' with Sergeant Hampton of 14 Intelligence Company, had presented him with a graphic picture of a city at war with itself. Yet it had not led to actual engagement with the enemy. Now all that was about to change and he wondered how he would deal with it when push came to shove.

*You'll be OK*, he told himself.

Danny had wanted to be a special kind of soldier since his schooldays – thinking first about the French Foreign Legion, then about becoming a mercenary, but eventually accepting that it had to be legitimate and so deciding on joining the army, in order to serve his requisite two years and then apply for the SAS. Having decided, he had done it and never regretted it, feeling that he was born to be a soldier. Now here he was, about to fire his first shots in anger, thankfully with Dead-eye by his side. That made him feel good.

After an hour or so of waiting, hearing nothing but the birdsong and the occasional car passing on the road below, Danny had an almost uncontrollable urge to break the silence by asking Dead-eye about the Telok Anson swamp. Unfortunately, though he had managed to screw up the courage, he was too far away to do it without shouting, which he knew would anger the experienced sergeant.

Dead-eye had placed them about fifteen metres apart, with Martin the highest up, Dead-eye closest to the road, therefore to Quinn's cottage, and Danny in the middle. This would give them a triangular field of fire homing in on where Dead-eye had calculated the ASU would be compelled to set up the RPG 7 for the required elevation. Clearly, he knew what he was doing, though it did prevent them from passing the time with conversation. Not that Dead-eye ever talked much anyway.

Frustrated, Danny contented himself by studying the scenery – the tree-lined, bright green, alluvial fields; sunlight glinting off a stretch of sea, glimpsed beyond the distant hills; birds winging through a jigsaw of blue sky and patchy clouds – and by dwelling on how different it was from the bleak, terraced streets of Kingswinford, where he grew up. It was hard to imagine, when you looked at this scenery, that Belfast lay just beyond the hills and its streets were even worse than those in Kingswinford – worse to look at and infinitely more dangerous to live in. It was hard to imagine what was happening here, with the British fighting a mean war on British soil. Of course, the Irish didn't think it was British soil – which explained the war.

Danny was almost lost in thoughts of this kind when a red Ford came in sight, from the direction of Belfast, and pulled into a lay-by just around a slow bend in the road. Although he could see the car clearly from his vantage point halfway up the hill, Danny realized that it would be out of sight of the OP. Knowing that this must have been deliberate, he instinctively tensed, preparing himself for action.

Three men got out of the car, leaving the driver behind the wheel, presumably to do the talking should an Army or RUC patrol come along. The men were wearing normal civilian clothing: corduroy trousers or denims, jackets and open-necked shirts. One of them lay on his belly, groped under the car, and eventually withdrew a long object wrapped in some kind of covering – the RPG 7, Danny surmised. Another leaned back into the rear of the vehicle, as if groping around beneath the seats, and eventually withdrew two more long parcels – probably wrapped rifles or sub-machine-guns. The third man, meanwhile, was leaning into the rear door at the other side.

Eventually he straightened up, holding a canvas bag, which Danny assumed was filled with magazines for the weapons.

After conversing briefly with the driver, the man holding the wrapped RPG 7 led the other two through a gateway in the high fuchsia hedges and wooden fence bordering the road, into the field at a location approximately forty-five degrees east of the line-of-sight of the OP. The men then made their way alongside the road, but were shielded from it by the high hedge. They were also hidden from the OP by an abrupt dip in the ground where the field ran down steeply before levelling out near the fence.

They were able to clamber a good twenty metres up that steep, lower stretch of the hill while remaining out of view of the OP and without being seen by the few cars passing by. When eventually they chose the spot from which to launch their attack, they were just below Dead-eye, obliquely to the right of Martin and Danny.

Hidden in the hedge, Danny set the M203 grenade launcher to fire, judged the angle of elevation required, then held the M16 steady.

The red Ford remained where it was – parked just around the bend in the road, out of sight of the OP.

The man with the wrapped RPG 7 looked at his watch, then said something to the other two, who immediately began unwrapping the parcels.

The large parcel was, indeed, a wrapped RPG 7

rocket launcher and the other two were Russian 7.62mm AK-47 automatic rifles, beloved of terrorists everywhere and instantly recognizable, even from this distance, because of the unusually curved 30-round box magazine.

When the weapons were unwrapped, the man with the canvas bag opened it and started handing out ammunition, including magazines for the AK-47s and a 2.25kg missile for the RPG 7.

Danny glanced sideways and saw Dead-eye's hand thrusting out of the hedge, about to give the signal to fire.

The man with the RPG 7 checked his watch again, then glanced back over his shoulder, down the hill and across the road to Quinn's cottage. Shaking his head from side to side, as if exasperated, he loaded the 2.25kg missile into the launcher, then glanced back over his shoulder again.

A grey removal truck came along the road from the direction of the nearby border, and pulled into the driveway. Four men got out, glanced up the hill in the general direction of the covert OP, and waved.

Obviously knowing that his comrades would be seen by the OP, the man knelt in the firing position and aimed the RPG 7.

Still looking sideways, Danny saw Dead-eye drop his hand, signalling, 'Open fire.' Leaning forward into the stock of his M16, Danny fired the M213 grenade launcher.

His head was ringing from the noise, his body jolting from the backblast, as the two grenades – one fired by Martin, located higher up the hill – exploded at the same time on either side of the three men, with soil and buckshot spewing up and outwards through boiling columns of black smoke.

Even as the smoke was still obscuring the men, the shocking roar of the GPMG firing from the OP joined the harsh chatter of the M16s, as well as Dead-eye's Colt Commando.

Danny had switched to the M16 automatically, hardly aware that he had done so, and was firing rapidly repeated three-round bursts into the swirling smoke from the buckshot grenades.

One of the men was already down, bowled sideways by the blast. The other two were dancing wildly in a convulsion of spitting earth created by the combined fire-power of the GPMG and three M16 assault rifles. Taken by surprise, and confused as to where the firing was actually coming from, the remaining two didn't even have time to fire their weapons before they were cut to shreds and collapsed.

As the two men fell, the red Ford screeched into life, reversed out of the lay-by, and raced back around the bend, returning to Belfast.

At the same time, the men in the cottage, seeing what had happened, raced across the driveway to get back into the removal van.

As Jock's GPMG trailed off into silence, Dead-eye leapt out of the hedge and raced across the field, his Colt Commando in one hand, a Landmaster III transceiver in the other. As he knelt down to examine the bloody ASU team, speaking into the transceiver at the same time, the removal van lumbered out of Quinn's driveway. One of the men, however, obviously senseless with anger, bellowed a string of abuse in a broad Ulster accent, then raced across the road and clambered over the fence. He dropped down the other side, took aim with his pistol, and fired at Dead-eye.

Stepping out from the hedge, Danny adopted the kneeling position, took aim with his M16 and fired a couple of three-round bursts. The man was punched backwards so hard that he smashed through the fence, falling to the ground.

'Stop that van!' Dead-eye bellowed, pointing down the hill, then speaking again into the transceiver.

Danny switched back to the M203 and loaded a grenade while running a few more yards down the hill, followed by Martin, who was holding his M16 in the Belfast Cradle. The removal van had just driven out through the gates of the cottage and was turning into the road, in the direction of the border, when Danny calculated the angle of elevation and fired a fragmentation grenade. The backblast rocked his shoulder and his head rang from the noise. Then the grenade exploded just in front of the truck, practically under the left wheel, shattering the windscreen and lifting the whole vehicle up on to two wheels. It slammed back down again, but careered across the road, bouncing over a ditch, then smashed through the fence and embedded itself deep in the hedgerow.

Martin was already racing past Danny when first one, then two of the men in the crashed van jumped down to the ground, before straightening up and firing their pistols.

Martin fired on the run and Danny fired a second later. One of the men jerked spasmodically, dropped his pistol, fell back, and shuddered wildly against the side of the van as more bullets stitched him. He was sliding to the ground, leaving a trail of blood on the side of the van, as the other man backed across the road, firing as he retreated. He had almost reached the fence of the cottage when a combined burst from Martin and Danny nearly cut him in two, then picked him up and slammed him back on to the fence, which immediately buckled under his falling body. Pouring blood from his chest and stomach, the man rocked like a see-saw for a couple of seconds, then slowly fell backwards, into the driveway. Meanwhile, Martin and Danny were racing down the hill to check the dead and the wounded.

The only wounded was the driver of the van, his eyes bloodied and blinded by shards of glass from the shattered windscreen, his forehead split open, his nose broken by impact with the steering wheel. He was unconscious, but groaning.

The other men, including the one across the road, had been torn to shreds by the high-velocity 5.56mm bullets of the M16s. Soaked in blood, with bone gleaming through gristle, they were certainly dead.

'Let's check the house,' Martin said.

Slightly shaken by the terrible wounds inflicted on the dead, but also feeling pure and bright, as if illuminated from within, Danny followed Martin along the gravel driveway to the front of Quinn's hideaway. Obviously excited, Martin smashed the lock on the door with a single burst from his M16, then led Danny inside.

The hall was filled with wooden crates containing guns and ammunition. So was the living room. Explosives of every kind were stacked up in the kitchen, and more weapons, ammunition and explosives were found in the back room.

'Some haul!' Martin said softly.

At that moment, he was buzzed on his walkie-talkie. When he had turned it on and identified himself, the voice of Dead-eye informed him that he was to remain in the cottage until Sappers – already called up by Dead-eye – arrived to remove the weapons, ammunition and explosives for transfer to Bessbrook. Danny, Dead-eye said, was to stand guard over the crashed removal van until an ambulance, also from Bessbrook, arrived to take away the dead and wounded. A REME team had also been called up to remove the crashed, badly damaged van.

'OK, boss,' Martin said. 'We've got you. Over and out.' He switched the walkie-talkie off and grinned at Danny. 'You get the stiffs and the truck,' he said, then waved his right hand, indicating the crates piled up all around him in the living room, 'and I get all this. Let's do what the man says.'

Leaving Martin in the relative warmth of the house, Danny stepped out into the biting cold, glanced uneasily at the bloody body lying face up by the fence, then crossed the road to the crashed removal van. The driver was still unconscious, but had mercifully stopped groaning and was now lying with his forehead resting on the steering wheel, which was covered in a mass of congealed blood, some of which had dripped from his blinded eyes. Since there was little he could do for him, Danny left him as he was and went around to stand guard by the side of the van, facing the road leading to Belfast.

From where he was standing, he could see that Jock had left the OP to join Dead-eye over the bodies of the three dead terrorists, in the dip near the bottom of the hill. Dead-eye had put his Landmaster III away and was talking to Jock while scanning the Belfast road, obviously impatient for the medics, REME team and Sappers to come and clean up the mess. Eventually, they did so – first the ambulance, then the REME breakdown truck and mechanics, and finally the Sappers with their own trucks. The medics removed the dead and the one wounded man, the REME truck removed the crashed van, and the Sappers transferred the weapons, ammunition and explosives from the cottage to their vehicles, then drove back to Bessbrook. When they had all gone, Danny and Martin joined Jock and Dead-eye outside the OP.

'You men did a good job,' Dead-eye said. 'I have no complaints.'

Though swelling with pride, Danny asked quietly: 'What about the man in the red Ford?'

'I gave the car's details to Bessbrook and they set up a roadblock and helicopter recce to bring him in. They've just told me they caught him.'

'What happens now?' Martin asked.

'We demolish this OP,' Dead-eye said, 'and return to Bessbrook. A chopper will lift us off at three p.m. – precisely one hour from now.'

'A hot bath and a cold beer,' Jock said. 'Back to civilization.'

'You'll be lucky,' Dead-eye said without humour.

They packed up their kit, demolished the OP and were lifted off the hill an hour later by a Gazelle. Ten minutes later they were back in Bessbrook, watching their beer being poured in the NAAFI canteen.

'Gimme, gimme!' Jock said.

# 13

Lieutenant Cranfield was wearing a pinstripe suit when he met Margaret Dogherty, coming off the Dublin train at Belfast Central Station. Margaret was wearing a knee-length Wallis overcoat of grey, understated elegance, with high heels emphasizing the curves of her already long legs. Her auburn hair was falling down around her face, which was pale-skinned, smooth and surprisingly delicate, except for a latent hardness, or world weariness. Though only twenty-five, she somehow looked older, though she was still an exceptionally attractive woman.

'Have you come?' she said to Cranfield, using that oddity of greeting peculiar to the Ulster Irish.

'Yes,' Cranfield replied. 'You look wonderful. Let me carry that bag.'

She handed him the travelling bag, then took his arm and let him lead her out of the busy station.

'That's a very nice pinstripe,' Margaret said. 'Sure it makes you look like some ponce from the Civil Service.' Her Ulster accent had effectively been erased by five years in London, then another three in Dublin, but she still used certain oddities of the vernacular.

'It makes me feel so respectable,' Cranfield said, 'when I'm out of uniform. Besides, I thought you might like it. Having a gentleman on your arm, instead of some rag-and-bone man like Michael O'Leary.'

Her sideways glance was one of mockery at his arrogance. 'What does that mean?'

'He said he had to visit someone in Dublin before we lifted him out. Given the danger to him the longer he remains here, I could only imagine him taking the risk for the woman he loves.'

Margaret smiled as they left the station, heading for the taxi rank by the pavement. 'He loves my body,' she said. 'He loves what it does to him.'

'He came to it pretty late, my dear, which is why he's besotted.'

'And you're not?'

'Not with that particular kind of passion. I'm a married man, after all.'

As they slipped into the back of the black taxi, which Cranfield refused to share with other passengers, as was the local custom, he realized that he hadn't been home for two months, though it seemed a lot longer than that. Back in Eaton Bishop, nothing would have changed much. His wife Maria would be pottering about in the garden, as she did nearly every day, and his three children, Julia,

Tanya and Robert, seven, six and five respectively, would be attending private school in the soothing greenery of Hereford, free of IRA snipers and Army checkpoints. It was a nice, easy life there.

'A married man having his little bit of fun,' Margaret said as the taxi pulled away from the kerb. 'Have you no conscience, Randolph?'

'Not really. I have a happy family in Hereford. Being a good father goes a long way with most married women. Maria has few complaints.'

'Does she know you play around?'

'Of course not.'

'Does she suspect?'

'I doubt it.'

'I don't know how men can face their wives and kids after being with my kind.'

'It comes with practice, my dear.'

In fact, Cranfield enjoyed going home – it had a civilizing influence on him – but he only liked it for limited periods, invariably becoming bored and restless if there too long. He was not a man for family life, let alone monogamy, though he'd always been careful to hide that side of himself from his wife. Now, as he sat beside Margaret in the black cab, aware of the heat of her soft thigh against his own, he was free of the slightest trace of guilt, at ease with himself.

'So *did* O'Leary visit you in Dublin?' he asked her.

'Yes. Sure he wanted me to marry him. Said he

was on his way to Australia – that you were fixing it up for him. Said we could begin a new life there, free of the IRA.'

'And you said?'

'No thanks. I had my own life to live, like. I told him he'd get over me in time and find someone better. When that didn't work, I reminded him that I did this for a livin' and now know nothing else. He left with tears in his eyes.'

'Does he know we put you in his path?'

'Sure he hasn't a clue.'

'We're lifting him out a week from now – all the way to Sydney via Bangkok, with a new identity and a healthy pension. Perhaps you should have said yes.'

'I'd have to be skint to consider that. Maybe in my old age.'

'A long time to go yet,' Cranfield said.

It did not, however, take long to reach the Europa Hotel. Leaving East Bridge Street, the taxi was soon passing the back of the imposing City Hall and its lovely gardens. Again, Cranfield was struck with how attractive the centre of Belfast would be were it not for the high steel fences and Army checkpoints that blocked off the main shopping precincts.

To most of the English, Belfast was a dreadful place of slums and bricked-up houses, but these were in the minority and the city was actually very appealing, with its stately Victorian architecture, the pastoral River Lagan, numerous parks and surrounding mountains, green hills and farmlands. If Belfast was sometimes not a pretty sight, it had been scarred by the very people laying claim to it.

Even as Cranfield was dwelling on this truth, the car turned off Howard Street, down Brunswick, then made a double right through Amelia and into Great Victoria Street. The Europa Hotel was almost immediately on the left, facing the pub where Cranfield had met his Protestant tout, Norman Reid.

The taxi pulled up in front of the security huts by the electronically controlled gates of the forecourt. Cranfield and Margaret climbed out. When Cranfield had paid the driver and picked up Margaret's bag, they entered the front door of the security hut. As he checked the contents of Margaret's bag, the private security guard asked her why she was bringing it into the hotel.

'I've just arrived from Dublin,' she told him, 'but me and my fiancé' – she grinned at Cranfield – 'are staying here for the afternoon. You understand, Mister?'

The security guard didn't smile. Instead, he zipped up the bag, then briskly, efficiently frisked Cranfield. A security woman did the same to Margaret, then they were waved through the inner door of the hut, out into the courtyard with its well-guarded, wire-fenced car park.

'There's nothing like this in Dublin,' Margaret

said, shaking her head in amazement. 'Belfast's a whole other world.'

'Would you like a drink first?' Cranfield asked as they entered the lobby of the hotel.

'No. I only have a couple of hours to spare. Let's have drinks in the room. Have you signed in already?'

'Yes.'

'What a bright wee boy you are!'

Cranfield collected the key, ordered a bottle of dry white wine to be sent up, waved the bellboy away, and led Margaret into the elevator, then along to their room. Once inside, he went to the window and glanced down on Great Victoria Street, with the Crown Liquor Saloon directly across the road.

An armoured pig had just stopped to let the soldiers check a parked car. If they couldn't locate the owner, or if the car was locked, they would assume there was a bomb planted in it and call the Sappers to blow it up. In the event, even as Cranfield was looking down, a harassed businessman rushed out of the Crown and started talking frantically to the soldiers, explaining why the car was parked there. Cranfield glanced left and right along the road, instinctively looking for trouble, then, feeling foolish, turned back to the room.

Margaret was sitting on the edge of the bed and kicking off her high heels.

'So what are you doing back in Belfast?' Cranfield asked.

'My mother's dyin',' she replied, 'so I've come to stay until it's all over.'

'I'm sorry to hear that.'

'You don't give a damn and neither do I. I can't stand the old cow. She's made my life miserable.'

'Still, she's dying.'

'Ach, we all go sometime.'

'You're just here until it's over?'

'Right.'

'How long do you think it'll be?'

Margaret shrugged. 'I don't know. It's the cancer. It could take days or weeks. Sure there's no way of knowin'.'

'Where do you plan staying?'

'In the family house in Conway Street, where I was born and grew up.'

'That's off the Falls, isn't it?'

'Aye. One of the places hit hardest when the Troubles began back in sixty-nine.'

'Is it near where O'Leary lives?'

'A couple of streets away.'

'You might bump into him.'

'When did you say he's leavin'?'

'A week today.'

'I'll avoid him for as long as I can. If I see him, I'll say I'm here because of my mum. That's one truth that should work, since Irishmen, if they don't respect other women, have a fearful respect for their mothers.'

The bell on the door rang. When Cranfield asked who it was, a voice said: 'Room Service.' The young man who came in was carrying a tray containing a bottle of chilled white wine and two glasses. Cranfield tipped him handsomely, then walked behind him back across the room and locked the door when he left.

He turned back to Margaret, who had taken off her coat, as well as her shoes, and was unbuttoning her dress down the front.

'Do you enjoy this?' she asked him as he removed his coat and tie, revealing the holstered Browning beneath. 'Fucking the woman that poor bastard thinks he loves?'

'I'll admit, it amuses me,' Cranfield replied.

'You think he's a poor dumb paddy. Is that it?'

'There's a lot of them about.'

'So says the high and mighty, over-educated Englishman. Here to protect the Irish from themselves.'

'With the help of the Irish, don't forget. At least the Irish like you. What a strange lot you are.'

'You don't know anything about the Irish,' Margaret told him. 'Coming over here to fight your colonial war, you see nothing but bottle-throwing Fenians, ferocious housewives in curlers and kids who've known nothing but the violence you helped to create. I was born and raised here and what I see is what you English are destroying. This is a lively, cultured city of the kind that could put most English towns to shame – but you think of it exactly as the Protestant invaders did when they sailed up the Lagan to take over – as a place filled with simple-minded bog-men who can't count without using their fingers. Well, it isn't. It's a place of imagination, which is what you pragmatic English don't understand. Fuck me, Cranfield, but don't try to fuck with me, because I won't play that game. Now take what you paid for.'

Cranfield had his way with her, enjoying it more because of her anger, feeling, as he strained up her body, that he was fighting another war. It was something he needed, the thrill of conflict, a sense of danger, and he found it in his dealings with this woman who whored for a living and, as a lucrative sideline, risked her life by seducing men in the IRA in order to set them up as patsies for British intelligence, as she had done with O'Leary.

She did it for money, but also out of vengeance, because, as she had told him, she didn't have too much time for men in general, let alone the terrorists or so-called freedom fighters on either side. She could do it, she'd told Cranfield, because she despised all such men. Thus she rendered them faceless.

When Cranfield had asked if she included him in that, she confirmed that she did. This revelation only increased his curiosity and sexual excitement.

Now, when he had finished and rolled off her sweat-slicked body, he asked what had made her hate men so much and, in particular, his own kind – those who lived and fought in the killing grounds of what had once been her home.

'If you despise men like me so much,' he said, 'why do you then betray your own? What made you turn and work for us? It can't just be the money.'

Still naked, she turned away to light a cigarette. When he passed her a glass of chilled white wine, she blew smoke in his face.

'When the Troubles first flared up in the Bogside, I was only eighteen and didn't have a clue what was going on. The Prods came stormin' down our street, throwing Molotov cocktails and swingin' wooden stakes with nails embedded in them. They smashed heads and windows, set houses on fire, and drove most of my neighbours from their homes – so I wasn't in love with them. Then the British Army arrived. It was like Armageddon. They came in to separate the Catholics from the Prods, but instead they made enemies of both. The Falls became a war zone.'

She inhaled, blew another cloud of smoke, then sipped her wine.

'I was thick as two planks,' she said. 'Hardly knew my own name. Thinkin' that some of the British soldiers were lovely, I fancied that one would fall for me and take me out of this place. I wasn't the only one, believe me. A lot of us were like that.

We'd throw stones during the day and fraternize with them at night, when they were wearin' their civvies. Of course that was my downfall.'

She rolled over and swung her legs out of the sheets, to sit on the edge of the bed. The sight of her took Cranfield's breath away, but he knew enough to keep his hands off her now.

'Once the Army settled in,' she continued, sounding faraway, 'the Catholic hard men came out of the woodwork and took over the streets. They also took over our lives, spyin' on us, demandin' protection money and punishin' those seen to go against them – with beatings, kneecappings and executions. At first it was mostly men who were victims, but soon enough they got around to the women. Men always do, don't they?'

She inhaled deeply, blew a cloud of smoke, then stubbed out her half-finished cigarette. Shuddering, she had another drink of wine, then placed the glass on her bare thigh.

'Me and my girlfriend, Peggy – she was only seventeen – were caught drinkin' with some Brits in a pub at the lower end of Grosvenor Street, in what we innocently thought was neutral territory. The two soldiers, sweet lads, were in civvies, but that only made matters worse. They were badly beaten, dragged out of the pub, then had their throats cut with a butcher's knife. I know this because me and Peggy were dragged out of the pub and forced to look at their dead, bloody bodies.

Then we were beaten up as well and sent home black and blue.'

She reached for another cigarette, changed her mind, and finished off her glass of wine instead. Cranfield silently topped up her glass and let her continue.

'Me and Peggy, God help us, were in a state of shock, but thought that at least the worst was over. Unfortunately, it wasn't. In fact, for us it was just beginning. For the next couple of days, when we dared to venture out, the men in the street would shout filthy comments and often spit at us. Naturally, when the men did it enough, the women followed suit. After a couple of days of this, we were both terrified to go out – we lived practically door-to-door – but on the fourth day the bastards came for us.'

She had another drink, almost finishing it all. As Cranfield topped her up, she lit another cigarette, inhaling deeply and exhaling as if she couldn't breathe properly. Eventually, back in control, she continued her dreadful tale.

'They dragged the two of us out of our houses at the same time. They were like one of those lynch mobs you see outside British courts when someone's raped or murdered a child – all punching, spitting, trying to tear our hair out. In the event, with regard to our hair, they were wasting their time.'

She had another drink, took a deep breath, let it out with a shuddering sigh.

'We were tied to lampposts. One of our neighbours, a woman, hacked our hair off with scissors, leaving both of us practically bald. Then a man came along with a bucket of hot tar and painted us with it – head, face, neck, arms and body, even our bare legs. When he had finished, his cronies, brave men one and all, threw bucketfuls of chicken feathers over us, until we were thoroughly tarred and feathered. They left us there, tied to the lampposts, for the passers-by to enjoy.'

'Christ!' Cranfield whispered.

'Ironically, it was a British Army patrol who released us, though they weren't sympathetic. "Fenian whores!" one of them muttered as he cut through the ropes. "You fucking deserve what you get." My mother, when she found out what had happened, said practically the same thing. So did Peggy's mother. That was what we got for bein' too young and not all that bright. It traumatized me for years.'

She stood up, drained her glass and set it back on the table, then turned to face Cranfield. 'I never forgave my mother for that. Never did, never will. Nor did I forgive those bastards who tarred and feathered me, then left me tied to that lamppost, for everyone to laugh at. When I'd recovered from my shock – and that took months, not days – I packed up and went alone to London, to make a new life for myself. I ended up, wouldn't you know, as just another Irish tart at King's Cross, doing lots for a little. Then I got my senses back, moved down to Mayfair, and learnt that being a whore for the wealthy was a lot easier, and certainly more lucrative, than spreadin' my legs for the poor. One of the people I fucked in my Mayfair flat was from British Intelligence.'

'Which gets you to me,' Cranfield said.

'Right. After getting rid of my accent – the last reminder of my roots – I moved to Dublin, did the tourist and middle-class trade, and picked up a few wee jobs for your fine friends in Whitehall. I returned to get my own back on the bastards . . . and that's why I'm here with you.'

'But you don't have to be here with me,' Cranfield told her. 'As you well know, it isn't a job requirement.'

'I like to make my own choices occasionally . . . though I never do it with men I might care for.'

'That puts me in my place.'

'Yes, Randolph, it does. You're my little convenience.'

Leaving him flushed with anger, she went into the bathroom, took her time showering, then returned to the bedroom and got dressed. As she was doing so he cooled down and soothed his wounded pride by watching her put her clothes on, piece by piece. It was as good as a striptease.

'Going back home could be dangerous,' he told her. 'You'd better be careful.'

'It won't be dangerous if you lift O'Leary out. In

that sense, his concerns are mine. I don't want him talkin'.'

'He's as good as gone,' Cranfield said.

Dressed and with hair combed, Margaret picked up her travel bag and walked up to the bed, where Cranfield was stretched out on top of the sheets, still completely naked.

'Are you stayin' here?' Margaret asked him.

'Only long enough to finish the wine,' he said, 'and get my breath back.'

She smiled, then leaned down to kiss him lightly on the lips. Straightening up, she said: 'You take care, Randolph.'

'I will,' Cranfield replied.

Margaret nodded and left the room.

Cranfield looked at his watch. Seeing that it was just after noon, he picked up the telephone. Calling a direct line to Lisburn HQ, he used a code-name that got him Captain Dubois.

'Cranfield here,' he said. 'What's happened at lunchtime?'

'A good lunch was had by all,' Dubois replied, 'and only one guest was missing.'

'Do you think it worth collecting him?' Cranfield asked, knowing that Dubois was referring to Michael Quinn.

'I think he has a lot to answer for,' Dubois replied, 'so you should go and fetch him.'

'Will do,' Cranfield said. Grinning like a Cheshire cat, he put down the receiver, hurried into the bathroom, showered, dressed and left the room – still carrying his Browning in the cross-draw position under the jacket of his immaculate pin-stripe suit.

Once outside the hotel, he caught a taxi to the Stanley Street RUC Station, by the Grosvenor Road, where a Q car, driven by Sergeant Lovelock, was waiting to take him to the lower Falls and Quinn's house.

'You got here just in time,' Sergeant Lovelock informed him as soon as he was in the car. 'Quinn's discovered the OP opposite his house and all hell's broken loose.'

'Damn!' Cranfield exclaimed softly, feeling fear for the first time, realizing, as the Q car shot out of the car park, that everything that could possibly go wrong was about to do so.

This time he had pushed his luck too far.

# 14

'I can smell something, I'm telling you,' Taff insisted, whispering, crouched up on the floor of O'Leary's loft and looking around him as if doubting his own sanity. 'I've smelt it for the last couple of days. It's the smell of . . .'

'You're just imagining it,' Lampton replied, also whispering. 'It's because we've been cooped up here so long. We haven't had a wash or a shave, we shit and piss in those plastic bags, and on top of all that, we haven't slept properly for days, so naturally we're inclined to think we can smell ourselves. You're just . . .'

'I don't think he's imagining it,' Gumboot said. 'I think I smell it as well.'

'Has anyone shit their pants?' Ricketts asked bluntly.

'No!' they all said in turn.

Ricketts glanced around the loft space, which remained surprisingly neat, considering how long the four of them had been secretly living up there. The Nikon F3HP heavy-duty camera with long-distance lens and D image intensifier, mounted on a tripod, was positioned just to the left of the peephole, being used only on special occasions. The STG laser surveillance system, tuned in to the probe in the wall adjoining Quinn's house across the street, was still at the peep-hole and working all the time, except when one of the men removed it temporarily to check the street or use the Thorn EMI 5kg hand-held thermal imager presently strung around Lampton's neck. Four sets of Gore-tex-lined Danner boots were standing in neat rows along one wall, as the need for silence had forced the men to remove them.

Even though they had been compelled to eat, wash, urinate and defecate up there, the wrappers from the only kind of food they had been able to have – the dry, high-calorie rations normally kept in their Escape Belts, such as biscuits, cheese, chocolate and sweets – as well as from moisturizing cloths, disposal towels and toilet paper, had been placed carefully in a large plastic bag hung from a nail on one of the walls and tied with string around the top. The vacuum flasks, now all empty, and water bottles, most of them nearly empty, were stacked neatly with the remainder of the rations in a noise-cushioning blanket in a corner of the loft. Most important, the sealed plastic bags for their excrement, urine and used toilet paper were in three larger plastic bags resting on the floor of the adjoining loft, which they had used as a toilet.

It was to the latter that Ricketts now cast his experienced eye.

'The bags?' he asked.

'They were all sealed after being used,' Gumboot said, 'and I personally examined every one of them.'

'Anyone piss and shit in the same bag?' Lampton asked over his shoulder while eyeballing the street through the peep-hole.

'No,' Gumboot said.

'No,' Ricketts added.

There was an uncomfortable silence for a moment, then Taff said: 'Oh, Jesus, I did that the first time . . . before you told us that we should keep them apart. Christ, I . . .'

'Piss and shit mixed can sometimes make the bags burst,' Lampton reminded them. 'I hope to God . . .'

'Damn!' Ricketts exclaimed softly, then hurriedly crossed the loft, at the crouch and stepping carefully from beam to beam, until he reached the adjoining space. There, he bent over, sniffed at the large bags, then checked the floor directly below them. A mixture of excrement and urine was dripping out of one of the rubbish bags, on to the floor. It was then dripping down between the joists and soaking through to the ceiling of the house below. 'Damn!' Ricketts exclaimed softly again. He turned back to look at the others, including the stricken Taff. 'One of the disposal bags has leaked and soaked through the floor to the ceiling of the room directly below, in the house next door. That'll give us away, I fear.'

'It already has,' Lampton replied, still at the peep-hole. 'One of the neighbours has just crossed from this side of the street – I think from the house next door – and is talking to Quinn. She's jabbing her finger in this direction.'

'Bloody 'ell!' Taff exclaimed softly. 'I didn't mean . . .'

'It's not your fault,' Lampton replied firmly. 'I should have told you about that deadly mixture before you used the first bag. My fault, Taff. My apologies, men.' He glanced through the peep-hole again, took a deep breath, then said: 'Yes, damn it, she's obviously told Quinn about the stain on her ceiling. He's just shouted into his own house, to call out a whole bunch of his hard men – four men. An ASU, no doubt. Yep, they all have guns. They're crossing the street to the house next door.' Lampton took another deep breath, then let it out again. 'Fuck! They've just gone out of view. That means they're entering the house.' Turning back to face his men, he said: 'Get on that radio, Gumboot, and call up a QRF to help bail us out of here. Ricketts, you keep the trapdoor in that next loft covered with your Browning. That's where they'll be coming up. But don't shoot unless someone aims at you – we don't want a riot. Taff, while Ricketts holds them at bay – which can only be temporary – you and I will have to pack up this equipment and have it ready for moving out. OK, men, shake out!'

Gumboot was already on the radio, calling for back-up from a QRF, or Quick Reaction Force, when Ricketts clambered over the joists to press his back against the bricks, raise his knees and aim his handgun two-handed at the trapdoor of the adjacent loft. Even before Lampton and Taff had begun dismantling and repacking the audiovisual surveillance equipment, Ricketts heard footsteps coming up the stairs from below, then the whispering of men on the landing directly below the trapdoor. Something clattered then squeaked – obviously a stepladder – prompting Ricketts to release the safety-catch of his Browning and hold the handgun firmly, applying pressure equally between the thumb and fingers of the firing hand. Waiting for the first man to appear, he took controlled, even breaths.

Completely ignoring Ricketts, Lampton and Taff got on with the business of dismantling the surveillance equipment and placing it back in reinforced canvas carriers. As they did so, Gumboot finished relaying his message to the Stanley Street RUC station, switched the set to 'Receive', then slithered sideways to glance down through the peep-hole. After noticing only that many of the neighbours were coming out of their homes to see what was happening, he withdraw his handgun and aimed it at the trapdoor in the adjoining loft, determined, on the one hand, to give covering to Ricketts, and on the other to keep his eye out for the arrival of the badly needed QRF.

The trapdoor squeaked, shook, then was suddenly flipped over by a human hand. A man's face appeared, his eyes too wide as they adjusted to the sudden gloom, then his second hand appeared, trying to aim his Webley.

'Halt!' Ricketts bawled. 'Security forces!'

A single shot from the man's pistol reverberated through the loft and the bullet ricocheted off the wall high above Ricketts's head. The man was firing wild and blind, but that made him no less dangerous, so Ricketts returned the fire with a double tap, which sounded like a deafening thunderclap in the confined space. The man's hand seemed to explode, spurting blood, bone and flesh. He screamed, dropped his pistol, then dropped back down through the trapdoor, knocking the steel ladder over as he crashed to the floor below. The other men down there cursed and bellowed instructions at one another. A woman further down screamed. Then a fusillade of pistol fire, shot vertically by the men below, straight up through the ceiling, turned the floor of the loft into a convulsion of spitting wood and billowing dust.

Ricketts pressed himself into the wall, then inched his way around it until he was closer to the open trapdoor. He leaned forward and emptied the rest of his 13-round magazine, aiming down through the trapdoor. There were more shouts and screams.

He pressed himself back against the wall and reloaded with a full magazine as the anticipated volley of return fire came from below, with the bullets smashing up through the floor in more spewing dust and wood chips, then ricocheting off the roof above his head. Even as Ricketts leaned forward to shoot down through the trapdoor hole again, Gumboot was inching forward with his High Power in one hand and a Royal Ordnance G60 stun grenade in the other.

Ricketts nodded.

Gumboot pulled the pin, dropped the grenade down through the hole, then threw himself back just as more shots were fired up through the ceiling. Dust and wood splinters spat up from the floor of the loft as the stun grenade exploded below with a loud bang and a blinding flash, leading to the cessation of the gunfire and a lot more cursing. Before the PIRA team could recover from the shock – for the stun grenade is essentially a diversionary device – Gumboot had shuffled forward again with another grenade in his hand.

'Smoke grenade,' he whispered.

Ricketts nodded again, then glanced at Lampton as Gumboot pulled the pin of the smoke grenade and dropped it down through the opening. Exploding almost instantly, the grenade filled the hallway below with smoke, which had everyone coughing even before it drifted up into the loft. Seeing what was happening, Lampton, who had just finished packing the surveillance equipment, nodded and picked up another canvas bag, from which he withdrew four SF10 respirators. When the men had put them on, to protect themselves from the smoke, which contained elements of burning CS gas, Lampton returned to the peep-hole, looked down on the street below, then stuck his thumb up in the air, indicating that the QRF force had arrived.

Wearing his respirator, and with his Browning ready to be fired single-handed, Ricketts moved forward to the opening and looked down into the smoke-filled hallway. The ladder was lying on its side where it had fallen, but otherwise the hallway was empty. From the ground floor, Ricketts could hear the hysterical babble of a woman – obviously the housewife – and more cursing and coughing from the PIRA men.

Ricketts dropped down through the hole and landed in the hallway just as gunshots were fired out in the street. He moved quickly along the passage, holding the Browning two-handed, kicking the two bedroom doors open, one after the other, and turning into the rooms ready to fire.

Both bedrooms were empty.

As Gumboot dropped down behind him, likewise wearing his respirator and holding his Browning two-handed, Ricketts hurried down the stairs, to the short hallway with the front door at one end and the living-room door to the side. As the door was open he went in, still preparing to fire. The room was empty, though filled with smoke and CS gas, so he checked the kitchen and back door, finding the latter locked. Satisfied that the house was empty, he hurried out to the hallway, just as Gumboot was pressing himself to the wall, his Browning still held two-handed, to tentatively stick his head around the door frame and look out into the street.

More gunshots rang out.

Gumboot disappeared outside and Ricketts followed him out, dropping low as he burst out of the front door, swinging the handgun from left to right, covering a wide arc. Women screamed, men hollered, and the spectators scattered. One woman was coughing and wiping her streaming eyes with a handkerchief, a man was squatting on the pavement with blood streaming from his head and shoulders – the results, so Ricketts surmised, of his own blind shots through the trapdoor hole – and a QRF team composed of British soldiers and RUC officers, all wearing flak jackets and carrying assault rifles and truncheons, were pouring out of Saracens to take command of the street.

Two other QRF teams had also arrived. One, consisting entirely of British Army troops, was rushing into O'Leary's house to help Lampton and Taff carry out their kit and equipment as quickly, and as securely, as possible. The other, composed of flak-jacketed RUC officers, was returning the gunfire of two PIRA men who were covering Quinn as he pushed the struggling O'Leary into the back of his car and followed him in with a pistol to his head. One of the PIRA gunmen managed to get into the car also, but the second was cut down as it roared off along the street and disappeared around the corner.

When the people saw the dead PIRA man, the feared riot began.

As the dead PIRA gunman was picked off the road by two RUC officers, the watching women started screaming abuse and the men – mostly youths, including some known dickers – started throwing stones and every other kind of debris. No sooner had they started than an armoured pig came along the street to disgorge special riot-control Army troops, wearing their familiar, still frightening flak jackets, perspex-visored helmets and reinforced leg and arm pads, who charged the crowd while holding up large shields and swinging their truncheons wildly.

Ricketts tugged the respirator off his face and let it hang loose just below his chin. Standing beside him, Gumboot did the same.

'Fuck it,' Gumboot said, 'they got O'Leary. They'll make that poor sod talk.'

'Let's protect the door,' Ricketts said.

Together they backed up to the door of O'Leary's house, since that was the one the QRF team had entered, probably under instructions. While stones and other debris drummed against the shields of the riot-control troops, who were now breaking up to swarm through the crowd and pick off certain individuals, Ricketts and Gumboot stood guard, both with their Brownings at the ready. Within minutes, even as the street battle raged, the soldiers who had rushed into O'Leary's house emerged again, this time in a protective circle around Lampton and Taff, both of whom were carrying packed-up surveillance equipment, as were some of the soldiers.

As Lampton and Taff were rushed to a waiting Saracen, a Q car pulled up and Lieutenant Cranfield climbed out, followed by Sergeant Lovelock. The latter was wearing a corduroy jacket and trousers, and an open-necked shirt. Cranfield was dressed in a black-leather jacket over what looked suspiciously like pinstripe trousers.

'Where's Quinn?' Cranfield asked.

Filled with a sudden, all-consuming rage, Ricketts raised his Browning, as if wanting to use it as a hammer, then walked purposefully up to Lieutenant Cranfield. Luckily, Lampton hurried back from the Saracen to push Ricketts back.

'That won't help,' he whispered.

'You heard the surveillance tapes,' Ricketts said. 'We both know what O'Leary did. We know what those PIRA fuckers'll do to him and who put him on that spot. We also know how many people will get hurt when O'Leary starts talking. We know who the big timer is.'

Ricketts started forward again, but again Lampton stopped him. 'One more move, Ricketts, and I swear I'll take *my* handgun and blow you to Kingdom Come. This won't wash. It's not your concern.'

'We're supposed to be the SAS,' Ricketts said. 'Not MI5.'

'I know,' Lampton said. 'Quiet now.' He turned to Cranfield, who took a step back and instinctively placed his hand inside his black-leather jacket, onto his Browning. 'Quinn got away,' Lampton said quietly, 'and he took O'Leary with him. He obviously guessed, from the location of our OP, that O'Leary had let us up there. He'll make him talk, Lieutenant.'

'It's time for a Chinese Parliament,' Cranfield replied, showing little emotion. 'Let's get the hell out of here.'

'Yes, boss,' Lampton said.

They all went their separate ways, heading back to Bessbrook in their own transport, leaving the QRF teams and riot-control soldiers to contain the continuing street violence.

The Saracen transporting Ricketts and Gumboot was stoned as it turned out of the street and headed back to Armagh.

'What a fucking war!' Gumboot said.

# 15

Cranfield knew he was in trouble as soon as he saw Captain Dubois' face. The Army intelligence officer was standing behind his desk, looking down through the window at the high-walled courtyard of Lisburn HQ, smoking a cigarette and radiating tension with every move of his body. When Cranfield entered the office, Dubois did not immediately turn to face him, but simply inhaled on his cigarette again, as if taking a deep breath to control himself.

Cranfield was already feeling shaky from the barrage of criticism he had received from, notably, Sergeant Lampton and Corporal Ricketts, at the Chinese Parliament, the informal meeting convened only an hour ago in the troop's sleeping quarters in Bessbrook.

Ricketts, in particular, had been incensed over what he had learnt about Cranfield's activities, from the conversations of Quinn and his spies, during his long surveillance in the OP above O'Leary's house. From those conversations, recorded over a period of five days, Ricketts and the others had learnt about Cranfield's illegal 'snatch' raids across the border, sometimes with, sometimes without, Captain Dubois; his killing of O'Halloran in his home in the Republic; and his exploitation of O'Leary's personal financial problems with PIRA.

Neither Ricketts nor Lampton were particularly concerned with the role of Dubois in all this, because Dubois was regular Army, not an SAS officer. They were, however, incensed that Cranfield, SAS, had overstepped the bounds of the Regiment's unwritten laws and, even worse, failed to consult any of his superiors before striking out on his own.

'It's out of order,' Sergeant Lampton had told him, 'and now we're paying the price for it. To the locals, we've become the new Black and Tans, while to the media we're a bunch of murderous cowboys. This is your fault, Lieutenant.'

As Cranfield knew only too well, regular Army officers entering the SAS for the first time invariably have to go through a painful period of adjustment when they discover that being limited to three-year stints deprives them of any real influence on the ethos of the Regiment; that the NCOs, who can remain in the Regiment for as long as their careers last, are actually the ones who will select or reject the officer entrants; and that even if selected, the officers will be treated with sly contempt by the NCOs and judged as short-term 'Ruperts' of dubious merit.

The SAS's Chinese Parliament, so alien to the regular Army, had sprung out of this unusual reversal of military rank and authority. They were, therefore, remarkably informal meetings – usually held before an operation, not after – at which everyone, from the commander down, could pitch in with his own ideas or criticisms. Apart from its recognition that the ordinary soldier can have as much to contribute as the officers, the Chinese Parliament is a regular, healthy reminder that the SAS scorns the notion of class.

While this attitude normally appealed to Cranfield, it had rebounded on him badly when, during that meeting, he had been so thoroughly lambasted by the contemptuous Lampton and Ricketts.

'You were grandstanding,' Sergeant Lampton had told him. 'Being a big timer. You wanted to fight this war on your own, but in the Regiment we work as a team. We're anonymous and you couldn't stand that, so you went out to be known. In doing that, you exposed us all.'

'Bullshit,' Cranfield had replied, trying to sound a lot more confident than he felt.

'No,' Ricketts had said. 'Not bullshit. Sergeant Lampton is right. It was your illegal snatch raids that brought you to the attention of Quinn and eventually made him go all-out to get you. That shouldn't have been the case. You should have played the game by the rules and remained anonymous, thus avoiding this range war with PIRA. It was also your cross-border raids that encouraged those dumb troopers on the Dublin road OP to pursue Quinn's arms dealers across the border, driving straight into a Gardai checkpoint, a highly publicized night in an Irish jail and subsequent deportation to Hereford. It's because of those men that Quinn learnt about the existence of the OPs overlooking his cottage in Armagh. And it's because of *that* discovery that Quinn learnt that we were after his hide and sent his men out to get us. Finally, it's because you insisted on inserting an OP facing Quinn's Falls Road home, in the house of your tout, O'Leary, that Quinn learnt he was helping us and took him away. When that poor bastard's tortured, he'll talk, blowing everything sky-high.'

'All of this, if I may say so,' Lampton had said icily, 'is because of your actions, which were based on self-interest and divorced from the best interests of the SAS.'

'We don't like big timers in this Regiment,' Ricketts had added, 'but that's what you were doing, Lieutenant – big timing all the way. Now the shit's hit the fan.'

Cranfield had argued his case, of course, but it hadn't cut much ice and when he left them it was with the knowledge that his reputation had been badly dented and possibly was now in ruins.

On the other hand, Lampton and Ricketts still

didn't know just how far he had gone to trap O'Leary in his web – namely, his use of Margaret Dogherty to get the Irishman in even more debt, thus encouraging him, with a little coaxing from Margaret, to turn to British Intelligence for financial assistance in return for information.

Thank God, they still didn't know about that.

Nevertheless, after that acrimonious, damning Chinese Parliament, Cranfield wasn't feeling too confident about this meeting with Captain Dubois. In fact, for the first time since childhood, he was feeling distinctly nervous. This feeling was not eased when Dubois turned around to face him, looking drawn and almost white with anger.

'Ah,' he said, sounding stiff. 'Lieutenant Cranfield!'

'Yes,' Cranfield said.

'Yes, *sir*!' Dubois corrected him.

'We use "boss" in the SAS.'

'You do realize, do you not, that although you're in the SAS, you come under the authority of the combined Intelligence and Security Group in this province?'

'Yes, boss, I realize that.'

'That means you must do as you're told. As an Army officer – your *senior* officer – I'm ordering you to address me as you would if in the regular Army. In other words, you address me as "sir".'

'Yes, sir,' Cranfield said, torn between anger and admiration for Dubois' surprising display of strength. Dubois, he suddenly realized, would have made a superb SAS officer. It made him like Dubois more.

Dubois nodded. 'You've taken a barrel of dynamite,' he said, 'and set a match to it. You've blown up the whole works. Do you understand that, Lieutenant?'

The use of his rank, instead of his first name, confirmed for Cranfield that Dubois was really, deeply upset with him. Nevertheless, unable to accept that he was wrong, he replied: 'No, I don't understand. I did what I thought was the best thing – and at least we've got Quinn on the run.'

'At what cost, Lieutenant?'

'Sorry?'

'The SAS is renowned not only for its skills in combat, but also for its use of psychological warfare when required – as it was in Malaya and Oman. The Regiment was brought here to use those same skills, but it made the mistake of bringing you with it, and what you've done, while very flamboyant, has caused more harm than good. Single-handedly you've destroyed the anonymity of the Regiment, risked the lives of a lot of other people, and set yourself up as PIRA's number one target, thus placing the SAS centre-stage. Do you understand now?'

'No,' Cranfield said. 'I think I've brought the worms out of the woodwork and given us a chance to get at them. Nothing comes without cost. I also think that I'm getting the blame for a lot of things I didn't do.'

Shaking his head in disbelief, Dubois took the chair behind his desk and folded his hands under his chin. He studied his desk for some time, then looked back up at Cranfield.

'This morning,' he said, 'another IRA terrorist, Sean McKee, in custody after being captured in south Armagh, supposedly by the RUC, claimed in court that in fact he'd been woken in his bed in the Republic by a British soldier holding a pistol to his head. That soldier, along with some of his friends, drove McKee back across the border and handed him over to the RUC. When the men responsible for this illegal act were named – and turned out to be some of your SAS troopers – they insisted that McKee was lying; that in fact he'd stumbled, drunk, into their foot patrol just this side of the border. McKee strongly denied this and stuck to his story, even as he was led away, thumbs defiantly in the air, to twenty-five years' imprisonment.'

Cranfield shrugged. 'McKee was high on a list of wanted men handed to us on our arrival in the area. We got him the only way we knew how.'

'The royal "we",' Dubois said sardonically.

Cranfield shrugged again. 'All right: I.'

Dubois nodded, then continued: 'With help from an informer, two others were arrested in the Republic and likewise handed over to the RUC – and again, the SAS was fingered.'

'I'm not responsible for them all,' Cranfield replied with his singular brand of sincerity. 'Some of my men are inclined to get impatient and take the initiative.'

'Having you as a bad example,' Dubois said.

'Naturally, I don't agree with that,' Cranfield said, holding his ground. 'And I really don't see how these cases, genuine though they are, can be used as examples of how I'm endangering the lives of other people. To join the SAS is to court danger – that's a weakness, or a perversion, shared by our officers, NCOs and troopers alike. So why blame me when what I do places my men in danger? It comes with the territory, Captain, so I've no guilt on that count.'

'Danger is one thing. *Unnecessary* danger is another, and that's what you brought about. Even worse, you didn't limit the danger to your SAS troopers; nor did you limit yourself to proper rules of engagement. Instead, you used a well-known local whore, Margaret Dogherty, to entrap that PIRA bookkeeper, Michael O'Leary, and make him turn into a Fred, doing so with scant regard for what might happen, should the couple be caught out.'

Cranfield opened his mouth to protest, but Dubois silenced him with a pointing index finger, then continued: 'Even worse, having already ignored the danger, in particular to O'Leary, you then offered him a lift-off to Australia in return for the use of his house for a covert OP – one inserted to watch the very man who could do O'Leary most damage, namely Michael Quinn. In doing so, you practically guaranteed that O'Leary's turn would be exposed – and in doing *that* you also virtually guaranteed that all those connected with O'Leary would be taken down with him. In the event, that's what happened.'

Suddenly, Cranfield felt his blood turning cold, some instinct telling him that he was about to hear something he would never forget.

'O'Leary's body has already been picked up from waste ground near the Divis flats,' Dubois said. 'First they gave him a six-pack with a pistol – elbows, kneecaps and ankles. Then they dropped concrete blocks on his shins. Then, while he was pinned down by the concrete blocks, they put a plastic bag over his head, kicked his ribs in, tortured him with a knife; and finally, presumably when he had talked, they blew his brains out. You can tear up his ticket to Australia – it's no use to him now.'

Suddenly feeling light-headed, Cranfield closed his eyes, took a deep breath and tried to control the racing of his heart. Realizing that this might be misconstrued as a sign of weakness, he opened his eyes again and said, as calmly as he could manage: 'O'Leary did what he did of his own accord and for his own benefit. He took his chances and paid the price. We all run that risk.'

There was silence for much longer than Cranfield could take comfortably, but eventually Captain Dubois, after another loud sigh, said: 'Yes, I suppose so. There's a certain truth in that. If you hadn't gotten to him first, his theft from the PIRA funds would have been discovered anyway, resulting in something rather similar to his ultimate fate.' He paused deliberately, tormentingly, but eventually added with chilling softness: 'We'll conveniently ignore the fact that your way of helping O'Leary out was to force him into becoming a turncoat. He was, after all, a member of PIRA and therefore, in the strictest sense of the term, still one of the enemy.'

'Correct,' Cranfield said, instantly feeling better.

'Unfortunately,' Dubois continued with soft-voiced, remorseless logic, 'that doesn't absolve you from the charge that your exploitation of O'Leary, and subsequent carelessness regarding him, put the lives of a lot of others in danger.'

'If you're talking about the OPs,' Cranfield said, already getting his confidence back, 'I'd remind you that they were manned by the SAS – and those men *expect* danger.'

'Not danger brought about by carelessness.'

'The use of that word is debatable.'

'Then what about the many others who might have been exposed by what O'Leary has revealed under torture?'

'What others?'

'The many who passed him information or were party to your entrapment and subsequent use of him.'

'Such as?'

'Let's suggest Margaret Dogherty. The woman with whom you've been having an affair . . .'

'You've had me watched?' Cranfield asked, taken by surprise, shocked, and flushed with anger.

'Of course. We keep our eye on our own men – particularly when they're involved in clandestine surveillance.'

'You bastard!'

'And in doing so,' Dubois continued with a slight, deadly smile, 'we learnt of your affair with Miss Dogherty. As that lady had already worked for us in London and Dublin, we weren't amused to find you becoming involved with her, far beyond the call of duty. It was completely out of order. Even more out of order, if I may say so, was getting her killed.'

The shock jolted through Cranfield like a bolt of electricity, first burning him, then turning him to ice, finally leaving him numb, with only a racing heart to remind him that he was still made of flesh and bone.

'What . . .?' He had to take a deep breath and let the word out when exhaling, but he simply couldn't finish his question, already dreading the answer.

'When O'Leary was tortured,' Dubois said with deadly calm, 'he must have confessed to pilfering the PIRA money. In doing so, he would also have told them that Margaret Dogherty had introduced him to you and that you had offered to replace the money if he became your tout. Given that Margaret Dogherty was, for reasons known to all the locals, not sympathetic to the local PIRA, who had once feathered and tarred her, Michael Quinn and his hoodlums would soon have put two and two together and gone in search of the lady, seeking revenge.'

Cranfield felt that he was choking, or about to be ill, but he managed to croak out: 'So what . . .?'

'We received the call this afternoon. She was shot in her own home. She was looking after her terminally ill mother when the men rang her doorbell. When she answered it, they emptied their pistols into her, killing her instantly. At the same time, all across the city, other people were murdered – seven in all. Our records show that they were all connected with O'Leary – and through him, to us.' Dubois paused, then offered his penultimate, lacerating statement: 'Yes, O'Leary talked . . . and nine people died. Congratulations, Lieutenant.'

Cranfield didn't ask permission to leave. He just did an abrupt about-turn and walked to the door, not sure if his legs would carry him there. In the event, they did. As he opened the door and started out, he was stopped by Dubois' voice.

'You've not only done irreparable damage to yourself, but also to the whole SAS. This time, if you try to make amends, don't make a mistake.'

'Go to hell,' Cranfield said.

Then he walked out, slamming the door behind him, determined to find Quinn.

# 16

Darkness had fallen when Cranfield, dressed in mismatching civilian clothing, including baggy brown-corduroy trousers, scuffed black shoes, threadbare coat, open-necked checkered shirt and stained navy-blue pullover, drove out of Bessbrook in a Q car, heading for the border.

His Browning was holstered to the side of his right leg and a Fairburn-Sykes Commando knife was strapped to the other, both up under his trousers.

Soon he was driving ever deeper into the country, along narrow, winding lanes lined with high hedgerows. Given the fiasco of this whole day, including the Chinese Parliament and his meeting with Dubois, he knew that what he was doing was a final, desperate gamble that would either redeem him or destroy him. Nevertheless, so great was his present humiliation that he felt he had finally to get Quinn or concede victory to him.

Lambert and Ricketts, he knew, would be even more infuriated if they discovered that he had struck out on his own again – and, even worse, taken another dangerous chance – but Cranfield just didn't give a damn, since apart from the humiliations already heaped upon him, not least by Lampton and Ricketts, he now had to contend with Dubois' parting shot: 'This time, if you try to make amends, don't make a mistake.'

*Well,* Cranfield thought grimly, *if I make a mistake this time I won't live long enough to be haunted by it. This time it's for keeps.*

Stopped once by an Army foot patrol, he showed his genuine identity papers and was allowed to drive on. Soon after, he was parking his unmarked car outside a Republican bar located halfway between the border and Quinn's cottage. It was a picturesque little place, with leaded-glass windows, now emitting light from inside, doors of solid oak, and a thatched roof. Smoke was coming out of its single chimney, indicating that an open fire was burning. When Cranfield rolled down the window of his car, he heard the distinctive sound of Irish music coming from inside.

Although Quinn would certainly not be found in this pub, it was one he had frequented during his visits to south Armagh, and therefore one in which he had many friends. Cranfield hoped to pick something up from them, then take it from there. It was a hellishly dangerous thing to attempt, but he felt he had no choice. He would not return to Bessbrook empty-handed. The very thought was unbearable.

After turning off the ignition and headlights, he took his genuine ID from his inside pocket and slipped it under the rubber mat on the floor. He then checked that his false ID was still in his inside pocket and double-checked his wallet, making sure that it contained only false credit cards and other personal items, with nothing that might give him away as an Englishman. According to his false ID, credit cards and even a letter from an invented mother, he was Bobby Duncan from Balkan Street, Belfast – a hard Republican street.

Satisfied, Cranfield climbed out of the car, locked it, took a few deep breaths, then walked across the gravelled forecourt and entered the pub. It was small, warm and noisy, with a beamed ceiling, a brass-and-wood bar, a four-piece Irish band – autoharp, fiddle, flatpick guitar, mandolin and singer – a postage-stamp dance floor, already busy, and pink-faced men and women packed into seats around the walls, drinking, smoking, talking, and joining the singer as chorus on patriotic songs.

Nobody stopped what they were doing when Cranfield walked in, but he sensed a lot of eyes turning towards him and tried to ignore them. Walking to the bar, he said with an Ulster brogue: 'A lively wee place you've got here. Sure I picked a good place to stop off. Pour me a Guinness, thanks.' Turning to the man beside him, he said: 'Sure it warms the belly all of a winter's night. It's quare good when yer travellin'.'

'Aye,' the man replied, smoking his pipe and puffing a cloud of blue smoke. 'Sure that's a fact, Mister. Ya be just passin' through then?'

'On m' way back to Belfast from Dublin after one of them ijit sales conventions. I'm in linens, like. A grand place, that Dublin, but quare expensive. I'll be glad to get back t' Balkan Street an' put m'feet up.'

'Sure there's nothin' like home'n hearth,' the man replied, blowing another cloud of smoke across the bar. 'I'd say that's a fact of life.'

The barman placed Cranfield's Guinness on the counter. Cranfield thanked him, paid, had a good drink, then engaged the man beside him in conversation.

'Sure that's a quare wee band they have up there. And that singer's real grand.'

'Ach, he's not bad. Gets them all goin' at it. By closin' time they'll have to read the Riot Act. It's a right wee place, this 'un.'

'Ach, it is,' Cranfield said. 'Sure I'm havin' a grand time already.'

Cranfield was proud of his Ulster accent and vernacular, but knowing it wasn't perfect, he was depending on the general, noisy level of conversation to hide any slight mistakes he might make. 'Here,' he said to the man beside him. 'Let me get you another. I'm Bobby Duncan, by the way.'

'Sure that's quare decent of you, Bob.' The man stuck his hand out. 'Mick Treacy.' They shook hands, then Cranfield ordered the man a Guinness. The singer had stopped singing and was telling a few jokes while the fiddler tuned up behind him. The men and women in the pub roared with laughter at the jokes, their faces flushed with drink and good humour. 'In the palm of his hand,' Cranfield said. 'Sure 'e knows what 'e's doin'.'

'Aye, he's a rare turn,' Mick replied. 'Alus good for a laugh. Lives local, like.'

'You'd all be locals here,' Cranfield said.

'All exceptin' the odd traveller like yerself. It's not a place you'd seek out.'

The band started up again, with the singer launching into 'Provie Birdie', a song about three Provos who, in real life, were lifted out of Mountjoy prison by helicopter, right under the noses of the guards. It was clear from the number of customers who joined in the chorus that the song was widely known and popular.

While engaging the amiable Mick in conversation, Cranfield sipped his Guinness and studied the smoky pub over the rim of his glass. The customers were a mixture of heavy housewives, working men in peaked caps, a few country-squire types, and, at the bar, on both sides of Cranfield, single men, most edging towards middle age. The younger men, most of whom were not too bright and undoubtedly in the Provisionals, had congregated along the pine-board wall between the bar and the door and were being fêted by teenage girls attracted to the excitements of terrorism. It was the young men, trying to impress the girls, who acted most like hard men and looked with blatant suspicion upon strangers. Seeing them, and the sideways glances they gave him, Cranfield sensed trouble.

'Sure have another Guinness on me,' Mick said as Cranfield turned back to face the bar. 'With perhaps a wee Bushmills.'

'That sounds great,' Cranfield said.

The round led into a second, helping to pass the next hour, then a friend of Mick's joined them at the bar and insisted on buying a third round. Conversation flowed thick and fast, bouncing from one subject to another, though most of it was about the Troubles in Belfast, Londonderry and south Armagh. The 'Brits' were reviled as bastards, but deemed ignorant rather than evil. Opinions about the IRA, its vices and virtues, were surprisingly varied.

The latter fact surprised Cranfield, as he had expected more unanimity in favour of the IRA – based on fear of reprisals, if nothing else – but everyone seemed to have his own opinion and felt free to air it.

The arguments grew more lively, the band played ever louder, the husbands and wives along the walls continued to sing uninhibitedly, and soon all conversations were being shouted from flushed, sweaty faces, through blue-grey veils of swirling cigarette smoke.

Eventually, just before closing time – which, as Cranfield knew, meant closing only the front door – the name of Michael Quinn was finally raised.

'Sure, the Troubles could be on yer doorstep,' Cranfield said, 'and you wouldn't even be knowin' it. At least not here in the country. Not like in the Falls.'

'Ach, aye,' Mick replied, polishing off a quick Bushmills. 'Take that incident yesterday – that to-do at Michael Quinn's place. Sure you never see the man hereabouts, 'cept on weekends, and then the Brits shoot up the place, killin' some lads into the bargain, and find the walls stacked high with weapons, ammunition an' s'plosives. Enough to blow up this whole village, so I've heard. Sure, it makes yer hair stand on end, it does.'

'Killed some lads, did they?' Cranfield asked rhetorically. 'Sure them bastards would kill their own mothers.'

'Aye, they would,' Mick replied, 'but they didn't get Quinn. It's been said he was in the Falls at the time an' didn't know what was goin' on.'

'Didn't know, my arse!' It was Mick's friend Kevin talking. 'That stuff didn't get into Quinn's house by accident. He had to know what was goin' on.'

'A lot of poor lads kilt.'

'All Provos,' Kevin said. 'As for Quinn, he was hidin' out there in the Falls until the milit'ry went for him.'

'Did they catch him?' Cranfield asked.

'Sure he took off like a bat out of hell an' hasn't been seen since. Ask me, he's hidin' out in Sean Doyle's house, just two miles down the road. That's the safe house he alus used for his PIRA mates, so that's where he'd stop first.'

Mick sighed. 'Sure you could be right there. As Bobby said' – Mick beamed a big smile at Cranfield – 'the Troubles could be right on yer doorstep and you wouldn't even know it. Aye, he could be right there in Doyle's place.'

'Let them British bastards worry about it,' Cranfield said. 'It's their concern, not ours.' He glanced at his watch and looked shocked. 'Bejasus! It's near midnight already! Me missus will kill me if I don't get back soon. Sorry, lads, but I'm goin' t' have t' go. What a quare good night that was.' He finished off his Guinness, shook hands all round, then had the usual trouble saying goodbye in Ireland, but finally managed it.

'You drive carefully now,' Mick advised him. 'Sure you've had a right few.'

'Ach, I'll be all right,' Cranfield said, waving again and heading for the door. 'Sure we salesmen are used t' this. Good night, Mick.'

'God bless.'

Gratefully leaving the bar, with his stomach tightening but excitement lancing through him, Cranfield hurried back across the dark courtyard to his parked Q car.

He was about to open the door when a young man stood up, where he had been kneeling at the other side, and aimed a Webley pistol held with both hands.

'Bobby Duncan, my arse,' he said.

Before Cranfield could think of what to do, he heard the scuffle of many feet behind him. Glancing back over his shoulder he saw the youths from the pub hurrying towards him – at least six or seven of them. Cranfield just had time to return his gaze to the youth aiming the pistol at him – long unwashed hair, fashionable 'designer' stubble, hollow cheeks, eyes shadowed; wearing a black leather jacket and blue denims – then the other youths rushed up to surround him. One of them pushed him in the face. Another flung him forward face first against the car, brutally punched his spinal column, kicked his ankles apart and snarled: 'Open those fuckin' legs, you English cunt!'

Cranfield did as he was told. The first youth frisked him, running his hands over his shoulders, down his chest, across his stomach, around his waist, up his spine, then back around his body to reach in and pull out his wallet.

'No weapon,' he said. 'Fuckin' amazin'! Let's see what we have here. Hey, you, turn aroun'!'

Before Cranfield could do so, someone grabbed him by the hair, jerked his head back, slapped his face, then grabbed his shoulder, spun him around and slammed him backwards into the car, letting him see all their faces. They were definitely the youths he had seen inside the pub – deprived, not too bright, clearly desperate for self-esteem – and all of them shared the same smirk of combined hatred and nervousness.

One of them, the one who'd reached Cranfield first, was examining his wallet.

'I don't fuckin' believe it,' he exclaimed, turning over Cranfield's false ID, credit cards and varied papers to examine them thoroughly. 'This bastard is genuine!'

'No, he's not,' a more mature, familiar voice said. 'He's just a Brit tryin' t' be clever. Let's check his car.'

Glancing over the shoulder of the youth with his wallet, Cranfield saw the amiable Mick Treacy. Returning Cranfield's stare, he said: 'You think I'm a fuckin ijit, you British turd? *Good night*, indeed! Who says "good night" around here? You were good, Mister, at playin' an Ulsterman, but not *that* fuckin' good. OK, lads, get 'is car keys.'

'In my right trouser pocket,' Cranfield said, since he had nothing to lose.

'Well, isn't he a quare wee lad?' Mick said sarcastically as one of the youths jammed his hand into Cranfield's pocket and pulled out his keys. 'So helpful an' all! They breed the wee uns like that in the Falls Road – as polite as the English. Right, Jim-boy, search the car.'

The youth with the Webley pistol walked around the car, grabbed Michael by the shoulder, dragged him off a few feet, and slammed him backwards into the trunk of a tree. Then he placed the barrel of the pistol against his forehead, right above the bridge of the nose.

'One fuckin' move and you get it. Not one tremor, cunt.'

Cranfield remained against the tree, trying to keep his breathing steady, but unable to stop the racing of his heart as the youths searched his Q car. They did it thoroughly, with growing excitement, as if doing even that turned them on and encouraged their violence. One opened the glove compartment, another searched through the back, two more checked the cluttered boot, one looked under the bonnet. Finding nothing, they became frustrated, smashing windows, slashing the seats, until finally, to Cranfield's despair, one of them ripped the rubber mat away and saw the ID beneath it.

He picked the ID up. After examining it with the aid of a pencil torch, he walked across to Mick and handed it to him.

'Fucking British Army,' he said. 'You were right again, Mick.'

'Mmmmm,' Mick said, examining the ID, then looking directly at Cranfield and offering a slight smile. 'Sure the Troubles could be on yer door-step and you wouldn't even be knowin' it,' he repeated sardonically. 'Isn't that the truth, Lieutenant Cranfield? Now we have the proof of it. After Michael Quinn, were ya?'

'Yes,' Cranfield said.

'Well, let's not disappoint ya.'

When Mick nodded at the gang of youths, they closed in on Cranfield, some grinning like idiots, others breathing deeply, all of them excited to be given something worthwhile to do. They punched him and kicked him, head-butted him, spat on him, tore his clothes, tugged at his hair and trampled on his toes. When he started falling, they held him up; when they had him upright, they punched him down; and when finally he could stand up no longer, they used their boots on him.

At first Cranfield felt sharp pain – each single blow, every kick – then the jolting, individual bolts of pain spread out through him to become a generalized agony that throbbed throughout his whole being. When he finally collapsed, stretched out on grass and gravel, where they kicked the hell out of him, his nausea overwhelmed the pain and made him throw up.

'God!' a youth said in disgust, then kicked Cranfield as punishment. 'Puked over m'boots! Take that you filthy English bastard!' Cranfield was kicked again and rolled over to look up at the stars, his head filled with a dreadful, tightening pain as his vision blurred badly.

'Right, lads, that's enough,' the amiable Mick

Treacy said. 'Let's get him into the van . . . Jim-boy, you've still got his keys?'

'Yeah, Mick.'

'Then drive his car away to where we can best make use of it later on. Sure this git won't be needin' it.'

Only dimly aware of what was happening, Cranfield was thrown into the back of the van, landing in a mess of tyres, tools and rope, then followed in by most of the youths. Mick Treacy sat up front beside the youth who had examined Cranfield's wallet and was now their driver.

'Quickly now,' Treacy told him.

The journey did not take long. Slowly getting his senses back, feeling battered and bruised, Cranfield reasoned that the safe house hiding Quinn was indeed only two miles away. Certainly, after rattling and bouncing over what was obviously a crude, country track, the van finally arrived at its destination and ground to a halt.

When the back doors were opened, most of the youths climbed out. Cranfield was picked up by the two remaining, dragged halfway out, then thrown off the back of the van. Hitting the ground, he almost cried out with the pain, but managed to stifle it. He was picked up again, punched two or three times, then dragged across grassy earth, on to a strip of gravel, and finally through the front door of a small cottage, into a warm, brightly lit room.

Picked up a third time, he was placed on a hard

wooden chair. His arms were pulled roughly, painfully, over the back of the chair, then his wrists and shoulders were strapped to it. His ankles were tied to the legs of the chair – luckily, the ropes were just above the ankles, well below the holstered gun and knife, which were not detected – then the youths stepped away to smirk at him.

A man who had been sitting in an armchair in front of the open fire, stood up, walked forward and stopped in front of him.

The man had a head of healthy grey hair and a hard, angry face.

'Who's this?' he asked Mick Treacy while looking at Cranfield.

Mick handed the man Cranfield's ID. The man studied it at length, first thoughtfully, then incredulously, finally with a thin, cruel smile. He leaned down to Cranfield, studied him intently, then slapped his face with his own ID and said: 'Lieutenant Cranfield of the fucking SAS! Sure isn't this a pleasant wee surprise! And you look just like yer picture.'

'What picture?' Cranfield asked, getting his senses back and desperate to hear the sound of his own voice, which might help calm his growing fears. 'You mean on the ID?'

Again the man slapped Cranfield's face with the ID, saying: 'No, I don't mean this shit. Sure we had yer photo taken by some of our own boyos and I've had many a good gander at it. I'd recognize you,

Lieutenant, with yer feet stickin' out of a barrel. Sure it's a pleasure to meet you.'

'You're Michael Quinn,' Cranfield said, trying to keep his voice steady.

'The one an' only,' Quinn replied. He studied Cranfield's ID, nearly threw it into the fire, changed his mind and carefully put it back into Cranfield's jacket pocket. 'By the time we finish with you they won't recognize you, so you might as well have some identification.' He straightened up to grin first at Mick Treacy, then at the assembled youths. 'So what'ya think of the brave SAS lieutenant?'

One of them spat in Cranfield's face and said: 'Whoever had this bastard would drown nothin'.'

'A mother's love is blind,' Mick Treacy informed him. 'You'll learn that when yer older.'

Some of the youths laughed nervously. Michael Quinn just smiled. It was a smile that made Cranfield feel more frightened that he'd imagined he could be.

*It's not real*, he thought desperately. *Stay calm. Don't make any mistakes. It all depends on what you say or don't say, so don't let them trick you. Don't panic. Don't break.*

'So what where ya doin' in my pub?' Quinn asked. 'Apart from havin' the Guinness. Lookin' for me, were you?' When Cranfield didn't immediately reply, Quinn slapped him viciously with the back of his hand, then said, 'Well, were you?'

'Yes,' Cranfield said.

Quinn straightened up, looking pleased. 'Why?'

Cranfield found it hard to breathe. 'I think you know why,' he replied.

'Gonna put a British bullet into my head. Was that what you were plannin'?' When Cranfield didn't reply, Quinn slapped him again and said, 'Well, was it?'

'Yes,' Cranfield said.

'Now why would ya want to be doin' that? Was it because of O'Leary?'

'My name is Randolph Cranfield,' Cranfield said. 'My rank is . . .'

Quinn's hand pressed over his mouth and pushed his head back until the wood of the hard chair was chopping painfully into his neck.

'When we want your name, rank, serial number and date of birth we'll ask for it,' Quinn said. Removing his hand, he continued: 'It was O'Leary. Sure don't I know that, Lieutenant? You came to get me for what I did to that weak, treacherous shite. Well, O'Leary's dead and buried, Lieutenant, an' he sang like a bird. That's why him and his whore were killed – along with a bunch of other shites. He was a tout, a turncoat, your wee Fred, so he had to be put down.'

'You could have just killed him,' Cranfield said. 'You didn't have to . . .'

Quinn's fist smashed into his face, making his head explode with pain. When he recovered, he found it difficult to breathe and felt blood on his face. Quinn had broken his nose.

'Of course we had to,' Quinn said. 'He had a mouth like a torn pocket. Every time he opened his mouth he took a wrong step. What was wrong was right for us and he sang like a canary. He gave us a lot of important names and made our hearts leap for joy. Now what about Margaret Dogherty?'

'My name is . . .'

Quinn pressed the palm of his hand against Cranfield's broken nose and squeezed until even Cranfield couldn't hold back the tears nor prevent himself screaming. When Quinn thought he'd had enough, he removed his hand and smiled a thin smile. 'You and her were thick, were you?'

'We shared a bed a few times,' Cranfield acknowledged, though he found breathing difficult.

'You'll be sharin' a fucking grave with her soon,' Quinn responded, 'though you won't be goin' as quick as she did. Twelve bullets she had in 'er. From the guns of two men. She went quicker than the clap of a duck's wing. You should be so lucky.'

'Fuck you,' Cranfield said.

Quinn punched him so hard that the chair went over backwards and the back of his head smashed into the floor. Pains darted across his forehead, exploded behind his nose, spread out across the back of his head, and shot down from his shoulder blades to his pinioned arms. He was temporarily blinded – by tears as well as pain – when someone pushed the chair upright again, returning him to the sitting position, where his breathing was anguished.

'I don't think he's feeling too well,' Mick Treacy said.

'Ach, he'll be all right when he's better,' Quinn replied. 'Sure he belongs to the SAS. A quare bunch of boys they are.' He leaned forward, no longer smiling, and stared directly into Cranfield's weeping eyes. 'We don't want yer fucking name, rank, serial number or date of birth. What we want is a lot of information about you and your friends in British Intelligence. We ask. You answer. Is that understood?'

'My name is . . .'

The pain was excruciating, exploding from his genitals, almost too much to bear yet becoming even worse when Quinn squeezed his testicles even harder. Cranfield screamed without thinking. He almost came off the chair, but was held down by the ropes. He would have lifted the chair off the floor, but one of the youths held him down. When Quinn released him, letting the pain subside a little, he could not stop the shaking of his body nor stem the pouring of sweat.

'What do you expect?' Quinn asked rhetorically. 'You want mercy, Lieutenant? Yer thinkin' I can't be that bad and won't go any further? Well, don't kid yourself, you ijit. I'll do more than you can imagine. I've lost two childern and a lot of friends to the Brits an' been tortured myself. First Crumlin Road jail. Then fucking Long Kesh. The Brits have their own wee ways in there – and none of 'em pleasant. Mercy, Lieutenant? Sure I'm not interested. I could have stayed sane in Long Kesh if I'd had children to think about, but my childern were killed by British bullets in what was classed as an accident. Of course I still had a wife. We used to live in Conway Street. We were there in sixty-nine when the Prods wrecked the place while the RUC looked the other way. Our house was fire-bombed. My children were in hysterics. A Prod with a baseball bat that had nails stickin' out of it smashed my missus over the head an' ran off down the street. My missus died that day. She became someone else. She was so crazed, she terrified the kids an' they had to take 'er away. Then the British Army took over, searched our houses, controlled our streets. They swore at our women, fired rubber bullets at our children, and treated us as if we were animals, only fit for the slaughterin'. One day, when they weren't firin' rubber bullets, they fired at my kids, killin' both of them outright. They said it was an accident, the bastards, an' left it at that. But I didn't. I won't. So don't ask me for mercy. You came here to put a bullet through my head, but instead you'll just talk. You know the Irish, don't you? We all like to talk – a good bit of crack to pass the time – so start talkin', Lieutenant. If you don't, we have our own wee ways. Now here's the first question . . .'

'My name is . . .'

There is pain and there is pain, some of which is beyond describing. What Cranfield endured over the next few hours was beyond comprehension. He heard his own screaming, reverberating through his head. It wasn't a sound that he recognized as his own, but it opened doors that led into hell. There were punches and kicks. Sharpened blades cut through to bone. The first gunshot, which filled the room like thunder, took his kneecap away.

'God,' Cranfield gasped, licking his tears from his upper lip as they dripped from his dazed eyes down his cheeks. 'My name is . . .'

He lost a second kneecap. The gun's roaring, which was deafening, did not drown out his screaming, which seemed to reverberate through his head to leave it ringing and spinning. At some point he vomited. He then dry-retched for some time. His stomach was in knots and his heart was racing, waiting for the next torment.

He smelt it before he felt it. Burning flesh and bodily hair. They stubbed their cigarettes out on his chest, against his nipples, in his ears, then a cigarette lighter was ignited and held under his nostrils.

Pain became his whole world.

*It's not real*, he thought, trying to stop himself from shivering, trying to choke back his vomit, determined in some buried cell of himself to hold on to his dignity. *Bear in mind that nothing is real, that nothing can break you. Just don't make a mistake.*

'My name is . . .'

Finally, he was on the floor, rolling about on the tiles, not feeling the cold because he was burning, immunized by the pain to the hardness, floating out of himself. There is pain and there is pain, he now knew, but there was none he had not felt.

'Sure I'll give you this,' Quinn said, standing over him and kicking his broken ribs with no great deal of hope, 'you're one tough, tight-lipped, determined bastard. A man has to admire that.'

'So what now?' Mick Treacy asked.

'Do you think this bag of shit and piss will talk?'

'He's beyond talkin', Michael.'

'Then let's take 'im out and put an end to 'im an' we'll still come out winners.'

'Achay, that's the ticket! Let's make fertilizer out of the shite an' help Ireland's green grass grow.'

'Hood 'im,' Quinn said.

A hood was slipped over Cranfield's head and tightened around his neck with a cord, making him feel claustrophobic and totally blind. A spasm of terror whipped through him, then passed away again.

*Breathe deeply and evenly*, he thought. *You're not going to choke. They're just trying to panic you.*

They picked him off the floor, forgetting about his smashed kneecaps. When he screamed and started falling again, they cursed and let him fall, then caught him by the shoulders and dragged him backwards across the brightly lit room. Someone opened the front door, letting freezing air rush in, then they dragged him across the dark courtyard and threw him back into the van. When he hit the tyres, tools and ropes, practically bouncing off the former, his smashed knees exploded with more pain and his broken ribs screamed – or he screamed – or some animal screamed.

*That wasn't me*, he decided.

'Don't vomit,' Mick Treacy said helpfully, 'or you'll just choke t' death. Sure it's real messy, that is.'

The van kicked into life and trundled off the forecourt. It bounced a little, then turned on to the narrow road that led into the countryside. The journey, which seemed to take for ever, took only a few minutes. The van stopped in a lay-by at the foot of a gentle hill. The wind moaned through the trees.

'Sure this is as good as any place,' Mick said in his amiable way. 'Let's drag the sack of spuds out.'

'Right,' Quinn said, 'let's do that.'

They dragged Cranfield to the rear of the van, then just rolled him off the edge. He hit the ground with a thud and let his scream wipe out the pain, then he felt the ground under his stomach and thighs as they dragged him across a stretch of sharp stones and eventually on to wet grass. It was easier on the grass, less painful, though cold, and he knew that he was being dragged uphill, out into the windy field.

When they'd dragged him another ten yards or so, they released him again. He fell face down in the grass, then rolled on to his back.

'Sit up,' Quinn said.

Cranfield took a deep breath, tried to sit up, but fell back. A youth cursed and grabbed him by the shoulders and propped him upright. Cranfield was finding it hard to breathe, but he clung to his dignity.

'I don't need the hood,' he said.

There was silence for a moment, as if they were deciding, then eventually the cord around his throat was loosened and the hood was tugged off.

He saw Quinn's healthy head of grey hair and his hard, angry face. Behind him were the amiable Mick Treacy and two of the youths. All of them were holding Webley pistols. All were aiming at him. The wind was howling across the dark field and there were stars in the cloudy sky.

'That's the only kind of mercy you'll get,' Michael Quinn told him. 'Do you have any last words?'

Cranfield thought of his wife and children, his many years in the army, his more admirable days with the SAS and all it had taught him. He hadn't completely failed. He'd just made a few mistakes. As Lampton and Ricketts had said, he'd big-timed too many times; but for all that, he'd done a good job and had only one left to do. He didn't know that it was possible to do it now, but he would certainly try.

'Fuck off,' he said.

Quinn kicked him in the ribs and cracked his head with his pistol, making him fall back and roll a few feet back down the hill, deeper into the darkness.

'Fuckin' British shite!' Quinn said, then started forward.

Cranfield rolled farther away and tugged his trouser leg up. He grabbed the Browning, jerked it out of its holster, and rolled on to his back to aim it two-handed at Quinn as he advanced with his pistol raised.

Quinn stopped, eyes widening, and started aiming his pistol, even as Cranfield fired his first shots in a precise double tap.

Quinn was stopped dead in his tracks, jolting as if electrocuted. He jerked back as if tugged on a string and thudded into the earth.

Even before Quinn hit the ground, Cranfield was swinging the handgun elsewhere, managing to put a burst into Mick Treacy before the two youths returned his fire.

He saw Treacy step backwards, a surprised look on his face, then the bullets from the Webleys smashed his chest and made his insides explode.

He saw stars between the clouds, then the stars, then a big star, then a white light.

Cranfield died in that radiance.

# 17

The news came into Bessbrook just after Cranfield's men had left the base for a raid on a housing estate in the Falls.

Captain Dubois had been informed by the 'green slime' that a couple of IRA men were being hidden in the estate and preparing to snipe on a British Army foot patrol. Short of his own soldiers, he had hauled the SAS troop out of their bashas at first light and told them to prepare for an assault. They were on the road within ten minutes, but without Lieutenant Cranfield, who hadn't been seen since storming out of Dubois' office the previous afternoon.

When the telephone rang, Dubois, wondering where Cranfield had gone this time, though certainly suspecting what he was up to, was watching the armoured pig containing the SAS troops leaving its parking bay below. He turned away from the window, picked up the phone, and listened to the person speaking on the other end of the line, first with disbelief, then with growing awareness, and finally with a look of deep thoughtfulness.

'And you're sure one of the dead men was Quinn?'

'Yes,' his caller, an RUC officer, said. 'The bodies were brought back and positively identified.'

'Excellent,' Dubois said. 'Thank you.'

He put the phone down and returned to the window just as the armoured pig left through the guarded gates of the compound, heading for Belfast.

'Well, well,' Dubois whispered to himself, 'he actually did it. It worked!' Returning to his desk, he picked up the phone, dialled HQ Lisburn, and used a code-name to get his MI5 associate. When the agent came on the line, Dubois said: 'It worked. The price was high, but he succeeded. Michael Quinn and his PIRA friend, Mick Treacy, were both found dead this morning in a field in south Armagh, shot fatally with 9mm bullets. A total of thirteen shots. Cranfield took them out before being mortally wounded. His own killers are unknown.'

Dubois stopped speaking to listen to the response. When the agent congratulated him, he smiled and hung up, clasped his fingers beneath his chin, pursed his lips for a moment, then smiled again and pressed the button on his intercom.

'It's going to be a nice day,' he told his secretary. 'I'll have tea and biscuits now.'

'Yes, sir,' she replied.

Pleased, Dubois released the intercom button and

leaned back in his chair.

'A *very* nice day!' he whispered.

Sitting between his mates in the cramped rear of the armoured pig taking them along the M1, secure in his body armour, checking his Heckler & Koch MP5 and adjusting his respirator, Ricketts glanced out the back and saw the sun rising over the soft, green hills on both sides of the motorway. He also saw the Gazelles coming down on the overt OPs, bringing resups and replacement troops, before lifting off the men who had been there all night or, in certain cases, for many days and nights. Ricketts still found it hard to believe that those lovely hills were a killing ground and that of all the places he had fought in, this was the worst. Luckily, he was fighting it with some good mates, which made all the difference.

'Are you OK?' Lampton asked him.

'Yes, Frank, I'm fine. A rude shock to have this unexpected call, but I'm waking up now.'

'I'd love to know where Cranfield is.'

'He's been missing since yesterday.'

'I asked Captain Dubois and he said that it wasn't my business. I felt like smacking his face.'

'An Army ponce,' Gumboot said. 'He's never been in the SAS. He still thinks the lower ranks and NCOs should be kept in their place. Little does he know.'

'A good soldier, though,' Martin said. 'I mean he

has a good record. He's been in Northern Ireland a long time and done a lot of good.'

'We did a lot of good in Oman,' Gumboot replied, 'but no one's singing *our* praises.'

'You know what I mean,' Martin said.

'Och, aye,' Jock cut in with an exaggerated Scottish accent. 'We all know that him and Cranfield are your heroes. That must mean you're officer material and all set to move on. The best o' luck, laddy.'

'Leave him alone,' Lampton said. 'Martin's earned his badge just by being here. He's also proven himself to be a good soldier, so let him have heroes. And let him be a good officer if that's what he wants.'

'Sure, boss,' Jock replied, rolling his eyes, shaking his head and flashing Gumboot a 'What more can I say?' look. 'Anything you say, boss.'

But no matter how much they mocked him, Martin was pleased to hear Sergeant Lampton speaking about him that way. He was proud of how he had behaved here – particularly during the first encounter with PIRA youths from the Divis flats – though he knew that not everyone in the Troop thought that highly of him.

He didn't mind being sneered at by the likes of Jock and Gumboot – he knew they were working-class, in the SAS for life, and highly resentful of most officers – whom they termed 'short-term Ruperts' – as well as of Troopers who aspired to be one of that class. No, what bothered Martin most was when

Troopers his own age – and, like him, only recently badged – behaved exactly the same way.

Officers like Cranfield and Dubois were indeed what Martin aspired to be. They represented his future. The other men, Martin realized, didn't understand such ambitions and strongly resented anyone who harboured them.

'I think Cranfield's gone looking for Michael Quinn,' Martin said distractedly, still thinking about the wedge his ambition drove between him and the other Troopers.

'Probably,' Taff Burgess said. 'Our surveillance proved that he had a bug about him – you know, Public Enemy Number One. He was stung that Quinn managed to get away, so he's probably gone after him.'

'The dumb shit,' Dead-eye said. They were the first words he had spoken. 'You ask me, *all* officers are dumb shits.' He shrugged. 'Who gives a fuck?'

'I do,' Lampton replied. 'I don't like big-timers. To tell you the truth, Lieutenant Cranfield has me worried. Where the fuck is he?'

'Somewhere he shouldn't be,' Ricketts replied. 'You can bet your life on it.'

'I don't bet,' Dead-eye said.

Danny looked with admiration at the expressionless Dead-eye and finally got up the courage to ask his burning question.

''Scuse me, Sergeant, do you mind if I ask you something?' Dead-eye just stared flatly at him, not responding at all, so Danny took a deep breath and came right out with it: 'What kind of experience did you have in the Telok Anson swamp in Malaya?'

The ensuing silence was filled only by the low growling of the armoured pig's engine and the wind roaring outside. Jock glanced at Gumboot, who rolled his eyes and whistled softly. Ricketts and Lampton exchanged glances, then lowered their heads to grin. Taff Burgess, who was terrified of Dead-eye, looked down at his boots, while Martin, who was also frightened of him, looked on, fascinated.

Eventually, after what seemed like an eternity, Dead-eye, staring flatly at Danny, said: 'What do you mean, kid?'

Danny cleared his throat, stoking his courage. 'I mean, you're really quiet, you know? And really good – a great soldier. I mean, you never say nothing – you just *do* it – but you do it so well and you learnt it all in that swamp in Malaya. I hear it changed you . . . you were changed in that jungle. What happened there, Sarge?'

Dead-eye stared at Danny for a long time, his eyes as flat as two stones; then speaking in what sounded like the voice of the walking dead, he said: 'It rained and it was hot and it stank and it was dark; and we lived off the jungle and shat and pissed in the water and fought the fucking guerrillas as ordered. What more do you need to know?'

'Nothing.'

'Good,' Dead-eye said.

No one spoke after that.

As the armoured pig trundled off the A1, cut through the Broadway, and turned into the Falls Road, Ricketts was reminded again of just how much he detested being in Northern Ireland. This wasn't a real war with an enemy to respect, but a dirty game of hide and seek, a demeaning police action, a bloody skirmish against faceless killers, mean-faced adolescents, hate-filled children and contemptuous housewives. Christ, he loathed it.

Ricketts was filled with this disgust as the armoured pig took him through the mean streets of Belfast in dawn's pale light, past terraced houses with doors and windows bricked up, pubs barricaded with concrete blocks and off-licences, betting shops and all kinds of shops protected by coils of barbed wire. He did, however, manage to swallow his bile when they neared the estate and Sergeant Lampton, now his best friend, started counting off the distance to the leap: 'Two hundred metres . . . one hundred . . . fifty metres . . . *Go! Go! Go!*'

The armoured pig screeched to a halt, its rear doors burst open, and the men, including Ricketts, leapt out one by one, carrying their weapons in the Belfast Cradle, then raced across the debris-strewn lawns in front of the bleak blocks of flats, still wreathed in the early-morning mist.

Ricketts raced ahead with Lampton, across the

lawn, into the block, along the litter-filled walkway, even as someone shouted a warning – a child's voice, loud and high-pitched – and a door slammed shut just above.

Up a spiral of steps, along a covered balcony, boots clattering on the concrete, making a hell of a racket, then Lampton was at the door in front of Ricketts, taking aim at the lock with his Remington 870 pump-action shotgun.

The noise was ear-splitting, echoing under the balcony's ceiling, as the wood around the Yale lock splintered and the door was kicked open. Lampton dropped to his knees, lowering the Remington, taking aim with his Browning High Power as Ricketts rushed into the room, his Heckler & Koch MP5 at the ready, bawling: 'Security Forces! Don't move!' even as he hurled a stun grenade to confuse those inside.

The grenade exploded, cracking the walls and ceiling, but when its flash had faded away an empty room was revealed.

Cursing, Ricketts and the others rushed through the poky rooms, tearing down the curtains, kicking over tables and chairs, ensuring that no one was hiding anywhere, then covering each other as they backed out again, cursing in frustration.

'Let's try the flats next door!' Gumboot bawled, his voice distorted eerily by the respirator. 'The fuckers on either side!'

But before they could do so, other doors opened

and housewives stepped out, still wearing their nightdresses, curlers in their hair, swearing just like the SAS men, and bending over to drum metal dustbin lids on the brick walls and concrete floor of the balcony.

The noise was deafening, growing louder every second, as more women emerged to do the same, followed by their children.

Their shrieked obscenities added dramatically to the general bedlam until, as Ricketts knew would eventually happen, the first bottle was thrown.

'Damn!' Lampton said, glancing up and down the walkway, then over the concrete wall, the shotgun in one hand, the Browning in the other, but briefly forgetting all he had been taught and failing to watch his own back. 'Let's get the hell out of here.'

It was his first and last mistake.

A ragged, gaunt-faced adolescent had followed them up the stairs and now stepped out of the stairwell with his Webley pistol aimed right at Lampton. He fired three times, in rapid succession, and Lampton was thrown back, bouncing against the concrete wall, even as the kid disappeared again.

Lampton dropped both his weapons and quivered epileptically, blood bursting from his respirator, and was falling as Ricketts raced to the stairs, bawling: 'Christ! Pick him up and let's go!' Then, as bottles burst about him, with drumming binlids and shrieked obscenities resounding in his head, he chased the assassin, plunging into the dangerous gloom of the stairwell without thinking about it.

The stairwell was almost dark, littered with rubbish, stained with piss, its concrete walls covered with graffiti, much of which was political. It was dangerously narrow, each flight of steps short, and Ricketts knew that he was running down blind, with the kid likely to step out from around a corner and blow his head off.

He didn't give a damn. This was a shocking revelation. The strain of the Falls Road OP had already taken its toll, straining his nerves to the limit, and now the shooting of Lampton, his best friend, had made him explode. He knew it, but he couldn't stop himself, so he kept running down the stairs.

'Phil!' Gumboot bellowed from up above.

Ricketts burst out of the stairwell, back into the morning light, just as someone on a balcony above dropped another bottle.

It exploded into a searing, crackling wall of yellow flame about ten metres away. A Molotov cocktail.

The kid with the gun had vanished. Ricketts cursed. When another Molotov cocktail exploded to his right, he glanced up and saw a bunch of dickers hanging over the wall of the balcony, some throwing more bottles. The bottles, which were more home-made petrol bombs, smashed on the ground along the bottom of the block of flats, creating a long wall of yellow fire.

'Shit!' Ricketts said, removing the respirator from his face and letting it dangle under his chin. 'Murderous little bastards!'

He was shocked by the realization that he had almost lost control of himself for the first time since joining the SAS.

'Damn!' he said. 'What the . . .?'

Gumboot came rushing out of the stairwell, crouched low, his Colt Commando at the ready.

'Jesus, Ricketts!' he exclaimed. 'What the hell do you think you're doing, going down the stairwell without back-up? You could have got yourself killed.'

'Sorry. I lost my head for a moment. Is Lampton . . .?'

Before Gumboot could reply, Jock McGregor appeared, carrying the blood-soaked Lampton over his shoulders.

'He's dead,' Gumboot said.

Ricketts felt terrible grief and rage, one emotion at odds with the other, but before he could think about it the wall beside him exploded, spitting dust and pulverized mortar, and he realized that he'd heard a rifle firing.

'Sniper!' Gumboot bellowed, dropping to his knees and scanning the waste ground as Jock hurried towards the armoured pig, still carrying Lampton. 'Some bastard up on the roof! Let's get the fuck out of here!'

Ricketts glanced back at the flats and saw smoke

billowing up from the balconies, forcing the dickers and housewives to scatter, many of them obviously choking and trying to cover their streaming eyes and noses. The roaring of sub-machine-guns suddenly came from the stairwell, then Danny and Taff came backing out, firing as they retreated.

'What's happening?' Ricketts shouted.

'We were covering Jock,' Taff said, 'as he carried Lampton down, with Dead-eye and Martin trying to hold back those stupid bastards on the second floor. They'd started throwing Molotov cocktails and instead of getting us they set fire to their own bloody flats. We backed down the stairs as Dead-eye and Danny threw some CS grenades and fired some rubber bullets, trying to hold the mob back. Then, just as we reached the stairwell leading down from the first floor, another bunch – hard men, not kids – carrying spiked clubs and chains, came along the first-floor balcony. Some followed us down the stairwell; the others went up to the second floor. Now Dead-eye and Martin are trapped up there, caught between the two groups. I think we have to go back up.'

Ricketts glanced back at the armoured pig to see Jock leaning forward, into the open rear doors, letting Lampton's body roll into the vehicle. 'Come on, Gumboot, let's go,' he shouted.

'What about us?' Danny asked.

Ricketts glanced at the wall of flame that ran

along the front of the building, sending up a great column of black smoke.

'There should be another entrance at the far end of the block,' he said to Danny. 'Go along there, take the stairs to the second floor, and come up behind those damned kids.'

'How do I stop them?'

'No bullets. Use a combination of smoke and stun grenades to put them out of action. If necessary, use the butt of your gun to beat the shit out of them.' He glanced back towards the pig and saw Jock at the PRC 319 radio. 'Jock's calling for back-up,' he said. 'It'll come from the nearest RUC station, which is just down the Falls, so it shouldn't take long. Now get up there and calm them down.'

'Right, boss,' Danny said.

While Danny and Taff ran towards the far end of the block of flats, Ricketts and Gumboot rushed back into the stairwell, holding their weapons at the ready, wondering what they would find there.

In fact, the stairwells were empty and they soon reached the second floor.

Martin felt as if he had wings and was taking flight. Standing beside Dead-eye, in the narrow, litter-strewn balcony, caught between the bottle-hurling youths at one end, the screaming housewives in their doorways, the wooden doors set alight by the hastily thrown Molotov cocktails, and the gang of hard men advancing from the other end with spiked clubs and bicycle chains, he was too enraptured with the sheer excitement of it all to feel any fear. This is what he had joined the SAS for and it was more than enough.

He was standing back to back with Dead-eye, facing the oncoming youths as Dead-eye prepared to tackle the hard men. The screaming housewives were dousing the fires with buckets of water, creating more smoke.

Martin asked: 'Do we fire or not, Sarge? I say let's shoot a few of the bastards and set an example.'

'Stop talking shit,' Dead-eye said, sounding calm. 'Shoot one of these bastards and the rest will go mad. Put your respirator on and then throw a couple of hand grenades – a stun grenade, followed by CS. That should dampen their spirits.'

An egg broke against Martin's face. It was followed by some tomatoes. A fat whore of a housewife threw a pile of rubbish at him and someone else deluged him in cold water. His rage came out of nowhere.

'Bugger this,' he said. 'I'm not playing with rubber bullets. If these paddies want to behave like pigs, then I'll treat them that way. I'm not taking this shit!'

'No real bullets!' Dead-eye hissed, as his stun grenade exploded just in front of the hard men, blinding them with light, deafening them, making them reel drunkenly and fall against the walls. It was followed instantly by the CS grenade, which obscured them in a chemical smoke that burned their throats and eyes, hurt their ears and made them choke and vomit.

When one of the youths aimed a pistol at Martin, he let rip with his short-barrelled Sterling sub-machine-gun, firing a short, deadly burst of 9mm bullets.

'No!' Dead-eye bawled.

The young man flung his hands up, looking very surprised, then back-flipped into the group bunched up behind him, parting them like skittles as he crashed backwards on to the concrete floor, his chest pumping blood.

The other youths looked down at him, briefly shocked into immobility, then, realizing that he was already dead, rushed as one at Martin. Being too surprised to fire his weapon a second time, the trooper let them swarm all over him before he could decide what to do.

By then it was too late.

The sub-machine-gun was torn from his hands. His respirator was torn off. He was punched and kicked, then picked up and spun around. He caught a brief glimpse of Dead-eye, whose back was still turned to him, heading boldly into the clouds of CS gas, to beat his way out through the crowd of choking, vomiting hard men.

Martin caught this glimpse of Dead-eye before he was turned away, balanced precariously on the hands of the bawling youths. Then he saw the balcony wall, the ground far below, and knew, with a terrible, lacerating fear, what they were going to do.

He couldn't believe it.

His own scream was the last thing he heard as they heaved him over the balcony and he plunged to the ground.

'Oh, my God!' Taff exclaimed just as he and Danny reached the second floor. 'They've thrown someone off the bloody balcony. Oh, Christ, it's a trooper!'

Danny glanced over the wall and saw the soldier on the ground, face down and not moving a muscle, looking like a rag doll. When he stared along the balcony, he saw some youths running towards him, out of a cloud of CS gas, choking, coughing, wiping their eyes and noses, some falling against the walls, others collapsing, writhing on the ground in their own vomit. Beyond them, Dead-eye was making his escape, beating his way through a gang of older men, all of whom were also suffering badly from the clouds of CS gas.

Clearly, Dead-eye was all right.

When a rifle shot rang out from the roof, Jock twisted sideways, grabbed his left arm, fell to his knees and shook his head as if dazed.

'Go back down and look after them,' Danny said. 'I'm going up on the roof.'

'What?'

'There's a sniper up there and I'm going to get him.'

'I'll come with you.'

'No. You go back down and look after those two.'

'OK,' Taff said. 'Be careful.'

'I will,' Danny replied.

While Taff hurried back down, Danny took the stairs to the roof. It was another three flights up and he passed a few people – two housewives and a pimply-faced youth who wanted to see what was happening. Danny simply brushed past them, pretending they weren't there; but when an older man, bumping into him near the top of the last stairwell, tried to stop him from going further, Danny belted him in the stomach with the stock of his sub-machine-gun, then thumped him on the side of the head and the back of the neck. When the man collapsed, groaning, Danny jumped over him and continued on up the stairs until he burst out on to the roof.

It was a broad, flat expanse filled with water tanks, TV aerials and litter. Plaster had fallen off the brick walls and thick dust covered all.

The sniper was leaning on the front wall, peering into the sights of his .303 Lee Enfield bolt-action sniper rifle. So dedicated was he, so intent on his work, that he didn't even hear Danny's approach until he was practically standing over him.

'Security Forces,' Danny said. 'Don't move!'

The man jerked his head around and looked up in surprise. He was a hard man, all right, with a scarred face and gelid gaze, his surprise soon giving way to fearless contempt. He studied Danny for a moment, taking note of his baby face, then grinned crookedly and said: 'Who the fuck are you kidding, boyo? Could you shoot me this close up?'

'I just might,' Danny said, lowering his sub-machine-gun and removing his Browning from its holster. He raised the handgun and aimed it right between the man's eyes. 'What do *you* think?' he asked.

Still kneeling on the ground, the man turned away from the wall. He deliberately swung the barrel of his rifle towards Danny, resting the stock against his hip for support.

'I think you're about eighteen years old and couldn't shoot someone this close.'

'You may be right,' Danny said.

When the man swung the barrel up higher, preparing to fire, Danny calmly squeezed the trigger of his Browning, putting a burst into the man's chest, directly over the heart. He was punched into the wall, his rifle clattering to the floor, and was dead before the reverberation of the gunshots had faded away.

Danny holstered his handgun, put down his sub-machine-gun, searched the dead man, carefully removing any papers that would help to identify him, then picked his sub-machine-gun up again and walked slowly, cautiously, back down the stairs.

Ricketts and Gumboot had also just reached the second floor when they saw an SAS trooper being flung off the roof and crash with a dreadful thud on to the concrete sixty feet below. They stopped momentarily, frozen with shock, as Jock raced away from the protection of the armoured pig, across the open road, to check that the fallen man was actually dead. Then the sniper fired again, wounding Jock in the arm, making him jerk violently sideways and fall to his knees.

'Oh, those bastards!' Gumboot exclaimed softly. 'I better go back down.'

'No,' Ricketts said. 'Taff's beaten you to it. He'll take care of Jock and . . .' He couldn't finish the sentence, not yet knowing exactly who'd been thrown off the roof, so he just shook his head and said: 'Come on. Let's get the hell up there.'

They ran up the remaining stairs and arrived at the third floor just as Dead-eye was advancing towards them. His face was covered with a respirator and he was using the butt of his Colt Commando to beat his way through a crowd of men who were coughing and vomiting in clouds of CS gas. Some of them were falling to the ground and gasping like beached fish.

When Dead-eye reached Ricketts and Gumboot,

just out of range of the CS gas, he removed the respirator from his face and said: 'They threw Martin off the roof when he shot and killed one of them.'

'He killed one?' Ricketts asked.

'Yes,' Dead-eye said. 'A kid.'

'Oh, Christ!' Ricketts said 'This could cause a lot of trouble.'

'We can counterbalance the kid's death with the story of our man thrown off the roof,' Dead-eye said in a cold-blooded, pragmatic manner. 'That should make them shut up.'

'Fuck,' Ricketts said, feeling shocked and unsure of himself. 'This is one filthy war.'

'It's a pisser,' Gumboot said, 'but we're stuck with it. Now let's get the hell out of here before those bastards recover.' He nodded towards the hard men now choking, vomiting and collapsing in the gas-filled walkway.

'Right,' Dead-eye said. 'Let's go.'

They hurried back down the stairs and out into the road where the fires from the Molotov cocktails were flickering out and two RUC trucks were disgorging men wearing flak jackets and carrying anti-riot shields and truncheons.

As the Quick Reaction Force men raced into the block of flats, sealing off both exits, Jock climbed shakily to his feet, holding his wounded arm, and Taff carried Martin's dead, smashed-up body back to the armoured pig.

Ricketts, Dead-eye and Gumboot formed a protective circle around Jock as he crossed the dangerous stretch of open ground.

They broke apart and spun around, preparing to fire, when they heard the sound of gunfire on the roof.

'That fucking sniper!' Gumboot exclaimed.

'No,' Ricketts said. 'It was a weapon firing on the roof, but it wasn't aimed at us.'

'It was either Danny firing at the sniper,' Taff explained, 'or the sniper firing at him.'

'He's a good kid,' Dead-eye said with a rare, if veiled, display of admiration. 'He'll be OK.'

Dead-eye was rarely wrong.

When Danny materialized, smiling shyly as he told them that the sniper was dead, they all piled gratefully into the armoured pig and were driven back to Bessbrook.

There, while still trying to adjust to the deaths of Frank Lampton and Martin Renshaw, they learned from Captain Dubois that Lieutenant Cranfield had been found at first light, his body riddled with bullets, lying near the dead bodies of PIRA activists Michael Quinn and Mick Treacy.

As the latter pair had been killed with 9mm bullets, six in Quinn, the other seven in Treacy, it was believed that they had both been shot by Cranfield just before he was killed.

It was also believed that Cranfield's Browning,

which had not been found at the scene of the killings, had been stolen by his executioners.

The identity of Cranfield's executioners had yet to be ascertained.

'Last but not least,' Dubois told the assembled men, 'I should inform you that for reasons to do with recent events, you will all soon be transferred back to Hereford. D Squadron will arrive a few weeks later and take over your duties. That's all. Dismissed.'

'Thanks a million,' Jock whispered.

The men left the briefing room, went straight to the NAAFI canteen, steadily drank themselves into a state of sleep-inducing oblivion, then staggered back to their makeshift beds in the Portakabin being used as sleeping quarters. By lights out, they were snoring.

All except Ricketts.

Deeply shocked by the death of Lampton, his best friend since Oman, and also disturbed by the manner of Renshaw's death, Ricketts had trouble sleeping. When at last he did so, after much tossing and turning, he had the first of the nightmares that would haunt him for years to come.

# 18

The remaining members of the SAS troop were shipped out of Belfast as quietly as they had been shipped in and returned to their Hereford HQ. A few weeks later, when the shock waves from the death of Lieutenant Cranfield had died away, the full complement of D Squadron 22 SAS arrived in Belfast amid a great deal of publicity designed to intimidate the IRA.

The two PIRA youths responsible for Cranfield's death were later caught, convicted and jailed in the Republic. In prison, one of the assassins admitted to Cranfield's controller that he had been present at the ghastly torture of Cranfield, but that the SAS officer had bravely refused to talk.

This knowledge went a long way to restoring Cranfield's tarnished reputation with the other members of the Regiment.

Having learnt from the mistakes of the first small group of SAS men in Northern Ireland, D Squadron chalked up a more satisfying record of counter-terrorist successes, reaping a rich harvest from the seeds sown by their relatively inexperienced, path-finding predecessors. Nevertheless, things did not go smoothly at first, even for D Squadron.

In April 1976 a four-man SAS team was set up in two OPs for surveillance of the house of Peter Cleary, an IRA 'staff captain' who lived near the border. During their many long days and nights in the OPs, the four soldiers had very little sleep and were exposed to the bitter elements.

Early one evening, shortly after a helicopter landing at Crossmaglen was attacked by the IRA with rockets and machine guns, the troopers arrested Cleary in his house near Forkhill, a mere fifty metres north of the border.

Cleary was taken to a nearby field with a five-man SAS escort, to await the arrival of another helicopter. According to one of the soldiers, all of the SAS men but one were used to help guide the chopper down with the aid of torches, which meant that Cleary was being guarded by just one trooper. Seeing his opportunity, he grabbed the soldier's rifle by the barrel and tried to pull it away. The soldier squeezed the trigger three times, hitting Cleary in the chest and killing him instantly.

As being 'shot while trying to escape' is an old military cliché often covering summary execution, few Republicans believed the SAS version of Cleary's death. Though the authorities put the death down to 'insufficient manpower' and 'a lack of handcuffs', the IRA alleged that Cleary had been murdered.

This was another set-back for the SAS.

D Squadron, however, then scored a major victory over the IRA. In early 1977, a young lance-corporal of the Royal Highland Fusiliers was killed by an IRA mortar bomb at Crossmaglen. The only clue to the identity of the killers was a dark-blue Datsun with a black vinyl roof, seen in the vicinity at the time of the incident and believed to be a scout vehicle for the ASU mortar team.

Midway through that month, late one Sunday afternoon, the vehicle was spotted again near the border. A hooded man carrying a bandolier of ammunition and a sawn-off shotgun got out of the car and walked in the direction of the hidden SAS patrol set up to entrap him. When one of the patrol rose to challenge the man, he raised his shotgun to fire. The SAS trooper opened fire first, killing the terrorist.

Immediately, the SAS trooper came under fire from a number of hidden gunmen using high-velocity Armalite rifles. The shots missed their target and the trooper ducked for cover. At the same time, other members of the SAS patrol fired back, aiming at the muzzle-flash of the enemy weapons and eventually forcing the IRA men to flee. When the SAS team went in pursuit of them, they found a trail of blood beside the road.

The man they had shot turned out to be a

twenty-year-old labourer, Seamus Harvey, from nearby Drummakaval. He died less than 200 yards from the site of an ambush in which three British soldiers had been killed just before the SAS arrived to set up their OP.

According to one unnamed source, some of Harvey's wounds were caused by an IRA Armalite rifle later used to murder a UDR corporal.

Because of these operations, IRA attacks in south Armagh ended for almost a year.

The SAS soldiers who had been caught by the Gardai when trying to cross the border into the Republic were returned from Hereford by RAF transport to be put on trial in Dublin. Throughout the trial, they were guarded by a senior SAS officer who let it be known that he feared for their lives. After a tense two days in the courtroom, three judges found the men guilty of entering the Republic without permission, but cleared them on the more serious charge of possessing firearms to endanger life. The weapons used as evidence during the trial were therefore returned to the SAS and the troopers were freed and flown back to Hereford, via RAF Northolt.

This was another victory for the SAS.

Celebrating in the bar at Hereford, Sergeant 'Dead-eye Dick' Parker, Corporal Phil Ricketts, and Troopers 'Jock' McGregor, 'Gumboot' Gillis, 'Taff' Burgess and Danny 'Baby Face' Porter raised their glasses in a toast. Then, though they normally didn't discuss the dead, or those who 'beat the clock', they somehow raised the name of Lieutenant Cranfield, agreeing that although he had certainly been a 'big-timer', he had made amends for it by showing exemplary courage during his final, terrible hours.

'He was a decent man at heart,' Ricketts said, 'but too wayward, or impulsive, for his own good – or for the good of the Regiment.'

'I agree,' Jock said. 'Even if he'd survived, he'd never have been invited back to the Regiment after serving out his first three-year stint.'

'No way,' Gumboot said.

Perhaps in order to avoid the names of the late Frank Lampton and Martin Renshaw, the former widely respected, the latter more reservedly so, they discussed the relationship between the SAS and the intelligence services in Northern Ireland. Their conclusion was that it was complex, bewildering, sometimes unsavoury, and too often deadly.

This led them back to Captain Dubois of 14 Intelligence Company and the mystery of his love-hate relationship with Lieutenant Cranfield.

'That Captain Dubois outsmarted Cranfield,' Ricketts explained, giving utterance at last to one of the many thoughts that had haunted him in past months and led to an increasing number of nightmares. 'I think he knew what he was doing all along. He understood that Cranfield was an unusual kind of SAS officer – impetuous, sometimes thoughtless, prepared to break all the rules – so he set him up to take out Michael Quinn . . . and to do so in a way that would make us look culpable, while absolving the Army from all blame.'

'Well, he certainly succeeded,' Taff offered. 'You've got to admire him.'

'Who dares wins,' Dead-eye said.

# SOLDIER F: SAS

# GUERRILLAS IN THE JUNGLE

Shaun Clarke

# Prelude

The guerrilla camp had been hacked out of the dense jungle and could be seen only from the air. Its centrepiece was a roughly levelled parade ground, about the size of a tennis court, though such a game was unknown to these people. Built in the natural caverns of red and ochre rock camouflaged by the overhanging foliage, the camp quarters consisted of a lean-to thatched with *atap* palm, with kitchen, lecture room, and sleeping benches for about sixty newcomers. The older hands were housed in an *atap* further up the hill, above the boulder and overlooking the parade ground.

A babbling stream, providing water for the camp, snaked around the boulder, past the parade ground and back into the dense, steaming jungle. The latrines were built further away, near to where the stream entered the jungle, carrying the excrement and urine to the isolated dwellings that used the same water for washing and drinking. The latrines themselves consisted of a thatched lean-to over a pit full of seething maggots. The stench was atrocious.

Few of the guerrillas were more than twenty-five years of age, most were under twenty, and a surprising number were little more than children. Some of the males wore khaki shorts, shirts and military caps, but most wore no item of uniform and were either dressed like coolies or wearing white shirts, grey trousers and felt hats. Most of them were barefoot, though some wore *terumpas* – wooden clogs held on by rubber straps.

Almost without exception, the women were in long-sleeved, high-necked white smocks and wide black trousers. All had bobbed hair and used no make-up. The better-educated taught Mandarin and singing; the others worked in the kitchen and did their fair share of the dirtiest, heaviest male chores. Though all of them acted as nurses, seamstresses and general domestics, they expected to be treated just like the men and could be just as merciless when it came to the treatment of prisoners or traitors.

The daily schedule was strict and demanding. Reveille was at first light, 5.30 in the morning, when the crying of gibbons and the clicking of cicadas dominated the chatter of the jungle. At 6.00, when the guerrillas had bathed and brushed their teeth, they took part in the flag-raising ceremony, singing 'The Red Flag'. Roll-call was followed by a communal reading of the laws and regulations of the Malayan Races' Liberation Army (MRLA). Calisthenics lasted until 6.30, followed by a cup of tea and a rest period.

At 7.00 they started drilling with weapons. This included practice in jungle-warfare tactics, racing up and down hills, climbing trees and learning various jungle ambush positions. At 8.30 they washed and rested, then had a breakfast of boiled tapioca or rice with greens – fern tops or sweet-potato leaves – followed by a second rest period.

Classes began at 10.00 sharp, with political and military lessons on a daily alternating basis, the former covering Marxism–Leninism, the writings of Mao Tse-tung and the current international situation; the latter, map-reading, tactical theory, lessons in the tactics of the Russian and Chinese armies, and the general principles of guerrilla warfare.

Depending on the length of the lectures, these classes would last until approximately noon, when the guerrillas would break for a snack of biscuits and hot water, with a rest period lasting until 1.00 p.m. From then until 3.00 they would have individual assignments: special instruction in Mandarin or general study groups for the new recruits; preparation for the next lectures by the instructors; jobs around the camp – collecting firewood, cleaning up, ministering to the many sick – then, at 3.00, another arduous hour of drilling with weapons. This was followed by a thirty-minute wash period and, at 4.30, the 'evening' meal, not much different from breakfast.

Even during the so-called 'free period' lasting until 6.00, they would be compelled to study or practice their drills.

At 6.00, after coffee, there was a parade of all hands to take down the colours and sing 'The Red Flag' again. Then the 'political research' would begin, with experienced political warriors leading group discussions about the doctrines of Communism. These discussions would include 'self-criticism' and 'mutual criticism' designed to eradicate the ego. No one smiled. Jokes were rarely made. Throughout every activity, they would repeatedly give one another the clenched-fist salute.

When the discussions ended, at 9.00 p.m. sharp, they went straight to bed.

Given such a harsh, undeviating routine, to be called upon to join a patrol into the jungle often seemed like a blessing.

* * *

All of the men and women in that particular morning's patrol were Chinese Malays. While some had been born in Malaya, others in China and a few in Hong Kong, Borneo or Sumatra, they all spoke Kuo-yü, the national dialect of China and the lingua franca of the jungle. They spoke in a whisper, and then only for the first few minutes; once away from the camp, deep in the jungle, they maintained a resolute silence, communicating only with hand signals.

Their armament for the patrol consisted of a British Bren gun, three antiquated tommy-guns, ten rifles, five shotguns, five pistols and a *parang*, or Malay jungle knife, shaped like a machete, one of which was carried by each member of the patrol.

From the vegetable gardens and rubber trees at the edge of the camp, they plunged straight into the darkness of the jungle. The ground was covered with a thick carpet of dead leaves and seedling trees, though no grass or flowers were to be seen. A dense undergrowth of young trees and palms of all kinds climbed to a height of about twelve feet, obscuring the giant roots of the trees. Out of the tangled green undergrowth, however, the countless tree trunks rose straight upwards for 150 feet, where they formed a solid canopy of green that almost entirely shut out the sky. The tree trunks, though similar in that they were all of a uniform thickness and straining up towards the light, were of every colour and texture: smooth and black, scaly and ochre-red, pale grey or green with moss, some as finely dappled as a moth's wing.

The trunks were often hidden by a network of creepers which in places broke out into enormous leaves. Elsewhere, the vines and creepers hung straight down from the branches to the ground, where they had taken root again, looping themselves from tree to tree like a ship's rigging. Up in the treetops, where the great trunks suddenly burst into branches, were huge hanging gardens of moss and ferns, themselves covered in tangled webs of liana and creepers. This dense canopy of constantly rotting, regenerating, intertwining foliage provided a few windows through which the sky could be glimpsed, but it served mostly to keep out the sunlight.

In this jungle, then, the average visibility for two men standing up was at most only twenty-five yards, varying slightly from place to place. Any confidence that this might have given to the guerrillas was soon lost when they had to leave the jungle and cross a large area of open paddy-fields, where they would have been easy targets for enemy snipers.

Grateful to reach the far side of the fields, they slipped through the open trees of a rubber estate, where sunlight and fresh air were allowed in. In these isolated patches, rattans and other thorns flourished, and the palms, ferns, bracken and seedling trees became so dense that the guerrillas, male and female, had to hack their way through with their *parangs* – an exhausting task.

By midday the humidity was making them all pour sweat, and when not protected by trees they were exposed to a heat that not only beat down upon their heads but also rose in suffocating waves from the parched ground.

They soon plunged back into the jungle where, though they were protected from direct sunlight, the humidity was even more suffocating. In fact, this jungle was even worse than the one they had left. Known as *belukar*, it was land that had once been cleared but gone back to secondary jungle, with swampy thickets of thorn, bracken and bamboo even more dense and impenetrable than the original growth. Also, it contained vast stretches of swampy jungle covered with *mengkuang*, a gargantuan leathery grass with sharp blades, about twenty feet long and four or five inches wide, with a row of curved thorns along each edge. In one hour of back-breaking work, only a hundred yards would be covered.

Nevertheless, though exhausted, sweating, sometimes bleeding, and constantly attacked by vicious red ants, the patrol thought of only one thing: the successful completion of their task.

Soon they came to the outer edge of the paddy-fields, where the *kongsi*-house, or company house, of the *towkay*, the merchant who owned the estate, was located, raised high on stilts. At a nod from the leader, two of the guerrillas entered the *kongsi*-house and dragged the terrified, struggling Chinese man out. They threw him on the ground, kicked him a few times, jerked him to his knees, then bound his hands together behind his back. In this position he was given a short speech about the glories of Communism, informed that he was being punished for his anti-Communist greed, then despatched with a bullet through the head.

This first job completed, the guerrillas took a short break, during which they relaxed in the grass, eating bananas and pineapple, watching the bee-eaters and bulbuls searching for flies overhead. When the break was over, the guerrillas, who had scarcely cast a nod in the direction of the dead man, marched around the edge of the bright-green paddy-field to the kampong itself, which consisted of a few thatched houses on stilts in a grove of coconut palms, fruit trees and hibiscus flowers.

There, they forced the head of the village to provide them with a proper cooked meal – a chicken curry with *brinjol* (aubergine), eggs, fried salt fish, rice and several vegetables – followed by coffee and sweetmeats. Afterwards they tied the headman's hands behind his back, made him kneel on the ground, roped his bound hands to his tethered ankles, then made the rest of the villagers gather around him.

A couple of male guerrillas entered the headman's house and emerged carrying a table between them. Two of the females then went in and dragged out his struggling, sobbing wife.

'This man,' the leader of the guerrillas said, pointing to the trembling headman, 'is an informer who must be punished for his crimes. You will all remain here and bear witness to his punishment. Anyone who tries to leave, or turns his head away, will be shot.'

While the terrified villagers and the shocked headman looked on, the latter's wife, eight months pregnant, was thrown on to her back on the table and held down by four guerrillas. The leader of the guerrillas then withdraw his *parang*, stood at the end of the table, between the woman's outstretched feet, and raised the gleaming blade above his head.

Knowing what was about to happen, the woman writhed frantically, sobbed, vomited and gibbered like a crazed animal. She was practically insane with fear even before she felt the first, appalling cut of the blade, making her release a scream that did not sound remotely human but chilled the blood of all those who heard it.

When the patrol's leader had finished his dreadful business, leaving a horrendous mess of shredded flesh and blood on the table, he and his men melted back into the jungle.

The guerrilla leader's name was Ah Hoi, but everyone knew him as 'Baby Killer'.

# 1

The man emerged from the trees and stood at the far side of the road, ghostly in the cold morning mist. It was just after first light. Having been on duty all night, the young guard, British Army Private John Peterson, was dog-tired and thought he was seeing things, but soon realized that the man was real enough. He was wearing jungle-green drill fatigues, standard-issue canvas-and-rubber jungle boots and a soft jungle hat. He had a machete on one hip, an Owen sub-machine-gun slung over one shoulder and a canvas bergen, or rucksack, on his back. Even from this distance, Private Peterson could see the yellow-and-green flash of the Malayan Command badge on the upper sleeve of the man's drill fatigues.

'Jesus!' Peterson whispered softly, then turned to the other soldier in the guardhouse located to one side of the camp's main gate. 'Do you see what I see?'

The second soldier, Corporal Derek Walters, glanced through the viewing hole of the guard-house.

'What . . .? Who the hell's *that*?'

After glancing left and right to check that nothing was coming, the ghostly soldier crossed the road. As he approached the guardhouse, it became clear that he was shockingly wasted, his fatigues practically hanging off his body, which was no more than skin and bone. Though he was heavily bearded and had blue shadows under his bloodshot eyes, both guards recognized him.

'Well, I'll be damned!' Private Peterson said. 'He actually made it!'

'Looks like it,' Corporal Peterson murmured. He opened the door of the guardhouse and stepped outside where the skeletal figure had just reached the barrier and was waiting patiently in the morning's brightening sunlight. 'Captain . . . Callaghan?' the guard asked tentatively.

'Yes, Trooper,' the captain said. 'How are you this morning?'

'Fine, boss.' Corporal Peterson shook his head in disbelief. 'Blimey, boss! You've been gone . . .'

'Three months. Raise the barrier, thanks.' When Corporal Peterson raised the barrier, Captain Patrick Callaghan grinned at him, patted him on the shoulder, then entered the sprawling combined

Army and Air Force base of Minden Barracks, Penang, where the recently reformed 22 SAS was temporarily housed.

*Not that you'd know it*, Callaghan thought as he walked lazily, wearily, towards headquarters where, he knew, Major Pryce-Jones would already be at his desk. While in Malaya, the SAS concealed their identity by discarding their badged beige berets and instead going out on duty in the blue berets and cap badges of the Manchester Regiment. Now, as Callaghan strolled along the criss-crossing tarmacked roads, past bunker-like concrete barracks, administration buildings raised off the ground on stilts, and flat, grassy fields, with the hangars and planes on the airstrip visible in the distance, at the base of the rolling green hills, Captain Callaghan saw men wearing every kind of beret and badge except those of the SAS.

In fact, the camp contained an exotic mix of regiments and police forces: six battalions of the Gurkha Rifles, one battalion each of the King's Own Yorkshire Light Infantry, the Seaforth Highlanders and the Devon Regiment, two battalions of the Malay Regiment, and the 26th Field Regiment of the Royal Artillery.

*And that's only this camp*, Callaghan thought. Indeed, just before he had left for his lone, three-month jungle patrol, a battalion of the Royal

Inniskilling Fusiliers had arrived from Hong Kong and the 2nd Guards Brigade had been sent from the United Kingdom. Subsequently, elements of other British regiments, as well as colonial troops in the form of contingents from the King's African Rifles and the Fijian Regiment, had joined in the struggle. There were now nearly 40,000 troops committed to the war in Malaya – 25,000 from Britain, including Royal Navy and Royal Air Force personnel, 10,500 Gurkhas and five battalions of the Malay Regiment.

In addition, there were the regular and armed auxiliary policemen, now totalling about 100,000 men. Most of these were Malays who had joined the Special Constabulary or served as Kampong Guards and Home Guards. The additional trained personnel for the regular police consisted mainly of men who had worked at Scotland Yard, as well as former members of the Palestine police, experienced in terrorism, men from the Hong Kong police, and even the pre-war Shanghai International Settlement, who spoke Chinese.

*It's not a little war any more*, Callaghan thought as he approached the headquarters building, *and it's getting bigger every day. This is a good time to be here.*

Not used to the bright sunlight, having been in the jungle so long, he rubbed his stinging eyes, forced himself to keep them open, and climbed the steps to the front of the administration block. There were wire-mesh screens across the doors and windows, with the night's grisly collection of trapped, now dead insects stuck between the wires, including mosquitoes, gnats, flies, flying beetles and spiders. An F-28 jet fighter roared overhead as Captain Callaghan, ignoring the insects' graveyard, pushed the doors open and entered the office.

With the heat already rising outside, it was a pleasure to step indoors where rotating fans created a cooling breeze over the administrative personnel – male and female; British, Malay, and some Eurasian Tamils – who were already seated at desks piled high with paper. They glanced up automatically when Callaghan entered, their eyes widening in disbelief when they saw the state of him.

'Is Major Pryce-Jones's office still here?' Callaghan asked.

'Yes, sir,' a Gurkha corporal replied. 'To your left. Down the corridor.'

'Thanks,' Callaghan replied, turning left and walking along the corridor until he came to the squadron commander's office. When he stopped in the doorway, the major raised his eyes from his desk, looked Callaghan up and down, then said in his sardonic, upper-class manner: 'It's about time you came back. You look a bloody mess, Paddy.'

'Sorry about that,' Callaghan replied, grinning broadly. He lowered his bergen and sub-machine-gun to the floor, then pulled up a chair in front of Pryce-Jones's desk. 'You know how it is.'

'If I don't, I'm sure you'll tell me in good time. Would you like a mug of hot tea?'

'That sounds wonderful, boss.'

'MARY!' Pryce-Jones's drawl had suddenly become an ear-shattering bellow directed at the pretty WRAC corporal seated behind a desk in the adjoining, smaller room.

'Yes, boss!' she replied, undisturbed.

'A tramp masquerading as an SAS officer has just entered the building, looking unwashed, exhausted and very thirsty. Tea with sugar and milk, thanks. Two of.'

'Yes, boss,' Mary said, pushing her chair back and disappearing behind the wall separating the offices.

'A sight for sore eyes,' Callaghan said.

'Bloodshot eyes,' Major Pryce-Jones corrected him. 'Christ, you look awful! Your wife would kill me for this.'

Callaghan grinned, thinking of Jennifer back in their home near Hereford and realizing that he hadn't actually thought about her for a very long time. 'Oh, I don't know, boss. She thinks I'm just a Boy Scout at heart. She got used to it long ago.'

'Not to seeing you in this state,' Pryce-Jones replied. 'Pretty rough, was it?'

Callaghan shrugged. 'Three months is a long time to travel alone through the jungle. On the other hand, I saw a lot during my travels, so the time wasn't wasted.'

'I should hope not,' Pryce-Jones said.

After spending three months virtually alone in the jungle, living like an animal and trying to avoid the murderous guerrillas, most men would have expected slightly more consideration from their superior officers than Callaghan was getting. But he wasn't bothered, for this was the SAS way and he certainly had only admiration for his feisty Squadron Commander. For all his urbane ways, Pryce-Jones was a hard-drinking, hard-fighting idealist, a tough character who had won a double blue at Cambridge and given up a commission early in World War Two in order to join a Scots Guards ski battalion destined for Finland. His wartime service included three years in Burma, much of it behind Japanese lines. He had then commanded an SAS squadron in north-west Europe from late 1944 until the regiment was disbanded in 1945.

Pryce-Jones was a stranger to neither the jungle nor danger. In fact, in 1950, General Sir John

Harding, Commander-in-Chief of Far East Land Forces, had called him for a briefing on the explosion of terrorism in Malaya, asking him to produce a detailed analysis of the problem. In order to do this, Pryce-Jones had gone into the jungle for six months, where he had hiked some 1,500 miles, unescorted, in guerrilla-infested territory, and talked to most of those conducting the campaign. Though ambushed twice, he had come out alive.

According to what he had later told Callaghan, much of his time had been spent with the infantry patrols trawling through the jungle in pursuit of an 'invisible' enemy. Because of this, he had concluded that the only way to win the war was to win the hearts and minds of the population, rather than try to engage an enemy that was rarely seen. The Communist Terrorists, or CT, were following Mao Tse-tung's philosophy of moving through the peasant population like 'fish in a sea', then using them as a source of food, shelter and potential recruits. What the British had to do, therefore, was 'dry up the sea'.

To this end, Pryce-Jones's recommendation was that as many of the aboriginals as possible be relocated to villages, forts, or kampongs protected by British and Federation of Malaya forces. By so doing they would win the hearts and minds of the people, who would appreciate being protected, while simultaneously drying up the 'sea' by depriving the guerrillas of food and new recruits.

When his recommendations had met with approval, Pryce-Jones, as the OC (officer commanding) of A Squadron in Minden Barracks, had sent Callaghan into the jungle to spend three months supervising the relocation of the kampongs and checking that the defence systems provided for them and the hearts-and-minds campaign were working out as planned.

Throughout that three months Callaghan had, like Pryce-Jones before him, travelled alone, from one kampong to the other, avoiding guerrilla patrols and mostly living off the jungle, covered in sweat, drenched by rain, often waist-deep in the swamps, drained of blood by leeches, bitten by every imaginable kind of insect, often going hungry for days, and rarely getting a decent night's sleep.

In fact, it had been a nightmare, but since Pryce-Jones had done the same thing for twice that long, Callaghan wasn't about to complain.

'It wasn't that difficult,' he lied as the pretty WRAC corporal, Mary Henderson, brought in their cups of tea, passed them out and departed with an attractive swaying of her broad hips. 'Although there are slightly over four hundred villages, most are little more than shanty towns, inhabited by Chinese squatters. Before we could move them, however, we had to build up a rapport with the aboriginals – in other words, to use *your* words, win their hearts and minds. This we did by seducing them with free food, medical treatment, and protection from the CT. Medical treatment consisted mainly of primitive clinics and dispensing penicillin to cure the aborigines of yaws, a skin disease. The kampongs and troops were resupplied by river patrols in inflatable craft supplied by US special forces, or by fixed-wing aircraft, though we hope to be using helicopters in the near future.'

'Excellent. I believe you also made contact with the CT.'

'More than once, yes.'

'And survived.'

'Obviously.'

Pryce-Jones grinned. 'Men coming back from there brought us some strange stories.'

'Oh?'

'Yes. Your clandestine warfare methods raised more than a few eyebrows back here – not to mention in Britain.'

'You mean the prostitutes?'

'Exactly.'

'The best is the enemy of the good. We did what we had to do, and we did our best.'

Pryce-Jones was referring to the fact that some

of the kampong prostitutes had been asking their clients for payment in guns, grenades and bullets instead of cash, then passing them on to the guerrillas in the jungle. Learning of this, Callaghan had used some of his SF (Security Forces) troops, there to protect the kampongs, to pose as clients in order to 'pay' the prostitutes with self-destroying weapons, such as hand-grenades fitted with instantaneous fuses that would kill their users, and bullets that exploded in the faces of those trying to fire them.

'What other dirty tricks did you get up to?' Pryce-Jones asked.

'Booby-trapped food stores.'

'Naturally – but what about the mail? I received some garbled story about that.'

Now it was Callaghan's turn to grin. 'I got the idea of mailing incriminating notes or money to leading Communist organizers. The poor bastards were then executed by their own kind on the suspicion that they'd betrayed their comrades.'

'How perfectly vile.'

'Though effective.'

'Word about those dirty tricks got back to Britain and caused a great deal of outrage.'

'Only with politicians. They express their outrage in public, but in private they just want us to win, no matter how we do it. They always want it both ways.'

Pryce-Jones sighed. 'Yes, I suppose so.' He sipped his steaming tea and licked his upper lip. 'But *are* we winning?' he asked.

'Yes,' Callaghan replied without hesitation. 'The war in the jungle's definitely turned in our favour. The CT groups have become more fragmented. An awful lot of their leaders have been captured or killed. Food's scarce outside the protected kampongs and the CT are therefore finding it more difficult to find recruits among the aboriginals, most of whom are now siding with us and clinging to the protection of our secured villages and forts. Unfortunately, now that the CT propaganda has failed, they're turning to terror and committing an increasing number of atrocities.'

'You're talking about Ah Hoi.'

'Yes. Only recently that bastard disembowelled an informer's pregnant wife in front of the whole damned village. He left the villagers terrified. Now he's rumoured to be somewhere south-west of Ipoh and we'll soon have to pursue him. What shape are the men in?'

'Better than the first bunch,' Pryce-Jones replied.

Callaghan knew just what he meant. After Pryce-Jones had submitted his recommendations regarding the war, Lieutenant-Colonel 'Mad Mike'

Calvert, veteran of the Chindit campaigns in Burma and commander of the World War Two SAS (Special Air Service) Brigade, had been asked to create a special military force that could live permanently in the jungle, to deny the guerrillas sanctuary or rest. That special force, based on the original World War Two SAS, was known as the Malayan Scouts.

Some of those who volunteered for the new unit were useful veterans of the SOE (Special Operations Executive), the SAS and the Ferret Force, the latter being a paramilitary unit drawn from Army volunteers, and former members of SOE's Force 136. The 'Ferret' scouts had led fighting patrols from regular infantry battalions, making the first offensive sweeps into the jungle, aided by forty-seven Dyak trackers, the first of many such Iban tribesmen from Borneo. Though doing enough to prove that the British did not have to take a purely defensive position, the Force was disbanded when many of its best men had to return to their civilian or more conventional military posts.

Unfortunately, too many of the men recruited in a hurry were either simply bored or were persistent troublemakers whose units were happy to see them go elsewhere. One group had even consisted of ten deserters from the French Foreign Legion who had escaped by swimming ashore from a troop-ship conveying them to the war in Indo-China. To make matters worse, due to the speed with which the Malayan Emergency built up, there was little time to properly select or train them.

Shortly after the arrival of that first batch, there were official complaints about too much drunkenness and the reckless use of firearms on the base. According to Pryce-Jones, such charges had been exaggerated because of the nature of the training, which was done under dangerously realistic conditions. Nevertheless, if not as bad as described, the first recruits were certainly rowdy and undisciplined.

Some of the wilder men had eventually been knocked into shape, but others had proved to be totally unsuitable for the special forces and were gradually weeded out. Seeking a better class of soldier, 'Mad Mike' Calvert had travelled 22,000 miles in twenty-one days, including a trip to Rhodesia which led to the creation of C Squadron from volunteers in that country. From Hong Kong he brought Chinese interpreters and counter-guerrillas, who had served with him in Burma, to join his Intelligence staff. Another source was a squadron of SAS Reservists and Territorials (many of whom had served under David Stirling), which had formed up in 1947 as 21 SAS Regiment. Most of those men had been of much better calibre and proved a worthy catch when, in 1952, the

Malayan Scouts were renamed as the 22nd Special Air Service Regiment (22 SAS).

The original three squadrons, A, B, and C, that had formed 22 SAS, had been augmented by a fourth, D Squadron, before Calvert left for the UK. By 1956 a further squadron, the Parachute Regiment Squadron, was raised from volunteers drawn from the Paras. That same year, C Squadron returned to Rhodesia to become the Rhodesian SAS and was replaced by a New Zealand squadron. This Kiwi connection meant that a number of Fijians joined the Regiment.

'Do you still have problems controlling them?' Callaghan asked. 'If you do, they'll be no good in the jungle. The CT will just eat them up.'

'There's still a lot of hard drinking and the occasional fragging of officers,' Pryce-Jones replied, 'but the lack of discipline has been corrected and replaced with excellent soldiering. Unfortunately, it'll be a long time yet before we live down the reputation we acquired during those early years. Not that it bothers me. We're supposed to be different from the greens, so let's keep it that way.'

'Hear, hear,' Callaghan said, mockingly clapping his hands together. 'The question is, can we actually *use* them or are they still being used for policing duties?'

'Things have greatly improved on that front,'

Pryce-Jones told him. 'Due to the recent expansion of the Federation of Malaya Police and the creation of Home Guard units and a Special Constabulary, the Army is increasingly being released from its policing obligations and given more time and means to fight the CT. The men are all yours now.'

'They'll need to be separated from the greens,' Callaghan said, referring to the green-uniformed regular Army, 'and preferably trained in isolation.'

'I've anticipated that. A new Intelligence section has been opened in Johore. It's filled with men experienced in jungle operations from the time they worked with me in Burma. I've included Hong Kong Chinese to act as interpreters. The head of the section is Major John M. Woodhouse, Dorset Regiment. As so much of the SAS work involves a hearts-and-minds campaign, which requires Intelligence gathering of all kinds, and since we'll need Chinese speakers, the Regiment will be flown to Johore, where a special training camp is already in the process of completion. The men can complete their preliminary training here, then move on to Johore a week from now.'

'Excellent,' Callaghan said. Restless already, even though exhausted, he stood up and went to the window behind the major's desk. Looking out, he saw a Sikh foreman supervising some Malay coolies in the building of a sangar at the edge of the runway containing rows of Beverley transports and F-28 jets. The sun was rising quickly in the sky, flooding the distant landscape of green hills and forest with brilliant light.

'I want to get that bastard Ah Hoi,' he said.

'You will in due course,' Pryce-Jones replied. 'Right now, you need a good meal, a hot shower and a decent sleep. And I need to work. So get out of here, Paddy.'

'Yes, boss,' Captain Callaghan said. He picked up his soaked, heavy bergen and camouflaged sub-machine-gun, then, with a blinking of weary eyes, walked out of the office.

'You can smell him from here,' Mary said, when Callaghan had left.

'A rich aroma,' Pryce-Jones replied.

# 2

As Captain 'Paddy' Callaghan was having a good sleep after showering three months of jungle filth off his emaciated body, the latest influx of recently badged troopers to 22 SAS were settling in for a week of initial training in Minden Barracks, before being flown on to Johore. Though just off the Hercules C-130 transport aircraft which had flown them all the way from Bradbury Lines, Merebrook Camp, Worcestershire, via RAF Lyneham, Wiltshire, the men were in a good mood as they adjusted to the brilliant morning sunshine and rising heat of the mainland, just across the Malacca Straits, facing the lively town of Penang.

'I've heard all about that place from an RAF buddy stationed at Butterworth,' Trooper Dennis 'the Menace' Dudbridge said, as the Bedford truck transported them away from the airstrip to the barracks at the far side of a broad, flat field. Formerly of the Gloucestershire Regiment, he was short, broad-shouldered, and as feisty as a bantam cock, with a permanently split lip and broken nose from one too many pub fights. 'He said the whores all look as sexy as Marilyn Monroe.'

'If a different colour and a bit on the slit-eyed side,' Corporal 'Boney Maronie' Malone reminded him.

'I get a hard-on just *thinking* about Marilyn Monroe,' Trooper Pete Welsh informed them in his deadly serious manner.

'Put splints on it, do you?' Boney Maronie asked him.

'We can't all walk around all day with three legs,' Pete replied, brushing his blond hair from his opaque, slightly deranged blue eyes. 'Not like you, Boney.'

'He doesn't need splints,' Trooper Alf Laughton observed. 'He needs a sling to keep it off the fucking ground when it sticks out too far. Isn't that true, Boney?'

'Some of us just happen to be well endowed. Not that I'm one to boast, lads, but you just don't compare.'

'I trust you'll put it to good use in Penang,' Dennis the Menace said.

'If we get there,' Boney replied. 'I've heard they're not giving us any time off before they send us into that fucking jungle to get bled dry by leeches.'

'They wouldn't dare!' Alf Laughton exclaimed. With flaming red hair and a face pitted by acne, Laughton looked like a wild man. He had been here three years ago, with the King's Own Yorkshire Light Infantry, and still had fond memories of George Town when the sun had gone down. 'We're entitled to a little fun and games before they work us to death.'

'We're entitled to Sweet FA,' Pete Welsh said, 'and that's what we'll get.'

Though they had all been badged recently, most of these men were experienced and had come to the SAS from units active in other theatres of operation. Some had come from the Long Range Desert Group (LRDG) and the wartime SAS, others had been recruited by 'Mad Mike' Calvert from British forces stationed in the Far East; and many, including a number of National Servicemen, were skilled soldiers who had volunteered to avoid the discipline of the more conventional regular Army. At least one of them, Sergeant Ralph Lorrimer, now sitting up front beside the driver of the Bedford, had experience in guerrilla warfare gleaned from wartime operations in North Africa, and as a member of Force 136, the clandestine resistance force set up by the SOE in Malaya during the Japanese occupation. Most of them, then, were experienced men.

Indeed, one of the few with no previous experience in warfare was the recently badged Trooper Richard Parker, already nicknamed 'Dead-eye Dick' because of his outstanding marksmanship, as displayed not only during his three years with the 2nd Battalion, Royal Regiment of Fusiliers, but also on the firing range of the SAS base at Merebrook Camp, Malvern. Brown-haired, grey-eyed and almost virginally handsome, Dead-eye was as quiet as a mouse, every bit as watchful, and very keen to prove himself with the SAS. Perhaps it was because his quiet nature seemed at odds with his remarkable skills as a soldier, which included relentless tenacity as well as exceptional marksmanship, that the men had taken him up as a sort of squadron mascot and were inclined to be protective of him, particularly when out on the town. Even the traditional bullshit, when it flew thick and fast, landed lightly on young Trooper Parker.

'Hey, Dead-eye,' Boney Maronie said to him, 'when they give us some time off I'll take you into George Town and find you a nice Malayan girl who likes breaking in cherry-boys.'

'I'm not a cherry-boy,' Parker replied quietly as the Bedford bounced over a hole on the road leading to the barracks. 'I've had my fair share.'

'Oh, really?' Boney asked with a broad grin. He was six foot tall, pure muscle and bone, and sex-mad. 'Where and when was that, then?'

Dead-eye shrugged. 'Here and there. Back home. In West Croydon.'

'In your car?'

'I've never had a car.'

'So where did you do it?'

'None of your business, Boney. Where I did it and who I did it with is my concern, thanks.'

'You're a cherry-boy. Admit it!'

'I'm not,' Dead-eye replied. 'It's just something I don't talk about. I was brought up that way.'

'You bleedin' little liar,' Boney said. 'If you've got as far as squeezing a bit of tit, I'd be bloody amazed.'

Dead-eye shrugged, but said no more. The conversation was beneath him. In fact, he was attractive, girls liked him a lot, and he'd practised sex with the same clinical detachment he brought to everything else, getting his fair share. He just didn't think it worth boasting about. Being a soldier, particularly in the SAS, was much more important.

'It's the quiet little buggers like Dead-eye,' Dennis the Menace said to Boney Maronie, 'who get their oats while blow-hards like you are farting into the wind. I know who *I'd* bet on.'

'Hey, come on . . .' Boney began, but was rudely interrupted when the Bedford ground to a halt outside the barracks and Sergeant Lorrimer bawled: 'All out back there! Shift your lazy arses!'

The men did as they were ordered, hopping off the back and sides of the open Bedford MK four-ton truck. When they were assembled on the baking-hot tarmac in front of the barracks, Sergeant Lorrimer pointed to the unattractive concrete blocks and said: 'Argue among yourselves as to who gets what basha, then put your kit in the lockers and have a brief rest. I'll be back in about thirty minutes to give you further instructions.'

'The man said *a brief rest*,' Pete Welsh echoed, 'and he obviously means it.'

'You have a complaint, Trooper?' Sergeant Lorrimer placed his large hands on his hips and narrowed his eyes. He was sweating and his beefy face was flushed.

'Complain? I wouldn't dream of it, boss! Thirty minutes is much too long.'

'Then we'll make it twenty,' Lorrimer said. 'I take it you agree that's in order?'

'Absolutely!' Welsh glanced uneasily left and right as the rest of the men groaned audibly and glared at him. 'No problem here, boss.'

'I could do with some scran,' Dennis the Menace said.

'You'll get a proper meal tonight,' Sergeant Lorrimer replied, 'when you've been kitted out and had a sermon from the OC. Meanwhile, you'll have to content yourself with a breakfast of wads and a brew up. And since you've only got twenty minutes to eat and drink, I suggest you get started.'

Sergeant Lorrimer jumped back up into the Bedford while the men moaned and groaned. Even as the truck was heading away towards the administration buildings located along the edge of the airstrip, the men continued complaining.

'Your bloody fault, Pete,' Dennis the Menace said. 'We could have had all of thirty minutes – now we're cut down to twenty. You should've known better.'

'I only said . . .'

'One word too many.' Alf Laughton was disgusted with him. 'You know what Sergeant Lorrimer's like when he gets too much sunshine. His face turns purple and he can't stand the bullshit.'

'You're all wasting time talking,' Dead-eye pointed out with his usual grasp of the priorities. 'If you keep talking you'll waste more of your twenty minutes and won't have time for breakfast. Let's pick beds and unpack.'

The accommodation consisted of rectangular concrete bunkers surrounded by flat green fields, slightly shaded by papaya and palm trees. The buildings had wire-mesh and wooden shutters instead of glass windows. The shutters were only closed during tropical storms; the wire-mesh was there to keep out the many flying insects attracted by the electric lights in the evenings. Likewise, because of the heat, the wooden doors were only closed during storms.

From any window of the barracks the men could see the airstrip, with F-28 jets, Valetta, Beverley and Hercules C-130 transports, as well as Sikorski S-55 Whirlwind helicopters, taking off and landing near the immense, sun-scorched hangars. Beyond the airstrip was a long line of trees, marking the edge of the jungle.

After selecting their beds and transferring personal kit to the steel lockers beside each bed, the men hurriedly unwrapped their prepacked wads, or sandwiches, and had hot tea from vacuum flasks.

'Christ, it's hot,' Pete Welsh said, not meaning the tea.

'It's hardly started,' Alf Laughton told him. 'Early hours yet. By noon you'll be like a boiled lobster, no matter how you try to avoid the sun. Fucking scorching, this place is.'

'I want to see Penang,' Dennis the Menace said. 'All those things you told us about it, Alf. All them Malay and Chinese birds in their *cheongsams*, slit up to the hip. George Town, here I come!'

'When?' Boney Maronie asked. 'If we're not even getting lunch on our first day here, what hope for George Town? We're gonna be worked to death, mates.'

'I don't mind,' Dead-eye said, stowing the last of his personal gear in his steel locker. 'I came here to fight a war – not to get pissed and screw some whores. I want to see some action.'

Dennis the Menace grinned crookedly and placed his hand affectionately on Dead-eye's head. 'What a nice lad you are,' he said, only mocking a little. 'And what a good trooper! It's good to see you're so keen.'

'You'd see action if you came with me to George Town,' Boney Maronie informed him. 'You'd see a battle or two, mate.'

'Not the kind of battle Dead-eye wants to see,' Dennis the Menace said. 'This kid here has higher aims.'

'That's right,' Dead-eye said.

Boney Maronie was rolling his eyes in mock disgust when the red-faced Sergeant Lorrimer returned, this time in an updated 4×4 Willys jeep that had armoured perspex screens and a Browning 0.5-inch heavy machine-gun mounted on the front. Hopping down, leaving the driver behind the steering wheel, Lorrimer bawled instructions for the men to assemble outside the barracks in order of height. When they had done so, he marched them across the broad green field bordered with papaya and palm trees to the quartermaster's store, to be kitted out with everything they needed except weapons, which could only be signed for when specifically required.

The standard-issue clothing included jungle-green drill fatigues, a matching soft hat and canvas-and-rubber boots. The men were also supplied with special canvas bergens which looked small when rolled up, but enormous when filled. The contents of each individual bergen included a sleeping bag of hollow-fill, man-made fibre; a bivi-bag, or waterproof one-man sheet used as a temporary shelter; a portable hexamine stove and blocks of hexamine fuel; an aluminium mess tin, mug and utensils; a brew kit, including sachets of tea, powdered milk and sugar; matches in a waterproof container and flint for when the matches ran out; needles and thread; a fishing line and hooks; a pencil torch and batteries; a luminous button compass; signal flares; spare radio batteries; fluorescent marker panels for spotter planes in case of rescue; a magnifying glass to help find splinters and stings in the skin; and a medical kit containing sticking plasters, bandages, cotton wool, antiseptic, intestinal sedative, antibiotics, antihistamine, water-sterilizing tablets, anti-malaria tablets, potassium permanganate, analgesic, two surgical blades and butterfly sutures.

'Just let me at you,' Dennis the Menace said, waving one of his small surgical blades in front of Boney's crutch. 'The world'll be a lot safer if you don't have one, so let's lop it off.'

'Shit, Dennis!' Boney yelled, jumping back and covering his manhood with his hands. 'Don't piss around like that!'

'You think this is funny, Trooper?' Sergeant Lorrimer said to Dennis the Menace. 'You think we give you these items for your amusement, do you?'

'Well, no, boss, I was just . . .'

'Making a bloody fool of yourself, right?' Lorrimer shoved his beetroot-red face almost nose to nose with the trooper. 'Well, let me tell you, that where you're going you might find a lot of these items useful – particularly when you have to slice a poisonous spike or insect out of your own skin, or maybe slash open a snake bite, then suck the wound dry and suture it yourself without anaesthetic. Will you be laughing then, Trooper?'

'No, boss, I suppose not. I mean, I . . .'

'Damn right, you won't, Trooper. A joker like you – you'll probably be pissing and shitting yourself, and crying for your mummy's tit. So don't laugh at this kit!'

'Sorry, boss,' Dennis the Menace said. 'Hear you loud and clear, boss.'

'At least I know you clean the wax from your ears,' Lorrimer said, then bellowed: 'Move it, you men!'

Once the squadron had been clothed and kitted out in order of size, they were marched back across the broad field, which, at the height of noon, had become a veritable furnace that burned their skin and made them pour sweat. To this irritation was added the midges and mosquitoes, the flies and flying beetles, none of which could be swotted away because every man, apart from being burdened with his heavy bergen, also had his hands engaged carrying even more equipment. When eventually they reached the barracks, their instinct was to throw the kit on the floor and collapse on their bashas. But this was not to be.

'Right!' Sergeant Lorrimer bawled. 'Stash that kit, have a five-minute shower, put on your drill fatigues, and reassemble outside fifteen minutes from now. OK, you men, *shake out*!'

The latter command was SAS slang for 'Prepare for combat', but the men knew exactly what Lorrimer meant by using it now: they were going to get no rest. Realizing that this time they didn't even have time to complain or bullshit, they fought each other for the few showers, hurriedly dressed, and in many cases were assembling outside without having dried themselves properly, their wet drill fatigues steaming dry in the burning heat. They were still steaming when Lorrimer returned in the jeep, but this time he waved the jeep away, then made the men line up in marching order.

'Had your scran, did you?' he asked when they were lined up in front of him.

'Yes, boss!' the men bawled in unison.

'Good. 'Cause that's all you're going to get until this evening. You're here to work – not wank or chase skirt – and any rest you thought you might be having, you've already had in that Hercules. OK, follow me.'

He marched them across the flat field, through eddying heatwaves, all the way back to the armoury, located near the quartermaster's stores. There they were given a selection of small arms, including the M1 0.3in carbine with 30-round detachable magazines, which was good for low-intensity work at short range, but not much else; the 9mm Owen sub-machine-gun, which used 33-round, top-mounted box magazines, could fire at a rate of 700 rounds per minute, and was reliable and rugged; the relatively new 7.62mm semi-automatic SLR (self-loading rifle) with 20-round light box magazines, which had yet to prove its worth; and the standard-issue Browning 9mm High Power handgun with 13-round magazines and Len Dixon holster.

When the weapons had been distributed among the men, each given as much as he could carry, Lorrimer pointed to the Bedford truck parked near by.

'Get in that,' he said. 'After the weather in England, I'm sure you'll appreciate some sunshine. All right, *move it*!'

When they had all piled into the Bedford, they were driven straight to the firing range, where they spent the whole afternoon, in ever-increasing heat, firing the various weapons – first the M1 carbine, then the Owen sub-machine-gun and finally the unfamiliar SLR. The heat was bad enough, but the insects were even worse, and within an hour or two most of the men were nearly frantic, torn between concentrating on the weapons and swotting away their tormentors. When they attempted to do the latter, they were bawled at by the redoubtable Sergeant Lorrimer. After two hours on the range, which seemed more like twelve, their initial enthusiasm for the sunlight, which had seemed so wonderful after England, waned dramatically, leaving them with the realization that they had been travelling a long time and now desperately needed sleep, proper food, and time to acclimatize to this new environment.

'What the fuck's the matter with you, Trooper?' Sergeant Lorrimer demanded of Pete Welsh.

'Sorry, boss, but I just can't keep my eyes open.'

'A little tired after your long journey from England, are you?' Lorrimer asked sympathetically.

'Yes, boss.'

'So what are you going to do in the jungle, Trooper, when you have to sleep when standing waist-deep in water? Going to ask for tea and sympathy, are you? Perhaps some time off?'

'I'm not asking now, boss. I'm just having problems in keeping my eyes open. It's the sunlight, combined with the lack of sleep. We're all the same, boss.'

'Oh, I see,' Lorrimer said. 'You're *all* the same. Well, that makes all the difference!' He glanced melodramatically around him, at the other men lying belly-down on the firing range, half asleep when not being tormented by mosquitoes and other dive-bombing tormentors. 'Need sleep, do you?' he asked.

'Yes, boss!' they all bawled simultaneously.

'If you sleep before bedtime,' Lorrimer explained,

'you'll all wake up in the middle of the morning, so you'd best stay awake. *On your feet, Troopers*!'

When they jumped to their feet, shocked by the tenor of Lorrimer's voice, he ran them a few times around the firing range, which was now like God's anvil, and only let them rest again when at least one of them, the normally tough Alf Laughton, started swaying as if he'd been poleaxed.

'Get back in the Bedford,' Lorrimer said, addressing the whole group. 'You're just a bunch of pansies.'

Breathless, pouring sweat, hardly able to focus their eyes, they piled into the Bedford, were driven back to the armoury, lined up for what seemed like hours to return their weapons, then were allowed to make their own way back to the barracks. There, in a state of near collapse, most of them threw themselves down on their steel-framed beds.

No sooner had they done so than Sergeant Lorrimer appeared out of nowhere, bawling, 'Off your backs, you lot! You think this is Butlins? Get showered and change into your dress uniforms and be at the mess by 5.30 sharp. Any man not seen having dinner will be up for a fine. Is that understood? *Move it*!'

They did so. In a state of virtual somnambulism, they turned up at the crowded mess, where Sergeant Lorrimer was waiting to greet them.

'Spick and span,' he said, looking them up and down with an eagle eye. 'All set for scran. OK, go in and get fed, take your time about it, but make sure you reassemble back out here. No pissing off to the NAAFI.'

'The day's over after din-dins,' Dennis the Menace said.

'It is for the common soldier,' Lorrimer replied, 'but not for you lot.' He practically purred with anticipation. 'You lot are *privileged*!'

They soon found out what he meant. After dinner, which few of them could eat, being far too exhausted, they were marched back to the barracks, told to change back into their already filthy drill fatigues, then driven out of the camp in a Bedford. A good ten miles from the camp, in an area notable only for the anonymity of its jungle landscape – no towns, no kampongs – they were dropped off in pairs, each a few miles from the other, none having the slightest clue where they were, and told that if they wanted a good night's sleep, they had to make their own way back to the camp as best they could. If they were not back by first light, when Reveille would be called, they would be RTU'd – sent straight back to Blighty.

'Do we get even a compass?' Boney Maronie asked. He and Pete Welsh were one of the first pairs to be dropped off.

'No,' Lorrimer replied. 'What you get is the information that the camp is approximately ten miles north, south, east or west. The rest you have to find out for yourself. Have a nice evening, Trooper.'

'Thanks, boss. Same to you.'

In fact, all of them made it back, though by very different means. Boney Maronie and Peter Welsh marched until they came to a main road – an hour's difficult hike in itself – then simply hitched a lift from a Malay banker whose journey home took him straight past the camp. Dennis the Menace and Dead-eye Dick had checked the direction of their journey in the Bedford, so they simply used the moon to give them an east-west reference and used that to guide them back the way they had come. After a walk that took them well past midnight, they came to a kampong where the headman, obviously delighted to have a chat with strangers, gave them dinner then drove them back to the base, depositing them there two hours before first light. Alf Laughton, dropped off with a recently badged trooper, formerly of the King's Own Scottish Borderers, became disgusted with his young partner, deliberately lost him, then waylaid a passing cyclist, beat him unconscious, stole his bicycle and cycled most of the way back. Just before reaching the main gate of the camp, he dumped the bicycle and walked the rest of the way, thus ensuring that neither the assault nor the theft could be traced back to him.

Others did even worse than Alf Laughton and, being found out, were RTU'd, as was Laughton's unfortunate young partner.

The rest, getting back successfully without committing any known criminal act, collapsed immediately on their beds and slept as long as they could. The ones who had the longest sleep were Boney Maronie and Pete Welsh, who had managed to get back two hours after leaving, earning almost a whole night in a proper bed.

Few others were so lucky. Typical were Dennis the Menace and Dead-eye Dick, who, having not slept since leaving England nearly twenty-six hours earlier, managed to get two hours sleep before Reveille, at first light. After that, the whole murderous routine was repeated again – for seven relentless, soul-destroying days.

All of this was merely a build-up to Johore, where, so Sergeant Lorrimer assured them, the 'real' jungle training would be done.

Johore loomed like a nightmare of the kind that only this breed of man could fully understand and hope to deal with.

# 3

The troopers coped with the forthcoming nightmare of Johore by fantasizing about the great time they would have when they were given the mandatory weekend off and could spend it on the island of Penang. This fantasy was fuelled by the stories of Alf Laughton, who, having been in Malaya before, when serving with the King's Own Yorkshire Light Infantry, still recalled vividly his wild evenings in George Town, with its trishaws, taxis, steaming food stalls, colourful markets and bazaars, sleazy bars, grand hotels and, of course, incredibly beautiful Eurasian women in sexy *cheongsams*.

Alf Laughton had the rest of them salivating.

The first seven days, which seemed like seven years, ended on a Friday and most of them, though exhausted beyond what they could have imagined, were looking forward to their great weekend in Penang, after their briefing by Major Pryce-Jones, which took place, helpfully, at six in the evening, when the sun was going down and the humid air was cooling.

'First, a bit of background,' Pryce-Jones began. He was standing on a raised section of the floor at one end of the room, in front of a large map of Malaya. Captain Callaghan was seated in a chair to the side of the raised area. In the week he had been back, he had already put on weight and was looking more his normal, healthy self. 'The Communist Party has existed here in a small way since the 1930s,' Pryce-Jones continued, 'when this was a prosperous place. Unfortunately, we then made the mistake of arming the Communist guerrillas during the war, to enable them to fight the Japanese. It never entered our heads that after the war those same weapons would be turned against us. In the event, they were. Once the guerrilla supremo, Chin Peng, had been awarded an OBE in the Victory Honours, he formed his 1,200 wartime guerrillas into ten regiments and used his 4,000 captured British and Japanese weapons to mount a campaign of terror against the Malays. They publicly executed rubber plantation workers, lectured the horrified onlookers on the so-called war against Imperialism, then melted back into the jungle.'

After pausing to let his words sink in, Pryce-Jones

tapped the blackboard beside the map, where someone had scrawled in white chalk: '*Kill one, frighten a thousand:* Sun-Zu.'

'These are the words of the old Chinese warrior Sun-Zu, and Chin Peng's guerrillas live by them. For this reason, once they had struck terror into the hearts of the Malays, they turned on the Europeans, mostly British plantation managers. Two were bound to chairs and ritually murdered. After that, the war escalated dramatically and British forces were brought in.'

Pryce-Jones put the pointer down and turned away from the blackboard. 'By early 1950, the Communist Terrorists had killed over 800 civilians, over 300 police officers and approximately 150 soldiers. We can take comfort from the fact that over 1,000 CT have been killed, over 600 have been captured, and nearly 400 have surrendered so far. Nevertheless, there's no sign of an end to the war, which is why you men are here.'

'Lucky us!' Dennis the Menace exclaimed, copping a couple of laughs.

'The CT attacks,' Pryce-Jones continued when the laughter had died away, 'are mostly against kampongs, isolated police stations, telecommunications, railways, buses, rubber estates, tin mines, and what they term the "running dogs of the British" – namely, us, the Security Forces. British infantry, however, with the help of Gurkha and police patrols, have managed to cut off food supplies going to the CT in the jungle. They've also booby-trapped supplies of rice, fish and other foods found prepared for collection by the CT. With the removal of over 400 Chinese squatters' villages from the edge of the jungle to wire-fenced enclosures defended by us, the CT have been deprived of yet another source of food, supplies and manpower. For this reason, they've moved deeper into the jungle, known to them as the *ulu*, where they're attempting to grow their own maize, rice and vegetables. In order to do this, they have to make cleared spaces in the *ulu* – and those spaces can be seen from the air. Unfortunately, it takes foot patrols days, sometimes weeks, to reach them. Which is where you come in.'

'Here it comes!' Boney Maronie chimed.

'The hard sell,' Dennis the Menace added.

'All right, you men, be quiet,' Sergeant Lorrimer told them. 'We don't have all night for this.'

Looking forward to the first evening of their free weekend, which most would spend in Penang, the men could only agree with Sergeant Lorrimer, and settled down quickly.

'To win the cooperation of the local tribesmen,' Pryce-Jones continued, 'we established a number of protected kampongs. Attracted by free food and medical treatment, as well as by the idea of protection from the atrocities of the CT, the tribesmen gradually moved into the kampongs and set up their bashas next to those of our troops. Medical supplies were dropped by the RAF and treatment given by doctors and Royal Army Medical Corps NCOs attached to the SAS. Once an individual settlement was established with a full quota of tribesmen, it became permanent and was placed under the control of the police or Malayan security forces. We'd then move on to build another elsewhere until we had a whole chain of such "forts" down the centre of the country, effectively controlling the area, keeping the terrorists out.'

'The hearts-and-minds campaign,' young Dead-eye said, having already done his homework.

'Correct. The campaign was successful in winning the trust of the tribesmen. They responded by becoming our eyes and ears in the *ulu*, passing on information on the whereabouts and movements of the CT.'

'So what's our place in all this?' Boney Maronie asked.

'You'll be called upon to be part of patrols based for long periods in the jungle,' Pryce-Jones replied. 'There you'll make contact with the aboriginals, the Sakai, who're being coerced by the terrorists into providing them with food. Once contact is made, you'll attempt to win their trust by supplying them with penicillin and other medicines, by defending their kampongs from the CT and in any other way you can.'

'Bloody nursemaids again!' Dennis the Menace groaned.

'Is staying for long periods in the jungle feasible for anyone other than the aboriginals?' Dead-eye asked quietly.

'Yes,' Captain Callaghan said. 'It's a daunting task, but it *can* be done. Indeed, at a time when seven days was considered the absolute limit for white men, one of our Scout patrols spent 103 days in there. The CC' – Callaghan nodded in the direction of Major Pryce-Jones –'has spent six months alone in the *ulu* and, as you know, I've just returned from a three-month hike through it. So it can be done.'

'If the Ruperts can do it,' Alf Laughton said, using the SAS nickname for officers, 'then I reckon we can too.'

'As Trooper Dudbridge has expressed his disdain for the hearts-and-minds side of the operation,' Pryce-Jones cut in, 'I should inform you that your main task will be to assist the Malay Police Field Force at kampongs and in jungle-edge patrols. You'll also send out small patrols from your jungle base to ambush the CT on the tracks they use to get to and from their hide-outs.'

'That sounds more like it,' Pete Welsh said, grinning as his wild blue eyes flashed from left to right and back again. 'Doing what we've been trained to do.'

'You've also been trained in hearts-and-minds tactics,' Sergeant Lorrimer reminded him, 'so don't ever forget it.'

'Sorry, boss,' Welsh replied, grinning lopsidedly and rolling his eyes at his mates. 'No offence intended.'

'Good.' Lorrimer turned away from him and spoke to Major Pryce-Jones instead. 'Will we be engaged *only* in jungle-edge patrols?'

'No,' Captain Callaghan replied after receiving the nod from Pryce-Jones. 'It's true that in the past we've avoided deep-penetration raids, but because of the increasing success of our food-denial operations, the CT are now heading deeper into the *ulu*. Unfortunately for them, in order to grow their own food they have to fell trees and make clearings. As our Company Commander has rightly pointed out, such clearings can be spotted from the air, which means they're vulnerable to attack. We'll therefore attack them. We'll do so by parachuting – or tree-jumping, which you're about to learn – into a confined Dropping Zone near the area. Then we'll place a cordon around the clearing. It won't be easy and certainly it will be dangerous, but in the end we'll win.'

'We're going to parachute into the *jungle*?' Alf Laughton asked, sounding doubtful.

'Yes,' Captain Callaghan answered. 'If I can do it, anyone can do it – and believe me, I've done it.'

'Is that one of the things we'll learn in Johore?'

'Correct,' Callaghan replied.

'I can't wait,' Pete Welsh said sarcastically. 'The top of a tree right through my nuts. I'll be back in the boys' choir.'

'Assuming that Trooper Welsh doesn't lose his precious nuts on a tree,' Sergeant Lorrimer said, 'and we all make it down to the DZ in one piece, what problems can we expect to find in that terrain?'

'Most of the country is dense and mountainous jungle,' Captain Callaghan replied, 'considered habitable only by aboriginal peoples, such as the Sakai. The hill contours make for steep, slippery climbs, while the routes off the paths are dense with trees that can trip you up and break your ankles. Nevertheless, as the few paths are likely to be mined or ambushed, you'll have to avoid them and instead move over uncharted ground. The terrorists have a network of jungle informers and will be using them to keep track of your movements, which will help them either to attack or avoid you. Finding them before they find you won't be made any easier by the difficulties of navigating in the jungle. You will, however, be aided by Dyak trackers, Iban tribesmen from Sarawak, all experts in jungle tracking and survival.'

'We go out in small patrols?' Dead-eye said.

'Yes. Three- or four-man teams. In the words of the founder of the Malayan Scouts, Lieutenant-Colonel Calvert: "The fewer you are, the more frightened you are, therefore, the more cautious you are and, therefore, the more silent you are. You are more likely to see the enemy before he will be able to see you." We abide by those words.'

'What's our first, specific mission?' Boney Maronie asked.

Callaghan stepped aside to let Major Pryce-Jones take the centre of the raised platform and give them the good news.

'Aerial reconnaissance has shown that the CT are growing food in a clearing in the Belum Valley, a remote, long mountain valley located near the Thai border. That valley will be searched by Gurkha, Commando and Malaya Police patrols, all moving in on foot, which should take them five days but gives them the advantage of being more difficult to spot. You men will form the stop, or blocking, party, parachuting in a day's march from the RV.

This operation will commence once you've completed your extensive jungle training in Johore.'

'When do we leave, boss?' Dennis the Menace asked.

'Tonight.'

# 4

The camp in Johore was a primitive affair, shared between Gurkhas, Royal Marines, RAF, British Army REME, Kampong Guards from the Federation of Malaya Police and SAS personnel. Hastily thrown together in a clearing in the jungle, it was surrounded by coconut palms, papaya trees and deep monsoon drains, with rows of wood-and-thatch barracks, latrines, open showers, a mess hut, armoury, quartermaster's store, motor pool, administrative block, NAAFI shop, airstrip for fixed-wing aircraft and helicopters, and a centrally located 'sports ground' with an obstacle course at one end, used for everything from weapons training to Close Quarters Battle (CQB) and unarmed combat.

'They don't even give us one night in Penang,' Alf Laughton complained as they were selecting their camp-beds and settling into the barracks, 'and now they plonk us down in this dump. A diabolical liberty!'

'More dust, heat, flies and mosquitoes,' Dennis the Menace said. 'Welcome to Paradise!'

'You know why these barracks are raised off the ground, don't you?' Pete Welsh asked rhetorically, having the answer all prepared. 'Because this place is crawling with scorpions, centipedes and snakes, every one of 'em poisonous.'

'It's crawling with everything except women,' Boney Maronie said, 'which is why they should have given us at least one night out in Penang. I think I'm getting ready to explode. I'll drench the whole fucking ceiling.'

'Boasting again,' Dennis the Menace said. 'You haven't really got it in you. But that obstacle course out there looks like hell. A few runs over that fucker and you'll soon get rid of all your excess energy. By the time you've finished, you won't remember what a woman is, let alone what she feels like.'

'Tree-jumping,' Dead-eye said. 'That's what bothers me. Those trees are 150 feet high and pretty damned dense. I don't fancy climbing those with a bergen, rifle and knotted rope, let alone parachuting into them.'

'Piece of piss,' Pete Welsh said, his grin making him look slightly crazy. 'You just spread your legs and get spiked through the balls by the top of a tree. If you miss that, you crash down through the branches and get all smashed to hell. Failing that, you snag your chute on the branches and possibly hang yourself. Sounds like a joyride.'

'I can't wait,' Alf Laughton said.

Once settled in, the men were gathered together in the briefing room, given a brief lecture on the history and habits of the jungle natives, told not to call them 'Sakai', which meant 'slave', and informed that they would be receiving a two-hour lesson in the native language every day. The first such lesson began immediately and was very demanding.

When it had ended, at 10 a.m., the men were allowed a ten-minute tea break, then marched to the armoury, where they were given a selection of weapons, including those fired on the range of Minden Barracks: the M1 0.3in carbine, the 9mm Owen sub-machine-gun, the 7.62mm semi-automatic SLR and the Browning 9mm High Power handgun. They were also given a Fairburn-Sykes commando knife and a machete-like *parang*.

Having already tested the men's skills on the range at Minden Barracks, Sergeant Lorrimer knew precisely who was best at what and distributed the weapons accordingly, with the Owen sub-machine-guns going to those he was designating as scouts, or 'point men', in his patrols.

'Here,' he told the men assembled outside the armoury in the already fierce heat, 'you won't have to sign the weapons in and out. Instead, you'll keep them with you at all times, either on your person or in your lockers. If any man loses a weapon or ammunition he'll be RTU'd instantly.'

From that moment on, though the men were trained together, they were broken up into four-man teams, first devised by David Stirling in World War Two as a means of combining minimum man-power with maximum surprise. The four-man team was deemed to be the most effective because members could pair up and look after each other, both tactically and domestically, sharing duties such as brewing up, cooking meals, erecting shelters or camouflaging their position. Also, soldiers have a natural bonding instinct and divide into pairs to tackle most tasks.

Though every member of the four-man patrols had been trained in signals, demolition and medicine, and was presently learning the rudiments of the local language, each individual had to specialize in one of these. Trained to Regimental Signaller standard in morse code and ciphers, the team's specialist signaller was responsible for calling in aerial resup (resupply) missions, casevac (casualty evacuation) and keeping contact with base. While all of the team had been trained in demolition, the team's specialist in this skill was responsible for either supervising, or carrying out, major sabotage operations. The job of the language specialist was to converse with the locals, on the one hand gaining their trust as part of the hearts-and-minds campaign, on the other gleaning from them whatever information he could. The specialist in medicine would not only look after the other members of his patrol, but also attempt to win the trust of the locals by treating them for stomach pains, toothache, tuberculosis, malaria, scurvy or any other illnesses, real or imagined.

'Though the basic unit will be the four-man team,' Captain Callaghan told them when they were kneeling in the dirt at the edge of the sports ground, in the murderous heat, assailed constantly by flying insects, 'we have three different kinds of patrol here. First is the reconnaissance patrol, usually a four-man team, which is tasked with observation and intelligence gathering, including topographical info; the selecting of sites for RVs, helicopter landings and good ambush positions; location of the enemy; and the checking of friendly defences, such as minefields. Second is the standing patrol, which can be anything from a four-man team to a troop or more. The standing patrol provides a warning of enemy advance and details of its composition, prevents enemy infiltration and directs artillery fire or ground-attack aircraft on to enemy positions. Finally, we have the fighting patrols, composed of either two four-man teams or an entire troop, depending on the nature of the mission. The job of the fighting patrol is to harass the enemy; conduct raids to gain intelligence or capture prisoners; carry out attacks against specific targets; and prevent the enemy from obtaining info about friendly forces in a given area. Sooner or later, each of you will take part in all three types of patrol. First, however, you'll undergo a weapons training programme more rigorous than anything you've imagined in your worst nightmares. They're all yours, Sergeant Lorrimer.'

Callaghan was not exaggerating. While the normal SAS training programme was the most demanding of any in the armed forces, even that had not prepared the men for the merciless demands that were now placed upon their physical stamina and skill. They were called upon not only to perform target practice in the scorching heat while being assailed by bloated flies, kamikaze mosquitoes and a host of other insects driven mad by the smell of human sweat, but also to carry out numerous tactical movements designed to meet the special requirements of jungle warfare.

Thus, when Sergeant Lorrimer was satisfied that each man had proven himself a crack shot, he moved on to lessons in the actions and drills to be carried out in case of contact with the enemy, the proper order of march when in the jungle, the silent signals required when changing formation, the various drills for encounters with natural and man-made obstacles, and, most important, the Head-On Contact Drill.

'The HOCD,' he explained as they were getting their breath back after an exhausting 'shoot and scoot' exercise, 'is the Standard Operating Procedure, or SOP, devised specially for four-man patrols on the move. When contact is made with the enemy, each member of the patrol will move instantly into a position that allows him to open fire without hitting a comrade. You four,' he said, jabbing his finger at Dennis the Menace, Boney Maronie, Dead-eye Dick and Alf Laughton. 'Stand up.'

'Jesus, boss,' Dennis the Menace complained as he wiped the sweat from his sunburnt face, 'we've just sat down for a so-called break.'

'The break's over, so get to your feet.' When the foursome were standing at the edge of the sports ground, near one of the deep monsoon drains, Lorrimer made them move into position to demonstrate a particular HOCD. He placed Dead-eye well away from the others, at the front as lead scout. Pushing the others closer together as carelessly as if they were shop-window dummies, he said: 'So! If the patrol is moving in file, these three men behind the lead scout will break left and right as they bring their weapons to bear on the enemy . . . *Break, damn it! Break!*'

Though already exhausted from their last exercise, Dennis the Menace, Boney Maronie and Alf Laughton had to quickly break apart while swinging their weapons up into the firing position.

'The patrol now has the option of advancing on the enemy or withdrawing,' Lorrimer continued. 'Should they choose the latter option, two of them will lay down covering fire . . . *Go on, then!*' he bawled at Dead-eye and Dennis the Menace, now forming a couple. '*Get on with it!*' When they had done as they were told, dropping into the kneeling position required for covering fire, then pretending to fire, much to the amusement of the onlookers, Lorrimer continued: 'So while these two are laying down covering fire, the other two will withdraw a distance . . . *Come on, you two, withdraw!*' he bawled at Boney Maronie and Alf Laughton. When they had done as ordered, withdrawing a few yards and taking up firing positions, he went on: 'The second two, as you can see, are now in a covering position, allowing the first pair to fall back – *Come on, fall back, you two!* – and so on. They keep repeating this movement until they're out of range of the enemy. You got that?'

'*Yes, boss*!' the men bawled in unison, some breaking into applause and laughter when the four returned sheepishly to the main group.

'You, you, you and you,' Lorrimer said, jabbing his finger at another four troopers. 'Get up and let's see you do it.'

That wiped the grins off their faces.

Every day was a relentless routine of early Reveille, hurried breakfast, the two-hour language lesson, ten-minute tea break, two hours on the firing range, an hour for lunch, two hours of battle tactics, both theoretical and physical, a ten-minute tea break, another two hours of Close Quarters Battle (CQB) and hand-to-hand combat, an hour for dinner, then an evening filled with map-reading, medical training, signals training and demolition.

Second best was not good enough. They had to be perfect at everything and were pushed relentlessly hard until they were.

Sergeant Lorrimer was a former Dorset Regiment and Force 136 NCO who was scarcely interested in drill and uniform, but hated sloppiness where battle discipline was concerned. When one soldier accidentally opened fire with a rifle, Lorrimer took the rifle off him, removed the safety-pin from a hand-grenade, then handed the soldier the grenade.

'Carry that for the rest of the day,' he said. 'By which time you should know how to handle a rifle.'

Lorrimer was also of the school which believes that discipline can be imposed in the good old-fashioned way – with fists – instead of with the rule book. More than once, instead of placing insolent troopers on a charge, he told them to 'step outside' to settle the matter with fisticuffs. So far, no one had managed to beat him and all of them, even when making fun of him, respected him for it.

For the most part the training was dangerously realistic. It included throwing grenades and diving for cover in the deep monsoon drains running through the area around the camp. This was only one of several lessons with live ammunition that disregarded the normal safety rules for field firing ranges. Since there was neither the time nor the facilities for such routines, all training had to take place on the parade ground and other clear spaces near the camp.

The working day usually ended at 10 p.m., leaving the men a couple of hours in which to do as they wished. As there was nowhere to go – outside the camp there was only jungle – they drank a lot of beer, became drunk quite quickly after the heat and exertion of the day and often got up to boyish pranks and fights.

The latter appeared to be the speciality of Pete Welsh and Alf Laughton, both of whom were hot-tempered and given to violent outbursts of the kind that would soon be outlawed by the Regiment.

'I'd trust those two fuckers about as far as I could throw them,' Dennis the Menace said. 'The NCOs in their parent regiments encouraged them to apply for the SAS just to get rid of them. A pair of troublemakers, if you ask me.'

'I'm not asking,' Boney Maronie replied. 'The less we know, the better, mate.'

Often, when there were fights, they were broken up by Sergeant Lorrimer, whose offer to try their luck with him outside would nearly always turn the men's anger into laughter and usually lead them to shake hands. Nevertheless, he complained privately to Captain Callaghan about the number of unsuitable men they had had wished upon them.

'We're gradually weeding them out,' Callaghan reassured him, 'but it's going to take a bit more time. In the meantime, we have to deal with what we've got and just pray that they don't cause too much trouble.'

'I don't believe in prayer,' Lorrimer replied, 'and I still think we're taking a big chance with some of those men.'

A week after arriving at Johore, with their preliminary training completed successfully, the men were moved out of the camp to live in primitive conditions and acquire new skills from the indigenous aboriginals and from Iban trackers brought to Malaya from Sarawak. Their first lessons were in the use of the *parang*, which was indispensable for hacking a path through dense undergrowth. Its use called for a surprisingly high degree of skill, and in the course of learning this many of the men cut themselves badly.

Wounded or not, they were then taught tracking in the jungle and swamps. This was a particularly exhausting business, requiring constant observation and concentration. While a top speed of approximately a mile an hour could be attained in a jungle environment, this was discouraged as it could mean missing vital clues about the passage and location of the enemy. Instead, a slow, cautious, ever-vigilant advance in single-file formation was the order of the day, with the lead scout taking the 'point' out front, followed by the Patrol Commander, or PC, and the Signaller, and the second-in-command, or 2IC, bringing up the rear as 'Tail-end Charlie'. The scout had the Owen sub-machine-gun, the PC had an SLR, and the other two men carried M1 carbines or Browning 12-gauge autoloader shotguns.

For the purposes of training, one four-man team would head into the jungle and make camp at a preselected RV, or rendezvous point. The second group then had to track them down. This they did with the aid of an experienced Iban tracker, who showed them what to look for by way of tell-tale signs such as broken twigs, faded footprints, or threads and cotton from drill fatigues that had been caught on branches when the first group, posing as the 'enemy', had passed by. The tracker also taught them how to magnetize a needle for use as a compass by rubbing it across a piece of silk and dangling it from a string, how to do the same with a razor blade by stropping it against the palm of the hand, and in general how to navigate in the jungle using the minimum of either natural or artificial aids.

Finally, although the men had already been trained in map-reading and the use of the standard-issue prismatic compass, they were taught how to judge distance in the jungle, how to use maps in relation to thick, impenetrable forest, how to use compass bearings and 'pacing' (counting the number of footsteps required) to reach a given destination, and how to take bearings and triangulate by means of the prismatic compass in daylight or darkness.

The Iban trackers came into their own with silent killing techniques and makeshift weapons. The SAS troopers had already been trained in various methods of the former, including martial-arts blows to the heart, lungs, liver, larynx, subclavian artery and spinal column and, of course, the cutting of the jugular vein with a knife. The trackers, however, showed them how to make spears by binding a knife to a 3-foot staff, shape a spear-thrower from a tree limb, make a compound bow and improvise weapons such as a sharpened wooden stake, a bone knife, a sock filled with soil and a garrotte made with two short wooden handles attached one to each end of a length of razor wire.

'Cut your fucking head clean off, that would,' Dennis the Menace said.

'They say a severed head remains conscious for up to twenty seconds after being lopped off,' Dead-eye solemnly informed them.

'My worst nightmare,' Boney Maronie said, 'is the twenty seconds of conversation I'd get after I'd garrotted Dennis. One second is bad enough.'

Back in the camp they had learnt special jungle preventative medicine from Royal Army Medical

Corps medics, but now, in the jungle, the aboriginals showed them many improvised medical techniques; these included cleaning wounds with urine (an extremely sterile liquid) where hot water is not available; packing infected wounds with maggots, which will eat only the 'dead' tissue; removing worms from the system by swallowing a small amount of petrol or kerosene; suturing severe cuts with needle and thread, making each suture individually; and improvising a splint with sticks rolled in cloth, a stretcher from tree branches rolled in blankets, or a jungle 'litter', or dangling stretcher, from bamboo or saplings bound together with creepers and suspended beneath a long pole. They also learned to improvise a tourniquet by wrapping a cloth three times around the limb, tying it with a half knot, placing a stick over the knot and securing it with a double knot, then twisting the stick until the cloth tightened enough to stop the bleeding.

Once they had mastered these jungle survival skills, the troopers, already worked to near exhaustion by daily practice on the firing range, were kept in the jungle to learn specialist jungle fighting tactics, such as ambush fire-control procedures, contact drills, fire and movement when breaking contact (or 'shoot and scoot') and firing at close range or in darkness.

When they emerged from the jungle they had all lost weight but gained an awful lot of knowledge.

Returning to the base, the men underwent the most frightening part of their training: tree-jumping, or parachuting into dense jungle, where the canopy was in some cases 150 feet high. Though this technique had not actually been tried before, the instructors were aware of three specific dangers: when a man crashed into the treetops, his parachute could snag, he could be smashed into thick branches or he could plummet through to the dense scrub below. As even the instructors had no experience to help them deal with such eventualities, they could do no more than remind the troopers to stay calm and use their common sense.

The training began with a static-line course which focused on the ground work, learning to deal with any problems that might arise during freefall and landing – for example, what to do if the soldier's 130lb of equipment sent him into an uncontrollable spin, or how to disentangle a parachute caught in branches. These lessons were followed by experimental climbs into the treetops while carrying 100 feet of rope, knotted every 18 inches. They would then tie one end of the rope to the canopy, let the other end fall to the ground, up to 150 feet below, and lower themselves by abseiling down the knotted rope. The stomach-churning climbs were followed by a series of experimental freefall jumps, carrying a rifle and a bergen strapped below the parachute, from a variety of aircraft into thinly wooded areas, leaving the aircraft at an altitude of 30,000 feet and opening the chute at 2,500 feet.

As High Altitude Low Opening (HALO) jumps into densely wooded areas had never been done before, even the parachute instructors could not help, so this phase of the training was ignored. Nevertheless, by the end of the extensive static-line training and fifty freefall jumps, some from high altitudes, others from dangerously low altitudes, the men were as prepared as they were ever likely to be.

'When do we do some *real* work?' Dennis the Menace asked.

'Tomorrow,' Sergeant Lorrimer replied.

# 5

'Ah Hoi's CTs are trying to grow food in a clearing in the Belum Valley, near the Thai border,' Major Pryce-Jones informed the men at the briefing that took place just after first light, 'and our job is to advance on that clearing and take out the guerrillas.'

'The real world at last!' Dennis the Menace said.

'Gurkhas, Royal Marine Commandos, Malaya Police and two squadrons of SAS are already approaching the site on foot,' Pryce-Jones continued as if he hadn't heard Dennis, though he threw a quick grin to Captain Callaghan, who was sitting in a chair to the side, smoking a cigarette. 'While they're doing so, you men will parachute into a confined DZ near the area and advance to the RV from there. The DZ will have been previously located and marked by Auster light observation aircraft flown by the Army Air Corps. It has to be assumed that when you parachute down, some of you will land in the trees. In such an event, we're hoping that the canopies will snag the branches firmly enough to belay you safely. With this in mind, you'll each be given, apart from your weapons, 100 feet of rope and some sound advice about tying knots.'

'Should have joined the bloody Navy!' Boney Maronie exclaimed to hoots of laughter.

'Don't forget, however,' Pryce-Jones continued when the laughter had died away, 'that if you land in bamboo it'll splinter and cut you to pieces. Also rocky areas, or spiky and weakened trees, can break bones and necks. In other words, when you're parachuting down, keep your eye on the treetops and manoeuvre away from anything too tricky. You'll embark on the march to the RV when you're all on the ground.'

'How long's the march, boss?' Dead-eye asked.

'That depends entirely on the terrain, which can't be gauged accurately from aerial photos. I'd estimate anything from a few days to a fortnight and either way you're in for a rough time. You'll have to hack your way through the undergrowth. You might find your way blocked by swamps. The rains can be so heavy they'll practically wash you away. Even in good weather, the *ulu* canopy is so thick that little light reaches the jungle floor and visibility is rarely more than fifty metres. Also, no matter how tough you are, you may find yourselves having to overcome a natural fear of the jungle environment, which is claustrophobic in the extreme and can cause severe lethargy. Even if you avoid that, you'll find that movement in the *ulu* is agonizingly slow and dangerous. Last but not least, enemy ambushes are likely to be mounted along rails and on crossing-points, which means you'll always have to opt for the more obscure, therefore more difficult and dangerous route. Given all these negative factors, it's an unpredictable scenario.'

'What about supplies?' Pete Welsh asked.

'Well, 55 Company Royal Army Service Corps are normally responsible for despatching supply containers to the ground forces from RAF aircraft, but as they've so far lost over a hundred men – killed when their planes crashed into the jungle – it's evident that resups aren't always easy to deliver in this environment. If absolutely necessary, resups will be dropped by Blackburn Beverleys or Valettas, but even when the planes manage to make their drops, the stores and equipment often becomes trapped high up on the jungle canopy, and have to be carried down by the troops on the ground, which merely makes for an additional hazard and a lot of wasted time. Therefore, for this operation we're introducing a special seven-to-fourteen-day patrol ration, so that you can operate for up to two weeks without resups.'

'What happens when we reach the RV?' Dead-eye asked in his usual serious manner. 'Do we take them out or hold them?'

'I'd rather have them alive than dead,' Pryce-Jones replied. 'The "green slime" can make use of them for intelligence purposes, then we can possibly convert them. On the other hand, the main purpose of the mission is to take them out and destroy their crops. How you do that will be decided on the spot by your Squadron Commander, Captain Callaghan. Any more questions?'

'Yes, boss,' Alf Laughton said. 'Since we've been deprived of our weekend in Penang, is there any chance of finding a decent bit of skirt in the jungle?'

Pryce-Jones answered the question dead-pan: 'In fact, a lot of the guerrillas are women and many of them are very attractive. But they all carry knives, know how to use them, and are quick to do so – particularly on the throats of "white devils". Any *more* questions?'

Everyone glanced at everyone else, but no one ventured another question. Taking note of their silence, Callaghan pushed his chair back and stood up, saying, 'Excellent. As you're all free of doubts or regrets, let's go and get kitted out.'

'Good luck,' Major Pryce-Jones said as the fifty-four men stood up and started out of the briefing room. He then nodded at Captain Callaghan, who nodded in turn at Sergeant Lorrimer.

'I'll follow you in a short while,' Callaghan said. 'Meanwhile, take care of them.'

'Right, boss,' Lorrimer said, then followed the other men out of the briefing room.

'Well, lads,' he heard Dennis the Menace say up ahead, as the men were crossing the sunny green field that led to the quartermaster's stores and armoury, 'that was an encouraging little briefing, was it not? Cut to pieces by bamboo, broken bones and necks, dense undergrowth, swamps and rain, no light, claustrophobia, and ambushes by female CT who cut white throats for breakfast. The boss sure knows how to cheer his men up!'

'Didn't bother me none,' said Pete Welsh, grinning crazily. 'I can take anything that's thrown at me. No sweat on *this* brow, mate!'

'You're sweating,' Alf Laughton told him. 'I can see you fucking sweating. It's pouring down your face like jungle rain. We can *all* see it, can't we, boys?'

'Yeah!' two or three chimed in.

'That's the heat,' Welsh shot back, still beaming. 'It's not a racing heart.'

'You don't have a fucking heart,' Dennis the

Menace said, 'so I suppose we've gotta believe you.'

The bullshit continued until they reached the quartermaster's stores, which was in a concrete block that included the armoury and radio store, all surrounded by papaya palms and neat hedgerows. The men were already wearing their rubber-and-canvas boots and special olive-green (OG) shirt and trousers, the former with long sleeves and manufactured from cellular-weave cotton, the latter of a heavy-duty cotton. The full-length tails of the shirt and high waist of the trousers were designed, when combined, as protection from the *ulu's* numerous disease-carrying insects and leeches, as well as from the sharp spikes and edges of rattan, bamboo and palms, which could inflict serious wounds on bare skin. The only extra item of clothing required, therefore, was a soft green bush hat, to be worn in place of the beige beret.

As they had also already been supplied with their *parangs* and personal weapons, their main purpose at the quartermaster's stores was to pick up, along with the usual kit, special waterproof jungle bergens, cosmetic camouflage cream, dulling paint and strips of camouflage cloth for their weapons, lengths of para-cord to replace their weapons' standard-issue sling swivels, a plentiful supply of Paludrine, salt tablets, sterilization tablets, and a

Millbank bag, the latter being a canvas container used to filter collected water, which was then sterilized with the tablets.

'I'd be careful if I was you,' Dennis the Menace said helpfully to Boney Maronie as he packed his supply of tablets into a side-pocket of the bergen. 'These tablets are a con. They're actually filled with bromide. They don't stop the shits or sterilize water; they just deaden the sexual impulse, which the Ruperts think makes for a better soldier – one not distracted by thoughts of tit and arse. By the time you come out of that jungle, you won't know what a hard-on is.'

'Ha, ha, very funny,' Boney Maronie responded, trying to look unconcerned, though he couldn't help staring at the boxes of tablets in a questioning manner.

'What the fuck are you doing, Trooper?' Sergeant Lorrimer bawled at him. 'Are you in a trance there? Get on with your packing!'

'Yes, boss!' Boney Maronie snapped and got on with his packing as Dennis the Menace cackled beside him.

From the quartermaster's stores they marched the few yards to the armoury, where, since they already had their personal weapons, they picked up additional fire-power, including light machine-guns, mortars, fragmentation and smoke grenades, magazines of tracer bullets (to identify enemy positions in a fire-fight), flares, a couple of crossbows with lightweight alloy bolts and arrows, used for silent killing, and even some air rifles that fired darts which, though unlikely to kill, could cause painful minor wounds.

'Robin Hood and his Merry Men,' Boney Maronie said, inspecting the crossbow, which would be in his charge. 'It makes me feel like a kid again.'

'The guy who gets one of those bolts through him won't feel like a kid,' Dead-eye said. 'He'll feel a lot more than that.'

'If *you* fire it,' Dennis the Menace said, 'he won't feel a damned thing. He'll be dead in a second.'

'True enough,' Dead-eye said.

To their impressive collection of personal rifles they added the M16 assault rifle. Weighing only 3.72mg with a 30-round magazine, and fully automatic, it was able to put down a considerable amount of fire-power in a short space of time. Its main advantage, however, lay in its slightness, which enabled each member of the patrol to carry more ammunition. Also, it had a diverse range of attachments: a bayonet for close-quarters combat; a bipod for accuracy when firing from the prone position over longer ranges; and telescopic sights and night-vision aids. The M16 could also be fitted with an M203 40mm grenade-launcher, attached beneath the stock extending under the barrel, with a separate trigger mechanism forward of the magazine, capable of firing a variety of 40mm grenades including smoke, high-explosive (HE) and phosphorus, to a maximum accurate range of just under 40m.

Also picked up were a couple of L4A4 Bren guns with curved, 300-round box magazines of .303in bullets raised on the top, a swivel-down bipod located under the barrel, a mounting pin for use with a tripod, a pistol grip just behind the trigger and a carrying handle.

'I've fond memories of this little beauty,' Sergeant Lorrimer said, inspecting one of the L4A4s. 'It was a weapon much appreciated by the Maquis during World War Two. We also used it a lot in Africa, when with the Long Range Desert Group. Simple, old-fashioned and reliable.'

'Just like you, Sarge,' Boney Maronie quipped.

Lorrimer sighed. 'Yes, I suppose so.'

When all the weapons had been collected, the men moved along to the radio store, where they signed for their Clansman High-Frequency (HF) radio sets, one for each of the four-man teams. More commonly known as the PRC 320, the radio had dipoles, or horizontal antennae, rather than vertical aerials, as the latter could disclose a troop's position to the enemy. When used by ground troops the sets operated on compact batteries, but as this was a deep-penetration operation, each patrol also carried a lightweight, hand-powered generator to recharge the batteries, should the need arise.

Although the PRC 320 had a voice/speech capability, it was also used as a Morse or continuous-wave (CW) transmitter through a headset, which made it undetectable by the enemy. When using a whip antenna, it had a maximum range of 100km (voice), but the range became virtually limitless when the set was operating on CW in the sky-wave mode, where the operator's signal literally bounced off the earth's atmosphere.

Finally, each man collected his relatively simple World War Two Irvin X-Type model parachute, which he had to strap immediately to his back, so that he could carry the packed bergens and weapons by hand.

'We've got so much gear here,' Pete Welsh said in disbelief, 'the fucking Beverley probably won't be able to lift off.'

'We should be so lucky,' Dennis the Menace said.

'Stop moaning like a bunch of geriatrics,' Sergeant Lorrimer said, 'and hump all that stuff back to the spider.'

'Yes, boss!' Boney Maronie said, setting a good

example by somehow managing to get all of his gear into his bear-like arms and heading off across the sunlit field.

The 'spider' is the eight-legged dormitory-style sleeping quarters used by the SAS back in Britain, but the term was often applied to barracks elsewhere. Now, as Boney Maronie marched towards the barracks, all the other men followed him.

Entering the building, which in fact did not have eight legs but consisted of one long room with opposite rows of steel-framed beds and lockers, they went to their respective bashas, where they packed their kit properly. When this was done, the men painted their weapons with quick-drying green camouflage paint, then wrapped them in the strips of cloth specially dyed to match the jungle background and disguise their distinctive shape, taking great care not to let the paint or strips of cloth interfere with the weapons' working parts or sights. After wrapping masking tape around the butts, pistol grips and top covers, they replaced the noisy sling swivels with para-cord, which made no sound at all.

With the weapons camouflaged, the men's last job was to camouflage themselves, applying the 'cam' cream and black 'stick' camouflage to the exposed areas of their skin, including the backs of their hands, wrists, ears and neck. The facial camouflage was applied in three stages: first dulling the features with a thin base coating diluted with water (they would use their own saliva when in the jungle); then making diagonal patterns across the face to break up the shape and outline of the features; finally darkening the areas normally highlit, such as forehead, nose, cheek bones and chin. To complete this effect, areas normally in shadow were left a lighter shade.

When applying personal camouflage the patrol members paired off to check each other's appearance and ensure that nothing had been missed. This led, as usual, to a stream of bullshit.

'Do I look pretty?' Dennis the Menace asked.

'As sexy as a duck's arse,' Boney Maronie replied.

'If that were true, you'd be up me so fast my head would be spinning.'

'Give me a kiss, Dead-eye.'

'Knock it off, Pete.'

'When I see you with that eye-shadow, kid, I melt with love. Or at least I get an instant hard-on.'

'You should have worn a skirt and joined the WRAC. You'd be in good company there.'

'Oh, the kid has a tongue!'

'I wouldn't mess with him if I were you,' Alf Laughton said. 'That kid's sweet face is a mask for deadly talents. He's the kind to explode.'

'That he does every night,' Boney Maronie cut in, 'which is why his sheets are soaked in more than sweat.'

'Aw, knock it off!' Dead-eye exclaimed, his blushes hidden by the dark camouflage. 'Why don't you blokes be serious?'

Before anyone could reply, Sergeant Lorrimer appeared in the doorway to bawl: 'All right, you limp dicks! Are you ready?'

'Yes, boss!' came the reply from many voices.

'Then pick your kit up and let's go.'

Heavily burdened, the fifty-four men left the gloom of the spider and marched into the rising heat of the early morning. A couple of Bedford three-tonners had been driven across from the motor pool and were waiting outside, but before the men could board they were inspected personally by Captain Callaghan. Satisfied that everything was in order, he gave them permission to board the Bedfords. The trucks then transported them to the airstrip, where three Vickers Valetta twin-engine aircraft, known affectionately as 'flying pigs' because of their bulbous shape, were waiting to fly them into the interior. Almost as soon as the men and their equipment had been transferred from the Bedfords to the Valettas, the aircraft took off.

Wedged tightly together and hemmed in by their weapons, bergens and supplies, the men joked and laughed for a few minutes after take-off. Eventually, tired of having to shout against the steady roar of the Valettas' twin Bristol Hercules turboprops, they fell silent, each preparing himself in his own way for what was to come. Some slept, others read, a few chewed gum or ate fruit. A few glanced out of the windows, fixing their eyes on the jungle far below, wondering what it would be like to parachute down into what looked like an almost solid, vibrant-green canopy of densely packed treetops.

'Ten minutes to go!' the Army Air Corps Loadmaster called out, perhaps sounding so cheerful because he would not be one of those parachuting down into that deceptively lovely jungle.

The men checked each other's gear. Some were restless and checked it twice. Not knowing when they would get the chance to eat again, a couple of them ate hurried last-minute snacks of apples, oranges, or bananas. Few had bread or biscuits because already their throats were dry from the heat inside the plane and, as they knew, the humidity of the jungle would be even worse.

'Dropping Zone, two minutes to go,' the Loadmaster informed them. 'Your altitude is 225 metres.'

Sergeant Lorrimer was the first to stand up, placing himself where all the men could see and hear him. 'Two-twenty-five metres,' he repeated. 'That means you'll have less than a minute to spot and steer for a solid tree, so keep your wits about you.'

'Stand up!' the Loadmaster bawled, opening the large boom door and letting the slipstream roar in. 'Action stations!'

The men stood in two lines, to the left and right of the boom door. As the Irvin X-Type model parachute had to be opened by hand, they did not have to connect static lines to the plane.

The first man out was Sergeant Lorrimer, who was acting as 'drifter' to discover the strength and direction of the wind. Though the veteran of more than 100 descents, he was still wary of tree-jumping and nervous of the odds-on chance that he would find himself dangling in a treetop with broken limbs or, even worse, a fractured spine. First swept sideways in the slipstream in the combined roaring of the wind and the aircraft's engines, he suddenly fell vertically, popped the parachute, was jerked back up for a moment, then fell more gently as the chute billowed open above him like a great, white mushroom. In just under a minute the jungle canopy was rushing up towards him and he found himself spinning rapidly into a tree. But he was lucky: although his feet and body smashed into the branches, the chute caught and held him.

Lorrimer was dangling about 150 feet above the ground. All he could see through the branches and leaves was thick undergrowth. Above him, the Valetta, which had been circling until the pilot saw him land, began its first run in over the DZ. As the aircraft came towards him, Sergeant Lorrimer disentangled himself from the branches, unwound his knotted rope, tied one end to a secure branch, let the other fall, and began to lower himself to the ground.

Having checked the strength and direction of the wind from Lorrimer's descent, the pilot slightly altered the course of the Valetta to allow for a more accurate fall. Inside the plane, the green light flashed again above the door and the SAS paratroopers prepared to jump. They went out one by one, but in 'sticks' of three from the left and right of the large boom door, as the Loadmaster patted each of them on the shoulder, bawling: '*Right, right, right!*'

Standing in the doorway, even Dead-eye was nervous, though he knew there was no turning back now. So, when he felt the Loadmaster's tap on his shoulder and heard him bawl '*Right!*', he didn't hesitate. As he launched himself into the slipstream, there was a sudden roaring, and the breath was sucked from his lungs. The next thing he knew, he was floating down through the air, looking first at the vast blue sweep of the sky, then at the approaching sea of green jungle, and feeling almost magically alive.

He was descending beautifully, steering for the middle of the trees. Then a gust of hot air made him swing violently, as if a giant had caught hold of him and was shaking him. Remaining calm, he let the air spill out of the chute and began to look for a healthy tree. This he found impossible, however – the jungle canopy was too dense – until he was only a few feet above the canopy. By then it was too late and he smashed into a tangle of treetops, came to a brief halt, already feeling battered and bruised, then heard the branch snapping and suddenly hurtled down, crashing through more branches and thinking he was being smashed to pieces. He came to a shuddering halt, snared in a lower branch, from which he wriggled free and dropped the last few feet.

Already on the ground, Sergeant Lorrimer grinned with contentment, but not everyone made it down that easily. Swinging from the top of one tall tree, as the last of the other parachutists descended successfully, was Boney Maronie. Temporarily paralysed with fear at being so high up, he tried to disguise it by lighting a cigarette. He gave up in this endeavour – his hands were shaking so much he couldn't light it – and eventually, when the last of the other parachutists had landed and everyone began to shout at him to come down, he fixed his knotted rope to the treetop, separated the parachute container from his bergen, secured the bergen to his shoulders, then abseiled down the tree on the knotted rope, dropping the last five or six feet in his desperate need to feel the ground beneath his feet.

'Spot of bother up there?' Sergeant Lorrimer asked him when the cheering and applause of the troopers had finally died down.

'Piece of piss,' Boney Maronie said. 'I was just having a rest.'

'Very wise,' Captain Callaghan said. 'OK, men, let's move out.'

They headed into the darkness of the jungle.

## 6

Captain Pryce-Jones had been right: the *ulu* closed in on them so fast that most of them suffered an initial claustrophobia and panic that had to be overcome. It was related to the extraordinary height of the trees, the seemingly solid nature of the canopy high above, the absence of light on the jungle floor, the dense, almost impenetrable undergrowth, the knowledge that poisonous snakes, centipedes and scorpions could fall on them from the overhanging foliage or crawl over their booted feet. Last but not least was the appalling humid heat, which instantly made all of the men sweat profusely and some of them feel almost suffocated.

As the Malayan jungle is evergreen, none of the varieties of trees sheds all its leaves at once, which explains the unusual density of the canopy and the gloomy, colourless nature of the jungle floor, which was covered in a thick carpet of dead leaves and seedlings, lying around the giant roots and thick creepers of the soaring trees, entwined with vines and lianas. The *ulu* is constantly rotting and regenerating, with ferns, mosses and herbaceous plants pushing through the leaves and fungi growing thickly on leaves and fallen tree trunks. Colouring the canopy, however, was a mass of white, yellow, pink, or scarlet blossom, often so sweetly scented that even the jungle far below was filled with the fragrance of the invisible flowers high above. This sickly-sweet smell made some of the men feel even more suffocated as they made their agonizingly slow advance.

The general feeling of tension was increased in other ways. As each man had been equipped with one magazine full of tracer bullets, which were to be used to identify enemy positions in a fire-fight, they were all uneasily conscious of the unseen enemy. Also, Captain Callaghan had made them place the magazines in their ammunition pouches upside down, with the bullets pointed away from the body in case they were hit by enemy fire and injured the wearer. Likewise, to ensure that they would not make good targets for the enemy, hand-grenades were not carried on the chest as they would have been in other environments. All of this simply served to highlight the nerve-racking fact that the enemy could be anywhere in the *ulu*, preparing an ambush.

Not allowed to talk or trade bullshit while on the march, forced to communicate only with hand signals, the troopers could not ignore the sounds of the jungle and therefore were prone to imagine things, which made for even more nervous tension.

In the daytime, the jungle was relatively quiet, but they would occasionally hear the hornbill, whose loud, discordant voice resembles that of a heron. They would also hear the rhythmic, noisy beating of its wings and, if there happened to be a break in the treetops, they would see its huge, black, ungainly form and its bizarrely shaped white head. It was the only living thing they had seen so far.

As the men would soon discover, the patrol would be on the move ten hours a day with only occasional breaks and brief halts. Their advance took them alternately from the humid swamp of the jungle to open river beds, where the harsh sun temporarily dried their sweat-soaked fatigues, but then baked their bodies and feet in fierce dry heat, which in some ways was even worse.

The burden of their weapons, radios, other items of equipment and supplies was a source of considerable frustration and led to a torrent of whispered obscenities. The weapons in particular were covered with knobs, swivels, handles, catches, guards and other protuberances which, however they were carried, scraped and bruised the hip bone, dug into the ribs and caught on every twig and creeper in the undergrowth, sometimes tugging the unwary owner practically off his feet.

Using a map in combination with aerial photographs of the terrain, Captain Callaghan managed to locate a watercourse that he hoped would provide a relatively easy route to a Sakai village, where he planned to pick up some guides. Unfortunately, when they reached the watercourse, they discovered that it was too deep and rough to follow easily, with sides so steep and so covered with bamboo, thorns and thickets of every kind that their progress was even slower than it had been in the jungle. To make matters even worse, where the ground of the watercourse was still wet, they found it almost impossible to keep their feet on the steep traverses and repeatedly, painfully tore their hands when clutching at twigs to prevent themselves from falling.

They camped that first evening on a sandbank several feet above the water-line, this being the only level place they could find. It was a relief in more ways than one, particularly as they could bathe, eat, drink and talk again, reasonably confident that the guards located far out on all four points would give them fair warning of any advancing enemy troops.

'The worst of all is not being able to talk,' Dennis the Menace said as he started stripping off his sweat-soaked clothing to dive naked into the river. 'When all you can listen to is this fucking jungle, you keep hearing things that aren't there.'

'You're a nutcase,' Boney Maronie said. 'I always knew it; now I've got solid proof.'

'There speaks the brave,' Dennis said. 'He was so scared on the top of that bloody tree, he almost shook the whole damned thing down.'

'Bullshit,' Boney Maronie retorted. 'I told you – I was just resting up until the latecomers landed on the DZ.'

'So how come you didn't light the cigarette that fell down from the treetops? The shakes, was it?'

'Fuck you, Dennis, I . . . *Shit!*' Stripped to the waist, Boney Maronie now saw what they were all suddenly noticing – that clusters of bloated leeches were stuck to various parts of their bodies. 'Jesus Christ!' Boney Maronie exclaimed in revulsion.

'Fucking hell,' chimed in Dennis the Menace, stripping off his OG trousers and standing in his pants to display a body completely covered in blood-sucking leeches. 'I've been pulling the bastards off me all day, so I didn't expect to find more. I'm being sucked dry!' He sat down again, lit a cigarette, inhaled and blew a cloud of smoke. 'Little fuckers!' he said, studying the glowing end of his cigarette.

Dead-eye Dick had also pulled off scores of leeches during the day and did not know that others had crawled through his clothing until he felt the blood running down his chest. Now, as he and his fellow troopers tried queasily to remove the bloodsuckers, Dennis the Menace started stubbing the end of his cigarette on to those clinging to his bared thighs, making them sizzle, smoke and shrivel up.

'God!' Pete West exclaimed, turning up his nose, 'that's bloody disgusting!'

'Disgusting to you,' Dennis the Menace said, 'but it makes sense to me. If you pull these little fuckers off, their teeth stay in and fester. Nope, you should only remove them by touching them with salt, tobacco, a solution of areca nut or a cigarette end.' To prove his point, he eagerly scorched another of the creatures.

'Aw, knock it off, Dennis!' Alf Laughton complained.

'It's the only sensible way, mate.'

'That's bullshit,' Boney Maronie said, wincing each time he pulled a leech off a bleeding wound. 'I've been told that removing leeches that way is no better than any other. The wounds bleed just as much and they're just as likely to become infected. Might as well just pull them off like this.' He pulled another insect off and winced again, putting on a brave show.

'Doesn't matter how you get rid of 'em,' Pete Welsh said, 'as long as you do it.' He, too, was smoking, touching his burning cigarette to the leeches on his body one by one, grinning dementedly as they sizzled. 'A lot of people have actually died from leeches – from the swelling that comes from their bites.'

'Crap,' Dead-eye said.

'It's bloody not. The wounds from leeches sometimes swell so much that they block the body's orifices and cause a slow, agonizing death.'

'What orifices?' Dead-eye asked sceptically.

'Lips, nostrils, arse-hole and the eye of your dick.'

'Ah, God!' Boney Maronie cried. 'Knock it off! I can't bear even thinking about that.'

Then, stripped completely naked and having nothing to hide, he jumped into the river.

Now naked as well, though not so keen to flaunt it, Dennis the Menace wrapped a towel around his waist, hurried to the river bank and tentatively waded in.

'What was that dangling between your legs?'

Boney Maronie asked when he surfaced. 'Another leech, was it?'

'Go fuck yourself,' Dennis the Menace said, sinking gratefully chest-deep in the water, soon followed by Dead-eye, Pete Welsh, Alf Laughton and an increasing number of the other men, all desperately grateful to have the sweat and the blood of the many leeches washed off them.

As the men were stopping at this location for only one night, they did not make up proper shelters, just personal Laying Up Positions, or LUPs, consisting mainly of uncovered shallow 'scrapes' in which they unrolled their hollow-fill sleeping bags on plastic sheeting. Above these simple beds they raised a shelter consisting of a waterproof poncho draped over wiring stretched taut between two Y-shaped sticks, making a triangular shape with the apex pointing into the wind.

Reasonably sure that there were no CT in the vicinity, and knowing that the camp was being guarded on all sides, they were confident enough to prepare hot food with the aid of portable hexamine stoves, followed by a much-appreciated brew-up and, for many, a 'smoko'.

As clothes saturated with sweat would quickly rot, Callaghan ordered some of the men to make a 'trench fire'. This they did by digging a trench about a foot deep, lining the bottom with rocks and stones from the river and lighting a fire of sticks and hexamine blocks on top of the rocks. As the flames were protected from any wind and could not set the surrounding foliage alight, the trench fire was ideal for drying out the troopers' soaked fatigues.

'We should raise these bashas off the ground,' Dead-eye said, 'to make sure the spiders, scorpions, centipedes and snakes don't get at us.'

'Oh, thanks very much,' Dennis the Menace said, as he unrolled his sleeping bag, 'for giving us all something to think about when we try to get some shut-eye.'

'I only meant . . .'

'I know what you mean and I know you're right, but I still don't want to hear it, kid,' the older man interrupted. 'We can't raise the bashas off the ground without building platforms of bamboo and thatch, but that's too much work for this short time. So here we are and here we stay for the night. Don't give us bad dreams, Dead-eye.'

Nevertheless, knowing that the creepy-crawlies were more likely to be drawn to dry clothing and footwear, they quickly constructed a simple raised platform by weaving elephant grass and palm leaves through cross-pieces of branches supported on four lengths of split bamboo. They piled their dried clothing and jungle boots up on the platform, which had been constructed, for additional protection, near the all-night trench fire.

'That takes care of the clothes and boots,' Dead-eye said, not concerned about the guerrillas, though he was clearly still wary of insects. 'But what about us?'

'Smear yourself with mud from the river,' Sergeant Lorrimer told him and the others, 'then cover your sleeping bags with leaves. You should all have sweet dreams.'

This they did, but it meant that they would have to sleep without moving much, which ensured that sleep did not come easily. There was another bar to sleeping. As darkness closed in, the jungle chorus, which had been hushed during the day, came to life and built up in an almost deafening crescendo, with every imaginable species of grasshopper, cicada and tree frog competing in a musical, rhythmic, discordant, cacophonous medley. Some sounded like alarm clocks, others like tinkling bells, yet others like hunting horns, a few like distant pneumatic drills. There were yodelling, clicking, gargling and rattling sounds and, worst of all, a pervasive humming that sounded like millions of insects imprisoned and going frantic in glass jars.

By night, the jungle was a symphony that could drive a man mad.

It was at night, too, that the insects ruled over their own domain. In the daytime, they did not trouble the men too much, but at night they were insatiable, driven frantic by the need for the salt in human sweat, relentlessly whining around the men's ears and biting them constantly, no matter how much they were slapped away.

Even worse than the mosquitoes were the midges, which made no noise but gave a bite that itched like a nettle sting and kept the victim awake throughout the night.

As a result of the many bites they received in the night, the men's faces in the morning were so swollen and distorted that they were, in many cases, almost unrecognizable. Indeed, some had cheeks so swollen that their eyes were closed and they couldn't see until they bathed them in cold water.

For most of the men, that first night was one of the worst they had ever experienced. Nevertheless, they moved out the next day – only to find it even more difficult than the first.

In the depths of the jungle, the limit of visibility was reduced to between 50 and 100 yards. Even when they were on a steep hillside, where a small landslide had opened up a window through which they could catch a glimpse of another tree-covered hillside, surmounted by sheer blue sky, they were none the wiser about their whereabouts, one hill looking exactly like another. There were no landmarks – and even if there were, they could not be seen. Another difficulty was that the scouts, or point men, had no way of judging distance: it took them three days to realize they were taking eight hours to travel one mile on the map instead of the three or four miles they had imagined, judging by the amounts of energy they were expending. Also, they were continually forced off their course by swamps, thickets, precipices, outcrops of rock and rivers. It was impossible even to follow a ridge unless it was very steep and clearly marked.

Sometimes they clambered up hills so steep that they had to hold on to the vegetation with both hands to pull themselves up, and on the descents had to lower themselves carefully from branch to branch. On such arduous climbs and descents they met every kind of prickly thicket, and sometimes came across rhododendron, coarse shrubs and moss so thick that they clambered over the top of them without actually touching the ground.

The worst going of all, however, consisted of whole valleys filled with huge granite boulders half-covered with a slippery layer of moss and with treacherous roots, so that a false step was liable to land them in the stream below. Their bergens seemed to get heavier and heavier; their weapons, snagging everything, became close to unbearable.

Even worse was the number of times the lead man, unless carefully watched, would turn through half a circle in a few minutes without being in the least aware of it, as he could not see the sun and there were no landmarks, apart from the interminable tree trunks, from which to take his bearings. When Captain Callaghan realized this was happening, he devised a new system.

'In future the man at the front won't carry his Owen sub-machine-gun. Instead, he'll use his *parang* to cut a path that he can pass through, even if just about. The second man will then widen the track and mark the route more clearly by bending saplings down or blazing tree trunks, and the third man will then follow through and check the course with a compass.'

'That sounds like hell for the first man,' Sergeant Lorrimer said.

'It will be,' Callaghan replied. 'For that very reason, the men will change places every half hour.'

The new approach worked well, though it exhausted the men hacking their way through the undergrowth and there were many minor wounds because of their inexperience with the razor-sharp *parang*, even after their training in Johore. Nevertheless, it hastened their advance and so they stuck to it. They were grateful, however, when, after four days on the march, they finally reached a Sakai village, where a couple of the aboriginals, known to Captain Callaghan, agreed to act as their guides to the RV.

'That's a relief,' Callaghan said to Lorrimer as they sat in the shade of one of the raised thatched huts, enjoying a brew-up and a cigarette. 'We seem to be taking longer every day, so I'm glad the Sakai are on board at last.'

'Bloody amazing, isn't it?' Lorrimer replied. 'You do all that training back at base, but once you're in the actual jungle, most of the training comes to nought. The *ulu* is so damned unpredictable.'

'Well, not *all* of the training comes to nought, Sarge. In fact, most of it holds up very well, if these men are anything to judge by. They've adapted remarkably quickly, when all's said and done. They've endured an awful lot in four days.'

'That's true enough. Even you, I suppose, couldn't have survived three months on your own if it hadn't been for your special jungle training.'

'No. I'll be eternally grateful for it.'

'You weren't so grateful when I was one of the directing staff.'

Callaghan chuckled at his recollection of Sergeant Lorrimer as a particularly ruthless DS during his personal training course in Johore. 'God, you were tyrannical, Sarge! A real bloody monster.'

'The proof is in the pudding,' Lorrimer said. 'I take that as a compliment.'

They moved out shortly after, this time with the Sakai guides out front, instead of SAS point men. Nevertheless, the hike through the jungle was no easier and, at times, even worse.

Every evening, when they stopped to make camp, the men de-leeched themselves and washed away the clotted blood. Then, as the noisy, biting insects became intolerable, they made a fresh leaf-shelter for the night. They soon became adept at this. Usually, they made a low framework with a sloping roof and lashed it firmly in place with vines. After collecting the largest leaves available, they thatched them into the framework of the roof. They then made a huge pile of branches and leaves as a mattress, put on all their clothes, smeared themselves with mud, if available, and finally covered themselves with groundsheets.

'I'm actually getting used to this,' Dennis the Menace said. 'Last night I almost had a whole night's sleep.'

'You still woke up looking like Bela Lugosi,' Boney Maronie said, laughing. 'Your face was bitten all to hell and your eyes were puffed up.'

'That's how he looks every morning,' Pete Welsh

said, 'even back in Blighty. That's why his wife ran away with the milkman.'

'How did you know that?' Dennis the Menace replied. 'I never told a soul about it.'

'Pete was the milkman,' Boney Maronie said.

'Seriously, though, lads,' Dennis the Menace said, 'it's amazing how you can learn to be comfortable even in these conditions – smeared with mud and covered with leaves and shrubbery. I'm almost getting to like it.'

'The mud helps a bit,' Alf Laughton said. 'At least the midges bite less. But it doesn't kill the whining of those fucking mosquitoes. I think they go even more frantic when they can't get at your bare skin. Their whining drives me insane.'

'Really?' Boney Maronie said. 'I hadn't noticed. You haven't changed at all, Alf.'

'Go and screw yourself, Boney!'

'Real cosy in here,' Dennis the Menace said, practically purring. 'I know I'm in for a good night.'

The rain came. It poured down like a waterfall. Though they had been told that bamboo always burns, no matter how wet, they learnt the hard way that this is true only when the fire is already burning. Thus, when the rain came unexpectedly – as it did – they could neither start a fire nor burn the hexamine stoves, and so were not only drenched, but had to eat cold tinned rations instead of hot food. It was a fierce, noisy tropical cloudburst that almost washed them away.

'Fucking hell!' Boney Maronie exclaimed as he huddled up beside Dennis the Menace, both wrapped in their ponchos. 'This is bloody terrible.'

'Noah's Ark should pass by any minute now.'

'I'm soaked to the bloody skin.'

'So am I. Even the leeches are drowning.'

'It's so noisy!' Dead-eye exclaimed, his voice muffled by the poncho covering his face. 'It sounds like jungle drums.'

'I hate this kind of racket,' Pete Welsh said. 'It gets on my nerves.'

'Tropical rains don't last long,' Alf Laughton said, 'so this should stop pretty soon.'

He was wrong. In fact, the rain was merely the prelude to the violent gale known as *Sumatras* – a terrifying experience that began as a loud roaring in the distance, but gradually increased in volume until it sounded like a squadron of fighter aircraft flying overhead.

In fact, thinking it was an air raid, some of the men instinctively dived for cover, including Dennis the Menace, Boney Maronie and Dead-eye. Face down in the mud, they soon realized that they were wrong – they weren't hearing aircraft, but something much worse. Sitting up again, they squinted into the rain and saw, through a narrow window in the rain-lashed, wind-blown trees, a boiling mass of black clouds streaked by jagged fingers of lightning. The roaring sound was a fearsome combination of thunder and wind.

'Shit,' Boney Maronie whispered, 'that wind is fierce!'

'*Sumatras*!' the Sakai guide nearby exclaimed in a hoarse, frightened whisper.

'*Take cover*!' Captain Callaghan bawled, before disappearing behind an enormous tree.

The storm exploded over them with awesome force, tearing the trees to shreds, filling the air with flying debris, picking some of the men up and flinging them back down like rag dolls. The noise was terrifying, and bolts of lightning daggered down into the forest like crooked fingers of silvery fire. The wind hurled the rain before it, turning it into a deluge, creating a whirlpool filled with flying foliage, including sharp-edged palms that slashed like razors across the upraised arms and hands of some of the men. They were screaming with pain even as a couple of trees toppled over, crashing down through the other trees, tearing the great branches off, creating a torrent of branches, vines, lianas, creepers and giant leaves, which rained down to add their own noise to the bedlam.

Far louder, great trees smashed down through smaller ones and crashed into the forest floor, right across the path of the patrol. Then the storm passed on as quickly as it had arrived, leaving an eerie silence.

When eventually the men crawled out of where they had been hiding, the first thing they saw, among the piled-up and widely strewn debris, was the decapitated head of one of the Sakai guides. What was left of his body was buried deep in the mud under the fallen truck of a giant tree.

'We'll never be able to dig him out,' Captain Callaghan said, 'so just bury his head.'

While most of the men looked on, hardly believing what they were seeing, the remaining Sakai guides buried the head, then held a funeral ceremony around the small mound of earth, all of them bowed low in prayer as the sodden trees dripped over their already soaked bodies.

First bogged down by the storm, then, when it abated, by the sea of mud, fallen trees and scattered foliage of its aftermath, the men took a long time in pulling themselves together. Nevertheless, hearing over the PRC 320 that the foot patrols consisting of Gurkhas, Royal Marine Commandos, Malaya Police and two squadrons of SAS were nearing the

RV, they were encouraged enough to move on into the drying, steaming jungle.

Their damaged morale was not boosted when one of the troopers complained of a terrible pain behind his eyes, aching in all his joints and alternating spasms of fever and freezing cold. When examined by the doctor, he was found to be running a temperature of 103 degrees and was diagnosed as suffering from benign tertiary – a virulent, though not serious, form of malaria.

A few hours later, the doctor was called upon to attend a trooper who had contracted blackwater fever, brought on when he had developed chronic malaria and failed to take enough quinine to combat it. As well as the symptom from which the disease derives its name, the trooper suffered relentless vomiting and dysentery, accompanied by such agonizing pains in the small of his back and across his pelvis that he complained about feeling as if all his bones were coming apart. Eventually, he had to be held down by two other troopers to counteract the violence of the spasms. After these had subsided, he was rolled on to a makeshift stretcher and carried the rest of the way.

The storm having blown itself out, the men moved on and found themselves facing a series of parallel rivers, which they crossed on bamboo rafts quickly built with the help of the Sakai.

Four feet wide and 30 feet long, the rafts were made by lashing together a double layer of 4-inch bamboos. The central third was raised by lashing on an additional deck of shorter poles, and the load was placed there, amidships, where it kept comparatively dry. As soon as it was light enough to see the feathery bamboo groves overhanging the bank, the men started poling the raft down-river to the RV, now only a few miles away.

As they travelled down the river, between high banks of mud and papaya trees, they learnt over the PRC 320 that the foot patrols, which had been marching for seven days, had finally reached Ah Hoi's jungle hide-out – only to discover that the guerrilla chief had fled with his men and the camp was empty.

'They must have been warned of our approach by the Communist agents in the villages along the route,' SAS Captain Tony Lidgate explained over the radio.

'We haven't spotted any CT either,' a disappointed Captain Callaghan informed him. 'Not one. Not a shadow.'

'They must have spotted the Valetta circling over the DZ,' Lidgate said.

Callaghan sighed, glancing around him at the exhausted men squatting on the raft. 'We can destroy the camp and farm,' he said, 'but it seems like a great deal of effort for such a small gain. A damned waste of time, in fact.'

'Not necessarily. We've just been in contact with Johore and been informed by the CO that we're to remain in the CT camp and turn it into a Forward Operating Base.'

'A good idea,' Captain Callaghan said, feeling the return of enthusiasm. 'An FOB in that location could be invaluable.'

'We're settling in already,' Lidgate said, 'and should have the tea on the brew by the time you get here. I'll see you then, Captain. Over and out.'

Callaghan switched the microphone off and handed it back to the radio operative, then he looked along the river to where it curved away between green walls of undergrowth and soaring trees. When the rafts turned that bend in the river, they saw the thatched huts and lean-tos of the abandoned CT camp, now filled with Gurkhas, Royal Marine Commandos, Malaya Police, Sakai and Iban trackers, and the two squadrons of SAS troopers.

'Home sweet home,' Captain Callaghan murmured, grinning at Sergeant Lorrimer as the rafts were poled to the shore.

# 7

When the men were at last resting gratefully on thatched mats in the shade of the lean-tos, some eating, some having a brew-up, others urgently cleaning themselves and shaving with the aid of hand mirrors, they were astonished to discover how much weight they had lost in a mere five days in the jungle. In fact, their bones stuck out everywhere and their skin, except where it was mottled with the purple spots of hundreds of leech bites, was a sickly yellow. Their clothes were in ragged tatters, and their hands, knees and faces were covered with a network of cuts and thorn scratches, as well as the larger cuts inflicted upon some by flying sharp-edged leaves during the terrifying *Sumatras*. The Royal Marine Commandos, Malaya Police and other two squadrons of SAS troopers did not look much better, though the Gurkhas, Sakai and Iban trackers looked much as usual.

Not far from where some of the men were resting, at the edge of the jungle just beyond the perimeter of the camp, a gibbon – a *wah-wah* in Malay – was swinging from branch to branch with its long arms.

'That,' Alf Laughton said, 'is the only animal we've seen throughout the whole march. Considering the jungle's supposed to be full of them, I think that's bloody amazing.'

'Well, I'm bloody amazed,' Pete Welsh said sarcastically.

While the men were resting up, Captain Callaghan exchanged reports with the other squadron commander, Captain Lidgate, then used the PRC 320 to contact Johore and arrange for supplies to be dropped. Later that afternoon, these were dropped by parachute from a Blackburn Beverley, which, with its payload capacity of 20,500kg, was able to deliver a substantial amount.

After their lengthy hike, or 'tab', through the jungle, the men were allowed to rest for most of the day. However, once the Beverley had flown overhead, their rest period ended and they were sent off in various directions to bring in the supplies that had fallen both in and outside the camp. When they had done this, stacking the supplies up in the middle of the compound, they were allocated various small tasks that would see them through the first night in some comfort: first washing themselves in the river, then the construction of trench fires for the cooking of some decent food, then a late-evening dinner, followed by beer and a smoko, and finally the preparation of temporary bashas.

Early next morning, however, they all took part in the construction of a proper FOB.

The guerrillas' camp had consisted of not much more than a few thatched lean-tos scattered around the clearing near open trenches filled with human excrement, urine and many thousands of seething, stinking maggots. The SAS plan was to construct a fully circular base camp surrounded by a cleared track, hemmed in with wire, and protected by Claymore mines and sentry posts.

First, though, they had to get rid of the maggots, which were giving even the most hardened troopers the shivers. They disposed of them by pouring kerosene into the trenches and setting light to it, creating half-a-dozen bonfires. While the bonfires burned, the rest of the work began in earnest.

As it was vitally important that the FOB could be defended by a fraction of the men while the majority of them were on patrol, the camp was designed within a circular cleared track that divided it from the surrounding jungle. This track, dug out of the ground over several days by SAS troopers with shovels and spades, formed an 'open' area that would have to be crossed by anyone, friend or enemy, wanting to enter the camp.

As some of the troopers were clearing the track, others were digging a series of defensive slit trenches at regular intervals around the camp, on the inner side of the circle, to be used as permanent sentry positions that would face out in every direction. The defensive trenches were similar to rectangular observation posts, or OPs, in that they had room for at least four men and shallow 'resting up' scrapes. However, unlike long-term OPs, they were open to the air.

At the same time, other trenches were being dug out in a smaller circle near the centre of the compound where the Sakai were constructing a large headquarters, which would be surrounded by similar constructions to be used as living quarters, cookhouse, mess hall, stores, and even a small area for football and general exercise. As the camp would have no vehicles, there was no need for a motor pool, but a helicopter landing pad was being levelled in the south-east corner of the circular compound.

The Sakai were expert at constructing the buildings and did so with the aid of curious SAS troopers. The framework of each building was made from poles of green timber, 6 inches in diameter. The stronger timber from standing trees was used to support the main beam of the roof. As most of the Sakai were expert axemen, they felled and trimmed the poles while the SAS troopers went out collecting the rattan required to bind the joints.

The rattan is a creeper that can grow to hundreds of feet in length, coiling along the ground before climbing to the summit of the tallest trees, where it bursts into a huge umbrella of giant leaves. Some rattan are two inches thick, but the ideal thickness for jungle constructions is one-third to half an inch. When one of suitable size was found, two or three troopers would pull it out of the ground or down from the trees. As the jointed green cane of the rattan is protected by a thorny shell, this would be stripped off, then the pliable stem would be coiled up like a rope and carried back to the Sakai in charge of the construction. Using a small, sharp knife, the Sakai would then split each rattan into two separate parts or, for finer lashings, into strips, then he would cut away and discard the inner pith.

While some of the Sakai were building the framework of the huts or splitting the rattan, others were teaching the SAS troopers to plait *atap* for the roofing material. Large clumps of *atap* were to be found near by, with drooping fronds 20–30 feet long. The fronds were pulled down with a crook and the top 8 feet of the pithy stalk cut off, stacked in special racks to prevent the leaves being damaged, then carried back to the camp in bundles. To plait the *atap*, all the leaves on one side starting at the base had to be bent back sharply, then threaded under and over the leaves on the other side of the central stem, thus giving a plaited surface 6–8 inches wide.

The *atap* was placed horizontally on the framework of the roof, starting at the bottom. It was then lashed in two places with fine rattan to the vertical members of the roof, which had been cut from the lower stems of *atap*. The *atap* was placed so that every part of the roof was covered by about eight thicknesses of plaited leaf, presenting on the outside an even surface of downwards-pointing leaf ends. At the apex of the roof a number of plaited *atap* were laid along the join of the two sides and pegged beneath the roof beam. The gables of the huts were filled in with *atap*, forming an unbroken surface, with the sides and ends left entirely open.

As for the bashas, where the SAS men slept, an aisle about 6 feet wide was left down the centre of each hut, with the timber-framed beds, or sleeping-benches, on either side raised about a couple of feet off the ground. The beds themselves consisted of elephant grass and palm leaves woven through cross-pieces of branches supported on pieces of split bamboo. Some of the troopers were able to sleep comfortably on these; others rolled their sleeping bag out and used it as a mattress.

All the buildings were raised off the ground on stilts to lessen the chance of invasion by poisonous snakes, centipedes, scorpions and giant jungle rats.

When the fires in the latrine trenches had stopped burning, thatched lean-tos were raised over the separate latrines, with bamboo walls between each, thus granting a modicum of privacy to the users. The trenches were filled with a mixture of quicklime and kerosene to prevent the return of the hideous maggots.

By this time the cleared path around the compound had been completed and was lined with a barbed-wire fence in which there were two openings, one as a Patrol Route Entry, the other as a Patrol Route Exit. The defensive trenches spaced at regular intervals around the inner side of the fence were manned permanently by SAS teams with tripod-mounted Bren guns and 3-inch mortars.

Claymore mines were laid around the camp, just outside the perimeter, on the other side of the cleared path, except for the areas directly facing both the Patrol Route Entrance and Exit. Set to be activated manually, or when someone stepped on them, they were shaped like concave plates which, on exploding, would fire around 350 metal balls over a fan-shaped area, shredding anyone within their range of 100 metres.

The circular compound was now a well-defended combination of base camp and Forward Operating Base.

The camp's construction had taken many days, during which time some of the men, getting their weight, strength and energy back, began to betray their restlessness by playing pranks, first on one another, then on the officers. These began as harmless jokes, usually occurring after an evening of swilling beer, but soon they had become more dangerous.

At first, the most popular pranks were placing a dead snake or jungle rat in someone's basha or sleeping bag, which would only be found when the victim slipped under the sheets or into the bag; putting a decapitated snake's head, amputated rat limb, a few maggots, worms, or dead centipedes or scorpions in someone's bowl of soup, which would only be spotted when the soup was almost finished; or emptying half the water out of someone's full water bottle and filling it up with captured mosquitoes, midges, flies or even wasps, which would frantically burst free when the cap was unscrewed, causing a shock, if not bites or stings, to the victim.

When such pranks became all too easy to anticipate, the more insatiable pranksters, such as Pete Welsh and Alf Laughton moved on to more questionable activities. *Live* snakes, scorpions, centipedes or giant spiders were placed in troopers' kit or weapons, where they could clearly be seen but had to be removed at great personal risk, often when the soldier was in a hurry to report for duty. Minute traces of gunpowder were poked into cigarettes to make them explode when lit, which led to one trooper's face being slightly burned. Seeds that caused unbearable itching were sprinkled inside underclothes and drill fatigues, driving some of the victims frantic when they were on guard or on the firing range. Stinging ants were hidden in soft jungle caps, boots, the pockets of bergens, and even the breeches of weapons, thus causing serious discomfort, often dangerously close to the eyes, sometimes when the victims were in the middle of important activities such as guard duty or jungle patrol.

Great or small, the pranks were not always taken in good spirit and often led to fist fights that had to be broken up by Sergeant Lorrimer. Before long, Lorrimer came to believe that new forms of discipline would have to be imposed and that the men had to be given more to do than simply act as a forward observation unit checking on an enemy that was, to all intents and purposes, invisible.

'Some of the pranks are getting out of hand,' he informed Captain Callaghan, 'and they're the work of men who probably shouldn't have been in this Regiment in the first place – men who transferred for the wrong reasons or were encouraged to do so by NCOs and officers who simply wanted to get shot of them because they were trouble. Unfortunately, we're lumbered with them for now.'

'What men?'

'Troopers Welsh and Laughton, for a start. They play a lot of the pranks, are involved in a lot of fights, and are clearly in the Regiment for the wrong reasons.'

'What reasons?'

'They mistake our lack of authoritarianism, or rather our democratic ways of operating – the Chinese Parliaments and so forth – for a complete lack of discipline. They're cowboys, always looking for some action, and not too fussy about how they get it. They could be trouble, boss. In fact, they already are.'

They were sitting on the verandah under the

overhanging roof of the new HQ building, looking out on the compound where SAS troopers, Gurkhas, Royal Marine Commandos, Sakai labourers, and Iban trackers were either going about their various activities or resting. Some were cleaning weapons, cooking over trench fires, reading maps, writing letters. Others were on guard in the defensive trenches around the camp's perimeter, their Bren guns and M1 carbines aimed at the solid wall of the jungle, just beyond the clear track that ran around the camp and the unseen, deadly Claymore mines placed between the track and the jungle. A football match was in progress in the sports area just west of the HQ. The smoke from the trench fires billowed up and was blown back by the wind, bringing the smell of grilling fish and boiling soup to the nostrils of the hungry Captain Callaghan and Sergeant Lorrimer. The former was smoking a cigarette, sighing as he exhaled.

'It *is* unfortunate,' he said, 'that because of the speed with which the Emergency built up we weren't allowed the luxury of more carefully selecting who we took on. This is now being rectified, but in the meantime, as you rightfully say, we're lumbered with the few remaining undesirables. When this op is over they'll be weeded out and a more stringent selection process applied. For now, I suppose, we'll just have to live with it.'

'I'm worried that the pranks will get worse and the fights more frequent. Either that or one of the pranksters will go too far and do some serious damage.'

'I'm worried about that as well,' Callaghan said.

In fact, they had due cause for concern. As this was a makeshift base camp, there was only one mess, used alike by officers, NCOs and troopers. A couple of days after the completion of the camp, SAS Captain Tony Lidgate was recalled to Johore and due to be lifted out by helicopter the following morning. That evening, he had farewell drinks with Captain Callaghan and other officers and NCOs in the mess, which doubled as a bar and was also filled with hard-drinking troopers. While Lidgate and his friends were standing in a group, drinks in hand, having an animated conversation, not far from a table where Dennis the Menace, Boney Maronie and Dead-Eye were also boozing, a group of SAS troopers, led by Pete Welsh and Alf Laughton, were getting very drunk in their bashas. Knowing what was going on in the mess, they decided to have some sport at the expense of their officers and NCOs.

'Let's scare the shit out of 'em,' Pete Welsh said, 'and set off a little explosion by the mess. They'll jump out of their boots!'

In fact, this had begun when Welsh, a former Sapper with the operational arm of No. 101 Special Training School, Singapore, now the explosive specialist in his four-man team, had been drunkenly boasting about the various ways in which he and other 3rd Corps soldiers had blown up railways and bridges here in Malaya, during the war against the Japanese. When Alf Laughton scoffed at some of the methods described by Welsh, the latter, slurring badly, said he would give them all a demonstration.

While Laughton and the others downed more beer and looked on, Welsh, grinning crazily, removed a small amount of PE (Plastic High-Explosive) from where he had been keeping it, in secret, in his bergen. He also removed a short piece of narrow copper tubing, a phial of acid, a piece of fine wire attached to a simple spring mechanism, a percussion cap and an instantaneous fuse.

'Dead-simple delayed-action device,' he slurred, 'known as a time pencil.'

'Right,' Alf Laughton said, nodding solemnly, 'you mentioned that, mate.'

Welsh nodded as well. They nodded in unison. 'Right,' Welsh slurred, awkwardly making up the simple bomb with blurred vision and shaky hands. 'A time pencil. Dead simple. Put the wire through the tube like this, see? With the spring sticking out one end, right? Then put the phial of acid in the tube as well, see? Like this. Now when I'm ready to set it off, I'll fix the striker to the percussion cap like this. Then I'll squeeze the copper tube to break the phial of acid inside. The acid will eventually eat through this piece of fine wire. When the wire dissolves, the spring will be released and force the striker against the percussion cap – here, see? – which will then ignite the instantaneous fuse and – *voilà*! – up she fucking goes, mate, in fire and smoke. Come on, let's go try it out on those Ruperts over in the mess hut.'

Picking up his home-made bomb and starting out of the basha, Welsh was tugged back by the equally drunken Alf Laughton. 'Hold on,' Laughton said, still holding his bottle of Tiger beer. 'Are we going to have time to get away, Pete?'

'Think I'm fucking dumb? Of *course* we'll've time to get away! The length of delay's reg'lated . . . regalate . . . 'scuse me, regulated by the thickness of the wire – this, see? – and I've chosen a wire that gives the min'im . . . min'mum . . . *minimum* period.'

'Whassat, den?' Laughton could hardly speak.

'Thirty minutes.'

'Even *you* can crawl away from the mess in that

time,' Trooper Jack Clayton told him, then broke down in giggles.

'Come on, you dumb cunts, let's go,' Welsh said, staggering out of the basha, carrying his DIY bomb. When the others followed him out, they crossed the dark compound, under the stars that could be seen above the clearing, and made their way, crouched low, often drunkenly falling over, to the 6-foot legs of the raised mess hut.

Huddling under the hut, they tried to stifle their giggling.

'Here,' someone whispered, 'give me a slug from that bottle.'

'Right, mate. That's what friends are for.'

The lights of the hut were filtering out from between the closed shutters, illuminating the hundreds of insects caught and dying in the wire-mesh coverings. They could hear Elvis Presley singing – obviously a radio playing – and loud conversation and laughter from the men.

'Having a fucking good time up there,' Laughton whispered.

'They'll warm up even more,' Welsh replied, 'when this little darlin' goes off. Here, hold my bottle.'

While Laughton held his bottle of Tiger beer, Welsh, still grinning, tied the bomb to one of the legs of the hut, wrapping the string around two or three times, then tugging the knot tight. After checking that the charge was firmly attached, he smirked even more insanely, and said to Laughton: 'Do you want the honour, mate?'

'Yeah,' Laughton slurred. 'Terrific. What I . . .?' He shook his head a few times, blinked rapidly, then cleared his throat and concentrated on his speech. 'What I do, mate?'

Welsh took hold of his right hand and placed it against the narrow copper tube. 'Just squeeze it like you're squeezing a nice piece of tit,' he said. 'Let go when you hear the phial of acid breaking. That's all there is to it.'

'Like this?'

'S'right,' Welsh informed him, still slurring.

Laughton squeezed the phial of acid until he heard it breaking. The sound gave him a bit of a shock and made him jerk his hand away, half expecting the bomb to go off immediately. When it didn't, the other men giggled uncontrollably and Laughton looked at Welsh. 'That it?'

Welsh nodded, grinning like a lunatic. ''At's it, mate,' he slurred. 'Now we better get the fuck out of it.'

They were only halfway back across the compound when the bomb exploded with a roar, blowing the leg to pieces, causing the whole mess hut to keel over like a sinking ship, and instantly setting fire to the timber wall and thatched roof.

The men inside were bawling, rolling across the tilting floor, bouncing off one another or into the tables and chairs that had toppled over and were also on the move. As the flames licked higher and the hut tilted more steeply, some of the men inside burst through the front door or clambered out through windows to drop to the ground, thinking they were being attacked by the CT.

Thinking the same, the men in the defensive trenches opened fire on the dark jungle with their Bren guns and M1 rifles.

The warning siren went off, adding to the general bedlam.

Having thrown themselves to the earth when hearing the explosion, Welsh, Laughton and the other men turned around and sat up, staring in amazement as yellow flames flickered along the wall of the mess hut, then engulfed the thatched roof.

'Shit!' Welsh hissed.

'Jesus Christ!' Laughton whispered.

'We're in for it now,' Jack Clayton said. 'That fucking bomb *worked*, mate!'

When Welsh saw Sergeant Lorrimer walking grimly towards him, he offered his crazy grin.

The next morning, when a surprisingly urbane, even amused, Captain Lidgate had been lifted off by an Army Air Corps Weston Dragonfly helicopter, Callaghan, having assumed command, took the unusual step of holding a disciplinary hearing and fining all of the men known to be involved in the explosion.

While it seemed lenient, the system of fines was one of the punishments Callaghan had decided would be more apt in this particular environment, where being 'confined to barracks' had no relevance whatsoever and imprisonment was out of the question.

Though he intended getting rid of the ringleaders, Welsh and Laughton, when the Regiment returned to Johore, Callaghan withheld this information on the grounds that it would adversely effect their performance while in the *ulu*. Nevertheless, he was now aware that something *had* to be done – as Sergeant Lorrimer had told him more than once.

'There's a lot of energy out there,' Sergeant Lorrimer said after the bombing, 'bottled up and about to explode. That's what caused that unholy prank last night.'

'Then let's give them something to do,' Callaghan replied. 'Let's start the deep reconnaissance patrols. That should burn up their energy.'

'And hopefully kill the bastards,' Lorrimer said. 'That might be a blessing.'

'God's will be done.'

# 8

The policy of cutting off food and ensuring political isolation had been successful in driving the CT deeper into the jungle. The Security Forces were therefore obliged to pursue the enemy there, which gave the SAS a second chance to prove its value and, at the same time, enabled Captain Callaghan to find work for his more troublesome men.

While relatively orthodox units, such as the Gurkha, Malay, African and Fijian battalions, concentrated on harrying the guerrillas of Johore, Callaghan's men were making their first serious contact with the aboriginal tribes of the interior. Their main task was to protect the Sakai jungle-dwellers, who, being completely at the mercy of the guerrillas, had been forced deeper into their service as a source of food and reluctant manpower. Now Callaghan's men, moving out from the base camp, or Forward Observation Base – for it was, indeed, a combination of both – began to win over these nomad tribesmen, often staying with them for considerable periods of time, sometimes as long as thirteen weeks, before being relieved by other men from the base camp.

One of their main tasks was to build landing strips or helicopter landing pads to enable the aboriginals to sell their supplies. They also brought them medical and engineering aid. In particularly dangerous situations, where the CT were terrorizing a village, the SAS simply moved the whole village and helped the natives rebuild a new home elsewhere. These 'new' communities became known, simply and logically, as 'New Villages'.

Generally speaking, the New Villages needed a remote part of the jungle, well away from any paths which might be used by prying Malays, yet not too far from the kampongs which would supply them with food. A good defensive position was needed for the guard post, if possible on the only way into the camp. Water, and *atap* for thatching, had to be near at hand.

Most of these New Villages, in effect kampongs, all took similar form: a small piece of ground capable of being levelled for a parade ground and a sports ground: two long huts near by for the men: a smaller headquarters housed a little back from the others, a cookhouse, preferably beside a stream, and communal latrines. The villages were then turned into fortresses, in which police posts and even artillery were established.

Much of the success of these New Villages depended on the few lone SAS troopers who lived in them for long periods to sell the aboriginals the idea of self-defence. This was part of the battle for hearts and minds.

For a couple of months Callaghan engaged his SF in Operation Spiderweb, designed to saturate a known CT area with troops so that the guerrillas' mode of life would be disrupted. A concentrated programme of police checks on roads and New Villages was put into action, forcing the bandits to retreat and use up their invaluable food reserves, which were always hidden deep in the *ulu*. When this campaign was in progress, more military units moved in to specific areas where it was hoped, by intensive ambushes and patrols, to force the terrorists out into the open or into the many 'stop' or ambush points established on tracks in the *ulu*.

Helping the SAS were Gurkhas, Royal Marine Commandos, twenty-two Jungle Companies of the Malayan Field Police Force, and Iban trackers from Sarawak, former headhunters who, though fierce fighters, had to be trained by the SAS in the fundamentals of modern soldiering. Now formally recognized as a locally raised unit of the British Army and named the Sarawak Rangers, they were issued with rifles which they used with more enthusiasm than skill. Nevertheless, they were invaluable as trackers and guides.

Thus, because of Operation Spiderweb, the SAS was living more and more in the jungle, engaging in a series of long, arduous, and usually dangerous operations that certainly burned off the excess energy of the SAS troublemakers.

A typical CT 'cleansing' operation was a joint effort between the RAF and the SF. When the enemy was identified as being concentrated in a particular area, the RAF would mount a heavy bombing raid of the jungle location by RAF Lincolns. A couple of SAS squadrons would then parachute into the area cleared – or more accurately, devastated – by the bombing. They would then either take out the surviving CT or, if the survivors had fled, take command of the area, ensuring that any remaining crops were destroyed, to further deprive the CT of food.

'The system obviously works,' Captain Callaghan said to Sergeant Lorrimer during a meeting in the wood-and-thatch HQ in the jungle base camp, 'but I view it as an indiscriminate use of air power, as likely to kill aboriginals as guerrillas. It is, therefore, in the long run, counterproductive, so I think we should find a better way.'

'I agree. Those bombing raids cause shocking destruction and do often kill the very people we're trying to protect.'

'Any ideas?'

'My belief is that instead of depending on the RAF to clear the way for us, we should concentrate even more on putting small groups of men into the *ulu*. We leave them there for as long as they're required to relay back all the intelligence they can gather on the guerrillas, when not actually harassing them with various acts of sabotage or raids on their camps. They can wage a hearts-and-minds campaign at the same time, thus doubling their effectiveness.'

'I agree with you in principle, but I'm not at all sure how long a small team left to their own devices would remain effective in the *ulu*. They might even go mad.'

'You did it alone for three months. Major Pryce-Jones did it for six. If you can do it, a team of four or five men, even only two, should find it less difficult.'

Callaghan laughed. 'I thought you were going to say easier.'

Lorrimer shook his head, grinning. 'I wouldn't dare.'

'I sometimes think I *did* go mad in that bloody jungle.'

'Not that you'd notice, boss.'

Callaghan grinned and nodded, as if agreeing with Lorrimer's judgement, then became more thoughtful again. 'Well, maybe it's actually easier to do it alone. At least you can only fight with yourself. On the other hand, four or five men, even two, locked together in that isolation, might more quickly get on one another's nerves.'

'I think if we select the right kind of men, we'd be OK. Types like young Parker.'

'Dead-eye Dick.'

'Yes. He hasn't seen action before, but he's a natural if ever I saw one. His endurance during his jungle training was phenomenal. His skill with shotguns and rifles is already the talk of the Regiment, and he can use that crossbow like nobody's business. He also appears to have nerves of steel. What's more, he's modest to the point of shyness.'

'A shy killer,' Callaghan suggested.

'He could be,' Lorrimer replied. 'I've known his type before. There were quite a few in the Long Range Desert Group and we had at least one in Force 136. Modest men, decent in every other respect, but able to kill without qualms. The two combined – the modesty and the killer instinct – make them invaluable.'

'What are you driving at, Sarge?' Callaghan was grinning. 'What are you after?'

'I'm suggesting you let me take a two-man team into the *ulu* and see just how far I can push it, how much we can do.'

'Anything else?'

'Well, I *have* been thinking of our conversation about the lack of time we had to properly pick the kind of men we need for the Regiment. Obviously, we can fix that by weeding out the last of the bad apples, but I still believe that by the time we return to England, we should have evolved a specific, very rigorous selection and training programme that'll ensure only the best make it through. Selection, training, then further training in highly specialized areas. So part of the reason for this jungle hike is to find out just what kind of training will be involved.'

'Right, Sergeant, I'll buy that. Who do you want?'

'Just two men and a Sakai guide, who we'll pick up *en route*. But initially, just two men. Me and . . .'

'Dead-eye Dick.' Callaghan's soft chuckle cut him short. 'Oh, you *are* subtle, Sergeant!'

Now Lorrimer chuckled. 'Well, a man has his reasons.'

'No one else?'

'No. Let's begin modestly to minimize possible damage. Dead-eye's perfect for this.'

'OK, you've got him. When do you want to leave?'

'Tomorrow,' Lorrimer said.

'Aren't you the keen one?' Callaghan sighed, perhaps wishing he could go as well. 'So how do you plan to insert?'

'By parachute.'

'Tree-jumping.'

'Yes.'

'I think we should stop that.'

'There's no other way.'

Callaghan sighed again, this time sadly. 'No, I suppose not.'

By now the SAS had made frequent parachute jumps into the *ulu* and suffered many casualties in their dangerous attempts to perfect tree-jumping. These casualties had occurred mainly because of the unpredictable behaviour of the parachutes as they were 'bounced' by the thermal effect of air above the trees. However, in the view of many officers, including Callaghan, the technique of abseiling out of the trees was also proving to be more dangerous than it was worth.

In theory, the soldier detached himself from his parachute, lashed a long webbing strap to a branch, and descended safely to the ground.

In practice, however, the webbing often bulged at intervals, where it had been stitched, and therefore snagged at high speed as it travelled through the D-rings on the soldier's harnesses. All too frequently this would jerk him to a violent halt, sometimes smashing him against the tree, resulting in broken bones or even death, the latter usually occurring when the parachutist, badly hurt and unable to stand the pain, cut himself loose from his snagged harness and fell at least 100 feet to the forest floor. Nevertheless, as tree-jumping was the only way to get into the areas cleared by the RAF bombing raids, it remained the Standard Operating Procedure of the campaign.

'Well,' Lorrimer said after a long silence, 'do I have your permission?'

'If you're going to do it, I suppose you're going to do it. The quicker the better, Sarge. Tomorrow it is.'

'Thanks, boss,' Lorrimer said, beaming with pleasure. 'I'd better get started straight away then; fix things up with Dead-eye.'

'Yes, Sergeant, you do that.'

Lorrimer left the HQ, almost dancing down the steps of the verandah under the overhanging roof of thatched palms, then walked the short distance to the radio shack. Once there, he had the on-duty trooper, Trooper Jack Clayton, radio back to Johore to say that he would require a Beverley for a two-man parachute jump, taking off approximately at first light. Leaving the radio shack, he went to the nearby helicopter landing pad where the pilot, Lieutenant Ralph Ellis of the Army Air Corps, was, as usual, lovingly tending his Sikorski S-55 Whirlwind.

'Pissing around as usual, are you, boss?' Sergeant Lorrimer said in the informal manner already ingrained in the SAS.

Lieutenant Ellis grinned. 'Keeps me busy, Sarge. What can I do for you?'

'I need to be flown back to Johore with another man tomorrow morning, a couple of hours before first light.

Ellis winced. 'You mean I have to get out of bed?'

''Fraid so, boss.'

'Four a.m.?'

'That sounds reasonable.'

'Who's the other man?'

'Trooper Richard Parker.'

'Dead-eye.'

'Correct.'

'What are you two up to, Sarge?'

'We're making a jump into the *ulu* and the Beverleys can't land here.'

'That's why I love my helicopter,' Ellis said,

stroking the green-painted fuselage of his beloved Whirlwind. 'She can go fast or slow, move up or down, take any number of positions. She's a real little beauty.'

Lorrimer grinned at the sexual connotations. 'No wonder you guys are glamorous to the ladies. I'm in the wrong business.'

'I would have to agree, Sarge.'

'Four a.m.?'

'I'll be here,' Ellis said.

'Good. See you then, boss.' Lorrimer turned away and crossed the sports ground to the spider, which, like the other buildings, was raised off the ground and made from timber and palm leaves and thatched with *atap*. On the sports ground near the barracks a few of the troopers, stripped to the waist and gleaming with sweat, were kicking a football between them in a desultory manner. Some of their mates were sitting around slugging Tiger beer from bottles and either idly watching their friends playing or enjoying the sunset. Gurkhas were relaxing on the verandah of their own barracks, as were the few remaining Royal Marine Commandos. The small group of Sarawak Rangers had their own quarters: a thatched house of the kind they would have lived in in Borneo and which they had constructed themselves. Trench fires were smoking around the sports ground and the inviting smell of cooking food filled the cooling evening air, doubtless tormenting the men in the defensive trenches located around the circular compound and facing out towards the jungle.

Entering the gloomy spider, which now had fans in the ceiling and was therefore much cooler than outside, Lorrimer marched between the facing rows of timber-and-thatch bashas, nodding at some of the men as he passed. Pete Welsh was lying flat on his back, stark naked, with an impressive erection, listening to Elvis Presley singing about teddy bears on the radio. On the bed beside him, Alf Laughton, completely ignoring Welsh's erection, was biting his lower lip as he concentrated on writing a letter home. Other men were also listening to radios, writing letters, leafing through pin-up magazines or books, smoking or checking their personal kit.

Lorrimer stopped when he came to young Dead-eye, who was sitting on the edge of his bed, meticulously cleaning his standard-issue M1 carbine. His 9mm Browning High Power handgun was lying on the bed, polished and oiled. Also on the bed, all polished, were his bayonet, Fairburn-Sykes commando knife and *parang*. Dead-eye, it was clear, took good care of his personal equipment.

'Hi, boss,' he said, looking up at Lorrimer with his steady, oddly opaque grey gaze and hesitant smile. 'You want me?'

'I'm thinking of going for a little hike into the jungle. Long-term. Just you and me. Doing anything and everything. It's kind of an experiment, so you don't have to come if you don't want to. You have to volunteer, kid.'

'I volunteer,' Dead-eye said.

'We leave for Johore by chopper at four in the morning, then fly in by Beverley from there.'

'Tree-jumping?'

'Yes.'

'What do I need?'

'What you've got here, plus a full kit, smoke, phosphorus and fragmentation grenades, flares, PRC 319, SARBE beacon, a 9mm Owen submachine-gun, a Browning 12-gauge autoloader shotgun and the crossbow.'

'Sounds like fun,' Dead-eye said.

'It just might be. Do you have any questions?'

'No,' Dead-eye said. 'Four a.m. at the chopper pad, then.'

'That's it. But make sure you collect those other weapons tonight.'

'Will do, Sarge.'

Lorrimer was walking back out of the barracks

when Dennis the Menace and Boney Maronie entered, both stripped to the waist and covered in sweat. Lorrimer stopped to ask: 'What have you two been up to? You look all hot and bothered. Having a little hanky-panky, were you?'

'Hey, give us a break, Sarge!' Boney Maronie said, outraged. 'I'm as straight as they come.'

'Not as straight as that erection on Pete Welsh,' Lorrimer said. 'He must have it up for sale.'

Both men glanced along the spider at Pete Welsh's impressive erection, which Welsh himself was ignoring.

'Mmmmm,' Boney Maronie said. 'About half the size of mine. He wants someone to give it a tug and make it grow bigger.'

'Why don't you help him out instead of making each other sweat in mysterious ways?'

'Football,' Dennis the Menace said firmly. 'No more and no less, Sarge. We were both playing football. So what are you doing here?'

'I came to invite Dead-eye for an extended trip into the jungle.'

'Extended? How long?'

'Two or three weeks. Maybe longer.'

'Just you and Dead-eye?' Boney Maronie asked.

'That's right.'

'Sounds real cosy,' Dennis the Menace said with

a wicked grin. 'Going to work up a sweat between you, are you?'

'*Touché*,' Lorrimer said, grinning and waving his right hand as he left the spider.

# 9

Looking down through one of the many windows of the almost empty Beverley, Dead-eye could see the canopy of the jungle, stretching out to the horizon like a green sea gaining colour in the brightening pearly-grey light of dawn. The trees looked impenetrable, like an almost solid mass. It was hard to believe that beneath them were streams, waterfalls, swamps, a myriad of wildlife, thriving Sakai kampongs – and approximately 2,000 Communist guerrillas. It was also hard to believe that you could actually parachute down and find enough space between the trees to reach the ground. Nevertheless, that was what he would be doing in a few minutes' time.

'We're coming in low,' the RAF Loadmaster said. 'Three hundred and fifty metres, to be precise. So you better be quick, boys.'

'No sweat,' Sergeant Lorrimer said. 'We've often

come in even lower than that, so we're not so concerned.'

'The brave lads of the SAS,' said the Loadmaster in an ironic voice. 'I'd like to recommend my mother-in-law to the Regiment. I desperately need to get rid of her.'

It was a backhanded compliment that made Lorrimer grin, while also reminding him and Dead-eye that the jump they were about to make was not without danger.

'You OK?' Lorrimer asked.

'Sure,' Dead-eye replied, meaning it, secretly thrilled that Lorrimer had chosen him above all the others for this special task.

Inevitably, the rest of the lads had given him a terrible ribbing the night before, making the anticipated jokes about 'hot-bedding' with Sergeant Lorrimer and how older men lusted after white-cheeked cherry boys. It was all good-natured fun and Dead-eye didn't mind it a bit, though he wished they'd stop calling him a 'cherry boy', which was a George Town whore's term for a male virgin. He didn't have a steady girlfriend, but Dead-eye was no virgin.

In fact, he'd lost his virginity at sixteen to an older woman, a so-called 'aunt', actually a girlfriend of his father's. Since then he'd had it pretty regularly, occasionally with girls his own age, but mostly with rather older women, whom he found were content with the sex and didn't expect too many sweet words from him.

Dead-eye was uncomfortable with conversation in general, but even more so with the endearments that most girls of his own age expected. Having spent his formative years watching his father beat his mother, he didn't have much faith in romantic love.

His father was a long-distance lorry driver, born and bred in West Croydon, which he had never left, except when driving across Britain or on the Continent. Parker senior was an alcoholic who liked football, darts, horse-racing, the dogs and women, in that order; but his wife came last on his long list of the latter.

Dead-eye had spent most of his childhood huddling in corners in his parents' house on a West Croydon council estate, looking on in terror and incomprehension as his father, roaring drunk, took out his spleen with fist and boot on his wife. Eventually, when Dead-eye was twelve or thirteen, he attempted to defend his mother and was pummelled almost senseless for his troubles.

Thereafter, like a wild animal smelling blood, Dead-eye's father started beating him instead of his mother. The teenager took this as a kind of victory, but when he received no thanks from his mother – who by now was deadening her pain by joining her husband in his drinking binges – he retreated into himself and gazed out upon the world with gravely suspicious eyes.

By the time he was eighteen, Dead-eye had realized that the only way he could retain his dignity was to leave home for good. Wanting to travel but not having the money to do so, needing adventure but not knowing how to find it, he took the only option that someone with his education, or lack of it, could take: he enlisted in the Army.

It was the best thing he could possibly have done. After passing his three months of basic training with flying colours, he was posted to the 2nd Battalion, Royal Regiment of Fusiliers, where his prowess on the firing range soon became almost legendary. Gratified by this, gaining pride and dignity from it, he realized that while he loved being a soldier, he still needed to do more than he was doing, which was basically an uninspiring routine of drill, training, and guard duties. So, when he heard that the renowned World War Two regiment, the SAS was being reformed to fight the war, or the Emergency, in Malaya, he applied to join. Though the selection process was brutally hard, he again passed with flying colours and soon found himself on a Hercules C-130, bound for Malaya. He had never been happier.

Now, sitting beside Sergeant Lorrimer in the otherwise empty hold of the Beverley, he felt that he was in very good company.

He was well aware of the fact that Lorrimer, apart from being a naturally likeable man, was a veteran of World War Two, a former member of the legendary Long Range Desert Group, then of the original 1 SAS, also in North Africa, and finally of Force 136, the clandestine resistance unit set up by the Special Operations Executive during World War Two for operations in Japanese-occupied Malaya.

In fact, Lorrimer was the kind of soldier that Dead-eye eventually wanted to become. Admiring and respecting the older man, he was truly proud to have been picked to be his partner for this dangerous mission.

'Stand up!' the Loadmaster bawled, opening the starboard door in the fuselage and letting the slipstream roar in. 'Action stations!'

'Hi, ho,' Sergeant Lorrimer said. 'On your feet, kid.'

'Aye, aye, boss.'

Dead-eye and Lorrimer stood up together, both heavily burdened with their parachutes, packed bergens, bandoliers, webbing and weapons.

'I'll go out first as the drifter,' Sergeant Lorrimer said to Dead-eye as the Loadmaster, whipped by the roaring slipstream, placed the boxed supplies by the open door, preparing to parachute them down into the jungle. 'Stay close behind me and as soon as I go out, place yourself on the ramp and wait until you see my parachute open. Only jump when you've checked the strength and direction of the wind from my decent.'

'Right, boss, I've got it.'

'I'm not finished yet.' Sergeant Lorrimer was being serious. 'When you're descending and have popped your parachute, keep your eyes on the jungle canopy, as well as on me, to ensure that you not only fall close to me, but drop down through a clearing in the forest. The supplies will go down first and we'll pick them up when we land. Have you got that?'

'Yes, Sarge.'

Lorrimer patted Dead-eye on the shoulder. 'I'm sure you have,' he said, then turned away to take his position behind the boxed supplies piled up near the open door.

The Loadmaster raised the thumb of his right hand, then pushed the wooden crates out. Being on static lines, the parachutes on the crates would be deployed at a predetermined height by a line connected to the aircraft. When the Loadmaster had checked that the chutes had opened successfully, he disconnected the static lines and waved

Lorrimer forward. Using standard-issue Irvin-X Type parachutes, Lorrimer and Dead-eye would have to 'pop' them themselves.

Lorrimer braced himself on the rim of the doorway, his body being whipped by the roaring slipstream. When the Loadmaster patted him on the shoulder and bawled 'Right!', Lorrimer threw himself out.

As soon as Lorrimer had disappeared, Dead-eye took his place on the edge of the doorway, holding on to the sides to keep the roaring wind from sucking him out. Looking down, he saw Lorrimer being swept briefly, violently sideways on the slipstream, above the already opened parachutes of the supply crates; then, escaping from it, dropping like a stone towards the jungle canopy 1,000 feet below. Almost immediately – or, to be more precise, as soon as he fell vertically – Lorrimer released his parachute. Dead-eye saw it billowing up like a white flower in that sea of sun-streaked greenery. Both the Loadmaster and Dead-eye watched Lorrimer's descent, gauging from it the strength and direction of the wind; then, as if thinking in tandem, the Loadmaster patted Dead-eye's shoulder, bawled 'Right', and Dead-eye threw himself out.

There was an even louder roaring. The breath was dragged from his lungs. The next thing he knew – though by now he was getting used to it – he was free of the slipstream, releasing his parachute, and floating down through the air, dazzled by the vast blue sweep of the morning sky, then by the approaching sea of green jungle, feeling magically, even transcendentally, alive.

Immediately below him, he saw the billowing white flower of Sergeant Lorrimer's parachute. Below that, he saw the smaller chutes of the supply crates – at least they looked smaller because they were further down – already nearing the dense jungle canopy.

As the first of the supply crates made contact with the canopy, either becoming tagged on the treetops or smashing on down to the jungle floor, Dead-eye used the strings on his chute to manoeuvre in the direction of Lorrimer. The descent was very quick, leaving little time for calculation, and Lorrimer was already disappearing through the treetops when Dead-eye managed to head in his direction. By the time Lorrimer had disappeared, the trees were rushing up at Dead-eye ever faster. He saw a gap and tried to manoeuvre into it, but hit the treetops anyway.

The former silence of his descent exploded with the sounds of his fall, as huge palm leaves, branches, creeping vines and creepers tried to ensnare him, then broke and gave way to let him fall through. He was trapped, stopped, broke free, fell again, then heard a snapping, cracking and hissing as he bounced, twisted and fell through showering leaves, flowers, broken branches and tendrils of rattan. He stopped about 30 feet above the ground, span rapidly, smashed into sharp branches and thorns, then came to a standstill, dangling in mid-air on the end of his harness.

Dazed, he blinked repeatedly, breathed deeply, then looked down at the jungle floor.

Lorrimer, already divested of his parachute and bergen, was looking up at him from a dark hole that Dead-eye soon realized was just the ground way below.

'Are you all right?' Lorrimer bawled.

'Yes!' Dead-eye bawled back.

'You'll have to abseil the rest of the way. Come on, kid, get moving!'

Feeling that he was being dragged down by the weight of his combined parachute, packed bergen, webbing, bandoliers and strapped-on weapons, Dead-eye was convinced he was about to fall. In the event, he didn't. Extremely calmly and carefully, he uncoiled his knotted rope, tied it around a particularly thick branch, let the rest of it drop down to the jungle floor, then used his commando knife to cut his parachute harness away from the foliage and started lowering himself down on the rope, using the knots as convenient grips. The combined weight of his bergen and other kit caused him agony, but eventually, when only 10 feet above the ground, he was able to let the rope go and drop the rest of the way. He fell in a clattering tangle of kit and weapons, feeling battered and bruised, into a thick carpet of dead leaves and seedling trees.

Picking himself up, he saw Lorrimer grinning at him.

'About bloody time,' the Sergeant said. 'The supplies all dropped in the vicinity, so let's go and collect them.'

'Yes, boss,' Dead-eye said.

# 10

Lone men in the jungle require the skills of the hunter: concealment, tracking, endurance, coolness and a lethally accurate shot. All of these were abilities perfected by Sergeant Lorrimer during his time with Force 136 in Malaya in 1943. Combined with them were a quick intelligence, relentless determination, and a good ear for foreign languages. As the admiring Dead-eye soon found out, the Yorkshireman could fire his Browning 12-gauge autoloader shotgun with high accuracy at a speed which made the first half-dozen shots seem like one. He could also speak fluent Malay, Chinese and Siamese, which gave him another advantage in the *ulu*.

Indeed, their first stop after the first day's gruelling hike through the gloomy, humid jungle, heavily burdened with their overpacked bergens, weapons and supplies, was a Sakai house which, like all such houses, was built on a slope to ensure that the front was high above the ground. It consisted of one large room, about 30 feet square, under a single ridge of *atap* thatching, with each gable extended to form lengthy extensions to the main room. Except for the uprights of the house, the whole framework was of bamboo. The floor was of symmetrical slats of bamboo lashed with fine rattan to the floor joists with a 'breathing' space between each slat. The main part of the house was surrounded by a balustrade of flattened bamboo surmounted by a single large bamboo, which fenced off the extensions so that they resembled loose boxes. They were used as guest rooms. The ridge of *atap* thatch that extended over the railing at night was rolled back during the day to let in cool air and light.

The house belonged to the village head, Abang Kasut, an old friend of Lorrimer's from the days when they had fought the Japanese together. Abang was a well-fed, amiable man who looked slightly licentious and self-satisfied. This could have been because he had a very large family, including many wives, all of whom were bare-breasted, wearing only a *sarong* of cloth or bark. Some had red, white or ochre paint smeared on their faces, and a few were ornamented with a matchstick thrust through the piece of flesh below and between the nostrils. All were smoke-stained and unwashed, but a few were beautiful, with luxuriant black hair tied in a bun held up with a bamboo comb. Their children, with round, dark eyes and pot bellies, seemed very happy.

'You live in the wrong country, my young friend,' Abang informed Dead-eye, noting how he could hardly take his eyes off the bare-breasted women. 'A man requires so many different things in a woman, he is hardly likely to find it in one, so he needs many wives. This is more civilized, yes?'

'I'm not sure that the wives would agree,' Dead-eye replied.

'Of course they do,' Abang insisted. 'Having to share my attentions with all the others removes the great burden of a single wife's servitude. They are happier this way.'

'And I'm sure *you're* not suffering, Abang,' Sergeant Lorrimer said.

The aboriginal roared with laughter, slapped his own pot belly, then poured liquid from a jar into three glasses. 'Here,' he said, handing a glass each to Lorrimer and Dead-eye, 'have a drink of *samsu*. It will make you feel less tired.'

In certain ways, being in this village was like returning to the Stone Age. The youths and older men carried 8-foot blow-pipes with bamboo quivers for poisoned arrows ornamented with strange conventional designs. Dressed only in a scanty loincloth, each carried on his back a small bag closely woven with fine rattan to hold his tobacco, flint, steel and tinder. The older men also carried an apparatus for preparing betel nut for chewing. Many of them wore strings of coloured beads looped over their shoulders, crossing front and behind, with more beads or an amulet of some kind around their necks. Some also wore a circle of woven and patterned bark to keep their hair in place, invariably with bright flowers tucked into it.

Lorrimer and Dead-eye spent the night in the headman's house, enjoying a lengthy meal of turtle soup followed by a combination of pig, *kijang* (barking deer), monkey and snake meat, with side dishes of sweet potatoes, lizard eggs, mixed vegetables with spices and ginger, and fried rice. This gourmet banquet was washed down with more *samsu*, a strong spirit distilled from rice, which soon got them drunk, encouraging Lorrimer and Abang to reminisce fondly about old times.

It did not escape Dead-eye's attention that when they discussed the fate of old friends from the war, both British and Sakai, a surprising number of them – indeed, the majority – had been captured and beheaded by the Japanese.

Nevertheless, clearly inspired by such recollections to have another adventure, Abang agreed to join them the next morning as their guide through the jungle.

'It will make me feel young again,' he said. 'I grow fat and lazy in this village, being served hand and foot. You come here to save me from myself, so how can I say no?'

Though stowing a lot of their gear in a covered trench beneath Abang's raised house, where it would not be found if the CT turned up, they moved out at first light still carrying 25-pound loads each, including a 9mm Owen sub-machine-gun, one Browning 12-gauge autoloader shotgun, full magazines for both weapons, the crossbow with 24 lightweight slim alloy bolts and arrows, six No. 80 white phosphorus incendiary hand-grenades, 9mm Browning High Power handguns, a week's food, water bottles, one change of clothes, groundsheets without blankets, a pair of field-glasses, a button compass and small-scale maps, *parangs*, commando knives, fishing line and hooks, and a basic medical kit that included antibiotics, antihistamine, water-sterilizing tablets, anti-malaria tablets, painkillers, and a good supply of waterproof plasters and bandages.

'No condoms,' Sergeant Lorrimer joked to Dead-eye. 'That means you're in for some real work.'

It did not take long for Dead-eye to understand why they needed an aboriginal guide, no matter how well they had been trained at Johore. Born and bred in the *ulu*, Abang had a keen eye for the most minute traces of human movement through the jungle, such as dislodged pieces of bark, broken branches, twisted leaves, threads of clothing caught on twigs, and even broken spiders' webs. Sometimes the terrorists would deliberately go without shoes in the hopes of making the Security Forces think the footprints were those of aboriginals, but Abang could tell the difference because, as he informed Lorrimer and Dead-eye, the aboriginals had splayed toe-prints whereas the terrorist footprint revealed toes cramped in by being normally encased in shoes or boots. Abang even showed them where some terrorists had attempted to blur their tracks by treading lightly in the footmarks of an elephant.

'They often use the footmarks of a *seladang* as well,' he said. 'The wild ox or bison of Malaya. Unless you look with extreme care, you will see only the footmark of the animal, not of the man.'

'This information is invaluable,' Sergeant Lorrimer told him. 'However, our first requirement is for a long-term hide-out from which we can forage through the *ulu* at will.'

'I have just the place,' Abang replied with confidence.

He led them upstream, across a high pile of fallen

trees, along a side stream, and through a bamboo thicket which retained no footprints. Following a narrow track slightly uphill, they came to a trench about 6 feet deep, 3 feet wide and 30 feet long, opening at its far end into a chamber about 12 feet square and 10 feet high, hollowed out of a steep bank of red clay and scrub-covered rock. This natural cave was covered by a belt of tangled bamboo 40 feet high, which would hide the smoke of a camp-fire. Surprisingly, the hollow was filled with old packing crates.

'I lived here for months,' Abang explained, 'to avoid the Japanese during the war. Later, I used it to hide from Ah Hoi's guerrillas. I am still alive, so it must be a safe place.'

Using a *changkol* – the large hoe which replaces the spade in Malaya – each of the men dug himself a scrape to lie in. A large tent was raised over the three scrapes. The *changkol* was also used to level a platform outside the tent, where they placed a crude table and chairs made from the packing crates. Over this they placed bamboo split in half and laid alternate ways up to make a covering against the rain. In a small patch of garden, they found plenty of edible tapioca.

Lorrimer and Dead-eye then settled in to learn about survival in this alien environment. They were taught well by Abang.

For the first few meals they caught fish by dropping small charges of gelignite into the pools. The tiny explosions dazed the fish, which could then be lifted out by hand – a process that required no great skill and was known to most of the SAS troopers. Later, however, when Abang took them over, they explored the jungle in search of pig, *kijang* and even monkeys. The pigs were scarce, but they managed to shoot a few barking deer.

To attract the deer, Abang would hide in the jungle and give out a piercing scream with the aid of a small section of bamboo split in a traditional Sakai manner. If there were any *kijang* within earshot, they would reply with their harsh bark and come closer, doing so each time Abang gave out his scream, until finally they were in range of Lorrimer's shotgun.

Dead-eye began using his standard-issue M1 carbine for anything larger than monkeys, though in the jungle, as he soon noticed, you rarely get a good shot at anything over fifty yards away. Nevertheless, he soon became as good as Lorrimer, and between them, with Abang's expert guidance, they shot, cooked and ate a wide variety of animals, including pigs, deer and monkeys, although the latter were low on their list of truly tasty food.

In the swamps there were a great many mud turtles, which are about the size of half a football.

Abang taught Lorrimer and Dead-eye to look for a slight cloudiness in the mud, which was an indication of the movement of a turtle just below the surface. When they saw the movement, they simply scooped the turtle up with their hands. The resulting soup was delicious – it included lichens and mosses soaked overnight in clean water – and the meat, when served on its own, was very tender and tasty.

Though less fun to catch or cook, snakes also made excellent food, being similar in taste and texture to a mixture of chicken and lobster. After Abang had removed the poisonous secretions on the skin or the venom glands from the head (in the latter case he removed the entire head) the snakes were gutted, then cooked in their skins by being placed on hot embers and turned constantly. When the heat caused the skin to split, the meat was removed and boiled. Cooked in a similar manner was the monitor lizard – a reptile 6 or 7 feet in length – whose eggs were also delicious and could be used in mixed-vegetable salads. Frogs, which had poisonous skins, were first skinned, then gutted and roasted on sticks.

On the ground of the jungle were snakes, centipedes, scorpions and giant spiders. These were dangerous. Just as dangerous, however, was the *seladang*, the wild ox or bison, which would attack humans on sight. Nevertheless, with Abang's help, they managed to shoot one and found, to their surprise, that the meat went down well with rice, sweet potato and vegetables, preferably followed by sweet coffee, *samsu* and a good cheroot. Finally, on the correct assumption that meat would not always be available, Abang taught them how to pick out edible fungi, leaves, nuts, roots, berries, and fruit from the *ulu*'s wide variety of produce, much of which was poisonous. The more edible fruits and plants had to be brought down from the jungle canopy, which entailed an arduous, dangerous climb and descent, though they soon mastered this without the aid of their abseiling ropes.

'Living off the fat of the land,' Dead-eye said after one particularly enjoyable meal of turtle soup, snake stew, wild figs, mango and coconut juice mixed with *samsu*. 'This is better than life back at home.'

Sergeant Lorrimer did not reply. He was too busy jotting down notes for the report which, as he had explained, would be the basis for a more rigorous SAS Selection, Training and Cross-Training programme, to be introduced when the Regiment was back in England.

'What's Cross-Training?' Dead-eye asked.

'Such innocence!' Sergeant Lorrimer replied. 'You're already doing it, kid.'

Before setting out on patrols in search of the CT, Lorrimer, Dead-eye and Abang practised walking and running past each other to make sure that no bit of metal caught the light and nothing could betray them by its rattle, such as ammunition, metallic kit or half-used boxes of matches. They even wrapped their weapons in adhesive tape to stop them shining in the moonlight.

With a little practice, they learned to walk heel first on hard ground and toe first on softer ground, so that they passed absolutely silently and were, with their camouflaged clothes and darkened faces, virtually invisible.

To walk in this way required much practice. As it called for the use of muscles not normally used, it was initially exhausting, though eventually it became second nature to them.

To follow a jungle path, even on a moonlit night, it was necessary to use light of some sort, so they put a green leaf inside the glass, not only to make the torch less bright, but to accustom their eyes to a dim light. If the battery ran out, a few fireflies or luminous centipedes in the reflector of the torch gave just enough light to read a map, lay a charge or even follow a path through the *ulu*.

The three of them temporarily gave up smoking because the use of tobacco affects one's sense of smell – and that was often the first means they had of detecting a nearby enemy. Also, they evolved a special system of signals that made talk unnecessary. One was a clicking noise between the upper teeth and side of the tongue – the sound used to encourage a horse. This was an excellent signal, being made very softly yet carrying a great distance on a still night. Even if the enemy heard it, they would probably mistake it for a bird, an insect or a rubber nut falling off a tree. A single click meant 'Stop' or 'Danger'.

The only other signal they needed was a rallying cry. For this they imitated the hunting cry of Britain's tawny owl, a piercing sound which carries a great distance even in thick woodland. It cannot be confused with any other cry heard in the Malayan jungle, yet to the uninitiated it passes without notice in the wide variety of weird nocturnal sounds.

Occasionally they would catch a brief glimpse of a jungle tiger, a few leaf-eating monkeys or some noisy gibbons. There were abundant signs of pig in the deep, muddy puddles which were their wallows, and where the rivers were bordered by meadows of green grass, kept short by water buffalo, or Chinese vegetable gardens.

The leeches, which were everywhere, were tormenting. By now, however, Lorrimer and Dead-eye had become inured to them (Abang hardly noticed them) and followed the Chinese custom of putting a pinch of their reddish fine-cut tobacco on each bite. This congealed the blood and stopped it flowing, but before long their legs, particularly the shins and ankles, were covered in suppurating, stinking sores about an inch across and a quarter of an inch deep. Pus poured out of them and, as a result of infection, the lymphatic glands in their groins became so painful and swollen that at times they could hardly walk, much less go hunting or on recce patrols. When sulphathiazole powder had also failed to cure them, they managed to draw the pus from the wounds by smearing the tar-like Chinese substance, *kow-yok*, on a piece of cloth and covering the wounds with it. This treatment also protected the wounds from the water.

Once on patrol, they were surprised by the number of rivers they had to cross. The jungle sometimes rose to hundreds of feet, from which altitude, through windows in the jungle wall, they could see its sheer extent, as well as the many rubber estates further west. Those steep hills, however, also turned some of the many rivers into foaming torrents that rushed, roaring, between boulders, slabs of granite and high mud banks.

Sometimes they took boats, less than 10 feet long and pointed at each end. With the two bergens in the stern, the three men could fit in, one behind the other, if they stretched out their legs on either side of the man in front. Abang also taught them to build two different kinds of jungle raft.

The bamboo raft consisted of two layers of thick bamboo in lengths of 10 feet. Holes were pierced through the bamboo canes near both ends and in the middle. Thin stakes were passed through the holes to connect the bamboo canes together. The canes were then lashed to the stakes with twine, rattan or strong vines. The second deck of the raft was made exactly the same way and laid on top of the first. The two layers were then lashed together.

The gripper bar raft, which was even quicker to build, required logs for the deck and four thick, slightly pliable stakes, long enough to overlap the width of the deck. Two of the stakes were placed on the ground, spaced apart to make a distance slightly shorter than the length of the logs. The logs were laid over the stakes, overlapping to similar lengths each end. The other stakes were placed on top of the logs, parallel with the stakes on the bottom. Each pair of stakes was tied firmly together on one side. A man standing on the logs then held the stakes down on the other side while a second man lashed them together so that the logs were gripped firmly between them.

Both rafts could be steered with the aid of a simple paddle rudder mounted on an A-frame near one end of the deck. The A-frame was secured to the four corners of the raft with guy ropes and the rudder was tied to the A-frame to prevent it from slipping. The rudder could then also be used as a 'sweep' for propulsion. Though primitive, both rafts were perfectly adequate for travel on all but the most violent of rivers.

Often, after coming in off the cooling river or emerging soaked in sweat from the *ulu*'s dreadful humidity, they would spend the night in a deserted Sakai village, where all the houses were made of bamboo and raised on stilts.

'The villages are deserted,' Abang explained, 'either because the Sakai are up on high ground, clearing the jungle to grow tapioca and maize, or because they're fleeing from Ah Hoi's guerrillas. Ah Hoi is committing dreadful atrocities to terrorize the whole *ulu*.'

Many of the Malay kampongs, also, were deserted and once or twice the three-man team spent the night there. One night was spent in a deserted charcoal-burner's hut, drinking *samsu*; another in a coffee house run by a wizened old

Chinese man whose coffee was strongly alcoholic. They slept drunkenly and soundly those nights.

For spying purposes, Lorrimer and Dead-eye would sometimes pass themselves off as Malays or Chinese. But the easiest way was to disguise themselves as Indians and dress like Tamils, wearing the standard white shirt, a *dhoti* or *sarong* around the waist, and a white cloth, deliberately dirtied, around the head and hanging down behind. Their complexions were darkened with a mixture of coffee, lamp-black, iodine and potassium permanganate. On such missions, they always kept a pistol and a hand-grenade tucked into the tops of their *sarongs* in case of emergency.

Often, they saw Malay cyclists or Tamil bullock-carts moving along the muddy, narrow paths by the river. Following the tracks of these people invariably brought them to a Sakai village or Malay kampong where they would pick up more info on the movements of Ah Hoi's guerrillas. Though Ah Hoi's main body of guerrillas seemed to be truly invisible, the three-man team often came across isolated bands of roving guerrillas or, possibly, bandits who had to be 'neutralized', 'taken out' or 'despatched' with ruthless efficiency. This Lorrimer and Dead-eye did with the Browning Autoloader shotgun, the M1 carbine, No.

80 white-phosphorus incendiary hand-grenades, home-made bombs, and even, on occasions when silent killing was necessary, with their Fairburn-Sykes commando knives or the crossbow.

Dead-eye was the one who always used the crossbow and he was deadly with it, usually putting the lightweight slim alloy bolt and arrow into his victim's heart, or through the back or side of his neck, with unerring accuracy.

'You have the eyes of a fucking hawk,' Lorrimer told him, 'and you're just as deadly.'

When engaged in their murderous activities, the team's routine was to leave the hide-out at last light, with their faces and hands darkened, wearing battledress carefully camouflaged with patches of mud. Each of them carried a main weapon, such as the 9mm Owen sub-machine-gun, the M1 carbine or the Browning shotgun. They also carried a 9mm Browning High Power handgun and a couple of No. 80 grenades or home-made bombs. The latter were made by putting a stick of gelignite, with detonator and fuse attached, inside a tin or a section of bamboo, then filling it up with several pounds of road metal. The fuse was lit by pressing a small igniter in a copper tube, obviating the need for matches. One great advantage of making their own was that they could vary the length of the fuses, so that the explosions would continue for some time after they left the scene. This would keep the guerrillas from answering their fire or following them until they were well away from the scene.

Once, encouraged by Abang, they followed the tracks of four men for five days until they spotted the hut occupied by the guerrillas. Settling down a good distance away, they waited for an impending rainstorm to arrive. When, as they had anticipated, the sentries took shelter from the rain, Abang, Lorrimer and Dead-eye crept up to within five yards of the soaked, still smouldering camp-fire. Lorrimer then pressed the igniter on a home-made bomb and lobbed it straight through the open entrance of the thatched hut. The guerrillas screamed in panic just before the bomb exploded, destroying most of the hut and setting what was left of it on fire. When two of the four guerrillas staggered shrieking from the swirling smoke and flames, both of them on fire, they were cut down by Dead-eye, who used his M1 with methodical, fearsome efficiency.

Occasionally the team separated to pursue guerrillas who had deliberately split up to elude them. Lorrimer would not normally have done this, but he made an exception in Dead-eye's case, confident that the young man was at his best when left to himself.

He was correct in this assumption. Armed with his M1, which he could now fire as rapidly and accurately as Lorrimer fired his Browning shotgun, and employing the aboriginal tracking knowledge he had gleaned from Abang, Dead-eye pursued his quarry relentlessly through the jungle, from early afternoon to last light. Finally realizing that he could not elude this mad dog of an Englishman, the guerrilla turned around to face him in a jungle clearing. The two men were barely 20 yards apart. Dead-eye fired six rapid repeat shots with his M1, so fast they were like a single shot, and the guerrilla was picked up and slammed back down on the jungle floor, his hand frozen around his unfired weapon.

Dead-eye didn't even bother to check that the man was dead; he just turned away and retraced his own route back through the trees.

'You're pretty good,' Lorrimer said, when Dead-eye had finished reporting to him in their hide-out. 'You're almost as quick as me now.'

'Quicker,' Dead-eye firmly corrected him, without a trace of irony.

'If you say so, kid.'

The truth of this assertion became plain when, on the next patrol, Lorrimer insisted that Dead-eye act as back-marker to him and Abang, who was at the front as tracker. When they encountered a guerrilla, who burst out of the jungle firing from the hip, Dead-eye instantly fired over Lorrimer's shoulder, cutting the terrorist down while Lorrimer was still taking aim.

'Shit,' Lorrimer acknowledged, 'either I'm getting old before my time or you're a phenomenon.'

'I'm pretty good,' Dead-eye said.

Lorrimer roared with laughter and slapped Dead-eye on the shoulder, though he knew that he had just been beaten at his own game. Thereafter he treated the young with the kind of respect he usually reserved only for veterans as old and experienced as himself.

'The kid's a natural,' he said privately to Abang.

'A born killer,' Abang said.

Just after last light on their final evening in the *ulu* they came across an encampment of guerrillas who seemed surprisingly unconcerned about guarding themselves. When Lorrimer looked closer, he noticed that the few guerrillas not sleeping were smoking from what could only be opium pipes.

'*Is* it opium?' he asked Abang in a whisper.

Abang nodded his confirmation. 'Look,' he said, pointing to the guerrilla's messy lean-tos. 'They are living in squalor. That suggests they are not CT, but renegade guerrillas, now living as outlaws –

the kind who rape and pillage in the name of Communism.' Abang pointed at the guerrillas' women, all of whom were equally slovenly, and either drunk on *samsu* or drugged from constantly smoking opium. 'Those women are not trained CT. They're just jungle whores. The men are *orang jahat* – bad men. We should neutralize them.'

'Then let's do it,' Lorrimer said.

The few bandits still awake, though unguarded, were surrounded by weapons which they would doubtless use if disturbed. Lorrimer therefore decided to disturb them permanently by blowing them to Kingdom Come. For this purpose he used another home-made bomb, lobbing it high to ensure that it fell close to the lean-to. It bounced into the soft earth near one of the men smoking opium. He removed the pipe from his lips, stared uncomprehendingly at the bomb, and was turning his head lazily, in an opium daze, to gaze questioningly at the others when the bomb exploded with a thunderous clap. It caused a violent eruption of soil, loose leaves and smoke that blew the kneeling group apart and set fire to the collapsing roof and walls of the lean-to.

Even before the smoke had cleared away, Dead-eye was firing at the shadowy figures crawling and screaming on the ground. He adjusted his aim by the lines of spurting soil stitched by the bullets.

When one of the bandits actually managed to raise himself to his knees, swinging a British tommy-gun up into the firing position, Sergeant Lorrimer nearly cut him in two with a couple of bursts from his Browning autoloader. The man quivered like a bowstring, appeared to bow politely, then fell face first into the leaf-covered earth beside the still-burning fire. Another burst from Lorrimer's autoloader blew the fire apart.

Running forward, Lorrimer, Dead-eye and Abang between them checked the state of the bandits, men and women. All except one were dead. The survivor, a woman, had lost half her face and was bleeding profusely and clearly dying. Leaning over her, Abang snapped in Mandarin: 'Ah Hoi! Baby Killer! Where is he?'

The woman opened her mouth to speak, but instead coughed up blood. When Abang had wiped the blood away with an oily rag, he repeated his question: 'Ah Hoi! Baby Killer! Where is he?'

The woman coughed more blood, this time mixed with phlegm, thus clearing her throat, and eventually managed to get the words out.

'Telok Anson,' she whispered.

She coughed blood for the third and final time, then closed her dazed eyes and died.

'The Telok Anson swamp,' Abang repeated to

Lorrimer and Dead-eye. 'That place is a nightmare.'

'Our work's finished here,' Lorrimer said.

After six long, hard weeks in the *ulu* with Abang, and having finally learnt where Ah Hoi, 'Baby Killer', was hiding with his guerrillas, Lorrimer decided that they had learnt all they needed to know there and should start back to the base camp as soon as possible.

The following day, they broke up their jungle hide-out, carefully hid all traces of their presence, then hiked back to Abang's village, where they used the PRC 319 to call in the chopper of Army Air Corps pilot Lieutenant Ellis.

When the familiar, green Sikorski S-55 Whirlwind arrived, Ellis could find no space to land, but he threw down a rope ladder and Lorrimer and Dead-eye – their loads a lot lighter than when they had arrived, but still heavily laden with packed bergens and weapons – waved goodbye to Abang and hauled themselves up the ladder.

The helicopter flew them back to the base camp in no time at all.

# 11

'What I learnt,' Sergeant Lorrimer told Captain Callaghan as they sat side by side in wicker chairs on the covered verandah of the base camp's timber-and-thatch administration building, 'is that once we've weeded out the last of the cowboys, we have to implement a completely different kind of training programme. We can attempt the basics of that programme here – trying it out, as it were – before we enter the Telok Anson swamp, but a proper, full-length programme can only be put into operation once we're back in England.'

'What kind of programme?' Callaghan asked.

'I'm thinking of something more extensive than standard military training. Some form of cross-training. What we need, I believe, are men who're particularly good at most kinds of military activity – weapons, battle strategy, teamwork, endurance – but also have specialist training in other areas that ensure they're ready for just about any kind of environment or physical challenge – heat, cold, jungle, mountain, rivers, the sea, the air – at least, with regard to the latter, parachute inserts, such as our tree-jumping.'

'The men already do that in a way. Certainly each member of the four-man teams is cross-trained in signals, demolition, medicine and basic languages.'

'Correct, but only since coming here. We have to make such training the *modus operandi* of the Regiment and implement the training back in England. The men have learned those subjects here almost by accident; picked up as and when necessary, but we should teach them in depth and expand the curriculum to include specialist techniques relating to survival in jungles and deserts, at sea and on snow-covered mountains, and of course in the air. What the men have learned here so far relates only to Malaya, which means they only have an expedient, basic knowledge of it. In future, they should be prepared for all contingencies and environments before they even leave the base in England. Combined with that, there should be a much more rigorous selection programme.'

'Are you doing a report on this?'

'Yes, boss.'

'I look forward to reading it, but give me a summary.'

'I'm thinking basically about a three-part selection and training programme. First is Selection. We only consider men with at least two years' service in another regiment and who, while being self-sufficient, will have no record of troublemaking and can still work well in a team. The selection will be based on a three-week training period tougher than any devised so far, concentrating on physical stamina and endurance, as well as determination and exceptional skills at map-reading and cross-country navigation. This will be followed by a week of rigorous mental and physical testing. Those who fail, even by injury, will be returned to their original units without recourse to appeal.'

'That's pretty rough,' Callaghan said.

'That's the idea,' Lorrimer replied. 'It will rid us at an early stage of those who're psychologically and physically unsuitable, leaving only the *crème de la crème*.'

'OK, what next?'

'Those passing Basic Training and Selection go on to a few months of further training – or Continuation Training as I've called it. This consists of patrol tactics for every conceivable situation and environment, including jungle, desert, mountain and sea; advanced signalling; demolition; first-aid and combat survival. Anyone failing at any point is RTU'd instantly.'

'Aye, aye, aye!' Callaghan whispered, shaking his right hand as if in agony. 'It hurts just to think of it, but what happens next?'

'The survivors . . .'

'Good word!'

'. . . go on to special, extensive jungle training, learning in detail everything we've learnt here in Malaya, preferably in a real jungle, followed by a static-line parachute course and a set number of actual jumps.'

'Still being RTU'd at any point if they don't come up to scratch.'

'Exactly.'

'And those passing are finally allowed to wear the beige beret and Winged Dagger badge.'

'Yes . . . but their training isn't over yet.'

'Lord have mercy! Continue.'

'Once badged, they go on to Cross-Training proper, including Escape and Evasion (E & E) and Resistance-to-Interrogation (R & I) exercises; High Altitude Low Opening, or HALO, insertion techniques; special boat skills for amphibious warfare and insertions; lessons in the driving and maintenance of every kind of military vehicle, including motor-bikes; and Close Quarters Battle (CQB) skills in a so-called 'killing house' designed just for that, with pop-up targets and false decoys; and, finally, fully comprehensive lessons in medicine and languages relevant to anywhere we might be sent in the next decade. By the time they finish that lot, your SAS troopers will be the finest in the world – and no bad apples.'

'Major Pryce-Jones will be pleased. He's already been talking about extensive Cross-Training, with all the men capable of doing all jobs, but some specializing in some more than the others. He's working on the possibility of dividing the four Sabre Squadrons of the Regiment into four 16-man troops, each of which, while manned by men with multi-skills, will have its own specialist role. So far he's thought of a Mobility Troop, specializing in operations in Land Rovers, fast-attack vehicles and motor-bikes; a Boat Troop, specializing in amphibious warfare and insertions; a Mountain Troop, specializing in mountain and Arctic warfare; and an Air Troop to be used for freefall parachuting, tree-jumping and HALO insertions. All of these men will, of course, be interchangeable as the need arises – so your ideas for a special SAS Selection and Training course should go down nicely with the OC.'

'Good.'

Even as they were talking, a distant growling in the sky announced the arrival of a four-engined Blackburn Beverley transport plane. As it appeared west of the base camp, bringing the fortnightly resups, a bunch of REME (Royal Electrical and Mechanical Engineers) men, all stripped to the waist and already sweating, but wearing shorts and jungle boots with rolled-down socks, piled into a Bedford van that had been parachuted in two weeks earlier. The van immediately roared into life and was driven out of the camp, heading for the smaller cleared area being used as a Drop Site. Less than a minute later the Beverley passed over the DS and began dropping supplies out of its rear door. The parachutes blossomed into white flowers that drifted down against the sheer blue sky towards the green canopy of the jungle.

'How was Dead-eye?' Callaghan asked.

'Perfect. A natural if ever I saw one. He made his first CT killing with a crossbow and didn't even flinch. I've never seen anything quite like. He's so nice otherwise.'

'A freak of nature,' Callaghan said. 'They're bound to pop up in this business. I'm glad he's on our side. I'm surprised, by the way, that you and Dead-eye lost so little weight.'

'That's because Abang taught us how to live properly off the jungle, which is what we've got to teach the men when back in England, and weed out the unsuitable. Any problems in that regard?'

Callaghan sighed. 'We've reason to believe that

Trooper Laughton, when making his way back during that field exercise in Penang, beat a Malay student unconscious, then stole his bicycle, cycled back to the base, dumped the bicycle just before reaching the main gates and walked the next few hundred yards back to the camp. The student has since lodged a protest and we've been forced to deny that it was one of our men. But some locals saw Laughton on the student's bicycle shortly after the beating, so naturally we weren't given an easy ride. Laughton's best pal, Trooper Welsh, isn't much better.'

'Oh? What makes you say that?'

'You're not going to believe it.'

'Try me, boss.'

Callaghan had trouble keeping back his grin. 'The night before you left for the interior with Dead-eye, Pete Welsh was, reportedly, lying on his bed in the spider, deep in drunken slumber, with an erection that nearly went through the ceiling.'

Sergeant Lorrimer burst out laughing. 'Yes,' he said, when he'd settled down, 'I remember it well. He had that erection even as I was talking to Dead-eye.'

'Then obviously you missed the best part,' Callaghan said.

'Do tell.'

Callaghan chuckled, shaking his head in disbelief. 'Apparently Dennis the Menace and Boney Maronie entered the barracks and saw Pete Welsh's whopper of an erection. Knowing that Welsh had no sense of humour, Dennis the Menace got a pink ribbon – don't ask me where – and wrapped it around the tip of Welsh's erection, then tied it in a big bow. Welsh was so deep in drunken slumber he didn't even wake up. Boney Maronie then got out his camera and took a couple of nice Kodacolor pictures of the erection wearing its big pink-ribbon bow, making sure that Welsh could also be recognized. When the pictures were developed, he pinned them up in the mess hall for every man in the camp to see when he came in for his scran.'

Callaghan had to stop talking until Lorrimer got over his fit of laughter.

'Can I continue?' Callaghan asked.

'Yes, boss.'

'When Welsh entered the mess to a round of applause, then saw the candid photos of himself, he guessed immediately who'd done it and went for Dennis the Menace. A riot ensued. The mess was taken apart. Amazingly, Dennis the Menace, who's only half the size of Welsh, beat the blazes out of the latter, but not until the mess was half demolished. Eventually, they were separated, with Welsh made to stay a few days in the barracks of the Royal Marine Commandos. He is, however, now back in the SAS spider, though we've only managed to keep him apart from Dennis the Menace and Boney Maronie by sending them out on separate jungle patrols. It's funny, I know . . . – ' Callaghan saw the big grin on Lorrimer's pink face – 'but it's also a further indication that we need a more disciplined bunch of men than those we have here.'

'Which just goes to prove what I'm saying,' Lorrimer replied. 'We need a much tougher selection and training programme to ensure that only the cream of the crop get into the Regiment – and the programme I'm suggesting will do just that.'

'I think you're right,' Callaghan said. 'In the meantime, we'll have to go on keeping these bastards busy by giving them as much jungle training as we can possibly manage – of the kind you've just described – before we send them into that swamp to take out Ah Hoi.'

'I'll second that motion,' Lorrimer said. 'Just let me at them.'

'Go to it, Sarge.'

Lorrimer went at it. For the next ten days the men were put through a punishing routine of daily training that would prepare them for the Telok Anson swamp. Basing the training very much on what he and Dead-eye had learned from Abang during their own sojourn in the *ulu*, Lorrimer concentrated on jungle tracking, living off the land, primitive medicine, the construction of shelters, silent killing techniques, Standard Operating Procedures (SOPs) designed specially for the *ulu*, raft building and manoeuvring, and basic phrases in Mandarin and Malay, the former for communication with the CT, the latter to aid the campaign to win the 'hearts and minds' of the Sakai and Malay *ulu* dwellers. All of this was in addition to their normal military training in weapons maintenance and firing, camouflage, Close Quarters Battle, hand-to-hand fighting, tree-jumping and abseiling.

The training lasted from first to last light each day, with minimal breaks in between, the longest being the forty minutes allocated for a packed lunch. By the time the men had finished their evening meal in the mess back in the base camp, it was time to hit their bashas for a brief, usually sweaty and restless sleep. Nevertheless, though all this was demanding enough, other aspects of the course caused even more concern.

'I can't even *touch* a snake,' Dennis the Menace complained, studying the piece of skinned, boiled snake on the pointed end of his fork, 'let alone eat one of the fuckers! Who wants my share?'

'Sorry, can't help you,' Boney Maronie said, looking dubiously into the steaming pot he was stirring in the temporary camp they had made in the jungle just outside the base camp. 'I'm too busy trying to digest this stew composed of the meat of a constipated monkey and various herbs, leaves and vines from the *ulu*. It looks a lot better than it smells, but my lips remain sealed.'

'Eat it,' Dead-eye told him. 'It's OK, believe me. I had it myself lots of times and it was really quite good.'

'West Croydon,' Dennis the Menace said, tentatively nibbling at his cooked snake. 'That's where this poor unfortunate comes from and we all know what that means. They'd eat the fucking carpet off the floor, the poor sods are so poor.'

Boney Maronie burst out laughing. 'Christ, man,' he said, watching Dennis the Menace nervously sinking his teeth into his piece of hot snake, 'you look like you're being forced to suck cock. Just take a good fucking bite, man!'

'I'll take a good bite of this if you take a decent swallow of that soup. Come on, big mouth, let's see you!'

'I'm just waiting for it to cool down,' Boney Maronie said. 'That's all that's holding me back, mate.'

'*Hey, you two*!' Sergeant Lorrimer bawled, emerging from the head-high grass beside the river they had just come along on their imperfect bamboo rafts. 'What the hell are you doing sniffing around that scran like we've got all fucking day? Eat the food you cooked – eat it all – or deal with me. Get it?'

'Yes, boss!' Dennis the Menace and Boney Maronie chanted in unison.

'And swop,' Lorrimer told them. 'Dennis the Menace has some soup and Boney Maronie has some snake, and if any of you throw it back up you'll get my boot up your arse. *Eat, damn it! EAT*!'

The two troopers bolted down their food and didn't find it half bad, though both later confessed that they had felt a little queasy.

'A purely psychological reaction,' Dennis the Menace said later, as they poled their home-made rafts down the river, balanced precariously. 'It was no more than that.'

'As psychological as my nausea when this fucking raft rolls from side to side,' Boney Maronie replied, awkwardly handling the paddle rudder, located just behind Dennis. 'I feel sick each time this river turns rough.'

'Rough?' Dead-eye said, surprised. 'This river never does more than ripple!'

'Those aren't ripples, Dead-eye. They're fucking great waves.'

'Where? I don't see any waves?'

'That doesn't matter a shit.' Boney Maronie worked the rudder, heading in towards the river bank. 'It's all psychological, after all. If I feel waves, there *are* waves.' He manoeuvred the raft into the high, muddy bank, allowing the other men to gratefully pile off and return to the temporary camp to have a brew-up. 'And that river, believe me, was fucking rough. That's why I felt seasick.'

'What bullshit!' Pete Welsh said later, when he overheard Boney Maronie discussing the perils of river navigation. Welsh was on his knees in the small clearing near the river, finishing off his jungle lean-to. Stripped to the waist and pouring sweat, he looked like he'd been swimming. 'An arse-hole like you, mate – you probably get seasick playing with your toy duck in the bath.'

'My duck's bigger than yours, chum, which makes it worth playing with.'

Welsh laughed at that, though he still didn't feel too friendly. Since the riot in the mess hall, after he had seen the photos of the pink ribbon on his manhood, he had kept a fair distance from both Dennis the Menace and Boney Maronie. The tension was still there, bubbling under the surface, but right now he was grinning in that way that made him seem decidedly crazy.

'Oh, yeah!' he said. 'Right!'

'How's the lean-to going?' Sergeant Lorrimer asked, stepping out of nowhere as usual and looking red-faced.

'Fine, boss,' Welsh replied.

'It doesn't look fine to me. A bloody breeze, never mind a *Sumatras*, would blow that rubbish away.' Lorrimer walked up to the shelter that Welsh had spent three hours building and kicked one of the bamboo struts away, making the whole thing collapse. 'See?' he said, as Welsh's sweaty face turned purple with rage. 'A passing rat could have knocked that garbage over. Start building again.'

'I could kill that bastard,' Laughton said later to Welsh as the latter, still flushed with anger, laboriously rebuilt his jungle basha.

'Surprise, surprise,' Welsh replied sarcastically. 'What's got *you* going?

Laughton knelt on the leafy ground beside Welsh. 'I'm tracking through the *ulu*, right? I've been at it for five hours. Up and down hills that were practically vertical, across rock-strewn rivers, through snake-infested swamps, taking care to cover all my own tracks. Suffocating in the heat, sweating like a pig. Not a second's break, not a drink, not a smoko; just going like the clappers and obviously catching up on them, about half an hour to the RV. Then – would you believe it? – that bastard Lorrimer comes out of nowhere – just parts the fucking foliage and steps out like an elephant – and bellows: 'You dumb bastard! You've just torn off a twig and broken a spider's web, letting any halfwit follow your trail. You're going to be fined for this, Trooper, so you might as well turn back.' Half an hour to the RV! Can you fucking believe it?'

'Did you have a weapon with you?'

'M1 carbine.'

'Should have used it and blamed it on the CT. Shut that bastard up proper.'

'Christ, Pete, you sound like you mean that.'

Welsh just laughed manically.

They were made to spend nights sleeping in the *ulu*, under their temporary bashas, first shaking out their kit to check for creepy-crawlies, then covering themselves in mud to keep off the clouds of noisily whining insects, then listening to the unholy roar of the jungle's nocturnal chorus, and always whispering the kind of bitter complaints that actually expressed pride.

'Fucking Mandarin and Malay!' Dennis the Menace complained in a resounding whisper from his bivi-bag, stretched out beside Boney Maronie under their basha of bamboo, *atap* and rattan.

'It'd be easier to learn Swahili from a retarded deaf-mute born in Lapland. I mean, why do we have to learn *their* bloody language? They all speak English anyway.'

'Not here, they don't.' Boney was being philosophical. 'This is the *ulu*, mate, the *real* jungle – not bloody Singapore – and most of the prats here have never been to school, let alone learnt decent English. Of course, I don't mind the language classes myself, being pretty good at it.'

'Hey, Dead-eye, you hear that?' Dennis the Menace was outraged. 'Boney Maronie, who can't order a Tiger beer in a Chinese bar, thinks he's fluent in Chinese and Malay. Am I dreaming, or what?'

'He didn't say "fluent", Dennis.'

'He *implied* it,' Dennis insisted.

'I only said . . .'

'Bullshit!' Dennis the Menace said. 'That's bloody nonsense, Boney. I don't give a bugger what you say, you can't speak Chinese for shit. As for Malay – well, I don't care what you say, mate, I've heard you trying to speak it in those classes and it's just embarrassing. Isn't that right, Dead-eye?'

'Well, I . . .'

'See? Dead-eye agrees with me! What more can you say? Nothing! Not a damned thing! Just put a plug in it, Boney!'

'I don't think he has to,' Dead-eye said. 'I think he's sleeping already.'

'Fucking berk!' Dennis the Menace said.

The training continued.

After a fortnight of what many of them described proudly as 'Hell on earth' they were called to the briefing room in the bamboo-and-thatch HQ and informed by Captain Callaghan that the training had ended and they were about to go on a very important op. The men burst into applause.

'All right, all right!' Callaghan said, waving his hands to silence them. 'I'm delighted that you're delighted. But calm down and let me get on with this briefing.'

'With you, boss!' Dennis the Menace called out.

'Just let us loose!' Boney Maronie bawled.

'*Shut your mouths*,' Sergeant Lorrimer bellowed, 'and let the boss speak!'

That shut them all up.

'The reason you've had such intensive jungle training,' Callaghan said, 'is that tomorrow we're going into the Telok Anson swamp to take out the CT leader, Ah Hoi, also known as "Baby Killer", and his gang of guerrillas.'

The men cheered again, but were soon silenced by the red-faced glare of Sergeant Lorrimer.

'Getting rid of Ah Hoi is very important,' Callaghan said, 'and a little background may explain why.'

'No explanations required, boss,' Welsh said. 'Just let us at him.'

'Anyone ask you to speak, Trooper?' Lorrimer asked.

'No, Sarge.'

'To date,' Callaghan continued, 'we've managed to kill, capture or forced to surrender over 9,000 CT, leaving only a hard core of about two thou' still in the jungle. Because of our hearts-and-minds campaign, those remaining have lost the support of the aboriginals and other village communities. Realizing that they can no longer rule even a single region, the CT still left are widely scattered into groups whose only recourse is savage terrorism without any political objective. They are therefore in a greatly weakened position and should be relatively easy to capture or wipe out.'

'We've heard *that* one before,' Laughton said.

'One more word out of you, Trooper,' Lorrimer said, 'and I'll beat you so hard around the ears you'll be deaf for the rest of your worthless life.'

'Hear you loud and clear,' Laughton replied.

'The most influential of the numerous CT leaders,' Callaghan continued, as if such interruptions were perfectly normal, 'is Ah Hoi, whose disembowelment of a pregnant woman in front of her husband, a headman, and his villagers was merely the first in a long line of increasingly hideous atrocities that have succeeded in terrifying the aboriginals into doing anything he demands of them. For that very reason, we have to get rid of him.'

'Do you dick-heads understand that?' Lorrimer asked in a calmer voice.

'Yes, Sarge!' the men responded in unison.

'Good,' Lorrimer said, then turned to Callaghan. 'OK, boss, continue.'

'Presently,' Callaghan went on, trying to hide his smile, 'Ah Hoi and his guerrillas, being located little over a day's march through rubber plantations from Kuala Lumpur, are emerging regularly from the *ulu* to murder and pillage. Apart from the sheer horror of many of their atrocities, they're damaging us by causing too many of our Security Forces to be tied up in guard duties around the plantations. Our task, therefore, is to enter the Telok Anson swamp and bring out that murderous bastard and his men.'

There was a brief, thoughtful silence, until Deadeye asked: 'What's the swamp like?'

'Swamp-like.' Everyone laughed, but then Callaghan became serious. 'Approximately 18 miles by 9 miles – about the size of central London. Dense jungle, a maze of rust-brown water, mangroves and glutinous mud. Lots of rain and heat combined, making for dreadful humidity. Leeches galore. Every kind of bug, insect, and venomous creepy-crawly known to man. I'm sure you'll enjoy it.'

'How do we insert?' Boney Maronie asked.

'A secret parachute drop from a Beverley to the jungle canopy 3 miles west of the swamp. After the tree-jump, we march east into the swamp itself. Once in the swamp, we'll be waist deep in water all day and sleeping by night in hammocks or on improvised rafts. Now you know why you've been worked so relentlessly over the past two weeks.'

'We insert by Beverley?' Dennis the Menace asked.

'Yes. You'll be choppered back to Johore tomorrow morning, then flown in a Beverley back to the jungle in the afternoon. You won't have time for any fun in Johore, so don't even think of it. You touch down and take off again.'

'Gee, boss, you're so kind,' Welsh said.

'The Irish are an emotional race,' Callaghan said, 'so you're lucky to have me. Are there any more questions?' The silence was resolute. 'Right,' Callaghan said. 'We rise at first light, have breakfast, get kitted out, then get lifted off in sticks of ten, which should take all morning. Once in Johore, we transfer to the Beverleys and fly on to the DZ. As I'm coming with you I won't wish you good luck. Thank you, gentlemen. Class dismissed.'

Obviously pleased that the bullshit was over and the real work about to begin, the troopers pushed their chairs back and hurried out of the briefing room.

'About time!' Dead-eye whispered.

He couldn't wait to get stuck in.

# 12

The thirty-seven men selected to go into the swamp rose at first light, jolted themselves awake with a quick shower, put on their OGs, jungle boots and soft green bush hats, then went to the mess for an early breakfast, during which the confidence-boosting bullshit flew thick and fast.

The banter continued as they were marched by Sergeant Lorrimer to the quartermaster's stores and armoury, located mercifully in the shade of a copse of papaya palms. There, in groups of ten, they picked up, along with their usual kit, special waterproof jungle bergens, cosmetic 'cam' cream, dulling paint and strips of camouflage cloth for their weapons, lengths of para-cord to replace their weapons' standard-issue sling swivels, a plentiful supply of Paludrine, salt tablets, sterilization tablets, and a Millbank bag to filter water.

From the quartermaster's stores the first group marched the few yards to the armoury where, since they already had their personal weapons, they picked up additional fire-power, including L4A4s with curved 300-round box magazines of .303-inch bullets, fragmentation and smoke grenades, magazines of tracer bullets, flares, a couple of crossbows with lightweight alloy bolts and arrows, and some air rifles that fired darts instead of bullets. These were complemented by 5.56mm M16 assault rifles with attachments, including bayonet, bipod, telescopic sights, night-vision aids, 40mm M203 clip-on grenade-launchers, and 40mm grenades for the launcher, including smoke, HE and phosphorus.

When the weapons had been collected, the ten men moved along to the radio store where they signed for their PRC 320 radio sets, one for each of the four- or five-man teams, plus lightweight, hand-powered generators to recharge the batteries and spare compact batteries for emergencies. Finally, each man collected his Irvin X-Type model parachute.

Returning to the spider, already sweating from humping their heavy gear, the men packed their kit and camouflaged their weapons with quick-drying green paint. When the final task, camouflaging themselves, was complete, they made their way, heavily burdened, to the helicopter landing pad, where the familiar face of Lieutenant Ralph Ellis greeted them. The Army Air Corps pilot was preparing his beloved Sikorski S-55 Whirlwind for take-off.

'Morning, ladies,' Ellis said, taking note of the camouflage make-up. 'Nice to see you all looking so pretty for our nice Sunday outing.' When the anticipated ribaldry had subsided, the pilot continued: 'I'll be lifting you off in sticks of ten, which will take four flights, so you're all going to have to be patient. Given the time required for lift-off, flight, putting down and return flight, I'd estimate no later than noon to have you all on the ground at Johore. OK, in you go.'

The first ten, including Callaghan, clambered into the chopper and took their seats with some difficulty, hampered by the sheer bulk of their combined bergens, parachutes, weapons and other kit.

'Bit cramped in here, boss,' Dennis the Menace said as he adjusted the straps of his parachute pack and bergen so that he could actually sit on the seat. 'Not exactly first class.'

'If I had first-class passengers,' Ellis replied, 'I'd try to improve things – but you know how it is.'

Dennis gave a hollow laugh.

'Where's Sergeant Lorrimer?' Laughton asked. 'Still snoring his head off in his basha?'

'He's still at the armoury,' Callaghan explained, 'and will leave with the last batch of men. I know you can't live without him, Laughton, but I'm sure you can wait.'

'For ever,' Welsh said.

'Have you men all settled in?' the Loadmaster enquired. 'We're about to take off.'

'Let us pray,' Boney Maronie said.

The sudden roaring of the Whirlwind's Wright R-1300 800-hp engine put a stop to any further conversation. The noise increased when the props started spinning, creating a whirlwind of fine soil, loose leaves and seedlings. The chopper lifted off the ground, swayed briefly from side to side, rose vertically to an altitude of about 1,500 feet, then flew horizontally towards Johore.

Suddenly, the vast canopy of the jungle was spread out below, an alluvial green sea, with the sun rising above the eastern horizon like a great silvery bowl.

It was a spectacular flight, but it took only thirty minutes, then the base camp came into view, rapidly spreading out below them, with its wood-and-thatch buildings encased in the cleared jungle clearly outlined from the sky by a great rectangle of coconut palms, papaya trees and inky-dark monsoon drains.

As the Whirlwind descended the men could make out the latrines, open showers, a motor pool packed with Bedford trucks and Jeeps, and an airstrip lined with Valetta and Beverley transports, as well as Whirlwind, Dragonfly and Sycamore helicopters. It looked like a busy base.

When the chopper touched down, the troopers piled out and gathered together just beyond the pull of the slipstream whipped up by the props, which were still spinning, though in neutral and slowing down. When Ellis cut the engine, the props gradually stopped turning and a refuelling tanker, which he had called up by radio, came across the airstrip to fill up the Whirlwind's tanks, enabling him to take off again.

Feeling hot and sweaty already, Dennis the Menace and Boney Maronie started slipping off their parachute packs and bergens, in order to rest on the grassy verge at the edge of the tarmac.

'Something wrong with you, gentlemen?' Captain Callaghan asked them.

'Sorry, boss,' Dennis replied. 'What's that?'

'Why are you sitting down? Are you feeling ill?'

'Well, no, boss . . .' Dennis glanced at Boney Maronie. 'We're just waiting for the others to arrive. I mean . . .'

'So you thought you'd sit on your fat arses twiddling your thumbs. Well, lads, you won't. Get those parachutes and bergens back on your shoulders, pick up your kit, and follow me across the airstrip to the Beverley. You can pass the time by putting your kit on the plane and then helping the Loadmaster with the supplies. OK? On your feet!'

With much moaning and groaning the men did as they were told, humping the parachute packs and bergens on to their backs, then following Callaghan across the sunbaked airstrip to where the RAF Beverley was being prepared for its flight to Telok Anson, south-west of Ipoh.

'Flight-Sergeant Norton?' Callaghan asked of the big man who was standing by the open boom door at the rear of the aircraft, wearing shorts, with rubber flip-flops on his feet. Stripped to the waist, he was gleaming with sweat and supervising the loading being done by a bunch of Chinese coolies.

'Yes, sir,' the man replied, sounding as if he'd smoked too many cigarettes. 'Flight-Sergeant Norton. That's me.'

'This is the first batch of troopers for the parachute jump into Telok Anson. They can load their own kit and then give you any other help you need.'

'That might speed things up,' Norton said, smiling at the troopers. 'OK, you men, clamber up here and make your way through to the passenger hold. When you've dumped your gear, come back and see me and I'll keep you busy.'

'You're too kind,' Boney Maronie said.

'Heart of gold,' Norton replied. 'Now get your lazy arses on this aircraft and let's see some work done.'

With the help of the reluctant, moaning SAS troopers the coolies were able to complete the loading of the supplies a lot sooner than expected, which allowed everyone to have an early break. When the SAS men had been picked up in a Bedford and driven back to their quarters, the coolies were finally allowed to sit on the grassy verge to await the arrival of the next stick of ten men.

'We've been in that FOB for less than two months,' Welsh said, 'but it seems *years* since we passed through *this* hole. It's changed a lot since we left.'

'Yeah,' Laughton agreed, squinting against the dazzling sunlight as he gazed across the airstrip, past the parked aircraft and helicopters, to the sports ground, row of barracks and line of jungle at the other side. 'It's become a regular Piccadilly Circus – a helluva lot of movement and noise.'

This was true enough. Valettas, other Beverleys, and a variety of helicopters – Whirlwinds, Dragonflys and Sycamores – were taking off and landing at regular intervals, creating huge clouds of swirling dust and debris. Bedford trucks and jeeps were racing along the roads of the base, transporting troops and supplies. A squadron of Gurkhas was engaged in rifle drill on the sports area. The wired perimeter was being patrolled by Kampong Guards from the Malaya Police, while the guardhouses were manned by RAF MPs and covered by the Royal Marines manning the Bren guns and 3-inch mortars in the sangars on either side of the gates.

'All it needs is a brothel,' Boney Maronie said, 'filled with nice girls from George Town.'

'If they were nice girls they wouldn't work in a brothel,' Dennis the Menace pointed out. 'Though that fact isn't likely to put *you* off, mate.'

'I just follow my God-given instincts. What's wrong with that?'

'You haven't followed them for weeks,' Welsh said. 'Nor has anyone else. I can take everything they throw at me in this filthy hole, except being deprived of my bit of tail.'

'I can't remember what a bit of tail looks like,' Dennis the Menace confessed.

'Since there's no brothel here, that's academic,' Laughton observed. 'Christ!' he added as an afterthought. 'I feel horny all of a sudden! Stop talking about it.'

The morning passed slowly, with the sun growing

stronger. Lolling about on the grass, the men began to feel soporific. Eventually, however, two more sticks of ten men and the final stick of seven, including Sergeant Lorrimer and Trooper 'Dead-eye' Parker, were brought in on three separate flights of the Whirlwind. By then it was just after noon and ferociously hot.

The men took their places in the Beverley and the aircraft took off. As a Beverley can carry 70 parachutists at a time, the 37 SAS paratroopers were all going to make the jump at the same time. It was a blessing that the flight took only thirty minutes, as the interior of the aircraft was suffocatingly hot and humid at that time of day. The men were therefore relieved when Norton opened the port and starboard doors, as well as the large boom door, letting cooler air come rushing in.

'OK, men,' Captain Callaghan said, standing up and adjusting the straps of his combined parachute pack and strapped-on bergen. 'I'll be going out first as the drifter. You men will follow on the command of Flight-Sergeant Norton. You'll go out in sticks of four from the port and starboard doors, and left and right of the boom door. The DZ is located in the bush about 12 miles from the edge of the swamp. The supplies will be dropped in the same area. Once we've collected and shared out the supplies, we'll march east and enter the swamp.'

'*Action stations!*' Flight-Sergeant Norton bawled.

'OK, men,' Callaghan said briskly. 'Stand up.' When the men had done so, he sorted them into four queues of nine men each, each lined up at one of the four chosen exits. He then took his position at the big boom door, holding onto the side and waiting for the overhead green light to flash. Looking down he saw the brilliant-green jungle canopy, stretching out to the curved line of the sheer blue horizon. It seemed like a long way down.

'Right!' Norton bawled and tapped him on the shoulder.

Callaghan threw himself out, was swept away on the roaring slipstream, escaped and started dropping like a stone, then tugged on the parachute cord. He was jerked back up, swung like a pendulum, then started drifting down towards the jungle, through a silence only broken by the wind whipping under the parachute. Though heavily burdened with his parachute back-pack, bergen, bandoliers and weapons, he felt as light as a feather.

As the jungle canopy came up towards him, gaining light and shade and dimension, he saw the relatively clear area of stunted grass and bush designated as the DZ, and using the lines of his chute, steered himself in that direction. Shaken by a gust of wind, he saw the treetops suddenly racing up towards him. He steered himself to the west, missed the dense, dangerous canopy, then plunged down a deep well of blurred greenery on to grass-covered earth.

When his feet hit the ground, he let his legs buckle, then rolled over with the parachute tugging at him. He reined the lines in, then popped the chute, feeling a sense of freedom when it broke loose from his bergen. At that point he stopped rolling.

Looking up, he saw the Beverley circling high above, dull grey against the blue sky, with sticks of men spilling out in four different directions and plunging towards the chutes billowing open below him. Before the last men reached the first batch, their own opening chute would pull them back up, then let them drift down above the others. It all looked rather beautiful.

The first men started landing in the bush around Callaghan, some having a clear fall, others tumbling down through the branches of the trees, still others snagged in the branches and uncoiling their knotted ropes to abseil the rest of the way down.

Callaghan wrapped up his chute, buried it in

the undergrowth, then, holding his Owen sub-machine-gun at the ready, went to join the men landing nearest to him.

The supplies, also being parachuted down, were falling over a fairly wide area, but well within the expected circular range.

As Callaghan hurried across the bush towards the nearest men, he saw one of those still coming down smashing brutally into the treetops. Caught by his own webbing, he was flipped over like a rag doll, smashed backwards into another thick branch, screamed in agony, then fell when the canopy collapsed. He bounced off more branches, smashed noisily through others, and eventually landed with a thud on his back – after a fall of over 100 feet. When he tried to call for help, the words came out as a shuddering, breathless wail of pain that did not sound human.

Callaghan turned around and headed in that direction, followed by some of the other grounded troopers. When they reached the man, it was immediately clear that he had seriously damaged his spine and was unable to move himself below the waist.

'Medic!' Dennis the Menace bawled.

Luckily, most of the men had landed already and a medic was among them. Responding promptly to the call, he checked the man's reactions, soon saw that he could feel nothing in his lower half and turned to whisper to Callaghan that he had broken his back.

'He has to be casevacked,' the medic said. 'This man can't be carried.'

'Damn!' Callaghan whispered.

Dead-eye, meanwhile, having fallen wide of the DZ and into the jungle canopy, found himself once more dangling by his parachute harness from one of the stronger branches of a tree. In fact, his fall had been stopped only 15 feet from the ground. Unable to shake the harness free, he released the bergen from the parachute back-pack and let it fall, rattling and banging its way down through the branches before hitting the soft carpet of leaves. Dead-eye was then able to wriggle out of the harness, freeing first one arm, then the other, and balancing himself precariously on the thick branch upon which he found himself sitting.

He was just about to lower himself to the ground when some bushes parted and a Chinese-looking man, obviously attracted by the noise of the falling bergen, entered the small clearing below. In his mid-twenties, he was barefoot and wearing khaki shorts, a shirt and military cap. And he was holding a British tommy-gun. He advanced on the tree, then stopped to stare down at the bergen. When he saw what it was, he froze on the spot, then glanced left and right, behind him and to the front. Then he knelt to examine the bergen.

Dead-eye was about to remove his 9mm Browning High Power handgun from its holster when he checked himself, for the sound of the shot would alert any other CTs in the vicinity. Changing his mind and moving as quietly as possible, he unsheathed his Fairburn-Sykes commando knife, gripped it tightly in his right hand, took a deep breath, then let himself slide off the thick branch and drop to the jungle floor.

He landed right beside the guerrilla, sliding his left arm around him as he did so, pulling him off his feet, and slashing the blade of the knife across his throat even as they both fell backwards into the leaves. The man could make no sound as his vocal cords had been cut, but he frantically kicked his legs, shuddered like an epileptic, and soaked Dead-eye's right hand in blood before gargling, choking and, after what seemed like an eternity, breathing his last.

Dead-eye slithered out from under him, checked that he was dead, closed and sheathed the commando knife, then picked his kit off the forest floor, slipped the straps of the heavy bergen over his shoulders, tightened them and checked all the weapons. Satisfied that everything was in order, he hurried off through the jungle, towards the clearing where the DZ was located and where most of the other men had dropped successfully.

Most, but not all. When Dead-eye arrived in the thinner forest of the bush, he found the squadron already engaged in the task of creating a temporary LZ for a helicopter.

'What's going on?' he asked Boney Maronie.

'Trooper Clayton broke his back when landing and is going to be casevacked back to Johore.'

'He didn't get far,' Dead-eye said.

'Where on earth did *you* land?' Captain Callaghan asked.

'Over there,' Dead-eye replied, waving his hand to indicate the nearby jungle. 'I got stuck halfway down a tree, but directly above an armed guerrilla. But don't worry, boss. I handled the situation.'

'You neutralized him?'

'Yes, boss.'

'Are you sure he was a guerrilla?' Callaghan asked.

'Absolutely. He was Chinese, wore one of those military caps, and was carrying a British tommy-gun.'

Sergeant Lorrimer had joined them to listen in on the conversation. When Dead-eye had finished talking, Lorrimer glanced automatically at the jungle.

'Well, well,' he said. 'We've had contact already.

Do you think there are any more in that bit of jungle?'

'No, I don't think so, Sarge. I made a hell of a racket coming down, yet that guerrilla was the only one to appear. I think he was some kind of point man, just looking around. The rest are probably still in the swamp.'

'Let's hope so,' Lorrimer said. He turned away to speak to Alf Laughton, who was in charge of a radio set. 'Did you manage to get in contact with Johore?'

'Yes, Sarge. The chopper's on its way and should be here any minute now.'

'Excellent.' Lorrimer turned back to Dead-eye. 'Since you've been a good boy, you can take your pick: either help clear an LZ for that chopper or give a hand with bringing in the supplies.'

'I'll bring in the supplies.'

'Go to it, kid.'

While half of the men were using their *parangs* to hack a clearing large enough for the chopper to land, the other half spread out to bring in the crates scattered around the DZ. After smashing open the wooden crates and metal containers that had come down on parachutes, they piled the supplies in a heap just outside the area being cleared for the LZ, completing the job just as an RAF Sycamore search-and-rescue helicopter came in to pick up the casualty.

The clearing made so hastily in the bush was just enough to allow the helicopter's rotor blades to miss the surrounding foliage. But it was still impossible to land because of the swampy terrain. Nevertheless, in an impressive display of flying skill, the pilot brought the helicopter into the small clearing, its rotors virtually scraping the trees, and hovered just above the swampy ground, with one wheel resting on a log, while the casualty, now strapped to the stretcher, was loaded aboard. Less than a minute later, the helicopter lifted off again, soon vanishing beyond the canopy of trees, leaving an ominous silence in its wake.

The spare weapons, ammunition and supplies were distributed among the men; then, as heavily burdened as pack mules, they marched east, towards the beckoning nightmare of the Telok Anson swamp.

# 13

It looked normal at first. To get to the swamp they had to pass through the stretch of jungle where Dead-eye had despatched the lone guerrilla. The corpse would have looked peaceful had it not been for the ghastly mess of congealed blood around the slashed throat and the black clouds of flies that were frantically trying to feed off it. Though the instinctive reaction of everyone was to ignore the grisly scene, Callaghan ordered that the corpse be buried in case any other guerrillas were in the vicinity and might be tipped off, by the discovery of the dead man, to the presence of the SAS here in the swamp. Using *changkols*, or large hoes, previously purchased from the Sakai, a couple of the troopers soon scooped out a shallow grave, threw the dead guerrilla into it, replaced the soil, then sprinkled loose leaves over the ground to make it look the same as before. The patrol then moved on.

The first hour was easy, a casual stroll in

single file through the jungle, kicking up the loose leaves, feeling grateful for the shade. Then they reached the edge of the swamp and everything changed.

The trees seemed to close in upon them, behind them, in front of them, forming an impenetrable living wall that had to be hacked away with the *parangs*. The ground became more marshy, squelching underfoot, making walking more laborious and exhausting. After only thirty minutes in the swamp, the sky was blocked out, the air had become appallingly humid and, even worse, was filled with whining flies, mosquitoes, midges, flying beetles, the occasional hornet and other equally ravenous winged insects of a type the troopers had never seen before. They all attacked noisily, viciously and constantly, further distracting the men from what they were doing.

Soon the wet ground became even more marsh-like, turning to mud, slopping over their boots, soaking their trouser legs and giving the impression that it was trying to suck them down like quicksand. Walking became monstrously difficult and soon left most of them breathless.

Unlike the jungle, the swamp offered a constant chorus of croaking, squawking, clicking, drumming, and sudden, startling rustling in the undergrowth. The latter, in particular, made the men jumpy, even causing them to suddenly raise their weapons, ready to fire.

Within an hour, the mud had turned to rust-brown water that became deeper with every step they took. Three hours later, when every man was running with sweat, he was also soaked up to the hips with water and forced to hold his personal weapon either across his chest or above his head. Both positions placed tremendous strain on the arms, causing sharp pains to dart along them, from shoulder to wrist.

With the water came the leeches. Already the trek was leading them along river banks and through more muddy water, the depths of which varied from shin to neck-high. Those parts of the body that were submerged were the prey for fat swamp leeches, which, as most of the men now knew, could consume half a pint of blood before being detected. And then, as if to ensure that there would be no reprieve for the struggling men, when they came to high ground that brought them out of the water they instantly became the target for the malarial mosquito and other insects. Before long, even the toughest soldier was beginning to think he was in hell on earth.

Their trials were made no easier by the fact that they were not allowed to speak on the march for fear either that some lurking guerrilla might overhear them or that their own voices would hide the sounds of an approaching enemy. Using only sign language, they were forced in on themselves, and thus distracted even more by the sounds all around them, particularly the sudden, sharp rustling which indicated sudden movement in the undergrowth. Usually these were caused by snakes, jungle pigs, monkeys or rats as big as rabbits.

By mid-afternoon the heat and humidity were appalling, making them pour more sweat and feel nauseous or nearly suffocated. Combined with the constant gloom caused by the dense jungle canopy, the sticky, oppressive heat made them feel unreal, disorientated, less capable of coherent thought and quick reactions. This only made many of them more anxious about the unseen CTs and suspicious of every sound in the teeming undergrowth.

In that state, it was easy for them to imagine that the jungle had a life of its own and was deliberately tormenting them. This seemed to be particularly true when they emerged from a swampy area to what at first sight appeared to be relatively clear, dry ground. Invariably, however, this turned out to be *belukar*, or secondary jungle, with thickets of thorn, bracken and bamboo more impenetrable than ever and covered with *mengkuang*, a gargantuan leathery grass with pointed blades. In one hour of back-breaking work, they would cover a mere hundred yards.

Before nightfall, they looked for somewhere to lay up, but where the water was not a couple of feet deep, the ground was too marshy to be used. They therefore looked for an area where the trees were close enough, and strong enough, to hold hammocks. Sleeping in this manner, swaying precariously above the snake-infested water or mud, was not made any easier by the jungle's nocturnal racket, nor by the countless insects that buzzed and whined all night, diving repeatedly at the frustrated men to get at their sweat and blood. It was also impossible to get rid of the leeches that had clung to their bodies, beneath the clothes, when they were wading chest-deep in the water. A final bar to sleep was the constant fear, encouraged by the ceaseless rustling of the undergrowth, that snakes, poisonous spiders or other venomous creatures would drop on to them from the branches directly above.

The second day, given the men's state of exhaustion, proved even more difficult. Subsequent days, during which they found no trace of a terrorist, were worse still, because the deeper into the swamp they went, the more nightmarish it became.

Each day, from the steamy mists of dawn to the damp, chilling sunrise, they had to force their way through stinking mud, rotting vegetation and thorny branches, sometimes wading up to their necks in the marsh channels, at other times practically swimming across open water, under drooping coils of vine, rattan and giant, razor-sharp leaves which cut their arms and faces, so driving the insects into a feeding frenzy and giving the growing number of fat leeches even more blood to feed upon.

Within a couple of days each man smelt of the swamp, his rotting clothes adding to the general stench of the place and hanging ever more loosely on his shrinking frame. This loss of weight was made worse by the fact that they were unable to cook decent food in the swamp and so had to rely on their dry, tasteless, high-calorie rations.

Though none of them actually hallucinated, all of them were driven back into themselves and spent a lot of time blocking out the horrors they were going through with memories of where they had come from and what they held most dear.

Try as he might not to become too distracted, Captain Callaghan found himself yearning for the sunny hills of Sicily and Italy, where he had served with Special Raiding Squadron, the renamed 1 SAS, in 1943. The gloomier the jungle became, the more vividly Callaghan saw the sun-scorched plains of Enna; the filthier the swamp became, the more colourful became his recollections of the Adriatic coast and Anzio. Callaghan had enjoyed the war, even the unsuccessful raids, feeling only half alive during the immediate post-war years when he returned to No. 3 Commando and divided his time between his family – he had two teenage daughters – and the dreary routine of a peacetime Army. He had been very glad, therefore, to be posted to Malaya at the start of the Emergency, for he was revitalized by fighting in the jungle. Nevertheless, though he basically loved being here, this present murderous hike, in pursuit of an 'invisible' enemy, left him no recourse but to escape from the horrors of the swamp by recalling the sunnier climates he had fought in during the war.

Similarly, Sergeant Lorrimer often found himself recalling the wide, open spaces of the North African desert, where he had been one of the first members of the SAS to go out on patrol with the Long Range Desert Group. Lorrimer had loved the desert, with its silence and space and vast, open sky; completely different from this filthy swamp with its noise, humidity and constant gloom. Waist-deep in water, ducking low to avoid drooping vines, he consoled himself by reliving the many daring raids he and his fellow SAS troopers had made in jeeps against enemy airfields around Benghazi, Bagoush and Sidi Haneish. He also thought occasionally of his wife in their small house in Runcorn, Cheshire, and of his children, a boy and two girls, now all grown up and married; but what he most remembered, as he sweated and stank in this filthy swamp, was the feel of the wind against his face and the sun dazzling his vision, as the jeeps tore across the desert plains to hit another German airfield. Now, more than ever, he yearned to feel and see that again, but instead there was only suffocating humidity and unrelieved gloom.

Trooper Dennis 'the Menace' Dudbridge was thinking a lot about drinking bitter in his local in Bristol. Before joining the regular Army, he had worked as a labourer in the docks at Avonmouth, where the men liked rough fun and games, particularly drinking and fighting. Dennis had been a heavy drinker from the minute he first set foot in a pub. He had also been quick to use his fists, which accounted for his broken nose and scarred upper lip. Married at eighteen after getting his girlfriend pregnant, he had sired four more kids, found home life increasingly irksome, and finally decided to escape it by joining the Army. Transferred to the Gloucestershire Regiment after his basic training, he had thoroughly enjoyed being away from home and was even more pleased when posted to West Berlin. There, when not on pointless manoeuvres or on guard duty at the Wall, he had lived the life of a hard-drinking bachelor. This did not change when his tour of duty ended and he returned to England.

Never much of a womanizer, Dennis liked his beer, darts, and macho conversation, preferably in a noisy, smoky pub. As he disliked being at home, he was happy enough to be in Malaya, but he didn't like this filthy swamp one bit.

Corporal 'Boney Maronie' Malone blocked out the horrors of the swamp with visions of the various women he'd had since losing his virginity at the relatively late age of twenty-three. He had, however, made up for lost time by sampling as many women as possible since then. Now twenty-nine and still a single man, he wanted no more out of life than a bit of nooky, a fast car, plenty to eat and drink, and a fair amount of lawful adventure with the SAS.

He required this colourful way of life because his mother had died when he was five years old, his father was a decent, deeply religious but dried-up bookkeeper for a firm of accountants in Coventry, where Boney Maronie had been born and bred, and his whole childhood and adolescence in the cathedral city had been lonely and boring beyond belief.

Boney Maronie's need for the fast lane explained his love of the SAS; yet even he was having difficulty in maintaining his enthusiasm while dragging his feet through mud, wading chest-deep in water, breathing humid air and the stench of natural decay, fighting off crazed insects, and keeping on the alert for poisonous snakes, scorpions, centipedes, hornets and the even more dangerous CT. Boney attempted to maintain his enthusiasm and ignore the swamp's vileness by recalling the many women he had known and then reducing them in his fevered imagination to mere artefacts composed of sweat-slicked skin, heaving breasts, erect nipples, moist, pouting lips and long hair tangled beautifully across eyes luminous with lust. Even being eaten alive by mosquitoes and midges, Boney Maronie could get an erection that made him feel superhuman.

Alf Laughton kept going by pretending that any minute now they were going to be lifted out of the swamp and deposited in Penang, which he remembered so vividly, having been there in 1953 with the King's Own Yorkshire Light Infantry. Born in Birkenhead, Merseyside, one of the five children of married publicans who worked night and day, Laughton felt at home as one of a large group and perhaps had gravitated to the Army for that very reason. Receiving little parental affection and largely ignored by his brothers and sisters, he soon devised various ways of getting himself attention, which mainly meant creating mischief. An inveterate troublemaker at school, he was not much better when he went to work, which he did at fourteen, as an apprentice welder in the shipyard. Eventually fired for bad behaviour, including dangerous practical jokes, he enlisted in the regular Army, which guaranteed him a better time than he would have had doing his National Service.

Given his dreary background, it was perfectly natural that he should find life in the Army more satisfying than Civvy Street and his first posting overseas, to Butterworth, Malaya, was the most exotic experience he'd had to date. Spending most of his spare time in Penang, a brief ferry cruise across the Strait of Malacca, he soon came to love the place, with its trishaws, *sampans*, bars, brothels, bazaars, markets, and beautiful women in figure-hugging *cheongsams*. Depressed when his tour of duty was over and he had to return to England, he played one too many practical jokes on his fellow soldiers, had one too many drinks, got into one too many fights, and was encouraged to join the newly reformed SAS by an NCO sick of the sight of him.

Now, here he was, pleased to be back in Malaya, but not so pleased to be slogging through this dark, dank, mosquito-infested swamp. He therefore dreamt of being lifted out and set down in the exotic, familiar streets of Penang.

Laughton's mate, Trooper Pete Welsh, was keeping going by ignoring the filth and dangers of the swamp and dreaming of revenge against all those in the squadron who had slighted him or otherwise riled him. An illegitimate child, he had been raised in Finsbury Park, North London, where his prostitute mother worked the pubs and brought the men back to her squalid bedsit, earning her money while he looked on, learning the facts of life in the most direct, brutal way possible. An alcoholic who was often beaten up by her clients, his mother just as frequently took her revenge out on her son, leaving him black and blue, traumatized by grief and fear. She would then weep tears of drunken remorse and try to buy his forgiveness with the presents he never received on Christmas or for his birthdays.

Welsh had suffered all this quietly until he was conscripted, trained as an explosives expert and posted to No. 101 Special Training School, Singapore. From there he transferred to the 3rd Corp, where, with other Sappers, he harassed the Japanese by blowing up railroads and bridges of strategic importance.

Though an excellent soldier, he never settled down and exploded at the slightest provocation, having violent fights that landed him in the cells. Nevertheless, he loved what he was doing – the war turned him on – and so he decided to go straight from National Service into the regular Army. Informed by his NCOs that the most expedient way of doing this was by signing up for the recently reformed SAS, which was desperate for volunteers and not yet vetting them too closely, Welsh did just that and soon found himself back in Malaya.

So here he was, slogging through a swamp that most of the other men thought was a nightmare, though it was, to Welsh, merely another place where he could take his revenge on the world in general and Dennis the Menace in particular.

No way in the world would Welsh let someone tie a pink bow on his cock, much less take a photograph of it, to be pinned up on the notice board in the mess.

He would have his revenge.

Welsh's energy was fuelled by the rage he was secretly nurturing as he slogged through the filth of the swamp.

His time would come soon.

Adding to the increasing anger, despair and frustration of the men was their continuing lack of contact with the enemy. Frequently they came across camps recently vacated by the terrorists, but the guerrillas themselves were as invisible as most of the alien wildlife in the undergrowth.

'Ah Hoi knows he's being followed,' Callaghan told Lorrimer as they studied a site littered with the shells of turtles eaten by the terrorists. 'I think the casevac of Trooper Clayton must have alerted them to our presence here. Now they're keeping ahead of us.'

'Then we have to block off their escape,' Lorrimer replied.

'Exactly. I think I should get on the radio and ask for another squadron to be dropped east of the swamp, to form a cordon around the eastern perimeter, then move in towards us, catching the guerrillas in the middle.'

'Those bastards are like swamp rats,' Lorrimer replied, 'knowing every tree, every bend in every river, every way out. So I don't think that one squadron will be enough to keep them in, though a pincer movement will certainly help when it comes to finishing them off.'

'You think we need even more men?'

'I think we should ask for that squadron to be dropped east of the swamp as you suggested. At the same time, however, the whole swamp should be encircled by a military and police cordon, with barbed wire placed along the coast, to prevent anyone coming in or out that way. Keep the bastards trapped in here and, with that pincer movement, we should trap them eventually.'

'Agreed,' Callaghan said. As Major Pryce-Jones was now based in Johore, Callaghan asked Laughton to get him on the blower. When the trooper had done so, Callaghan made his request. After listening attentively, he handed the microphone back to Laughton. 'He's OK'd it,' he said to Lorrimer, 'but insists that it'll take another few days. Most of the men are already out on jungle patrols around Johore. But he's going to call in D squadron and send them out as soon as they're organized, which should be two days from now. In the meantime we're to continue advancing towards the centre of the swamp.'

'It's going to be one hell of a hike, Captain.'

'Who dares wins,' Callaghan said.

Their route across the swamp was taking them alongside the Tengi River. Checking by the side of the river, Dead-eye, now an expert tracker after his training with Abang, noted a series of broken branches and leaves directly over where footsteps had been covered with leaves, indicating that some men in bare feet had hiked east, obviously heading for the centre of the swamp.

'The CT,' Lorrimer deduced. 'Ah Hoi's men.'

'Right,' Callaghan said. 'As we thought, they're

retreating back into the swamp, trying to cover their tracks.'

'Then let's follow them,' Dead-eye said.

'No,' Callaghan replied. 'This is a relatively dry area, so I think we should stay here for the night and move on in the morning. While we're setting up camp, you can go out alone and check if any CT are in the area. They can't be too far ahead of us now, but we don't want to run into them without warning. Ok, Dead-eye, get going.'

Because of his frail physique, Dead-eye, weighed down with a bergen that included full camping gear and an arsenal of spare grenades and ammunition, looked even more heavily burdened than the others. This impression was only emphasized by the fact that he was carrying a 5.56mm M1 assault rifle with the bayonet, telescopic sight and 40mm M203 grenade-launcher already fixed to it. Also, strapped down the back of his bergen, was the crossbow with a belt of lightweight alloy bolts and arrows. In fact, Dead-eye looked like a bizarre Quasimodo as he turned away and headed deeper into the jungle, leaving the rest of the squadron behind to fix up the camp.

'You go with him,' Callaghan said to the nearest trooper, Neil Moffatt. 'Keep his back covered.'

'Right, boss,' Moffatt said, picking up his Owen

sub-machine-gun and following Dead-eye into the jungle.

'OK, Sarge,' Callaghan said to Lorrimer, now confident that the CT were heading west and that it was safe to camp there. 'Tell the men to make up their bashas for the night. They can talk, wash themselves in the river and even have something to eat and drink. But they still can't light fires.'

'Right, boss, I'll tell them.'

Delighted to be given a break on what amounted to solid ground, instead of in mud or water, the men enthusiastically washed themselves in the river, ate their cold, high-calorie rations, then created their own personal style of basha. One made a root shelter by packing soil between the extended roots of a tree, thus turning it into a little cave. Another made a bough shelter by unrolling his bivi-bag under the outspread branches of a fallen tree, which formed a natural ceiling. A third made a sapling shelter by draping his waterproof poncho over a series of horseshoe-shaped branches and weighting down the ends of the poncho with stones.

Other men made a variety of triangular shelters with groundsheets and stick supports, fixing the ends of the groundsheets with string and short, wooden stakes. A few of the more energetic made shelters from simply woven *atap*, elephant grass, palm leaves or bamboo. Captain Callaghan and

Sergeant Lorrimer, being more experienced in jungle survival, built bamboo rafts and slept on the river, tying the rafts to the base of the tree trunks on the bank. In doing this, they solved the problem of the creepy-crawlies on the ground while also ensuring that the river breeze would keep them cool. For this the other men envied them.

Not too many would have envied Dead-eye. Leaving the relatively open, dry ground near the river bank and heading into the *ulu*, he ran almost immediately into a stretch of *belukar*, or secondary jungle, where the thickets of thorn, bracken and bamboo, almost impenetrable in themselves, were covered with the gargantuan leathery *mengkuang*, the pointed blades of which slashed his face and hands, soaking him in his own blood.

Thirty minutes later, just as the blood was congealing, he sank chest-deep in muddy water and felt the leeches sticking to his legs, hands and body. Continuing to wade through the water, holding his M1 above his head, he temporarily froze when a geometrically patterned snake, the venomous Malay pit viper, emerged from the vegetation by his right elbow, slithered across the branch floating in the water directly in front of him, practically brushing his chest as it crossed his path, then disappeared back into the dense foliage to his left.

Releasing the breath he had been holding in, Dead-eye continued wading and was relieved when the ground beneath his feet turned upwards, letting him rise out of the water as he advanced. Eventually back on marshy land, he moved deeper into the *ulu*, tormented even more now by the many leeches clinging to him and sucking on his blood, but unwilling to stop to remove them, which would have taken too long. Instead, he kept advancing, checking every leaf and branch, only detouring when faced with something hideous in the undergrowth – another snake, a venomous spider, sleeping vampire bats, 10-inch centipedes and nests of hornets whose sting, when not actually fatal, was more painful than being pierced by hot rivets.

Dead-eye braved all of this and stopped only when he suddenly saw the back of a man kneeling on the bank at the other side of a short stretch of leaf-covered swamp water, examining the ground around his bare feet. Though dressed like a Chinese coolie, but with a military cap on his head, he was carrying a British M1 rifle, which marked him as one of Ah Hoi's guerrillas.

Not wanting to fire his own M1 carbine and alert other CT in the area, Dead-eye decided to use his crossbow. Removing it as quietly as possible from where it was strapped across his bergen, he knelt on the grass, cocked the weapon, inserted a lightweight alloy bolt and arrow, then prepared to fire.

At that moment, a large spider, of a species unknown to Dead-eye but about the size of his outspread hand and looking rather like a tarantula, materialized eerily from under the leaves and crawled over his boot. Paralysed with the kind of fear that no human could cause in him, feeling goose pimples all over, his heart suddenly racing, Dead-eye watched as the enormous spider crossed over the toe of his boot, moved up the laces and onto his leg, just above the ankle, then mercifully changed its mind and turned back down, sliding off the other side of the boot and disappearing under the carpet of leaves as eerily as it had first appeared.

Letting his breath out, then sucking in another lungful of air, Dead-eye waited until his racing heart had settled down, then looked at the man across the short stretch of swamp. The man was still kneeling, carefully studying the ground around him.

Dead-eye took aim along the sights of the crossbow, then squeezed the trigger, sending the alloy bolt and arrow racing through the air and straight into the nape of the guerrilla's neck.

The man quivered violently as if whipped, then stood up and turned around to face the river, looking very surprised. He gripped the bolt in his right hand, pulled a little, winced and stopped, then opened and shut his mouth a few times, as if checking if he had feeling left in his neck. He touched the bolt again, winced, shuddered violently, then sank unsteadily to his knees. He tried to pull the bolt out, convulsed in agony, then fell face down in the mud. He shook for a few seconds like an epileptic having a violent fit, then was still.

At that moment, Dead-eye heard a loud rustling in the undergrowth a good distance behind him. Spinning around, he was relieved to see a sweaty Trooper Moffatt blundering like an elephant from the jungle, just south of the route Dead-eye had taken.

Angry at Moffatt's amateurish and noisy advance, Dead-eye was about to wave him down when, to his horror, he saw that an enormous log impregnated with six-inch nails and sharpened hardwood spikes had been suspended above the trail on a rope that formed a trip-wire to release the log. It was, Dead-eye recognized instantly, the hideous booby-trap known as the Chinese Chopper.

'Freeze!' Dead-eye bawled.

Startled, Moffatt froze momentarily, but when he recognized Dead-eye, his evident relief made him forget the warning and he stepped forward again. He tripped over the rope and stumbled a little as the rest of the rope rapidly unravelled and the immense, spiked log fell upon him.

Hearing the noise of snapping branches, Moffatt just had time to glance up before the log smashed down on him, crushing him, piercing him with multiple stab wounds and finally pinning his mangled body to the ground. He hadn't even had time to scream.

'Shit!' Dead-eye whispered, then advanced, crouched low, now checking his surroundings even more carefully, until he reached Moffatt's body. The young trooper had been flattened beneath the log, pressed deeply into the mud. He was covered with an appalling amount of blood and more was squirting out of his numerous wounds.

Dead-eye didn't have to check that Moffatt was dead, but he did look for his weapon, failed to find it, and realized that it must have been buried under him. Knowing that there was little more he could do, Dead-eye headed back the way he had come, not stopping until he reached the camp by the river.

Dead-eye found most of the men asleep in their jungle bashas, with Callaghan and Lorrimer sleeping on bamboo rafts in the middle of the narrow river. Entering the river, which came up to his chest, Dead-eye waded up to Callaghan's raft, shook him awake and told him about the loss of Moffatt.

'If they left that booby-trap,' Captain Callaghan responded pragmatically, 'they've surely left others – and that means the bastards know we're pursuing them. No point in being too careful now. We'll just go in and finish them off. Get a good night's sleep, Trooper.'

'Yes, boss,' Dead-eye said. He waded back to the grassy bank, rolled his bivi-bag out on a soft carpet of leaves, then, no longer concerned about creepy-crawlies, fell into a deep, helpful sleep. When he woke at dawn, he felt older and wiser.

# 14

When the men moved out the next morning, Dead-eye went on point to lead them through the hellish swamp to where the dead Moffatt was still pinned beneath the fatal log, his body now rendered even more hideous by being covered in bloated flies and red ants.

No one really wanted to touch the bloody, crushed, stabbed corpse but some of the men, at Callaghan's insistence, rolled the log off and buried the trooper in a shallow grave, being forced to beat the flies off as they did so.

Once the body was covered up, the patrol moved on across the short stretch of swamp to where the guerrilla was still lying face down in the mud with the alloy bolt and arrow through his neck, protruding front and rear, the congealed blood around it attracting swarms of flies and an army of ants. More grisly still, some animal from the *ulu* had fed off the corpse, tearing an arm from the shoulder and carrying it off to its lair. The bloody stump of the arm had become an ants' nest being attacked by many different kinds of insects.

'I'm fucked if I'm burying him,' Welsh said. 'Let the animals have him.'

'Why not?' Laughton replied. 'What's left of him will disappear soon enough. Hey, Dead-eye, good shot!'

'Thanks,' Dead-eye said.

'Fucking Robin Hood,' Dennis the Menace said. 'I wouldn't invite that little bastard to a game of darts. You'd be pinned to the fucking board.'

'Do you play darts?' Boney Maronie asked.

'No,' Dead-eye replied. 'I don't drink, so I never go to pubs and have never played darts.'

'Let's all say our thanks,' Boney Maronie said. 'God's still on our side.'

They marched on, deeper into the swamp, leaving the dead guerrilla well behind and keeping their eyes peeled for other booby-traps. In fact, they had only marched another hour when Dead-eye, still on point, saw another Chinese Chopper across the trail. Boney Maronie put it out of action by tearing the rope to shreds with a hail of 9mm bullets from his Owen sub-machine-gun, causing the viciously spiked log to crash to the ground.

'Nice one,' Dennis the Menace said.

An hour later the real nightmare began. First,

they came across a thatch-and-palm lean-to once used by some guerrillas, as could be seen from a pile of ant-covered chicken bones, turtle shells covered in swarms of flies, decaying vegetables and a couple of line drawings showing various routes through the swamp. Excited, Trooper Frank Turner snatched up the maps.

'*Don't touch them*!' Sergeant Lorrimer bellowed – too late. He then threw himself out of the lean-to as a hidden fragmentation grenade, detonated by a trip-wire fixed to the phoney maps, exploded with a deafening roar, hurling Turner backwards in a fountain of loose soil, his flesh shredded by razor-sharp, red-hot shrapnel, and setting fire to the few parts of the lean-to not blown apart.

The scorched, shredded Turner was lying on his back, shuddering spasmodically and screaming like an animal as Lorrimer picked himself up and wiped soil from his face.

'Damn!' he exclaimed, then turned to the other men. 'Don't ever touch anything!' he bawled. 'Check everything first!' He knelt beside the screaming man, saw the scorched and shredded flesh, and was still deciding what to do about him when the man coughed up a mess of blood and phlegm, then shuddered, evacuated his bowels and died.

'Do you want me to call up for a casevac?' Laughton asked.

'What for? He's dead.'

'Just thought you might want the body flown home, Sarge.'

'We'd have to clear an LZ and that would take half the day,' Lorrimer told him, glancing at Callaghan for support and receiving it in the shape of a slight nod. 'Let's bury him here and move on. We're running out of supplies.'

While some of the men were given the unpleasant detail of digging a grave for Turner, Lorrimer took Callaghan aside. 'Do you think D Squadron and the others will be dropped today as agreed?'

'I don't see why not, but I'll get on the blower and check.'

'Can they drop us resups at the same time?'

'I don't think so, Sarge. They're going to need all the space they can get for the men being brought in.'

'My sentiments exactly. And this is our seventh day in this filthy swamp, which means we've run out of half our rations. The men are also running out of patience. I say we wait until we know the others have been dropped, throw a cordon around the swamp, then move in and don't stop until this bloody business is ended, no matter how difficult it is or how bad the casualties.'

'I think you're right,' Callaghan said. 'If we hold back too long, this swamp will do us in before the CT do, so let's go for broke. I'll get on to Major Pryce-Jones and see what he has to say.' Callaghan crossed to where Laughton was kneeling on the swampy ground with his PRC 320 beside him. 'Get me Major Pryce-Jones,' Callaghan said. When Laughton had made contact, Callaghan asked his fellow officer when the drop was going to commence.

'The Kampong Guards of the Malaya Police are on their way right now,' Pryce-Jones replied, 'and I'm just about to head for the airstrip to join the rest of D Squadron. The Kampong Guards are going to block off the coast and we'll be cordoning off the eastern perimeter of the swamp to prevent the CT from getting out that way. We'll work our way into the swamp to link up with you. Have you located them yet? Over.'

'We know they're heading upriver, towards the centre of the swamp and possibly further, so you could make contact before us. Over.'

'OK. We'll send up a flare if we do. You do the same. Good luck, Captain. Over and out.'

The patrol moved on, heading east on a compass bearing, picking an ever more cautious way through the swamp, noses alert for the smell of guerrilla fire smoke or cooking, ears straining through the cacophony of bullfrog croaks for the sound of a human voice, eyes straining in the gloom to see snakes, poisonous spiders, wild boar or more booby-traps. They saw all of those.

Forced to follow the river, they encountered a lot of snakes where they were sheltering in the relative cool of the muddy banks. Most of the snakes slithered away at the sight or sound of booted feet, but some of them were particularly aggressive, rising up in the air and darting forward with their venomous fangs spitting. As it was now clear that the CT knew the British were here – and as their constant use of the *parangs* to hack away the dense foliage was creating a racket anyway – the men were no longer concerned with maintaining silence and either despatched the aggressive snakes with a short burst from their semi-automatic weapons or by slicing through them with the *parangs*. They were often amazed, in the latter case, when the two halves of the bisected reptile wriggled off in separate directions for a considerable distance before finally surrendering to death's stillness.

Welsh had no compunction about breaking the silence when he had to pass under a branch on which was resting an enormous, hairy spider. Pete despatched it – and the branch – with a sustained burst from his Owen.

When an enormous *seladang* virtually exploded out of the undergrowth and charged, bellowing angrily, at some of the men, the wild ox was not stopped by a couple of shots from Deadeye's M1 carbine, but only by a sustained burst from Lorrimer's more powerful Browning 12-gauge autoloader shotgun. This did not quite lift the huge animal off its feet – as it would have done a man – but it certainly stopped its ferocious advance, made its legs buckle as its intestines slopped out, and finally caused it to sink bloodily to the marshy earth.

Trooper Jimmy Ashman was the first man to see the next Chinese Chopper. Grinning like a schoolkid because he'd seen it before it trapped him, he skirted around it – and tripped over another string stretched along both sides of the narrow track.

His scream was dreadful as he staggered back from the impact of the spear that was suddenly thrusting out of his chest. It had been fired from a bow concealed in the earth and operated by a trigger mechanism set off by the hidden trip-cord. Ashman kept screaming as he dropped his M1, staggering backwards as if punch-drunk, and instinctively tried to jerk the spear out of his smashed chest and pierced heart. He was dying even as he was attempting this and dead by the time he fell backwards into a pool of mud.

Welsh automatically sub-machine-gunned the

activating cords of the booby-trap, then also peppered the area on both sides of the track, just to be sure. When they knew the ground was safe, the men dug a shallow grave for Ashman, buried him, conducted a simple ceremony and then continued their march.

About an hour later, when they had managed to hack their way through another 500 yards of murderously dense secondary jungle, Lorrimer and Dead-eye, sharing point duty together, spotted three guerrillas about 50 yards away across a stretch of open, rust-brown water.

After using a hand signal to tell the rest of the squadron to drop to the ground, Lorrimer indicated that Dead-eye should follow him. He discarded his bergen and other kit, slipped into the water, holding his Browning shotgun above his head, waited for Dead-eye to follow suit, then grabbed a floating log. With the log in front of them, they both inched through the water, resting their weapons near the top of the log, though slightly behind it, so that only the log would have been seen if the guerrillas had turned around. When they neared the other side of the stretch of open water, both still hidden by the log and about 50 yards from the bank, they saw that the guerrillas were two men and a woman.

As they were quietly bringing their weapons up

into the firing position, resting the barrels on the floating log, they heard the distant rumble of aircraft and saw the guerrillas pointing at the sky.

A Beverley was flying overhead. Even as they all looked up, four separate sticks of men dropped out in different directions – from the port and starboard doors; left and right of the boom door – and their parachutes billowed out, one after the other, to let them descend silently onto the eastern side of the swamp. Though neither Lorrimer nor Dead-eye said a word, they both knew the men descending on the parachutes were the Kampong Guards, to be followed shortly by SAS D Squadron.

Lorrimer nodded at Dead-eye, then aimed along the upraised sights of his Browning shotgun. Dead-eye did the same with his M1 carbine. They opened fire simultaneously, taking out the two men, who convulsed in a dramatic explosion of spitting soil and foliage. The woman, however, jumped to her feet and fled into the jungle.

'Damn!' Lorrimer exclaimed. 'Let's go get her!' Pushing the log aside, they both waded to the bank, scrambled out, dripping wet, and raced into the jungle after the woman. She disappeared like a wisp of smoke, as if she had never been. 'Damn!' Lorrimer said again. Returning to the stretch of water, they checked the dead guerrillas, found nothing of importance on them, so slipped back into the water and waded back to the other side, holding their weapons above their heads. As they were scrambling up the far bank, a second Beverley flew overhead, disgorging another group of paratroopers to the east.

'D Squadron,' Lorrimer said.

'Good,' Dead-eye replied. 'We'll soon have the CT boxed in, then this'll be over in no time.'

'I wouldn't count on it,' Lorrimer warned.

They then hacked their way through the dense foliage, back to the main party.

By the following morning, the Kampong Guards had laid barbed wire along the coast, thus blocking all entrances to the area from the east. Simultaneously, D Squadron had tightened the cordon around the guerrillas by moving to a point on the River Tengi several miles upstream from Callaghan's group. The two groups were now closing towards one another in a pincer movement around the CT. Even more effectively, the Kampong Police, with the aid of Royal Marine Commandos, also threw a huge cordon around the whole swamp perimeter and arranged for helicopters to fly over the area, scanning the open spaces in the watery swamp for signs of Ah Hoi and his guerrillas.

It was now fifteen days since the SAS had dropped into the swamp and all the men were suffering from prickly heat and a variety of infections. Many had legs and arms ripped by thorns, with the wounds infected and badly ulcerated. Nevertheless, when Major Pryce-Jones contacted Captain Callaghan to inform him that the rest of D Squadron, under his command, was presently marching from the eastern perimeter into the swamp, Callaghan pressed his men on for the final push against the CT.

As they neared the centre of the swamp, they had to watch out for an increasing number of booby-traps, as well as actual guerrillas. The latter suddenly started appearing in the undergrowth just long enough to fire quick bursts from their assault rifles or tommy-guns before disappearing again. When this happened, the SAS troopers broke from their lengthy single file and instead fanned out across the *ulu* to form a broad cordon composed of two- or four-man teams, from which the CT could not escape.

Aware that they were now hedged in on all sides, the CT responded by attempting a suicidal last-ditch stand.

Captain Callaghan stuck close to Trooper

Laughton, who had the PRC 320, through which he kept in regular contact with Major Pryce-Jones as the latter advanced into the swamp from the east.

When the first CT jumped up from behind some foliage just ahead, firing his tommy-gun and wounding one SAS trooper, Callaghan sent up a flare. The CT sniper disappeared as quickly as he had materialized, but Dead-eye switched to the M203 grenade-launcher on his M1 and fired a 40mm shell where the guerrilla had been, blowing the foliage to pieces and setting fire to the bark of a tree. When the smoke cleared, the sniper's scorched, shredded body was revealed, sprawled brokenly over a fallen tree trunk.

'Advance!' Sergeant Lorrimer bawled, then jumped up and ran, leaping over the dead guerrilla and rushing into the jungle, though safely at the half-crouch, with Dead-eye coming up close behind him. When another guerrilla appeared, taking aim with a Belgian FN assault rifle, Lorrimer fired his Browning shotgun from the hip, three shots in quick succession, and the guerrilla was picked up and punched back into the shrubbery with half of his chin gone, his throat a bloody mess and the bones of his chest exposed through the gashes in his tunic.

He had hardly hit the ground when two more

guerrillas jumped up, to be despatched by a fusillade from Dead-eye's deadly accurate M1 carbine. Dead-eye then switched again to the grenade-launcher, firing on a trajectory that landed the grenade just beyond the men he had killed. The explosion was catastrophic – more than the grenade warranted – and he realized even before the flames had flickered out and the smoke had dispersed that he had set off another booby-trap, probably some kind of land-mine.

'Booby-traps!' he bawled. His warning, however, was too late for one trooper, who dived for the cover of a small sapling, shaking it enough to dislodge the mortar shell lodged loosely in its branches. Dead-eye saw it falling and threw himself to the ground just in time to avoid the deafening blast of the explosion. When the showering debris had settled down, he looked to the side and saw a severed leg pumping blood onto the green grass only yards away. Jumping back to his feet, he saw the rest of the trooper, a leg here, an arm there. Realizing that nothing could be done, he raced on, attempting to catch up with Lorrimer, who was directly ahead, with Dennis the Menace and Boney Maronie directly behind him, and a grim-faced Welsh bringing up the rear.

By now the jungle was filled with smoke and

reeking of cordite, reverberating with the sounds of explosions and the screams of wounded or dying men. Dropping to one knee to replace his empty magazine, Dead-eye almost choked on the smoke. He wiped tears from his eyes, then saw an SAS trooper tripping over a hidden rope, thus releasing a springing shaft with a wooden spear lashed to its tip. Impaled through the stomach, the soldier was punched violently backwards. He stared down in shock at the spear, almost collapsed, but was held up by the springing shaft. He screamed in agony, then died there on his feet. He remained that way, held upright even in death, as Dead-eye jumped up and advanced again into the smouldering, smoke-wreathed *ulu*.

Dennis the Menace and Boney Maronie, working as a team, were advancing at the half-crouch just ahead of Dead-eye when they saw another guerrilla pop up from behind some undergrowth to take a shot at them. They dropped to the ground and the bullets whistled over their heads, but a second burst kicked up a line of spitting soil between them, making them roll apart.

The ground caved in under Boney and he disappeared from view, then let forth a dreadful, anguished scream.

Shocked, Dennis the Menace released the pin on a fragmentation grenade and hurled it towards the guerrillas. He covered his ears while it exploded, sending foliage and loose soil geysering skyward, then wriggled across to where Boney Maronie had disappeared and was still screaming dreadfully. Finding a hole in the ground – previously covered by a false surface raised on breakable supports – he looked down to see his friend writhing on a bed of wooden stakes that had been sharpened and then smeared with excrement to cause maximum damage.

'Punji pit!' Dennis bawled like a madman. 'Help! For God's sake!'

Callaghan and Laughton appeared out of swirling smoke to kneel beside Dennis the Menace and look down into the pit.

'Dear God!' Callaghan exclaimed softly while Laughton winced.

Welsh dropped down beside them and also looked into the punji pit, where Boney Maronie was still writhing and screaming. 'Fucking hell!' Welsh groaned. 'What a way to go!'

Outraged, Dennis the Menace dived at Welsh, but was hauled back by Captain Callaghan. 'What the hell do you think you're doing, Trooper?'

'He said . . .'

'Never mind, damn it,' Callaghan interjected sharply. 'Let's get that man out of there.'

'How?' Laughton asked.

Sergeant Lorrimer and Dead-eye emerged from the swirling smoke and dropped to their knees beside Captain Callaghan.

'Cover us,' Callaghan said. 'We've got to get Boney out of that pit, so I'm going down into it. Make sure no one gets near us.'

'Right, boss,' Sergeant Lorrimer replied, then pointed his index finger at Laughton. 'Lay down covering fire with that Bren gun,' he said, 'and keep firing until we tell you to stop.'

'Will do,' Laughton said, unstrapping the Bren gun from his bergen, releasing the tripod, mounting the gun and aiming along the sights at the undergrowth straight ahead. When he saw the undergrowth shifting, he opened fire and kept firing, the gun making a sustained roaring sound. Lorrimer did the same with his Browning shotgun, blasting the foliage to shreds, and Dead-eye fired one shot after the other, his hawk eyes picking out every movement of foliage and never failing to find the guerrilla causing it.

'Keep it up!' Callaghan bawled over the din as he dropped his bergen and webbing to the muddy ground. Freed of all encumbrances, he lay belly-down on the grass, slithered backwards, and very carefully lowered himself into the punji pit, where Boney Maronie was still pinioned on the excrement-smeared wooden stakes. Boney had stopped moving to prevent further injury and anguish, and was breathing heavily while staring up at Callaghan with terrified eyes.

Callaghan carefully placed his feet between the stakes, steadied himself, then leant over Boney.

Pain and fear had made the trooper almost unrecognizable. Blood was pouring profusely from the many wounds in his back and legs. He was doomed, but he still had to be rescued.

'Captain . . .' he managed to croak, then sucked in some more air.

'This is going to hurt terribly,' Callaghan said, 'but you'll just have to endure it.'

'Yes, Cap'n. Oh, God!'

A mortar shell exploded near the men above, causing loose soil and foliage to rain down over Callaghan's head and Boney Maronie's sweating, frightened face. When the debris finally settled, Callaghan checked that the men above were still firing their weapons – obviously unhurt, they were – then took a deep breath, leaned over Boney Maronie, and said: 'OK, bite your lower lip. This'll hurt like hell.'

He took hold of Boney Maronie's shoulders and eased him up off the sharpened stakes. When Boney Maronie started screaming, Callaghan stopped being gentle and hauled him upright as fast as he could. Boney Maronie screamed even louder, his body quivering like a bowstring. When he was free of the stakes he collapsed into Callaghan's embrace and clung sobbing to him.

'It's not over yet,' Callaghan said, 'and you can't let me down. Scream as much as you want, lad.' He glanced directly above him. Welsh was looking down. The others were continuing to pour gunfire into the jungle where the guerrillas were lurking. 'OK, Welsh,' Callaghan said. 'You've got to haul Boney Maronie up. It doesn't matter how much it hurts him, nor how much he screams – you've just got to do it.' Still holding Boney Maronie in his arms, he repeated: 'You scream as much as you want, lad. But try to climb out of here. OK, let's do it.'

Callaghan released Boney Maronie and patted him on the cheek. Boney just stood there, his feet between the stakes, swaying, a dazed look in his eyes, his back and legs pouring blood.

'Yes, boss,' he managed to croak.

'Raise your hands as high as you can,' Callaghan said. Boney did as he was told. Welsh grabbed his hands, glanced at Captain Callaghan, received his nod and started pulling Boney Maronie up. Boney screamed like an animal, being torn apart by pain, but Callaghan pushed as Pete Welsh pulled . . . and eventually Boney was out of the pit, face down on the ground.

Though no longer screaming, he was sobbing like a child, helplessly, shamelessly, hardly aware of himself. Captain Callaghan leaned forward, stroked the back of his head, and said, 'We've got to leave you for now, Boney. We can't casevac you yet. We'll call in a chopper just as soon as this is over, but in the meantime you'll just have to endure it. There's no more we can do.'

'The pain,' Boney groaned. 'God, the pain.'

'I'm going to give you some morphine,' Callaghan said. 'That's all I can do for now.'

'Yes, boss. Jesus, yes!'

The number and depth of the wounds, combined with the excrement left in them from the stakes, convinced Callaghan that Boney could not survive. Nevertheless, he put him out of his pain by injecting him with morphine, smeared the areas between the wounds with river mud, which would help to keep away the insects, and finally covered him with a waterproof poncho that would help to keep his temperature even.

'Right,' he said, speaking loudly against the roaring of the combined weapons of Lorrimer, Deadeye, Laughton and Dennis the Menace. 'That's all I can do. We have to go on now.'

'No, boss,' Boney managed to say, still being face down in the grass because he couldn't possibly lie on his badly wounded back. 'The guerrillas might pass through here. Please, God, boss, you know what . . .'

He didn't have to say more. Callaghan removed his own 9mm Browning High Power handgun from its holster and laid it on the grass by Boney's fingers, to enable him to join the 'Exit Club', should the guerrillas find him still alive.

'OK, Boney, good luck.'

Dennis the Menace stopped firing and turned around. 'We just leave him?' he asked, sounding choked.

'We've no choice,' Callaghan said. 'Now get up and advance to the east and don't look back, Trooper.'

'Yes, boss,' Dennis the Menace said. He turned away to hide his tears and said, 'OK, Dead-eye, are you all set?'

'Yes,' Dead-eye said, sounding as cool as a block of ice. 'Let's put an end to this shit.' He stood up, switched his M1 to the grenade-launcher, inserted a 40mm shell, then fired it at the undergrowth straight ahead. When the shell exploded, tearing the foliage apart, setting some of it on fire, and filling the area with smoke, he and the others raced on at the half-crouch, leaving Boney Maronie to his fate.

Dennis the Menace, determined not to show his tears, was racing out ahead, though still a good way behind Welsh.

When a flare exploded over the *ulu* to the east, indicating that the rest of D Squadron had made contact with the CT, the men knew they were close to the guerrillas' camp.

Welsh saw his chance then. Consumed with the rage that had fuelled most of his life, landing him in trouble time after time, but making him a good soldier if not a good SAS trooper, he wanted to wreak his revenge on Dennis the Menace.

He didn't care what chances he took to do it – he just had to do it – so he raced on ahead, taking point, but suicidally, crashing through the undergrowth, firing his sub-machine-gun from the hip, lobbing hand-grenades at anything that moved, and running into the blinding smoke like a man both invisible and invincible. He managed to kill quite a few of the guerrillas, but no one touched him.

Eventually arriving at a trampled track that sloped downhill into a low, sheltered area, Welsh suspected that the CT might be down there, preparing to make their last stand. Knowing from experience that sloping ground was the ideal place for a spike trap – where man or beast would step down harder than normal, thus making the false surface cave in – he carefully checked the track, convinced that it would be booby-trapped, and did indeed find the false surface of a spike trap, covered with loose soil and leaves.

Stepping carefully around it, he deliberately knelt on the ground at the other side, facing downhill.

Dennis the Menace was the first to emerge from the smoke-wreathed forest at the top of the gentle rise. When he saw Welsh, he stopped, glanced left and right, then waited for the nod indicating 'Advance'. When he received it, he advanced at the half-crouch down the hill, not seeing the spike trap.

Welsh smiled grimly as Dennis the Menace hurried down the slope and approached the murderous spike trap.

Just before he reached the trap, however, a guerrilla stepped out from the trees behind him and took aim with a British tommy-gun.

Without even thinking, Welsh opened fire with his Owen, swinging it in an arc, cutting across the guerrilla, throwing him into convulsions, practically lifting him off his feet and hurling him backwards into the undergrowth.

Dennis the Menace froze, glanced back over his shoulder, then turned to the front again as Welsh, hardly believing that he was hearing his own voice, bawled: 'Spike trap! Get off the track! Come down through the undergrowth!' As Dennis the Menace did just that, the others emerged from the jungle behind him and Welsh shouted out the same warning. When they had all passed the spike trap and were looking downhill, Captain Callaghan patted Welsh on the shoulder, saying: 'Good man. Now are those commie bastards down there or not?'

'I think they're down there,' Welsh said quietly.

'Then let's go and get them.'

They advanced down the hill and reached a stretch of sheltered flatland that ended back at the bank of the curving river.

The CTs had moved on.

# 15

The woman emerged from the trees and stood at the far side of the river, ghostly in the cold morning mist. It was just after first light. Having been on guard duty all night, Dead-eye was dog-tired and thought he was seeing things, but soon realized that the woman was real enough. She was tiny, emaciated, wearing an olive-green uniform, standing in bare feet, with her black hair pulled up and tied in a pony tail at the back of her head.

Having emerged from the *ulu*, she stood for a moment on the far bank and looked directly at Dead-eye. He was aiming his M1 carbine at her from behind the wall of loose branches and leaves he had built as a jungle variation on the normal loose-stoned sangar. Seemingly unconcerned that Dead-eye might fire at her, the woman stepped down into the river, then waded across, clambered out the other side and walked right up to him.

Only about 4 feet 6 inches tall, she was practically skeletal and suffering from beri-beri, with a visible puffiness around her knees, ankles and wrists. But she must have once been pretty.

'My name is Ah Niet,' she said. 'I come with a message from Ah Hoi. Take me to your leader.'

Climbing to his feet, Dead-eye crossed a few yards of grass to shake Dennis the Menace awake. 'Come on, Dennis, wake up!' When Dennis had rubbed his eyes and was looking reasonably alert, Dead-eye pointed backwards to the tiny female guerrilla, saying: 'We've got a visitor. She's come from Ah Hoi with a message. I'm going to take her to Callaghan, so take over my guard duty.'

Dennis the Menace looked in surprise at the short, wasted Chinese woman, rubbed his eyes again, then picked up his M1 carbine and climbed to his feet. 'Surprise, surprise,' he said. 'She looks like she hasn't eaten a good meal in months.'

'She probably hasn't,' Dead-eye said. 'Take over my sangar.'

'Right,' Dennis the Menace said and walked back to the branch-and-palm sangar, where the woman was patiently waiting for him.

'She speaks English?' Dennis the Menace asked.

'Yes,' Dead-eye said.

'A little,' the woman corrected him.

'That's enough. Come with me.' As Dennis

settled into Dead-eye's thatched sangar, the latter led Ah Niet across the clearing, through the trees and back to another part of the river bank, where Captain Callaghan was wisely sleeping on his floating bamboo raft tethered to some branches. When Dead-eye called out to him, he opened his eyes. Seeing the woman, he used the rope to pull the raft to the bank, then clambered on to the grassy verge. He studied the woman thoughtfully.

'This lady is called Ah Niet,' Dead-eye said. 'She claims to be a messenger from Ah Hoi.'

'Is this true?' Callaghan asked.

'Yes, sir,' Ah Niet replied.

'Where's Ah Hoi now?'

The woman waved her hand vaguely in the direction of the jungle on the other side of the river. 'Over there. Deeper in *ulu.* Near heart of swamp. It hard for you there.'

'I'm sure,' Callaghan replied smoothly. 'So what's the message?'

'Ah Hoi is willing to come out of swamp if you give compensation. For each of his men. Also amnesty for those now in prison.'

'Compensation? Do you mean money?'

'Yes, sir. A sum to be kindly agreed between us.'

'Wait here,' Callaghan said. 'Dead-eye, give her

something to eat and drink. Your emergency rations will do.'

'That's *my* rations we're talking about, boss.'

'I'm a generous man with other men's scran. Now I'm off to talk to Major Pryce-Jones on Trooper Laughton's radio. I'll be back in a minute.'

While Callaghan was away, talking to Pryce-Jones on the PRC 320, Dead-eye told the clearly exhausted Ah Niet to rest on the grass. When she was sitting at his feet, he knelt beside her, gave her some chocolate from his escape belt, then poured water from his bottle into a tin mug and handed it to her. She wolfed the chocolate down and drank the water greedily, confirming that she had gone hungry for some time. A few minutes later, Callaghan returned, now accompanied by a sleepy Lorrimer.

'No deal,' Callaghan said when the woman stood to face him. 'No money, no amnesty. Tell Ah Hoi he's surrounded. The whole swamp has been encircled by Kampong Guards and another squadron of SAS troopers is moving in on your encampment from the east, to form a cordon completed by this group. Your leader has a choice between surrendering within twelve hours or death in the swamp. If our foot soldiers fail in this task, the RAF will bomb him out of hiding. That's the message you're taking back.'

'Yes, sir.' Ah Niet pointed to the south. 'Paddy-field over there. If Ah Hoi comes out, he surrenders in paddy-field. Thank you, sir. I say goodbye.'

She waded back across the river, then dissolved into the *ulu* like a ghost.

'Alert the men,' Callaghan said. 'We're going to move out and set up our camp in that paddy-field. Let's pray he comes out.'

After being wakened, the men were allowed to wash in the river and have a breakfast of high-calorie rations. When ready, they demolished their wide variety of jungle shelters, shook out and rolled up their ponchos, packed their bergens, strapped them to their backs, then picked up their personal weapons and moved out one by one, first wading across the river, holding their weapons above their heads, then falling into a single file that snaked through the *ulu*, heading south towards the distant paddy-field.

It was not a long journey in terms of distance – only two miles – but that part of the *ulu*, being near the swamp's centre, was a vile combination of swamp and murderously dense *belukar*. The swamp water, which usually came up to the men's chests, was filled with snakes, leeches, floating logs and broken, obstructive branches. Its brown, moss-covered surface was covered constantly with swarms of noisily buzzing flies, midges, whining mosquitoes and hornets whose stings were agonizing. Before long, some of the men had eyes so swollen from mosquito bites that they could hardly see.

When not being tormented in the chest-deep water, the men were faced with the dreaded *belukar*, which, with its thick, tangled *mengkuang* grass and razor-sharp giant leaves, had to be hacked away with *parangs* and sometimes even uprooted by hand. The first mile took the men almost four hours of unremitting labour and when eventually they were allowed to stop for a rest, they were kept busy removing the bloodsucking leeches from their bruised skin, either by burning them off with cigarettes or by sprinkling them with salt and then pulling them off. Both ways left them a tremendous number of cuts and scars, many of which were already suppurating.

Having removed the leeches, the troopers then had to plunge back into the water, where they were attacked all over again. Emerging from the water about half an hour later, again covered in leeches, they had to hack their way through another long stretch of *belukar*, which left them exhausted and bathed in sweat. By last light, when they were emerging from the swamp to the wide, relatively cool paddy-field, most of them had lost pounds in weight and were looking as bad as they felt.

Mercifully, they could rest while waiting to see whether or not Ah Hoi would emerge with his guerrillas before the twelve-hour deadline was up. Constructing another wide variety of shelters around the edge of the dry paddy-field, the men settled in gratefully, some even managing to sleep, but most of them just resting until they were called for guard duty or to go out on point.

At dusk, a few hours before the deadline, the lights of many torches appeared in the *ulu* at the far side of the paddy-field, weaving to and fro like stars in the night sky as a large group advanced. Captain Callaghan immediately ordered his men out of their shelters, then formed them into a defensive cordon along their side of the paddy-field, with the field covered by tripod-mounted Bren guns and personal weapons.

The guerrillas, men and women, emerged from the jungle with their weapons strapped across their backs, one hand raised in a sign of surrender, the other holding a torchlight.

The woman, Ah Niet, was at the head of the group, beside a short, tubby man wearing a grey jacket with high collar, grey trousers, a military cap and a pair of *terumpas*, the wooden clog held on by rubber straps.

'That must be Ah Hoi,' Callaghan whispered to Lorrimer.

'Let's hope so, boss.'

The man was, in fact, Ah Hoi, and introduced himself thus when he and Callaghan met in the middle of the paddy-field. When Callaghan saluted him, Ah Hoi simply nodded by way of response. He was short, fat and rather arrogant, but nothing about him suggested the kind of man who could personally disembowel a woman in her eighth month of pregnancy.

'This is not a surrender,' he said, speaking Mandarin, which Callaghan understood. 'I am simply avoiding the senseless slaughter of my honourable forces. We will win in the end.'

'Ask your men to hand over their weapons,' Captain Callaghan replied, ignoring Ah Hoi's humourless propaganda.

'Of course,' Ah Hoi said with a wintry smile. When he nodded at his men, not saying a word, they unstrapped their weapons, removed them from their backs, and reverentially laid them on the dry paddy-field. At a command from Lorrimer, some of the SAS men started picking up the weapons while ordering the unarmed guerrillas to squat on the ground.

Callaghan, meanwhile, was using Laughton's radio to contact Major Pryce-Jones, presently still moving in from the east with D Squadron. After being informed of Ah Hoi's surrender, Pryce-Jones promised to send over some helicopters to lift off the guerrillas and transfer them to the camp in Johore.

When Callaghan had finished speaking to Pryce-Jones, he ordered flares to be set off to mark the paddy-field as the LZ for the choppers. When this had been done, he turned back to Ah Hoi, who had remained standing, as still as a statue, beside the diminutive Ah Niet.

'Are all your men here?' Callaghan asked.

'No,' Ah Hoi replied. 'Another group is located at another camp, deeper in the jungle. As they have no radios, we could not communicate, but Ah Niet will take you to them and help you bring them back out.'

'She doesn't look fit enough to survive another journey into the swamp.'

'She will do as ordered.'

'Good,' Callaghan said. In fact, being already drained of blood by the leeches and covered in the sores they had inflicted, he dreaded going back into the swamp. Nevertheless, it had to be done, so when a combination of RAF and Army Air Corps Whirlwind, Dragonfly and Sycamore helicopters had started lifting the guerrillas, including Ah Hoi, off the paddy-field, he let his own men rest while he returned to the swamp with Ah Niet, Lorrimer, Dead-eye and Dennis the Menace.

This final hike was hellish.

It soon became clear to Callaghan and the others that Ah Niet had been seriously weakened by the beri-beri and was having considerable trouble in breathing, let alone guiding them through the swamp, which consisted, in this area, mostly of muddy water covered in white pollen and green moss. It was also filled with drifting logs, thorny branches and cutting leaves, as well as being covered with the usual swarms of noisy, aggressive insects. Water snakes, many venomous, glided by just under the surface too often for comfort. Even more debilitating was the fact that the group was forced to virtually swim most of the way, the men holding their weapons above their heads. This caused cramp, other darting, distracting pains and general exhaustion.

Though clearly very ill, Ah Niet led the way, swimming in total silence, but stopping frequently to get her breath back. She vomited three times and coughed up blood twice, yet when Callaghan asked her if she wanted to turn back, she shook her head and said they had to go on as Ah Hoi had ordered.

'Such devotion!' Lorrimer whispered.

'Yeah,' Dennis the Menace replied. 'Makes you want to puke, don't it?'

Finally, as they were approaching what Ah Niet

claimed was the location of the other guerrillas, her strength gave out completely, she had a dreadful coughing fit, bringing up blood and phlegm, and then, before anyone could catch her, splashed face first into the water, sank beneath the surface, and was carried away under some drifting foliage. When she surfaced, about 20 yards away, she was no longer breathing.

'Fucking hell,' Dennis the Menace said. '*Now* what do we do?'

'We leave her here,' Captain Callaghan said pragmatically. 'There's nothing else we *can* do. Our job is to find the rest of the guerrillas and bring them out of the swamp. According to Ah Niet, they're somewhere around here, so let's go and find them.'

'If we go without Ah Niet,' Dead-eye said, 'we might not be welcome.'

'We'll know soon enough,' Callaghan said.

Indeed, they had walked only a few yards after clambering out of the swamp when the jungle exploded with the roaring of the guerrilla's rifles and tommy-guns. Up at the front on point, Dennis the Menace took the brunt of the fire, performing a St Vitus dance in the middle of a violent convulsion of exploding foliage, then falling backwards into prickly shrubbery, pumping blood from a great many bullet wounds.

As Dennis the Menace was dying, Lorrimer was retreating backwards the way they had just come, firing his Browning shotgun from the hip at the guerrillas he saw perched in the trees. Branches and leaves were blown apart, almost as if dynamited, and some guerrillas screamed and plunged to the ground in a noisy shower of foliage.

Dead-eye, meanwhile, had run to Dennis the Menace, where he lay on his back across some bushes, curved like a bow, but with most of his insides turned out by a hail of bullets. Discovering that his friend was dead, Dead-eye was filled with cold rage and advanced fearlessly on the guerrillas, firing his M1 carbine at anything that moved. He then switched to the M203 grenade-launcher, tearing a line of jungle to shreds with a series of fragmentation grenades, all aimed with devastating accuracy.

Even as the wounded guerrillas were screaming in agony, and while smoke and flames were curling in bright-yellow and blue tendrils through the dark-green foliage, now curtained in black smoke, Dead-eye was fixing his bayonet to the barrel of his M1 and preparing to engage in hand-to-hand combat, which would have been suicidal.

Luckily, he was stopped from doing so by Callaghan, who pulled him back, bawling: 'Don't be a damned fool! We've got to return to the paddy-field and call in the RAF. Come on, Dead-eye, let's go!'

'No, damn it!'

'*Let's go!*'

Even as Callaghan was pulling Dead-eye back to the bank of the river running through the swamp, Lorrimer was being attacked by a female guerrilla swinging a *parang*. Momentarily startled to see a woman in front of him, Lorrimer was slower than usual in getting off a shot from his Browning, thus giving her time to swing her *parang* in a horizontal sweep, lopping off his head as precisely as if it had been guillotined.

The head flew through the air, spewing blood in its wake, and landed on the marshy ground a few feet from where Callaghan and Dead-eye were making their retreat, firing on the move.

When Dead-eye saw the severed head, he thought he was hallucinating. It was the right way up, resting on a neck that was pouring blood into the grass. Even more ghoulish and terrifying, Lorrimer's eyes were actually moving in their sockets, first left, then right, but eventually turning up to focus on Dead-eye in an oddly pleading, demented, then dazed manner. Just as Dead-eye understood what he was actually seeing, the eyes in the severed head rolled in their sockets, then froze in the finality of death.

Dead-eye let out a low, gargling sound, then went cold all over.

'Let's go!' Callaghan snapped, ignoring the severed head and tugging Dead-eye towards the river bank. When Dead-eye failed to move, Callaghan brutally slapped his face and snapped: 'Come on, damn it!'

Jerked free from his shocked reverie, Dead-eye turned away from the river, dropped to one knee, then again switched on the M203 grenade-launcher and began to inflict as much damage as humanly possible on the jungle within his line of vision. While Callaghan looked on, not daring to stop him, Dead-eye used up his whole supply of grenades, causing dreadful devastation, fire and smoke and much screaming. When he had run out of grenades, he switched back to the rifle mode and repeated the same, coldly methodical performance, emptying one magazine, changing it for another, emptying that and changing again until nothing was left. He then stood up, stared coldly at Callaghan, and said in a hoarse, emotionless whisper: 'OK, boss, it's done. Let's get the hell out of here.'

Both men plunged back into the swamp and, mostly wading, but sometimes actually swimming, defying the river snakes and ignoring the swarming insects, made their way back to the moonlit paddy-field. There, the last of the guerrillas had been lifted off and the evacuation of the SAS troops was beginning.

'I want that man to have priority,' Callaghan said, pointing at Dead-eye. 'Get him back to Johore and let him sleep until he awakens. I want him looked after.'

'Yes, boss,' Lieutenant Ralph Ellis said. 'Hear you loud and clear, boss.' The pilot helped Dead-eye into his Sikorski S-55 Whirlwind, then flew him back to Johore.

Twenty-four hours later, the few guerrillas remaining in the *ulu* emerged to surrender.

# 16

Once the remaining CTs had emerged from the swamp, a group of SAS troopers went back in to recover the body of Dennis the Menace and the severed head and body of Sergeant Lorrimer.

Simultaneously, another group retraced their own footsteps to pick up Boney Maronie, dead or alive. In fact, he was dead. He had not been forced to join the 'Exit Club' – committing suicide to prevent himself from falling into the hands of the enemy – but had bled to death from the many wounds inflicted on him by the punji pit.

His body, along with those of the others, was shipped back to England for proper burial.

The surrender of the Communist Terrorists in the Telok Anson swamp marked the beginning of the end of the Emergency in Malaya. Shortly after being taken into captivity, Ah Hoi was given the choice between prison or exile in China. Choosing the latter, he was flown out of Malaya. When he had gone, the SAS, no longer needing to fight in the jungle, concentrated on the hearts-and-minds campaign, proving once and for all that they had a long-term future as a regiment with unusual capabilities, ranging from the military to the diplomatic.

Once back in Britain, Major Pryce-Jones and Captain Callaghan set about the creation of the Selection and Training programme they had discussed at great length in Malaya. By 1960 when the Regiment was transferred from Merebrook Camp, Malvern, Worcestershire, to what would become its permanent home at Bradbury Lines, Redhill, Hereford, the 'bad apples' had been weeded out and the more stringent mental and physical tests applied to all new applicants, ensuring that they were the *crème de la crème* of the military services.

Pete Welsh and Alf Laughton, formerly considered 'bad apples' but having proved themselves in Malaya, actually survived the weeding-out process for the revitalized SAS and went on to become reliable NCOs. The former lost his life in Borneo in 1964; the latter survived that same campaign and returned to Bradbury Lines to become a ruthlessly efficient member of the Directing Staff (DT) at 22 SAS Training Wing, Hereford.

Major Pryce-Jones was RTU'd to the Scots

Guards, but eventually returned to the SAS as a Commanding Officer at Stirling Lines, Hereford, retiring shortly after his successful involvement in the Falklands War of 1982.

Captain Callaghan, promoted to Major shortly after the Regiment transferred to Bradbury Lines, Hereford, went on to lead D Squadron during the Borneo campaign of 1964, where the former 'troublemakers', Pete Welsh and Alf Laughton, both served well under him.

Trooper Richard 'Dead-eye Dick' Parker was psychologically scarred for all time by his experiences in the Telok Anson swamp, yet was, also, oddly enhanced by them. Though haunted by the deaths of Dennis the Menace and Boney Maronie, as well as suffering repeated nightmares about the severed head of Sergeant Lorrimer – whom he had respected so much, almost like a father figure – he soon realized that he had never been happier than when in Malaya and was, for better or worse, a natural soldier.

Apart from being in the SAS, he had no interest in life.

This was proven in 1961 when, after three years of monumental boredom with a peacetime fighting force, he married a girl he had met in Hereford, had a few good months in bed with her, then realized that they had nothing to say to one another when they were not actually making love. By 1963, when Dead-eye was posted with the squadron to Borneo, the marriage was over.

Having seen so many die, mostly those whom he respected, Dead-eye, when he returned from Borneo in 1966, stopped socializing and spent most of his spare time alone, reading books on military theory. He was a man who loved war and understood at the same time that what he most loved would inevitably kill those he loved the most. He therefore decided to protect himself from that kind of pain. His isolation protected him.

By 1972, when Dead-eye was serving in Oman, in the Arabian Gulf, he had become one of the most private, feared and respected members of the SAS. This was appropriate, for by that time the SAS had become the most private, feared and respected body of fighting men in the world.

Dead-eye, an island unto himself, was proud to be part of it.